THE PAPERS OF
Thomas Jefferson

CHARLES T. CULLEN,
EDITOR

SECOND SERIES

THE PAPERS OF THOMAS JEFFERSON

SECOND SERIES

Jefferson's Extracts from the Gospels

"The Philosophy of Jesus" and
"The Life and Morals of Jesus"

DICKINSON W. ADAMS,
EDITOR

RUTH W. LESTER,
ASSISTANT EDITOR

INTRODUCTION BY
EUGENE R. SHERIDAN

PRINCETON UNIVERSITY PRESS
PRINCETON, NEW JERSEY

Printed in the United States of America by
Princeton University Press,
Princeton, New Jersey

CONTENTS

FOREWORD

THE INTRODUCTION to the first volume of *The Papers of Thomas Jefferson* announced that a second series would be published, containing "those materials which seem most naturally to permit a classified arrangement." Starting in 1954, the list of abbreviations found in the front of each volume contains a reference to the Second Series, described as "the topical series to be published at the end of this edition. . . ." The decision to launch this important part of Jefferson's papers while the chronological series progressed was made sometime in the 1960s, and work is now well under way on Jefferson's parliamentary writings, his account books, and his literary commonplace book. The present volume inaugurates what we expect will be a significant and important complement to Jefferson's letters and related papers found in the chronological series.

Dickinson W. Adams became interested in Jefferson's examinations of Christianity as a doctoral student at Brown University. In correspondence with Julian Boyd he received encouragement to pursue a detailed study of the biblical compilations, only one of which is extant. As work progressed, Mr. Boyd invited him to publish his finished work in the Second Series. Boyd and Adams were discussing revisions of the submitted manuscript when Adams died at the end of 1977. It was Mr. Boyd's plan to devote his attention to this material as soon as he completed work on Volume 20, but he left both unfinished when he died in 1980.

Having discussed this volume with him in the months before his death, and having reviewed his notes afterwards, I was aware of the numerous details that needed attention before the manuscript could be submitted for publication. As soon as Eugene Sheridan assumed his duties as associate editor of *The Papers of Thomas Jefferson*, he accepted the assignment of writing a new introduction, and in the process of editing Adams' manuscript, we revised the appendix somewhat from the plan originally agreed upon by Adams and Boyd. In short, the primary documents in this volume were edited by Dickinson Adams, but Julian Boyd and Eugene Sheridan made changes here and there, some of which were first recommended by Mr. Boyd and approved by Mr. Adams and some of which resulted from the final review of the manuscript by the present Jefferson Papers staff. Because neither the original editor nor the former general editor could respond to questions that arose upon review, final responsibility for the quality and accuracy of the volume must, in this case, fall more heavily than usual on the present general editor of *The Papers of Thomas Jefferson.*

The present volume provides all sources from the Jefferson papers that relate to the compilation of the Gospel extracts. This material should help answer questions about Jefferson's religious beliefs, which he himself always refused to discuss publicly, even after it became an issue in the presidential election of 1800. No previous edition of these extracts has ever provided the context of Jefferson's biblical criticism; indeed, most have confused "The Philosophy of Jesus" and "The Life and Morals of Jesus." The former disappeared not long after Jefferson's death and is reconstructed herein by Dickinson Adams for the first time. His dedicated work and Julian Boyd's guidance over almost a decade demonstrate the impressive accomplishments made possible by skilled documentary editing. Their achievement provides the editors of Jefferson's papers with an impressive beginning of our Second Series.

Charles T. Cullen

April 13, 1982

ACKNOWLEDGMENTS

I T IS a pleasure to acknowledge the assistance I have received in preparing this volume for publication. My foremost obligation is to Julian P. Boyd, who first advised me to study Jefferson's biblical compilations for my doctoral dissertation at Brown University and then encouraged me to prepare this volume for the Second Series in *The Papers of Thomas Jefferson*. I am also deeply grateful for the help extended me by Ruth W. Lester, Assistant Editor of *The Papers of Thomas Jefferson*, and by David Billington, my former research assistant at Princeton. Princeton University and the National Historical Publications and Records Commission both provided funds that enabled me to do research on this volume.

The staff of the Manuscript Division at the University of Virginia has been unfailingly helpful. I owe particular debts of gratitude to William G. Ray for supplying copies of numerous documents relevant to my work; to John C. Wyllie for helping me in my regrettably unsuccessful search for the original "Philosophy of Jesus"; and to Anne Freudenberg for her excellent work in supervising the photostating of the New Testaments from which Jefferson actually clipped the passages he used in his first biblical compilation. James A. Bear, Jr., resident director at Monticello, suggested valuable leads for further research and helped me tentatively to identify the holograph of a crucial document, the Table of Texts for "The Philosophy of Jesus," in the Edgehill-Randolph Papers at the University of Virginia.

I am indebted to the staff of the National Museum of History and Technology, Smithsonian Institution, for numerous services. Keith E. Melder and Silvio A. Bedini were especially helpful in providing me with microfilm copies of "The Life and Morals of Jesus" as well as of the English New Testaments Jefferson used to compile this work. In addition, the Smithsonian's Division of Political History answered numerous inquiries and volunteered much useful information.

I have also benefited from the aid of the dedicated staffs of the British Library, the Monticello Association, and Brown University Libraries. In regard to the last of these, I am especially grateful to M. F. Gross for her typing assistance.

Although it would be impossible for me adequately to thank everyone who has assisted me with my work, I must single out several individuals whose help has been particularly beneficial. Wil-

ACKNOWLEDGMENTS

liam G. McLoughlin of Brown University supervised the doctoral dissertation on which this volume is based. Hyatt Waggoner gave me continual support during my graduate years at Brown. Neda M. Westlake of the University of Pennsylvania more than once made available to me a copy of the same edition of the very rare 1804 English New Testament Jefferson used in "The Life and Morals of Jesus." Ciran Mac an Aili of Dublin supplied a copy of the same edition of the 1799 New Testament used by Jefferson to compile "The Philosophy of Jesus," thereby making an essential contribution to the authenticity of the reconstructed text of that work presented in this volume.

The contribution of Elizabeth Brown Adams to this work has extended far beyond the usual patience and understanding of the wife of a scholar who seems to be permanently in his study. She helped me immensely by discussing this work with me and contributed substantially to the reorganization and rewriting of several drafts.

Dickinson W. Adams

North Dartmouth, Massachusetts
August 20, 1975

JEFFERSON'S
EXTRACTS FROM
THE GOSPELS

INTRODUCTION

"Fix reason firmly in her seat, and call to her tribunal every fact, every opinion," Thomas Jefferson advised one of his nephews in the course of a disquisition on religious education. "Question with boldness even the existence of a god; because, if there be one, he must more approve the homage of reason, than that of blindfolded fear."[1] This critical attitude, typical of the Age of Enlightenment, characterized Jefferson's approach to religion, as to all other problems, from his youth. But unlike many other adherents of the Enlightenment, especially those in France, Jefferson's rationalism led him ultimately to an affirmation of faith rather than a rejection of religious belief. Jefferson's rational religion was perhaps nowhere better expressed than in his two compilations of extracts from the New Testament—"The Philosophy of Jesus" (1804) and "The Life and Morals of Jesus" (1819-1820?). Since coming to public attention in the mid-nineteenth century, these efforts by Jefferson to ascertain the authentic acts and teachings of Jesus have been surrounded by much confusion.[2] Some scholars have confused "The Philosophy of Jesus" with "The Life and Morals of Jesus," a few even failing to realize that they are two distinct works. Others have accepted uncritically the subtitle of "The Philosophy of Jesus," concluding that Jefferson prepared it for the use of the Indians. And still others have assumed that Jefferson produced both compilations strictly for his personal edification, thereby dismissing evidence which suggests that the composition of "The Philosophy of Jesus" was motivated in part by his apprehensions over the future of republicanism in the United States.[3] Most of this confusion stems

[1] TJ to Peter Carr, 10 Aug. 1787.

[2] Henry S. Randall, *The Life of Thomas Jefferson* (Philadelphia, 1858), III, 654-58, was the first to reveal the existence of two separate compilations. Before then, "The Philosophy of Jesus" had been a matter of public knowledge after the 1829 publication of TJ's 12 Oct. 1813 letter to John Adams in Thomas Jefferson Randolph, ed., *Memoir, Correspondence, and Miscellanies, from the Papers of Thomas Jefferson* (Charlottesville, 1829), IV, 222-26, where it is misdated 13 Oct. 1813. This letter is also printed in the Appendix of the present volume.

[3] The following accounts of TJ's religion are especially significant: Dickinson Ward Adams, "Jefferson's Politics of Morality: The Purpose and Meaning of His Extracts from the Evangelists 'The Philosophy of Jesus of Nazareth' and 'The Life and Morals of Jesus of Nazareth' " (Ph.D. diss., Brown University, 1970); C. Randolph Benson, *Thomas Jefferson as Social Scientist* (Cranbury, N.J., 1971), p. 188-211; Daniel J. Boorstin, *The Lost World of Thomas Jefferson* (Boston, 1948), p. 151-66; Gilbert Chinard, "Jefferson among the Philosophers," *Ethics*, LIII (July 1943), 255-68; Bernhard Fabian, "Jefferson's *Notes on Virginia*: The Genesis of Query XVII, *The different religions received into that State?*" *William and Mary Quarterly*, 3d ser., XII (Jan. 1955), 124-38; Henry W. Foote, *The Religion of Thomas Jefferson* (Boston, 1947); same, ed., *The Life and Morals of Jesus of Nazareth* (Boston, 1951), p. 7-32; William D. Gould, "The Religious Opinions of Thomas Jefferson," *Mississippi Valley Historical Review*, XX (Sep. 1933), 191-208; Leslie J. Hall, "The Religious Opinions of Thomas Jefferson," *Sewanee Review*, XXI (Apr. 1913), 164-76; Robert M. Healey, *Jefferson on Religion in Public Education* (New Haven, 1962); William B. Huntley, "Jefferson's Public and Private Religion," *South Atlantic Quarterly*, LXXIX (Summer 1980), 286-301; George M. Knoles, "Religious Ideas of Thomas Jefferson," *MVHR*, XXX (Sep. 1943), 187-204; Adrienne Koch, *The Philosophy of Thomas Jefferson* (New York, 1943), p. 23-39; Fred C. Luebke, "The Origins of Thomas Jefferson's Anti-Clericalism," *Church History*, XXX (Sep. 1963), 344-56; Dumas

from the unfortunate disappearance of Jefferson's first biblical compilation. A careful reconstruction of the text of "The Philosophy of Jesus" and the collection of Jefferson's papers at one place now make it possible to place that manuscript and "The Life and Morals of Jesus" in their proper historical context by tracing the development of Jefferson's religious attitudes, describing the genesis of both documents, and discussing their significance in the evolution of his religious beliefs.

I

Jefferson's religion has long fascinated and vexed students of his career. Always reticent about his private life, Jefferson was especially reluctant to reveal his religious beliefs. Indeed, so firmly was he convinced that religion was essentially a private affair between each person and his God that he studiously avoided religious discussions even with members of his own family lest he have undue influence upon their views.[4] "Say nothing of my religion," he admonished a correspondent who was seeking information on his personal beliefs for a biographical sketch. "It is known to my god and myself alone."[5] Although Jefferson did in fact discuss his religious beliefs in a few letters written late in life, before then he rarely touched on this subject in his surviving correspondence. Nevertheless, enough evidence has survived to make possible a reliable reconstruction of the main lines of his religious development before he became president.

Jefferson came of age at a critical point in the religious history of the Western world. By the middle of the eighteenth century the Enlightenment was in full swing in Europe and America. The Enlightenment was a highly complex movement that went through several different stages of development and varied in emphasis and strength from country to country, but in general it represented a decisive shift, at least among the educated elite, from a predominantly theological to a fundamentally secular world view. Inspired by the successes of the Scientific Revolution and weary of a long series of inconclusive religious wars and doctrinal disputes between Catholics and Protestants, enlightened

---

Malone, *Jefferson the President: First Term, 1801-1805* (Boston, 1970), p. 190-205; M. J. Mehta, "The Religion of Thomas Jefferson," *Indo-Asian Culture*, VI (Jan. 1967), 95-103; Royden J. Mott, "Sources of Jefferson's Ecclesiastical Views," *Church History*, III (Dec. 1934), 267-84; Merrill D. Peterson, *Thomas Jefferson and the New Nation, A Biography* (New York, 1970), p. 46-56, 955-61; Randall, *Life of Jefferson*, III, 553-61; Herbert W. Schneider, "The Enlightenment in Thomas Jefferson," *Ethics*, LIII (July 1943), 246-54; and Constance B. Schulz, "The Radical Religious Ideas of Thomas Jefferson and John Adams, A Comparison" (Ph.D. diss., University of Cincinnati, 1973), p. 176-264.

[4] One of TJ's grandsons, who was very close to him, testified as to his reticence with his family regarding his religion: "Of his peculiar religious opinions, his family know no more than the world. If asked by one of them, his opinion on any religious subject, his uniform reply was, that it was a subject each was bound to study assiduously for himself, unbiased by the opinions of others—it was a matter solely of conscience; after thorough investigation, they were responsible for the righteousness, but not the rightfulness of their opinions; that the expression of his opinion might influence theirs, and he would not give it!" Thomas Jefferson Randolph to Henry S. Randall, undated, Randall, *Life of Jefferson*, III, 672.

[5] TJ to Joseph Delaplaine, 25 Dec. 1816.

thinkers scorned metaphysical and theological speculation as useless and concentrated instead on the rational investigation of nature and society, making their main goal the improvement of man's lot in this life rather than the preparation of souls for salvation in a life to come. The rationalistic spirit that animated the Enlightenment inevitably brought it into conflict with organized Christianity, whose emphasis on the value of supernatural revelation, tradition, and ecclesiastical authority was rejected by those who insisted that religion, like all other institutions, had to be justified instead on the twin grounds of reasonableness and social utility. The Enlightenment's demand for the rationalization and demystification of religion evoked a variety of responses. Latitudinarians sought to prove the reasonableness of Christianity, Deists preached the sufficiency of natural religion, and skeptics and atheists rejected religion as superstition—and these beliefs all coexisted in many quarters with a continued defense of Christian orthodoxy on traditional grounds. The rationalistic critique of Christianity was far less prominent in the American Enlightenment than in its European counterpart owing to the high degree of religious toleration that existed in the British colonies. In the case of Jefferson, however, who in this respect was more closely attuned to the European Enlightenment than most of his American contemporaries, the tension between the spirit of critical analysis and the tenets of traditional Christianity was the central theme of his religious history.

The precise details and chronology are still somewhat obscure, but it seems clear that at some point during the 1760s Jefferson experienced a religious crisis in the course of which he rejected his ancestral Anglican creed and embraced instead a vaguely defined natural religion. This religious transformation was apparently caused by Jefferson's inability "from a very early part of my life" to accept the central Christian doctrine of the Trinity owing to the "difficulty of reconciling the ideas of Unity and Trinity" in the godhead.[6] His rationalism led him, in the words of a contemporary Virginian, to repudiate "as falsehoods things unsusceptible of strict demonstration."[7] Having rejected the dogma of the Trinity as a logical absurdity that could not be reconciled with human reason, Jefferson then subjected the rest of Christianity to the test of rational analysis and concluded that its basic doctrines were simply unacceptable to an enlightened man living in the eighteenth century. "The person who becomes sponsor for a child, according to the ritual of the church in which I was educated," he later explained in declining a French friend's request that he serve as godfather to his son, "makes a solemn profession, before god and the world, of faith in articles, which I had never sense enough to comprehend, and it has always appeared to me that comprehension must precede assent."[8]

The process by which Jefferson came to reject the validity of Christianity can be traced in part through an analysis of the passages from the works of Henry St. John, Viscount Bolingbroke, the rakish Tory political leader and man of letters, that Jefferson laboriously entered into his so-called "Literary Bible," a commonplace book consisting of extracts from the writings of various ancient and modern dramatists, philosophers, and poets, compiled largely in

[6] TJ to J. P. P. Derieux, 25 July 1788.

[7] Edmund Randolph, *History of Virginia*, ed. Arthur H. Shaffer (Charlottesville, Va., 1970), p. 183.

[8] TJ to J. P. P. Derieux, 25 July 1788.

the 1760s and early 1770s.[9] Bolingbroke's philosophical writings, which are a veritable *summa* of rationalistic criticisms of revealed religion, constitute by far the longest single entry in the "Literary Bible," running to almost sixty pages in manuscript, and are the only works therein that deal specifically with the subject of Christianity. It is therefore highly significant that Jefferson turned to these writings during what was evidently a period of intellectual turmoil in his youth, and it is almost certain, in view of his later remarks on religion, that the extracts he made from them reflect his own views. These selections, some of which he copied verbatim and others of which he paraphrased, suggest that Jefferson, like Bolingbroke, felt obliged to reject as contrary to human reason the basic foundations of Christianity. Thus, the Bible was not the inspired word of God because, as Bolingbroke argued, inspiration itself is a concept that cannot be proved by evidence "such as no reasonable man can refuse to admit" and also because the scriptures contain many "gross defects and palpable falsehoods . . . such as no man who acknowleges a supreme all-perfect being can beleive to be his word."[10] The Christian scheme of divine revelation was likewise objectionable inasmuch as it postulated that for centuries the one true God had restricted knowledge of himself to a small nation on the eastern rim of the Mediterranean while leaving the rest of the world in a spiritual void— "it is impossible to conceive, on grounds of human reason, to what purpose a divine economy, relative to the coming of Christ, should have confined the knowledge of the true god to the Jews, and have left the rest of mankind without god in the world."[11] No less absurd were the Christian plan of redemption and the doctrine of the fall of man upon which it was predicated. In regard to the latter, it was "in all circumstances, absolutely irreconcileable to every idea we can frame of wisdom, justice, and goodness, to say nothing of the dignity of the supreme being"; and as for the former, it was simply inconceivable that a just God "sent his only begotten son, who had not offended him, to be sacrificed by men, who had offended him, that he might expiate their sins, and satisfy his own anger."[12] In fact, Bolingbroke decided, God had not sent his son to redeem the world because Jesus was not divine. The miracles Jesus supposedly worked "were equivocal at best, such as credulous superstitious persons, and none else, believed, such as were frequently and universally imposed by the first fathers of the christian church, and as are so still by their successors, wherever ignorance or superstition abound"; he failed to reveal "an entire body of ethics, proved to be the law of nature from principles of reason, and reaching all the duties of life"; and the history of the development of Christian doctrine after his death indicated that the "system of belief and prac-

[9] Gilbert Chinard, ed., *The Literary Bible of Thomas Jefferson* (Baltimore, 1928). The original manuscript of this commonplace book is in DLC; a new edition of it is being prepared in this series. The specific works TJ extracted were Bolingbroke's posthumously published religious and philosophical essays. See *The Works of Lord Bolingbroke* (London, 1844), vols. III and IV. For the edition of Bolingbroke's works owned by TJ, see E. Millicent Sowerby, comp., *Catalogue of the Library of Thomas Jefferson* (Washington, D.C., 1952-59), No. 1265. Bolingbroke's religion and philosophy are analyzed in Walter M. Merrill, *From Statesman to Philosopher: A Study in Bolingbroke's Deism* (New York, 1949). See also Merrill D. Peterson, "Thomas Jefferson and the Enlightenment: Reflections on Literary Influence," *Lex et Scientia*, XI (1975), 103-7.

[10] Chinard, ed., *Literary Bible*, p. 40-41, 70.

[11] Same, p. 46-47.

[12] Same, p. 56-57.

tise" he taught were not "complete and perfect," forcing one to "assume that the son of god, who was sent by the father to make a new covenant with mankind, and to establish a new kingdom on the ruins of paganism, executed his commission imperfectly."[13] Finally, Bolingbroke was repelled by the nature of the God who was revealed in the Bible. In the Old Testament this deity was "partial, unjust, and cruel; delights in blood, commends assassinations, massacres and even exterminations of people," while in the New Testament he "elects some of his creatures to salvation, and predestinates others to damnation, even in the womb of their mothers."[14] In sum, traditional Christianity was unacceptable to a rational man because its fundamental doctrines were basically mysteries that could not be comprehended by human reason, and "No man can beleive he knoweth not what nor why."[15]

It is evident from random comments in Jefferson's writings that these selections from Bolingbroke's works accurately reflect his own considered opinion of Christianity before the late 1790s. For example, the Bible, far from being the revealed word of God, was for Jefferson merely a human "History" that he advised one of his nephews to read "as you would read Livy or Tacitus."[16] Instead of being the son of God, Jesus was only "a man, of illegitimate birth, of a benevolent heart, enthusiastic mind, who set out without pretensions to divinity, ended in believing them, and was punished capitally for sedition by being gibbetted according to the Roman law."[17] Rather than an inspiring chapter in the development of mankind, Jefferson saw in the history of Christianity a gloomy chronicle of successive "corruptions" of its pristine "Purity" and a series of misguided efforts to impose doctrinal uniformity upon the world, which had stifled free thought, led "Millions of innocent men, women, and children" to be "burnt, tortured, fined, imprisoned," and made "one half the world fools, and the other half hypocrites."[18] In fact, Jefferson confided to an English correspondent on the eve of the French Revolution, in one of his harshest criticisms of orthodox Christianity, most forms of Christian worship were nothing less than "demonism."[19]

As in the case of many other enlightened eighteenth-century thinkers, the young Jefferson turned to natural religion after discarding his inherited Christian faith. Calvin "was indeed an Atheist, which I can never be," Jefferson confided late in life to John Adams, thereby revealing the limits of his religious skepticism, "or rather his religion was Daemonism. If ever man worshipped a false god, he did."[20] For Jefferson, human reason, not supernatural revelation or ecclesiastical authority, henceforth became the sole arbiter of religious truth. Thus, through rational investigation he came to believe in a supreme being who created the universe and continued to sustain it by means of fixed, math-

[13] Same, p. 47-48, 50-51.

[14] Same, p. 64.

[15] Same, p. 49-50.

[16] TJ to Peter Carr, 10 Aug. 1787. See also TJ to Robert Skipwith, 3 Aug. 1771, where in the appended list of books the Bible is entered under "History" rather than "Religion."

[17] TJ to Peter Carr, 10 Aug. 1787.

[18] TJ, Outline of Argument in Support of His Resolutions for Disestablishment in Virginia, [Oct.-Dec. 1776]; Thomas Jefferson, *Notes on the State of Virginia*, ed. William Peden (Chapel Hill, N.C., 1955), p. 159-60.

[19] TJ to Richard Price, 8 Jan. 1789.

[20] TJ to John Adams, 11 Apr. 1823 (Appendix).

ematically precise natural laws—"the Creator and benevolent governor of the world."[21] Disdaining miraculous interventions in human affairs, this benevolent being revealed himself to all men at all times and in all places through the natural wonders of the created universe and was therefore infinitely superior to the arbitrary, jealous, mysterious, and vindictive deity that Jefferson perceived in the Old and New Testaments. "The missionary of supernatural religion appeals to the testimony of men he never knew, and of whom the infidel he labors to convert never heard, for the truth of those extraordinary events which prove the revelation he preaches . . . ," Jefferson quoted approvingly from Bolingbroke. "But the missionary of natural religion can appeal at all times, and every where, to present and immediate evidence, to the testimony of sense and intellect, for the truth of those miracles which he brings in proof: the constitution of the mundane system being in a very proper sense an aggregate of miracles."[22]

In addition to substituting the God of nature for the God of revelation, Jefferson also found a new basis for morality to replace the traditional spiritual sanctions of Christianity. Under the influence of the writings of the Scottish philosopher Henry Home, Lord Kames, Jefferson concluded that God had endowed each person with an innate faculty for distinguishing right from wrong, known as the moral sense. The moral sense performed this function, he believed, by making virtue pleasing and vice displeasing to men, nature having "implanted in our breasts a love of others, a sense of duty to them, a moral instinct in short, which prompts us irresistibly to feel and succour their distresses."[23] At the same time, by directing men to differentiate between good and evil on the basis of social utility, the moral standards prescribed by this faculty varied from age to age and culture to culture—a species of relativism Jefferson accepted with equanimity. The moral sense did not work automatically, however. It had to be instructed by education and example to incline a person toward right conduct. In order therefore to cultivate and nurture his own moral sense, Jefferson as a young man turned to the ethical precepts of the classical Epicurean and Stoic philosophers, thereby seeking to achieve the good life as defined by the former through the stern self-discipline enjoined by the latter. For at that time he wholeheartedly agreed with the contention of his intellectual mentor Bolingbroke that a "system of ethics . . . collected from the writings of antient heathen moralists of Tully, of Seneca, of Epictetus, and

[21] Same.

[22] Chinard, ed., *Literary Bible*, p. 49.

[23] TJ to Thomas Law, 13 June 1814 (Appendix). TJ also discussed the moral sense in letters to Robert Skipwith, 3 Aug. 1771; to Martha Jefferson, 11 Dec. 1783; to Peter Carr, 10 Aug. 1787; and to John Adams, 14 Oct. 1816. See also Koch, *Philosophy of Jefferson*, p. 15-22, and Morton White, *The Philosophy of the American Revolution* (New York, 1978), p. 113-27, for more detailed analyses of TJ's concept of the moral sense, with the former stressing the influence of Kames and the latter that of Jean Jacques Burlamaqui. Sowerby, comp., *Catalogue*, No. 1254, offers evidence which seems to indicate that TJ was more heavily influenced by Kames than by Burlamaqui. Garry Wills' *Inventing America: Jefferson's Declaration of Independence* (New York, 1978), p. 200-206, argues that Francis Hutcheson decisively influenced TJ's concept of the moral sense. Ronald Hamowy, "Jefferson and the Scottish Enlightenment: A Critique of Garry Wills's *Inventing America: Jefferson's Declaration of Independence*," *WMQ*, 3d ser., xxxvi (Oct. 1979), 503-23, refutes Wills' thesis. It is also notable that TJ referred to Kames, but not to Hutcheson, in his letter to Thomas Law on the moral sense.

others, would be more full, more entire, more coherent, and more clearly deduced from unquestionable principles of knowledge" than that taught in the New Testament by Jesus of Nazareth—a judgment Jefferson radically revised during his administration as president.[24]

Jefferson's early rejection of traditional Christian doctrine and adoption of natural religion left him with a lifelong belief in the need for freedom of thought and the primacy of morality over dogma in religious affairs. Each person, he decided, had a natural right to worship—or not to worship—God as he pleased. Since the very essence of religion was the free assent of the human mind to what it deemed to be God's truth, no one could be forced to believe what his intellect rejected, for coercion produced hypocrisy rather than conviction and was thus an affront to God and man alike. Everyone, therefore, must be free to decide for himself the truth or falsity of the claims of particular religions— hence the fervor with which Jefferson threw himself into the struggle during the American Revolution to disestablish the Anglican Church in Virginia.[25] By the same token, Jefferson welcomed the diversity of religious views that freedom of inquiry entailed. Although he personally rejected supernatural rev- elation and church authority as valid sources of religious truth, his deep com- mitment to freedom of conscience led him to respect the opinions of those who did accept them. For in regard to religion what ultimately mattered to him was the quality of a person's life, not the truth of the doctrines in which he believed or the nature of the church to which he belonged. In New York and Pennsylvania, he wrote in *Notes on Virginia*, "Religion is well supported; of various kinds, indeed, but all good enough; all sufficient to preserve peace and good order."[26] His manner of expression in this case was unusually harsh, and elsewhere he expressed the same sentiment in milder terms. But the main point is clear: the best measure of the efficacy of any religion is the character of the moral standards it instills in its adherents rather than the substance of the theological doctrines it teaches. Whereas in his opinion dogma dealt with mat- ters that were beyond human understanding and that historically had provoked bitter strife, morality regulated human relations in the social world to which men had been destined by nature, and had the potential to generate harmony in society—a key element in the Jeffersonian hierarchy of values. "Reading, reflection and time have convinced me," he noted shortly after his retirement from the presidency, expressing a long-held view, "that the interests of society require the observation of those moral precepts only in which all religions agree, (for all forbid us to murder, steal, plunder, or bear false witness) and

[24] Chinard, ed., *Literary Bible*, p. 50. The preponderance of ancient over Christian moralists is evident in the reading lists appended to or contained in the letters of advice TJ wrote to Robert Skipwith, 3 Aug. 1771; and to Peter Carr, 19 Aug. 1785 and 10 Aug. 1787. TJ's indebtedness to classical culture is discussed in Karl Lehmann, *Thomas Jefferson, American Humanist* (Chicago, 1947), and Louis B. Wright, "Thomas Jefferson and the Classics," American Philosophical Society, *Proceedings*, LXXXVII (Apr. 1943), 223-33. For an exposition of the way in which the tension between classicism and Christianity helped to produce the Enlightenment, see Peter Gay, *The Enlightenment: An Interpretation. The Rise of Modern Paganism* (New York, 1966), p. 207-419.

[25] TJ, Outline of Argument in Support of His Resolutions for Disestablishment in Virginia, [Oct.-Dec. 1776]; TJ, Bill for Establishing Religious Freedom, [1779]; *Notes on Virginia*, ed. Peden, p. 158-61; Willibald M. Ploechl, "Thomas Jefferson, Author of the Statute of Virginia for Religious Freedom," *The Jurist*, III (Jan. 1943), 3-51.

[26] *Notes on Virginia*, ed. Peden, p. 161.

that we should not intermeddle with the particular dogmas in which all religions differ, and which are totally unconnected with morality."[27] Thus Jefferson's religion was basically moralistic in emphasis, as befitted one whose controlling purpose in life was the improvement of man and society in this world rather than the next.

Despite the leading role Jefferson played in the campaign to separate church and state in Virginia, his own religious views did not become a major public issue until the time of the bitter party conflict between Federalists and Republicans in the late 1790s. After leveling sporadic allegations of infidelity against Jefferson beginning as early as the election of 1796,[28] Federalist leaders and their clerical supporters in New England and the middle states made this theme the centerpiece of a powerful propaganda offensive that was designed to blacken his character and destroy his electoral support during the presidential campaign of 1800. As Jefferson's prospects for winning the presidency in 1800 increased, some Federalists, desperately eager to retain control of the executive branch of government, unleashed a frenzied barrage of vituperative attacks upon his personal character and public record. They poured scorn on him for his alleged cowardice as governor of Virginia. They heaped ridicule on him as an unworldly philosopher and scientist who was unfit to conduct weighty affairs of state. They denounced the imprudent letter to his Italian friend Philip Mazzei in which he suggested that Washington was an apostate to revolutionary principles. They charged that he was an undiscriminating Francophile whose inordinate sympathy for the French Revolution would bring the worst excesses of Jacobinism to the United States. They warned that he was an enemy of the federal Constitution who wanted to undo the work of the Philadelphia Convention. And they argued that he was a narrow-minded agrarian who was irrationally hostile to the interests of commerce and industry. But most of all the Federalists and their ministerial allies arraigned Jefferson before the bar of public opinion as an unbeliever who was unworthy to serve as chief magistrate of a Christian nation.[29]

Since Jefferson had carefully concealed his private religious views from the public, his critics seized upon selected passages from *Notes on Virginia*, his first and only published book, to prove their contention that he was fundamentally hostile to religion. Hence they charged that his refusal to admit that a "universal deluge" was a sufficient explanation for the presence of shells high atop the Andes was a veiled attack upon the account of the flooding of the world in Genesis, which made the Virginia leader a party to that "war upon revelation [in which] infidels have levelled their batteries against the miraculous *facts* of the scripture: well knowing that if its historical truth can be overturned, there is an end to its claim of inspiration."[30] They pointed to his "suggestion" that

[27] TJ to James Fishback, 27 Sep. 1809 (Appendix).

[28] William Loughton Smith, *The Pretensions of Thomas Jefferson to the Presidency Examined; and the Charges against John Adams Refuted, Part 1* (Philadelphia, 1796), p. 14, 36-40.

[29] Charles O. Lerche, Jr., "Jefferson and the Election of 1800: A Case Study in the Political Smear," *WMQ*, 3d ser., v (Oct. 1948), 467-91. Linda Kerber, *Federalists in Dissent: Imagery and Ideology in Jeffersonian America* (Ithaca, N.Y., 1970), p. 53-56, and Richard Buel, Jr., *Securing the Revolution: Ideology in American Politics, 1789-1815* (Ithaca, N.Y., 1972), p. 231-34, also deal with Federalist criticism of TJ's religion.

[30] John M. Mason, *The Voice of Warning, to Christians, on the Ensuing Election of a President of the United States* (New York, 1800), p. 9-14.

blacks might have been originally created as a distinct race as proof of his disbelief in the biblical account of the creation of man and argued that if Jefferson's hypothesis were correct it would mean that "the history of the bible, which knows of but *one* [race], is a string of falsehoods from the book of Genesis to that of Revelation; and the whole system of redemption, predicated on the *unity* of the human race, is a cruel fiction."[31] They construed his remark that farmers were the chosen people of God "if ever he had a chosen people" to signify that he rejected the providential role of the Jews in the Christian scheme of salvation history, and they contended that his proposal not to teach the Bible to young children indicated his opposition to religious education in general.[32] But worst of all, in the opinion of Jefferson's critics, was his argument that the state should refrain from interfering with religion because, among other things, "it does me no injury for my neighbor to say there are twenty gods or no god. It neither picks my pocket nor breaks my leg."[33] Instead of indicating Jefferson's tolerance for divergent religious points of view, they insisted that at the very least this statement revealed a disturbing indifference to religion that could have profoundly dangerous social consequences. "Let my neighbor once persuade himself that there is no God," a New York minister warned, "and he will soon pick my pocket, and break not only my *leg* but my *neck*. If there be no God, there is no law, no future account; government then is the ordinance of man only, and we cannot be subject for conscience sake."[34]

In the light of this evidence, Jefferson's opponents triumphantly proclaimed, the conclusion was clear. Jefferson was an atheist, an infidel, or at best a deist (in their zeal to undermine his popular support his critics frequently sacrificed analytical rigor to rhetorical effect) who was hostile to Christianity and therefore unworthy to serve in the highest office possible for the American people to bestow upon a fellow citizen. Elect Jefferson to the presidency, they warned, and dire consequences would ensue for the fledgling republic. His victory would arouse the wrath of God himself, "destroy religion, introduce immorality . . . loosen all the bonds of society," and undermine the standing of the United States among the nations of the world. "Can serious and reflecting men look about them and doubt," asked "A Christian Federalist," conjuring up an awful vision of the apocalypse that was bound to result from the triumph of the allegedly irreligious Republican leader, "that if Jefferson is elected, and the Jacobins get into authority, that those morals which protect our lives from the knife of the assassin—which guard the chastity of our wives and daughters from seduction and violence—defend our property from plunder and devastation, and shield our religion from contempt and profanation, will not be trampled upon and exploded."[35]

The object of this relentless wave of criticism steadfastly refused to reply to his critics during the election of 1800, believing as a matter of principle that he was accountable to God alone for his religious convictions and realizing as a practical matter that nothing he could say would silence his detractors. As a

---

[31] Same, p. 17.

[32] Same, p. 17-18; William Linn, *Serious Considerations on the Election of a President: Addressed to the Citizens of the United States* (New York, 1800), p. 14-16.

[33] *Notes on Virginia*, ed. Peden, p. 159.

[34] Linn, *Serious Considerations*, p. 19.

[35] "A Christian Federalist" to the Voters of Delaware, 21 Sep. 1800, printed in *History of American Presidential Elections, 1789-1968*, ed. Arthur M. Schlesinger and others (New York, 1971), I, 150.

result, charges that he was an irreligious enemy of Christianity plagued Jefferson throughout his administration as president and especially during his first term. As his popularity rose and as the power of the Republican party increased throughout the Union, the Federalists and their supporters among the clergy found that the accusation of infidelity was one of the few weapons they could still use against him with some hope of success. Moreover, although later attacks on Jefferson's views of religion never again reached the intensity of those in 1800, the technique of criticism, at least on the level of published discourse, continued to focus on his *Notes on Virginia*. For example, a New York minister, known more familiarly as the author of a famous yuletide poem, published a pamphlet during the election of 1804 in which he examined the same parts of this book and arrived at the same conclusion as his predecessors four years before. "But can any person who believes the testimony of his senses and reason," he asked, "deny that the book which offers a theory of the earth contrary to the scripture account of creation; which denies the possibility of a universal deluge; which considers the Bible history as no better than ordinary tradition; which extols Voltaire and the French Encyclopedists, the imps who have inspired all the wickedness with which the world has of late years been infested; which says that the natives of America are older than those of Asia, though scripture says that the world was peopled from one pair, placed in Asia; which considers it as a doubtful matter whether the blacks be really men, or only an intermediate grade between us and the brutes; and which esteems all religions 'good enough'; can he deny that this book is an instrument of infidelity?"[36]

By that time, however, Jefferson had in fact responded to accusations that he was irreligious and hostile to Christianity, though, characteristically, he did so privately rather than publicly.

II

The charges of infidelity that were hurled against Jefferson by his Federalist and clerical adversaries set in motion a train of events that led him to compose his famous "Syllabus . . . of the merit of the doctrines of Jesus" in 1803 and its less well known successor, "The Philosophy of Jesus," in the following year.

[36] Clement C. Moore, *Observations upon Certain Passages in Mr. Jefferson's Notes on Virginia, which Appear to Have a Tendency to Subvert Religion, and Establish a False Philosophy* (New York, 1804), p. 29. The Rev. Mr. Moore later wrote *The Night before Christmas.*

Luebke, "Origins of Jefferson's Anti-Clericalism," p. 344-54, argues that TJ's hostility to the clergy originated in response to ministerial attacks on his religious views during the presidential election campaign of 1800. It would be more accurate to say that these attacks merely brought to the surface a long-standing animosity against the clergy that TJ had theretofore managed to keep to himself. As early as 1775, for example, in an analysis of the relationship between Christianity and the common law, he had criticized English judges for being "accomplices in the frauds of the clergy; and even bolder than they are." Gilbert Chinard, ed., *The Commonplace Book of Thomas Jefferson* (Baltimore, 1926), p. 362. It is true that TJ was more open in expressing his anticlericalism after 1800 than before, but it is equally indubitable that his anticlerical sentiments long predated the electoral contest of that year. It is also interesting that TJ's anticlericalism did not distinguish between Congregationalist and Episcopal ministers, who were the most outspoken in their criticism of him on religious grounds, and Baptist and Methodist ministers, who generally supported him because of his advocacy of religious freedom.

In compiling these two works, Jefferson was motivated by more than just a simple wish to rebut those who were assailing his character on religious grounds. He was also responding to another problem that was of deep concern to him: how to guarantee the perpetuation of republican government in the United States at a time when, as it seemed to him, political factionalism and social disharmony were threatening to undermine its basic foundations. Jefferson's solution to this problem was an effort to foster the social harmony that he considered essential for the survival of America's republican experiment by formulating a moralistic version of Christianity on which all men of good will could agree. Thus, in addition to demonstrating to a select group of relatives and friends that he was indeed a good Christian according to his own lights, Jefferson also wrote the "Syllabus" and compiled "The Philosophy of Jesus" to set forth a demystified form of Christianity that he deemed appropriate for a society that had chosen to live according to republican principles. Typically, he went to great lengths to present that version of Christianity to his countrymen through the medium of an author other than himself.

Jefferson's apprehensions over the future of republicanism in the United States grew markedly in the 1790s as political life in the new nation was polarized by the rise of two national parties with sharply opposing principles and policies. As the country divided along Republican and Federalist lines, Jefferson became increasingly convinced that the very future of popular government in America was the central issue at stake between the two parties. The institution of the Hamiltonian fiscal system, the adoption of a foreign policy that seemingly appeased aristocratic Britain while affronting republican France, the employment of military force in Pennsylvania to suppress popular discontent, the creation of a large standing army during the XYZ crisis, and the use of the Sedition Act to silence Republican political criticism of the Adams administration—these things portended nothing less to Jefferson than a settled Federalist design to create a monarchical government in the United States.[37] Nor was this a passing mood. Jefferson remained convinced until the end of his life that only the triumph of the Republican party in 1800 had prevented the Federalists from carrying out this nefarious design and thereby assured the continuance of America's experiment in republicanism. Just a few months before his death he pointed with pride to his leadership of the Republican cause during the bitter party battles of the 1790s as the most important public service he had ever rendered the nation, and he claimed that the "spirits of the people were so much rendered desperate by the X.Y.Z. imposture, and other stratagems and machinations," that if it had not been for his own efforts and those of his supporters "they would have sunk into apathy and monarchy, as the only form of government which could maintain itself."[38]

At the same time that Jefferson became apprehensive over putative Federalist threats to the survival of republican government in the new nation, he repeatedly

---

[37] TJ's fear that the Federalists intended to establish a monarchical form of government is a recurrent theme in his correspondence from the early 1790s onward. See, for example, TJ to George Washington, 23 May 1792; to Lafayette, 16 June 1792; to Philip Mazzei, 24 Apr. 1796; to Charles Pinckney, 29 Oct. 1799; and to John Dickinson, 23 July 1801. For an analysis of the ideological presuppositions that inclined TJ and his fellow Republicans to view Federalist policies in this light, see Lance Banning, *The Jeffersonian Persuasion: Evolution of a Party Ideology* (Ithaca, N.Y., 1978).

[38] TJ, "Thoughts on Lotteries," [Feb. 1826].

lamented that political differences between adherents of the two parties were becoming so acrimonious that they were undermining the social harmony and tolerance he thought essential for a republic. Differences of opinion over political issues were only to be expected in a free government and might even lead to sharp debate between the contending sides. But if such disputes became so intense as to destroy social harmony, there would be no possibility of compromise to the satisfaction of all the parties involved. Society would then become divided into hostile classes and interests, with each one striving to advance its goals at the expense of the others instead of all cooperating together harmoniously to achieve the public good. "The passions are too high at present, to be cooled in our day," he wrote to a southern supporter soon after taking office as vice-president, in a frank revelation of his fear of the corrosive impact of partisan strife on social harmony. "You and I have seen warm debates and high political passions. But gentlemen of different politics would then speak to each other and separate the business of the Senate from that of society. It is not so now. Men who have been intimate all their lives, cross the streets to avoid meeting, and turn their heads another way, lest they should be obliged to touch their hats. This may do for young men with whom passion is enjoyment. But it is affecting to peaceable minds."[39] Since Jefferson believed that the preservation of harmonious social relations was to a large extent a matter of personal morality and character, it is not surprising that as the eighteenth century drew to a close he began to be interested in a moral system that would be more efficacious for this purpose than that offered by the classical philosophers who had hitherto been his main ethical guides.

Jefferson's growing concern during the 1790s with the need to preserve social harmony in the midst of sharp partisan conflicts coincided with a significant shift in his personal attitude toward Christianity. Ironically, at the very time public attacks on him as an enemy of Christianity were mounting, Jefferson was in the process of adopting a much more sympathetic view of that religion than he had previously entertained. This change came about largely as a result of the influence of Dr. Joseph Priestley's *An History of the Corruptions of Christianity*, a two-volume work that Jefferson acquired and read sometime after 1793. Priestley, a noted English chemist and Unitarian theologian, set forth a highly demythologized version of Christianity in these tomes, which so impressed Jefferson that he adopted key parts of it and later described the work itself as the "groundwork of my view of this subject" and as one of the bases "of my own faith."[40] The English champion of Unitarianism, who became one

[39] TJ to Edward Rutledge, 24 June 1797. TJ also revealed the high value he placed on social harmony in republics in a letter to Elbridge Gerry: "It will be a great blessing to our country if we can once more restore harmony and social love among its citizens" (TJ to Gerry, 29 Mch. 1801). Indeed, a recent study of TJ's presidency argues that "the fundamental characteristic of Jefferson's personality seems to have been an ardent desire for harmony, in both his public and his private life" (Robert M. Johnstone, Jr., *Jefferson and the Presidency: Leadership in the Young Republic* [Ithaca, N.Y., 1978], p. 34).

[40] TJ to Martha Jefferson Randolph, 25 Apr. 1803; TJ to John Adams, 22 Aug. 1813 (Appendix). Although *Corruptions of Christianity* was originally published in Birmingham in 1782, TJ owned a 1793 edition printed in London, suggesting that he probably read it at some point in the mid-1790s (Sowerby, comp., *Catalogue*, No. 1526).

In addition to *Corruptions of Christianity*, TJ listed three other works in his 22 Aug. 1813 letter to John Adams, which together, he claimed, formed "the basis of my own

of Jefferson's friends after moving to the United States in 1794 to escape political persecution in his native land, argued that Christianity was originally a simple religion that had been corrupted by the early church in a misguided effort to make it intellectually respectable to pagans and by later churchmen for the less edifying purpose of increasing their power over the laity. The essence of true Christianity, Priestley insisted, could be summed up in a few plain propositions. There was but one God, and he had given Jesus the special mission of revealing his true nature to the world and of teaching men how to lead virtuous lives on earth so that they would be rewarded rather than punished in the life to come. Jesus was not a member of the godhead, nor did he ever claim to be. Nevertheless, God signified his approval of Jesus' teachings by enabling him to perform miracles and to rise from the dead, thereby making him the greatest moral teacher who had ever lived. As a result, mankind was obliged to worship the one true God and to follow the moral teachings of Jesus. Virtually everything else in orthodox Christianity—doctrines like the Trinity, the atonement, and original sin, as well as devotional practices like the veneration of relics and saints—was a corruption of the primitive purity of the Christian message and had to be discarded so as to restore Christianity to its pristine simplicity and thus make it acceptable to modern men, who were otherwise inclined to reject it as a mass of superstitions.[41]

Priestley's work made a deep and lasting impression on Jefferson. It convinced him that the early Christians had a Unitarian concept of God and that therefore one like himself could be a true Christian without being a Trinitarian. It persuaded him that Jesus had never laid claim to divinity, which to him made Jesus more credible as a great moral teacher. It increased his appreciation of Christian morality by demonstrating to his satisfaction that the dogmas that had led him to reject the validity of Christianity in his youth were in fact

---

faith." These works were Priestley's *History of Early Opinions Concerning Jesus Christ*, 4 vols. (London, 1786); Conyers Middleton's *A Letter from Rome* (London, 1729); and Middleton's *A Letter to Dr. Waterland* (London, 1731). (Sowerby, comp., *Catalogue*, Nos. 1525, 1527.) Of the four, *Corruptions of Christianity* undoubtedly had the most crucial impact on the development of TJ's demythologized Christian faith. *Early Opinions Concerning Jesus Christ* merely elaborated Priestley's view of Jesus as a human reformer who acted under a special mandate from God, and was not acquired by TJ until after he had written the "Syllabus" in April 1803, by which time he had formed a basic attitude toward Christianity that remained essentially unchanged until the time of his death in 1826 (Sowerby, comp., *Catalogue*, No. 1527). In contrast, the two works by Middleton, an iconoclastic English scholar who was perhaps best known for his attack on the validity of miracles in the post-apostolic age, almost certainly did more to induce TJ to adopt a skeptical approach to religious problems than to inspire any positive spiritual beliefs in him. Whereas the *Letter from Rome* was a study of the pagan origins of many Roman Catholic practices, the *Letter to Waterland* was basically a critique of belief in the literal inerrancy of the Bible. Furthermore, as Peterson, *Jefferson*, p. 51, points out, it is virtually certain that TJ read Middleton before the American Revolution, thus confirming Priestley's pivotal importance in the emergence of TJ's demystified variant of Christianity. See also n. 42 below.

[41] Priestley summarized his primary thesis in *Corruptions of Christianity*, II, 440-66. See also Ira T. Brown, "The Religion of Joseph Priestley," *Pennsylvania History*, XXIV (Apr. 1957), 85-100, and Caroline Robbins, "Honest Heretic: Joseph Priestley in America," Am. Phil. Soc., *Procs.*, CVI (Feb. 1962), 60-76.

perversions of the primitive Christian message rather than integral parts of it.[42] Rejecting Priestley's Socinianism, he still refused to entertain the possibility that Jesus had performed miracles or risen from the dead because these actions contravened what he understood to be the unvarying character of the laws of nature. Otherwise, he fully accepted Priestley's contention that true Christianity was basically a simple religion whose original emphasis on the unity of God and the primacy of morality over dogma had been perverted through the course of history by the development of metaphysical and theological doctrines no human mind could understand and by the introduction of forms of worship no rational man could practice without degrading himself. Unlike his English intellectual mentor, however, Jefferson most frequently attributed these corruptions to the sinister machinations of the clergy, who, he believed, deliberately sought to make religion as mysterious as possible in order to render themselves indispensable to the people over whom they presumed to exercise spiritual authority. "The mild and simple principles of the Christian philosophy," he argued shortly after being sworn in as president for the first time, "would produce too much calm, too much regularity of good, to extract from it's disciples a support for a numerous priesthood, were they not to sophisticate it, ramify it, split it into hairs, and twist it's texts till they cover the divine morality of it's author with mysteries, and require a priesthood to explain them."[43] Jefferson had long suspected that primitive Christianity had been corrupted in the course of history, but it remained for Priestley to enable him to work out the full implications of this insight.[44] Thus, by presenting him with a demystified form of Christianity that comported with his rationalistic world view, Priestley made it possible for Jefferson to regard himself as a genuine Christian and launched him on the quest for the authentic teachings of Jesus that was to lead in time to the "Syllabus" and "The Philosophy of Jesus."

As Jefferson's view of Christianity was changing under the impact of the writings of Dr. Priestley, he began to consider the relationship between republicanism and Christianity under the influence of that perennial gadfly, Dr. Benjamin Rush. Jefferson first became friendly with the noted Philadelphia physician and social reformer during the Revolution, when, as fellow members of the Continental Congress, they had worked together to advance the twin causes of American independence and union. Although both men remained convinced republicans, their paths had later diverged owing to their sharply differing perceptions of the ultimate significance of America's republican destiny. Whereas the philosophically rationalistic Jefferson regarded republicanism as basically a secular movement that was designed to improve humanity and society by restoring the natural rights of man and expanding the scope of self-government, the theologically universalist Rush considered it as essentially a religious movement that was part of a divine plan to bring about the kingdom

[42] The impact of *Corruptions of Christianity* on TJ can readily be seen by comparing his view of Jesus before and after he read this work. Thus, in 1787, TJ believed that Jesus had had "pretensions to divinity," whereas in 1803 he maintained that Jesus had never claimed to be divine (TJ to Peter Carr, 10 Aug. 1787; TJ to Benjamin Rush, 21 Apr. 1803, Appendix).

[43] TJ to Elbridge Gerry, 29 Mch. 1801.

[44] TJ, Outline of Argument in Support of His Resolutions for Disestablishment in Virginia, [Oct.-Dec. 1776]; Notes on Heresy, [Oct.-Dec. 1776]; *Notes on Virginia*, ed. Peden, p. 159.

of God on earth by freeing mankind from the burden of royal and ecclesiastical oppression through the spread of the principles of human equality and Christian charity.[45] Thus Rush believed that Christianity and republicanism, far from being antithetical, actually stood in a symbiotic relationship with each other. The progress of both was necessary to achieve the millennium to which he looked forward. "Republican forms of government are the best repositories of the Gospel," he declared in 1791. "I therefore suppose they are intended as preludes to a glorious manifestation of its power and influence upon the hearts of men."[46] Convinced that Jefferson's secular outlook on life was blinding him to the most vital dimension of America's republican experiment, the zealous Rush characteristically took it upon himself to set forth his alternative view of the matter to his erring Virginia friend.

Rush began to carry out his self-appointed mission after Jefferson emerged from retirement and returned to Philadelphia in 1797 to serve as vice-president. During the next several years the two men discussed the subject of Christianity in a series of conversations, which, Jefferson later recalled, "served as an Anodyne to the afflictions of the crisis through which our country was then labouring.[47]" In view of Jefferson's reluctance to discuss his religious beliefs, it seems plausible to assume that it was Rush who initiated these talks. At any rate, in the course of the conversations Jefferson denied Federalist charges that he was hostile to Christianity and indicated that although he accepted certain Christian doctrines he did not believe in the divinity of Jesus.[48] Rush welcomed these professions of support for Christianity, all the more so since he had suspected Jefferson of infidelity, but he was disappointed by Jefferson's unwillingness to go even further and acknowledge that Christ was divine. In order to correct this deficiency Rush urged Jefferson to read William Paley's *A View of the Evidences of Christianity*, a widely used handbook of orthodox criticisms of Deism by a noted English moralist and theologian, and extracted a promise from him to provide a written statement on his religious beliefs for

[45] Julian P. Boyd, "Thomas Jefferson's 'Empire of Liberty,' " *Virginia Quarterly Review*, xxiv (Autumn 1948), 538-54; Donald J. D'Elia, "The Republican Theology of Benjamin Rush," *Pa. History*, xxxiii (Apr. 1966), 187-204; D'Elia, "Jefferson, Rush, and the Limits of Philosophical Friendship," Am. Phil. Soc., *Procs.*, cxvii (Oct. 1973), 333-43.

[46] Benjamin Rush to Elhanan Winchester, 12 Nov. 1791, *Letters of Benjamin Rush*, ed. L. H. Butterfield (Princeton, 1951), i, 611.

[47] TJ to Benjamin Rush, 21 Apr. 1803 (Appendix).

[48] According to an autobiographical account by Rush, TJ assured him that "he believed in the divine mission of the Saviour of the World, but he did not believe that he was the Son of God in the way in which many Christians believed it," that "he believed further in the divine institution of the Sabbath, which he conceived to be a great blessing to the world, more especially to poor people and slaves," and that "he believed likewise in the resurrection and a future state of rewards and punishments." *The Autobiography of Benjamin Rush*, ed. George W. Corner (Princeton, 1948), p. 152. Rush's testimony cannot be accepted at face value. To be sure, TJ's implicit rejection of Jesus' divinity and avowed belief in life after death comport with what is known about his religious beliefs, and his statement about the Sabbath sounds plausible (TJ to Rush, 21 Apr. 1803, and accompanying "Syllabus," Appendix). Otherwise, it is highly unlikely that he literally believed Jesus was the "Saviour of the World," since he consistently described him as nothing more than a great Jewish moral reformer, and it is virtually certain he did not believe in Jesus' resurrection, since he specifically rejected it as a corruption of Christianity (TJ to William Short, 31 Oct. 1819, n. 3, Appendix).

Rush's perusal. But Jefferson found himself unable at this time to state his view of Christianity in a way that would satisfy Rush, and therefore he hesitated to fulfill his pledge.[49]

Personal conversation having failed to achieve the desired objective, the indefatigable Rush next resorted to epistolary persuasion. As the presidential campaign of 1800 progressed and the prospect of a Republican electoral triumph grew more probable, he addressed two important letters to Jefferson at Monticello, stressing the theme that Christianity and republicanism were organically related. Writing in August, Rush first reminded Jefferson of his promised statement on religion and then, in an obvious effort to instruct him as to the real significance of America's republican experiment, emphasized that true Christianity was the firmest guarantee for the success of republican government. "I have always considered Christianity as the *strong ground* of Republicanism," he observed to the man he now thought was most likely to become the nation's next chief magistrate: "Its Spirit is opposed, not only to the Splendor, but even to the very *forms* of monarchy, and many of its precepts have for their Objects republican liberty and equality, as well as simplicity, integrity, and Œconomy in government. It is only necessary for Republicanism to ally itself to the christian Religion, to overturn all the corrupted political and religious institutions in the world."[50]

At first Jefferson was unresponsive to Rush's exposition of the interrelationship between republicanism and Christianity. In replying to his Philadelphia correspondent he firmly maintained that his attitude toward Christianity would "displease neither the rational Christian or Deist; and would reconcile many to a character they have too hastily rejected." Nevertheless, he pleaded that he still needed more time to produce a satisfactory statement of his religious creed. Then, ignoring the main point of Rush's letter, he lashed out at his clerical tormentors, charging that they were secretly bent upon making Christianity the legally established religion of the United States.[51] Fearing that the entire thrust of his argument had been misunderstood, Rush hastened to reassure Jefferson that an established church was the farthest thing from his mind. It was not through a union of church and state that Christianity would advance the cause of republicanism, Rush wrote in October, since that would only corrupt religion and politics alike. Rather, this advancement would come about through the voluntary acceptance by a free people of the "simple doctrines and precepts of Christianity," doctrines and precepts which, he readily admitted, had been "dishonoured by being mixed with human follies and crimes by the corrupted Churches of Europe," but which, when purged of centuries of accumulated dross and restored to their primitive simplicity, would, he was certain, eventually lead to the spread of true Christianity and republican forms of government throughout the globe.[52]

Although Jefferson did not reply to Rush's second letter, in the end the Philadelphian's proselytizing efforts enjoyed a limited success. By forcing Jefferson to confront the issue of the relationship between Christianity and republicanism at a time when his attitude toward the former was undergoing a significant change, Rush was instrumental in inducing him to take a view of

[49] Benjamin Rush to TJ, 22 Aug. 1800 (Appendix).
[50] Same.
[51] TJ to Benjamin Rush, 23 Sep. 1800 (Appendix).
[52] Benjamin Rush to TJ, 6 Oct. 1800 (Appendix).

the subject that was somewhat in accord with his own. To be sure, Jefferson always remained immune to Rush's extravagant millennial hopes, and he refused to follow him in accepting such fundamental Christian doctrines as the divinity of Jesus. But he did decide that Christian morality could serve as one of the basic foundations of the country's republican experiment by promoting the social harmony among the citizenry that he considered essential for the survival of the republic. The "Christian religion," he told one of his New England supporters soon after taking over the reins of government from John Adams, "when divested of the rags in which [the clergy] have inveloped it, is a religion of all others most friendly to liberty, science and the freest expansions of the human mind."[53] It would be wrong to attribute Jefferson's new appreciation of the role of Christian morality in a republican society exclusively to Rush's influence, but it would also be unfair to underestimate the Philadelphia doctor's role in its development.

Thus as Jefferson began his first term as president several factors had converged to arouse his interest in ascertaining the true teachings of Jesus. Public criticism of his alleged atheism and infidelity had caused him to reexamine his attitude toward Christianity. The fierce party conflicts of the 1790s had disrupted the social harmony he valued as one of the main pillars of republicanism and made him sensitive to the need for a more effective system of ethical principles to inform the moral sense of the new nation than the one provided by his classical Epicurean and Stoic guides. The writings of Dr. Priestley had offered him a version of Christianity that was well suited to his rationalistic frame of mind. And his exchanges with Dr. Rush had heightened his awareness of the social utility of Christian morality. Yet for a number of reasons two more years were to pass before he openly formed these disparate elements into a coherent system. To begin with, his electoral victory over John Adams convinced him that the specter of monarchical government in the United States had been banished and temporarily soothed his fears about the threat posed to social harmony by severe partisan conflicts. Accordingly, by adopting a conciliatory policy toward the defeated Federalists, he hoped to entice the bulk of their followers to enlist under the Republican banner, and by scrupulously respecting the right of all citizens to religious freedom, he sought to disarm those who claimed that he was an enemy of Christianity.[54] In addition, he still had not found a way of reconciling his acceptance of Christian morality with his rejection of Christian dogma that might satisfy those who differed with him. Thus he had a further incentive for maintaining a discreet silence on the subject of his religious beliefs. As a result, it required the appearance of another timely work by Priestley, coupled with a revival of Jefferson's concern about preserving social harmony in the young republic and a sharp rise in public criticism of him on religious grounds, to impel him to produce a formal statement of his view of the Christian religion and to make his first compilation of passages from the New Testament.

[53] TJ to Moses Robinson, 23 Mch. 1801 (Appendix).

[54] For typical expressions of TJ's hope of detaching the main body of Federalists from their leaders, see his letters to James Monroe, 7 Feb. [Mch.] 1801; to Horatio Gates, 8 Mch. 1801; and to William Branch Giles, 23 Mch. 1801. For a summary statement of his policy of noninterference in religious affairs, see his letter to the Baptist Committee of Danbury, Conn., 1 Jan. 1802. Both issues are discussed in Malone, *Jefferson the President: First Term*, p. 69-89, 108-9.

The work by Priestley that had such a catalytic effect on Jefferson was an otherwise modest publication entitled *Socrates and Jesus Compared.* In this sixty-page pamphlet, published in Philadelphia early in 1803, Priestley sought to demonstrate that revealed religion was superior to natural religion by assessing the relative merits of the founder of Christianity and the man the Unitarian leader regarded as the crowning glory of ancient philosophy. Socrates and Jesus, Priestley argued, each had certain personal characteristics in common. Both were wise men who led temperate private lives. Both were virtuous men who strove to persuade other men to act virtuously. Both were religious men who submitted to a higher power. Both were poor men who shunned riches, and both were honest men who displayed great courage throughout their lives, especially in the face of death.[55] Yet, ultimately, their differences far outweighed their similarities. Jesus was a monotheist who taught humanity to worship the one true God, whereas Socrates was a polytheist who had no notion of the unity of God. Jesus emphasized that "great sanction of virtue,"[56] the doctrine of rewards and punishment in the life to come, whereas Socrates was uncertain whether there was life after death. Jesus stressed that piety consisted of inner reverence for God, and morality of obedience to his unchanging laws, whereas Socrates equated the former with the observance of frequently licentious public rituals and the latter with conformity to mutable human laws. Jesus, though less well educated than Socrates, exuded greater authority and dealt with more important subjects in his teachings, the primary object of which was "to inculcate a purer and more sublime morality respecting God and man than any heathen could have a just idea of."[57] Jesus was more forthright and fearless in denouncing all forms of vice; Socrates preferred to express his disapproval indirectly through ridicule and was regrettably deficient in opposing sexual laxity. Jesus preached his moral doctrines for all mankind, reaching out to high and low, rich and poor, male and female alike, whereas Socrates confined his teachings to the upper classes, thus making Christian morality more useful to a republican society inasmuch as it was expressed in a "language suited to the equal nature, and equal rights of all men."[58] Finally, Jesus worked miracles and rose from the dead, thereby demonstrating that his teachings were specially approved by God, though he himself was only a man.[59] In Priestley's opinion there was only one way to explain why Jesus had purer notions of God, morality, and life after death than the better educated Athenian. "In comparing the characters, the moral instructions, and the whole of the history, of Socrates and Jesus," he concluded, "it is, I think, impossible not to be sensibly struck with the great advantage of revealed religion, such as that of the Jews and the christians, as enlightening and enlarging the minds of men, and imparting a superior excellence of character. This alone can account for the difference between Socrates and Jesus, and the disciples of each of them; but this one circumstance is abundantly sufficient for the purpose."[60]

Jefferson was immediately impressed by both the message and the methodology of *Socrates and Jesus.* He received a copy of the pamphlet from Priestley

[55] Joseph Priestley, *Socrates and Jesus Compared* (Philadelphia, 1803), p. 1-3, 33-34.
[56] Same, p. 20.
[57] Same, p. 38-39.
[58] Same, p. 46.
[59] Same, p. 33-47.
[60] Same, p. 48.

near the end of March 1803, just as he was about to leave Monticello for Washington, and read it with growing interest on his way back to the capital. Although he was unconvinced by Priestley's contention that the founder of Christianity had been divinely inspired and endowed with supernatural powers, he agreed wholeheartedly that "the moral precepts of Jesus . . . as taught by himself and freed from the corruptions of latter times" were unquestionably superior to any other system of morality and particularly appropriate for a republican society dedicated to the principles of liberty and equality.[61] He especially appreciated the way in which Priestley weighed the advantages of Christianity against the shortcomings of ancient philosophy without denigrating the genuine achievements of the classical philosophers, whom the president continued to admire. Indeed, Jefferson was so impressed by Priestley's use of the comparative method in *Socrates and Jesus* that he decided it would also be an excellent way for him to present his own unorthodox religious views. Thus, inspired by the example of Priestley's pamphlet, Jefferson quickly made two important and, for him, unprecedented decisions. He decided to reveal his view of the Christian religion to a small circle of relatives and friends in the form of a comparative analysis of the moral teachings of the classical philosophers, the Jews, and Jesus so as to convince them that he was not irreligious and hostile to Christianity. In addition, he resolved to use Priestley as the instrument for propagating this view of Christianity among the general public in order to foster the social harmony he cherished as one of the bulwarks of the American republic.[62]

Socrates and Jesus galvanized Jefferson into action because it appeared during a period of unusually intense partisan conflict and exceptionally severe attacks on the president's putative infidelity. Spain's retrocession of Louisiana to France and the suspension by Spanish authorities of the American right of deposit at New Orleans had led, during the winter of 1802-1803, to an upsurge of war fever in the normally Republican West, which the Federalists tried to turn to their advantage by sharply criticizing Jefferson for his apparent supineness in the face of a threat to a vital national interest and by loudly calling for the employment of military force to vindicate the country's treaty rights. Although Jefferson allayed Western fears and overcame the immediate crisis by dispatching James Monroe on a special diplomatic mission to France in January 1803, this episode still stood as a stark reminder to him of the dangers that extreme partisanship posed to the often fragile ties that bound together the new nation and once again made him sensitive to the problem of maintaining social harmony in a republican society.[63] Furthermore, while Federalist leaders were calling for war in the West, they and their clerical supporters were also busily denouncing Jefferson as an archenemy of religion with even greater

[61] TJ to Edward Dowse, 19 Apr. 1803 (Appendix).

[62] TJ to Joseph Priestley, 9 Apr. 1803, and to Benjamin Rush, 21 Apr. 1803 (Appendix).

[63] For TJ's apprehensions over the possible repercussions of Federalist machinations during the New Orleans crisis, see his letters to James Monroe, 10 Jan. 1803 and 13 Jan. 1803; and to Robert R. Livingston, 3 Feb. 1803. Several Republican congressmen voiced similar concerns during this period. *Circular Letters of Congressmen to Their Constituents, 1789-1829*, ed. Noble E. Cunningham, Jr. (Chapel Hill, N.C., 1978), I, 311-13, 323-27, 347-51. See also Malone, *Jefferson the President: First Term*, p. 239-83.

vehemence than usual owing to the return of Thomas Paine to America in October 1802 after a tempestuous absence of fifteen years in Europe. The arrival of the author of the notoriously anti-Christian *Age of Reason* and the warm welcome he received from the president could mean only one thing, the Federalists and their ministerial allies repeated over and over again: Jefferson had brought Paine back to America so that Paine could subvert Christianity in the United States as he supposedly had done in France. A Republican congressman from Virginia vividly described the opposition's onslaught on the president to his constituents several weeks before Jefferson read *Socrates and Jesus*: "The federalist, like a bear with a sore head, or robbed of her whelps, would go all lengths to plunge our happy country into a war, take all occasions to inflame the minds of the people, by doing which they think they can draw the President into contempt; their necromantic art is easily seen through, for though they cry out war, war; and that nothing but war is to secure the port of New-Orleans, in the next breath they say they have no confidence in the President; if war was to be the result, that the President is a coward, a jacobin and infidel; that he is a deist, and all the republican party, or the leaders of them; that the President sent to France for Thomas Paine to destroy religion—this Paine is the author of the Age of Reason."[64] Anxious to reduce the social disharmony caused by partisan and sectarian strife, and provoked beyond endurance by Federalist criticism of his religion, Jefferson welcomed the opportunity provided by *Socrates and Jesus* for revealing his view of Christianity directly to a small number of confidants and indirectly, through Priestley, to the public at large.

Jefferson wasted little time in urging Priestley to write an irenic work on Christianity that would reflect the president's view of the subject. A few days after reading *Socrates and Jesus*, he dispatched a carefully worded letter to Priestley in which he praised the pamphlet and entreated the author to deal with the same subject "on a more extensive scale." In order to facilitate Priestley's task, he proceeded to outline exactly the sort of work he himself would have liked to write but which, for lack of sufficient time and adequate knowledge, he wanted the Unitarian leader to publish instead. Thus he advised the aged controversialist to begin by examining the moral teachings of the leading Epicurean and Stoic philosophers of antiquity, noting the points in which they excelled as well as those in which they were deficient. This done, the next step was to describe what the president perceived to be the degraded condition of

[64] George Jackson to the Freeholders of the North Western Congressional District of Virginia, 22 Feb. 1803, *Circular Letters*, ed. Cunningham, I, 312. Robert Williams, a Republican congressman from North Carolina, also discussed the "considerable bickering against our present chief magistrate, with regard to his religious opinions" in a 28 Feb. 1803 circular letter (same, p. 327). It is significant that these are the only Republican rebuttals to opposition criticism of TJ on religious grounds in Cunningham's comprehensive edition of congressional circular letters—a telling sign of the intensity of this kind of attack at this point in TJ's presidency. See also Malone, *Jefferson the President: First Term*, p. 190-200, for a discussion of TJ's often strained relationship with Paine after the latter's return to America. TJ was undoubtedly even more sensitive than usual to public criticism of his private character in 1803 because in September of the previous year James Callender had published a series of articles in the *Richmond Recorder* accusing the president of carrying on a liaison with a slave named Sally Hemings. See Constance B. Schulz, " 'Of Bigotry in Politics and Religion': Jefferson's Religion, the Federalist Press, and the Syllabus," *VMHB*, XCI (Jan. 1983), 73-91.

the theology and ethics of the Jews so as to show the need for the reform of both on the eve of Jesus' birth. Only then, he believed, would it be possible to portray Jesus in his true historic role as a great moral reformer who, recognizing the inadequacies of the morality and theology of the Jews, "endeavored to bring them to the principles of a pure deism, and juster notions of the attributes of god, to reform their moral doctrines to the standard of reason, justice and philanthropy, and to inculcate the belief of a future state." Jefferson admonished Priestley to avoid the contentious issue of whether Jesus was a member of the godhead himself or merely a divinely inspired man, well knowing that even he and his Unitarian correspondent did not agree on that point. However, he strongly emphasized the need to point out the difficulties involved in ascertaining the true teachings of Jesus, since, in his view, they were first written down many years after Jesus' death by the "most unlettered of men" and were then further corrupted in the course of time by "those who pretend to be his special disciples." Yet, despite the disrepute into which orthodox Christianity had fallen, at least in Jefferson's opinion, he was confident that a work that accurately described the authentic doctrines of Jesus, restoring them to their original purity and simplicity and eliminating the corruptions of later ages, would convince even the most skeptical that Christian morality was superior to any alternative and that its founder was the "most innocent, the most benevolent the most eloquent and sublime character that ever has been exhibited to man." In addition to serving the cause of historical truth, however, Jefferson obviously hoped that a work such as the one he so painstakingly outlined to Priestley would promote harmonious social relations among the citizens of the young republic by emphasizing the moral imperatives of Jesus that united them rather than the dogmas of the churches that divided them, thereby making religion a centripetal rather than a centrifugal force in the new nation and thus eliminating what the president saw as one of the mainsprings of excessively divisive partisanship in the country.[65]

Less than two weeks after writing to Priestley, Jefferson described his attitude toward Christianity at greater length in a well-known letter to Dr. Rush and an accompanying "Syllabus of an Estimate of the merit of the doctrines of Jesus, compared with those of others."[66] In these two documents, which were written with considerable care, the president offered the first and only formal description of his demythologized Christian faith, which he had developed in part under the influence of Priestley's writings and to which he adhered for the rest of his life. In the letter Jefferson recalled his promise to provide Rush with a statement on his view of Christianity and apologized for taking so long to keep his pledge, citing in extenuation the press of public business as well as the difficulty of the subject. Despite Federalist charges to the contrary, Jefferson denied that he was averse to Christianity and claimed that in fact he was as good a Christian as anyone. But the Christianity he believed in was not the religion professed by the Christian churches. "To the corruptions of Christianity, I am indeed opposed," he confided to his Philadelphia friend, thereby revealing his continued distaste for orthodoxy, "but not to the genuine precepts of Jesus himself. I am a Christian, in the only sense in which he wished any one to be; sincerely attached to his doctrines, in preference to all others; ascribing to himself every human excellence, and believing he never claimed any

[65] TJ to Joseph Priestley, 9 Apr. 1803 (Appendix).
[66] TJ to Benjamin Rush, 21 Apr. 1803, and enclosed "Syllabus" (Appendix).

other." Although he realized this admission might disarm some of those who criticized him on religious grounds, he implored Rush to regard his letter as confidential lest it be construed to mean that he conceded to the public a right to scrutinize his religious beliefs.

Jefferson explained his concept of the "genuine precepts of Jesus" in the "Syllabus" that accompanied his letter to Rush. This document, cast in the form of a comparative analysis of the moral doctrines of the classical philosophers, the Jews, and Jesus, was in effect an elaboration of the views he had expressed in his recent letter to Priestley. Jefferson praised the ancients for their precepts regarding the achievement of self-discipline but found them seriously deficient with respect to man's social obligations. In particular, he criticized their failure to inculcate "peace, charity, and love to our fellow men" or to embrace "with benevolence, the whole family of mankind." Considering his belief in the necessity of maintaining social harmony to ensure the success of America's experiment in self-government, this evaluation was tantamount to admitting that the teachings of the Epicurean and Stoic moralists, which he had once valued above all others, were insufficient for guiding the moral sense of a republican nation. Turning to the Jews, Jefferson gave them due, if somewhat grudging, credit for being monotheists. Otherwise he faulted them for having deplorable ideas of the attributes of God and for adhering to a system of ethics that he judged to be irrational with respect to relations between individuals as well as antisocial in regard to intercourse between nations. As a result, they stood in need of "reformation . . . in an eminent degree" at the dawn of the Christian era.

Having thus set the stage, Jefferson next dealt with Jesus. In his view, the Nazarene was the foremost moral reformer of the Jews, and his teachings, he implied, were of universal significance owing to his highly developed moral sense, not his divinity or divine inspiration, neither of which Jefferson accepted. The president reduced the authentic doctrines of Jesus to three essential points. First, this "benevolent and sublime reformer,"[67] as Jefferson was wont to call him, confirmed the monotheism of the Jews while correcting their erroneous notions of the "attributes and government" of the one true God. Next, he preached a system of morality that was far superior to those of the ancients and the Jews in that it dealt with intentions as well as acts and instilled "universal philanthropy, not only to kindred and friends, to neighbors and countrymen, but to all mankind, gathering all into one family, under bonds of love, charity, peace, common wants, and common aids"—a system, in short, that was well designed to promote social concord among a citizenry whose commitment to republican principles and institutions was threatened, in Jefferson's opinion, by partisan and sectarian strife. Finally, he taught the doctrine of a life in the hereafter in order to encourage virtuous conduct in the here and now. Aside from these three points, Jefferson virtually stated that every other doctrine ascribed to Jesus was in reality a corruption of his original message that had resulted either from the unintentional misrepresentations of the Evangelists, who recorded his teachings long after his death, or from the machinations of his "schismatizing followers" who deliberately perverted his simple precepts to serve their own ends. Accordingly, the implied message of the "Syllabus" was that Christianity could only be made acceptable to rational men by purging

[67] TJ to Ezra Stiles Ely, 25 June 1819 (Appendix).

it of its corruptions and restoring the doctrines of Jesus to their pristine simplicity.[68]

Jefferson did not write his letter to Rush and the "Syllabus" simply to keep a promise to a friend. He also used them to convince a few relatives and confidants of the groundlessness of Federalist charges that he was an atheist and an infidel and to test the acceptability of his view of Christianity. At the same time that he dispatched these two documents to Rush, he also sent copies of them to his daughters (Martha Jefferson Randolph and Mary Jefferson Eppes),[69] to at least two members of his cabinet (Secretary of War Henry Dearborn and Attorney General Levi Lincoln) and probably to two more (Secretary of the Treasury Albert Gallatin and Postmaster General Gideon Granger),[70] and to Priestley.[71] Later in the year, moreover, he lent a copy of them to his boyhood friend, John Page, a prominent Episcopalian who was then serving as governor of Virginia.[72] Jefferson notified his daughters and his cabinet members that he wanted them to read the letter and the "Syllabus" so that they could judge for themselves the truth or falsehood of the charges made against him on religious grounds, but he made it clear that he wanted neither document to appear in print. Although Jefferson had no wish to publicize his religious beliefs directly, he was nevertheless eager for Priestley to publish a work on Christianity that would reflect his own views and promote social harmony, and therefore he sent both documents to the Unitarian for the express purpose of encouraging him to undertake this task.[73]

Reaction to the letter to Rush and the "Syllabus," though mixed, was generally encouraging. The response of Jefferson's daughters to them is unknown, but after reading the "Syllabus" Governor Page was pleased to inform Jefferson that he "was not mistaken in my opinion that the difference between us was not so great, as many have supposed."[74] Attorney General Lincoln praised the "Syllabus" as a "valuable compendium" and received permission from Jefferson to make a copy for his personal use, while Secretary of War Dearborn, mistakenly assuming that the president planned to publish this document to refute his religious critics, advised him to use somewhat more diplomatic language in characterizing the Evangelists.[75] Rush himself expressed pleasure at the discovery that Jefferson was "by no means so heterodox as you have been supposed to be by your enemies," and while rejecting the president's contention that Jesus was merely human, he assured him that he had long since ceased

---

[68] Chinard, "Jefferson among the Philosophers," p. 263-66, suggests that the views expressed in the "Syllabus" were inspired by TJ's reading of William Enfield, *The History of Philosophy . . . drawn up from Brucker's Historia Critica Philosophiae*, 2 vols. (Dublin, 1792). This hypothesis seems unlikely inasmuch as TJ did not order a copy of Enfield's work until 1805 and did not refer to it in his correspondence thereafter until 1813 (Sowerby, comp., *Catalogue*, No. 1337).

[69] TJ to Martha Jefferson Randolph, 25 Apr. 1803; TJ to Mary Jefferson Eppes, 25 Apr. 1803.

[70] TJ to Henry Dearborn and others, [23 Apr. 1803] (Appendix).

[71] TJ to Joseph Priestley, 24 Apr. 1803 (Appendix).

[72] John Page to TJ, 12 Sep. 1803, 16 Nov. 1803, 5 Dec. 1803; TJ to Page, 25 Nov. 1803.

[73] TJ to Joseph Priestley, 24 Apr. 1803 (Appendix).

[74] John Page to TJ, 16 Nov. 1803.

[75] Levi Lincoln to TJ, 24 Apr. 1803; Henry Dearborn to TJ, undated but endorsed as received 4 May 1803.

to regard theological exactitude "as the criterion of disposition and Conduct, and much less of our future acceptance at the bar of the supreme Judge of the World."[76] This point of view must have delighted Jefferson, but, as he later learned to his regret, it was not one to which Rush steadily adhered. Jefferson was probably most interested in Priestley's reaction to the letter and the "Syllabus," however, and this, though at first slightly disappointing, was in the end a source of great satisfaction to him. As might have been expected, Priestley vigorously rejected Jefferson's notion that Jesus had never claimed to be acting under a special mission from God, but he treated this as an honest difference of opinion and otherwise found nothing to criticize in Jefferson's view of Christianity. More importantly, although Priestley was initially reluctant to accept Jefferson's "flattering invitation to enter farther into the comparison of Jesus with other philosophers," he subsequently changed his mind and informed the president in December 1803 that he had decided to write such a comparative study after all.[77]

Jefferson was sufficiently encouraged by the response to the limited disclosure of his demythologized Christian faith to turn to the task of extracting the passages from the Gospels that he regarded as expressive of the authentic teachings of Jesus. Having decided that a rationalized variant of Christianity purged of what he saw as its corruptions was not only preferable to any other religion but also potentially one of the strongest unifying forces in a republican society, the naturally methodical Jefferson felt impelled to determine with exact precision the genuine moral precepts of Jesus, which for him constituted the heart of the Christian religion, and thereby rid them of the unpalatable mystifications with which Jesus' followers had allegedly surrounded them throughout history. Jefferson approached this task with his usual care and preparation. As early as 9 April 1803, the same day he had first urged Priestley to write a work on Christianity, he ordered from a Philadelphia bookseller two volumes by the Unitarian theologian that were well designed to facilitate his study of the Gospels—*A Harmony of the Evangelists in English* and *A Harmony of the Evangelists in Greek*. Then, after being informed that these works were not readily available, he renewed his request for them on 5 May, just as he was receiving the first reactions to the letter to Rush and the "Syllabus."[78] He finally obtained the *Harmonies* from Priestley himself, who, learning of Jefferson's failure to obtain them, sent him a personal copy of the two works in August, though it is uncertain exactly when they arrived.[79] For the remainder of the year Jefferson was too preoccupied with public business to pursue his biblical researches, and it seems that he did not begin this work in earnest until after he learned in December that Priestley had embarked on a study of classical and Christian morality. With the assistance of Priestley's *Harmonies*, Jefferson then started to examine the Gospels, distinguishing what he considered to be

[76] Benjamin Rush to TJ, 5 May 1803 (Appendix).

[77] Joseph Priestley to TJ, 7 May 1803 (Appendix); Priestley to TJ, 12 Dec. 1803.

[78] TJ to Nicholas G. Dufief, 9 Apr. 1803, 5 May 1803; Dufief to TJ, 13 Apr. 1803, 2 May 1803.

[79] John Vaughan to TJ, 1 Aug. 1803; TJ to Vaughan, 14 Aug. 1803. Vaughan was the intermediary through whom Priestley conveyed his *Harmonies* to TJ. TJ, who was at Monticello when he wrote to Vaughan, instructed him to forward Priestley's volumes to Washington, D.C., and probably did not receive them until after his return to the capital on 25 Sep. 1803.

the true from the false teachings of Jesus, until at length, by 20 January 1804, he decided he was ready to make a compilation in Greek and English of the biblical passages containing Jesus' genuine moral precepts. On that day he ordered "two copies of the New Testament in Greek or Greek and Latin, both of the same edition exactly; and two others in English, both also of the same edition and all four of the same format that they may admit of being bound up together."[80]

As Jefferson awaited the arrival of the New Testaments he had ordered, he hastened to apprize Priestley of what now appeared to him to be a serious omission in the concept of the work on Christianity that he had earlier outlined for the use of his Unitarian friend. In consequence of his study of the Gospels, Jefferson was now convinced that Priestley's work could best serve the twin causes of religious truth and social harmony if it contained an introductory section consisting of the moral teachings of Jesus as expressed in the *ipsima verba* of the great reformer himself. "I rejoice that you have undertaken the task of comparing the moral doctrines of Jesus with those of the ancient Philosophers," he wrote to Priestley near the end of January, adding: "I think you cannot avoid giving, as preliminary to the comparison, a digest of his moral doctrines, extracted in his own words from the Evangelists, and leaving out everything relative to his personal history and character. It would be short and precious."[81] Jefferson even intimated that he was willing to put aside his own plan to make a compilation of extracts from the Gospels if Priestley followed his suggestion. Priestley died on 6 February, however, before receiving the president's letter but after completing his comparative study of ancient and Christian morality, whereupon Jefferson decided to go ahead with his original plan.[82]

Jefferson completed his first collection of Gospel extracts—"The Philosophy of Jesus"—with remarkable dispatch. On 4 February 1804 he received two sets of the New Testament—a pair of virtually identical English editions published in Dublin by George Grierson in 1791 and 1799 as well as two copies of a Greek-Latin edition published in London by F. Wingrave and others in 1794—and by 10 March the compilation was finished and bound.[83] Little is known about the actual composition of this work. Jefferson apparently first made a list of the Gospel verses that seemed to him to contain the genuine moral teachings of Jesus, and then, over a period of several evenings, he clipped these passages from the Bible and added others as he went along, pasting them in double columns on 46 octavo sheets.[84] Contrary to his original design, he only used verses in English, evidently deciding that the press of public business left him with insufficient time to produce a bilingual text. Although many

[80] TJ to Nicholas G. Dufief, 20 Jan. 1804. TJ to Joseph Priestley, 29 Jan. 1804 (Appendix), clearly shows that TJ originally planned to compile "The Philosophy of Jesus" in Greek as well as English.

[81] TJ to Joseph Priestley, 29 Jan. 1804 (Apppendix).

[82] Thomas Cooper to TJ, 6 Feb. and 16 Feb. 1803, notified TJ of Priestley's death and the completion of his study of classical and Christian morality.

[83] Dufief transmitted the New Testaments to TJ with a letter of 28 Jan. 1804. TJ, Account with John Marsh, 10 Jan.-12 Mch. 1804, gives 10 Mch. 1804 as the date he was charged for the binding of "The Philosophy of Jesus."

[84] The Appendix of the present volume contains letters describing the compilation of "The Philosophy of Jesus" that TJ wrote to John Adams, 12 Oct. 1813; to Van der Kemp, 25 Apr. 1816; and to William Short, 31 Oct. 1819.

distinguished biblical scholars have been daunted by the challenge of disentangling the many layers of the New Testament, the rationalistic Jefferson was supremely confident of his ability to differentiate between the true and the false precepts of Jesus, observing on several occasions that the former were "as easily distinguishable as diamonds in a dunghill."[85] His first biblical compilation, he was convinced, contained nothing but "46. pages of pure and unsophisticated doctrines, such as were professed and acted on by the *unlettered* apostles, the Apostolic fathers, and the Christians of the 1st. century."[86] He entitled it "The Philosophy of Jesus of Nazareth extracted from the account of his life and doctrines as given by Mathew, Mark, Luke, and John. being an abridgement of the New Testament for the use of the Indians unembarrassed with matters of fact or faith beyond the level of their comprehensions." This subtitle was intentionally ironic. The "Indians" Jefferson had in mind were not the aboriginal inhabitants of North America. They were, rather, the Federalists and their clerical allies, whose political and religious obscurantism, as the president saw it, endangered the stability of the republic and needed to be reformed by a return to the simple, uncorrupted morality of Jesus.[87]

After finishing "The Philosophy of Jesus," Jefferson looked forward with anticipation to the appearance of Priestley's last work on Christianity. But when several months passed and the promised work still had not materialized, Jefferson felt impelled once again to test the acceptability of his rationalistic version of the Christian message. Accordingly, he wrote to Rush early in August 1804 and offered to let him read "The Philosophy of Jesus."[88] Jefferson may have hoped that if Rush approved of this compilation he could be induced to

[85] TJ to John Adams, 12 Oct. 1813 (Appendix). See also the letters from TJ to Van der Kemp and Short mentioned above in n. 84.

[86] TJ to John Adams, 12 Oct. 1813 (Appendix).

[87] Most writers on the subject assume TJ compiled "The Philosophy of Jesus" for the use of the Indians (Foote, *Religion of Thomas Jefferson*, p. 61; Gould, "Religious Opinions of Thomas Jefferson," p. 203; and Malone, *Jefferson the President: First Term*, p. 205). TJ consistently stated that he had made this biblical compilation for his personal use (see the letters cited in n. 84 above). For evidence that he used the term "Indians" as a code word for his Federalist and clerical adversaries during the time he prepared this manuscript, see his second inaugural address, delivered 4 Mch. 1805, wherein he ostensibly criticized the "habits" and "prejudice" of the aboriginal inhabitants of North America, but actually aimed these words at his political and ministerial opponents. He made this clear in notes he prepared regarding the draft of this address: "None of these heads needs any commentary but that of the Indians. This is a proper topic not only to promote the work of humanizing our citizens towards these people, but to conciliate to us the good opinion of Europe on the subject of the Indians. This, however, might have been done in half the compass it here occupies. But every respector of science, every friend to political reformation must have observed with indignation the hue and cry raised against philosophy and the rights of man; and it really seems as if they would be overborne and barbarism, bigotry and despotism would recover the ground they have lost by the advance of the public understanding. I have thought the occasion justified some discountenance of these anti-social doctrines, some testimony against them, but not to commit myself in direct warfare on them, I have thought it best to say what is directly applied to the Indians only, but admits by inference a more general extension" (DLC: TJ Papers, f. 25710). It seems clear, therefore, that the subtitle of "The Philosophy of Jesus" was deliberately ironic and that the work itself was never intended specifically for the aboriginal population of the United States.

[88] TJ to Benjamin Rush, 8 Aug. 1804 (Appendix).

publish a work embodying its view of Christianity. If this was indeed Jefferson's hope, Rush's reply must have come as a rude jolt. For, eschewing the spirit of doctrinal tolerance with which he had greeted the "Syllabus," Rush sternly informed the president that although he would "receive with pleasure the publication you have promised me upon the character of the Messiah . . . unless it advances it to divinity and renders his *death* as well as his *life* necessary for the restoration of mankind, I shall not accord with its author."[89] Since there was no way "The Philosophy of Jesus" could meet such an exacting standard, Jefferson decided not to send it to his Philadelphia friend after all and never again mentioned the subject in his correspondence with him.

Rush's lack of sympathy for Jefferson's demystified Christian creed was followed by an even more shattering blow to the president's hope of using Christian morality to foster social concord in the new nation. Near the end of 1804 Priestley's comparative analysis of classical and Christian morality was finally published under the title *The Doctrines of Heathen Philosophy, Compared with Those of Revelation*. This work, upon which Jefferson had placed so much hope, disappointed him greatly. It was long, diffuse, and badly written, reflecting the fact that Priestley had composed it while in poor health and facing the shadow of death. It was bogged down by lengthy discussions of often abstruse philosophical and theological points. It made no comparison between Judaism and Christianity, as Jefferson had suggested, and, worst of all from his point of view, it lacked a clear and compact description of the authentic teachings of Jesus. In short, it was useless as a means of promoting the rationalistic Christian faith Jefferson favored. "I apprehend however," he regretfully observed shortly after reading the *Doctrines of Heathen Philosophy*, "that [Priestley] meditated a 2d. part which should have given a view of the genuine doctrines of Jesus divested of those engrafted into his by false followers. I suppose this because it is wanting to compleat the work, and because I observe he calls what is published Part Ist."[90]

Rush's unsympathetic reaction to rationalistic Christianity and Jefferson's disappointment with Priestley's posthumously published work led him to abandon his rather naive hope of promoting social harmony in the young republic by exalting Christian morality over Christian dogma. Rush's response suggested the futility of trying to propagate a version of Christianity that sought to evade the central issue of Jesus' divinity, and Priestley's death deprived the president of the only trusted friend with theological ability who was sympathetic to his religious views. Jefferson himself continued to be averse to religious controversy and thus had no intention of personally publicizing his view of Christianity beyond the limited circle to which he had already revealed it. At the same time, Jefferson's overwhelming victory in the presidential election of 1804, coupled with the continued growth of the Republican party throughout the nation, temporarily allayed his apprehensions about the future of republicanism in the United States, while the various domestic and international crises that punctuated his second administration diverted him from further intensive study of the New Testament. Thus, although he remained deeply interested in ascer-

[89] Benjamin Rush to TJ, 29 Aug. 1804.
[90] TJ to Benjamin Smith Barton, 14 Feb. 1805 (Appendix). TJ received a copy of Priestley's *Doctrines of Heathen Philosophy* on 6 Feb. 1805 (Patrick Byrne to TJ, 2 Jan. 1805; TJ to Byrne, 14 Feb. 1805). He revealed his eagerness for its publication in letters to Henry Fry of 21 May 1804 and 17 June 1804.

taining the authentic moral teachings of Jesus, henceforth he pursued this subject for personal rather than public reasons. After 1804, except in a single instance discussed below, he used "The Philosophy of Jesus" strictly for his private moral instruction and edification, until at length he replaced it with a more ambitious compilation, "The Life and Morals of Jesus."

III

Aside from the fact that both were part of Jefferson's quest for the genuine doctrines of Jesus, in virtually every other important respect "The Philosophy of Jesus" and "The Life and Morals of Jesus" stand in sharp contrast to each other. The main focus of "The Philosophy of Jesus" is on the moral teachings of Jesus, whereas "The Life and Morals of Jesus" gives attention to the details of his career as well as the content of his doctrine. Jefferson compiled "The Philosophy of Jesus" in response to his personal religious needs and his concern with the problem of maintaining social harmony in a republican nation, but "The Life and Morals of Jesus" was strictly a product of his private search for religious truth. "The Philosophy of Jesus" is a unilingual compilation of Gospel verses in English, whereas "The Life and Morals of Jesus" is a multilingual collection of verses in Greek, Latin, French, and English (Jefferson did not read Hebrew or any other Semitic language). The provenance of "The Philosophy of Jesus" is fairly clear, and the date of its compilation can be determined with great exactitude; the background of "The Life and Morals of Jesus" is more obscure, and the precise date of its composition still cannot be established with any certainty. The steps that led Jefferson to compile "The Life and Morals of Jesus" continue to be somewhat unclear, but they include his correspondence with John Adams, an exchange of letters with the former secretary of the Continental Congress, the importunities of an immigrant Dutch scholar, Jefferson's interest in the progress of Unitarianism, and a chance remark by a man he had once cherished like a son.

Jefferson seems to have initially conceived the idea of making a quadrilingual compilation of Gospel verses shortly before he began his second term as president. In order to accomplish such a work he first had to acquire two copies of the New Testament in each of the languages he planned to use. This was of paramount importance because in the process of clipping verses from the Evangelists and pasting them on to blank sheets of paper it was inevitable that he would occasionally take some passages from one side of a given page and then later decide to use others on the reverse side of it, thus forcing him to have recourse to a second, unclipped copy of the same page. Accordingly, he instructed a Baltimore bookseller at the end of January 1805 to send him two copies of "le Nouveau testament corrigé sur le Grec in 12mo Paris. 1803," carefully noting that "a single one, or two of different editions would not answer to my purpose,"[91] and a few weeks later he ordered the same number of copies of "a tolerably decent edition of the New testament in 12mo." from a Philadelphia book dealer.[92] Since these orders were promptly filled, Jefferson had in his possession by the end of March dual copies of a French New Testament printed in Paris in 1802 by J. Smith and of an English New Testament printed

[91] TJ to J. P. Reibelt, 31 Jan. 1805.
[92] TJ to Mathew Carey, 7 Mch. 1805.

in Philadelphia in 1804 by Jacob Johnson.[93] These, together with the pair of identical Greek-Latin New Testaments he had acquired the year before in connection with "The Philosophy of Jesus," gave him the basic sources he needed to make a quadrilingual biblical compilation and were in fact the very same volumes he used to compile "The Life and Morals of Jesus" during his retirement at Monticello a decade and a half later.[94] Unfortunately, Jefferson never explained why, after having taken the trouble early in 1805 to gather the materials for a more linguistically comprehensive collection of extracts from the Gospels than that contained in "The Philosophy of Jesus," he put aside the projected work and did not take it up again in earnest for another fifteen years. He was probably too busy attending to affairs of state during his second administration as president to find time for further biblical research, and he apparently found "The Philosophy of Jesus" sufficiently satisfying as a source of moral instruction during the early years of his retirement from public life to obviate the need for another work of this sort.[95] In the absence of direct evidence, however, any account for this delay must be necessarily conjectural.

After he retired from the presidency, Jefferson's revived correspondence with John Adams was the next step in the path that eventually led to "The Life and Morals of Jesus." After a hiatus of eleven years caused by their political estrangement during the 1790s, the two ex-presidents resumed writing to each other in 1812, largely through the devoted efforts of their mutual friend, Benjamin Rush.[96] The subject of Christianity soon became one of the leading themes of their correspondence as a result of the printing of Jefferson's 9 April 1803 letter to Joseph Priestley in Thomas Belsham's *Memoirs of the Late Reverend Theophilus Lindsey*, a biography of one of the founding fathers of English Unitarianism that was published in London in 1812.[97] Adams, who had also rejected Christian orthodoxy as a young man,[98] read this letter in the following year and was favorably impressed by Jefferson's estimate of the merits of Christianity in relation to ancient philosophy and Judaism. Adams was unaware of the "Syllabus" or the posthumous publication of Priestley's *The Doctrines of Heathen Philosophy, Compared with Those of Revelation*, however, and he expressed regret that Jefferson had never elaborated his view of Christianity to Rush and that Priestley had failed to publish the comparative analysis of classical, Jewish, and Christian morality that Jefferson had urged him to write. Jefferson thereupon sought to dispel these misapprehensions by sending Adams a copy of the "Syllabus" and *The Doctrines of Heathen Philosophy* as well as by giving him the first detailed description of "The Philosophy of Jesus." Like

[93] J. P. Reibelt to TJ, 2 Feb. 1805, endorsed as received 3 Feb. 1805; and Mathew Carey to TJ, 19 Mch. 1805, endorsed as received 25 Mch. 1805, announced the fulfillment of TJ's orders for these books.

[94] Edgar J. Goodspeed, "Thomas Jefferson and the Bible," *Harvard Theological Review*, XL (Jan. 1947), 71-76, was the first to identify all the editions of the New Testament that TJ used in "The Life and Morals of Jesus."

[95] TJ to John Adams, 12 Oct. 1813 (Appendix), expresses satisfaction with "The Philosophy of Jesus." TJ first expressed dissatisfaction with this compilation in a 25 Apr. 1816 letter to Van der Kemp (Appendix).

[96] L. H. Butterfield, "The Dream of Benjamin Rush: The Reconciliation of John Adams and Thomas Jefferson," *Yale Review*, XL (Winter 1951), 297-319.

[97] See TJ to Joseph Priestley, 9 Apr. 1803, notes (Appendix).

[98] Schulz, "Radical Religious Ideas of Adams and Jefferson," p. 4-175, offers the most comprehensive survey and analysis of Adams' religion.

Jefferson, Adams was disappointed by Priestley's last book, but he admired the "Syllabus" and urged Jefferson several times to publish a comparative study of classical and Christian morality that would set forth his view of the authentic teachings of Jesus. But Jefferson deftly turned aside Adams' pleas, citing old age and insufficient knowledge of the subject in justification of his refusal to undertake this task, to which he also might have added his settled resolve never to reveal his religious beliefs to the public. "We must leave therefore to others, younger and more learned than we are," he informed Adams in the fall of 1813, "to prepare this euthanasia for Platonic Christianity, and it's restoration to the primitive simplicity of it's founder."[99] Despite Jefferson's refusal to write a book on religion in accordance with Adams' wishes, this episode led to a wide-ranging discussion of fundamental religious issues by the two elder statesmen that lasted almost until the time of their deaths. Both agreed that Christianity was originally a simple system of moral teachings that had to be purged of the dogmatic corruptions of later ages in order to be made intellectually respectable to rational men, thereby encouraging Jefferson to persist in his quest for the genuine doctrines of Jesus.[100]

Adams' repeated calls for Jefferson to publish a comparison of the moral doctrines of antiquity and Christianity did not fall upon entirely deaf ears. To be sure, Jefferson never planned to write a book on this subject for publication, but he did reexamine "The Philosophy of Jesus" and tentatively decide to revise it in a manner that somewhat reflected Adams' influence, having concluded by 1816 that it "was too hastily done . . . being the work of one or two evenings only, while I lived at Washington, overwhelmed with other business."[101] Jefferson first revealed this decision to his old friend Charles Thomson, who had served as secretary to the Continental Congress from its inception in 1774 to its demise in 1789 and then retired from politics to devote the rest of his life to biblical scholarship. He produced a highly regarded translation of the Bible that was published in 1808 and a *Synopsis of the Four Evangelists* that appeared seven years later.[102] Shortly after receiving a copy of the latter from his former colleague in the Old Congress, Jefferson thanked Thomson for the gift in a letter written early in January 1816, in which he briefly described "The Philosophy of Jesus," adducing it as "a document in proof that *I* am a *real Christian*, that is to say, a disciple of the doctrines of Jesus, very different from the Platonists, who call *me* infidel, and *themselves* Christians and preachers of the gospel, while they draw all their characteristic dogmas from what it's Author never said or saw." He then noted that if he could find the time he wanted to add to "The Philosophy of Jesus" the corresponding Greek, Latin, and French

[99] TJ to John Adams, 12 Oct. 1813 (Appendix). See also TJ to Adams, 22 Aug. 1813 (Appendix); and Adams to TJ, 29 May, 16 July, 18 July, 22 July, 9 Aug., 14 Sep., 22 Sep., 25 Dec. 1813.

[100] In addition to the letters cited above in n. 99, see TJ to Adams, 24 Jan. 1814, 8 Apr. 1816, 11 Jan. 1817, 5 May 1817, 17 May 1818, 14 Mch. 1820, 8 Jan. 1825; and Adams to TJ, 3 Mch. 1814, 20 June 1815, 3 May 1816, 30 Sep. 1816, 12 Dec. 1816, 19 Apr. 1817, 26 May 1817, 20 Jan 1820, 4 Sep. 1821, 15 Aug. 1823, 22 Jan. 1825, 23 Jan. 1825.

[101] TJ to Van der Kemp, 25 Apr. 1816 (Appendix).

[102] J. Edwin Hendricks, *Charles Thomson and the Making of a New Nation, 1729-1824* (Cranbury, N.J., 1979), p. 129-83. TJ had also acquired a copy of Thomson's translation of the Old and New Testaments (Sowerby, comp., *Catalogue*, No. 1474).

verses "in columns side by side," which would have entailed redoing the whole work since there was probably not enough room in the original compilation for three more columns of Gospel verses. He also wanted to subjoin to the revised compilation a translation of Pierre Gassendi's *Syntagma Epicuri Philosophiae*, a seventeenth-century volume by a French Catholic priest and philosopher that contained a Christianized version of Epicureanism that Jefferson greatly admired inasmuch as he regarded the teachings of Epicurus as "the most rational system remaining of the philosophy of the ancients, as frugal of vicious indulgence, and fruitful of virtue as the hyperbolical extravagancies of his rival sects."[103] If Jefferson had in fact altered "The Philosophy of Jesus" along these lines, the resulting work would have borne some resemblance to the comparative study of classical and Christian morality that Adams had urged him to produce, with the important exception that it would have been strictly for Jefferson's personal use. Jefferson informed another correspondent several months later that he definitely planned to revise "The Philosophy of Jesus" during the winter of 1816-17, but he failed to carry out this resolve for another three years, at which time he produced a much different biblical compilation.[104]

Jefferson's letter to Thomson unexpectedly turned out to be a source of unwelcome publicity for the former president. Thomson, who was old and not in complete possession of his mental faculties, led some of his friends in Pennsylvania to believe that Jefferson had embraced orthodox Christianity, and he inadvertently left the letter itself in the home of a friend in Philadelphia, who apparently allowed others to read it. Rumors thereupon began to circulate that Jefferson had accepted the divinity of Jesus and planned to publish a book on his moral teachings, in consequence of which he received a number of letters inquiring as to the veracity of these reports.[105] Jefferson was distressed by the disclosure of his letter to Thomson, though he generously refrained from criticizing his aged and infirm friend. On the other hand, he indignantly denied any suggestion that the letter signified an alteration in his religious views. "A change from what?" he asked one long-time friend who had written to him in the summer of 1816 regarding his reported conversion to Christian orthodoxy. "The priests indeed have heretofore thought proper to ascribe to me religious, or rather antireligious sentiments, of their own fabric, but such as soothed their resentments against the Act of Virginia for establishing religious freedom. . . . But I have ever thought religion a concern purely between our god and our consciences, for which we were accountable to him, and not to the priests."[106] He also rejected with equal vehemence the notion that he had written a book on Jesus' doctrines for public consumption. "I write nothing for publication, and last of all things should it be on the subject of religion," he wrote in the fall of the same year to a Philadelphian who had offered to print the work the ex-president had supposedly prepared for publication. "On the dogmas of re-

---

[103] TJ to Charles Thomson, 9 Jan. 1815 [1816] (Appendix). See also Thomas F. Mayo, *Epicurus in England (1650-1715)* (Dallas, Tex., 1934), p. 1-4.

[104] TJ to Van der Kemp, 25 Apr. 1816 (Appendix).

[105] Margaret Bayard Smith to TJ, 21 July 1816; George Logan to TJ, 16 Oct. 1816; Mathew Carey to TJ, 22 Oct. 1816; Joseph Delaplaine to TJ, 23 Nov. 1816. See also TJ to George Logan, 12 Nov. [1816], notes (Appendix); and TJ to Charles Thomson, 29 Jan. 1817 (Appendix).

[106] TJ to Margaret Bayard Smith, 6 Aug. 1816 (Appendix).

ligion as distinguished from moral principles, all mankind, from the beginning of the world to this day, have been quarrelling, fighting, burning and torturing one another, for abstractions unintelligible to themselves and to all others, and absolutely beyond the comprehension of the human mind. Were I to enter on that arena, I should only add an unit to the number of Bedlamites."[107] Jefferson's stern denials eventually laid to rest the rumors excited by his letter to Thomson, and after 1816 he was no longer troubled by queries about his alleged conversion to traditional Trinitarian Christianity. Nevertheless, this episode probably brought him closer to making a new collection of extracts from the evangelists by strengthening his resolve to produce a private work that embodied his demythologized view of the figure he regarded as the greatest moral teacher in human history rather than the more orthodox view that certain Christians had inferred from the letter to Thomson.

Jefferson was further impelled to compile "The Life and Morals of Jesus" by the failure of his efforts to induce another author to write a rationalistic biography of the founder of Christianity. The author in question was Francis Adrian Van der Kemp, a learned Dutch scholar, a former minister with a Unitarian theological outlook, a member of the American Philosophical Society and the American Academy of Arts and Sciences, and an enthusiastic supporter of American independence who had left his homeland to escape political oppression and settled in upstate New York in 1788.[108] The sexagenarian Van der Kemp was a good friend of John Adams and a sometime correspondent of Jefferson who had a penchant for conceiving grandiose works in history, theology, and natural philosophy and then failing to bring them to fruition—a personal foible of which Jefferson was as yet unaware. Van der Kemp did complete one manuscript life of Jesus, but it was never printed because the sole copy was lost in transit when he sent it to England for publication. Subsequently, in 1813, Adams allowed Van der Kemp to read the "Syllabus," disregarding a strict injunction from Jefferson to show it to no one else but Mrs. Adams, though Adams did refuse Van der Kemp's request for a copy of it.[109] This manuscript reawakened Van der Kemp's interest in writing another work on the same subject, and three years later, after having read Jefferson's 9 April 1803 letter to Priestley in Belsham's biography of Theophilus Lindsey, he decided to take direct action. Accordingly, he wrote to Jefferson in March 1816 and not only asked for a copy of the "Syllabus" to use in connection with a life of Jesus he planned to write, but also requested permission to publish the document, without attribution, in a Unitarian journal in England to promote a discussion of Jesus' true merits.[110]

Van der Kemp's announced intention to write a life of Jesus came as welcome news to Jefferson. The former president was still disinclined to publicize his own demystified view of the Nazarene, but he was eager for someone else to publish a book portraying Jesus as a great moral reformer rather than as the son of God, hoping thereby to advance the cause of rational religion and begin the process of ridding Christianity of what he deemed to be its corruptions. Unaware of the frequent disparity between Van der Kemp's scholarly goals

[107] TJ to Mathew Carey, 11 Nov. 1816.
[108] Henry F. Jackson, *Scholar in the Wilderness, Francis Adrian Van der Kemp* (Syracuse, N.Y., 1963).
[109] Van der Kemp to John Adams, 4 Oct. 1813, 28 Dec. 1813 (MHi: AM).
[110] Van der Kemp to TJ, 24 Mch. 1816 (Appendix).

and achievements, he somewhat naively concluded that the Unitarian scholar was well suited for this task and therefore went to great lengths to ensure that the projected study of Jesus conformed to his own view of the matter. Thus he gave Van der Kemp permission to publish in England the "Syllabus" and the accompanying 21 April 1803 letter to Benjamin Rush, subject to the stipulation that the authorship of both documents be concealed. He also offered to allow Van der Kemp to print both the "Syllabus" and "The Philosophy of Jesus" in his planned study of Jesus, again on condition that their author remain anonymous. "To this Syllabus and Extract ['The Philosophy of Jesus'], if a history of his life can be added, written with the same view of the subject," he assured this prospective biographer of Jesus, "the world will see, after the fogs shall be dispelled, in which for 14. centuries he has been inveloped by Jugglers to make money of him, when the genuine character shall be exhibited, which they have dressed up in the rags of an Impostor, the world, I say, will at length see the immortal merit of this first of human Sages."[111] Moreover, when Van der Kemp subsequently expressed doubt that he could write an adequate study of Jesus without dealing with a number of related historical and theological issues that he felt ill-equipped to handle, Jefferson sought to dispel his misgivings by urging him to focus his attention on the "mortal biography of Jesus," arguing that such a work, if "candidly and rationally written, without any regard to sectarian dogmas, would reconcile to his character a weighty multitude who do not properly estimate it; and would lay the foundation of a genuine christianity."[112]

Despite all of Jefferson's efforts, Van der Kemp bitterly disappointed his expectations. He did arrange for the publication of the "Syllabus" and the letter to Rush, both suitably altered to conceal the identity of their author, in the October 1816 issue of the *Monthly Repository of Theology and General Literature*, an English Unitarian periodical. Contrary to Jefferson's hopes, however, they failed to elicit any comment in England, and, evidently owing to an indiscretion by Van der Kemp, they were published with a prefatory statement by the editor of the periodical describing their author as "an eminent American Statesman" who was one of the "leading men in the American revolution."[113] This clue enabled John Quincy Adams, then serving as American ambassador to the Court of St. James, to identify Jefferson as the author of these documents and caused Jefferson to fear that his secret would become known to others— a fate he was spared thanks to the limited circulation of the *Monthly Repository*.[114] Furthermore, Van der Kemp failed to avail himself of Jefferson's invitation to use "The Philosophy of Jesus"—the second and last time that Jefferson offered to allow someone else to read this compilation—and never wrote his projected life of Jesus, adding yet another item to a long list of unexecuted scholarly plans. By the end of 1817, if not before, Jefferson realized that Van der Kemp was not going to produce a study of Jesus and that he himself was

---

[111] TJ to Van der Kemp, 25 Apr. 1816 (Appendix).

[112] TJ to Van der Kemp, 24 Nov. 1816 (Appendix). See also Van der Kemp to TJ, 1 Nov. 1816 (Appendix).

[113] *Monthly Repository of Theology and General Literature*, xi (Oct. 1816), 573-74.

[114] Van der Kemp to TJ, 4 June 1816, notes (Appendix); Jackson, *Scholar in the Wilderness*, p. 246-52.

the only one who could compile the "mortal biography" of the great reformer to his own satisfaction.[115]

Jefferson's view of the significance of the American Unitarian movement further persuaded him of the value of such a work. He carefully followed the controversy between Calvinists and Unitarians in New England, which became particularly acute after 1815, and rejoiced in any progress the latter made at the expense of the former. He welcomed the Unitarian rejection of the Trinity and its emphasis on the moral precepts of Jesus over the dogmas of the churches, seeing in this the harbinger of a return to the pristine purity of primitive Christianity—a prospect in which he took great pleasure. "The religion of Jesus is founded on the Unity of God, and this principle chiefly, gave it triumph over the rabble of heathen gods then acknoleged," he informed the Rev. Jared Sparks, a Unitarian minister. "Thinking men of all nations rallied readily to the doctrine of one only god, and embraced it with the pure morals which Jesus inculcated."[116] Jefferson was convinced that a similar process was at work in early nineteenth-century America, and therefore he predicted a much more glorious future for Unitarianism than it was in fact to enjoy. "The pure and simple unity of the creator of the universe is now all but ascendant in the Eastern states," he prophesied in 1822, "it is dawning in the West, and advancing towards the South; and I confidently expect that the present generation will see Unitarianism become the general religion of the United states."[117] Jefferson proved to be a poor prophet in this case, but his exaggerated estimate of Unitarianism's future prospects in America nevertheless played a significant part in the history of his biblical researches insofar as it convinced him that his demythologized view of Christianity was rapidly gaining ground and thereby led him to persist in his quest for Jesus' genuine acts and teachings.

Although several factors had conspired since 1813 to reawaken and sustain Jefferson's interest in making a new collection of extracts from the Gospels, it was actually a chance remark by William Short that eventually prompted him to begin work on "The Life and Morals of Jesus." Writing in October 1819, Short, who had served as Jefferson's private secretary in France over three

---

[115] TJ last mentioned Van der Kemp's proposed life of Jesus in TJ to Van der Kemp, 1 May 1817.

[116] TJ to Jared Sparks, 4 Nov. 1820 (Appendix).

[117] TJ to James Smith, 8 Dec. 1822 (Appendix). For other evidence of TJ's interest in the progress of Unitarianism, see the following letters in the Appendix: TJ to Salma Hale, 26 July 1818; to Thomas B. Parker, 15 May 1819; to Jared Sparks, 4 Nov. 1820; to Timothy Pickering, 27 Feb. 1821; to Thomas Whittemore, 5 June 1822; to Benjamin Waterhouse, 26 June 1822, 19 July 1822; to John Davis, 18 Jan. 1824; and to George Thacher, 26 Jan. 1824.

Conrad Wright, *The Beginnings of Unitarianism in America* (Boston, 1955), p. 201-2, points out that the two leading forms of anti-Trinitarianism among Unitarians were Arianism, which held that Jesus was less than a god but more than a man, and Socinianism, which held that Jesus was more than a man but less than a god—a crucial difference in emphasis. TJ was neither an Arian nor a Socinian. Unlike the Arians, he did not believe that God had created Jesus before the world, and, in contrast to the Socinians, he did not believe that Jesus was a divinely inspired moral teacher who had been empowered by God to work miracles and rise from the dead. On the contrary, TJ viewed Jesus in a humanistic light as a mortal man who was an inspired moral reformer endowed with great natural gifts, and thus he rejected the Trinity for reasons different from those advanced by most Unitarians of his time.

decades earlier and been regarded by him almost like a son, facetiously observed that the state of his own health was such that he had "so far adopted the principles of Epicurus . . . as to consult my ease towards the attainment of happiness in this poor world, poor even in making the best of it."[118] Aghast at this travesty of the teachings of one of his favorite philosophers, Jefferson chided Short for misunderstanding Epicureanism and took advantage of the occasion to make an extended comparison between various ancient moralists and Jesus, clearly awarding the latter the palm as the greatest moral teacher of all. He then revealed that he had been thinking of putting together a work consisting of a translation of the writings of the Stoic philosopher "Epictetus (for he has never been tolerably translated into English) . . . the genuine doctrines of Epicurus from the Syntagma of Gassendi, and an Abstract from the Evangelists of whatever has the stamp of the eloquence and fine imagination of Jesus."[119] This project, which he had reluctantly concluded to be impracticable, owing to his advancing years, would have gathered under one cover all that he most admired in the moral systems of antiquity and Christianity. But Short, who mistakenly assumed that Jefferson had been planning to publish a book, thereupon urged him in December to resume work on his projected "abstract from the Evangelists," arguing that it was high time someone separated the wheat from the chaff in the Gospels.[120] Short's plea was successful, for after reading it, Jefferson discarded the idea of a comparative collection of ancient and Christian morality and finally turned instead to the task of extracting from the Gospels for his own use those passages that seemed to him to contain the *ipsima acta et verba* of Jesus. Jefferson never explained why he decided to begin this work when he did, but he had been dissatisfied with "The Philosophy of Jesus" since at least 1816 and probably felt that he did not have much time left before his death to make another biblical compilation.

Relatively little is known about the actual composition of "The Life and Morals of Jesus." As in the case of "The Philosophy of Jesus," Jefferson first prepared a table of contents and then clipped and pasted the Gospel verses on to blank leaves of paper, once again occasionally adding new verses as he proceeded.[121] Starting from left to right, he inserted the Greek, Latin, French, and English verses in separate columns, presumably putting in the English column before the others on each page. Unlike "The Philosophy of Jesus," however, which concentrates primarily on the moral precepts of Jesus and is arranged in topical order, the second compilation is devoted to Jesus' actions as well as his teachings. Jefferson arranged them in chronological order, closely but not slavishly following the sequence of events given in Archbishop William Newcome's *A Harmony in Greek of the Gospels*, which was first published in Dublin in 1778.[122] In selecting passages for inclusion in his work, Jefferson treated the Gospels as ordinary secular histories and accordingly divided their

---

[118] William Short to TJ, 21 Oct. 1819. See also George G. Shackelford, "William Short, Jefferson's Adopted Son, 1758-1849" (Ph.D. diss., University of Virginia, 1955).

[119] TJ to William Short, 31 Oct. 1819 (Appendix).

[120] William Short to TJ, 1 Dec. 1819.

[121] This is the inescapable conclusion to be drawn from the surviving fragmentary draft table of contents for "The Life and Morals of Jesus" (DLC: TJ Papers, f. 42080).

[122] This conclusion is based on a careful comparison of "The Life and Morals of Jesus" with Archbishop Newcome's *Harmony in Greek*—a work that was part of TJ's last library (*Catalogue: President Jefferson's Library*, Washington, D.C., 1829, lot 507).

contents into three separate categories. The first consisted of verses made up of "a ground work of vulgar ignorance, of things impossible, of superstitions, fanaticisms, and fabrications," which he rejected as the falsifications of the Evangelists and therefore excluded from his work.[123] The second consisted of passages containing "sublime ideas of the supreme being, aphorisms and precepts of the purest morality and benevolence, sanctioned by a life of humility, innocence, and simplicity of manners, neglect of riches, absence of worldly ambition and honors, with an eloquence and persuasiveness which have not been surpassed"—passages that in his opinion could not have been invented by those "grovelling authors," Matthew, Mark, Luke, and John, and therefore must be included in his compilation.[124] The third category consisted of verses "not free from objection, which we may with probability ascribe to Jesus himself"—apparently those in which Jesus intimated he was acting under divine inspiration. Jefferson nevertheless included these on the ground that they accurately reflected the beliefs of a man who could not be expected to have been completely liberated from the superstitions of his people.[125]

It is impossible to be certain when Jefferson finished his second biblical compilation. He wrote two letters to Short in 1820—the first on 13 April and the second on 4 August[126]—in which, without ever mentioning "The Life and Morals of Jesus," he discussed the subject of Jesus in such a way as to justify the inference that the work was complete before the second letter was written. This inference is nevertheless purely speculative. In any event, he had the finished work bound by Frederick A. Mayo of Richmond, though once again it is impossible to determine when.[127]

If the completion date of "The Life and Morals of Jesus" remains a matter of conjecture, there can be no doubt that Jefferson compiled it strictly for his own moral and religious instruction. He never mentioned this collection of Gospel verses in his surviving correspondence, nor did he even reveal its existence to the members of his family. Only after his death did they become aware of it.[128] Until then, it was undoubtedly one of the works on morality that he read each evening, for, with the exception of a single important point of doctrine,[129] it was the one in which he finally established to his ultimate satisfaction the authentic deeds and principles of the man he esteemed as the master moral preceptor of the ages.

[123] TJ to William Short, 4 Aug. 1820 (Appendix).

[124] Same.

[125] Same.

[126] Both letters are in the Appendix.

[127] Mayo's label appears on the inner cover of the bound "Life and Morals of Jesus." Unfortunately, no mention of the binding of this work exists in the surviving correspondence between TJ and Mayo.

[128] Thomas Jefferson Randolph to Henry S. Randall, undated, Randall, *Life of Jefferson*, III, 672.

[129] The point in question was whether Jesus was a materialist or a spiritualist. TJ believed that Jesus was a spiritualist until Thomas Cooper convinced him otherwise in 1823 (TJ to William Short, 13 Apr. 1820 (Appendix); and TJ to Thomas Cooper, 11 Dec. 1823). Koch, *Philosophy of Jefferson*, p. 36, concludes that TJ's "understanding of materialism was not profound." TJ wrote in 1819 that "I never go to bed without an hour, or half hour's previous reading of something moral, whereon to ruminate in the intervals of sleep" (TJ to Vine Utley, 21 Mch. 1819).

IV

"The Philosophy of Jesus" and "The Life and Morals of Jesus" symbolize the point in Jefferson's religious development at which he professed to be a Christian. Consequently, the question naturally arises as to what he meant by this term. Jefferson has been alternately praised and damned by contemporaries and later scholars as a Unitarian, a Deist, a rationalist, and an infidel.[130] Accepting that Jefferson was not a systematic religious thinker, an analysis of the elements of his Christian faith reveals that there was both more to it than those who emphasize his rationalism have conceded and less than those who stress his religiousness have admitted. In fact, it seems best to describe Jefferson as a demythologized Christian—as one, that is to say, who rejected all myth, all mystery, all miracles, and almost all supernaturalism in religion and sought instead to return to what he perceived to be the primitive purity and simplicity of Christianity.

The cornerstone of Jefferson's religion was an unswerving commitment to monotheism. He firmly believed in the existence of one God, who was the creator and sustainer of the universe and the ultimate ground of being. He was convinced that this God revealed himself through the natural wonders of his rationally structured universe rather than through any special revelation imparted to man and written down in sacred scriptures. "The movements of the heavenly bodies," he once told John Adams, appealing to the traditional argument from design, "so exactly held in their course by the balance of centrifugal and centripetal forces, the structure of the earth itself, with it's distribution of lands, waters and atmosphere, animal and vegetable bodies, examined in all their minutest particles, insects mere atoms of life, yet as perfectly organised as man or mammoth, the mineral substances, their generation and uses, it is impossible, I say, for the human mind not to believe that there is, in all this, design, cause, and effect, up to an ultimate cause, a fabricator of all things from matter and motion, their preserver and regulator while permitted to exist in their present forms, and their regenerator into new and other forms."[131] As to the nature of this Supreme Being, Jefferson was of two minds. On the one hand, he sometimes thought that human reason (which he regarded as the only trustworthy source of religious truth) could know nothing about the divine nature; on the other hand, he lavishly praised Jesus for making the one true God worthy of human worship inasmuch as he took "for his type the best qualities of the human head and heart, wisdom, justice, goodness, and adding to them power, ascribed all of these, but in infinite perfection, to the supreme being."[132] There was one thing about the godhead of which Jefferson was certain, however: the one true God that man was obliged to worship and adore was not the triune deity of orthodox Christianity. Jefferson had nothing but scorn for the traditional doctrine of three persons in one God. He rejected it as a contradiction in terms, regretted it as a relapse into polytheism, and scoffed

---

[130] Gould, "Religious Opinions of Thomas Jefferson," p. 199, and Foote, *Religion of Thomas Jefferson*, p. 69-76, view TJ as a Unitarian; Koch, *Philosophy of Jefferson*, p. 37, and Schulz, "Radical Religious Ideas of Adams and Jefferson," p. 279, as a Deist; Knoles, "Religious Ideas of Thomas Jefferson," p. 188, as a rationalist; and Mason, *Voice of Warning*, p. 8, as an infidel.

[131] TJ to John Adams, 11 Apr. 1823 (Appendix).

[132] Same; TJ to William Short, 4 Aug. 1820 (Appendix).

at it as the "hocus-pocus phantasm of a god like another Cerberus with one body and three heads."[133] Of all the alleged corruptions of Christianity, this was the one he denounced with the greatest feeling and frequency.

Next in importance to the unity of God were the moral teachings of Jesus. Jefferson was convinced that Jesus had not left behind a complete system of morality. This was so, he believed, because Jesus died before reaching full intellectual maturity, because he never set down his doctrines in writing, and because his disciples first wrote them down many years after his death, "when much was forgotten, much misunderstood, and presented in very paradoxical shapes."[134] Yet he was equally convinced that the fragmentary teachings of Jesus that had survived constituted the "outlines of a system of the most sublime morality which has ever fallen from the lips of man."[135] He admired the ancient Epicureans and Stoics for showing man how to control himself, but he esteemed Jesus for teaching men to love all humanity, not just family, friends, and fellow countrymen. "Epictetus and Epicurus give us laws for governing ourselves," he noted, "Jesus a supplement of the duties and charities we owe to others."[136] It was the universal law of love, both among men and between nations, that constituted the peculiar excellence of Christianity in Jefferson's eyes and made it superior to any other moral system, ancient or modern. Although he sometimes insinuated that a number of Jesus' precepts and injunctions were valid only insofar as they were expressions of a universal moral law that predated Christianity and was common to all religions, he believed that Jesus' emphasis on man's obligations to be just and charitable to all human beings was his distinctive contribution to the moral development of mankind.[137]

Belief in the one true God and adherence to the morality of Jesus would lead, Jefferson hoped, to some sort of reward in a life after death. He praised Jesus for preaching the doctrine of a life in the hereafter to encourage virtue in the here and now and presumably accepted the teaching himself for this very reason. As he grew older, however, he looked forward to a life after death for another reason, and that was his wish to be reunited with his beloved wife and children.[138] He was occasionally troubled by doubts as to whether in fact there was a life to come, but, on the whole, hope triumphed over despair. "Adore God. Reverence and cherish your parents. Love your neighbor as yourself. Be just. Be true. Murmur not at the ways of Providence," he wrote the year before his death in a valedictory letter to the son of a friend. "So shall the life into which you have entered be the Portal to one of eternal and ineffable

[133] TJ to James Smith, 8 Dec. 1822 (Appendix). For other expressions of TJ's anti-Trinitarianism, see his letters to J. P. P. Derieux, 25 July 1788; to John Adams, 22 Aug. 1813; to William Canby, 18 Sep. 1813; to Francis Adrian Van der Kemp, 30 July 1816; to Timothy Pickering, 27 Feb. 1821; and to John Adams, 11 Apr. 1823 (Appendix).

[134] TJ to Joseph Priestley, 9 Apr. 1803 (Appendix); "Syllabus," [21 Apr. 1803] (Appendix).

[135] TJ to William Short, 31 Oct. 1819 (Appendix).

[136] Same.

[137] "Syllabus," [21 Apr. 1803] (Appendix); TJ to James Fishback, 27 Sep. 1809 (Appendix); TJ to John Adams, 11 Jan. 1817, 5 May 1817.

[138] "Syllabus," [21 Apr. 1803] (Appendix); TJ to John Adams, 13 Nov. 1818, 14 Mch. 1820, 8 Jan. 1825.

bliss."[139] Since Jefferson rejected the orthodox doctrine of hell but approved Jesus' teaching that God would mete out punishments as well as rewards after death, he presumably believed with the Universalists that in time all persons would be reconciled with the deity.[140]

Jefferson revered the founder of Christianity as the greatest moral teacher in history. He did not believe that Jesus was the son of God, nor did he think Jesus ever claimed to be that. He admitted that Jesus believed he was divinely inspired, but he excused this unfortunate lapse from grace as the inevitable result of Jesus' having been brought up among a superstitious people who regarded the "fumes of the most disordered imaginations . . . as special communications of the deity."[141] Instead, he admired Jesus as the preeminent reformer of the Jewish religion whose extraordinary moral sense had enabled him to enunciate universally valid truths. In Jefferson's considered judgment, Jesus was "the Herald of truths reformatory of mankind in general, but more immediately of that of his own countrymen, impressing them with more sublime and more worthy ideas of the Supreme being, teaching them the doctrine of a future state of rewards and punishments, and inculcating the love of mankind, instead of the anti-social spirit with which the Jews viewed all other nations."[142] But since in the end Jesus was, for Jefferson, merely a man, he felt under no obligation to accept all of his teachings, though he rarely specified which ones he rejected.[143]

Belief in the unity of God, acceptance of the moral precepts of Jesus, hope for a life after death, and reverence for Jesus as a great moral reformer—such were the constituent elements of Jefferson's Christian faith and, as he thought, the faith of primitive Christianity as well. Otherwise, he rejected the Bible as a source of divine revelation and regarded it as a mere human history. He dismissed the possibility of miracles as contrary to the laws of nature. He did not believe that Jesus had founded a particular church to safeguard and transmit his doctrines. He spurned the theological, metaphysical, and ecclesiological doctrines of traditional Christianity on the grounds that for the most part they dealt with matters beyond human understanding and were all corruptions of Jesus' original message. He cited the "immaculate conception of Jesus, his deification, the creation of the world by him, his miraculous powers, his res-

---

[139] TJ to Thomas Jefferson Smith, 21 Feb. 1825. Smith was the son of TJ's good friends Samuel Harrison Smith and Margaret Bayard Smith; see TJ to Margaret Bayard Smith, 6 Aug. 1816, notes (Appendix). Notice the element of ambiguity in a poem TJ wrote shortly before his death, which states in part: "I go to my fathers; I welcome the shore, / which crowns all my hopes, or which buries my cares" (TJ to Martha Jefferson Randolph, [2 July 1826]). See also Randall, *Life of Jefferson*, III, 545.

[140] TJ to Van der Kemp, 1 May 1817, explicitly rejects the traditional Christian concept of hell as a state of eternal punishment.

[141] TJ to William Short, 4 Aug. 1820 (Appendix).

[142] TJ to George Thacher, 26 Jan. 1824 (Appendix).

[143] TJ explicitly rejected Jesus' "spiritualism" and his willingness to accept "repentance" alone as sufficient for the forgiveness of sins. To the first TJ opposed his own materialism and to the second, his insistence on "a counterpoise of good works to redeem [sin]" (TJ to William Short, 13 Apr. 1820, Appendix). He also rejected by implication Jesus' doctrine that God punishes some sinners into eternity; see the letter to Van der Kemp cited above in n. 140. These are the only points on which TJ is known to have differed with what he regarded as Jesus' authentic teachings, as opposed to those of the various Christian churches.

[41]

urrection and visible ascension, his corporeal presence in the Eucharist, the Trinity, original sin, atonement, regeneration, election, orders of hierarchy, &c." as but the most flagrant examples of those "artificial systems, invented by Ultra-Christian sects, unauthorised by any single word ever uttered by [Jesus]."[144] Nor was there any doubt in his mind as to the origin of these so-called corruptions of Christianity. He was firmly convinced that they had been deliberately fabricated by the clergy to render lay people dependent upon them and thereby to increase their wealth and power. It was obvious, he stated in a letter that he decided not to send, "that but a short time elapsed after the death of the great reformer of the Jewish religion before his principles were departed from by those who professed to be his special servants, and perverted into an engine for enslaving mankind, and aggrandizing their oppressors in church and state: that the purest system of morals ever before preached to man has been adulterated and sophisticated by artificial constructions, into a mere contrivance to filch wealth and power to themselves, that rational men not being able to swallow their impious heresies, in order to force them down their throats, they raise the hue and cry of infidelity, while themselves are the greatest obstacles to the advancement of the real doctrines of Jesus, and do in fact constitute the real anti-Christ."[145] But much as he criticized orthodox Christianity in private, he never did so in public (except for a few general remarks in *Notes on Virginia*),[146] not only out of a sense of political prudence, but also because his deep commitment to religious freedom led him to respect the right of others to hold religious opinions different from his. For, ultimately, what most concerned him was how men acted in society, not what they believed in religion. If the acceptance of orthodox Christian doctrines produced virtuous lives, he welcomed the result without approving the cause. "I write with freedom," he informed a Kentucky Unitarian, "because, while I claim a right to believe in one god, if so my reason tells me, I yield as freely to others that of believing in three. Both religions I find make honest men, and that is the only point society has any authority to look to."[147] *Ecrasez l'infâme* was as foreign to his nature as *Credo quia impossibile*.

Jefferson's demythologized version of Christianity, like so many other aspects of his life and thought, resists easy historical categories. It was anti-Trinitarian in its concept of God, Christian in its acceptance of the morality of Jesus, skeptical in its rejection of biblical revelation and church dogma, deistic in its conviction that the clergy had deliberately corrupted the pure doctrines of Jesus to serve their selfish purposes, rationalistic in its assumption that human reason was the only valid source of religious truth, and humanistic in its equation of religion with morality. In the end Jefferson probably best described his peculiarly eclectic faith when he observed of himself: "I am of a sect by myself, as far as I know."[148] This demythologized creed is perfectly reflected in Jefferson's two compilations of extracts from the Gospels, in which, by excluding all mythic and miraculous events and concentrating instead on the moral precepts of Jesus, he offers his view of Jesus as the foremost moral reformer in human history.

[144] TJ to William Short, 31 Oct. 1819, n. 3 (Appendix).
[145] TJ to William Baldwin, 19 Jan. 1810 (Appendix).
[146] *Notes on Virginia*, ed. Peden, p. 159-61.
[147] TJ to James Smith, 8 Dec. 1822 (Appendix).
[148] TJ to Ezra Stiles Ely, 25 June 1819 (Appendix).

THE PHILOSOPHY OF JESUS

THE RECONSTRUCTION OF
"THE PHILOSOPHY OF JESUS"

The text of "The Philosophy of Jesus" presented in this volume is a reconstruction of the missing original copy of Jefferson's first compilation of verses
from the Evangelists. The fate of the original "Philosophy of Jesus" is wrapped
in mystery. Jefferson referred or alluded to this work in six different letters,
the first written in 1804 and the last in 1819—just before he began work on
"The Life and Morals of Jesus."[1] According to the testimony of his grandson,
Thomas Jefferson Randolph, "The Philosophy of Jesus" was still among Jefferson's effects at the time of his death in July 1826.[2] Yet, thirty-two years
later, Henry S. Randall stated in his noted biography of Jefferson that this
compilation was "not preserved in Mr. Jefferson's family, but his grandson,
Mr. George Wythe Randolph, has obtained for us a list of its contents. That,
in different languages ["The Life and Morals of Jesus"], is in the possession
of his oldest grandson, Colonel Thomas Jefferson Randolph."[3] What became
of "The Philosophy of Jesus" between 1826 and 1858 is as yet unknown.
Randall's statement that it was "not preserved in Mr. Jefferson's family" is
sufficiently ambiguous to permit one to infer that by 1858 it had been accidentally destroyed, inadvertently lost, deliberately stolen, or simply given to a
trusted friend of the family. But this is purely conjectural. What is beyond
dispute is that "The Philosophy of Jesus" was still in existence in 1826 but is
now no longer to be found, notwithstanding the best efforts of the editors of
the present volume to locate it.[4]

But if the original text of "The Philosophy of Jesus" has been lost, perhaps
beyond hope of recovery, there are still, thanks to Jefferson's methodical work
habits, four surviving pieces of evidence that can be used to reconstruct his
first collection of passages from the Gospels with a high degree of accuracy.
The first two items are the New Testaments from which he actually clipped
the verses he used in "The Philosophy of Jesus." Both volumes are editions of
the King James Version printed in Dublin by George Grierson, one in 1791
and the other in 1799. They were donated to the University of Virginia in

[1] See the letters printed in the Appendix from TJ to Benjamin Rush, 8 Aug. 1804;
to John Adams, 12 Oct. 1813; to Charles Clay, 29 Jan. 1815; to Charles Thomson, 9
Jan. 1815 [1816]; to Van der Kemp, 25 Apr. 1816; and to William Short, 31 Oct.
1819.

[2] Thomas Jefferson Randolph to Henry S. Randall, undated, Henry S. Randall, *The
Life of Thomas Jefferson* (Philadelphia, 1858), III, 671.

[3] Same, p. 452.

[4] Henry W. Foote, ed., *The Life and Morals of Jesus of Nazareth* (Boston, 1951), p.
22, erroneously states that "a few sheets" and the "title page" of the original "Philosophy
of Jesus" (hereafter referred to as PJ) were sold in New York in 1934. In fact, the items
in question were the copies of the title page and the table of texts of the compilation that
are referred to herein as the E-R MS. They were offered for sale in 1934 by TJ's
granddaughter thrice removed, Miss Olivia Taylor, but were withdrawn from auction
before purchase and were subsequently donated to the University of Virginia as part of
the Edgehill-Randolph Papers (American Art Association, Anderson Galleries Inc., sale
no. 4073, item 250; William G. Ray to the Editor, 12 Sep. 1967, Jefferson Editorial
Files).

1913 by Jefferson's great-granddaughter, Martha Jefferson Trist Burke. Before Mrs. Burke acquired them, the two mutilated volumes were held by her mother, Virginia Randolph Trist, a granddaughter of Jefferson; by Mrs. Trist's sister, Cornelia Jefferson Randolph; and presumably by Miss Randolph's mother, Martha Jefferson Randolph, the third president's daughter. Mrs. Burke, who may have been unaware of "The Philosophy of Jesus," assumed that Jefferson had used these New Testaments in preparing "The Life and Morals of Jesus," but internal evidence clearly demonstrates they were the ones he used to put together his earlier biblical compilation.[5]

The other two pieces of evidence used in reconstructing "The Philosophy of Jesus" are dual copies of the title page and the list of the Gospel verses Jefferson included in this work. The more important of the two copies is located in the Edgehill-Randolph Papers at the University of Virginia and is henceforth referred to as the E-R MS Table of Texts. It is not in Jefferson's holograph, but the copyist clearly tried to duplicate his handwriting and did such a creditable job that it is almost impossible to identify the writer with any certainty. This copy is probably the work of Jefferson's granddaughter, Cornelia Jefferson Randolph (1799-1871), who was also involved in making a transcript of the English text of the multilingual "Life and Morals of Jesus."[6] It is written on four pages of three leaves and is stitched together with copies, in the same hand, of Jefferson's 21 April 1803 letter to Benjamin Rush and the accompanying "Syllabus." All these documents, in turn, are bound together by a cover on which the same copyist wrote extracts from the purported deathbed speech of Julian the Apostate, as given in Jean Phillipe René de La Bletterie, *The Life of the Emperor Julian* (London, 1746).[7] Since Jefferson sold this book to the Library of Congress in 1815, it is possible that the E-R MS Table of Texts was transcribed before that year. Yet there is no other evidence that the quotations from La Bletterie's work might have been used by Jefferson himself, and it is entirely conceivable that they are completely unrelated to "The Philosophy of Jesus." In any event, the fact that the copyist took such pains to duplicate Jefferson's holograph strongly suggests that she (or he) worked from Jefferson's original Table of Texts for his first compilation of extracts from the Gospels. Moreover, since so much care was taken to make a facsimile Table of Texts by the only means generally available in the early nineteenth century, it seems safe to assume that the E-R MS is accurate.

The other copy of the title page and the Table of Texts for "The Philosophy of Jesus" is the one printed in Randall's 1858 biography of Jefferson.[8] As we have seen, Randall obtained this copy from George Wythe Randolph, Thomas Jefferson Randolph's younger brother. Randall did not specify where the younger

[5] Mrs. Burke made clear her belief that Jefferson had used these volumes to compile "The Life and Morals of Jesus" (hereafter referred to as LJ) in some notations she made in the 1799 New Testament and in the transcription of his second biblical compilation described in n. 6 below.

[6] This tentative attribution is based strictly upon a comparison of the E-R MS Table of Texts with samples of Cornelia Jefferson Randolph's handwriting. The transcript of LJ she helped to make is in ViU: TJ Papers. It was donated to the University of Virginia by Fraunces Maury Burke, Martha J. T. Burke's daughter.

[7] E. Millicent Sowerby, comp., *Catalogue of the Library of Thomas Jefferson* (Washington, D.C., 1952-59), No. 90.

[8] Randall, *Life of Jefferson*, III, 654-55.

Randolph obtained this transcript, but it seems very likely that what Randall printed was copied from the E-R MS Table of Texts, although there are a number of discrepancies between the two. In every case, however, the evidence found in the clipped 1791 and 1799 New Testaments attests to the accuracy of the E-R MS Table of Texts and suggests that the variations in the one printed by Randall are almost all the result of misreadings of the sometimes obscure text of the E-R MS. For example, the 3's in the E-R MS Table of Texts often resemble 9's, and it is often difficult to distinguish among commas, dashes, and periods. In addition, Randall's Table of Texts also contains several arbitrary changes and common errors of transcription. Thus, since Randall never corrects variations between the verses listed in the E-R MS Table of Texts and the ones Jefferson actually clipped from the New Testament, it is difficult to resist the conclusion that the E-R MS was the original source for his Table of Texts.

I

Such, then, are the items available for a reconstruction of the text of "The Philosophy of Jesus"—the E-R MS Table of Texts, of which Randall's Table is but an imperfect copy, and the mutilated 1791 and 1799 New Testaments from which Jefferson actually clipped the verses he included in this compilation. But none of these bears Jefferson's identifying holograph. Furthermore, some discrepancies exist between the E-R MS Table of Texts and the clipped New Testaments. Accordingly, it became necessary to find definite marks of Jefferson's handiwork in each of the main pieces of evidence.

In this regard, the first question that had to be answered was how Jefferson actually compiled "The Philosophy of Jesus." Since Jefferson's letters are disappointingly reticent on this vital question, the essential clue was provided by "The Life and Morals of Jesus." Unlike "The Philosophy of Jesus," the basic items Jefferson used to compile the English portion of "The Life and Morals of Jesus" are still extant, including a fragmentary draft list of contents,[9] the final Table of Texts,[10] and the two mutilated New Testaments from which he clipped the Gospel verses. Taken together, these items offer valuable hints as to how Jefferson made his second biblical compilation and, by extension, his first as well.

In brief, these materials show that in the process of compiling "The Life and Morals of Jesus," Jefferson first drew up a proposed table of contents and then proceeded to clip and paste the appropriate passages from the Evangelists, sometimes adding new verses as he went along. This conclusion was first suggested by the surviving draft table of contents. It was reinforced, moreover, by a comparison between the final Table of Texts and the main body of "The Life and Morals of Jesus." This comparison revealed three key points. To begin with, it showed that the page numbers for the Gospel verses listed in the Table of Texts almost invariably correspond to the pages on which the verses appear in the text itself, strongly suggesting that Jefferson first drew up the Table of Texts, then clipped and pasted the passages from the Evangelists, and lastly entered the appropriate page numbers in the Table. In addition, Jefferson made a number of alterations in the final Table of Texts, writing over some of the

[9] This fragment is in DLC: TJ Papers, f. 42080.
[10] This Table of Texts is part of the original LJ reproduced in this volume.

original verse entries and inserting additional verse numbers above others. It seems virtually impossible that he made these changes after finishing the main compilation but before making up the final Table of Texts. Rather, it is far more likely that he first drew up the Table of Texts and then made the changes as he was putting together the text itself and adding new verses not originally listed in the Table. This supposition is further borne out by the third major point that emerged from comparing the Table of Texts with the actual text of "The Life and Morals of Jesus"—namely, that several verses appear in the main body of this work, but not in the Table of Texts, and that one verse appears in the Table, but not in the text itself. These discrepancies can only be explained on the supposition that Jefferson added new verses to the text of "The Life and Morals of Jesus" after first having drawn up what he thought to be the completed Table of Texts.

Having established that in producing "The Life and Morals of Jesus" Jefferson first drew up a table of contents and then clipped and pasted the corresponding passages from the Gospels, adding new verses as he proceeded, it seemed reasonable to assume that he had used the same method with "The Philosophy of Jesus." Not only would this have been consistent with the high degree of system Jefferson brought to almost every task he undertook, but it also provides a solution to a riddle that has long tantalized scholars: how the third president could have finished "The Philosophy of Jesus" in the course of only several evenings at a time when his primary attention was devoted to transacting public business.[11] Even if one takes into consideration Jefferson's later admission that he did the work too hastily,[12] it is still difficult to believe that he was able both to decide upon the Gospel passages he wanted to include in "The Philosophy of Jesus" and to clip and paste them together in only two or three evenings in February 1804. But this difficulty disappears if one assumes that Jefferson first studied the New Testament for a while, next prepared a proposed Table of Texts, and then spent from one to three nights simply clipping the relevant passages from the Evangelists and pasting them on to blank sheets of paper, occasionally inserting new verses as he worked. In addition to being plausible, this assumption has the further merit of fitting in nicely with the fact that Jefferson is known to have carefully read Joseph Priestley's *Harmonies of the Evangelists* shortly before he began work on "The Philosophy of Jesus," which suggests that he had a good idea beforehand of what he wanted to include in his first biblical compilation.[13]

Thus, in reconstructing "The Philosophy of Jesus," it seemed safe to assume that Jefferson worked from a prepared Table of Texts that was drawn up before he clipped the verses from the Gospels which he included in that work. In order to make the reconstructed text as accurate as possible, however, it was necessary to discover precisely how Jefferson had constructed the original text. It is important to remember that Jefferson used two New Testaments to compile "The Philosophy of Jesus," since he realized in advance that after clipping and pasting a passage from one side of a page he would sometimes want to use another passage on the other side of it. But in examining a mutilated page in

[11] TJ to Van der Kemp, 25 Apr. 1816, and to William Short, 31 Oct. 1819 (Appendix). In the former letter TJ claimed to have completed PJ in "one or two evenings only," and in the latter he stated that he had finished it in "2. or 3. nights only."

[12] TJ to Van der Kemp, 25 Apr. 1816 (Appendix).

[13] TJ to Joseph Priestley, 29 Jan. 1804 (Appendix).

the 1791 or 1799 New Testament, it was frequently impossible at first glance to determine which side of it Jefferson had used in "The Philosophy of Jesus." Therefore, it became essential to ascertain whether Jefferson had followed any set procedure that would indicate which side of any given page in the New Testaments he was most likely to have used.

Once again "The Life and Morals of Jesus" and the clipped New Testaments Jefferson had employed to compile its English text provided the solution. Using photocopies of these two volumes, the Gospels were carefully reconstructed by pasting the clippings from the English text of this compilation into the appropriate gaps of the mutilated New Testaments. The result of this test was striking. It showed that Jefferson almost always took Gospel passages from one of these New Testaments and did not have recourse to the other unless he wanted to use a verse that appeared on the reverse side of a passage he had already clipped and pasted into "The Life and Morals of Jesus." A close inspection of the New Testaments from which Jefferson cut out extracts for "The Philosophy of Jesus" revealed that the 1799 volume was much more mutilated than the 1791 volume. It seemed safe to assume, therefore, that Jefferson had followed the same procedure in clipping Gospel verses for "The Philosophy of Jesus" as he did for "The Life and Morals of Jesus."

II

Thus, despite his silence on this crucial point, Jefferson's basic methodology in compiling "The Philosophy of Jesus" was established with the aid of his second biblical compilation. To begin with, he prepared a Table of Texts before clipping verses from the Gospels and probably added some new verses in the course of his work. In addition, he rarely cut a passage from the 1791 New Testament unless it had already been removed from the 1799 New Testament. It remained, then, to test the accuracy of these findings by doing precisely what Jefferson had done to compile his first collection of extracts from the Gospels.

In order to do this, unmutilated copies of the identical New Testaments Jefferson had used in the compilation had to be found. An extensive search located a copy of the 1791 edition in the British Library, and the only extant copy of the 1799 edition that could be found was owned by a book dealer in Dublin. Using photocopies of both, verses were clipped from the New Testaments in the order in which they appeared in the E-R MS Table of Texts. In almost every case, Jefferson's mutilated New Testaments made it possible to establish precisely which edition he had used for a given verse. The few exceptions came from pages Jefferson had already heavily clipped.

This step in the reconstruction of the text was especially important. Instead of simply taking the E-R MS Table of Texts at face value, the reverse side of each clipping was also considered for possible inclusion. Furthermore, each side of every page from the copy of the British Library's 1791 New Testament was carefully matched to determine exactly what portion on one side was eliminated by the use of a clipped passage on the other.

This test demonstrated beyond any reasonable doubt that Jefferson followed the same procedure in compiling "The Philosophy of Jesus" as he did in compiling "The Life and Morals of Jesus." With few exceptions, he did not clip a passage from the 1791 New Testament unless he had already removed a verse on the other side of it from the 1799 New Testament. Furthermore, this test proved conclusively that in every case where the Randall and the E-R MS Table of Texts varied the latter contained the accurate reading. In two instances, moreover, the New Testaments corrected both Tables. Randall and the E-R MS each list L18:9-14, but the mutilated New Testaments show that these verses were not clipped. They also list L23:23 twice. This verse is clipped from the 1799 New Testament, but not the 1791, and in fact Jefferson used parts of it in two places in "The Philosophy of Jesus."[14]

After all the discrepancies had been resolved and the verses listed in the E-R MS Table of Texts clipped, the two New Testaments used in the reconstruction were then compared with the ones actually employed by Jefferson. This showed that sixteen clippings still remained that are not listed in the Table of Texts, raising the question of which, if any, were included in "The Philosophy of Jesus." Jefferson seems to have intentionally clipped a number of the verses that do not appear in the Table of Texts. Since "The Life and Morals of Jesus" contains several verses not listed in its Table of Texts, it therefore seemed necessary to place relevant additional verses at appropriate points in "The Philosophy of Jesus." Of the sixteen clippings in question, seven and a half contain verses, or parallels of verses, that appear in "The Life and Morals of Jesus" and thus may be presumed to have been used in "The Philosophy of Jesus" as well. Four others, which are not in "The Life and Morals of Jesus," are nevertheless so consistent with the contents of "The Philosophy of Jesus" that they have been inserted at fitting points in the reconstructed text. The remaining four and a half clippings, however, consist of verses Jefferson is unlikely to have used and are thus excluded from the reconstructed text.[15]

The problem of the additional verses was not the only one encountered in reconstructing the text of "The Philosophy of Jesus." Certain verses are listed in both the E-R MS and the Randall Table of Texts that contain in part material that Jefferson probably would have excluded because of their miraculous or supernatural content. For example, Jefferson used L14:4 in both of his biblical compilations: "And they held their peace. And he took *him*, and healed him, and let *him* go."[16] But in "The Life and Morals of Jesus" he excluded the last sentence of this verse, which suggests that he might have done the same in "The Philosophy of Jesus." Since there is no way of ascertaining whether Jefferson did in fact omit it in his first biblical compilation, however, this sentence and others like it have been retained in the reconstructed text, and footnotes have been provided identifying portions of verses omitted in "The Life and Morals of Jesus" that may have been left out of "The Philosophy of Jesus" as well.

After having done virtually everything possible to ensure the reliability of the reconstructed text of "The Philosophy of Jesus," one further test was made to check the result. This was to ascertain how accurate a text of the English portion of "The Life and Morals of Jesus" would be produced if one tried to

[14] PJ, p. 45. References to page numbers in PJ are to those supplied by the editors in reconstructing the text and are found at the top of the pages in this volume.

[15] The additional verses excluded from the reconstructed text of PJ are: M8:9-10 (the cure of the centurion's servant); M9:33-34 (the casting out of a demon); M10:3-4 (the call of the apostles); M11:2-9 (Jesus and John the Baptist); and a duplicate of M11:9.

[16] PJ, p. 22; LJ, p. 40. References to page numbers in LJ are to those penned at the top of each page by Jefferson as he prepared the manuscript.

reconstruct it strictly on the basis of Jefferson's Table of Texts and the mutilated New Testaments he used to compile it. The results are as follows.

First, one verse, L14:15, is listed in the Table of Texts but is not in the text itself. The clipped New Testaments indicate this verse was not used.

Second, a number of small clippings, running to no more than two lines, were never pasted into "The Life and Morals of Jesus." These consist for the most part of chapter numbers and headings, which Jefferson usually did not use in the English portion of this compilation and therefore discarded.

Third, Jefferson used only parts of forty-six verses in "The Life and Morals of Jesus." All but ten of the unused portions of verses are unclipped, which means that more than 75 percent of the partially used verses would appear in a hypothetical reconstructed text.

Fourth, there are ten missing clippings of more than two lines. Four of these can be eliminated because for the most part they contain verses Jefferson actually listed in the Table of Texts. Two consist of verses which, if included in a reconstructed text, would not significantly alter its meaning because parallels to them exist in other parts of "The Life and Morals of Jesus." The remaining clippings include M7:2, M24:29, Mk14:53, and a fragment of M4:19. All four of these verses are in "The Life and Morals of Jesus" (though Jefferson lined out Mk14:53), but none is listed in the Table of Texts, and probably only M7:2 would have been included in a reconstructed text for stylistic reasons.[17]

Finally, a few other minor discrepancies between the original "Life and Morals of Jesus" and a hypothetical reconstructed text must be recognized. Jefferson made five slight changes in the English text of his second biblical compilation that would not be apparent to someone trying to reconstruct it solely on the basis of his Table of Texts and the clipped New Testaments. First, he changed "out" to "up" in L6:12.[18] Second, he cut out "as" in the first line of M24:38.[19] Third, he corrected the verse number for J7:53, which was misprinted "58."[20] Fourth, he pasted in and lined out Mk14:53, a verse that does not appear in the Table of Texts.[21] Finally, he inadvertently left out five lines of M19:12.[22] These variations are significant only insofar as they alert readers to the possibility that Jefferson may have made similar alterations in "The Philosophy of Jesus."

In summary, a reconstructed text of the English portion of "The Life and Morals of Jesus" would not differ greatly from the actual text of Jefferson's second biblical compilation. Some portions of verses would appear in the reconstructed compilation that are not in the original "Life and Morals of Jesus," suggesting that Jefferson might have excluded the same portions from "The Philosophy of Jesus." But the fact that Jefferson left part of a Gospel verse out of his second biblical compilation does not necessarily mean that he omitted it from his first as well. For example, in "The Life and Morals of Jesus," he used all of J18:4, which attributes to Jesus a knowledge of the future in which Jefferson personally did not believe, whereas he used only the last three words

[17] LJ, p. 13, 40, 63, 75.
[18] LJ, p. 5.
[19] LJ, p. 64.
[20] LJ, p. 36.
[21] LJ, p. 75.
[22] LJ, p. 51.

of it ("Whom seek ye?") in "The Philosophy of Jesus."[23] In any event, just as the reconstructed text of "The Philosophy of Jesus" contains some Gospel verses in full that a reconstructed text of "The Life and Morals of Jesus" would have only in part, so, too, the original text of Jefferson's second collection of extracts from the Evangelists contains several portions of Gospel verses that, according to the evidence of the clipped 1791 and 1799 New Testaments, he completely excluded from his first compilation.

III

Having discovered the basic procedures used by Jefferson in compiling "The Philosophy of Jesus" and having followed them in selecting and ordering the Gospel verses for the reconstructed text, there remained the question of whether he had arranged the verses in single- or in double-column format on the pages of this work. Happily, Jefferson himself seemed to provide the clues needed to solve this mystery, though one of them proved to be profoundly misleading. In 1813 Jefferson specifically described "The Philosophy of Jesus" as "an 8vo. of 46 pages," and in 1816 he stated, with reference to this work, that he hoped to "add to my little book the Greek, Latin and French texts, in columns side by side."[24] Since it would have been virtually impossible for Jefferson to add three more columns of verses to a page already containing two, he seemed to imply in his latter statement that "The Philosophy of Jesus" had only one column of text per page.

Yet it soon became apparent that this conclusion conflicted with Jefferson's description of "The Philosophy of Jesus" as an octavo volume of 46 pages. The normal size of an octavo page is eight inches long and six inches wide. However, it would require pages at least ten inches long to produce a 46-page volume in which one could fit, in single-column format, all the passages from the 1791 and 1799 New Testaments used in the reconstructed text of "The Philosophy of Jesus."[25] Furthermore, if Jefferson had actually revised this compilation by simply supplementing the original English text with the corresponding verses in Greek, Latin, and French, he would have needed pages at least seven inches wide, given the width of the columns of text in the dual pairs of New Testaments he had at his disposal in these languages for this task.[26] Neither measurement seemed consistent with the normal dimensions of an octavo page or with Jefferson's own description of "The Philosophy of Jesus" as "a wee little book."[27] In view of these considerations, it began to appear increasingly doubtful that Jefferson had in fact arranged the text of his first biblical compilation in the form of one column of Gospel verses per page. This skepticism was further strengthened by the fact that he never modified "The Philosophy of Jesus" as

[23] PJ, p. 42; LJ, p. 73.

[24] TJ to John Adams, 13 Oct. 1813, and to Charles Thomson, 9 Jan. 1815 [1816] (Appendix).

[25] The total length of all the passages from these two volumes included in the reconstructed text of PJ is 480 inches.

[26] The width of a column of text in both the 1791 and the 1799 New Testaments is two inches—the same width as a column of text in the English New Testaments Jefferson used to compile LJ. The corresponding measurements for the matched pairs of Greek-Latin and French New Testaments he also owned in 1816 are three inches and one and three-quarters inches, respectively.

[27] TJ to Charles Thomson, 9 Jan. 1815 [1816] (Appendix).

he had intended, but made an entirely different compilation instead, which lends credence to the view that the original "Philosophy of Jesus" did not have sufficient space for three additional columns of verses per page. In fact, it seemed far more likely that what Jefferson actually had in mind in 1816 was to produce a new volume for his own use consisting of the same English verses used in the original "Philosophy of Jesus," but with these verses taken from the English New Testaments he had acquired from Mathew Carey in 1805 and supplemented by the corresponding passages from the Gospels in Greek, Latin, and French.

After the single-column hypothesis was rejected as untenable, the reconstructed text was arranged on the basis of two columns of Gospel verses per page. The resulting text proved to be far more consonant with Jefferson's description of the physical dimensions of the original "Philosophy of Jesus" than the one produced by following the alternative hypothesis. By arranging the verses from the 1791 and 1799 New Testaments in two columns per page and by making each page of text an average of five and one-quarter inches long, a reconstructed text of "The Philosophy of Jesus" was created that was exactly 46 pages long. The average length per column was not altogether arbitrary inasmuch as the columns of text in the 1791 and 1799 New Testaments are six and six and one-quarter inches long, respectively. In consequence of this finding, the text of "The Philosophy of Jesus" presented here is arranged in double-column format, with the columns averaging five and one-quarter inches in length.

IV

The painstaking care taken in reconstructing the text of Jefferson's first biblical compilation should inspire confidence that, if and when the original is ever found, the substantial accuracy of the reconstructed text will be verified. Admittedly, Jefferson may only have used in part some of the Gospel verses printed in full in the reconstructed compilation. In this regard the annotation following the reconstructed "Philosophy of Jesus," particularly the notes identifying verses that appear in Jefferson's first collection of Gospel extracts but not in his second, should prove helpful to readers. But on the whole it seems reasonable to assert that the text of "The Philosophy of Jesus" presented here is substantially similar, if not virtually identical, to the missing original copy of this work.

The Philosophy

of Jesus of Nazareth.
extracted from the account of
his life and doctrines as given by
Mathew, Mark, Luke, & John.

being an abridgement of
the New Testament
for the use of the Indians
unembarrassed with matters of fact
or faith beyond the level of their
comprehension.

A Table of the texts extracted from the gospels, of the order in which they are arranged into sections. & the heads of each section.

§. I. Luke 2. 5— 7. 21. 22. 39— 49. 51. 52. } History of Jesus.
       3. 23.— 38.

II. Matt. 10. 5.— 31. 42. Precepts for the Priesthood.

III. Luke 22. 24 — 27. }
    John. 13. 4 — 17. } Preachers to be humble.

IV. John. 10. 1 — 16. }
    Luke. 11. 52. } false teachers.
       12. 13 — 15. }

V. John. 13. 34. 35. disciples should love one another.

VI. Matt. 13. 24 — 30. 36 — 43. Parable of the tares. a man not to judge for God.

VII. Matt. 20. 1 — 16. Parable of the laborers.

VIII. Mark. 2. 15 — 17. } Physicians are for the sick.
     Matt. 18. 10. 11 } Parables. of the lost sheep, the
     Luke 15. 3 — 32. } lost peice of silver the prodigal son.

IX. John. 8. 1 - 11.
    matt 18. 15 - 17. } the duty of mutual forgiveness
    Luke. 13. 6 — 9 } & forbearance.

X. matt. 5. 1 — 13. 19 — 48. }
      6. 1 — 34 } the Sermon in the mount.
      7. 1 — 27.

XXIV.   18. 1—8. Parable of the unjust judge.

XXV. Matt. 21. 33—41. Parable of the unjust husbandman & their lord.

XXVI. Luke. 17. 7—10. mere justice no praise.

XXVII   14. 12—14. the merit of disinterested good.

XXVIII. matt. 21. 28—31. acts better than proffessions.

XXIX.   22. 15—22. submission to magistrates.

XXX.   19. 9—12. the bond of mariage.

XXXI.   25. 14—30. the duty of emproving our talent.

XXXII. Luke. 12. 16—21. vain calculations of life.

XXXIII Matt. 25. 1—13, ⎞
                              ⎬ watch and be ready.
       Luke. 12   35—48 ⎠

XXXIIII John. 12. 24—28.   a future life.

XXXV matt 22. 23—32. the resurrection.

XXXVI.   23. 31—46.   the last judgement.

XXXVII.   13. 31—33. 44—52. the Kingdom of heaven

XXXVIII John. 4. 24. God.

XXXIX. John 18. 1.2.3. Matt. 26. 49. 50. John 18. 4. 5. 8.

       Matt. 26. 55. John. 18. 12. Matt. 26. 57.

       John. 18. 19—23. matt. 26. 59—62. Luke. 22. 67. 68. 70

       mark. 14. 60. 64. Luke. 23. 1—3. John 18. 36.

       Luke 23. 4—23. Matt 27. 24. 25. Luke 23. 23. 24.

       Matt 27. 26. John 19. 16. Luke 23. 33. 34.

       John 19. 25—27. matt 27. 46. John 19. 28—30.

death of Jesus.

XI. *Matt.* 19. 19 – 24. 29. 30 }
        22. 35 – 40 } general moral precepts.

XII.   12. 1 – 5. 11. 12. }
  Luke 14. 1 – 6 } the sabath.

XIII   11. 37 – 48. }
  matt. 15. 1 – 9. } deeds & not ceremonies avail.

XIV   10 – 20. }
    12. 33 – 37. } words the fruit of the heart.

XV.   13. 1 – 9. 18 – 23. Parable of the sower.

XVI. *Luke* 7. 36 – 47. }
  mark 12. 41 – 44. } the will for the deed.

XVII. *Matt.* 11. 28 – 30 General exhortation.

XVIII *Luke* 10. 25 – 37. Parable of the Samaritan true benevolence.

XIX *matt.* 23. 1 – 33. }
  Luke. 18. 9 – 14. } humility. pride hypocrisy.
  Matt 14. 7 – 11. } Pharisaism.
  Matt 18. 1 – 6 }

XX. *Luke* 16. 19 – 31. Dives & Lazarus }
  matt. 22. 1 – 14. the wedding supper } God no
    12. 46 – 50. } respecter
    8. 11. —— —— —— } of persons.

XXI. *Luke.* 13. 1 – 5. misfortune no proof of sin.

XXII.   14. 26 – 33. Prudence & firmness to duty

XXIII.   16. 1 – 13. Parable of the unjust steward. worldly wisdom

1

L

CHAP. II.

AND it came to pass in those days, that there went out a decree from Cesar Augustus, that all the world should be taxed.

2 (And this taxing was first made when Cyrenius was governor of Syria.)

3 And all went to be taxed, every one in his own city.

4 And Joseph also went up from Galilee, out of the city of Nazareth, into Judea, unto the city of David, which is called Bethlehem, (because he was of the house and lineage of David,)

5 To be taxed with Mary his espoused wife, being great with child.

6 And so it was, that while they were there, the days were accomplished that she should be delivered.

7 And she brought forth her first-born son, and wrapped him in swaddling-clothes, and laid him in a manger, because there was no room for them in the inn.

21 And when eight days were accomplished for the circumcising of the child, his name was called JESUS,

22 And when the days of her purification, according to the law of Moses, were accomplished, they brought him to Jerusalem, to present him to the Lord;

39 And when they had performed all things according to the law of the Lord, they returned into Galilee, to their own city Nazareth.

40 And the child grew, and waxed strong in spirit, filled with wisdom; and the grace of God was upon him.

41 Now his parents went to Jerusalem every year at the feast of the passover.

42 And when he was twelve years old, they went up to Jerusalem, after the custom of the feast.

43 And when they had fulfilled the days, as they returned, the child Jesus tarried behind in Jerusalem; and Joseph and his mother knew not of it.

44 But they supposing him to have been in the company, went a days journey: and they sought him among their kinsfolk and acquaintance.

45 And when they found him not, they turned back again to Jerusalem, seeking him.

L2

46 And it came to pass, that after three days they found him in the temple, fitting in the midst of the doctors, both hearing them, and asking them questions.

47 And all that heard him were astonished at his understanding and answers.

48 And when they saw him, they were amazed: and his mother said unto him, Son, why hast thou thus dealt with us? behold, thy father and I have sought thee sorrowing.

49 And he said unto them, How is it that ye sought me? wist ye not that I must be about my Fathers business?

51 And he went down with them, and came to Nazareth, and was subject unto them:

52 And Jesus increased in wisdom and stature, and in favour with God and man.

L3

23 And Jesus himself began to be about thirty years of age, being, (as was supposed) the son of Joseph, which was the son of Heli,

24 Which was the son of Matthat, which was the son of Levi, which was the son of Melchi, which was the son of Janna, which was the son of Joseph,

25 Which was the son of Mattathias, which was the son of Amos, which was the son of Naum, which was the son of Esli, which was the son of Nagge,

26 Which was the son of Maath, which was the son of Mattathias, which was the son of Semei, which was the son of Joseph, which was the son of Juda,

27 Which was the son of Joanna, which was the son of Rhesa, which was the son of Zorobabel, which was the son of Salathiel, which was the son of Neri,

28 Which was the son of Melchi, which was the son of Addi, which was the son of Cosam, which was the son of Elmodam, which was the son of Er,

29 Which was the son of Jose, which was the son of Eliezer, which was the son of Jorim, which was the son of Matthat, which was the son of Levi,

o Which was the son of Simeon, which was the son of Juda, which was the son of Joseph, which was the son of Jonan, which was the son of Eliakim,

L3

31 Which was *the fon of* Melea, which was *the fon* of Menan, which was *the fon* of Mattatha, which was *the fon* of Nathan, which was *the fon* of David,

32 Which was *the fon of* Jeffe, which was *the fon* of Obed, which was *the fon* of Booz, which was *the fon* of Salmon, which was *the fon* of Naaffon,

33 Which was *the fon* of Aminadab, which was *the fon of* Aram, which was *the fon* of Efrom, which was *the fon* of Phares, which was *the fon* of Juda,

34 Which was *the fon* of Jacob, which was *the fon* of Ifaac, which was *the fon* of Abraham, which was *the fon* of Thara, which was *the fon* of Nachor

35 Which was *the fon* of Saruch, which was *the fon* of Ragau, which was *the fon* of Phalec, which was *the fon* of Heber, which was *the fon* of Sala,

36 Which was *the fon* of Cainan, which was *the fon* of Arphaxad, which was *the fon* of Sem, which was *the fon* of Noe, which was *the fon* of Lamech,

37 Which was *the fon* of Mathufala, which was *the fon* of Enoch, which was *the fon* of Jared, which was *the fon* of Maleleel, which was *the fon* of Cainan,

38 Which was *the fon* of E-nos, which was *the fon* of Seth, which was *the fon* of Adam, which was *the fon* of God.

12 And it came to pafs in thofe days, that he went out into a mountain to pray, and continued all night in prayer to God.

13 ¶ And when it was day, he called unto him his difciples; and of them he chofe twelve, whom alfo he named apoftles:

14 Simon (whom he alfo named Peter) and Andrew his brother, James, and John, Philip, and Bartholomew,

15 Matthew, and Thomas, James *the fon* of Alpheus, and Simon called Zelotes,

16 And Judas *the brother* of James, and Judas Ifcariot, which alfo was the traitor.

5 Thefe twelve Jefus fent forth, and commanded them, faying, Go not into the way of the Gentiles, and into *any* city of the Samaritans enter ye not.

[L6: 12-16]

M10

M10

6 But go rather to the loft, sheep of the houfe of Ifrael.

7 And as ye go, preach, saying, The kingdom of heaven is at hand.

8 Heal the fick, cleanfe the lepers, raife the dead, caft out devils: freely ye have received, freely give.

9 Provide neither gold, nor filver, nor brafs in your purfes:

10 Nor ferip for your journey, neither two coats, neither fhoes, nor yet ftaves: (for the workman is worthy of his meat.)

11 And into whatfoever city or town ye fhall enter, enquire who in it is worthy, and there abide till ye go thence.

12 And when ye come into an houfe, falute it.

13 And if the houfe be worthy, let your peace come upon it: but if it be not worthy, let your peace return to you.

14 And whofoever fhall not receive you, nor hear your words; when ye depart out of that houfe, or city, fhake off the duft of your feet.

15 Verily I fay unto you, It fhall be more tolerable for the land of Sodom and Gomorrha, in the day of judgment, than for that city.

16 ¶ Behold, I fend you forth as fheep in the midft of wolves: be ye therefore wife as ferpents, and harmlefs as doves.

17 But beware of men, for they will deliver you up to the councils, and they will fcourge you in their fynagogues.

18 And ye fhall be brought before governors and kings for my fake, for a teftimony againft them and the Gentiles.

19 But when they deliver you up, take no thought how or what ye fhall fpeak, for it fhall be given you in that fame hour what ye fhall fpeak.

20 For it is not ye that fpeak, but the fpirit of your Father which fpeaketh in you.

21 And the brother fhall deliver up the brother to death, and the father the child: and the children fhall rife up againft their parents, and caufe them to be put to death.

22 And ye fhall be hated of all men for my name's fake: but he that endureth to the end, fhall be faved.

23 But when they perfecute you in this city, flee ye into another: for verily I fay unto you, ye fhall not have gone o

er the cities of Ifrael till the Son of man be come.

24 The difciple is not above his mafter, nor the fervant above his lord.

25 It is enough for the difciple that he be as his mafter, and the fervant as his lord: if they have called the mafter of the houfe Beelzebub, how much more *fhall they call* them of his houfhold ?

26 Fear them not therefore: for there is nothing covered, that fhall not be revealed: and hid, that fhall not be known.

27 What I tell you in darknefs, *that* fpeak ye in light: and what ye hear in the ear, *that* preach ye upon the houfetops.

28 And fear not them which kill the body, but are not able to kill the foul: but rather fear him which is able to deftroy both foul and body in hell.

29 Are not two fparrows fold for a farthing? and one of them fhall not fall on the ground without your Father.

30 But the very hairs of your head are all numbered.

31 Fear ye not therefore, ye are of more value than many fparrows.

34 Think not that I am come to fend peace on earth: I come not to fend peace, but a fword.

35 For I am come to fet a man at variance againft his father, and the daughter againft her mother, and the daughter in law againft her mother-in-law.

36 And a man's foes *fhall be* they of his own houfhold.

37 He that loveth father or mother more than me, is not worthy of me; and he that loveth fon or daughter more than me, is not worthy of me.

38 And he that taketh not his crofs, and followeth after me, is not worthy of me.

39 He that findeth his life, fhall lofe it: and he that lofeth his life for my fake, fhall find it.

40 ¶ He that receiveth you receiveth me; and he that receiveth me, receiveth him that fent me.

41 He that receiveth a prophet in the name of a prophet, fhall receive a prophet's reward; and he that receiveth a righteous man, in the name of a righteous man, fhall receive a righteous man's reward.

42 And whofoever fhall give to drink unto one of thefe little ones, a cup of cold water only, in the name of a difciple, verily I fay unto you, he fhall in no wife lofe his reward.

L22

24 ¶ And there was also a strife among them, which of them should be accounted the greatest.

25 And he said unto them, The kings of the Gentiles exercise lordship over them, and they that exercise authority upon them, are called benefactors.

26 But ye *shall* not *be* so: but he that is greatest among you, let him be as the younger: and he that is chief, as he that doth serve.

27 For whether *is* greater, he that sitteth at meat, or he that serveth ? *is* not he that sitteth at meat ? but I am among you as he that serveth.

J13

4 He riseth from supper, and laid aside his garments, and took a towel, and girded himself.

5 After that he poured water into a bason, and began to wash the disciples feet, and to wipe *them* with the towel wherewith he was girded.

6 Then cometh he to Simon Peter: and Peter said unto him, Lord, dost thou wash my feet ?

7 Jesus answered and said unto him, What I do, thou knowest not now ; but thou shalt know hereafter.

8 Peter saith unto him, Thou shalt never wash my feet. Jesus answered him, If I wash thee not, thou hast no part with me.

9 Simon Peter saith unto him, Lord, not my feet only, but also *my* hands and *my* head.

10 Jesus saith to him, He that is washed, needeth not, save to wash *his* feet, but is clean every whit : and ye are clean, but not all.

11 For he knew who should betray him ; therefore said he, Ye are not all clean.

11 So after he had washed their feet, and had taken his garments, and was set down again, he said unto them, Know ye what I have done to you ?

13 Ye call me Master, and Lord : and ye say well : for *so* I am.

14 If I then *your* Lord and Master, have washed your feet, ye also ought to wash one another's feet.

15 For I have given you an example, that ye should do as I have done to you.

16 Verily, verily I say unto you, The servant is not greater than his lord, neither he that is sent greater than he that sent him.

17 If ye know these things, happy are ye if ye do them.

J

CHAP. X.

VErily, verily I say unto you, He that entereth not by the door into the sheepfold, but climbeth up some other way, the same is a thief and a robber.

2 But he that entereth in by the door is the shepherd of the sheep.

3 To him the porter openeth; and the sheep hear his voice: and he calleth his own sheep by name, and leadeth them out.

4 And when he putteth forth his own sheep, he goeth before them, and the sheep follow him: for they know his voice.

5 And a stranger will they not follow, but will flee from him: for they know not the voice of strangers.

6 This parable spake Jesus unto them: but they understood not what things they were which he spake unto them.

7 Then said Jesus unto them again, Verily, verily I say unto you, I am the door of the sheep.

8 All that ever came before me, are thieves and robbers: but the sheep did not hear them.

9 I am the door: by me if any man enter in, he shall be saved, and shall go in and out, and find pasture.

10 The thief cometh not, but for to steal, and to kill, and to destroy: I am come that they might have life, and that they might have it more abundantly.

11 I am the good shepherd: the good shepherd giveth his life for the sheep.

12 But he that is an hireling, and not the shepherd, whose own the sheep are not, seeth the wolf coming, and leaveth the sheep, and fleeth: and the wolf catcheth them, and scattereth the sheep.

13 The hireling fleeth, because he is an hireling, and careth not for the sheep.

14 I am the good shepherd, and know my *sheep*, and am known of mine.

15 As the Father knoweth me, even so know I the Father: and I lay down my life for the sheep.

16 And other sheep I have, which are not of this fold: them also I must bring, and they shall hear my voice; and there shall be one fold, *and* one shepherd.

L11

52 Wo unto you, lawyers, for ye have taken away the key of knowledge: ye entered not in your selves, and them that were entering in, ye hindered.

L12

13 ¶ And one of the company said unto him, Master, speak to my brother, that he divide the inheritance with me.

14 And he said unto him, Man, who made me a judge, or a divider over you?

15 And he said unto them, Take heed, and beware of covetousness; for a man's life consisteth not in the abundance of the things which he possesseth.

J13

34 A new commandment give unto you, That ye love one another; as I have loved you, that ye also love one another.

15 By this shall all men know that ye are my disciples, if ye have love one to another.

M13

24 ¶ Another parable put he forth unto them, saying, The kingdom of heaven is likened unto a man which sowed good seed in his field:

25 But while men slept, his enemy came and sowed tares among the wheat, and went his way.

26 But when the blade was sprung up, and brought forth fruit, then appeared the tares also.

27 So the servants of the housholder came and said unto him, Sir, didst not thou sow good seed in thy field? from whence then hath it tares?

28 He said unto them, An enemy hath done this. The servants said unto him, Wilt thou then that we go and gather them up?

29 But he said, Nay; lest while ye gather up the tares, ye root up also the wheat with them.

30 Let both grow together until the harvest. and in the time of harvest I will say to the reapers, Gather ye together first the tares, and bind them in bundles to burn them, but gather the wheat into my barn.

36 Then Jesus sent the multitude away, and went into the house: and his disciples came unto him, saying, Declare unto us the parable of the tares of the field.

37 He answered and said unto them, He that soweth the good seed is the Son of man:

M13

38 The field is the world: the good feed are the children of the kingdom: but the tares are the children of the wicked one:

39 The enemy that fowed them, is the devil: the harveft is the end of the world: and the reapers are the angels.

40 As therefore the tares are gathered and burnt in the fire; fo fhall it be in the end of this world.

41 The Son of man fhall fend forth his angels, and they fhall gather out of his kingdom all things that offend, and them which do iniquity;

42 And fhall caft them into a furnace of fire: there fhall be wailing and gnafhing of teeth.

43 Then fhall the righteous fhine forth as the fun in the kingdom of their Father. Who hath ears to hear, let him hear.

M

C H A P. XX.

FOR the kingdom of heaven is like unto a man that is an houfholder, which went out early in the morning to hire labourers into his vineyard.

2 And when he had agreed with the labourers for a penny a day, he fent them into his vineyard.

3 And he went out about the third hour, and faw others ftanding idle in the marketplace,

4 And faid unto them, Go ye alfo into the vineyard, and whatfoever is right, I will give you. And they went their way.

5 Again, he went out about the fixth and ninth hour, and did likewife.

6 And about the eleventh hour he went out, and found others ftanding idle, and faith unto them, Why ftand ye here all the day idle?

7 They fay unto him, Becaufe no man hath hired us. He faith unto them, Go ye alfo into the vineyard, and whatfoever is right, *that* fhall ye receive.

8 So when even was come, the lord of the vineyard faith unto his fteward, Call the labourers, and give them *their* hire, beginning from the laft unto the firft.

9 And when they came that *were hired* about the eleventh hour, they received every man a penny.

10 But when the firft came, they fuppofed that they fhould have received more, and they likewife received every man a penny.

M20

11 And when they had received *it*, they murmured against the good man of the house,

12 Saying, these last have wrought but one hour, and thou hast made them equal unto us, which have borne the burden and heat of the day.

13 But he answered one of them, and said, Friend, I do thee no wrong: didst not thou agree with me for a penny?

14 Take *that* thine *is*, and go thy way: I will give unto this last, even as unto thee.

15 Is it not lawful for me to do what I will with mine own? is thine eye evil because I am good?

16 So the last shall be first, and the first last: for many be called, but few chosen.

Mk2

15 And it came to pass that as Jesus sat at meat in his house, many publicans and sinners sat also together with Jesus and his disciples: for there were many, and they followed him.

16 And when the scribes and Pharisees saw him eat with publicans and sinners, they said unto his disciples, How is it that he eateth and drinketh with publicans and sinners?

17 When Jesus heard *it*, **he** saith unto them, They that are whole have no need of the physician, but they that are sick: I came not to call the righteous, but sinners to repentance.

M18

10 Take heed that ye despise not one of these little ones; for I say unto you, that in heaven their angels do always behold the face of my Father which is in heaven.

11 For the Son of man is come to save that which was lost.

[M18: 12-14]

12 How think ye? if a man have an hundred sheep, and one of them be gone astray, doth he not leave the ninety and nine, and goeth into the mountains, and seeketh that which is gone astray?

13 And if so be that he find it, verily I say unto you, he rejoiceth more of that *sheep*, than of the ninety and nine which went not astray?

14 Even so it is not the will of your Father which is in heaven, that one of these little ones should perish.

C H A P. XV.

[L15:1]

THen drew near unto him all the publicans and sinners for to hear him.

[L15:2]

2 And the Pharisees and scribes murmured, saying, This man receiveth sinners, and eateth with them.

L15

3 ¶ And he spake this parable unto them, saying,

4 What man of you having an hundred sheep, if he lose one of them, doth not leave the ninety and nine in the wilderness, and go after that which is lost until he find it ?

5 And when he hath found it, he layeth it on his shoulders, rejoicing.

6 And when he cometh home, he calleth together his friends and neighbours, saying unto them, Rejoice with me, for I have found my sheep which was lost.

7 I say unto you, that likewise joy shall be in heaven over one sinner that repenteth, more than over ninety and nine just persons, which need no repentance:

8 ¶ Either what woman having ten pieces of silver, if she lose one piece, doth not light a candle, and sweep the house, and seek diligently till she find it ?

9 And when she hath found it, she calleth her friends and her neighbours together, saying, Rejoice with me, for I have found the piece which I had lost.

10 Likewise I say unto you, There is joy in the presence of the angels of God, over one sinner that repenteth.

11 ¶ And he said, A certain man had two sons :

12 And the younger of them said to his father, Father, give me the portion of goods that falleth to me. And he divided unto them his living.

13 And not many days after the younger son gathered all together, and took his journey into a far country, and there wasted his substance with riotous living.

14 And when he had spent all, there arose a mighty famine in that land ; and he began to be in want.

15 And he went and joined himself to a citizen of that country ; and he sent him into his field to feed swine.

16 And he would fain have filled his belly with the husks that the swine did eat; and no man gave unto him.

17 And when he came to himself, he said, How many hired servants of my father's have bread enough and to spare, and I perish with hunger!

18 I will arise, and go to my father, and will say unto him,

L15

Father, I have finned againft heaven, and before thee,

19 And am no more worthy to be called thy fon : make me as one of thy hired fervants.

20 And he arofe, and came to his father. But when he was yet a great way off, his father faw him, and had compaffion, and ran, and fell on his neck, and kiffed him.

21 And the fon faid unto him, Father, I have finned againft heaven, and in thy fight, and am no more worthy to be called thy fon.

22 But the father faid to his fervants, Bring forth the beft robe, and put it on him, and put a ring on his hand, and fhoes on his feet.

23 And bring hither the fatted calf, and kill it; and let us eat and be merry.

24 For this my fon was dead, and is alive again ; he was loft, and is found. And they began to be merry.

25 Now his elder fon was in the field : and as he came and drew nigh to the houfe, he heard mufick and dancing.

26 And he called one of the fervants, and afked what thefe things meant.

27 And he faid unto him, Thy brother is come ; and thy father hath killed the fatted calf, becaufe he hath received him fafe and found.

28 And he was angry, and would not go in : therefore came his father out, and intreated him.

29 And he anfwering, faid to his father, Lo, thefe many years do I ferve thee, neither tranfgreffed I at any time thy commandment, and yet thou never gaveft me a kid, that I might make merry with my friends :

30 But as foon as this thy fon was come, which hath devoured thy living with harlots, thou haft killed for him the fatted calf.

31 And he faid unto him, Son thou art ever with me, and all that I have is thine.

32 It was meet that we fhould make merry and be glad ; for this thy brother was dead, and is alive again, and was loft, and is found.

C H A P. VIII.

JEfus went unto the mount of Olives :

2 And early in the morning he came again into the temple, and all the people came unto him ; and he fat down, and taught them.

J

3 And the scribes and Pharisees brought unto him a woman taken in adultery; and when they had set her in the midst,

4 They said unto him, Master, this woman was taken in adultery, in the very act.

5 Now Moses in the law commanded us that such should be stoned: but what sayest thou?

6 This they said, tempting him, that they might have to accuse him. But Jesus stooped down, and with *his* finger wrote on the ground as though he heard them not

7 So when they continued asking him, he lifted up himself, and said unto them, He that is without sin among you, let him first cast a stone at her.

8 And again he stooped down, and wrote on the ground.

9 And they which heard *it*, being convicted by their own conscience, went out one by one, beginning at the eldest, *even* unto the last: and Jesus was left alone, and the woman standing in the midst.

10 When Jesus had lift up himself, and saw none but the woman, he said unto her, Woman, where are those thine accusers? hath no man condemned thee?

11 She said, No man, Lord. And Jesus said unto her, Neither do I condemn thee: go, and sin no more.

15 ¶ Moreover, if thy brother shall trespass against thee, go and tell him his fault between thee and him alone; if he shall hear thee, thou hast gained thy brother.

16 But if he will not hear *thee, then* take with thee one or two more, that in the mouth of two or three witnesses every word may be established.

17 And if he shall neglect to hear them, tell it unto the church: but if he neglect to hear the church, let him be unto thee as an heathen man and a publican.

6 ¶ He spake also this parable: A certain man had a fig-tree planted in his vineyard, and he came and sought fruit thereon, and found none.

7 Then said he unto the dresser of his vineyard, Behold, these three years I come seeking fruit on this fig-tree, and find none: cut it down, why cumbereth it the ground?

8 And he answering, said unto him, Lord, let it alone this year also, till I shall dig about it, and dung *it*.

L13

9 And if it bear fruit, *well :* and if not, *then* after that thou shalt cut it down.

M

CHAP. V.

AND feeing the multitudes, he went up into a mountain; and when he was fet, his difciples came unto him.

2 And he opened his mouth, and taught them, faying,

3 Bleffed *are* the poor in fpirit, for theirs is the kingdom of heaven.

4 Bleffed *are* they that mourn : for they fhall be comforted.

5 Bleffed *are* the meek: for they fhall inherit the earth :

6 Bleffed *are* they which do hunger and thirft after righteoufnefs : for they fhall be filled.

7 Bleffed *are* the merciful : for they fhall obtain mercy.

8 Bleffed *are* the pure in heart : for they fhall fee God.

9 Bleffed *are* the peacemakers : for they fhall be called the children of God.

10 Bleffed *are* they which are perfecuted for righteoufnefs fake : for theirs is the kingdom of heaven.

19 Whofoever therefore fhall break one of thefe leaft commandments, and fhall teach men fo, he fhall be called the leaft in the kingdom of heaven : but whofoever fhall do, and teach *them,* the fame fhall be called great in the kingdom of heaven.

20 For I fay unto you, That except your righteoufnefs fhall exceed *the righteoufnefs* of the Scribes and Pharifees, ye fhall in no cafe enter into the kingdom of heaven.

21 ¶ Ye have heard that it was faid by them of old time, Thou fhalt not kill : and whofoever fhall kill, fhall be in danger of the judgment.

22 But I fay unto you, That whofoever is angry with his brother without a caufe, fhall be in danger of the judgment : and whofoever fhall fay to his brother, Raca, fhall be in danger of the council : but whofoever fhall fay, Thou fool, fhall be in danger of hell-fire.

23 Therefore, if thou bring thy gift to the altar, and there rememberest that thy brother hath ought againft thee :

24 Leave there thy gift before the altar, and go thy way, firft be reconciled to thy brother, and then come and offer thy gift.

M5

25 Agree with thine adversary quickly, whiles thou art in the way with him: left at any time the adversary deliver thee to the judge, and the judge deliver thee to the officer, and thou be cast into prison.

26 Verily I say unto thee, Thou shalt by no means come out thence, till thou hast paid the uttermost farthing.

27 ¶ Ye have heard that it was said by them of old time, Thou shalt not commit adultery.

28 But I say unto you, That whosoever looketh on a woman to lust after her, hath committed adultery with her already in his heart.

29 And if thy right eye offend thee, pluck it out, and cast it from thee: for it is profitable for thee that one of thy members should perish, and not that thy whole body should be cast into hell.

30 And if thy right hand offend thee, cut it off, and cast it from thee: for it is profitable for thee that one of thy members should perish, and not that thy whole body should be cast into hell.

31 It hath been said, Whosoever shall put away his wife, let him give her a writing of divorcement.

32 But I say unto you, That whosoever shall put away his wife, saving for the cause of fornication, causeth her to commit adultery: and whosoever shall marry her that is divorced, committeth adultery.

33 ¶ Again, ye have heard that it hath been said by them of old time, Thou shalt not forswear thy self, but shalt perform unto the Lord thine oaths.

34 But I say unto you, Swear not at all, neither by heaven, for it is God's throne:

35 Nor by the earth, for it is his footstool: neither by Jerusalem, for it is the city of the great King.

36 Neither shalt thou swear by thy head, because thou canst not make one hair white or black.

37 But let your communication be, Yea, yea; Nay, nay: for whatsoever is more than these, cometh of evil.

38 ¶ Ye have heard that it hath been said, An eye for an eye, and a tooth for a tooth.

39 But I say unto you, that ye resist not evil: but whosoever shall smite thee on thy right cheek, turn to him the other also.

M5

40 And if any man will sue thee at the law, and take away thy coat, let him have thy cloke also.

41 And whosoever shall compel thee to go a mile, go with him twain.

42 Give to him that asketh thee, and from him that would borrow of thee, turn not thou away.

43 ¶ Ye have heard that it hath been said, Thou shalt love thy neighbour, and hate thine enemy:

44 But I say unto you, Love your enemies, bless them that curse you, do good to them that hate you, and pray for them which despitefully use you:

45 That ye may be the children of your Father which is in heaven; for he maketh his sun to rise on the evil and on the good, and sendeth rain on the just and on the unjust.

46 For if ye love them which love you, what reward have ye? do not even the publicans the same?

47 And if ye salute your brethren only, what do you more *than others?* do not even the publicans so?

48 Be ye therefore perfect, even as your Father which is in heaven is perfect.

CHAP. VI.

TAke heed that ye do not your alms before men, to be seen of them: otherwise ye have no reward of your Father which is in heaven.

2 Therefore, when thou dost *thine* alms, do not sound a trumpet before thee, as the hypocrites do, in the synagogues, and in the streets, that they may have glory of men. Verily I say unto you, they have their reward.

3 But when thou doest alms, let not thy left hand know what thy right hand doeth:

4 That thine alms may be in secret: and thy Father which seeth in secret, himself shall reward thee openly.

5 ¶ And when thou prayest, thou shalt not be as the hypocrites *are:* for they love to pray standing in the synagogues, and in the corners of the streets, that they may be seen of men. Verily, I say unto you, they have their reward.

6 But thou, when thou prayest, enter into thy closet, and when thou hast shut thy door, pray to thy Father which is in secret, and thy Father which seeth in secret, shall reward thee openly.

M

7 But when ye pray, use not vain repetitions, as the heathen do: for they think that they shall be heard for their much speaking.

8 Be not ye therefore like unto them: for your Father knoweth what things ye have need of, before ye ask him.

9 After this manner therefore pray ye: Our Father which art in heaven, Hallowed be thy name.

10 Thy kingdom come, Thy will be done in earth as *it is* in heaven.

11 Give us this day our daily bread.

12 And forgive us our debts, as we forgive our debtors.

13 And lead us not into temptation, but deliver us from evil: For thine is the kingdom, and the power, and the glory, for ever. Amen.

14 For, if ye forgive men their trespasses, your heavenly Father will also forgive you.

15 But if ye forgive not men their trespasses, neither will your Father forgive your trespasses.

16 ¶ Moreover, when ye fast, be not as the hypocrites, of a sad countenance: for they disfigure their faces, that they may appear unto men to fast.

Verily, I say unto you, they have their reward.

17 But thou, when thou fastest, anoint thy head, and wash thy face:

18 That thou appear not unto men to fast, but unto thy Father which is in secret: and thy Father which seeth in secret, shall reward thee openly.

19 ¶ Lay not up for your selves treasures upon earth, where moth and rust doth corrupt, and where thieves break through and steal.

20 But lay up for yourselves treasures in heaven, where neither moth nor rust doth corrupt, and where thieves do not break through nor steal.

21 For where your treasure is, there will your heart be also.

22 The light of the body is the eye: if therefore thine eye be single, the whole body shall be full of light.

23 But if thine eye be evil, thy whole body shall be full of darkness. If therefore the light that is in thee be darkness, how great *is* that darkness!

24 ¶ No man can serve two masters: for either he will hate the one, and love the other; or else he will hold to the one, and despise the other. Ye cannot serve God and mammon.

M6

25 Therefore I say unto you, Take no thought for your life, what ye shall eat, or what ye shall drink; nor yet for your body, what ye shall put on: Is not the life more than meat, and the body than raiment?

26 Behold the fowls of the air: for they sow not, neither do they reap, nor gather into barns; yet your heavenly Father feedeth them. Are ye not much better than they?

27 Which of you by taking thought can add one cubit unto his stature?

28 And why take ye thought for raiment? consider the lilies of the field how they grow; they toil not, neither do they spin.

29 And yet I say unto you, that even Solomon in all his glory was not arrayed like one of these.

30 Wherefore if God so clothe the grass of the field, which to-day is, and to-morrow is cast into the oven, *shall he not much more clothe you,* O ye of little faith?

31 Therefore take no thought, saying, What shall we eat? or what shall we drink? or wherewithal shall we be clothed?

32 (For after all these things do the Gentiles seek) for your heavenly Father knoweth that ye have need of all these things.

33 But seek ye first the kingdom of God, and his righteousness, and all these things shall be added unto you.

34 Take therefore no thought for the morrow: for the morrow shall take thought for the things of itself: sufficient unto the day is the evil thereof.

C H A P. VII.

M

Judge not, that ye be not judged.

2 For with what judgment ye judge, ye shall be judged: and with what measure ye mete, it shall be measured to you again.

3 And why beholdest thou the mote that is in thy brothers eye, but considerest not the beam that is in thine own eye?

4 Or how wilt thou say to thy brother, Let me pull out the mote out of thine eye; and behold, a beam *is* in thine own eye?

5 Thou hypocrite, first cast out the beam out of thine own eye; and then shalt thou see clearly to cast out the mote out of thy brothers eye.

6 ¶ Give not that which *is* holy unto the dogs, neither cast ye your pearls before swine, lest they trample them under

their feet, and turn again and rent you.

7 ¶ Afk. and it fhall be given you: feek, and ye fhall find: knock, and it fhall be opened unto you.

8 For every one that afketh, receiveth: and he that feeketh, findeth: and to him that knocketh, it fhall be opened.

9 Or what man is there of you, whom if his fon afk bread, will he give him a ftone?

10 Or if he afk a fifh, will he give him a ferpent?

11 If ye then being evil, know how to give good gifts unto your children, how much more fhall your Father which is in heaven give good things to them that afk him?

12 Therefore all things whatfoever ye would that men fhould do to you, do ye even fo to them: for this is the law and the prophets.

13 ¶ Enter ye in at the ftrait gate; for wide is the gate, and broad is the way, that leadeth to deftruction, and many there be which go in thereat:

14 Becaufe ftrait is the gate, and narrow is the way which leadeth unto life, and few there be that find it.

15 ¶ Beware of falfe prophets, which come to you in fheeps clothing, but inwardly they are ravening wolves.

16 Ye fhall know them by their fruits: Do men gather grapes of thorns, or figs of thiftles?

17 Even fo every good tree bringeth forth good fruit; but a corrupt tree bringeth forth evil fruit.

18 A good tree cannot bring forth evil fruit: neither can a corrupt tree bring forth good fruit.

19 Every tree that bringeth not forth good fruit, is hewn down and caft into the fire.

20 Wherefore by their fruits ye fhall know them.

21 ¶ Not every one that faith unto me, Lord, Lord, fhall enter into the kingdom of heaven; but he that doth the will of my Father which is in heaven.

22 Many will fay to me in that day, Lord, Lord, have we not prophefied in thy name? and in thy name have caft out devils? and in thy name done many wonderful works?

23 And then will I profefs unto them, I never knew you: depart from me, ye that work iniquity.

24 ¶ Therefore, whofoever heareth thefe fayings of mine,

M7

and doeth them, I will liken him unto a wife man, which built his house upon a rock:

25 And the rain descended, and the floods came, and the winds blew, and beat upon that house: and it fell not, for it was founded upon a rock.

26 And every one that heareth these sayings of mine, and doeth them not, shall be likened unto a foolish man, which built his house upon the sand:

27 And the rain descended, and the floods came, and the winds blew, and beat upon that house: and it fell, and great was the fall of it.

M7:28-29]

28 And it came to pass when Jesus had ended these sayings, the people were astonished at his doctrine.

29 For he taught them as one having authority, and not as the scribes.

[M8:1]

CHAP. VIII.

WHen he was come down from the mountain, great multitudes followed him.

M19

13 ¶ Then were there brought unto him little children, that he should put his hands on them, and pray: and the disciples rebuked them.

14 But Jesus said, Suffer little children, and forbid them

not to come unto me; for of such is the kingdom of heaven.

15 And he laid his hands on them, and departed thence.

16 ¶ And behold, one came and said unto him, Good Master, what good thing shall I do that I may have eternal life?

17 And he said unto him, Why callest thou me good? there is none good but one; that is God: but if thou wilt enter into life, keep the commandments.

18 He saith unto him, Which? Jesus said, Thou shalt do no murder, Thou shalt not commit adultery, Thou shalt not steal, Thou shalt not bear false witness,

19 Honour thy father and thy mother: and, Thou shalt love thy neighbour as thyself.

20 The young man saith unto him, All these things have I kept from my youth up: what lack I yet?

21 Jesus said unto him, If thou wilt be perfect, go and sell what thou hast, and give to the poor, and thou shalt have treasure in heaven: and come and follow me.

22 But when the young man heard that saying, he went away sorrowful: for he had great possession.

M19

23 ¶ Then said Jesus unto his disciples, Verily I say unto you, that a rich man shall hardly enter into the kingdom of heaven.

24 And again I say unto you, It is easier for a camel to go through the eye of a needle, than for a rich man to enter into the kingdom of God.

29 And every one that hath forsaken houses, or brethren, or sisters, or father, or mother, or wife, or children, or lands for my names sake, shall receive an hundred fold, and shall inherit everlasting life.

30 But many *that are* first, shall be last; and the last *shall be* first.

M22

35 Then one of them, *which was* a lawyer, asked *him* a question, tempting him, and saying,

36 Master, which *is* the great commandment in the law?

37 Jesus said unto him, Thou shalt love the Lord thy God with all thy heart, and with all thy soul, and with all thy mind.

38 This is the first and great commandment.

32 And the second *is* like unto it, Thou shalt love thy neighbour as thyself.

40 On these two commandments hang all the law and the prophets.

CHAP. XII.

AT that time Jesus went on the sabbath-day through the corn, and his disciples were an hungred, and began to pluck the ears of corn, and to eat.

2 But when the Pharisees saw *it*, they said unto him, Behold, thy disciples do that which is not lawful to do upon the sabbath-day.

3 But he said unto them, Have ye not read what David did when he was an hungred, and they that were with him,

4 How he entered into the house of God, and did eat the shew-bread, which was not lawful for him to eat, neither for them which were with him, but only for the priests?

5 Or have ye not read in the law, how that on the sabbath-days the priests in the temple profane the sabbath, and are blameless?

11 And he said unto them, What man shall there be among you, that shall have one sheep, and if it fall into a pit on the sabbath-day, will he not lay hold on it, and lift *it* out?

12 How much then is a man better than a sheep? wherefore it is lawful to do well on the sabbath-days.

L

C H A P. XIV.

AND it came to pass, as he went into the house of one of the chief Pharisees to eat bread on the sabbath-day, that they watched him.

2 And behold there was a certain man before him which had the leprosy.

3 And Jesus answering, spake unto the lawyers and Pharisees, saying, Is it lawful to heal on the sabbath-day?

4 And they held their peace. And he took *him*, and healed him, and let him go:

5 And answered them, saying, Which of you shall have an ass or an ox fallen into a pit, and will not straightway pull him out on the sabbath-day?

6 And they could not answer him again to these things.

L11

37 ¶ And as he spake, a certain Pharisee besought him to dine with him: and he went in, and sat down to meat.

38 And when the Pharisee saw *it*, he marvelled that he had not first washed before dinner.

39 And the Lord said unto him, Now do ye Pharisees make clean the outside of the cup and the platter; but your

inward part is full of ravening and wickedness.

40 Ye fools, did not he that made that which is without, make that which is within also?

41 But rather give alms of such things as you have: and behold all things are clean unto you.

42 But wo unto you, Pharisees; for ye tithe mint, and rue, and all manner of herbs, and pass over judgment and the love of God: these ought ye to have done, and not to leave the other undone.

43 Wo unto you, Pharisees: for ye love the uppermost seats in the synagogues, and greetings in the markets.

44 Wo unto you, scribes and Pharisees, hypocrites: for ye are as graves which appear not, and the men that walk over *them*, are not aware of *them*.

45 ¶ Then answered one of the lawyers, and said unto him, Master, thus saying, thou reproachest us also.

46 And he said, Wo unto you also, ye lawyers: for ye lade men with burdens grievous to be borne, and ye yourselves touch not the burdens with one of your fingers.

47 Wo unto you: for ye build the sepulchres of the prophets, and your fathers killed them.

L11

48 Truly ye bear witnefs that ye allow the deeds of your fathers: for they indeed killed them, and ye build their fepulchres.

M

CHAP. XV.

THen came to Jefus fcribes an Pharifees, which were of Jerufalem, faying,

2 Why do thy difciples tranfgref the tradition of the elders? for they wafh not their hands when they eat bread.

3 But he anfwered and faid unto them, Why do you alfo tranfgrefs the commandment of God by your tradition?

4 For God commanded, faying, Honour thy father and mother: and, He that curfeth father or mother, let him die the death.

5 But ye fay, Whofoever fhall fay to *his* father or *his* mother, It *is* a gift by whatfoever thou mighteft be profited by me,

6 And honour not his father or his mother, *he fhall be free.* Thus have ye made the commandment of God of none effect by your tradition.

7 Ye hypocrites, well did Efaias prophefy of you, faying,

8 This people draweth nigh unto me with their mouth, and honoureth me with their lips; but their heart is far from me.

9 But in vain do they worfhip me, teaching *for doctrines* the commandments of men.

10 ¶ And he called the multitude, and faid unto them, Hear and underftand.

11 Not that which goeth into the mouth defileth a man: but that which cometh out of the mouth, this defileth a man.

12 Then came his difciples, and faid unto him, Knoweft thou that the Pharifees were offended after they heard this faying?

13 But he anfwered and faid, Every plant which my heavenly Father hath not planted, fhall be rooted up.

14 Let them alone: they be blind leaders of the blind, And if the blind lead the blind, both fhall fall into the ditch.

15 Then anfwered Peter, and faid unto him, Declare unto us this parable.

16 And Jefus faid, Are ye alfo yet without underftanding?

17 Do not ye yet underftand, that whatfoever entereth in at the mouth, goeth into the belly, and is caft out into the draught?

18 But thofe things which proceed out of the mouth, come forth from the heart, and they defile the man.

M15

19 For out of the heart proceed evil thoughts, murders, adulteries, fornications, thefts, false witnefs, blafphemies.

20 Thefe are the things which defile a man: but to eat with unwafhen hands, defileth not a man.

M12

33 Either make the tree good, and his fruit good ; or elfe make the tree corrupt, and his fruit corrupt : for the tree is known by his fruit.

34 O generation of vipers, how can ye, being evil, fpeak good things ? for out of the abundance of the heart the mouth fpeaketh.

35 A good man out of the good treafure of the heart, bringeth forth good things : and an evil man out of the evil treafure, bringeth forth evil things.

36 But I fay unto you, that every idle word that men fhall fpeak, they fhall give account thereof in the day of judgment.

37 For by thy words thou fhalt be juftified, and by thy words thou fhalt be condemned.

C H A P. XIII.

THE fame day went Jefus out of the houfe, and fat by the fea-fide.

2 And great multitudes were gathered together unto him, fo that he went into a fhip, and fat, and the whole multitude ftood on the fhore.

3 And he fpake many things unto them in parables, faying, Behold, a fower went forth to fow.

4 And when he fowed, fome feeds fell by the way-fide, and the fowls came and devoured them up.

5 Some fell upon ftony places, where they had not much earth: and forthwith they fprung up, becaufe they had no deepnefs of earth :

6 And when the fun was up, they were fcorched, and becaufe they had not root, they withered away.

7 And fome fell among thorns : and the thorns fprung up and choked them.

8 But other fell into good ground, and brought forth fruit, fome an hundred-fold, fome fixty-fold, fome thirty-fold.

9 Who hath ears to hear, let him hear.

18 ¶ Hear ye therefore the parable of the fower.

19 When any one heareth the word of the kingdom, and underftandeth it not, then cometh the wicked one, and catch-

M

M13

eth away that which was fown in his heart : this is he which received feed by the way-fide.

20 But he that received the feed into ftony places, the fame is he that heareth the word, and anon with joy receiveth it :

21 Yet hath he not root in himfelf, but dureth for a while : for when tribulation, or perfecution arifeth becaufe of the word, by and by he is offended.

22 He alfo that received feed among the thorns, is he that heareth the word: and the care of this world, and the deceitfulnefs of riches choke the word, and he becometh unfruitful.

23 But he that received feed into the good ground, is he that heareth the word, and underftandeth it : which alfo beareth fruit, and bringeth forth fome an hundred-fold, fome fixty, fome thirty.

L7

36 ¶ And one of the Pharifees defired him that he would eat with him. And he went into the Pharifees houfe, and fat down to meat.

37 And behold, a woman in the city, which was a finner, when fhe knew that Jefus fat at meat in the Pharifees houfe,

brought an alabafter-box of ointment.

38 And ftood at his feet behind him weeping, and began to wafh his feet with tears, and did wipe them with the hairs of her head, and kiffed his feet, and anointed them with the ointment.

39 Now when the Pharifee which had bidden him faw it, he fpake within himfelf, faying, This man, if he were a prophet, would have known who and what manner of woman this is that toucheth him : for fhe is a finner.

40 And Jefus anfwering, faid unto him, Simon, I have fomewhat to fay unto thee. And he faith, Mafter, fay on.

41 There was a certain creditor, which had two debtors : the one owed five hundred pence, and the other fifty.

42 And when they had nothing to pay, he frankly forgave them both. Tell me therefore which of them will love him moft ?

43 Simon anfwered and faid, I fuppofe that he to whom he forgave moft. And he faid unto him, Thou haft rightly judged.

44 And he returned to the woman, and faid unto Simon,

L7

Seeſt thou this woman? I entered into thine houſe, thou gaveſt me no water for my feet; but ſhe hath waſhed my feet with tears, and wiped *them* with the hairs of her head.

45 Thou gaveſt me no kiſs: but this woman, ſince the time I came in, hath not ceaſed to kiſs my feet.

46 Mine head with oil thou didſt not anoint: but this woman hath anointed my feet with ointment.

47 Wherefore I ſay unto thee, her ſins, which are many, are forgiven; for ſhe loved much: but to whom little is forgiven, the ſame loveth little.

Mk12

41 ¶ And Jeſus ſat over againſt the treaſury, and beheld how the people caſt money into the treaſury: and many that were rich caſt in much.

42 And there came a certain poor widow, and ſhe threw in two mites, which make a farthing.

43 And he called unto him his diſciples, and ſaith unto them, Verily I ſay unto you, that this poor widow hath caſt more in, than all they which have caſt into the treaſury.

44 For all they did caſt in of their abundance: but ſhe of her want did caſt in all that ſhe had, *even* all her living.

M11

28 ¶ Come unto me, all ye that labour, and are heavy laden, and I will give you reſt.

29 Take my yoke upon you, and learn of me, for I am meek and lowly in heart; and ye ſhall find reſt unto your ſouls.

30 For my yoke is eaſy, and my burden is light.

25 ¶ And behold, a certain lawyer ſtood up, and tempted him, ſaying, Maſter, what ſhall I do to inherit eternal life?

L10

26 He ſaid unto him, What is written in the law? how readeſt thou?

37 And he anſwering, ſaid, Thou ſhalt love the Lord thy God with all thy heart, and with all thy ſoul, and with all thy ſtrength, and with all thy mind; and thy neighbour as thyſelf.

28 And he ſaid unto him, Thou haſt anſwered right: this do, and thou ſhalt live.

29 But he, willing to juſtify himſelf, ſaid unto Jeſus, And who is my neighbour?

30 And Jeſus anſwering, ſaid, A certain man went down from Jeruſalem to Jericho, and fell among thieves, which ſtripped him of his raiment, and wounded *him*, and departed, leaving *him* half dead.

L10

31 And by chance there came down a certain priest that way; and when he saw him, he paffed by on the other fide.

32 And likewife a Levite, when he was at the place, came and looked *on him*, and paffed by on the other fide.

33 But a certain Samaritan, as he journeyed, came where he was: and when he faw him, he had compaffion *on him*,

34 And went to him, and bound up his wounds, pouring in oil and wine, and fet him on his own beaft, and brought him to an inn, and took care of him.

35 And on the morrow, when he departed, he took out two pence, and gave *them* to the hoft, and faid unto him, Take care of him; and whatfoever thou fpendeft more, when I come again, I will repay thee.

36 Which now of thefe three, thinkeft thou, was neighbour unto him that fell among the thieves?

37 And he faid, He that fhewed mercy on him. Then faid Jefus unto him, Go, and do thou likewife.

C H A P. XXIII.

THEN fpake Jefus to the multitude, and to his difciples,

2 Saying, The fcribes and the Pharifees fit in Mofes' feat.

3 All therefore whatfoever they bid you obferve, *that* obferve and do; but do not ye after their works: for they fay, and do not.

4 For they bind heavy burdens, and grievous to be borne, and lay *them* on mens fhoulders, but they themfelves will not move them with one of their fingers.

5 But all their works they do for to be feen of men: they make broad their phylacteries, and enlarge the borders of their garments,

6 And love the uppermoft rooms at feafts, and the chief feats in the fynagogues,

7 And greetings in the markets, and to be called of men, Rabbi, Rabbi.

8 But be not ye called Rabbi; for one is your Mafter, *even* Chrift, and all ye are brethren.

9 And call no man your father upon the earth; for one is your Father which is in heaven.

10 Neither be ye called mafters: for one is your Mafter, *even* Chrift.

M

M23

11 But he that is greatest among you, shall be your servant.

12 And whosoever shall exalt himself, shall be abased; and he that shall humble himself, shall be exalted.

13 ¶ But wo unto you, scribes and Pharisees, hypocrites; for ye shut up the kingdom of heaven against men: for ye neither go in yourselves, neither suffer ye them that are entering, to go in.

14 Wo unto you, scribes and Pharisees, hypocrites; for ye devour widows' houses, and for a pretence make long prayers; therefore ye shall receive the greater damnation.

15 Wo unto you, scribes and Pharisees, hypocrites; for ye compass sea and land to make one proselyte, and when he is made, ye make him two-fold more the child of hell than yourselves.

16 Wo unto you, ye blind guides, which say, Whosoever shall swear by the temple, it is nothing; but whosoever shall swear by the gold of the temple, he is a debtor.

17 Ye fools, and blind: for whether is greater, the gold, or the temple that sanctifieth the gold?

18 And whosoever shall swear by the altar, it is nothing: but whosoever sweareth by the gift that is upon it, he is guilty.

19 Ye fools, and blind: for whether is greater, the gift, or the altar that sanctifieth the gift?

20 Whoso therefore shall swear by the altar, sweareth by it, and by all things thereon.

21 And whoso shall swear by the temple, sweareth by it, and by him that dwelleth therein.

22 And he that shall swear by heaven, sweareth by the throne of God, and by him that sitteth thereon.

23 Wo unto you, scribes and Pharisees, hypocrites; for ye pay tithe of mint and anise, and cummin, and have omitted the weightier matter of the law, judgment, mercy, and faith: these ought ye to have done, and not to leave the other undone.

24 Ye blind guides, which strain at a gnat, and swallow a camel.

25 Wo unto you, scribes and Pharisees, hypocrites; for ye make clean the outside of the cup, and of the platter, but within they are full of extortion and excess.

M23

26 Thou blind Pharifee, cleanfe firft that *which is* within the cup and platter, that the outfide of them may be clean alfo.

27 Wo unto you, fcribes and Pharifees, hypocrites ; for ye are like unto whited fepulchres, which indeed appear beautiful outward, but are within full of dead mens bones, and of all uncleannefs.

28 Even fo ye alfo outwardly appear righteous unto men, but within ye are full of hypocrify and iniquity. •

29 Wo unto you, fcribes and Pharifees, hypocrites : becaufe ye build the tombs of the prophets, and garnifh the fepulchres of the righteous,

30 And fay, If we had been in the days of our fathers, we would not have been partakers with them in the blood of the prophets.

31 Wherefore ye be witneffes unto yourfelves, that ye are the children of them which killed the prophets.

32 Fill ye up then the meafure of your fathers.

33 Ye ferpents, ye generation of vipers, how can ye efcape the damnation of hell ?

L14

7 ¶ And he put forth a parable to thofe which were bidden, when he marked how they chofe out the chief rooms; faying unto them,

8 When thou art bidden of any man to a wedding, fit not down in the higheft room : left a more honourable man than thou be bidden of him ;

9 And he that bade thee and him, come and fay to thee, Give this man place ; and thou begin with fhame to take the loweft room.

10 But when thou art bidden, go and fit down in the loweft room ; that when he that bade thee cometh, he may fay unto thee, Friend, go up higher : then fhalt thou have worfhip in the prefence of them that fit at meat with thee.

11 For whofoever exalteth himfelf, fhall be abafed ; and he that humbleth himfelf, fhall be exalted.

C H A P. XVIII.

M

AT the fame time came the difciples unto Jefus, faying, Who is the greateft in the kingdom of heaven ?

2 And Jefus called a little child unto him, and fet him in the midft of them,

3 And faid, Verily I fay unto you, except ye be converted, and become as little children, ye fhall not enter into the kingdom of heaven.

M18

4 Whofoever therefore fhall humble himfelf as this little child, the fame is greateft in the kingdom of heaven.

5 And whofo fhall receive one fuch little child in my name, receiveth me.

6 But whofo fhall offend one of thefe little ones which believe in me, it were better for him that a millftone were hanged about his neck, and *that he* were drowned in the depth of the fea.

L16

19 ¶ There was a certain rich man, which was clothed in purple and fine linen, and fared fumptuoufly every day.

20 And there was a certain beggar named Lazarus, which was laid at his gate full of fores,

21 And defiring to be fed with the crumbs which fell from the rich mans table: moreover, the dogs came and licked his fores.

22 And it came to pafs that the beggar died, and was carried by the angels into Abraham's bofom: the rich man alfo died, and was buried.

23 And in hell he lift up his eyes, being in torments, and feeth Abraham afar off, and Lazarus in his bofom.

24 And he cried, and faid, Father Abraham, have mercy on me, and fend Lazarus that he may dip the tip of his finger in water, and cool my tongue; for I am tormented in this flame.

25 But Abraham faid, Son, remember that thou in thy lifetime receivedft thy good things, and likewife Lazarus evil things: but now he is comforted and thou art tormented.

26 And befides all this, between us and you there is a great gulf fixed: fo that they which would pafs from hence to you, cannot; neither can they pafs to us, that *would come* from thence.

27 Then he faid, I pray thee therefore, father, that thou wouldeft fend him to my father's houfe:

28 For I have five brethren; that he may teftify unto them, left they alfo come into this place of torment.

29 braham faith unto him, They have Mofes and the prophets; let them hear them.

30 And he faid, Nay, father Abraham: but if one went unto them from the dead, they will repent.

31 And he faid unto him, If they hear not Mofes and the

L16:31

prophets, neither will they be perfuaded, though one rofe from the dead.

M

C H A P. XXII.

AND Jefus anfwered and fpake unto them again by parables, and faid,

2 The kingdom of heaven is like unto a certain king, which made a marriage for his fon,

3 And fent forth his fervants to call them that were bidden to the wedding : and they would not come.

4 Again he fent forth other fervants, faying, Tell them which are bidden, Behold, I have prepared my dinner : my oxen and *my* fatlings *are* killed, and all things are ready : come unto the marriage.

5 But they made light of *it*, and went their ways, one to his farm, another to his merchandize :

6 And the remnant took his fervants, and intreated *them* fpitefully, and flew *them*.

7 But when the king heard *thereof*, he was wroth : and he fent forth his armies, and deftroyed thofe murderers, and burnt up their city.

8 Then faith he to his fervants, The wedding is ready, but they which were bidden were not worthy.

9 Go ye therefore into the high-ways, and as many as ye fhall find, bid to the marriage.

10 So thofe fervants went out into the *high*-ways, and gathered together all as many as they found, both bad and good : and the wedding was furnifhed with guefts.

11 ¶ And when the king came in to fee the guefts, he faw there a man which had not on a wedding garment :

12 And he faid unto him, Friend, how cameft thou in hither, not having a wedding-garment ? And he was fpeech-lefs.

13 Then faid the king to the fervants, Bind him hand and foot, and take him away, and caft *him* into outer darknefs : there fhall be weeping and gnafhing of teeth.

14 For many are called, but few *are* chofen.

46 ¶ While he yet talked to the people, behold, his mother and his brethren ftood without, defiring to fpeak with him.

M12

47 Then one faid unto him, Behold thy mother and thy brethren ftand without, defiring to fpeak with thee.

48 But he anfwered and faid unto him that told him, Who is my mother ? and who are my brethren ?

M12

49 And he stretched forth his hand towards his disciples, and said, Behold my mother, and my brethren.

50 For whosoever shall do the will of my Father which is in heaven, the same is my brother, and sister, and mother.

M8

11 And I say unto you, that many shall come from the east and west, and shall sit down with Abraham, and Isaac, and Jacob in the kingdom of heaven:

L

CHAP. XIII.

THere were present at that season some that told him of the Galileans, whose blood Pilate had mingled with their sacrifices.

2 And Jesus answering, said unto them, Suppose ye that these Galileans were sinners above all the Galileans, because they suffered such things ?

3 I tell you, Nay : but except ye repent, ye shall all likewise perish.

4 Or those eighteen, upon whom the tower in Siloam fell; and slew them, think ye that they were sinners above all men that dwelt in Jerusalem ?

5 I tell you, Nay : but except ye repent, ye shall all likewise perish.

25 ¶ And there went great multitudes with him : and he turned, and said unto them,

[L14:25]

26 If any man come to me, and hate not his father, and mother, and wife, and children, and brethren, and sisters, yea, and his own life also, he cannot be my disciple.

L14

27 And whosoever doth not bear his cross, and come after me cannot be my disciple.

28 For which of you intending to build a tower, sitteth not down first, and counteth the cost, whether he have *sufficient* to finish *it?*

29 Lest haply after he hath laid the foundation, and is not able to finish *it*, all that behold *it*, begin to mock him,

30 Saying, this man began to build, and was not able to finish.

31 Or what king going to make war against another king, sitteth not down first, and consulteth whether he be able with ten thousand to meet him that cometh against him with twenty thousand ?

32 Or else, while the other is yet a great way off, he sendeth an ambassage, and desireth conditions of peace.

33 So likewise, whosoever he be of you that forsaketh not all that he hath, he cannot be my disciple.

L

CHAP. XVI.

AND he said also unto his disciples, There was a certain rich man which had a steward; and the same was accused unto him, that he had wasted his goods.

2 And he called him, and said unto him, How is it that I hear this of thee? give an an account of thy stewardship: for thou mayest be no longer steward.

3 Then the steward said within himself, What shall I do? for my lord taketh away from me the stewardship: I cannot dig, to beg I am ashamed.

4 I am resolved what to do, that when I am put out of the stewardship, they may receive me into their houses.

5 So he called every one of his lords debtors unto him, and said unto the first, How much owest thou unto my lord?

6 And he said, An hundred measures of oil. And he said unto him, Take thy bill, and sit down quickly, and write fifty.

7 Then said he to another, And how much owest thou? And he said, An hundred measures of wheat. And he said unto him, Take thy bill, and write fourscore.

8 And the lord commended the unjust steward, because he had done wisely: for the children of this world are in their generation wiser than the children of light.

9 And I say unto you, Make to yourselves friends of the mammon of unrighteousness; that when ye fail, they may receive you into everlasting habitations.

10 He that is faithful in that which is least, is faithful also in much; and he that is unjust in the least, is unjust also in much.

11 If therefore ye have not been faithful in the unrighteous mammon, who will commit to your trust the true *riches?*

12 And if ye have not been faithful in that which is another mans, who shall give you that which is your own?

13 ¶ No servant can serve two masters: for either he will hate the one, and love the other; or else he will hold to the one, and despise the other. Ye cannot serve God and mammon.

CHAP. XVIII.

AND he spake a parable unto them, *to this end,* that men ought always to pray, and not to faint;

L

L18

2 Saying, There was in a city a judge, which feared not God, neither regarded man.

3 And there was a widow in that city, and she came unto him, saying, Avenge me of mine adversary.

4 And he would not for a while; but afterward he said within himself, Though I fear not God: nor regard man;

5 Yet because this widow troubleth me, I will avenge her, left by her continual coming she weary me.

6 And the Lord said, Hear what the unjust judge faith.

7 And shall not God avenge his own elect, which cry day and night unto him, though he bear long with them?

8 I tell you that he will avenge them speedily.

M21

33 ¶ Hear another parable: There was a certain housholder which planted a vineyard, and hedged it round about, and digged a wine-press in it, and built a tower, and let it out to husbandmen, and went into a far country.

34 And when the time of the fruit drew near, he sent his servants to the husbandmen, that they might receive the fruits of it.

35 And the husbandmen took his servants, and beat one and killed another, and stoned another.

36 Again, he sent other servants, more than the first: and they did unto them likewise.

37 But last of all he sent unto them his son, saying, They will reverence my son.

38 But when the husbandmen saw the son, they said among themselves, This is the heir, come let us kill him, and let us seize on his inheritance.

39 And they caught him and cast him out of the vineyard, and slew him.

40 When the Lord therefore of the vineyard cometh, what will he do unto those husbandmen?

41 They say unto him, He will miserably destroy those wicked men, and will let out his vineyard unto other husbandmen, which shall render him the fruits in their seasons.

7 But which of you having a servant ploughing or feeding cattle, will say unto him by and by when he is come from the field, Go and sit down to meat?

L17

L17

8 And will not rather fay unto him, Make ready wherewith
I may fup, and gird thy felf
and ferve me till I have eaten
and drunken; and afterward
thou fhalt eat and drink;

9 Doth he thank that fer-
vant becaufe he did the things
that were commanded him? I
trow not.

10 So likewife ye, when ye
fhall have done all thofe things
which are commanded you,
fay, We are unprofitable fervants; we have done that which
was our duty to do.

L14

12 ¶ Then faid he alfo to
him that bade him, When thou
makeft a dinner or a fupper,
call not thy friends, nor thy
brethren, neither thy kinfmen,
nor *thy* rich neighbours; left
they alfo bid thee again, and
a recompenfe be made thee.

13 But when thou makeft a
feaft, call the poor, the maimed, the lame, the blind:

14 And thou fhalt be bleffed;
for they cannot recompenfe
thee: for thou fhalt be recom-
penfed at the refurrection of
the juft.

M21

28 ¶ But what think you?
A certain man had two fons,
and he came to the firft, and
faid, Son, go work to day in
my vineyard.

29 He anfwered and faid, I
will not: but afterwards he
repented, and went.

30 And he came to the fe-
cond, and faid likewife. And
he anfwered and faid, I *go*, fir;
and went not.

31 Whether of them twain
did the will of his father?
They fay unto him, The firft.
Jefus faith unto them, Verily
I fay unto you, that the publicans and the harlots go into
the kingdom of God before
you.

15 ¶ Then went the Phari-
fees, and took counfel how
they might entangle him in *his*
talk.

16 And they fent out unto
him their difciples, with the
Herodians, faying, Mafter, we
know that thou art true, and
teacheft the way of God in
truth, neither careft thou for
any man: for thou regardeft
not the perfon of men.

17 Tell us therefore, What
thinkeft thou? Is it lawful to
give tribute unto Cefar, or not?

18 But Jefus perceived their
wickednefs, and faid, Why
tempt ye me, ye hypocrites?

19 Shew me the tribute-
money. And they brought
unto him a penny.

M22

M22

20 And he faith unto them, Whofe is this image and fuperfcription?

21 They fay unto him, Cefar's. Then faith he unto them, Render therefore unto Cefar, the things which are Cefar's; and unto God, the things that are God's.

22 When they had heard thefe words, they marvelled, and left him, and went their way.

M19

3 ¶ The Pharifees alfo came unto him, tempting him, and faying unto him, Is it lawful for a man to put away his wife for every caufe?

4 And he anfwered and faid unto them, Have ye not read, that he which made them at the beginning, made them male and female?

5 And faid, For this caufe fhall a man leave father and mother, and fhall cleave to his wife, and they twain fhall be one flefh.

6 Wherefore, they are no more twain, but one flefh. What God therefore hath joined together, let no man put afunder.

7 They fay unto him, Why did Mofes then command to give a writing of divorcement, and to put her away?

8 He faith unto them, Mofes, becaufe of the hardnefs of your hearts, fuffered you to put away your wives: but from the beginning it was not fo.

9 And I fay unto you, Whofoever fhall put away his wife, except it be for fornication, and fhall marry another, committeth adultery; and whofo marrieth her which is put away, doth commit adultery.

10 His difciples fay unto him, If the cafe of the man be fo with his wife, it is not good to marry.

11 But he faid unto them, All men cannot receive this faying, fave they to whom it is given:

12 For there are fome eunuchs, which were fo born from their mothers womb: and there are fome eunuchs, which were made eunuchs of men: and there be eunuchs, which have made themfelves eunuchs for the kingdom of heaven's fake. He that is able to receive it, let him receive it.

14 ¶ For the kingdom of heaven is as a man travelling into a far country, who called his own fervants, and delivered unto them his goods:

15 And unto one he gave five talents, to another two, and to another one, to every

M25

M25 man according to his feveral ability, and ſtraightway took his journey.

16 Then he that had received the five talents, went and traded with the fame, and made *them* other five talents.

17 And likewife he that *had received* two, he alfo gained other two.

18 But he that had received one, went and digged in the earth, and hid his lord's money.

19 After a long time, the lord of thofe fervants cometh, and reckoneth with them

20 And fo he that had received five talents, came and brought other five talents, faying, Lord, thou deliveredſt unto me five talents : behold, I have gained befides them five talents more.

21 His lord faid unto him, Well done, thou good and faithful fervant; thou haſt been faithful over a few things, I will make thee ruler over many things : enter thou into the joy of thy Lord.

22 He alfo that had received two talents, came and faid, Lord, thou deliveredſt unto me two talents : behold, I have gained two other talents befides them.

23 His lord faid unto him, Well done, good and faithful fervant ; thou haſt been faithful over a few things, I will make thee ruler over many things : enter thou into the joy of thy Lord.

24 Then he which had received the one talent, came and faid, Lord, I knew thee that thou art an hard man, reaping where thou haſt not fown, and gathering where thou haſt not ſtrewed :

25 And I was afraid, and went and hid thy talent in the earth : lo, there thou haſt *that is* thine.

26 His lord anfwered and faid unto him, Thou wicked and ſlothful fervant, thou kneweſt that I reap where I fowed not, and gather where I have not ſtrewed :

27 Thou oughteſt therefore to have put my money to the exchangers, and then at my coming I ſhould have received mine own with ufury.

28 Take therefore the talent from him, and give it unto him which hath ten talents.

29 For unto every one that hath ſhall be given, and he ſhall have abundance : but from him that hath not ſhall be taken away even that which he hath.

M25

30 And caſt ye the unpro-
fitable ſervant into outer dark-
neſs: there ſhall be weeping
and gnaſhing of teeth.

L12

16 And he ſpake a parable
unto them, ſaying, The ground
of a certain rich man brought
forth plentifully.

17 And he thought within
himſelf, ſaying, What ſhall I
do, becauſe I have no room
where to beſtow my fruits?

18 And he ſaid, This will I
do: I will pull down my barns,
and build greater: and there
will I beſtow all my fruits and
my goods.

19 And I will ſay to my ſoul,
Soul, thou haſt much goods
laid up for many years; take
thine eaſe, eat, drink, and be
merry.

20 But God ſaid unto him,
Thou fool, this night thy ſoul
ſhall be required of thee: then
whoſe ſhall theſe things be
which thou haſt provided?

21 So is he that layeth up
treaſure for himſelf, and is not
rich towards God

CHAP. XXV.

M

THen ſhall the kingdom of
heaven be likened unto
ten virgins, which took their
lamps, and went forth to meet
the bridegroom.

2 And five of them were
wiſe, and five were fooliſh.

3 They that were fooliſh
took their lamps, and took no
oil with them:

4 But the wiſe took oil in
their veſſels with their lamps.

5 While the bridegroom
tarried, they all ſlumbered and
ſlept.

6 And at midnight there was
a cry made, Behold, the bridegroom cometh, go ye out to
meet him.

7 Then all thoſe virgins a-
roſe, and trimmed their lamps.

8 And the fooliſh ſaid unto
the wiſe, Give us of your oil,
for our lamps are gone out.

9 But the wiſe anſwered,
ſaying, Not ſo; leſt there be
not enough for us and you:
but go ye rather to them that
ſell, and buy for yourſelves.

10 And while they went to
buy, the bridegroom came,
and they that were ready went
in with him to the marriage,
and the door was ſhut.

11 Afterwards came alſo the
other virgins, ſaying, Lord,
Lord, open to us.

12 But he anſwered and
ſaid, Verily I ſay unto you, I
know you not.

13 Watch therefore, for ye

M25:13 know neither the day nor the hour wherein the Son of man cometh.

L12   35 Let your loins be girded about, and *your* lights burning.

36 And ye yourselves like unto men that wait for their Lord, when he will return from the wedding, that when he cometh and knocketh, they may open unto him immediately.

37 Blessed *are* those servants whom the Lord when he cometh shall find watching: verily, I say unto you, that he shall gird himself, and make them to sit down to meat, and will come forth and serve him.

38 And if he shall come in the second watch, or come in the third watch, and find *them* so, blessed are those servants.

39 And this know, that if the good-man of the house had known what hour the thief would come, he would have watched, and not have suffered his house to be broken through.

40 Be ye therefore ready also: for the Son of man cometh at an hour when ye think not.

41 ¶ Then Peter said unto him, Lord, speakest thou this parable unto us, or even to all?

42 And the Lord said, Who then is that faithful and wise steward, whom *his* Lord shall make ruler over his houshold, to give them *their* portion of meat in due season?

43 Blessed *is* that servant, whom his lord when he cometh shall find so doing.

44 Of a truth I say unto you, that he will make him ruler over all that he hath.

45 But and if that servant say in his heart, My lord delayeth his coming: and shall begin to beat the men-servants, and maidens, and to eat and drink, and to be drunken :

46 The lord of that servant will come in a day when he looketh not for him, and at an hour when he is not aware, and will cut him in sunder, and will appoint him his portion with the unbelievers.

47 And that servant which knew his lord's will, and prepared not *himself*, neither did according to his will, shall be beaten with many *stripes*.

48 But he that knew not, and did commit things worthy of stripes, shall be beaten with few stripes. For unto whomsoever much is given, of him shall be much required : and

L12:48

to whom men have committed much, of him they will ask the more.

J12

24 Verily, verily I fay unto you, Except a corn of wheat fall into the ground, and die, it abideth alone : but if it die, it bringeth forth much fruit.

25 He that loveth his life, fhall lofe it: and he that hateth his life in this world, fhall keep it unto life eternal.

M22

23 ¶ The fame day came to him the Sadducees, which fay that there is no refurrection, and afked him,

24 Saying, Mafter, Mofes faid, If a man die, having no children, his brother fhall marry his wife, and raife up feed unto his brother.

25 Now there were with us feven brethren, and the firft when he had married a wife, deceafed, and having no iffue, left his wife unto his brother.

26 Likewife the fecond alfo, and the third, unto the feventh.

27 And laft of all the woman died alfo.

28 Therefore in the refurrection, whofe wife fhall fhe be of the feven ? for they all had her.

29 Jefus anfwered and faid unto them, Ye do err, not knowing the Scriptures, nor the power of God.

30 For in the refurrection they neither marry, nor are given in marriage ; but are as the angels of God in heaven.

31 But as touching the refurrection of the dead, have ye not read that which was fpoken unto you by God, faying,

32 I am the God of Abraham, and the God of Ifaac, and the God of Jacob ? God is not the God of the dead, but of the living.

31 ¶ When the Son of man fhall come in his glory, and all the holy angels with him, then fhall he fit upon the throne of his glory.

M25

32 And before him fhall be gathered all nations ; and he fhall feparate them one from another, as a fhepherd divideth his fheep from the goats :

33 And he fhall fet the fheep on his right hand, but the goats on the left.

34 Then fhall the King fay unto them on his right hand, Come, ye bleffed of my Father, inherit the kingdom prepared for you from the foundation of the world.

35 For I was an hungred, and ye gave me meat : I was thirfty, and ye gave me drink : I was a ftranger, and ye took me in,

M25

36 Naked, and ye cloathed me : I was fick, and ye vifited me : I was in prifon, and ye came unto me.

37 Then fhall the righteous anfwer him, faying, Lord, when faw we thee an hungred, and fed *thee ?* or thirfty, and gave *thee* drink ?

38 When faw we thee a ftranger, and took *thee* in ? or naked and cloathed *thee ?*

39 Or when faw we thee fick, or in prifon, and came unto thee ?

40 And the King fhall anfwer, and fay unto them, Verily I fay unto you, Inafmuch as ye have done *it* unto one of the leaft of thefe my brethren, ye have done *it* unto me.

41 Then fhall he fay alfo unto them on the left hand, Depart from me, ye curfed, into everlafting fire, prepared for the devil and his angels.

42 For I was an hungred, and ye gave me no meat : I was thirfty, and ye gave me no drink :

43 I was a ftranger, and ye took me not in : naked, and ye clothed me not : fick, and in prifon, and ye vifited me not.

44 Then fhall they alfo anfwer him, faying, Lord, when faw we thee an hungred, or

athirft, or a ftranger, or naked, or fick, or in prifon, and did not minifter unto thee ?

45 Then fhall he anfwer them, faying, Verily I fay unto you, Inafmuch as ye did *it* not to one of the leaft of thefe, ye did *it* not to me.

46 And thefe fhall go away into everlafting punifhment : but the righteous into life eternal.

31 ¶ Another parable put he forth unto them, faying, The kingdom of heaven is like to a grain of muftard-feed, which a man took and fowed in his field.

M13

32 Which indeed is the leaft of all feeds : but when it is grown, it is the greateft among herbs, and becometh a tree : fo that the birds of the air come and lodge in the branches thereof.

33 ¶ Another parable fpake he unto them. The kingdom of heaven is like unto leaven, which a woman took and hid in three meafures of meal, till the whole was leavened.

34 All thefe things fpake Jefus unto the multitude in parables, and without a parable fpake he not unto them :

[M13:34]

M13

44 ¶ Again, the kingdom of heaven is like unto treasure in a field; which when a man hath found, he hideth, and for joy thereof goeth and selleth all that he hath, and buyeth that field.

45 ¶ Again, the kingdom of heaven is like unto a merchantman, seeking goodly pearls:

46 Who when he hath found one pearl of great price, he went and sold all that he had, and bought it.

47 ¶ Again, the kingdom of heaven is like unto a net that was cast into the sea, and gathered of every kind.

48 Which, when it was full, they drew to shore, and sat down, and gathered the good into vessels, but cast the bad away.

49 So shall it be at the end of the world : the angels shall come forth, and sever the wicked from among the just ;

50 And shall cast them into the furnace of fire : there shall be wailing and gnashing of teeth.

51 Jesus saith unto them, Have ye understood all these things ? They say unto him, Yea, Lord.

52 Then said he unto them, Therefore every scribe which

is instructed unto the kingdom of heaven, is like unto a man that is an housholder, which bringeth forth out of his treasure things new and old.

24 God is a Spirit, and they that worship him, must worship him in spirit and in truth.

J4

CHAP. XVIII.

J

WHEN Jesus had spoken these words, he went forth with his disciples over the brook Cedron, where was a garden, into the which he entered, and his disciples.

2 And Judas also which betrayed him, knew the place : for Jesus oft times resorted thither with his disciples.

3 Judas then having received a band of *men*, and officers from the chief priests and Pharisees, cometh thither with lanterns, and torches, and weapons.

49 And forthwith he came to Jesus, and said, Hail, Master; and kissed him.

M26

50 And Jesus said unto him, Friend, wherefore art thou come ? and Whom seek ye ?

J18:4

5 They answered him, Jesus of Nazareth. Jesus saith unto them, I am *he*. If therefore ye seek me, let these go their way :

J18

J18:8

M26:55

Are ye come out as againſt a thief with ſwords and ſtaves for to take me? I ſat daily with you teaching in the temple, and ye laid no hold on me.

J18

12 Then the band, and the captain and officers of the Jews, took Jeſus and bound him,

M26:57

led *him* away to Caiaphas the high prieſt, where the ſcribes and the elders were aſſembled.

J18

19 ¶ The high-prieſt then aſked Jeſus of his diſciples, and of his doctrine.

20 Jeſus anſwered him, I ſpake openly to the world; I ever taught in the ſynagogue, and in the temple, whither the Jews always reſort; and in ſecret have I ſaid nothing.

21 Why aſkeſt thou me? aſk them which heard me, what I have ſaid unto them: behold, they know what I ſaid.

22 And when he had thus ſpoken, one of the officers which ſtood by, ſtruck Jeſus with the palm of his hand, ſaying, Anſwereſt thou the high prieſt ſo?

23 Jeſus anſwered him, If I

have ſpoken evil, bear witneſs of the evil; but if well, why ſmiteſt thou me?

59 Now the chief prieſts and elders, and all the council, ſought falſe witneſs againſt Jeſus to put him to death.

60 But found none: yea, though many falſe witneſſes came, yet found they none. At laſt came two falſe witneſſes,

61 And ſaid, This *fellow* ſaid, I am able to deſtroy the temple of God, and to build it in three days.

62 And the high prieſt aroſe, and ſaid unto him, Anſwereſt thou nothing? what *is it which* theſe witneſs againſt thee?

Art thou the Chriſt? tell us. And he ſaid unto them, If I tell you, you will not believe.

68 And if I alſo aſk *you*, you will not anſwer me, nor let *me* go.

Again the high prieſt aſked him, and ſaid unto him, Art thou the Chriſt, the Son of the Bleſſed?

62 And Jeſus ſaid, I am:

70 Then ſaid they all, Art thou then the Son of God? And he ſaid unto them, Ye ſay that I am.

M26

L22:67

[Mk14: 61-62]

L22

Mk14

63 Then the high prieſt rent his clothes, and ſaith, What need we any further witneſ-ſes ?

64 Ye have heard the blaſ-phemy : what think ye ? And they all condemned him to be guilty of death.

[M27:1]

C H A P. XXVII.

WHEN the morning was come, all the chief prieſts and elders of the peo-ple, took counſel againſt Jeſus to put him to death.

C H A P. XXIII.

L

AND the whole multitude of them, aroſe, and led him unto Pilate.

2 And they began to accuſe him, ſaying, We found this *fel-low* perverting the nation, and forbidding to give tribute to Ceſar, ſaying, that he himſelf is Chriſt a king.

3 And Pilate aſked him, ſay-ing, Art thou the king of the Jews ? and he anſwered him, and ſaid, Thou ſayeſt *it.*

J18:36

My kingdom is not of this world :

L23

4 Then ſaid Pilate to the chief prieſts, and *to* the people, I find no fault in this man.

5 And they were the more fierce, ſaying, He ſtirreth up the people, teaching through-cut all Jewry, beginning from Galilee to this place.

6 When Pilate heard of Ga-lilee, he aſked whether the man were a Galilean.

7 And as ſoon as he knew that he belonged unto Herod's juriſdiction, he ſent him to Herod, who himſelf was alſo at Jeruſalem at that time.

8 ¶ And when Herod ſaw Jeſus, he was exceeding glad : for he was deſirous to ſee him of a long ſeaſon, becauſe he had heard many things of him ; and he hoped to have ſeen ſome miracle done by him.

9 Then he queſtioned with him in many words ; but he anſwered him nothing.

10 And the chief prieſts and ſcribes ſtood, and vehemently accuſed him.

11 And Herod with his men of war ſet him at nought, and mocked him, and arrayed him in a gorgeous robe, and ſent him again to Pilate.

12 ¶ And the ſame day Pi-late and Herod were made friends together ; for before they were at enmity between themſelves.

13 ¶ And Pilate when he had called together the chief prieſts, and the rulers, and the people,

L23

14 Said unto them, Ye have brought this man unto me as one that perverteth the people: and behold, I having examined *him* before you, have found no fault in this man, touching those things whereof ye accuse him;

15 No, nor yet Herod: for I sent you to him, and lo, nothing worthy of death is done unto him.

16 I will therefore chaftife him, and releafe *him*.

17 For of neceffity he muft releafe one unto them at the feaft.

18 And they cried out all at once, faying, Away with this *man*, and releafe unto us Barabbas:

19 (Who for a certain fedition made in the city, and for murder, was caft in prifon)

20 Pilate therefore, willing to releafe Jefus, fpake again to them.

21 But they cried, faying, Crucify *him*, crucify him.

22 And he faid, unto them the third time, Why, what evil hath he done? I have found no caufe of death in him: I will therefore chaftife him, and let *him* go.

23 And they were inftant with loud voices, requiring that he might be crucified;

24 ¶ When Pilate faw that he could prevail nothing, but that rather a tumult was made, he took water, and wafhed his hands before the multitude, faying, I am innocent of the blood of this juft perfon: fee ye *to it*.

M27

25 Then anfwered All the people, and faid, His blood *be* on us, and on our children.

and the voices of them, and of the chief priefts prevailed.

L23:23

24 And Pilate gave fentence that it fhould be as they required.

26 ¶ Then releafed he Barabbas unto them: and when he had fcourged Jefus, he delivered him to be crucified.

M27

16 Then delivered he him therefore unto them to be crucified. And they took Jefus, and led him away.

J19

17 And he bearing his crofs, went forth into a place called *the place* of a fkull, which is called in the Hebrew, Golgotha;

[J19:17]

33 And when they were come to the place which is called Calvary, there they cru-

L23

L23

cified him, and the malefactors: one on the right hand, and the other on the left.

34 ¶ Then said Jesus, Father, forgive them; for they know not what they do.

J19

25 ¶ Now there stood by the cross of Jesus, his mother, and his mother's sister, Mary *the wife* of Cleophas, and Mary Magdalene

26 When Jesus therefore saw his mother, and the disciple standing by, whom he loved, he saith unto his mother, Woman, behold thy son.

27 Then saith he to the disciple, Behold thy mother. And from that hour that disciple took her unto his own *home.*

M27

46 And about the ninth hour, Jesus cried with a loud voice, saying, Eli, Eli, lama sabachthani? that is to say, my God, my God, why hast thou forsaken me?

J19

28 ¶ After this, Jesus knowing that all things were now accomplished, that the scripture might be fulfilled, saith, I thirst.

29 Now there was set a vessel full of vinegar: and they filled a spunge with vinegar,

and put it upon hyssop, and put it to his mouth.

30 When Jesus therefore had received the vinegar, he said, It is finished: and he bowed his head, and gave up the ghost.

NOTES TO
"THE PHILOSOPHY OF JESUS"

The primary purpose of the notes to "The Philosophy of Jesus" (hereafter referred to as PJ) is to enable the reader to judge the accuracy of the reconstructed text. To this end, the following kinds of information are provided:

(1) When a verse in PJ does not appear also in "The Life and Morals of Jesus" (hereafter referred to as LJ), the notes indicate this and whether a parallel verse appears elsewhere in either document. If it is initially doubtful that a particular verse appeared in PJ, the inclusion of that verse, or a parallel, in LJ provided grounds for including it in PJ. The same assumption applies, of course, if the parallel of a doubtful verse appears elsewhere in PJ.

(2) The term "additional verses" is used to designate verses that TJ clipped from the 1791 or the 1799 New Testament (hereafter referred to as NT) that do not appear in either the Randall or the Edgehill-Randolph manuscript (E-R MS) Table of Texts. It does not apply to verses located on the reverse side of clippings TJ clearly used in PJ. In the notes, additional verses are set off from the other verses by brackets. Additional verses are discussed in the notes only when there is some likelihood that they appeared in PJ.

The notes are meant also to indicate variations between PJ and LJ, to discuss the ways in which TJ might have interpreted certain verses, and to resolve the differences between the E-R MS and the Randall Tables of Texts. References to Table of Texts, without one of these designations, are to the table that precedes the two sets of extracts printed herein. References to page numbers in PJ and LJ are to those appearing at the top of the pages in this volume, the former supplied by the editors in the reconstructed text, the latter penned by TJ when he prepared the manuscript.

To provide a fully documented case for the reliability of the reconstructed text presented here, the following items have been deposited in the Jefferson Papers Office at Princeton University: (1) photostats of the original 1791 and 1799 NTs clipped by TJ to compile PJ; (2) a copy of the text of PJ presented in this volume, with the origin of each clipping from the NTs specifically identified; and (3) annotated copies of the NTs clipped for the reconstruction.

L2:21: Portion of verse not used in PJ or LJ: "which was so named of the angel before he was conceived in the womb."

L2:22: Neither this verse nor any parallel appears in LJ.

L2:40: In LJ, TJ excluded the final phrase: "and the grace of God was upon him." He may have used this phrase in PJ because of a note in Joseph Priestley, *A Harmony of the Evangelists, in English* (London, 1780), p. 14, stating that it might be interpreted as "*an extraordinary grace* or *gracefulness*, the term *God* being used in this manner in Hebrew for a superlative, as mountains of God . . . meaning very high mountains."

L2:41: Neither this verse nor any parallel appears in LJ.

L2:42-49: TJ's use of these verses, even with L2:49 excluded in LJ, is note-worthy, given the nature of the incidents involved and the orthodox in-ference that they show either that Jesus was divine or that he had a special mission from God. In view of TJ's well known skepticism on both points, he probably included these verses as an expression of his personal belief that Jesus' "natural endowments [were] great" ("Syllabus," [21 Apr. 1803], Appendix). He may also have been influenced by the note on L2:46 in Priestley, *English Harmony*, p. 16, stating that: "The teachers of the law used to expound it to the young people in some apartments of the temple. There young men used to inquire of them, and to be examined by them concerning it. We are not, therefore, to suppose that Jesus, at the age of twelve years, assumed the character of an instructor, but that he attended to the instructions of those who were skilled in the law, and, for his information, asked pertinent questions."

NOTES FOR PAGE 2

L2:46-49: See preceding note.

L2:49: Neither this verse nor any parallel appears in LJ. TJ may have inter-preted the verse to mean that Jesus was merely surprised that his parents did not expect him to attend religious instruction. By excluding this verse in LJ, TJ presented Jesus in a more humble and submissive light.

L2:51: Portion of verse not used in PJ or LJ: "but his mother kept all these sayings in her heart." TJ omitted the entire verse in Greek and Latin in LJ.

L2:52: In LJ, TJ excluded the final phrase: "and in favour with God and man." This phrase is so susceptible to a figurative interpretation that it seems remarkable TJ took the trouble to exclude it from LJ. Its omission in LJ raises the possibility that TJ also omitted it in PJ.

L3:23-38: Except for a portion of L3:23 ("And Jesus himself began to be about thirty years of age"), LJ has neither these verses nor any parallels. At this point LJ diverges sharply from PJ to give accounts of Jesus' baptism by John, the first cleansing of the temple, and the execution of John the Baptist by Herod.

The clipped NTs leave little doubt that TJ used L3:23-38 in PJ. In view of TJ's generally low regard for the Old Testament, he probably included these genealogical verses to emphasize his belief that despite his great gifts Jesus was ultimately human rather than divine.

NOTES FOR PAGE 3

L3:31-38: See preceding note.

[L6:12-16]: Although they are not listed in the Table of Texts, these verses were clipped from an outer column of the 1791 NT and were almost certainly used here by TJ as a much-needed introduction to M10:5. TJ also used L6:12-16 in LJ, p. 5, though in a different context.

M10:7: This verse does not appear in LJ, and there is no parallel of it in PJ or LJ. But both compilations include numerous verses that refer to the "kingdom of heaven" and the "kingdom of God," for example, M13:24 (PJ, p. 8; LJ, p. 24) and M6:33 (PJ, p. 18; LJ, p. 12). Indeed, TJ entitled section xxxvii of PJ "the Kingdom of heaven."

M10:7-8: These verses, which are not in LJ, have M9:36 on their reverse side in the 1791 and 1799 NTs. Since M9:36 appears immediately before Mk6:7 and M10:5 in LJ, p. 28, it is possible that TJ used M9:36 before M10:5 in PJ. If so, TJ may not have included in PJ M10:7-8, the miraculous content of which was otherwise unacceptable to him.

M10:8: There is no parallel of this verse in PJ, and neither the verse itself nor any parallel appears in LJ. TJ might have made the verse acceptable to himself in a number of ways on the basis of notes in Priestley, *English Harmony*. He could have deleted the phrase "raise the dead"; *English Harmony*, p. 86, claimed that these words were not in many early manuscript NTs. He also could have interpreted the phrase "cast out devils" as did Priestley, who argued that Satan might be regarded as "an allegorical personage, or the principle of evil personified" (same, p. v). In a note on M10:28, moreover, Priestley asserted that when Jesus spoke of an immaterial soul and of demonic possession he was merely reflecting "the philosophical principles that perhaps began about that time to spread among the Jews" (same, p. 86).

M10:19-20: No parallel of these verses appears in PJ, and neither the verses themselves nor any parallels are in LJ. A note on the parallel verse M13:11 in Priestley, *English Harmony*, p. 196, may explain why TJ found these verses acceptable for PJ: "This promise was either confined to the apostolic age, or the meaning must be, that their circumstances, and the goodness of their cause, would be sufficient, without any supernatural assistance, to suggest what they ought to say, and therefore they did not need to be anxious about the matter."

M10:21: TJ excluded this verse from LJ and all other verses stating that loyalty to Jesus and his message would cause familial and social strife. But PJ has a number of verses expressing this sentiment, for example, L14:26-27 (PJ, p. 32). Priestley's note on L14:26 in *English Harmony*, p. 147, contains an interpretation that may have persuaded TJ to use that verse, as well as M10:21, in PJ: "*Hate not his father and mother*] The meaning is, that we should prefer the cause of Christ to all earthly considerations. So also when it is said, *Jacob have I loved and Esau have I hated*, the meaning is, I have loved Jacob more than Esau."

M10:22: There is no parallel of this verse in PJ, and neither the verse itself nor any parallel appears in LJ.

M10:23: No parallel of this verse appears in PJ or LJ. TJ excluded the words "for verily I say unto you, ye shall not have gone over the cities of Israel, till the Son of man be come" in LJ, p. 29. He may have included these words in PJ because of a paraphrase of them in Priestley, *English Harmony*,

p. 86: "Ye shall not have sufficiently preached the gospel in Judea before the destruction of Jerusalem."

M10:24: Although this verse is not in LJ, PJ and LJ both have parallels, for example, J13:16 (PJ, p. 6; LJ, p. 70).

M10:25: No parallel of this verse appears in PJ, and neither the verse itself nor any parallel is in LJ.

[M10:34-41]: Although not in the Table of Texts, these verses were clipped from the outer column of a 1799 NT page from which TJ also cut a number of other verses. Their inclusion in PJ is tentative, but it seems likely that TJ would have used at least M10:34-39. The absence of M10:34-41 from LJ is no reason for excluding them from PJ, for unlike LJ, PJ contains several verses which state that following Jesus' teachings will cause familial and social strife, for example, M10:21 (PJ, p. 4). TJ may have been influenced by the note on M10:34-37 in Priestley, *English Harmony*, p. 86: "*Think not that I am come to send peace*] Here our Lord foretels what would be the actual *consequence* of his preaching in the world, before the general acceptance of it, which would bring on a final state of peace and happiness."

PJ and LJ both have parallels to M10:39 (J12:25 in PJ, p. 40; L17:33 in LJ, p. 48). The inclusion here of M10:40-41, which suggest that Jesus had a divine mission, is more problematical, given TJ's skepticism on this point. However, there are other verses in PJ and LJ that carry the same suggestion (J10:1-5 in PJ, p. 7, and LJ, p. 37) and thus support the hypothesis that TJ used M10:40-41 in PJ.

M10:42: Neither this verse nor any parallel appears in LJ. PJ has several verses expressing a similar sentiment, for example, M18:5 (PJ, p. 30).

J13:11: TJ did not have to construe the words "For he knew who should betray him" to mean that Jesus had supernatural knowledge of the future. In Greek the passage reads literally: "for he knew him who was delivering up him." As a result, TJ could have taken the passage to mean no more than that Jesus was aware of Judas' true character or that he had actual knowledge of Judas' plan to betray him. In LJ, p. 68-69, the verses contained in section III of PJ are immediately preceded by accounts of Judas' agreement with the chief priests (M26:14-18) and of his reason for betraying Jesus (Mk14:1-8). PJ lacks both sets of verses as well as any parallels.

J13:13-14: TJ probably understood "Master" to mean "teacher" and "Lord" to signify that Jesus was superior to his disciples only in human terms.

NOTES

NOTES FOR PAGE 7

J10:6-10, 15: These verses are not in LJ, and there are no parallels of them in PJ or LJ. TJ probably included them in PJ, despite their intimation that Jesus had a special relationship with God, because of the different emphases he had in mind when he compiled this portion of PJ and LJ. He described this section of PJ as "false teachers" and the corresponding section of LJ as "the good shepherd." In LJ he also excluded the NT chapter heading "Christ the good shepherd."

J10:16: The use of this verse here and in LJ, p. 37, is noteworthy in view of TJ's strong belief in the inevitability and desirability of diverse religious opinions. Also included in PJ, p. 32, is M8:11, which echoes the sentiment of J10:16. TJ's use of these two verses (as well as J10:6-10) in PJ can best be explained by the supposition that he understood them to refer to Jesus's moral principles, whose spread he favored, rather than to the dogmas of the Christian churches, whose development he deplored.

NOTE FOR PAGE 8

L12:13-15: Randall's Table of Texts gives this entry as L12:13, 15, and the E-R MS Table of Texts as L12:13-15. The clipped 1799 NT indicates that the E-R MS is correct.

NOTE FOR PAGE 9

M13:39-43: Priestley, *English Harmony*, provided interpretations of some of the key words and phrases in these verses that might have made them acceptable to TJ. Priestley noted in regard to "angels" that "The Jews called every thing an *angel or messenger*, by which God acts" (same, p. 103). With respect to "Son of man," Priestley paraphrased M16:13 ("Whom do men say that I, the Son of man, am?") to mean: "I who am a man; on other occasions this phrase, having been applied by Daniel to the Messiah, was also used as a characteristic of him by the Jews. Perhaps it ought to be rendered, *Whom do men say that I am? Do they say I am the Son of man*, i.e. *the Messiah?*" (same, p. 115).

NOTES FOR PAGE 10

Section VIII, beginning with Mk2:15-17: The headings for this section differ in the E-R MS and the Randall Tables of Texts. The former reads "Physicians are for the sick" and "Parables of the lost sheep," whereas the latter reads "Physicians care for the sick" and "Parable of the lost sheep." In both cases the E-R MS appears to be the more accurate reading. The sense of the verses in Section VIII and the derivation of the descriptive phrase "Physicians are for the sick" from Mk2:17 both point to the use of "are" rather than "care," and "Parables" is more descriptive of the section than "Parable." Moreover, the entry in the Table of Texts for LJ, p. 43-44, is "Parables of the lost sheep and Prodigal son."

Mk2:15: In LJ, p. 27, TJ replaced "And it came to pass that as Jesus sat at meat in his house" with a comparable clause from L5:29: "And Levi made him a great feast in his own house: and."

M18:10: Neither this verse nor any parallel appears in LJ. PJ has several other verses expressing a similar sentiment, for example, M10:42 (PJ, p. 5).

M18:11: This verse does not appear in LJ, and there is no parallel of it in PJ or LJ.

[M18:12-14]: These verses are not listed in the Table of Texts. The 1799 NT indicates that TJ cut them out as part of a larger clipping that also included M18:10-11. The parallel verses L15:3-7 appear in PJ, p. 11, and LJ, p. 42. The fact that the additional verses M18:12-14 are parallel to L15:3-7, which immediately follow, does not necessarily mean that they were not used in PJ as shown. The sentiment expressed in M18:14 is repeated several times in Section VIII of PJ. If the additional verses L15:1-2 are placed as shown, M18:12-14 become highly appropriate, for then the objection of the Pharisees in L15:2 (PJ, p. 11) would be to Jesus' discourse in M18:10-14.

[L15:1-2]: These verses are not listed in the Table of Texts. TJ cut them from an outer column of the 1799 NT as part of a larger clipping that also included L15:3-8. In LJ, p. 42-44, TJ used L15:1-32 precisely as in PJ, without any intervening verses.

NOTE FOR PAGE 11

[L15:2]: See preceding note.

NOTES FOR PAGE 14

Section x, beginning with M5:1: The E-R MS Table of Texts gives the heading for this section as "Sermon in the mount," whereas the Randall Table of Texts gives it as "sermon on the mount." The E-R MS is probably correct inasmuch as TJ used "in" rather than "on" in the LJ Table of Texts.

M5:22: In addition to the fact that this verse can be interpreted figuratively rather than literally, Priestley provided a gloss on it that undoubtedly mitigated its harshness for TJ. Priestley interpreted "Raca" to mean "an empty or good for nothing fellow" and observed that if one person applied it to another without reason "his punishment will be as much greater, as that which is inflicted by the Sanhedrin for the most atrocious crimes exceeds the punishments that are inflicted by the inferior courts of Justice." He also construed "Thou fool" to mean "*rebel* or *apostate*" and noted that if one person called another "*a wicked abandoned wretch*, which reflects upon his moral character as well as his understanding, and all without reason, his punishment in a future life will be so great, that it may be compared to burning in the valley of Hinnom." Finally, Priestley maintained that the Greek term for "hell-fire" referred to the "valley of the son of Hinnom, which was a valley near Jerusalem, infamous for idolatry, and particularly burning of infants to Molock. . . . By the name of this horrid place the Jews, in our Saviour's time, represented the punishment of the wicked in another life, and he adopted it after them" *(English Harmony,* p. 42-43).

M5:39: Priestley, *English Harmony,* p. 44, claimed that "resist not evil" could not be taken literally, as Jesus and Paul "when they were actually smitten, did not voluntarily expose themselves to farther insults, but expostulated on account of those they had received. The precept can, therefore, only be intended to inculcate a meek and unrevengeful temper."

M5:40: Priestley, *English Harmony,* p. 45, paraphrased this verse as follows: "Also, in opposition to the covetous, and consequently litigious spirit of the Pharisees, I would advise you to suffer as far as possible, and by any means compose your differences in an amicable manner, rather than go to law with one another."

M5:48: TJ substituted L6:34-36 for M5:48 in LJ, p. 10, thereby emphasizing M5:44-46, especially the idea that one should not only love but actively aid one's enemies. It is also significant that whereas M5:48 enjoins men to imitate God's perfection, L6:36 urges them to imitate his mercy.

M7:3: In LJ, p. 13, TJ inserted part of L6:38 before this verse.

M7:6: Because of a typographical error in the 1799 NT, the last two words of this verse read "rent you" instead of "rend you."

M7:21-23: TJ substituted the quite different message of M12:35-37 in place of these verses in LJ, p. 14. However, PJ, p. 40-41, and LJ, p. 67-68, both have M25:31-46, which express virtually the same sentiment as M7:21-23. TJ probably excluded M7:21-23 from LJ because in them Jesus speaks in the first person when he discusses the day of judgment, whereas in M25:31-46, he refers to the "Son of man."

[M7:28-29; M8:1]: These verses, which are not in the Table of Texts, come from a leaf of the 1799 NT that was cut out at the gutter. If TJ used all three of these additional verses in PJ as shown here, he would have needed almost all of the other verses on that page for PJ, p. 19-20. The sole exception is M8:2, which would have been used instead for the material on the reverse, M8:11 (PJ, p. 32). Furthermore, these additional verses appear in LJ, p. 15, in precisely the same order as they are given here.

M19:29: There is no parallel of this verse in PJ, and neither the verse itself nor any parallel appears in LJ.

M19:30: Although this verse does not appear in LJ, the parallel verse, M20:16, is in both PJ (p. 10) and LJ (p. 53).

M22:35-39: In LJ, p. 60, TJ substituted the parallel verses Mk12:28-31.

L14:4: In LJ, p. 40, TJ left out the phrase "And he took *him*, and healed him, and let *him* go," in every language except French.

L14:5: In LJ, p. 40, TJ left out "And answered them, saying" and substituted "And he saith unto them" from M4:19.

L11:47-48: These verses do not appear in LJ. PJ, p. 29, and LJ, p. 62, have the parallel verses M23:29-30.

L11:48: See preceding note.

M15:1-20: Although none of these verses appears in LJ, the generally parallel verses Mk7:1-5, 14-23, are included there (p. 29-30).

M15:19-20: See preceding note.

M12:33: This verse does not appear in LJ. PJ, p. 19, and LJ, p. 14, have the almost parallel verses M7:16-18.

M12:34: There is no parallel of this verse in PJ, and neither the verse itself nor any parallel appears in LJ.

M13:4: In LJ, p. 22, this verse is complete except in English, where TJ intentionally left out the word "up" for stylistic reasons and to conform the text to the other languages.

M13:18-23: Randall's Table of Texts gives this selection as M13:18-29, whereas the E-R MS Table of Texts gives it as M13:18-23. The latter is undoubtedly correct inasmuch as M13:24-29 had previously been used in PJ, p. 8.

M13:20-23: See preceding note.

L7:39-40: The traditional interpretation of these verses assumes that the Pharisee merely protested mentally, making Jesus' reply a manifestation of his supernatural powers. TJ could have construed the verse differently. The Greek text can be interpreted to mean that the Pharisee "said quietly" so that Jesus heard him, or TJ might have decided that the Pharisee made his attitude evident to Jesus by his general demeanor. TJ could have cut out the words "within himself" in both PJ and LJ and thereby eliminated any implication that Jesus possessed supernatural powers. That he did not do so here, but that he did delete similar material in other cases, suggests that in this instance he was more interested in retaining the total drama of the incident than in making it conform to his humanistic understanding of Jesus' character and career.

NOTES FOR PAGE 26

L7:47: This verse, which has no parallel in PJ, does not appear in LJ. TJ's exclusion of it from LJ is remarkable inasmuch as it does not necessarily mean that Jesus forgave the woman's sin on his own authority. If TJ's description of this section as "the will for the deed" is any indication, he may have interpreted L7:36-47 as a case in which Jesus "preaches the efficacy of repentance towards forgiveness of sin" (TJ to William Short, 13 Apr. 1820, Appendix). In contrast, TJ noted in the same letter, "I require a counterpoise of good works to redeem [sin]." Thus TJ probably accepted Jesus' pronouncement in L7:47 as genuine but left it out of LJ because of his disagreement with the sentiments therein expressed.

L10:37: This verse is actually L10:27.

NOTES FOR PAGE 27

Section xix, beginning with M23:1: In the E-R MS Table of Texts all the selections for this section are joined by one brace, so that the entire heading is meant to apply to all the verses in it, though "humility, pride, hypocrisy" are entered opposite the second selection, L18:9-14, and "Pharisaism" is placed opposite the third and fourth. In contrast, Randall's Table of Texts has two braces for the selections, so that "humility, pride, hypocrisy" apply to M23:1-33 and L18:9-14 and "Pharisaism" to L14:7-11 and M18:1-6. In view of the contents of Section xix, the E-R MS appears to be correct.

The second digit of L18:9-14 is smudged in the E-R MS Table of Texts. The original entry might just as well have been L10 or L11. The figure 18 is entered above the original entry and provides the basis for the reading L18:9-14. Nevertheless, it is virtually certain that TJ did not use L18:9-14 in PJ. These verses are all unclipped in the 1791 NT, and L18:9-10 as well as the first two lines of L18:11 are uncut in the 1799 NT. TJ almost certainly clipped the 1799 NT page for L18:1-8, which are on the reverse side of L18:9-14 (PJ, p. 33-34). Since L18:9-14 do appear in LJ, TJ might have omitted them from PJ through inadvertence.

M23:8-10: TJ undoubtedly construed the phrase "one is your Master, *even* Christ" to mean that God was superior to Jesus as well as to the apostles and that therefore Jesus was not divine.

NOTES FOR PAGE 30

M18:5: Neither this verse nor any parallel appears in LJ. PJ, p. 5, has the parallel verse M10:[40].

[115]

M18:6: There is no parallel of this verse in PJ, and the verse itself does not appear in LJ. LJ, p. 47, has the parallel verses L17:1-2.

L16:19-31: The extent to which TJ accepted Jesus' teachings on hell is extremely problematical, given the skepticism with which he regarded it. For example, in responding to a correspondent who had referred him to a seventeenth-century work on demonology by Balthasar Bekker, TJ sarcastically observed, "I think Bekker might have demanded a truce from his antagonists, on the question of Hell, by desiring them first to fix it's geography. But wherever it be, it is certainly the best patrimony of the church, and procures them in exchange the solid acres of this world" (TJ to Francis Adrian Van der Kemp, 1 May 1817).

NOTE FOR PAGE 31

M12:46-50: There is no parallel of these verses in PJ, and the verses themselves do not appear in LJ. LJ, p. 16, has the parallel verses Mk3:31-35.

NOTES FOR PAGE 32

M12:49-50: See preceding note.

M8:11: PJ, p. 7, and LJ, p. 37, have the somewhat parallel verse J10:16. M8:11 does not appear in LJ.

L14:[25]: Although this verse is not listed in the Table of Texts, the 1791 NT shows that TJ removed L14:25-33 in one clipping and presumably used all the verses in PJ.

L14:26-27: Neither these verses nor any parallels appear in LJ. PJ has a number of parallels, however. See, for example, M10:21 (PJ, p. 4).

L14:33: PJ, p. 21, contains a rough parallel of this verse in M19:29. L14:33 does not appear in LJ, which has the somewhat parallel verses L9:57-62 (LJ, p. 26).

NOTE FOR PAGE 33

L16:1-13: In the Table of Texts this parable appears under the heading of "worldly wisdom," which suggests that TJ was not in accord with the traditional view that Jesus' purpose in it was to urge his disciples to exhibit the same prudence and foresight in spiritual matters that the unjust steward had exhibited in the pursuit of temporal matters.

NOTES FOR PAGE 34

M21:33: In LJ, p. 57, TJ used the phrase "Hear another parable" from M21:33 in place of the corresponding phrase in Mk12:1: "And he began to speak unto them by parables."

M21:33-41: Except as indicated above, TJ replaced these verses in LJ, p. 57, with the parallel verses Mk12:1-9.

NOTES

L14:14: In LJ, p. 41, TJ omitted the last part of this verse in French: "car tu en recevras la récompense à la résurrection des justes."

M22:15-22: TJ surely must have found in these verses more than what he conveyed in the heading he gave them in the Table of Texts: "submission to magistrates." In Jesus' reply to the question whether it was lawful for the Jews to pay tribute to the Romans, he must also have found support for his own belief in the need for an absolute separation between church and state. Considering the extent to which TJ was bedeviled by clerical criticism of his religion, it is not surprising that he felt compelled to stress the need for ministerial "submission to magistrates." Yet TJ must have also relished Jesus' injunction to render "unto God, the things that are God's," for he firmly believed that each person's religion was a private matter between himself and the deity.

M22:20-22: See preceding note.

M19:11-12: By adding these verses, which are not essential to the theme of Section xxx, "the bond of mariage," TJ seems to have gone out of his way to reject the idea that celibacy is superior to marriage.

M25:13: In LJ, p. 65, TJ used the words "Watch therefore" from this verse. PJ, p. 39, and LJ, p. 19, contain the parallel verse L12:40.

L12:37: The last word in this verse should read "them," "him" being a typographical error in the 1791 NT.

L12:46: In the English column of LJ, p. 20, TJ left out "and will appoint him his portion with the unbelievers."

J12:25: Although this verse does not appear in LJ, p. 48 contains the parallel verse L17:33.

M22:23-32: TJ used these verses here and in LJ, p. 59, in preference to the parallel verses Mk12:18-27 and L20:27-38, which are not in either compilation. TJ usually preferred Matthew over the other Evangelists, and in this case he probably preferred him for stylistic reasons alone. Yet this selection from Matthew is also the most neutral of the three descriptions of the nature of life after death and may have been chosen by TJ for that very reason.

M22:29-32: TJ possibly found the real attraction of these verses in the statement that "God is not the God of the dead, but of the living," which was congruent with his own cherished conviction that "the earth belongs in usufruct to the living" (TJ to James Madison, 6 Sep. 1789).

M25:31-46: These verses are designated as "the last judgment" in the Table of Texts for PJ and as "the day of judgment" in the Table of Texts for LJ. This does not signify any alteration in TJ's interpretation of these verses, which can only refer to a final general judgment. It may indicate, however, a wish to soften the impact of the verses that refer to "everlasting punishment." Priestley, *English Harmony*, p. 201, maintained that the Greek word that was translated as "everlasting punishment" really meant no more than "the punishment of an entire period, age, or dispensation." If TJ did believe in a last judgment, it was almost certainly one in which all men would be ultimately reconciled with God after a due period of punishment for their transgressions, a doctrine of universal salvation much favored by Priestley.

NOTES FOR PAGE 41

M25:36-46: See preceding note.

M13:31-32: There is no parallel of these verses in PJ. TJ substituted the parallel verses Mk4:30-32 for M13:31-32 in LJ, p. 26.

M13:33: There is no parallel of this verse in PJ, and neither the verse itself nor any parallel appears in LJ.

[M13:34]: This verse is not listed in the E-R MS or the Randall Tables of Texts, both of which give the verses as M13:31-33. But the last 3 in the E-R MS has been written over another, unidentifiable number, and M13:34 was cut from the outer column of a much-clipped 1791 NT page, raising the possibility that TJ used it in PJ as shown here. LJ, p. 26, has a parallel of this verse in Mk4:33-34, which are used with other verses parallel to M13:31-32.

NOTES FOR PAGE 42

M13:44[-]52: The Randall and the E-R MS Tables of Texts give this selection as M13:44, 52. In addition to the fact that the use of these two verses alone would make little sense, the clipped NTs show that TJ used M13:44-52 and indicate that the copyist who made the E-R MS erred in putting a comma rather than a dash between 44 and 52. PJ, p. 9, and LJ, p. 25, contain M13:40-43, which are parallel to M13:49-50.

J4:24: There is no parallel of this verse in PJ, and neither the verse itself nor any parallel appears in LJ. TJ emphatically rejected the notion that God was a "Spirit" in the sense of being incorporeal and doubted that Jesus meant the term to be understood in this way (TJ to John Adams, 15 Aug. 1820, Appendix).

J18:1-3: Randall's Table of Texts gives this selection as J18:12, 13, whereas the E-R MS Table gives it as J18:1-3. Undoubtedly the latter is correct. J18:12-13 make no sense at the start of Section XXXIX. Furthermore, J18:13 is unclipped in both NTs, and J18:12 is unclipped in the 1791

NT, having been cut from the 1799 NT for use in PJ, p. 43, where it is listed in both Tables of Texts and is appropriate. Finally, J18:1-3, which, according to Randall's table, TJ did not use, are cut from the 1799 NT.

M26:50: Portion of verse not used: "Then came they, and laid hands on Jesus, and took him."

J18:4: Portion of verse not used: "Jesus therefore knowing all things that should come upon him, went forth, and said unto them." TJ used the whole verse in LJ, p. 73.

J18:5: Portion of verse not used: "And Judas also which betrayed him, stood with them." TJ used the whole verse in LJ, p. 73.

J18:8: Portion of verse not used: "Jesus answered, I have told you I am *he*." TJ used the whole verse in LJ, p. 73.

NOTES FOR PAGE 43

M26:55: Portion of verse not used: "In that same hour said Jesus to the multitude." TJ used the whole verse in LJ, p. 73.

J18:12: This verse does not appear in LJ. Instead TJ used a parallel from the last sentence of M26:50 (LJ, p. 73).

M26:57: Portion of verse not used: "And they that laid hold on Jesus." TJ used the whole verse in LJ, p. 74.

M26:59-62: These verses do not appear in LJ. Instead TJ used parallel verses from Mk14:55-60 (LJ, p. 75).

L22:67: Portion of verse not used: "Saying." In LJ, p. 75, TJ left out the entire phrase: "Saying, Art thou the Christ? tell us."

[Mk14:61-62]: Portion of Mk14:61 not used: "But he held his peace, and answered nothing." TJ used the whole verse in LJ, p. 75.

Portion of Mk14:62 not used: "and ye shall see the Son of man sitting on the right hand of power, and coming in the clouds of heaven." TJ did not use any of this verse in LJ.

These two verses do not appear in the Table of Texts. TJ carefully clipped them from an inner column of a page of the 1799 NT from which he also took another clipping consisting of Mk14:63-64 (PJ, p. 44). The reverse side of the former clipping contained one or two words from Mk15:18 and all of Mk15:19. It is unlikely that TJ used Mk15:18-19, not only because he left parts of them in the NT, but also because there seems to be no appropriate place for them in PJ. The placement of Mk14:61-62 in PJ is necessarily conjectural, though it does conform somewhat to the arrangement of Mk14:61 in LJ, p. 75.

At first sight the inclusion of a direct assertion by Jesus that he was the "Son of the Blessed" appears to be at odds with TJ's belief that Jesus had "every human excellence, and . . . never claimed any other" (TJ to Benjamin Rush, 21 Apr. 1803, Appendix). But TJ probably understood this passage, as well as all others like it in PJ and LJ, to mean that Jesus was a man specially approved by God, a theme that Priestley had emphasized in *Corruptions of Christianity*.

Mk14:63-64: Randall's Table of Texts gives this selection as Mk14:60, 64, which is clearly an error, since Mk14:60 is unclipped in both NTs. In the E-R MS Table of Texts the entry for Mk14:63 is written over what appears to be an erased entry. Since the number 3 is almost closed on the left, it can easily be misread as a zero. TJ definitely cut out Mk14:63-64 from the 1799 NT in one clipping.

[M27:1]: This verse is not in the Table of Texts. It is not in LJ, nor is there any parallel of it in PJ or LJ. Yet it seems virtually certain that TJ used it here as shown because it is the only verse clipped out of one of the outer columns of the 1799 NT. TJ may have been persuaded to use the verse by a passage in Priestley, *A Harmony of the Evangelists, in Greek* (London, 1778), p. 115, wherein Priestley sought to reconcile the varying accounts in the Gospels of Jesus' trial by arguing that there had been two assemblies of the chief priests, one to try Jesus and the other to determine how to have him put to death: "Indeed, both Matthew (xxvii.1.) and Mark (xv.1) speak of an assembly of the chief priests when it was day; but this was after his examination, and was only for the purpose of consultating among themselves in what manner they should get their sentence put in execution; and therefore they make no mention of Jesus being brought before them at the time. The resolution which they came to at this second meeting, was to carry Jesus to Pilate, which they did immediately."

L23:1: There is no parallel of this verse in PJ, and the verse itself does not appear in LJ. TJ used the parallel verse J18:28 in LJ, p. 76.

L23:2: There is no parallel of this verse in PJ, and neither the verse itself nor any parallel appears in LJ. TJ did not include any verse in LJ in which the Jews specifically charge Jesus with forbidding the payment of tribute to Caesar or in which Jesus claims that he is Christ the king. But that compilation does have some verses which imply the Jews made this charge against Jesus, for example, J18:33 (LJ, p. 76). The charge of forbidding the Jews to pay tribute to the Romans is generalized in LJ. The Jews call Jesus a "malefactor" in J18:30 (LJ, p. 76), and Pilate observes in L23:14 (LJ, p. 77) that the Jews criticized Jesus as "one that perverteth the people."

L23:3: There is no parallel of this verse in PJ, and the verse itself does not appear in LJ. TJ used the parallel verses J18:33-34 in LJ, p. 76.

J18:36: Portion of verse not used: "Jesus answered . . . if my kingdom were of this world, then would my servants fight that I should not be delivered to the Jews; but now is my kingdom not from hence." TJ used the whole verse in LJ, p. 76.

L23:4: There is no parallel of this verse in PJ, and the verse itself does not appear in LJ. TJ used the parallel verse J18:38 in LJ, p. 76.

L23:14: For TJ's interpretation of the charge to which Pilate refers, see his note on this verse in LJ, p. 77.

L23:17-23: There is no parallel of these verses in PJ, and the verses themselves do not appear in LJ. TJ used the roughly parallel verses M27:15-23, 26 in LJ, p. 78.

L23:23: This verse is listed twice in the Table of Texts—the first time as shown here and the next time as following M27:24-25. But TJ could only have used the whole verse once, since it is unclipped in the 1791 NT. The clipped 1799 NT indicates that TJ divided the verse as shown here.

M27:24-25: There is no parallel of these verses in PJ, and neither the verses themselves nor any parallels appear in LJ.

L23:23-24: There is no parallel of these verses in PJ, and neither the verses themselves nor any parallels appear in LJ.

M27:26; J19:16: Although there is no positive evidence that TJ did not use both of these verses in their entirety, it seems unlikely that he did so because of the repetition that would have resulted from the use of the phrases "he delivered him to be crucified" in the former and "then delivered he him therefore unto them to be crucified" in the latter. If TJ eliminated either of these phrases, it was probably the one in M27:26. TJ apparently used M27:24-25 and J19:16 to fix the responsibility for Jesus' crucifixion on the Jews, as these are the only Gospel verses that can be construed to mean that Jesus was released to them. It seems significant that TJ used none of these verses in LJ. In that compilation TJ so arranged the verses as to show that although the Jewish priests and elders brought about Jesus' condemnation, he was actually crucified by the Romans.

[J19:17]: This verse is not in the Table of Texts, but TJ used it in LJ, p. 80. Even though it repeats some of the material contained in L23:33, TJ may have used it in PJ so that he could have both the terms "Golgotha" and "Calvary" in his text. TJ clipped J19:17 from the 1799 NT.

L23:33: There is no parallel of this verse in PJ, and the verse itself does not appear in LJ. TJ used the parallel verse J19:18 in LJ, p. 80.

NOTES FOR PAGE 46

L23:34: Portion of verse not used in PJ or LJ: "And they parted his raiment, and cast lots."

M27:46: In view of the enigmatic character of Jesus' exclamation, which was clearly derived from Psalm 22, the way in which TJ interpreted it is central to his understanding of Jesus' life and mission. TJ probably did not interpret Jesus' exclamation as a cry of despair, since he was fully conversant with the Psalms and knew that Psalm 22 ends triumphantly. Accordingly, he evidently considered M27:46 to be a symbolic expression of confidence by Jesus in the ultimate triumph of his moral teachings, an event to which TJ looked forward as well (TJ to Jared Sparks, 4 Nov. 1820; to Timothy Pickering, 27 Feb. 1821; and to Benjamin Waterhouse, 26 June 1822, Appendix).

J19:28: There is no parallel of this verse in PJ, and neither the verse itself nor any parallel appears in LJ. It seems unlikely that TJ used the phrase "that the scripture might be fulfilled," but there is no evidence that he did not.

J19:29: There is no parallel of this verse in PJ, and the verse itself is not in LJ. TJ used the parallel verse M27:48 in LJ, p. 81.

J19:30: There is no parallel of this verse in PJ, and the verse itself is not in LJ. TJ used the parallel verse M27:50 in LJ, p. 81.

THE LIFE AND MORALS
OF JESUS

"THE LIFE AND MORALS
OF JESUS":
A HISTORY OF THE TEXT

The text of "The Life and Morals of Jesus" presented in this volume is a newly made photoreproduction of the original compilation, which is now in the custody of the Smithsonian Institution. As was mentioned in the Introduction, Jefferson probably completed "The Life and Morals of Jesus" in the summer of 1820 and definitely kept its existence a secret from everyone but Frederick A. Mayo, who bound it. After his death in 1826, Jefferson's family discovered it, and it remained with them until almost the end of the nineteenth century. His only surviving child, Martha Jefferson Randolph, apparently took personal charge of "The Life and Morals of Jesus," even though in his will Jefferson had given custody of his papers to her son, Thomas Jefferson Randolph. With the aid of three of her daughters, Mrs. Randolph made a transcript of the English text of this compilation,[1] and in 1830, while living in Washington, D.C., she lent the original work itself to Jefferson's old friend, Margaret Bayard Smith, who returned it to her unharmed.[2] Thomas Jefferson Randolph assumed custody of "The Life and Morals of Jesus" after his mother's death in 1836 and kept it at his Edgehill, Va., estate. It was Colonel Randolph who gave Henry S. Randall permission to print the title page and the table of contents of this compilation in the final volume of his 1858 biography of Jefferson, which became the first public revelation of the existence of Jefferson's second collection of extracts from the Evangelists.[3] Colonel Randolph died in 1875, whereupon "The Life and Morals of Jesus" passed into the hands of his daughter, Sarah Nicholas Randolph, author of a noted study of Jefferson's family life.[4] Miss Randolph offered to sell the manuscript, together with a valuable collection of Jefferson's personal papers, to the federal government in 1890, but the Senate failed to approve a bill authorizing the purchase, notwithstanding the recommendation of the Librarian of Congress, Ainsworth R. Spofford.[5] Sarah Randolph died two years later, at which time her sister, Carolina Randolph, took possession of the volume.

The Jefferson family finally relinquished custody of "The Life and Morals of Jesus" as a result of the determined efforts of Cyrus Adler. Adler, who was Librarian of the Smithsonian from 1893 to 1908, first became interested in this document in 1886, when, while still a fellow at Johns Hopkins University, he discovered the two English New Testaments Jefferson had used to compile

---

[1] This transcript is now in ViU. Cornelia Jefferson Randolph, Mary Jefferson Randolph, and Virginia Jefferson Randolph also helped to transcribe it.

[2] Margaret Bayard Smith to Jane Kirkpatrick, 31 Mch. 1830, *The First Forty Years of Washington Society*, ed. Gaillard Hunt (New York, 1906), p. 315-16.

[3] Henry S. Randall, *The Life of Thomas Jefferson* (Philadelphia, 1858), III, 451-52, 655-58.

[4] Sarah N. Randolph, *The Domestic Life of Thomas Jefferson* (New York, 1871).

[5] [Cyrus Adler, ed.], *The Life and Morals of Jesus of Nazareth Extracted Textually from the Gospels in Greek, Latin, French, and English by Thomas Jefferson* (Washington, D.C., 1904), p. 10-11; Paul G. Sifton, "The Provenance of the Thomas Jefferson Papers," *American Archivist*, XL (Jan. 1977), 24-26.

it as he was "cataloguing a small but very valuable Hebrew library gathered together by Dr. Joshua I. Cohen."[6] These two volumes were subsequently acquired by the Smithsonian. In the meantime, Adler, his acquisitive instincts aroused, began to search for "The Life and Morals of Jesus." He contacted Sarah Nicholas Randolph, but she died before they could meet and discuss his wish to acquire the work. Undaunted by this setback to his hopes, Adler persisted in his quest until his efforts succeeded in 1895, when he purchased "The Life and Morals of Jesus" for the Smithsonian from Carolina Randolph for $400.[7] It has since remained at the Smithsonian.

The acquisition of "The Life and Morals of Jesus" by the Smithsonian prepared the way for its publication. John F. Lacey, a Republican politician born in Virginia who served in the U.S. House of Representatives as a member from Iowa between 1893 and 1907, read this compilation in 1900 and wrote a newspaper article about it that was widely reprinted. Two years later he arranged for the publication of a volume containing the English text of "The Life and Morals of Jesus," and in the same year he sponsored a resolution calling upon Congress to authorize the printing of a facsimile of the entire compilation.[8] This led to the publication in 1904, at government expense, of a facsimile edition of "The Life and Morals of Jesus" with an introduction by Adler describing the provenance of the work as it was known at that time.[9] Since then, a number of other editions of "The Life and Morals of Jesus" have appeared, some containing the original text in all four languages and others containing only the English text.[10] Whatever their other merits, all of these editions have two serious defects. They do not offer an adequately annotated text of "The Life and Morals of Jesus," and, in the absence of a reconstructed text of "The Philosophy of Jesus," they present only a partial view of Jefferson's quest for Jesus' authentic acts and doctrines.

[6] [Adler, ed.], *Life and Morals of Jesus*, p. 10.

[7] Same, p. 10; Cyrus Adler, *I Have Considered the Days* (Philadelphia, 1945), p. 58-59; Merrill D. Peterson, *The Jeffersonian Image in the American Mind* (New York, 1960), p. 301.

[8] The volume Representative Lacey arranged to have published appeared under the title *The Life and Morals of Jesus of Nazareth Extracted Textually from the Gospels, together with a Comparison of his Doctrines with those of Others* (St. Louis, 1902). See also Peterson, *Jeffersonian Image*, p. 301.

[9] [Adler, ed.], *Life and Morals of Jesus*.

[10] In addition to those cited above in n. 5 and n. 8, other editions of TJ's second biblical compilation include: *The Thomas Jefferson Bible . . . with a Valuable Appendix of Biblical Facts* (Chicago, 1904); Henry E. Jackson, ed., *The Thomas Jefferson Bible* (New York, 1923); *Life, Sayings and Words of Jesus. Selected and Arranged by Thomas Jefferson* (Cleveland, 1940); Douglas E. Lurton, ed., *The Jefferson Bible. Compiled by Thomas Jefferson* (New York, 1940); *The Life & Morals of Jesus Christ of Nazareth Extracted Textually from the Gospels of Matthew, Mark, Luke & John by Thomas Jefferson* (New York, 1946); Henry W. Foote, ed., *The Life and Morals of Jesus Extracted Textually from the Gospels of Matthew, Mark, Luke, and John, By Thomas Jefferson* (Boston, 1951); and O. I. A. Roche, ed., *The Jefferson Bible* (New York, 1964).

The

Life and Morals

of

Jesus of Nazareth

Extracted textually

from the Gospels

in

Greek, Latin

French & English.

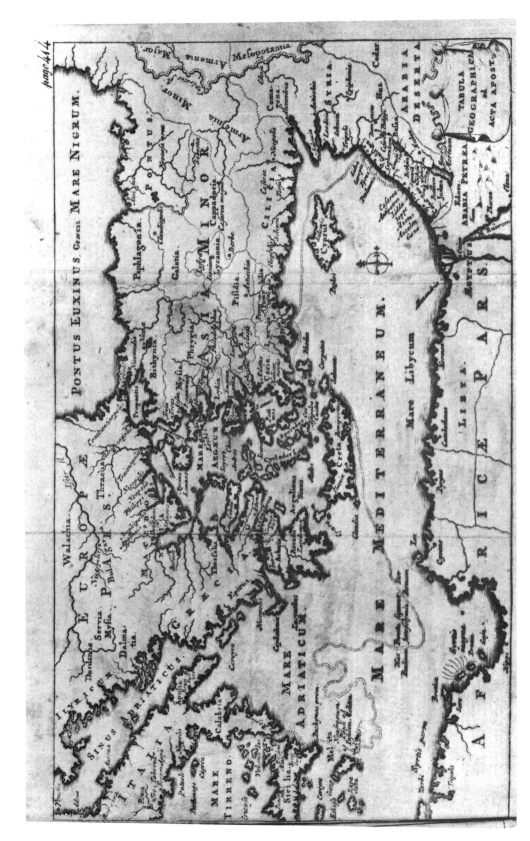

A Table

of the Texts ~~of this Extract~~ from the Evangelists, and of the order of their arrangement.

employed in this Narrative (above "Extract": *narrative*)

page	
1.	Luke. 2. 1—7. Joseph & Mary go to Bethlehem, where Jesus is born.
	21. 39. he is circumcised & named & they return to Nazareth.
	40. 42—48. 51. 52. at 12 years of age he accompanies his
2.	parents to Jerusalem and returns.
	L. 3. 1. 2. Mk. 1. a M. 3. 4. 5. 6. John baptises in Jordan.
	M. 3. 13. Jesus is baptised. L. 3. 23. at 30. years of age.
3.	J. 2. 12—16. drives the traders out of the temple.
	J. 3. 22. M. 4. 12. Mk. 6. 17—28. he *baptises but retires* into Galilee on the death of Joh.
4.	~~Mk. 1.~~ Mk. 1. 21. 22. he teaches in the Synagogue.
5.	M. 12. 1—5. 9—12. Mk. 2. 27. M. 12. 14. 15. explains the Sabbath.
	L. 6. 12 —17. call of his disciples.
6.	M. 5. 1—12. L. 6. 24. 25. 26. M. 5. 13— 47. L. 6. 34. 35. 36. M. 6. 1.—34. 7. 1.
to	L. 6. 38. M. 7. 3—20. 12. 35. 36. 37. 7. 24—29. the Sermon in the Moun.
15.	M. 8. 1. Mk. 6. 6. M. 11. 28. 29. 30. exhorts.
16.	L. 7. 36—46. a woman anointeth him.
17.	Mk. 3. 31—35. L. 12. 1—7, *13—15* precepts
18.	L. 12. 16.—21. parable of the rich man.
20	22—48. 54. 59. *L. 13. 1—5* precepts.
21.	L. 13. 6—9. parable of the fig tree.
22.	L. 11. 37—46. 52. 53. 54. precepts.
23.	M. 13. 1—9. Mk. 4. 10. M. 13. 18—23. parable of the Sower.
.25	Mk. 4. 21. 22. 23. precepts. M. 13. 24—30. 36—52. parable of the Tar…
.27	Mk. 4. 26—34. L. 9. 57—62. L. 5. 27—29. Mk. 2. 15—17 precepts
	L. 5. 36—39. parable of new wine in old bottles.
28	M. 13. 53—57. a prophet hath no honor in his own country.
29	M. 9. 36 Mk. 6. 7 M. 10. 5. 6. 9—18. 23. 26—31. Mk. 6. 12. 30. mission, instru, return again
30. 31.	J. 7. 1. Mk. 7. 1—5. 14—24. M. 18. 1—4. 7—9. 12—17. 21—22. 5 precepts.
.33.	M. 18. 23.—35. parable of the wicked servant.

54.	L. 10. 1 — 8. 10 — 12. mission of the LXX.
35.	J. 7. 2 — 16. 19 — 26. 32. 43 — 53. the feast of the tabernacles.
36.	J. 8. 1 — 11. the woman taken in Adultery.
37.	J. 9. 1. 2. 3. to be born blind no proof of sin.
	J. 10. 1 — 5. 11 — 14. 16. the good shepherd.
38.	L. 10. 25 — 37. love god & thy neighbor. parable of the Samaritan.
39.	L. 11. 1 — 13. form of prayer.
40.	L. 14. 1 — 6. the Sabbath.
41.	7 — 24. the bidden to a feast.
42.	28 — 32. precepts.
44.	L. 15. 1 — 32. parables of the lost sheep and Prodigal son.
45.	L. 16. 1 — 15. parable of the unjust steward.
46.	19 — 31. parable of Lazarus.
48.	L. 17. 1 — 4. 7 — 10. 20. 26 — 36. precepts to be always ready.
49.	L. 18. 1 — 14. parables of the widow & judge, the Pharisee & Publican.
51.	L. 10. 38 — 42. M. 19. 1 — 26. precepts.
52.	M. 20. 1 — 16. parable of the laborers in the vineyard.
54.	L. 19. 1 — 28. Zaccheus, & the parable of the talents.
56.	M. 21. 1 — 3. 6 — 8. 10. J. 12. 19 — 24. M. 21. 17. goes to Jerusalem & Bethany.
	Mk. 11. 12. 15 — 19. the traders cast out from the temple.
	Mk. 11. 27. M. 21. 27 — 31. parable of the two sons.
7.	M. 21. 33. Mk. 12. 1 — 9. [M. 21. 45. 46.] parable of the vineyard & husbandmen.
8.	M. 22. 1. — 14. parable of the king and wedding.
9.	15 — 33. tribute. marriage. resurrection.
60.	Mk. 12. 28 — 31. M. 22. 40. Mk. 12. 32. 33. the two commandments.
62.	M. 23. 1 — 33. precepts. pride. hypocrisy. swearing.
63.	Mk. 12. 41 — 44. the widow's mite.
64.	M. 24. 1. 2. 16 — 21. 32. 33. 36 — 39. 40 — 44. Jerusalem & the day of judgment.
	45 — 51. the faithful and wise servant.
65.	M. 25. 1 — 13. parable of the ten virgins.
66.	14 — 30. parable of the talents.
68.	L. 21. 34 — 36. M. 25. 31 — 46. the day of judgment.
69.	Mk. 14. 1 — 8. a woman anointeth him.

Mt. 26. 14 — 16. Judas undertakes to point out Jesus.

17 — 20. L. 22. 24 — 27. J. 13. 2. 4 — 17. 21 — 26. 31. 34. 35. Mt. 26. 31. 33.

L. 22. 33 — 34. Mt. 26. 35 — 45. precepts to his disciples, washes their feet trou — ble of mind and prayer.

J. 18 1 — 3. Mt. 26. 48 — 50. Judas conducts the officers to Jesus.

J. 18. 4 — 8. Mt. 26. 50 — 52. 55. 56. Mk. 14. 51. 52. Mt. 26. 57. J. 18. 15. 16. 18. 17. J. 18. 25. 26. 27. Mt. 26. 75. J. 18. 19 — 23. Mk. 14. 55 — 61. L. 22. 67. 68. 70. Mk. 14. 63 — 65. he is arrested & carried before Caiaphas the High priest & is condemned.

J. 18. 28 — 31. 33 — 38. L. 23. 5. Mt. 27. 13. is then carried to Pilate.

L. 23. 6 — 12. who sends him to Herod.

L. 23. 13 — 16. Mt. 27. 15 — 23. 26. recieves him back, scourges and delivers him to execution.

Mt. 27. 27. 29 — 31. 3 — 0. L. 23. 26 — 32. J. 19. 17 — 24. Mt. 27. 39 — 43. L. 23. 39 — 41. 34. J. 19. 25 — 27. Mt. 27. 46 — 55. 56. his crucifixion. death and burial.

J. 19. 31 — 34. 38 — 42. Mt. 27. 60. his burial.

1 Ἐγένετο δὲ ἐν ταῖς ἡμέραις ἐκείναις, ἐξῆλθε δόγμα παρὰ Καίσαρος Αὐγύςου, ἀπογράφεσθαι πᾶσαν τὴν οἰκουμένην.

2 (Αὕτη ἡ ἀπογραφὴ πρώτη ἐγένετο ἡγεμονεύοντος τῆς Συρίας Κυρηνίου.)

3 Καὶ ἐπορεύοντο πάντες ἀπογράφεσθαι, ἕκαςος εἰς τὴν ἰδίαν πόλιν.

4 Ἀνέβη δὲ καὶ Ἰωσὴφ ἀπὸ τῆς Γαλιλαίας, ἐκ πόλεως Ναζαρὲτ, εἰς τὴν Ἰουδαίαν, εἰς πόλιν Δαβίδ, ἥτις καλεῖται Βηθλεὲμ, (διὰ τὸ εἶναι αὐτὸν ἐξ οἴκου καὶ πατριᾶς Δαβίδ,)

* 5 ‡ Ἀπογράψασθαι ‡ σὺν Μαριὰμ τῇ ‡ μεμνηςευμένῃ αὐτῷ γυναικὶ, οὔσῃ ‡ ἐγκύῳ.

6 Ἐγένετο δὲ ἐν τῷ εἶναι αὐτοὺς ἐκεῖ, ἐπλήσθησαν αἱ ἡμέραι τοῦ τεκεῖν αὐτήν.

* 7 Καὶ ἔτεκε τὸν υἱὸν αὐτῆς τὸν πρωτότοκον, καὶ ‡ ἐσπαργάνωσεν αὐτὸν, καὶ ‡ ἀνέκλινεν αὐτὸν ἐν τῇ ‡ φάτνῃ· διότι οὐκ ἦν αὐτοῖς τόπος ἐν τῷ ‡ καταλύματι.

21 Καὶ ὅτε ἐπλήσθησαν ἡμέραι ὀκτὼ τοῦ περιτεμεῖν τὸ παιδίον, καὶ ἐκλήθη τὸ ὄνομα αὐτοῦ Ἰησοῦς.

39 Καὶ ὡς ἐτέλεσαν ἅπαντα τὰ κατὰ τὸν νόμον Κυρίου, ὑπέςρεψαν εἰς τὴν Γαλιλαίαν, εἰς τὴν πόλιν αὐτῶν Ναζαρέτ.

40 Τὸ δὲ παιδίον ηὔξανε, καὶ ἐκραταιοῦτο πνεύματι, πληρούμενον σοφίας·

42 Καὶ ὅτε ἐγένετο ἐτῶν δώδεκα, ἀναβάντων αὐτῶν εἰς Ἱεροσόλυμα κατὰ τὸ ἔθος τῆς ἑορτῆς·

43 Καὶ τελειωσάντων τὰς ἡμέρας, ἐν τῷ ὑποςρέφειν αὐτοὺς, ὑπέμεινεν Ἰησοῦς ὁ παῖς ἐν Ἱερουσαλήμ· καὶ οὐκ ἔγνω Ἰωσὴφ καὶ ἡ μήτηρ αὐτοῦ.

* 44 ‡ Νομίσαντες δὲ αὐτὸν ἐν τῇ ‡ συνοδίᾳ εἶναι, ἦλθον ἡμέρας ὁδὸν· καὶ ‡ ἀνεζήτουν αὐτὸν ἐν τοῖς ‡ συγγενέσι καὶ ἐν τοῖς ‡ γνωςοῖς.

45 Καὶ μὴ εὑρόντες αὐτὸν, ὑπέςρεψαν εἰς Ἱερουσαλήμ, ζητοῦντες αὐτόν.

---

1 FActum est autem in diebus illis, exiit edictum à Cæsare Augusto, describi omnem habitatam.

2 (Hæc descriptio prima facta est præside Syriæ Cyrenio.)

3 Et ibant omnes describi, unusquisque in propriam civitatem.

4 Ascendit autem & Joseph à Galilæa, ex civitate Nazaret, in Judæam, in civitatem David, quæ vocatur Bethlehem, propter esse ipsum ex domo & familia David,

5 Describi cum Maria desponsata sibi uxore, existente prægnante.

6 Factum est autem in esse eos ibi, impleti sunt dies parere ipsam.

7 Et peperit filium suum primogenitum, & fasciavit eum, & reclinavit eum in præsepi: quia non erat eis locus in diversorio.

21 Et quando impleti sunt dies octo circumcidendi puerulum, & vocatum est nomen ejus JESUS.

39 Et ut perfecerunt omnia quæ secundum legem Domini, reversi sunt in Galilæam in civitatem suam Nazaret.

40 At puer crescebat, & corroborabatur spiritu, plenus sapientia:

42 Et quum factus esset annorum duodecim, ascendentibus illis in Hierosolyma, secundum consuetudinem festi,

43 Et consummantibus dies, in reverti ipsos, remansit Jesus puer in Hierusalem: & non cognovit Joseph & mater ejus.

44 Existimantes autem illum in comitatu esse, venerunt diei iter: & requirebant eum in cognatis, & in notis.

45 Et non invenientes eum, regressi sunt in Hierusalem, quærentes eum.

The Roman empire taxed.

En ce tems-là, on publia un Edit de la part de César-Auguste, pour faire un dénombrement des habitans de toute la terre.

2. Ce dénombrement se fit, avant que Quirinus fût Gouverneur de Syrie.

3. Ainsi tous alloient pour être enregistrés, chacun dans sa ville.

4. Joseph aussi monta de Galilée en Judée, de la ville de Nazareth, à la ville de David, nommé Beth-léhem, parce qu'il étoit de la maison et de la famille de David;

5. Pour être enregistrés avec Marie son épouse, qui étoit enceinte.

6. Et pendant qu'ils étoient là, le tems auquel elle devoit accoucher arriva.

7. Et elle mit au monde son Fils premier-né, et elle l'emmaillotta, et le coucha dans une crèche, parce qu'il n'y avoit point de place pour eux dans l'hôtellerie.

21. Quand les huit jours furent accomplis pour circoncire l'enfant, il fut appelé JESUS,

39. Et après qu'ils eurent accompli tout ce qui est ordonné par la Loi du Seigneur, ils retournèrent en Galilée, à Nazareth, qui étoit leur ville.

40. Cependant l'enfant croissoit et se fortifioit en esprit, étant rempli de sagesse.

42. Et quand il eut atteint l'âge de douze ans, ils montèrent à Jérusalem, selon la coutume de la fête.

43. Lorsque les jours de la fête furent achevés, comme ils s'en retournoient, l'enfant Jésus demeura dans Jérusalem; et Joseph et sa mère ne s'en aperçurent point.

44. Mais pensant qu'il étoit en la compagnie de ceux qui faisoient le voyage avec eux, ils marchèrent une journée, et ils le cherchèrent parmi leurs parens et ceux de leur connoissance;

45. Et ne le trouvant point, ils retournèrent à Jérusalem, pour l'y chercher.

AND it came to pass in those days, that there went out a decree from Cesar Augustus, that all the world should be taxed.

2 (*And* this taxing was first made when Cyrenius was governor of Syria.)

3 And all went to be taxed, every one into his own city.

4 And Joseph also went up from Galilee, out of the city of Nazareth, into Judea, unto the city of David, which is called Beth-lehem (because he was of the house and lineage of David,)

5 To be taxed with Mary his espoused wife, being great with child.

6 And so it was, that, while they were there, the days were accomplished that she should be delivered

7 And she brought forth her first-born son, and wrapped him in swaddling-clothes, and laid him in a manger; because there was no room for them in the inn.

21 And when eight days were accomplished for the circumcising of the child, his name was called JESUS,

39 And when they had performed all things, according to the law of the Lord, they returned into Galilee, to their own city Nazareth.

40 And the child grew, and waxed strong in spirit, filled with wisdom;

42 And when he was twelve years old, they went up to Jerusalem, after the custom of the feast.

43 And when they had fulfilled the days, as they returned, the child Jesus tarried behind in Jerusalem; and Joseph and his mother knew not *of it*.

44 But they supposing him to have been in the company, went a day's journey; and they sought him among *their* kinsfolk and acquaintance.

45 And when they found him not, they turned back again to Jerusalem, seeking him.

46 Καὶ ἐγένετο, μεθ' ἡμέρας τρεῖς εὗρον αὐτὸν ἐν τῷ ἱερῷ καθεζόμενον ἐν μέσῳ τῶν διδασκάλων, καὶ ἀκούοντα αὐτῶν, καὶ ἐπερωτῶντα αὐτούς.

* 47 ‡ Ἐξίσταντο δὲ πάντες οἱ ἀκούοντες αὐτοῦ, ἐπὶ τῇ συνέσει καὶ ταῖς ‡ ἀποκρίσεσιν αὐτοῦ.

48 Καὶ ἰδόντες αὐτὸν ἐξεπλάγησαν. Καὶ πρὸς αὐτὸν ἡ μήτηρ αὐτοῦ εἶπε· Τέκνον, τί ἐποίησας ἡμῖν οὕτως; ἰδοὺ ὁ πατήρ σου κἀγὼ ὀδυνώμενοι ἐζητοῦμέν σε.

52 Καὶ Ἰησοῦς προέκοπτε σοφίᾳ καὶ ἡλικίᾳ.

‖ 1 Ἐν ἔτει δὲ † πεντεκαιδεκάτῳ τῆς † ἡγεμονίας Τιβερίου Καίσαρος, ‡ ἡγεμονεύοντος Ποντίου Πιλάτου τῆς Ἰουδαίας, καὶ † τετραρχοῦντος τῆς Γαλιλαίας Ἡρώδου, Φιλίππου δὲ τοῦ ἀδελφοῦ αὐτοῦ τετραρχοῦντος τῆς Ἰτουραίας καὶ Τραχωνίτιδος χώρας, καὶ Λυσανίου τῆς Ἀβιληνῆς τετραρχοῦντος,

2 Ἐπ' ἀρχιερέων Ἄννα καὶ Καϊάφα,

4 Ἐγένετο Ἰωάννης βαπτίζων ἐν τῇ ἐρήμῳ.

4 Αὐτὸς δὲ ὁ Ἰωάννης εἶχε τὸ ἔνδυμα αὐτοῦ ἀπὸ τριχῶν καμήλου, καὶ ζώνην δερματίνην περὶ τὴν ὀσφὺν αὐτοῦ· ἡ δὲ τροφὴ αὐτοῦ ἦν ἀκρίδες καὶ μέλι ἄγριον.

5 Τότε ἐξεπορεύετο πρὸς αὐτὸν Ἱεροσόλυμα, καὶ πᾶσα ἡ Ἰουδαία, καὶ πᾶσα ἡ περίχωρος τοῦ Ἰορδάνου,

6 Καὶ ἐβαπτίζοντο ἐν τῷ Ἰορδάνῃ ὑπ' αὐτοῦ,

13 Τότε παραγίνεται ὁ Ἰησοῦς ἀπὸ τῆς Γαλιλαίας ἐπὶ τὸν Ἰορδάνην πρὸς τὸν Ἰωάννην, τοῦ βαπτισθῆναι ὑπ' αὐτοῦ.

23 Καὶ αὐτὸς ἦν ὁ Ἰησοῦς ὡσεὶ ἐτῶν τριάκοντα ἀρχόμενος,

12 Μετὰ τοῦτο κατέβη εἰς Καπερναούμ, αὐτὸς καὶ ἡ μήτηρ αὐτοῦ καὶ οἱ ἀδελφοὶ αὐτοῦ καὶ οἱ μαθηταὶ αὐτοῦ· καὶ ἐκεῖ ἔμειναν οὐ πολλὰς ἡμέρας.

---

46 Et factum est, post dies tres invenerunt illum in templo sedentem in medio doctorum, & audientem illos, & interrogantem eos.

47 Stupebant autem omnes audientes eum, super intelligentia & responsis ejus.

48 Et videntes ipsum, attoniti fuerunt: Et ad illum mater ejus dixit: Fili, quid fecisti nobis sic? ecce pater tuus & ego dolentes quærebamus te.

52 Et Jesus proficiebat sapientia, & ætate.

1 IN anno autem quinto decimo imperii Tiberii Cæsaris, præsidente Pontio Pilato Judææ, & tetrarcha Galilææ Herode, Philippo autem fratre ejus tetrarcha Ituææ, & Trachonitidis regionis, & Lysania Abilenæ tetrarcha,

2 Sub principibus Sacerdotum Anna & Caiapha,

4 Fuit Joannes baptizans in deserto.

4 Ipse autem Joannes habebat indumentum suum è pilis cameli, & zonam pelliceam circa lumbum suum: esca autem ejus erat locustæ & mel silvestre.

5 Tunc exibat ad eum Hierosolyma, & omnis Judæa, & omnis circum vicinia Jordanis.

6 Et baptizabantur in Jordane ab eo.

13 Tunc accedit Jesus à Galilæa ad Jordanem ad Joannem, baptizari ab eo.

23 Et ipse erat Jesus quasi annorum triginta incipiens.

12 Post hoc descendit in Capernaum, ipse & mater ejus, & fratres ejus, & discipuli ejus, & ibi manserunt non multis diebus.

46. Et au bout de trois jours, ils le trouvèrent dans le Temple, assis au milieu des Docteurs, les écoutant et leur faisant des questions.	46 And it came to pass, that after three days they found him in the temple, sitting in the midst of the doctors, both hearing them, and asking them questions. L. 2
47. Et tous ceux qui l'entendoient étoient ravis de sa sagesse et de ses réponses.	47 And all that heard him were astonished at his understanding and answers.
48. Quand *Joseph et Marie* le virent, ils furent étonnés ; et sa mère lui dit : *Mon* enfant, pourquoi as-tu ainsi agi avec nous ? Voilà ton père et moi qui te cherchions étant fort en peine.	48 And when they saw him, they were amazed: and his mother said unto him, Son, why hast thou thus dealt with us? behold, thy father and I have sought thee sorrowing.
51. Il s'en alla ensuite avec eux, et vint à Nazareth, et il leur étoit soumis.	51 And he went down with them, and came to Nazareth, and was subject unto them:
52. Et Jésus croissoit en sagesse, en stature, et en grace.	52 And Jesus increased in wisdom and stature.
LA quinziéme année de l'empire de Tibère César, Ponce Pilate étant Gouverneur de la Judée, Hérode étant Tétrarque de la Galilée, Philippe son frère, Tétrarque de l'Iturée et de la province de la Trachonite, et Lysanias, Tétrarque d'Abilène ; 2. Anne et Caïphe étant Souverains Sacrificateurs,	NOW in the fifteenth year of the reign of Tiberius Cesar, Pontius Pilate being governor of Judea, and Herod being tetrarch of Galilee, and his brother Philip tetrarch of Iturea and of the region of Trachonitis, and Lysanias the tetrarch of Abilene, 2 Annas and Caiaphas being the high priests, L. 3
4. Jean baptisoit dans le désert,	4 John did baptize in the wilderness, M. 1
4. Ce Jean avoit un habit de poils de chameau, et une ceinture de cuir autour de ses reins, et sa nourriture étoit des sauterelles et du miel sauvage.	4 And the same John had his raiment of camels' hair, and a leathern girdle about his loins; and his meat was locusts and wild honey. M. 3
5. Alors ceux de Jérusalem, et de tout le pays des environs du Jourdain, venoient à lui.	5 Then went out to him Jerusalem, and all Judea, and all the region round about Jordan.
6. Et ils étoient baptisés par lui dans le Jourdain.	6 And were baptized of him in Jordan,
13. Alors Jésus vint de Galilée au Jourdain vers Jean, pour être baptisé par lui.	13 Then cometh Jesus from Galilee to Jordan unto John, to be baptized of him. M. 3
23. Et Jésus étoit *alors* âgé d'environ trente ans.	23 And Jesus himself began to be about thirty years of age. L. 3
12. Après cela, il descendit à Capernaüm, avec sa Mère, ses Frères, et ses Disciples : et ils n'y demeurèrent que peu de jours.	12 After this he went down to Capernaum, he, and his mother, and his brethren, and his disciples; and they continued there not many days. J. 2

3

13 Καὶ ἐγγὺς ἦν τὸ πάσχα τῶν Ἰουδαίων, ϗ ἀνέβη εἰς Ἱεροσόλυμα ὁ Ἰησῦ.

* 14 Καὶ εὗρεν ἐν τῷ ἱερῷ τὰς πωλῦντας ‡ βόας ϗ πρόβατα ϗ περιςεράς, ϗ τὰς † κερματιςὰς καθημένες.

* 15 Καὶ ποιήσας † φραγέλλιον ἐκ ‡ σχοινίων, πάντας ἐξέβαλεν ἐκ τῦ ἱερῦ, τά τε πρόβατα ϗ τὰς βόας ϗ τῶν κολλυβιςῶν ἐξέχεε τὸ † κέρμα, ϗ τὰς τραπέζας ἀνέςρεψε·

* 16 Καὶ τοῖς τὰς περιςερὰς πωλῦσιν εἶπιν· Ἄρατε ταῦτα ἐντεῦθεν· μὴ ποιεῖτε τὸν οἶκον τῦ πατρός με οἶκον † ἐμπορίε.

22 Μετὰ ταῦτα ἦλθεν ὁ Ἰησῦς, ϗ οἱ μαθηταὶ αὐτῦ εἰς τὴν Ἰεδαίαν γῆν· ϗ ἐκεῖ διέτριβε μετ᾽ αὐτῶν ϗ ἐβάπτιζε.

12 Ἀκούσας δὲ ὁ Ἰησῦς ὅτι Ἰωάννης παρεδόθη, ἀνεχώρησεν εἰς τὴν Γαλιλαίαν.

17 Αὐτὸς γὰρ ὁ Ἡρώδης, ἀποςείλας ἐκράτησε τὸν Ἰωάννην, ϗ ἔδησεν αὐτὸν ἐν τῇ φυλακῇ, διὰ Ἡρωδιάδα τὴν γυναῖκα Φιλίππε τῦ ἀδελφῦ αὐτῦ, ὅτι αὐτὴν ἐγάμησεν.

18 Ἔλεγε γὰρ ὁ Ἰωάννης τῷ Ἡρώδῃ· Ὅτι ἐκ ἔξεςί σοι ἔχειν τὴν γυναῖκα τῦ ἀδελφῦ σε.

19 Ἡ δὲ Ἡρωδιὰς ἐνεῖχεν αὐτῷ, ϗ ἤθελεν αὐτὸν ἀποκτεῖναι· ϗ ἐκ ἠδύνατο·

20 Ὁ γὰρ Ἡρώδης ἐφοβεῖτο τὸν Ἰωάννην, εἰδὼς αὐτὸν ἄνδρα δίκαιον ϗ ἅγιον· ϗ συνετήρει αὐτόν· ϗ ἀκέσας αὐτῦ, πολλὰ ἐποίει, ϗ ἡδέως αὐτῦ ἤκυε.

21 Καὶ γενομένης ἡμέρας εὐκαίρε, ὅτε Ἡρώδης τοῖς γενεσίοις αὐτῦ δεῖπνον ἐποίει τοῖς μεγιςᾶσιν αὐτῦ, ϗ τοῖς χιλιάρχοις, ϗ τοῖς πρώτοις τῆς Γαλιλαίας.

22 Καὶ εἰσελθούσης τῆς θυγατρὸς αὐτῆς τῆς Ἡρωδιάδος, ϗ ὀρχησαμένης, ϗ ἀρεσάσης τῷ Ἡρώδῃ ϗ τοῖς συνανακειμένοις, εἶπεν ὁ βασιλεὺς τῷ κορασίῳ· Αἴτησόν με ὃ ἐὰν θέλῃς, ϗ δώσω σοί.

23 Καὶ ὤμοσεν αὐτῇ· Ὅτι ὃ ἐάν με αἰτήσῃς, δώσω σοί, ἕως ἡμίσες τῆς βασιλείας μυ.

---

13 Et prope erat Pascha Judæorum, & ascendit Hierosolymam Jesus.

13 Et invenit in templo vendentes boves, & oves, & columbas, & numularios sedentes.

15 Et faciens flagellum ex funiculis omnes ejecit ex templo, & oves & boves : & numulariorum effudit monetam, & mensas subvertit.

16 Et columbas vendentibus dixit : Auferte ista hinc : ne facite domum patris mei domum mercatûs.

22 Post hæc venit Jesus & discipuli ejus in Judæam terram : & illic morabatur cum eis, & baptizabat.

12 Audiens autem Jesus quod Joannes traditus esset, secessit in Galilæam :

17 Ipse enim Herodes mittens prehendit Joannem, & vinxit eum in custodia, propter Herodiadem uxorem Philippi fratris sui, quia eam duxerat.

18 Dicebat enim Joannes Herodi : Quod non licet tibi habere uxorem fratris tui.

19 At Herodias insidiabatur illi : & volebat eum occidere, & non poterat.

20 Nam Herodes metuebat Joannem, sciens eum virum justum & sanctum : & conservabat eum, & audiens eum, multa faciebat, & suaviter eum audiebat.

21 Et facta die opportuna, quum Herodes natalitiis suis cœnam faciebat principibus suis, & tribunis, & primis Galilææ :

22 Et ingressa filia ipsius Herodiadis, & saltante, & placente Herodi & unà recumbentibus ait rex puellæ : Pete à me quicquid velis, & dabo tibi.

23 Et juravit illi : Quia quicquid petieris, dabo tibi, usque dimidium regni mei.

13. Car la Pâque des Juifs étoit proche ; et Jésus monta à Jérusalem.

14. Il trouva dans le Temple des gens qui vendoient des taureaux, des brebis et des pigeons, avec des changeurs qui y étoient assis.

15. Et ayant fait un fouet de petites cordes, il les chassa tous du Temple, et les brebis et les taureaux ; il répandit la monnoie dès changeurs, et renversa leurs tables ;

16. Et il dit à ceux qui vendoient les pigeons : Otez tout cela d'ici, et ne faites pas de la Maison de mon Père, une maison de marché.

22. Après cela, Jésus s'en alla en Judée avec ses Disciples, et il y demeura avec eux, et y baptisoit.

12. Or, Jésus ayant appris que Jean avoit été mis en prison, se retira dans la Galilée.

17. Car Hérode avoit envoyé prendre Jean, et l'avoit fait lier dans la prison, à cause d'Hérodias, femme de Philippe son frère, parce qu'il l'avoit épousée.

18. Car Jean disoit à Hérode : Il ne t'est pas permis d'avoir la femme de ton frère.

19. C'est pourquoi Hérodias lui en vouloit, et elle désiroit de le faire mourir ; mais elle ne pouvoit,

20. Parce qu'Hérode craignoit Jean, sachant que c'étoit un homme juste et saint ; il le considéroit, il faisoit même beaucoup de choses selon ses avis, et il l'écoutoit avec plaisir.

21. Mais un jour vint à propos, auquel Hérode faisoit le festin du jour de sa naissance, aux Grands de sa cour, aux officiers de ses troupes, et aux principaux de la Galilée.

22. La fille d'Hérodias étant entrée, et ayant dansé, et ayant plu à Hérode et à ceux qui étoient à table *avec lui*, le Roi dit à la jeune fille : Demande-moi ce que tu voudras, et je *te le* donnerai.

23. Et il le lui jura, *disant :* Tout ce que tu me demanderas je te *le donnerai*, jusqu'à la moitié de mon Royaume.

13 And the Jews' passover was at hand ; and Jesus went up to Jerusalem, J.2.

14 And found in the temple those that sold oxen, and sheep, and doves, and the changers of money, sitting :

15 And, when he had made a scourge of small cords, he drove them all out of the temple, and the sheep, and the oxen ; and poured out the changers' money, and overthrew the tables ;

16 And said unto them that sold doves, Take these things hence ; make not my Father's house an house of merchandise.

22 After these things came Jesus and his disciples into the land of Judea ; and there he tarried with them, and baptized. J.3.

12 Now, when Jesus had heard that John was cast into prison, he departed into Galilee : *Th. A.*

17 For Herod himself had sent forth, and laid hold upon John, and bound him in prison for Herodias' sake, his brother Philip's wife ; for he had married her. *Mk. 6.*

18 For John had said unto Herod, It is not lawful for thee to have thy brother's wife.

19 Therefore Herodias had a quarrel against him, and would have killed him ; but she could not :

20 For Herod feared John, knowing that he was a just man, and an holy, and observed him ; and when he heard him, he did many things, and heard him gladly.

21 And when a convenient day was come, that Herod, on his birthday, made a supper to his lords, high captains, and chief *estates* of Galilee ;

22 And when the daughter of the said Herodias came in and danced, and pleased Herod, and them that sat with him, the king said unto the damsel, Ask of me whatsoever thou wilt, and I will give *it* thee.

23 And he sware unto her, Whatsoever thou shalt ask of me, I will give *it* thee, unto the half of my kingdom.

α 24 Ἡ δὲ ἐξελθῦσα, εἶπε τῇ μητρὶ αὐτῆς· Τί αἰτήσομαι; Ἡ δὲ εἶπε· Τὴν κεφαλὴν Ἰωάννε τῦ βαπτιςῦ.

25 Καὶ εἰσελθῦσα εὐθέως μετὰ σπυδῆς πρὸς τὸν βασιλέα, ᾐτήσαλο, λέγυσα. Θέλω ἵνα μοι δῷς ἐξ αὐτῆς ἐπὶ πίνακι τὴν κεφαλὴν Ἰωάννε τῦ βαπτιςῦ.

26 Καὶ περίλυπΘ· γενόμενΘ· ὁ βασιλεὺς, διὰ τοὺς ὅρκυς ἢ τοὺς συνανακειμένυς οὐκ ἠθέλησεν αὐτὴν ἀθετῆσαι.

* 27 Καὶ εὐθέως ‡ ἀποςείλας ὁ ‡ βασιλεὺς ‡ σπεκυλάτωρα, ‡ ἐπέταξεν ‡ ἐνεχθῆναι τὴν κεφαλὴν αὐτοῦ.

* 28 Ὁ δὲ ἀπελθὼν ‡ ἀπεκεφάλισεν αὐτὸν ἐν τῇ φυλακῇ· ἢ ἤνεγκε τὴν κεφαλὴν αὐτοῦ ἐπὶ πίνακι, ἢ ἔδωκεν αὐτὴν τῷ κορασίῳ· ἢ τὸ κοράσιον ἔδωκεν αὐτὴν τῇ μητρὶ αὐτῆς.

24 Illa verò egressa, dixit matri suæ: Quid petam? Illa verò ait: Caput Joannis Baptistæ.

25 Et ingressa statim cum studio ad regem, petivit, dicens: Volo ut mihi des ex ipsa in disco caput Joannis Baptistæ.

26 Et contristatus factus rex, propter juramenta, & simul discumbentes, non voluit eam rejicere.

27 Et statim mittens rex speculatorem, injunxit afferri caput ejus. Ille autem abiens decollavit eum in carcere:

28 Et attulit caput ejus in disco, & dedit illud puellæ, & puella dedit illud matri suæ.

29 Et

21 Καὶ εἰσπορεύονlαι εἰς Καπερναύμ· ἢ εὐθέως τοῖς σάββασιν εἰσελθὼν εἰς τὴν συναγωγὴν, ἐδίδασκε.

22 Καὶ ἐξεπλήσσονlο ἐπὶ τῇ διδαχῇ αὐτῦ· ἦν γὰρ διδάσκων αὐτὲς ὡς ἐξυσίαν ἔχων, ἢ ἐχ ὡς οἱ γραμματεῖς.

21 Et ingrediuntur in Capernaum: & statim Sabbatis ingressus in synagogam, docebat.

22 Et percellebantur super doctrina ejus: Erat enim docens eos quasi auctoritatem habens, & non sicut Scribæ.

Κεφ. ιβ'. 12.

1 ἘΝ ἐκείνῳ τῷ καιρῷ ἐπορεύθη ὁ Ἰησῦς τοῖς σάββασι διὰ τῶν σπορίμων· οἱ δὲ μαθηταὶ αὐτῦ ἐπείνασαν, ἢ ἤρξαντο τίλλειν ςάχυας, ἢ ἐσθίειν.

2 Οἱ δὲ Φαρισαῖοι ἰδόνlες, εἶπον αὐτῷ· Ἰδὺ, οἱ μαθηταί συ ποιῦσιν ὃ ἐκ ἔξεςι ποιεῖν ἐν σαββάτῳ.

3 Ὁ δὲ εἶπεν αὐτοῖς· Οὐκ ἀνέγνωlε τί ἐποίησε Δαβὶδ, ὅτε ἐπείνασεν αὐτὸς, ἢ οἱ μετ' αὐτῦ;

4 Πῶς εἰσῆλθεν εἰς τὸν οἶκον τῦ Θεῦ, ἢ τὺς ἄρτυς τῆς προθέσεως ἔφαγεν, ὓς ἐκ ἐξὸν ἦν αὐτῷ φαγεῖν, ἐδὲ τοῖς μετ' αὐτῦ, εἰ μὴ τοῖς ἱερεῦσι μόνοις;

5 Ἢ ἐκ ἀνέγνωlε ἐν τῷ νόμῳ, ὅτι τοῖς σάββασιν οἱ ἱερεῖς ἐν τῷ ἱερῷ τὸ σάββατον βεβηλῦσιν, ἢ ἀναίτιοί εἰσι;

CAPUT XII.

1 IN illo tempore abiit Jesus Sabbatis per sata: at discipuli ejus esurierunt, & cœperunt vellere spicas, & manducare.

2 Verum Pharisæi videntes, dixerunt ei: Ecce discipuli tui faciunt quod non licet facere in Sabbato.

3 Ille verò dixit eis: Non legistis quid fecerit David, quando esuriit ipse & qui cum eo?

4 Quomodo intravit in domum Dei, & panes propositionis comedit, quos non licitum erat ei edere, neque his qui cum eo, nisi Sacerdotibus solis?

5 Aut non legistis in lege, quia Sabbatis Sacerdotes in sacro Sabbatum violant, & inculpati sunt?

24. Et étant sortie, elle dit à sa mère : Que demanderai-je ? Et *sa mère* lui dit : *Demande* la tête de Jean-Baptiste.

25. Et étant incontinent rentrée avec empressement vers le Roi, elle lui fit sa demande, et lui dit : Je voudrois que tout à l'heure tu me donnasses dans un bassin la tête de Jean-Baptiste.

26. Et le Roi en fut *triste* ; cependant à cause du serment, et de ceux qui étoient à table *avec lui*, il ne voulut pas la refuser.

27. Et il envoya incontinent un de ses gardes, et lui commanda d'apporter la tête de *Jean*.

28. *Le garde* y alla, et lui coupa la tête dans la prison ; et l'ayant apportée dans un bassin, il la donna à la jeune fille, et la jeune fille la présenta à sa mère.

21. Ensuite ils entrèrent à Capernaüm ; et Jésus étant d'abord entré dans la Synagogue le jour du Sabbat, il y enseignoit.

22. Et ils étoient étonnés de sa doctrine, car il les enseignoit comme ayant autorité, et non pas comme les Scribes.

EN ce tems-là, Jésus passoit par des blés un jour de Sabbat ; et ses Disciples ayant faim, se mirent à arracher des épis, et à en manger.

2. Les Pharisiens voyant cela, lui dirent : Voilà tes Disciples qui font ce qu'il n'est pas permis de faire le jour du Sabbat.

3. Mais il leur dit : N'avez-vous pas lu ce que fit David ayant faim, tant lui que ceux qui *étoient* avec lui :

4. Comment il entra dans la maison de Dieu, et mangea les pains de proposition, dont il n'étoit pas permis de manger, ni à lui, ni à ceux qui *étoient* avec lui, mais aux seuls Sacrificateurs ?

5. Ou n'avez-vous pas lu dans la Loi, que les Sacrificateurs, au jour du Sabbat, violent le Sabbat dans le Temple, sans être coupables ?

24 And she went forth, and said unto her mother, What shall I ask? and she said, The head of John the Baptist.

25 And she came in straightway with haste unto the king, and asked, saying, I will that thou give me, by and by in a charger, the head of John the Baptist.

26 And the king was exceeding sorry; *yet* for his oath's sake, and for their sakes which sat with him, he would not reject her.

27 And immediately the king sent an executioner, and commanded his head to be brought: and he went and beheaded him in the prison;

28 And brought his head in a charger, and gave it to the damsel: and the damsel gave it to her mother.

21 And they went into Capernaum; and straightway on the sabbath-day, he entered into the synagogue, and taught.

22 And they were astonished at his doctrine: for he taught them as one that had authority, and not as the scribes.

AT that time Jesus went on the sabbath-day through the corn; and his disciples were an hungered, and began to pluck the ears of corn, and to eat.

2 But when the Pharisees saw *it*, they said unto him, Behold, thy disciples do that which is not lawful to do upon the sabbath-day.

3 But he said unto them, Have ye not read what David did when he was an hungered, and they that were with him;

4 How he entered into the house of God, and did eat the shew-bread, which was not lawful for him to eat, neither for them which were with him, but only for the priests?

5 Or, have ye not read in the law, how that on the sabbath-days, the priests in the temple profane the sabbath, and are blameless?

9 Καὶ μεταβὰς ἐκεῖθεν, ἦλθεν εἰς τὴν συναγωγὴν αὐτῶν.

9 Et transiens inde, venit in synagogam eorum.

10 Καὶ ἰδοὺ, ἄνθρωπος ἦν τὴν χεῖρα ἔχων ξηράν· καὶ ἐπηρώτησαν αὐτὸν, λέγοντες· Εἰ ἔξεστι τοῖς σάββασι θεραπεύειν; ἵνα κατηγορήσωσιν αὐτοῦ.

10 Et ecce homo erat manum habens aridam, & interrogabant eum, dicentes, Si licet Sabbatis curare? ut accusarent eum.

11 Ὁ δὲ εἶπεν αὐτοῖς· Τίς ἔσται ἐξ ὑμῶν ἄνθρωπος, ὃς ἕξει πρόβατον ἕν, καὶ ἐὰν ἐμπέσῃ τοῦτο τοῖς σάββασιν εἰς βόθυνον, οὐχὶ κρατήσει αὐτὸ καὶ ἐγερεῖ;

11 Ipse autem dixit illis, Quis erit ex vobis homo qui habebit ovem unam, & si ceciderit hæc Sabbatis in foveam, nonne apprehendet eam & exiget?

12 Πόσῳ οὖν διαφέρει ἄνθρωπος προβάτου; ὥστε ἔξεστι τοῖς σάββασι καλῶς ποιεῖν.

12 Quanto igitur præstat homo ove? Itaque licet Sabbatis bona facere.

27 Καὶ ἔλεγεν αὐτοῖς· Τὸ σάββατον διὰ τὸν ἄνθρωπον ἐγένετο, οὐχ ὁ ἄνθρωπος διὰ τὸ σάββατον.

27 Et dicebat eis: Sabbatum propter hominem factum est, non homo propter Sabbatum.

14 Οἱ δὲ Φαρισαῖοι συμβούλιον ἔλαβον κατ' αὐτοῦ ἐξελθόντες, ὅπως αὐτὸν ἀπολέσωσιν.

14 At Pharisæi consilium ceperunt adversus eum, exeuntes, ut eum perderent.

15 Ὁ δὲ Ἰησοῦς γνοὺς ἀνεχώρησεν ἐκεῖθεν· καὶ ἠκολούθησαν αὐτῷ ὄχλοι πολλοί, καὶ ἐθεράπευσεν αὐτοὺς πάντας.

15 At Jesus cognoscens, recessit inde: & sequutæ sunt eum turbæ multæ, & curavit eos omnes:

* 12 Ἐγένετο δὲ ἐν ταῖς ἡμέραις ταύταις, ἐξῆλθεν εἰς τὸ ὄρος προσεύξασθαι· καὶ ἦν † διανυκτερεύων ἐν τῇ προσευχῇ τοῦ Θεοῦ.

12 Factum est autem in diebus illis, exiit in montem orare: & erat pernoctans in oratione Dei.

13 Καὶ ὅτε ἐγένετο ἡμέρα, προσεφώνησε τοὺς μαθητὰς αὐτοῦ· καὶ ἐκλεξάμενος ἀπ' αὐτῶν δώδεκα, οὓς καὶ ἀποστόλους ὠνόμασε·

13 Et quum factus esset dies, advocavit discipulos suos: & eligens ex ipsis duodecim, quos & Apostolos nominavit.

14 (Σίμωνα, ὃν καὶ ὠνόμασε Πέτρον, καὶ Ἀνδρέαν τὸν ἀδελφὸν αὐτοῦ, Ἰάκωβον καὶ Ἰωάννην, Φίλιππον καὶ Βαρθολομαῖον·

14 Simonem, quem & nominavit Petrum, & Andream fratrem ejus, Jacobum & Joannem, Philippum & Bartholomæum!

15 Ματθαῖον καὶ Θωμᾶν, Ἰάκωβον τὸν τοῦ Ἀλφαίου, καὶ Σίμωνα τὸν καλούμενον Ζηλωτήν.

15 Matthæum & Thomam, Jacobum Alphæi, & Simonem vocatum Zeloten.

16 Ἰούδαν Ἰακώβου, καὶ Ἰούδαν Ἰσκαριώτην, ὃς καὶ ἐγένετο προδότης·)

16 Judam Jacobi, & Judam Iscariotem, qui & fuit traditor.

* 17 Καὶ καταβὰς μετ' αὐτῶν, ἔστη ἐπὶ ‡ τόπου † πεδινοῦ, καὶ ὄχλος μαθητῶν αὐτοῦ, καὶ πλῆθος πολὺ τοῦ λαοῦ ἀπὸ πάσης τῆς Ἰουδαίας καὶ Ἱερουσαλήμ, καὶ τῆς † παραλίου Τύρου καὶ Σιδῶνος, οἳ ἦλθον ἀκοῦσαι αὐτοῦ, καὶ ἰαθῆναι ἀπὸ τῶν νόσων αὐτῶν·

17 Et descendens cum illis, stetit in loco campestri, & turba discipulorum eju-, & multitudo copiosa plebis ab omni Judæa, & Hierusalem, & maritima Tyri & Sidonis, qui venerunt audire eum, & sanari à languoribus suis:

I

9. Étant parti de-là, il vint dans leur synagogue.

10. Et il y trouva un homme qui avoit une main sèche; et ils lui demandèrent, pour avoir lieu de l'accuser : Est-il permis de guérir dans les jours de Sabbat?

11. Et il leur dit, Qui sera celui d'entre vous, qui ayant une brebis, si elle tombe au jour du Sabbat dans une fosse, ne la prenne et ne l'en retire?

12. Et combien un homme ne vaut-il pas mieux qu'une brebis? Il est donc permis de faire du bien dans les jours de Sabbat.

27. Puis il leur dit : Le Sabbat a été fait pour l'homme, et non pas l'homme pour le Sabbat.

14. Là-dessus les Pharisiens étant sortis, délibérèrent entr'eux comment ils le feroient périr.

15. Mais Jésus connoissant *cela*, partit de-là, et une grande multitude le suivit.

12. En ce tems-là, *Jésus* alla sur une montagne pour prier ; et il passa toute la nuit à prier Dieu.

13. Et dès que le jour fut venu il appela ses Disciples, et il en choisit douze d'entr'eux qu'il nomma Apôtres.

14. *Savoir*, Simon, qu'il nomma aussi Pierre, et André son frère, Jacques et Jean, Philippe et Barthelemi ;

15. Matthieu et Thomas, Jacques *fils* d'Alphée, et Simon appelé le Zélé ;

16. Jude, *frère* de Jacques et Judas Iscariot, qui fut celui qui le trahit.

17. Étant ensuite descendu avec eux, il s'arrêta dans une plaine, avec la troupe de ses Disciples, et une grande multitude de peuple de toute la Judée et de Jérusalem, et de la *contrée* maritime de Tyr et de Sidon, qui étoient venus pour l'entendre.

---

9 And when he was departed *M. 12.* thence, he went into their synagogue:

10 And, behold, there was a man which had *his* hand withered. And they asked him, saying, Is it lawful to heal on the sabbath-days? that they might accuse him.

11 And he said unto them, What man shall there be among you, that shall have one sheep, and if it fall into a pit on the sabbath-day, will he not lay hold on it, and lift *it* out?

12 How much then is a man better than a sheep? Wherefore it is lawful to do well on the sabbath-days.

27 And he said unto them, The *Mk. 2.* sabbath was made for man, and not man for the sabbath:

14 Then the Pharisees went out, *M. 12.* and held a council against him, how they might destroy him.

15 But when Jesus knew *it*, he withdrew himself from thence: and great multitudes followed him,

12 And it came to pass in those *L. 6.* days, that he went up into a mountain to pray, and continued all night in prayer to God.

13 And when it was day, he called *unto him* his disciples; and of them he chose twelve, whom also he named Apostles;

14 Simon, (whom he also named Peter,) and Andrew his brother, James and John, Philip and Bartholomew,

15 Matthew and Thomas, James *the son* of Alpheus, and Simon called Zelotes,

16 And Judas *the brother* of James, and Judas Iscariot, which also was the traitor.

17 And he came down with them, and stood in the plain; and the company of his disciples, and a great multitude of people out of all Judea and Jerusalem, and from the sea-coast of Tyre and Sidon, which came to hear him,

Κεφ. ε΄ 5.

1 Ἰδὼν δὲ τοὺς ὄχλους, ἀνέβη εἰς τὸ ὄρ⊕· κ̆ καθίσαντ⊕ αὐτοῦ προσῆλθον αὐτῷ οἱ μαθηταὶ αὐτοῦ·

2 Καὶ ἀνοίξας τὸ ςόμα αὐτοῦ, ἐδίδασκεν αὐτοὺς, λέγων·

3 Μακάριοι οἱ πτωχοὶ τῷ πνεύματι· ὅτι αὐτῶν ἐςιν ἡ βασιλεία τῶν οὐρανῶν.

4 Μακάριοι οἱ πενθοῦντες· ὅτι αὐτοὶ παρακληθήσονται.

5 Μακάριοι οἱ πραεῖς· ὅτι αὐτοὶ κληρονομήσουσι τὴν γῆν.

6 Μακάριοι οἱ πεινῶντες κ̆ διψῶντες τὴν δικαιοσύνην· ὅτι αὐτοὶ χορτασθήσονται.

7 Μακάριοι οἱ ἐλεήμονες· ὅτι αὐτοὶ ἐλεηθήσονται.

8 Μακάριοι οἱ καθαροὶ τῇ καρδίᾳ· ὅτι αὐτοὶ τὸν Θεὸν ὄψονται.

* 9 ‡ Μακάριοι οἱ † εἰρηνοποιοί· ὅτι αὐτοὶ υἱοὶ Θεοῦ κληθήσονται.

10 Μακάριοι οἱ δεδιωγμένοι ἕνεκεν δικαιοσύνης· ὅτι αὐτῶν ἐςιν ἡ βασιλεία τῶν οὐρανῶν.

11 Μακάριοί ἐςε ὅταν ὀνειδίσωσιν ὑμᾶς κ̆ διώξωσι, κ̆ εἴπωσι πᾶν πονηρὸν ῥῆμα καθ᾽ ὑμῶν, ψευδόμενοι, ἕνεκεν ἐμοῦ.

12 Χαίρετε κ̆ ἀγαλλιᾶσθε· ὅτι ὁ μισθὸς ὑμῶν πολὺς ἐν τοῖς οὐρανοῖς· οὕτω γὰρ ἐδίωξαν τοὺς προφήτας τοὺς πρὸ ὑμῶν.

24 Πλὴν οὐαὶ ὑμῖν τοῖς πλεσίοις· ὅτι ἀπέχετε τὴν παράκλησιν ὑμῶν.

* 25 ‡ Οὐαὶ ὑμῖν οἱ ‡ ἐμπεπλησμένοι· ὅτι πεινάσετε. Οὐαὶ ὑμῖν οἱ ‡ γελῶντες ‡ νῦν· ὅτι ‡ πενθήσετε κ̆ † κλαύσετε.

26 Οὐαὶ ὑμῖν ὅταν καλῶς ὑμᾶς εἴπωσι πάντες οἱ ἄνθρωποι· κατὰ ταῦτα γὰρ ἐποίουν τοῖς ψευδοπροφήταις οἱ πατέρες αὐτῶν.

13 Ὑμεῖς ἐςε τὸ ἅλας τῆς γῆς· ἐὰν δὲ τὸ ἅλας μωρανθῇ, ἐν τίνι ἁλισθήσεται; εἰς οὐδὲν ἰσχύει ἔτι, εἰ μὴ βληθῆναι ἔξω, κ̆ καταπατεῖσθαι ὑπὸ τῶν ἀνθρώπων.

14 Ὑμεῖς ἐςε τὸ φῶς τοῦ κόσμου. Οὐ δύναται πόλις κρυβῆναι ἐπάνω ὄρους κειμένη.

CAPUT V.

1 VIdens autem turbas, ascendit in montem: & sedente eo, advenerunt illi discipuli ejus.

2 Et apierens os suum, docebat eos, dicens:

3 Beati pauperes spiritu, quoniam ipsorum est regnum cælorum.

4 Beati lugentes, quia ipsi consolabuntur.

5 Beati mites, quoniam ipsi hæreditabunt terram.

6 Beati esurientes & sitientes justitiam, quoniam ipsi saturabuntur.

7 Beati misericordes, quoniam ipsi misericordiâ afficientur.

8 Beati mundi corde, quoniam ipsi Deum videbunt.

9 Beati pacifici, quoniam ipsi filii Dei vocabuntur.

10 Beati persecutione affecti propter justitiam, quoniam ipsorum est regnum cælorum.

11 Beati estis quum maledixerint vos, & persecuti fuerint, & dixerint omne malum verbum adversum vos, mentientes, propter me.

12 Gaudete & exultate, quoniam merces vestra multa in cælis, sic enim persequuti sunt Prophetas qui ante vos.

24 Veruntamen væ vobis divitibus, quia habetis consolationem vestram.

25 Væ vobis impleti: quia esurietis. Væ vobis ridentes nunc: quia lugebitis & flebitis.

26 Væ quum benedixerint vobis homines: secundum hæc enim faciebant pseudoprophetis patres eorum.

13 Vos estis sal terræ; si autem sal infatuatum sit, in quo sal etur? ad nihilum valet ultra, si non ejici foras, & conculcari, ab hominibus.

14 Vos estis lux mundi: non potest civitas abscondi supra montem posita.

CHAPITRE V.

Sermon sur la Montagne.

JÉSUS voyant tout ce peuple, monta sur une montagne ; et s'étant assis, ses Disciples s'approchérent de lui.

2. Et ouvrant sa bouche, il les enseignoit, en disant :

3. Heureux les pauvres en esprit ; car le Royaume des cieux est à eux.

4. Heureux ceux qui pleurent ; car ils seront consolés.

5. Heureux les débonnaires ; car ils hériteront la terre.

6. Heureux ceux qui sont affamés et altérés de la justice ; car ils seront rassasiés.

7. Heureux les miséricordieux ; car ils obtiendront miséricorde.

8. Heureux ceux qui ont le cœur pur ; car ils verront Dieu.

9. Heureux ceux qui procurent la paix ; car ils seront appelés enfans de Dieu.

10. Heureux ceux qui sont persécutés pour la justice ; car le Royaume des cieux est à eux.

11. Vous serez heureux, lorsqu'à cause de moi on vous dira des injures, qu'on vous persécutera, et qu'on dira faussement contre vous toute sorte de mal.

12. Réjouissez - vous alors, et tressaillez de joie, parce que votre récompense sera grande dans les cieux ; car on a ainsi persécuté les Prophètes qui ont été avant vous.

24. Mais malheur à vous, riches ; parce que vous avez déjà reçu votre consolation.

25. Malheur à vous, qui êtes rassasiés ; parce que vous aurez faim. Malheur à vous, qui riez maintenant ; car vous vous lamenterez et vous pleurerez !

26. Malheur à vous, lorsque tous les hommes diront du bien de vous ; car leurs pères en faisoient de même des faux Prophètes !

13. Vous êtes le sel de la terre ; mais si le sel perd sa saveur, avec quoi le salera-t-on ? Il ne vaut plus rien qu'à être jeté dehors, et à être foulé aux pieds par les hommes.

14. Vous êtes la lumière du monde : Une ville située sur une montagne ne peut être cachée.

AND seeing the multitudes, he went up into a mountain : and when he was set, his disciples came unto him :

2 And he opened his mouth, and taught them, saying,

3 Blessed *are* the poor in spirit : for their's is the kingdom of heaven.

4 Blessed *are* they that mourn : for they shall be comforted.

5 Blessed *are* the meek : for they shall inherit the earth.

6 Blessed *are* they which do hunger and thirst after righteousness : for they shall be filled.

7 Blessed *are* the merciful : for they shall obtain mercy.

8 Blessed *are* the pure in heart : for they shall see God.

9 Blessed *are* the peace-makers : for they shall be called the children of God.

10 Blessed *are* they which are persecuted for righteousness' sake : for their's is the kingdom of heaven.

11 Blessed *are* ye when *men* shall revile you, and persecute *you*, and shall say all manner of evil against you falsely, for my sake.

12 Rejoice, and be exceeding glad ; for great *is* your reward in heaven : for so persecuted they the prophets which were before you.

24 But woe unto you that are rich ! for ye have received your consolation.

25 Woe unto you that are full ! for ye shall hunger. Woe unto you that laugh now ! for ye shall mourn and weep.

26 Woe unto you when all men shall speak well of you ! for so did their fathers to the false prophets.

13 Ye are the salt of the earth : but if the salt have lost his savour, wherewith shall it be salted : it is thenceforth good for nothing, but to be cast out, and to be trodden under foot of men.

14 Ye are the light of the world. A city that is set on an hill cannot be hid.

15 Οὐδὲ καίουσι λύχνον, κỳ τι-
θέασιν αὐτὸν ὑπὸ τὸν μόδιον, ἀλλ'
ἐπὶ τὴν λυχνίαν, κỳ λάμπει πᾶσι
τοῖς ἐν τῇ οἰκίᾳ.

16 Οὕτω λαμψάτω τὸ φῶς ὑ-
μῶν ἔμπροσθεν τῶν ἀνθ. ὥπων, ὅπως
ἴδωσιν ὑμῶν τὰ καλὰ ἔργα, κỳ δο-
ξάσωσι τὸν πατέρα ὑμῶν τὸν ἐν
τοῖς οὐρανοῖς.

17 Μὴ νομίσητε ὅτι ἦλθον καταλῦσαι τὸν νόμον, ἢ τὰς προφήτας· ὐκ
ἦλθον καταλῦσαι, ἀλλα πληρῶσαι.

* 18 ‡ Ἀμὴν γὰρ λέγω ὑμῖν, ἕως
ἂν παρέλθῃ ὁ οὐρανὸς κỳ ἡ γῆ, † ἰῶτα
‡ ἓν ἢ ‡ μία ‡ κεραία οὐ μὴ
‡ παρέλθῃ ἀπὸ τοῦ ‡ νόμου, ἕως
ἀνπάντα γένηται.

19 Ὃς ἐὰν οὖν λύσῃ μίαν τῶν
ἐντολῶν τούτων τῶν ἐλαχίςων, κỳ
διδάξῃ οὕτω τοὺς ἀνθρώπους, ἐλά-
χις Θ· κληθήσεται ἐν τῇ βασιλείᾳ
τῶν οὐρανῶν· ὃς δ' ἂν ποιήσῃ κỳ διδάξῃ οὗΤΘ· μέγας κληθήσεται ἐν
τῇ βασιλείᾳ τῶν οὐρανῶν.

20 Λέγω γὰρ ὑμῖν, ὅτι ἐὰν μὴ
περισσεύσῃ ἡ δικαιοσύνη ὑμῶν
πλεῖον τῶν Γραμματέων κỳ Φαρισαίων, οὐ μὴ εἰσέλθητε εἰς τὴν
βασιλείαν τῶν οὐρανῶν.

21 Ἠκούσατε ὅτι ἐρρέθη τοῖς
ἀρχαίοις· Οὐ φονεύσεις· ὃς δ' ἂν
φονεύσῃ, ἔνοχ Θ· ἔςαι τῇ κρίσει.

* 22 Ἐγὼ δὲ λέγω ὑμῖν, ὅτι
πᾶς ὁ ‡ ὀργιζόμεν Θ· τῷ ἀδελφῷ
αὐτοῦ ‡ εἰκῆ, ἔνοχος ἔςαι τῇ κρίσει·
ὃς δ' ἂν ‡ εἴπῃ τῷ ἀδελφῷ αὐτοῦ
† ῥακά ἔνοχ Θ· ἔςαι τῷ συνεδρίῳ· ὃς
δ' ἂν εἴπῃ ‡ μωρέ, ‡ ἔνοχ Θ· ἔςαι
εἰς τὴς ‡ γέενναν τοῦ ‡ πυρός.

23 Ἐὰν οὖν προσφέρῃς τὸ δῶρόν σου
ἐπὶ τὸ θυσιαςήριον, κᾀκεῖ μνησθῇς,
ὅτι ὁ ἀδελφός σου ἔχει τὶ κ.ἰὰ σοῦ,

* 24 Ἄφε· ἐκεῖ τὸ δῶρόν σου ἔμπροσθεν τοῦ θυσιαςηρίου, κỳ ὕπαγε,
πρῶτον † διαλλάγηθι τῷ ἀδελφῷ
σου, κỳ τότε ἐλθὼν πρόσφερε τὸ
‡ δῶρ.ν σου.

15 Neque accendunt lucer-
nam, & ponunt eam sub mo-
dio, sed super candelabrum, &
lucet omnibus in domo.

16 Sic luceat lux vestra coram
hominibus, ut videant vestra
pulchra opera, & glorificent Patrem vestrum qui in cælis.

17 Ne putetis quod veni dissolvere legem, aut Prophetas;
non veni dissolvere, sed adim-
plere.

18 Amen quippe dico vobis,
donec prætereat cælum & terra,
jota unum, aut unus apex non
præteribit à lege, donec omnia
fiant.

19 Qui ergo solverit unum
mandatorum istorum minimorum, & docuerit sic homines,
minimus vocabitur in regno cælorum : qui autem fecerit & docuerit, hic magnus vocabitur in
regno cælorum.

20 Dico enim vobis, quòd si
non abundaverit justitia vestra
plus Scribarum & Pharisæorum;
non intrabitis in regnum cælorum.

21 Audistis quia pronunciatum est antiquis : Non occides :
qui autem occiderit, obnoxius
erit judicio.

22 Ego autem dico vobis, quia
omnis irascens fratri suo imme-
ritò, obnoxius erit judicio : qui
autem dixerit fratri suo Raca,
obnoxius erit confessui : qui autem dixerit fatue, obnoxius erit
in gehennam ignis.

23 Si ergo offers munus tuum
ad altare, & ibi recordatus fueris, quia frater tuus habet aliquid adversum te,

24 Relinque ibi munus tuum
ante altare, & vade, prius recon-
ciliare fratri tuo, & tunc veniens
offer munus tuum.

15. Et on n'allume point une chandelle pour la mettre sous un boisseau, mais *on la met* sur un chandelier, et elle éclaire tous ceux qui *sont* dans la maison.

16. Que votre lumière luise ainsi devant les hommes, afin qu'ils voient vos bonnes œuvres, et qu'ils glorifient votre Père qui *est* dans les cieux.

17. Ne pensez point que je suis venu abolir la Loi ou les Prophètes; je suis venu, non pour les abolir, mais pour les accomplir.

18. Car je vous dis en vérité, que jusqu'à ce que le ciel et la terre passent, il n'y aura rien dans la Loi qui ne s'accomplisse, jusqu'à un seul iota, et à un seul trait de lettre.

19. Celui donc qui aura violé l'un de ces plus petits commandemens, et qui aura ainsi enseigné les hommes, sera estimé le plus petit dans le Royaume des cieux; mais celui qui les aura observés et enseignés, celui-là sera estimé grand dans le Royaume des cieux.

20. Car je vous dis, que si votre justice ne surpasse celle des Scribes et des Pharisiens, vous n'entrerez point dans le Royaume des cieux.

21. Vous avez entendu qu'il a été dit aux Anciens: Tu ne tueras point; et celui qui tuera sera punissable par les Juges.

22. Mais moi, je vous dis, que quiconque se met en colère contre son frère, sans cause, sera puni par les Juges; et celui qui dira à son frère, Racha, sera puni par le Conseil; et celui qui lui dira, Fou, sera punissable par la géhenne du feu.

23. Si donc tu apportes ton offrande à l'autel, et que là tu te souviennes que ton frère a quelque chose contre toi;

24. Laisse là ton offrande devant l'autel, et va-t-en premièrement te réconcilier avec ton frère; et, après cela, viens et offre ton offrande.

15 Neither do men light a candle, and put it under a bushel, but on a candlestick, and it giveth light unto all that are in the house.

16 Let your light so shine before men, that they may see your good works, and glorify your Father which is in heaven.

17 Think not that I am come to destroy the law, or the prophets: I am not come to destroy, but to fulfil.

18 For verily I say unto you, Till heaven and earth pass, one jot or one tittle shall in no wise pass from the law, till all be fulfilled.

19 Whosoever, therefore, shall break one of these least commandments, and shall teach men so, he shall be called the least in the kingdom of heaven: but whosoever shall do, and teach *them*, the same shall be called great in the kingdom of heaven.

20 For I say unto you, That except your righteousness shall exceed *the righteousness* of the scribes and Pharisees, ye shall in no case enter into the kingdom of heaven.

21 Ye have heard that it was said by them of old time, Thou shalt not kill; and, whosoever shall kill, shall be in danger of the judgment:

22 But I say unto you, That whosoever is angry with his brother without a cause, shall be in danger of the judgment: and whosoever shall say to his brother, Raca, shall be in danger of the council: but whosoever shall say, Thou fool, shall be in danger of hell fire.

23 Therefore, if thou bring thy gift to the altar, and there rememberest that thy brother hath aught against thee;

24 Leave there thy gift before the altar, and go thy way; first be reconciled to thy brother, and then come and offer thy gift.

8

25 Ἴσθι † εὐνοῶν τῷ ‡ ἀντιδίκῳ
σου ‡ ταχὺ, ἕως ὅτου εἶ ἐν τῇ ὁδῷ
μετ᾽ αὐτοῦ μήποτέ σε παραδῷ ‡
ἀντίδικ⊙ τῷ ‡ κριτῇ, ϰ ὁ κριτής
σε παραδῷ τῷ ὑπηρέτῃ, ϰ εἰς φυλακὴν βληθήσῃ.

26 Ἀμὴν λέγω σοι, οὐ μὴ ἐξέλθῃς ἐκεῖθεν ἕως ἂν ἀποδῷς τὸν
ἔσχατον κοδράντην.

27 Ἠκούσατε ὅτι ἐῤῥέθη τοῖς
ἀρχαίοις· Οὐ μοιχεύσεις·

28 Ἐγὼ δὲ λέγω ὑμῖν, ὅτι πᾶς
ὁ βλέπων γυναῖκα πρὸς τὸ ἐπιθυ-
μῆσαι αὐτῆς, ἤδη ἐμοίχευσεν αὐτὴν ἐν τῇ καρδίᾳ αὐτοῦ.

29 Εἰ δὲ ὁ ὀφθαλμός σου ὁ δε-
ξιὸς σκανδαλίζει σε, ἔξελε αὐτὸν, ϰ
βάλε ἀπὸ σοῦ· συμφέρει γάρ σοι, ἵνα
ἀπόληται ἓν τῶν μελῶν σου, ϰ μὴ
ὅλον τὸ σῶμά σου βληθῇ εἰς γέενναν.

30 Καὶ εἰ ἡ δεξιά σου χεὶρ σκανδαλίζει σε, ἔκκοψον αὐτὴν, ϰ βάλε
ἀπὸ σοῦ· συμφέρει γάρ σοι, ἵνα ἀ-
πόληται ἓν τῶν μελῶν σου, ϰ μὴ
ὅλον τὸ σῶμά σου βληθῇ εἰς γέ-
ενναν·

31 Ἐῤῥέθη δὲ ὅτι ὃς ἂν ἀπολύσῃ
τὴν γυναῖκα αὐτοῦ, δότω αὐτῇ ἀ-
ποστάσιον·

32 Ἐγὼ δὲ λέγω ὑμῖν, ὅτι ὃς ἂν
ἀπολύσῃ τὴν γυναῖκα αὐτοῦ, πα-
ρεκτὸς λόγου πορνείας, ποιεῖ αὐτὴν
μοιχᾶσθαι ϰ ὃς ἐὰν ἀπολελυμένην
γαμήσῃ, μοιχᾶται.

* 33 Πάλιν ἠκούσατε ὅτι ‡ ἐῤῥέθη τοῖς ‡ ἀρχαίοις· Οὐκ † ἐπιορ-
κήσεις· ἀποδώσεις δὲ τῷ Κυρίῳ
τοὺς ὅρκους σου.

34 Ἐγὼ δὲ λέγω ὑμῖν, μὴ ὀμόσαι ὅλως· μήτε ἐν τῷ οὐρανῷ, ὅτι
θρόν⊙ ἐςὶ τοῦ Θεοῦ·

35 Μήτε ἐν τῇ γῇ, ὅτι ὑποπό-
διόν ἐςι τῶν ποδῶν αὐτοῦ· μήτε εἰς

---

25 Esto benefenciens adverfa-
rio tuo cito, dum es in via cum
eo: ne forte te tradat adverfarius
judici, & judex te tradat minif-
tro; & in cuftodiam conjiciaris.

26 Amen dico tibi, non exies
inde, donec reddas noviffimum
quadrantem.

27 Audiftis quia pronunciatum
eft antiquis: Non mœchaberis.

28 Ego autem dico vobis, quia
omnis confpiciens mulierem ad
concupifcendum eam, jam mœ-
chatus eft eam in torde fuo.

29 Si autem oculus tuus dexter
fcandalizat te, erue eum, & projice abs te: confert enim tibi ut
pereat unum membrorum tuorum, & non totum corpus tuum
conjiciatur in gehennam.

30 Et fi dextera tua manus
fcandalizat te, abfcinde eam, &
projice abs te: confert enim tibi
ut pereat unum membrorum tuorum, & non totum corpus
tuum conjiciatur in gehennam.

31 Pronunciatum eft autem,
quod quicumque abfolverit uxorem fuam, det ei repudium.

32 Ego autem dico vobis, quia
quicunque abfolverit uxorem fuam, excepta ratione fornicatio-
nis, facit eam mœchari: & qui
abfolutam duxerit, adulterat.

33 Iterum audiftis quia pronunciatum eft antiquis: Non
perjurabis: reddes autem Domino juramenta tua.

34 Ego autem dico vobis, non
jurare omninò, neque in cœlo,
quia thronus eft Dei:

35 Neque in terra, quia fca-
bellum eft pedum ejus: neque

25. Accorde-toi au plutôt avec ta partie adverse, pendant que tu es en chemin avec elle, de peur que ta partie adverse ne te livre au Juge, et que le Juge ne te livre au Sergent, et que tu ne sois mis en prison.

26. Je te dis en vérité, que tu ne sortiras pas de là, jusqu'à-ce que tu aies payé le dernier quadrain.

27. Vous avez entendu qu'il a été dit aux Anciens : Tu ne commettras point adultère.

28. Mais moi, je vous dis, que quiconque regarde une femme pour la convoiter, il a déjà commis l'adultère avec elle dans son cœur.

29. Que si ton œil droit te fait tomber *dans le péché*, arrache-le, et jette-le loin de toi ; car il vaut mieux pour toi qu'un de tes membres périsse, que si tout ton corps étoit jeté dans la géhenne.

30. Et si ta main droite te fait tomber *dans le péché*, coupe-la, et jette-la loin de toi ; car il vaut mieux pour toi qu'un de tes membres périsse, que si tout ton corps étoit jeté dans la géhenne.

31. Il a été dit aussi : Si quelqu'un répudie sa femme, qu'il lui donne la lettre de divorce.

32. Mais moi, je vous dis, que quiconque répudiera sa femme, si ce n'est pour cause d'adultère, il l'expose à devenir adultère; et que quiconque se mariera à la femme qui aura été répudiée, commet un adultère.

33. Vous avez encore entendu qu'il a été dit aux Anciens : Tu ne te parjureras point ; mais tu t'acquitteras envers le Seigneur de ce que tu auras promis avec serment.

34. Mais moi, je vous dis : Ne jurez point du tout; ni par le ciel, car c'est le trône de Dieu :

35. Ni par la terre, car c'est son

25 Agree with thine adversary quickly, whilst thou art in the way with him; lest at any time the adversary deliver thee to the judge, and the judge deliver thee to the officer, and thou be cast into prison.

26 Verily I say unto thee, Thou shalt by no means come out thence, till thou hast paid the uttermost farthing.

27 Ye have heard that it was said by them of old time, Thou shalt not commit adultery :

28 But I say unto you, That whosoever looketh on a woman, to lust after her, hath committed adultery with her already in his heart.

29 And if thy right eye offend thee, pluck it out, and cast *it* from thee : for it is profitable for thee, that one of thy members should perish, and not *that* thy whole body should be cast into hell.

30 And if thy right hand offend thee, cut it off, and cast *it* from thee : for it is profitable for thee, that one of thy members should perish, and not *that* thy whole body should be cast into hell.

31 It hath been said, Whosoever shall put away his wife, let him give her a writing of divorcement:

32 But I say unto you, That whosoever shall put away his wife, saving for the cause of fornication, causeth her to commit adultery : and whosoever shall marry her that is divorced, committeth adultery.

33 Again, ye have heard that it hath been said by them of old time, Thou shalt not forswear thyself, but shalt perform unto the Lord thine oaths:

34 But I say unto you, Swear not at all: neither by heaven; for it is God's throne :

35 Nor by the earth : for it is his

9

Ἱεροσόλυμα, ὅτι πόλις ἐςὶ τοῦ μεγάλου βασιλέως·

36 Μήτε ἐν τῇ κεφαλῇ σου ὀμόσῃς, ὅτι οὐ δύνασαι μίαν τρίχα λευκὴν ἢ μέλαιναν ποιῆσαι.

37 Ἔςω δὲ ὁ λόγ۔ ὑμῶν, Ναὶ ναί, Οὒ οὔ· τὸ δὲ περισσὸν τούτων, ἐκ τοῦ πονηροῦ ἐςιν.

38 Ἠκούσατε ὅτι ἐῤῥέθη· Ὀφθαλμὸν ἀντὶ ὀφθαλμοῦ, ᐤ ὀδόντα ἀντὶ ὀδόντ۔.

39 Ἐγὼ δὲ λέγω ὑμῖν, μὴ ἀντιςῆναι τῷ πονηρῷ· ἀλλ' ὅςις σε ῥαπίσει ἐπὶ τὴν δεξιάν σου σιαγόνα, ςρέψον αὐτῷ ᐤ τὴν ἄλλην.

40 Καὶ τῷ θέλοντί σοι κριθῆναι, ᐤ τὸν χιτῶνά σου λαβεῖν, ἄφες αὐτῷ ᐤ τὸ ἱμάτιον.

41 Καὶ † ὅςις σε † ἀγγαρεύσει † μίλιον ἓν, ὕπαγε μετ' αὐτοῦ δύο.

42 Τῷ αἰτοῦντί σε δίδου· ᐤ τὸν θέλοντα ἀπὸ σοῦ δανείσασθαι μὴ ἀποςραφῇς.

43 Ἠκούσατε ὅτι ἐῤῥέθη· Ἀγαπήσεις τὸν πλησίον σου, ᐤ μισήσεις τὸν ἐχθρόν σου.

44 Ἐγὼ δὲ λέγω ὑμῖν, ἀγαπᾶτε τοὺς ἐχθροὺς ὑμῶν, εὐλογεῖτε τοὺς καταρωμένους ὑμᾶς, καλῶς ποιεῖτε τοὺς μισοῦντας ὑμᾶς, ᐤ προσεύχεσθε ὑπὲρ τῶν ἐπηρεαζόντων ὑμᾶς ᐤ διωκόντων ὑμᾶς·

45 Ὅπως γένεσθε υἱοὶ τοῦ πατρὸς ὑμῶν τοῦ ἐν οὐρανοῖς, ὅτι τὸν ἥλιον αὐτοῦ ἀνατέλλει ἐπὶ πονηροὺς ᐤ ἀγαθοὺς, ᐤ βρέχει ἐπὶ δικαίους ᐤ ἀδίκους.

46 Ἐὰν γὰρ ἀγαπήσητε τοὺς ἀγαπῶντας ὑμᾶς, τίνα μισθὸν ἔχετε; οὐχὶ ᐤ οἱ τελῶναι τὸ αὐτὸ ποιοῦσι;

47 Καὶ ἐὰν ἀσπάσησθε τοὺς ἀδελφοὺς ὑμῶν μόνον, τί περισσὸν ποιεῖτε; οὐχὶ ᐤ οἱ τελῶναι οὕτω ποιοῦσιν;

in Hierosolyma, quia civitas est magni regis:

36 Neque in capite tuo juraveris, quia non potes unum capillum album aut nigrum facere.

37 Sit autem fermo vefter, Etiam, etiam, Non, non : quod autem abundans his, à malo eft.

38 Audiftis quia pronunciatum eft : Oculum pro oculo, & dentem pro dente.

39 Ego autem dico vobis, non obfiftere malo : fed quicunque te percufferit in dexteram tuam maxillam, verte illi & aliam.

40 Et volenti tibi judicium parari, & tunicam tuam tollere, dimitte ei & pallium.

41 Et quicunque te angariaverit milliare unum, vade cum illo duo.

42 Petenti te, da : & volentem à te mutuare, ne avertaris.

43 Audiftis quia pronunciatum eft, Diliges proximum tuum, & odio habebis inimicum tuum.

44 Ego autem dico vobis, Diligite inimicos veftros, benedicite maledicentes vos : benefacite odientibus vos, & orate pro infeftantibus vos, & infeftantibus vos,

45 Ut fitis filii Patris veftri qui in cælis, quia folem fuum producit fuper malos et bonos, & pluit fuper juftos & injuftos.

46 Si enim dilexeritis diligentes vos, quam mercedem habetis? nonne & publicani idem faciunt?

47 Et fi falutaveritis fratres veftros tantum, quid abundans facitis? nonne & publicani fic faciunt?

marchepied, ni par Jérusalem, car c'est la ville du grand Roi.

36. Ne jure pas non plus par ta tête; car tu ne peux faire devenir un seul cheveu blanc ou noir.

37. Mais que votre parole soit, Oui, Oui, Non, Non; ce qu'on dit de plus vient du malin.

38. Vous avez entendu qu'il a été dit: œil pour œil, et dent pour dent.

39. Mais moi, je vous dis, de ne pas résister à celui qui vous fait du mal; mais si quelqu'un te frappe à la joue droite, présente-lui aussi l'autre.

40. Et si quelqu'un veut plaider contre toi, et t'ôter ta robe, laisse-lui encore l'habit.

41. Et si quelqu'un te veut contraindre d'aller une lieue avec lui, vas-en deux.

42. Donne à celui qui te demande, et ne te détourne point de celui qui veut emprunter de toi.

43. Vous avez entendu qu'il a été dit: Tu aimeras ton prochain, et tu haïras ton ennemi.

44. Mais moi, je vous dis: Aimez vos ennemis, bénissez ceux qui vous maudissent, faites du bien à ceux qui vous haïssent, et priez pour ceux qui vous outragent et qui vous persécutent;

45. Afin que vous soyez enfans de votre Père qui *est* dans les cieux; car il fait lever son soleil sur les méchans et sur les bons, et il fait pleuvoir sur les justes et sur les injustes.

46. Car si vous n'aimez que ceux qui vous aiment, quelle récompense en aurez-vous? les péagers même n'en font-ils pas autant?

47. Et si vous ne faites accueil qu'à vos frères, que faites-vous d'extraordinaire? Les péagers même n'en font-ils pas autant?

footstool: neither by Jerusalem; for it is the city of the great King:

36 Neither shalt thou swear by thy head; because thou canst not make one hair white or black:

37 But let your communication be, Yea, yea; Nay, nay: for whatsoever *is* more than these cometh of evil.

38 Ye have heard that it hath been said, An eye for an eye, and a tooth for a tooth:

39 But I say unto you, That ye resist not evil: but whosoever shall smite thee on thy right cheek, turn to him the other also.

40 And if any man will sue thee at the law, and take away thy coat, let him have *thy* cloak also.

41 And whosoever shall compel thee to go a mile, go with him twain.

42 Give to him that asketh thee; and from him that would borrow of thee, turn not thou away.

43 Ye have heard that it hath been said, Thou shalt love thy neighbour, and hate thine enemy:

44 But I say unto you, Love your enemies, bless them that curse you, do good to them that hate you, and pray for them which despitefully use you, and persecute you;

45 That ye may be the children of your Father which is in heaven: for he maketh his sun to rise on the evil and on the good, and sendeth rain on the just and on the unjust.

46 For if ye love them which love you, what reward have ye? do not even the publicans the same?

47 And if ye salute your brethren only, what do ye more *than others?* do not even the publicans so?

34 Καὶ ἐὰν δανείζητε παρ᾽ ὧν ἐλπίζετε ἀπολαβεῖν, ποία ὑμῖν χάρις ἐςί; καὶ γὰρ οἱ ἁμαρτωλοὶ ἁμαρτωλοῖς δανείζουσιν, ἵνα ἀπολάβωσι τὰ ἴσα.	34 Et si mutuum dederitis à quibus speratis recipere, quæ vobis gratia est? Etenim peccatores peccatoribus fœnerantur, ut recipiant æqualia.
35 ‡ Πλὴν ‡ ἀγαπᾶτε τὰς ‡ ἐχθρὰς ὑμῶν, καὶ ‡ ἀγαθοποιεῖτε, καὶ ‡ δανείζετε ‡ μηδὲν † ἀπελπίζοντες· καὶ ἔςαι ὁ μισθὸς ὑμῶν πολὺς, καὶ ἔσεσθε υἱοὶ τοῦ ὑψίςου ὅτι αὐτὸς ‡ χρηςός ἐςιν ἐπὶ τὰς ‡ ἀχαρίςους καὶ ‡ πονηρούς.	35 Veruntamen diligite inimicos vestros, & benefacite, & mutuum date nihil desperantes: & erit merces vestra multa, & eritis filii Altissimi: quia ipse benignus est super ingratos & malos.
36 Γίνεσθε ἒν οἰκτίρμονες, καθὼς καὶ ὁ πατὴρ ὑμῶν οἰκτίρμων ἐςί.	36 Estote ergo misericordes, sicut & Pater vester misericors est.

Κεφ. ϛʹ. 6.	CAPUT VI.
1 Προσέχετε τὴν ἐλημοσύνην ὑμῶν μὴ ποιεῖν ἔμπροσθεν τῶν ἀνθρώπων, πρὸς τὸ θεαθῆναι αὐτοῖς· εἰ δὲ μήγε, μισθὸν οὐκ ἔχετε παρὰ τῷ πατρὶ ὑμῶν τῷ ἐν τοῖς οὐρανοῖς.	1 ATtendite misericordiam vestram non facere ante homines, ad spectari eis: si autem non, mercedem non habetis apud Patrem vestrum qui in cælis.
2 Ὅταν οὖν ποιῇς ἐλημοσύνην, μὴ σαλπίσῃς ἔμπροσθέν σου, ὥσπερ οἱ ὑποκριταὶ ποιοῦσιν ἐν ταῖς συναγωγαῖς καὶ ἐν ταῖς ῥύμαις, ὅπως δοξασθῶσιν ὑπὸ τῶν ἀνθρώπων· Ἀμὴν λέγω ὑμῖν, ἀπέχουσι τὸν μισθὸν αὐτῶν.	2 Cum ergo facis eleëmosynam, ne tuba clanxeris ante te, sicut hypocritæ faciunt in synagogis & in vicis, ut glorificentur ab hominibus: amen dico vobis, excipiunt mercedem suam.
3 Σοῦ δὲ ποιοῦντος ἐλημοσύνην, μὴ γνώτω ἀριστερά σου τί ποιεῖ ἡ δεξιά σου·	3 Te autem faciente eleëmosynam, nesciat sinistra tua quid faciat dextera tua.
4 Ὅπως ᾖ σου ἡ ἐλημοσύνη ἐν τῷ κρυπτῷ καὶ ὁ πατήρ σου ὁ βλέπων ἐν τῷ κρυπτῷ, αὐτὸς ἀποδώσει σοι ἐν τῷ φανερῷ.	4 Ut sit tua eleëmosyna in secreto: & Pater tuus videns in secreto, ipse reddet tibi in manifesto.
5 Καὶ ὅταν προσεύχῃ, οὐκ ἔσῃ ὥσπερ οἱ ὑποκριταί· ὅτι φιλοῦσιν ἐν ταῖς συναγωγαῖς καὶ ἐν ταῖς γωνίαις τῶν πλατειῶν ἑςῶτες προσεύχεσθαι, ὅπως ἂν φανῶσι τοῖς ἀνθρώποις. Ἀμὴν λέγω ὑμῖν, ὅτι ἀπέχουσι τὸν μισθὸν αὐτῶν.	5 Et quum ores, non eris sicut hypocritæ: quia amant in synagogis, & in angulis platearum stantes orare, ut appareant hominibus, amen dico vobis, quod excipiunt mercedem suam.
6 Σὺ δὲ ὅταν προσεύχῃ, εἴσελθε εἰς τὸ ταμιεῖόν σου, καὶ κλείσας τὴν θύραν σου, πρόσευξαι τῷ πατρί σου τῷ ἐν τῷ κρυπτῷ· καὶ ὁ πατήρ σου ὁ βλέπων ἐν τῷ κρυπτῷ, ἀποδώσει σοι ἐν τῷ φανερῷ.	6 Tu autem cum ores, intra in cubiculum tuum, & claudens ostium tuum, ora Patrem tuum qui in secreto: & Pater tuus conspiciens in secreto, reddet tibi in apparenti.
7 ‡ Προσευχόμενοι δὲ μὴ † βαττολογήσητε, ὥσπερ οἱ ‡ ἐθνικοί· ‡ δοκοῦσι γὰρ ὅτι ἐν τῇ † πολυλογίᾳ αὐτῶν ‡ εἰσακουσθήσονται.	7 Orantes autem ne inania loquamini, sicut ethnici, arbitrantur enim quod in multiloquio suo exaudientur.
8 Μὴ οὖν ὁμοιωθῆτε αὐτοῖς· οἶδε γὰρ ὁ πατὴρ ὑμῶν, ὧν χρείαν ἔχετε, πρὸ τοῦ ὑμᾶς αἰτῆσαι αὐτόν.	8 Ne igitur assimilemini eis: novit enim Pater vester quorum usum habetis, ante vos petere eum.

34. Et si vous ne prêtez qu'à ceux de qui vous espérez de recevoir, quel gré vous en saura-t-on ? puisque les gens de mauvaise vie prêtent aussi aux gens de mauvaise vie, afin d'en recevoir la pareille.

35. C'est pourquoi, aimez vos ennemis, faites du bien, et prêtez sans en rien espérer, et votre récompense sera grande, et vous serez les enfans du très-haut ; parce qu'il est bon envers les ingrats et les méchans.

36. Soyez donc miséricordieux, comme aussi votre père est miséricordieux.

PRENEZ garde de ne pas faire votre aumône devant les hommes, afin d'en être vu; autrement vous n'en aurez point de récompense de votre Père qui *est* aux cieux.

2. Quand donc tu feras l'aumône, ne fais pas sonner la trompette devant toi, comme font les hypocrites, dans les Synagogues et dans les rues, afin qu'ils *en* soient honorés des hommes. Je vous dis en vérité, qu'il reçoivent leur récompense.

3. Mais quand tu fais l'aumône, que ta main gauche ne sache pas ce que fait ta droite.

4. Afin que ton aumône se fasse en secret; et ton Père qui *te* voit dans le secret, te le rendra publiquement,

5. Et quand tu prieras, ne fais pas comme les hypocrites ; car ils aiment à prier en se tenant debout dans les Synagogues et aux coins des rues, afin d'être vus des hommes. Je vous dis en vérité, qu'ils reçoivent leur récompense.

6. Mais toi, quand tu pries, entre dans ton cabinet ; et ayant fermé la porte, prie ton père qui *est* dans ce *lieu* secret ; et ton père qui te voit dans le secret, te récompensera publiquement.

7. Or, quand vous priez, n'usez pas des vaines redites comme les Païens ; car ils croient qu'ils seront exaucés en parlant beaucoup.

8. Ne leur ressemblez donc pas ; car votre Père sait de quoi vous avez besoin, avant que vous *le* lui demandiez.

34 And if ye lend *to them* of whom ye hope to receive, what thank have ye? for sinners also lend to sinners, to receive as much again.

35 But love ye your enemies, and do good, and lend, hoping for nothing again : and your reward shall be great, and ye shall be the children of the Highest : for he is kind unto the unthankful, and *to* the evil.

36 Be ye, therefore, merciful, as your Father also is merciful.

TAKE heed that ye do not your alms before men, to be seen of them : otherwise ye have no reward of your Father which is in heaven.

2 Therefore, when thou doest *thine* alms, do not sound a trumpet before thee, as the hypocrites do in the synagogues, and in the streets, that they may have glory of men. Verily I say unto you, They have their reward.

3 But when thou doest alms, let not thy left hand know what thy right hand doeth :

4 That thine alms may be in secret : and thy Father, which seeth in secret, himself shall reward thee openly.

5 And when thou prayest, thou shalt not be as the hypocrites *are :* for they love to pray standing in the synagogues, and in the corners of the streets, that they may be seen of men. Verily I say unto you, They have their reward.

6 But thou, when thou prayest, enter into thy closet; and, when thou hast shut thy door, pray to thy Father which is in secret; and thy Father which seeth in secret, shall reward thee openly.

7 But when ye pray, use not vain repetitions, as the heathen *do:* for they think that they shall be heard for their much speaking.

8 Be not ye, therefore, like unto them : for your Father knoweth what things ye have need of, before ye ask him.

9 Οὕτως οὖν προσεύχεσθε ὑ-
μεῖς· ΠΑΤΕΡ ἡμῶν ὁ ἐν τοῖς οὐ-
ρανοῖς· ἁγιασθήτω τὸ ὄνομά σου·

10 Ἐλθέτω ἡ βασιλεία σου·
γενηθήτω τὸ θέλημά σου, ὡς ἐν
οὐρανῷ, καὶ ἐπὶ τῆς γῆς.

11 Τὸν ἄρτον ἡμῶν τὸν ἐπιού-
σιον δὸς ἡμῖν σήμερον.

12 Καὶ ἄφες ἡμῖν τὰ ὀφειλήματα ἡμῶν, ὡς καὶ ἡμεῖς ἀφίεμεν
τοῖς ὀφειλέταις ἡμῶν.

13 Καὶ μὴ εἰσενέγκῃς ἡμᾶς εἰς
πειρασμὸν, ἀλλὰ ῥῦσαι ἡμᾶς ἀπὸ
τοῦ πονηροῦ· ὅτι σοῦ ἐστιν ἡ βασιλεία, καὶ ἡ δύναμις, καὶ ἡ δόξα εἰς
τοὺς αἰῶνας· ἀμήν.

14 Ἐὰν γὰρ ἀφῆτε τοῖς ἀνθρώποις τὰ παραπτώματα αὐτῶν,
ἀφήσει καὶ ὑμῖν ὁ πατὴρ ὑμῶν ὁ οὐ-
ράνιος·

15 Ἐὰν δὲ μὴ ἀφῆτε τοῖς ἀνθρώποις τὰ παραπτώματα αὐτῶν,
οὐδὲ ὁ πατὴρ ὑμῶν ἀφήσει τὰ
παραπτώματα ὑμῶν.

16 Ὅταν δὲ νηστεύητε, μὴ γίνεσθε, ὥσπερ οἱ ὑποκριταί, σκυθρω-
ποί· ἀφανίζουσι γὰρ τὰ πρόσωπα
αὐτῶν, ὅπως φανῶσι τοῖς ἀνθρώποις νηστεύοντες· ἀμὴν λέγω ὑμῖν,
ὅτι ἀπέχουσι τὸν μισθὸν αὐτῶν.

17 Σὺ δὲ νηστεύων ἄλειψαί σου τὴν
κεφαλὴν, καὶ τὸ πρόσωπόν σου νίψαι·

18 Ὅπως μὴ φανῇς τοῖς ἀνθρώποις νηστεύων, ἀλλὰ τῷ πατρί σου
τῷ ἐν τῷ κρυπτῷ· καὶ ὁ πατήρ σου
ὁ βλέπων ἐν τῷ κρυπτῷ, ἀποδώσει
σοι ἐν τῷ φανερῷ.

* 19 Μὴ ‡ θησαυρίζετε ὑμῖν
‡ θησαυροὺς ἐπὶ τῆς ‡ γῆς, ὅπου
‡ σὴς καὶ ‡ βρῶσις ‡ ἀφανίζει, καὶ
ὅπου ‡ κλέπται ‡ διορύσσουσι καὶ
‡ κλέπτουσι·

20 Θησαυρίζετε δὲ ὑμῖν θησαυροὺς ἐν οὐρανῷ, ὅπου οὔτε σὴς οὔτε
βρῶσις ἀφανίζει, καὶ ὅπου κλέπται
οὐ διορύσσουσιν οὐδὲ κλέπτουσιν.

21 Ὅπου γάρ ἐστιν ὁ θησαυρὸς
ὑμῶν, ἐκεῖ ἔσται καὶ ἡ καρδία ὑμῶν.

22 Ὁ λύχνος τοῦ σώματός
ἐστιν ὁ ὀφθαλμός· ἐὰν οὖν ὁ ὀφθαλμός σου ἁπλοῦς ᾖ, ὅλον τὸ σῶμά
σου φωτεινὸν ἔσται.

9 Sic ergo orate vos: Pater
noster qui in cælis, sanctificetur
nomen tuum.

10 Adveniat regnum tuum:
Fiat voluntas tua, sicut in cælo,
& in terra.

11 Panem nostrum supersub-
stantialem da nobis hodie.

12 Et dimitte nobis debita
nostra, sicut & nos dimittimus
debitoribus nostris.

13 Et ne inferas nos in tentationem, sed libera nos à malo.
Quoniam tuum est regnum, &
potentia, & gloria in secula. A-
men.

14 Si enim dimiseritis hominibus lapsus eorum, dimittet &
vobis Pater vester cælestis.

15 Si autem non dimiseritis
hominibus lapsus ipsorum, nec
Pater vester dimittet lapsus vestros.

16 Quum autem jejunatis, ne
fiatis sicut hypocritæ, obtristati;
obscurant enim facies suas; ut
appareant hominibus jejunantes,
amen dico vobis, quia recipiunt
mercedem suam.

17 Tu autem jejunans, unge
tuum caput, & faciam tuam lava:

18 Ut ne appareas hominibus
jejunans, sed Patri tuo qui in secreto: & Pater tuus videns in
secreto, reddet tibi in mani-
festo.

19 Ne thesaurizate vobis thesauros in terra, ubi ærugo &
tinea exterminat, & ubi fures
perfodiunt, & furantur.

20 Thesaurizate autem vobis
thesauros in cælo, ubi neque
ærugo, neque tinea exterminat,
& ubi fures non effodiunt, nec
furantur.

21 Ubi enim est thesaurus
vester, ibi erit & cor vestrum.

22 Lucerna corporis est oculus; si igitur oculus tuus sim-
plex fuerit, totum corpus tuum
lucidum erit.

9 After this manner, therefore, pray ye: Our Father which art in heaven; Hallowed be thy name.

10 Thy kingdom come. Thy will be done in earth, as *it is* in heaven.

11 Give us this day our daily bread.

12 And forgive us our debts, as we forgive our debtors.

13 And lead us not into temptation; but deliver us from evil: For thine is the kingdom, and the power, and the glory, for ever, Amen.

14 For if ye forgive men their trespasses, your heavenly Father will also forgive you:

15 But if ye forgive not men their trespasses, neither will your Father forgive your trespasses.

16 Moreover, when ye fast, be not as the hypocrites, of a sad countenance: for they disfigure their faces, that they may appear unto men to fast. Verily I say unto you, They have their reward.

17 But thou, when thou fastest, anoint thine head, and wash thy face;

18 That thou appear not unto men to fast, but unto thy Father which is in secret: and thy Father, which seeth in secret, shall reward thee openly.

19 Lay not up for yourselves treasures upon earth, where moth and rust doth corrupt, and where thieves break through and steal:

20 But lay up for yourselves treasures in heaven, where neither moth nor rust doth corrupt, and where thieves do not break through nor steal:

21 For where your treasure is, there will your heart be also.

22 The light of the body is the eye: if, therefore, thine eye be single, thy whole body shall be full of light.

---

9. Vous donc, priez ainsi : Notre Père qui *es* aux cieux, ton nom soit sanctifié ;

10. Ton règne vienne ; ta volonté soit faite sur la terre comme au ciel ;

11. Donne-nous aujourd'hui notre pain quotidien ;

12. Pardonne-nous nos péchés, comme aussi nous pardonnons à ceux qui nous ont offensés ;

13. Et ne nous abandonne point à la tentation, mais délivre-nous du malin. Car à toi appartient le règne, la puissance, et la gloire à jamais : Amen.

14. Si vous pardonnez aux hommes leurs offenses, votre Père céleste vous pardonnera aussi *les vôtres* ;

15. Mais si vous ne pardonnez pas aux hommes leurs offenses, votre Père ne vous pardonnera pas non plus les vôtres.

16. Et quand vous jeûnez, ne prenez pas un air triste comme les hypocrites ; car ils se rendent le visage tout défait, afin qu'il paroisse aux hommes qu'ils jeûnent.

17. Mais toi, quand tu jeûnes, oins ta tête et lave ton visage ;

18. Afin qu'il ne paroisse pas aux hommes que tu jeûnes, mais *seulement* à ton Père qui *est* en secret ; et ton Père qui *te* voit dans le secret, te récompensera publiquement.

19. Ne vous amassez pas des trésors sur la terre, où les vers et la rouille gâtent tout, et où les larrons percent et dérobent ;

20. Mais amassez-vous des trésors dans le ciel, où les vers ni la rouille ne gâtent rien, et où les larrons ne percent ni ne dérobent point ;

21. Car où est votre trésor, là sera aussi votre cœur.

22. L'œil est la lumière du corps. Si donc ton œil est sain, tout ton corps sera éclairé ;

23 Ἐὰν δὲ ὁ ὀφθαλμός σου πονηρὸς ᾖ, ὅλον τὸ σῶμά σου σκοτεινὸν
ἔςαι. Εἰ οὖν τὸ φῶς τὸ ἐν σοὶ, σκό-
τ©· ἐςὶ, τὸ σκότ©· πόσον;

24 Οὐδεὶς δύναται δυσὶ κυρίοις
δουλεύειν. ἢ γὰρ τὸν ἕνα μισήσει,
κὶ τὸν ἕτερον ἀγαπήσει· ἢ ἑνὸς ἀνθέξεται, κὶ τοῦ ἑτέρου καταφρονή-
σει· οὐ δύνασθε Θεῷ δουλεύειν κὶ
μαμμωνᾷ.

25 Διὰ τοῦτο λέγω ὑμῖν, μὴ
μεριμνᾶτε τῇ ψυχῇ ὑμῶν, τί φάγητε κὶ τί πίητε· μηδὲ τῷ σώματι
ὑμῶν, τί ἐνδύσησθε· οὐχὶ ἡ ψυχὴ
πλεῖόν ἐςι τῆς τροφῆς, κὶ τὸ σῶμα
τοῦ ἐνδύματ©·;

26 Ἐμβλέψατε εἰς τὰ πετεινὰ
τοῦ οὐρανοῦ, ὅτι ὐ σπείρουσιν, οὐδὲ
θερίζουσιν, οὐδὲ συνάγουσιν εἰς ἀποθήκας, κὶ ὁ πατὴρ ὑμῶν ὁ οὐράν-
τρέφει αὐτά. οὐχ ὑμεῖς μᾶλλον
διαφέρετε αὐτῶν;

27 Τίς δὲ ἐξ ὑμῶν μεριμνῶν
δύναται προσθεῖναι ἐπὶ τὴν ἡλικίαν αὐτοῦ πῆχυν ἕνα;

* 28 Καὶ περὶ ‡ ἐνδύματ©· τί
μεριμνᾶτε; † καταμάθετε τὰ
‡ κρίνα τοῦ ‡ ἀγροῦ ‡ πῶς ‡ αὐξά-
νει· οὐ ‡ κοπιᾷ, ‡ οὐδὲ ‡ νήθει·

29 Λέγω δὲ ὑμῖν, ὅτι οὐδὲ Σολομὼν ἐν πάσῃ τῇ δόξῃ αὐτοῦ περιεβάλετο ὡς ἓν τούτων.

* 30 Εἰ δὲ τὸν ‡ χόρτον τοῦ
ἀγροῦ, σήμερον ὄντα, κὶ ‡ αὔριον εἰς
‡ κλίβανον βαλλόμενον, ὁ Θεὸς
‡ οὕτως ‡ ἀμφιέννυσιν, οὐ πολλῷ
μᾶλλον ὑμᾶς, ὀλιγόπιςοι;

31 Μὴ οὖν μεριμνήσητε, λέγον-
τες· Τί φάγωμεν, ἢ τί πίωμεν,
ἢ τί περιβαλώμεθα;

32 Πάντα γὰρ ταῦτα τὰ ἔθνη
ἐπιζητεῖ· οἶδε γὰρ ὁ πατὴρ ὑμῶν
ὁ οὐράν©· ὅτι χρῄζετε τούτων ἁ-
πάντων.

33 Ζητεῖτε δὲ πρῶτον τὴν βασιλείαν τοῦ Θεοῦ, κὶ τὴν δικαιο-
σύνην αὐτοῦ· κὶ ταῦτα πάντα
προςτεθήσεται ὑμῖν.

34 Μὴ οὖν μεριμνήσητε εἰς τὴν
αὔριον· ἡ γὰρ αὔριον μεριμνήσει
τὰ ἑαυτῆς· ἀρκετὸν τῇ ἡμέρα ἡ
κακία αὐτῆς. 29. † 3.

---

23 Si autem oculus tuus malus fuerit, totum corpus tuum
tenebrosum erit. si ergo lumen
quod in te, tenebræ sunt, tenebræ quantæ?

24 Nemo poteſt duobus do-
minis ſervire : aut enim unum
oderit, & alterum diliget : aut
unum amplexabitur, & alterum
deſpiciet. non poteſtis Deo ſervire & mammonæ.

25 Propter hoc dico vobis, ne
anxiemini animæ veſtræ, quid
manducetis, & quid bibatis : neque corpori veſtro, quid induamini. nonne anima plus eſt eſcâ,
& corpus indumento?

26 Inſpicite in volatilia cæli,
quoniam non ſeminant, neque
metunt, neque congregant in
horrea, & Pater veſter cæleſtis
paſcit illa, nonne vos magis ex-
cellitis illis?

27 Quis antem ex vobis anxia-
tus poteſt adjicere ad ſtaturam
ſuam cubitum unum?

28 Et circa veſtimentum quid
anxiamini? Obſervate lilia agri
quomodo augentur : non ſati-
gantur, neque nent.

29 Dico autem vobis, quo-
niam nec Salomon in omni
gloria ſua amictus eſt ſicut
unum iſtorum.

30 Si autem fœnum agri hodie exiſtens, & cras in clibanum
injectum, Deus ſic circumornat,
non multò magis vos, exiguæ
fidei?

31 Ne igitur anxiemini, dicentes : Quid manducabimus,
aut quid bibemus, aut quid cir-
cumamiciemur?

32 Omnia enim hæc gentes
inquirunt. Novit enim Pater
veſter cæleſtis quod opus habetis horum omnium.

33 Quærite autem primum
regnum Dei, & juſtitiam ejus,
& hæc omnia adponentur vobis.

34 Ne igitur anxiemini in
cras : nam cras curabit ſua ipſius : ſufficiens diei malitia ſua.

23. Mais si ton œil est mauvais, tout ton corps sera ténébreux. Si donc la lumière qui est en toi *n'est que* ténèbres, combien seront grandes ces ténèbres !

24. Nul ne peut servir deux maîtres ; car ou il haïra l'un, et aimera l'autre; ou il s'attachera à l'un, et méprisera l'autre: Vous ne pouvez servir Dieu et Mammon.

25. C'est pourquoi je vous dis: Ne soyez point en souci de votre vie , de ce que vous mangerez, ou de ce que vous boirez ; ni pour votre corps, de quoi vous serez vêtus. La vie n'est-elle pas plus que la nourriture ; et le corps plus que le vêtement ?

26. Regardez les oiseaux de l'air; car ils ne sèment , ni ne moissonnent , ni n'amassent *rien* dans des greniers , et votre Père céleste les nourrit: N'êtes-vous pas beaucoup plus excellens qu'eux ?

27. Et qui est-ce d'entre vous, qui , par son souci , puisse ajouter une coudée à sa taille ?

28. Et pour ce qui est du vêtement , pourquoi en êtes-vous en souci ? Apprenez comment les lis de champs croissent; ils ne travaillent ni ne filent.

29. Cependant , je vous dis , que Salomon même , dans toute sa gloire , n'a point été vêtu comme l'un d'eux.

30. Si donc Dieu revêt ainsi l'herbe des champs, qui est aujourd'hui, et qui demain sera jetée dans le four , ne vous *revêtira-t-il* pas beaucoup plutôt, ô gens de petite foi ?

31. Ne soyez donc point en souci, disant : Que mangerons-nous ? que boirons-nous ? Ou de quoi serons-nous vêtus ?

32. Car ce sont les Païens qui recherchent toutes ces choses ; et votre Père céleste sait que vous avez besoin de toutes ces choses-là.

33. Mais cherchez premièrement le Royaume de Dieu et sa justice , et toutes ces choses vous seront données par-dessus.

34. Ne soyez donc point en souci pour le lendemain ; car le lendemain aura soin de ce qui le regarde: A chaque jour suffit sa peine.

23 But if thine eye be evil, thy whole body shall be full of darkness. If, therefore, the light that is in thee be darkness, how great *is* that darkness ?

24 No man can serve two masters: for either he will hate the one, and love the other; or else he will hold to the one, and despise the other. Ye cannot serve God and mammon.

25 Therefore I say unto you, Take no thought for your life, what ye shall eat or what ye shall drink; nor yet for your body, what ye shall put on. Is not the life more than meat, and the body than raiment ?

26 Behold the fowls of the air: for they sow not, neither do they reap, nor gather into barns; yet your heavenly Father feedeth them. Are ye not much better than they ?

27 Which of you, by taking thought, can add one cubit unto his stature ?

28 And why take ye thought for raiment ? Consider the lilies of the field how they grow: they toil not, neither do they spin ;

29 And yet I say unto you, That even Solomon in all his glory was not arrayed like one of these.

30 Wherefore, if God so clothe the grass of the field, which to day is, and to morrow is cast into the oven, *shall he* not much more *clothe* you ? O ye of little faith ;

31 Therefore, take no thought, saying, What shall we eat? or, What shall we drink? or, Wherewithal shall we be clothed?

32 (For after all these things do the Gentiles seek:) for your heavenly Father knoweth that ye have need of all these things.

33 But seek ye first the kingdom of God, and his righteousness; and all these things shall be added unto you.

34 Take therefore no thought for the morrow: for the morrow shall take thought for the things of itself. Sufficient unto the day *is* the evil thereof.

13.

Κεφ. ζ. 7.

1 ΜΉ κρίνετε, ἵνα μὴ κρι-
θῆτε.

2 Ἐν ᾧ γὰρ κρίματι κρίνετε,
κριθήσεσθε· κỳ ἐν ᾧ μέτρῳ μετρεῖτε, ἀντιμετρηθήσεται ὑμῖν.

* 38 Δίδοτε, κỳ δοθήσεται ὑ-
μῖν· ‡ μέτρον καλὸν, † πεπιε-
σμένον κỳ ‡ σεσαλευμένον κỳ † ὑ-
περεκχυνόμενον δώσουσιν εἰς τὸν
‡ κόλπον ὑμῶν·

3 Τί δὲ βλέπεις τὸ κάρφⒼ τὸ
ἐν τῷ ὀφθαλμῷ τοῦ ἀδελφοῦ σου,
τὴν δὲ ἐν τῷ σῷ ὀφθαλμῷ δοκὸν
οὐ κατανοεῖς;

4 Ἢ πῶς ἐρεῖς τῷ ἀδελφῷ σου·
Ἄφες, ἐκβάλω τὸ κάρφⒼ ἀπὸ τοῦ
ὀφθαλμοῦ σου· κỳ ἰδοὺ ἡ δοκὸς ἐν
τῷ ὀφθαλμῷ σου;

* 5 Ὑποκριτὰ, ἔκβαλε πρῶτον τὴν ‡ δοκὸν ἐκ τοῦ ὀφθαλμοῦ
σου, κỳ τότε διαβλέψεις ἐκβαλεῖν
τὸ ‡ κάρφⒼ ἐκ τοῦ ὀφθαλμοῦ
τοῦ ἀδελφοῦ σου.

6 Μὴ δῶτε τὸ ἅγιον τοῖς κυσὶ,
μηδὲ βάλητε τοὺς μαργαρίτας ὑ-
μῶν ἔμπροσθεν τῶν χοίρων· μήποτε καταπατήσωσιν αὐτοὺς ἐν
τοῖς ποσὶν αὐτῶν, κỳ στραφέντες
ῥήξωσιν ὑμᾶς.

7 Αἰτεῖτε, κỳ δοθήσεται ὑμῖν·
ζητεῖτε, κỳ εὑρήσετε· κρούετε, κỳ
ἀνοιγήσεται ὑμῖν.

8 Πᾶς γὰρ ὁ αἰτῶν λαμβάνει,
κỳ ὁ ζητῶν εὑρίσκει, κỳ τῷ κρούοντι
ἀνοιγήσεται.

9 Ἢ τίς ἐστιν ἐξ ὑμῶν ἄνθρω-
πⓄ, ὃν ἐὰν αἰτήσῃ ὁ υἱὸς αὐτοῦ
ἄρτον, μὴ λίθον ἐπιδώσει αὐτῷ;

10 Καὶ ἐὰν ἰχθὺν αἰτήσῃ, μὴ
ὄφιν ἐπιδώσει αὐτῷ;

* 11 Εἰ οὖν ὑμεῖς, πονηροὶ ὄντες,
‡ οἴδατε ‡ δόματα ἀγαθὰ διδόναι
τοῖς τέκνοις ὑμῶν, πόσῳ μᾶλλον ὁ
πατὴρ ὑμῶν ὁ ἐν τοῖς οὐρανοῖς, δώσει ἀγαθὰ τοῖς αἰτοῦσιν αὐτόν;

12 Πάντα οὖν ὅσα ἂν θέλητε
ἵνα ποιῶσιν ὑμῖν οἱ ἄνθρωποι, οὕτω
κỳ ὑμεῖς ποιεῖτε αὐτοῖς· οὗτⒶ
γάρ ἐστιν ὁ νόμⒼ κỳ οἱ προφῆται.

CAPUT VII.

1 NE judicate, ut non judi-
cemini.

2 In quo enim judicio judica-
veritis, judicabimini : & in
qua mensurâ mensi fueritis, remetietur vobis.

38 Date, & dabitur vobis :
Mensuram bonam, confertam,
& coagitatam, & super fluen-
tem dabunt in sinum vestrum :

3 Quid autem intueris festucam
quæ in oculo fratris tui, at in tuo
oculo trabem non animadvertis?

4 Aut quomodo dices fratri
tuo : Sine ejiciam festucam de
oculo tuo, & ecce trabs in oculo
tuo ?

5 Hypocrita, ejice primùm
trabem de oculo tuo, & tunc
intueberis ejicere festucam de
oculo fratris tui.

6 Ne detis sanctum canibus,
neque mittatis margaritas vestras ante porcos, ne forte con-
culcent eas in pedibus suis, &
conversi dirumpant vos.

7 Petite, & dabitur vobis :
quærite, & invenietis : pulsate,
& aperietur vobis.

8 Omnis enim patens acci-
pit : & quærens invenit, &
pulsanti aperietur.

9 Aut quis est ex vobis homo,
quem si petierit filius suus
panem, nunquid lapidem dabit ei ?

10 Et si piscem petierit, nunquid serpentem dabit ei ?

11 Si ergo vos mali existen-
tes, nôstis data bona dare filiis
vestris, quanto magis Pater vester qui in cælis, dabit bona petentibus se ?

12 Omnia ergo quæcumque
vultis ut faciant vobis homines,
ita & vos facite illis. Hæc enim
est Lex & Prophetæ.

[158]

CHAPITRE VII.
Fin du Sermon sur la Montagne.

NE jugez point, afin que vous ne soyez point jugés.

2. Car on vous jugera du même jugement que vous aurez jugé ; et on vous mesurera de la même mesure que vous aurez mesuré *les autres.*

38. Donnez, et on vous donnera ; on vous donnera dans le sein une bonne mesure, pressée et secouée, et qui se répandra par-dessus ;

5. Et pourquoi regardes-tu une paille qui *est* dans l'œil de ton frère ; tandis que tu ne vois pas une poutre qui *est* dans ton œil ?

4. Ou comment dis - tu à ton frère, ne mets que j'ôte cette paille de ton œil, toi qui a une poutre dans le tien ?

5. Hypocrite, ôte premièrement de ton œil la poutre, et alors tu penseras à ôter la paille hors de l'œil de ton frère.

6. Ne donnez point les choses saintes aux chiens, et ne jetez point vos perles devant les pourceaux ; de peur qu'ils ne les foulent à leurs pieds, et que se tournant ils ne vous déchirent.

7. Demandez, et on vous donnera ; cherchez, et vous trouverez ; heurtez, et on vous ouvrira.

8. Car quiconque demande, reçoit ; et qui cherche, trouve ; et l'on ouvre à celui qui heurte.

9. Et qui sera même l'homme d'entre vous qui donne une pierre à son fils, s'il lui demande du pain ?

10. Et s'il lui demande du poisson, lui donnera-t-il un serpent ?

11. Si donc, vous., qui êtes mauvais, savez bien donner à vos enfans des bonnes choses, combien plus votre Père qui est dans les cieux, donnera-t-il des biens à ceux qui *les* lui demandent.

12. Toutes les choses que vous voulez que les hommes vous fassent, faites-*les*-leur aussi de même ; car c'est là la Loi et les Prophètes.

JUDGE not, that ye. be not *M. 7.* judged.

2 For with what judgment ye judge, ye shall be judged: and with what measure ye mete, it shall be measured to you again.

38 Give, and it shall be given unto you ; good measure, pressed down, and shaken together, and running over, shall men give into your bosom. *L. 6.*

3 **And why beholdest thou the mote that is in thy brother's eye, but considerest not the beam that is in thine** own eye ? *M. 7.*

4 Or how wilt thou say to thy brother, Let me pull out the mote out of thine eye ; and, behold, a beam *is* in thine own eye ?

5 Thou hypocrite ! first cast out the beam out of thine own eye ; and then shalt thou see clearly to cast out the mote out of thy brother's eye.

6 Give not that which is holy unto the dogs ; neither cast ye your pearls before swine, lest they trample them under their feet, and turn again and rend you.

7 Ask, and it shall be given you ; seek, and ye shall find ; knock, and it shall be opened unto you :

8 For every one that asketh, receiveth ; and he that seeketh, findeth ; and to him that knocketh, it shall be opened.

9 Or what man is there of you, whom if his son ask bread, will he give him a stone ?

10 Or if he ask a fish, will he give him a serpent ?

11 If ye then, being evil, know how to give good gifts unto your children, how much more shall your Father, which is in heaven, give good things to them that ask him ?

12 Therefore all things whatsoever ye would that men should do to you, do ye even so to them : for this is the law and the prophets.

13 Εἰσέλθετε διὰ τῆς ‡ στενῆς πύλης· ὅτι † πλατεῖα ἡ ‡ πύλη, κ̀ † εὐρύχωρG ἡ ‡ ὁδὸς ἡ ‡ ἀπάγουσα εἰς τὴν ‡ ἀπώλειαν, κ̀ πολλοί εἰσιν οἱ εἰσερχόμενοι δι᾽ αὐτῆς·

14 Ὅτι ςενὴ ἡ πύλη, κ̀ τεθλιμμένη ἡ ὁδὸς ἡ ἀπάγουσα εἰς τὴν ζωὴν, κ̀ ὀλίγοι εἰσὶν οἱ εὑρίσκοντες αὐτήν.

15 Προσέχετε δὲ ἀπὸ τῶν ψευδοπροφητῶν, οἵτινες ἔρχονται πρὸς ὑμᾶς ἐν ἐνδύμασι προβάτων, ἔσωθεν δέ εἰσι λύκοι ἅρπαγες.

16 Ἀπὸ τῶν καρπῶν αὐτῶν ἐπιγνώσεσθε αὐτούς. Μήτι συλλέγουσιν ἀπὸ ἀκανθῶν ςαφυλὴν, ἢ ἀπὸ τριβόλων σῦκα;

17 Οὕτω πᾶν δένδρον ἀγαθὸν καρποὺς καλοὺς ποιεῖ· τὸ δὲ σαπρὸν δένδρον καρποὺς πονηροὺς ποιεῖ.

18 Οὐ δύναται δένδρον ἀγαθὸν καρποὺς πονηροὺς ποιεῖν, οὐδὲ δένδρον σαπρὸν καρποὺς καλοὺς ποιεῖν.

19 Πᾶν δένδρον μὴ ποιοῦν καρπὸν καλὸν, ἐκκόπτεται, κ̀ εἰς πῦρ βάλλεται.

20 Ἄραγε ἀπὸ τῶν καρπῶν αὐτῶν ἐπιγνώσεσθε αὐτούς.

35 Ὁ ἀγαθὸς ἄνθρωπG ἐκ τῦ ἀγαθῦ θησαυρῦ τῆς καρδίας ἐκβάλλει τὰ ἀγαθά· κ̀ ὁ πονηρὸς ἄνθρωπG ἐκ τῦ πονηρῦ θησαυρῦ ἐκβάλλει πονηρά.

36 Λέγω δὲ ὑμῖν, ὅτι πᾶν ῥῆμα ἀργὸν, ὃ ἐὰν λαλήσωσιν οἱ ἄνθρωποι, ἀποδώσουσι περὶ αὐτῦ λόγον ἐν ἡμέρᾳ κρίσεως.

37 Ἐκ γὰρ τῶν λόγων σου δικαιωθήσῃ, κ̀ ἐκ τ λόγων σου καταδικασθήσῃ.

24 Πᾶς οὖν ὅςις ἀκούει μου τοὺς λόγους τούτους, κ̀ ποιεῖ αὐτοὺς, ὁμοιώσω αὐτὸν ἀνδρὶ φρονίμῳ, ὅςις ᾠκοδόμησε τὴν οἰκίαν αὐτῦ ἐπὶ τὴν πέτραν·

25 Καὶ κατέβη ἡ βροχὴ, κ̀ ἦλθον οἱ ποταμοὶ, κ̀ ἔπνευσαν οἱ ἄνεμοι, κ̀ προσέπεσον τῇ οἰκίᾳ ἐκείνῃ, κ̀ οὐκ ἔπεσε· τεθεμελίωτο γὰρ ἐπὶ τὴν πέτραν.

13 Intrate per angustam portam, quia lata porta & spatiosa via ducens ad perditionem, & multi sunt ingredientes per eam.

14 Quia angusta porta, & stricta via ducens ad vitam, & pauci sunt invenientes eam.

15 Attendite verò à falsis prophetis, quia veniunt ad vos in indumentis ovium, intrinsecùs autem sunt lupi rapaces.

16 A fructibus eorum agnoscetis eos. Nunquid colligunt à spinis uvam, aut de tribulis ficum?

17 Sic omnis arbor bona fructus bonos facit: at cariosa arbor fructus malos facit.

18 Non potest arbor bona fructus malos facere, neque arbor cariosa fructus pulchros facere.

19 Omnis arbor non faciens fructum pulchrum, exscinditur, & in ignem injicitur.

20 Itaque ex fructibus eorum agnoscetis eos.

35 Bonus homo de bono thesauro cordis ejicit bona: & malus homo de malo thesauro ejicit mala.

36 Dico autem vobis, quòd omne verbum otiosum quod loquuti fuerint homines, reddent de eo rationem in die judicii.

37 Ex enim verbis tuis justificaberis, & ex verbis tuis condemnaberis.

24 Omnis ergo quicunque audit mea verba hæc, & facit ea, assimilabo illum viro prudenti, qui ædificavit domum suam super petram.

25 Et descendit pluvia & venerunt flumina & flaverunt venti, & procuberunt domui illi, & non cecidit: fundata erat enim super petram.

13 Enter ye in at the strait gate; for wide *is* the gate, and broad *is* the way, that leadeth to destruction, and many there be which go in thereat:

14 Because strait *is* the gate, and narrow *is* the way, which leadeth unto life, and few there be that find it.

15 Beware of false prophets, which come to you in sheep's clothing, but inwardly they are ravening wolves.

16 Ye shall know them by their fruits. Do men gather grapes of thorns, or figs of thistles?

17 Even so, every good tree bringeth forth good fruit; but a corrupt tree bringeth forth evil fruit.

18 A good tree cannot bring forth evil fruit, neither *can* a corrupt tree bring forth good fruit.

19 Every tree that bringeth not forth good fruit is hewn down, and cast into the fire.

20 Wherefore by their fruits ye shall know them.

35 A good man, out of the good treasure of the heart, bringeth forth good things: and an evil man, out of the evil treasure, bringeth forth evil things.

36 But I say unto you, That every idle word that men shall speak, they shall give account thereof in the day of judgment.

37 For by thy words thou shalt be justified, and by thy words thou shalt be condemned.

24 Therefore whosoever heareth these sayings of mine, and doeth them, I will liken him unto a wise man, which built his house upon a rock:

25 And the rain descended, and the floods came, and the winds blew, and beat upon that house; and it fell not: for it was founded upon a rock.

13. Entrez par la porte étroite ; car la porte large et le chemin spacieux mènent à la perdition, et il y en a beaucoup qui y entrent.

14. Mais la porte étroite, et le chemin étroit mènent à la vie, et il y en a peu qui le trouvent.

15. Gardez-vous des faux Prophètes, qui viennent à vous en habits de brebis, mais qui au dedans sont des loups ravissans.

16. Vous les reconnoîtrez à leurs fruits : Cueille-t-on des raisins sur des épines, ou des figues sur des chardons ?

17. Ainsi tout arbre *qui est* bon porte de bons fruits ; mais un mauvais arbre porte de mauvais fruits.

18. Un bon arbre ne peut porter de mauvais fruits, ni un mauvais arbre porter de bons fruits.

19. Tout arbre qui ne porte point de bons fruits, est coupé et jeté au feu.

20. Vous les connoîtrez donc à leurs fruits.

21. Ceux qui me disent : Seigneur, Seigneur, n'entreront pas tous au Royaume des cieux ; mais celui-là seulement qui fait la volonté de mon Père qui *est* dans les cieux.

22. Plusieurs me diront en ce jour-là : Seigneur, Seigneur, n'avons-nous pas prophétisé en ton nom ? N'avons-nous pas chassé les Démons en ton nom ? Et n'avons-nous pas fait plusieurs miracles en ton nom ?

23. Alors, je leur dirai ouvertement : Je ne vous ai jamais connus : Retirez-vous de moi, vous qui faites métier d'iniquité.

24. Quiconque donc entend ces paroles que je dis, et les met en pratique, je le comparerai à un homme prudent, qui a bâti sa maison sur le roc.

25. Et la pluie est tombée, les torrens se sont débordés, et les vents ont soufflé, et sont venus fondre sur cette maison-là ; elle n'est point tombée, car elle étoit fondée sur le roc.

26 Καὶ πᾶς ὁ ἀκούων μου τοὺς λόγους τούτους, ᾗ μὴ ποιῶν αὐτοὺς ὁμοιωθήσεται ἀνδρὶ μωρῷ, ὅστις ᾠκοδόμησε τὴν οἰκίαν αὐτοῦ ἐπὶ τὴν ἄμμον·	26 Et omnis audiens mea verba hæc, & non faciens ea, affimilabitur viro ftulto, qui ædificavit domum fuam fuper arenam :
* 27 Καὶ ‡ κατέβη ἡ ‡ βροχὴ, ᾗ ἦλθον οἱ ποταμοὶ, ᾗ ‡ ἔπνευσαν οἱ ‡ ἄνεμοι, ᾗ ‡ προσέκοψαν τῇ ‡ οἰκίᾳ ἐκείνῃ ᾗ ἔπεσε, ᾗ ἦν ἡ ‡ πτῶσις αὐτῆς μεγάλη.	27 Et defcendit pluvia, & venerunt flumina, & flaverunt venti, & proruerant domui illi, & cecidit, & fuit cafus illius magnus.
28 Καὶ ἐγένετο ὅτε συνετέλεσεν ὁ Ἰησοῦς τοὺς λόγους τούτους, ἐξεπλήσσοντο οἱ ὄχλοι ἐπὶ τῇ διδαχῇ αὐτοῦ·	28 Et factum eft, quum confummaffet Jefus fermones hos, ftupebant illum turbæ fuper doctrina ejus.
29 Ἦν γὰρ διδάσκων αὐτοὺς ὡς ἐξουσίαν ἔχων, ᾗ οὐχ ὡς οἱ γραμματεῖς. 22. † 2.	29 Erat enim docens eos ut auctoritatem habens, & non ficut Scribæ.
Κεφ. η. 8.	**CAPUT VIII.**
1 ΚΑταβάντι δὲ αὐτῷ ἀπὸ τοῦ ὄρους, ἠκολούθησαν αὐτῷ ὄχλοι πολλοί.	1 DEfcendente autem eo de monte, fecutæ funt eum turbæ multæ.
Καὶ περιῆγε τὰς κώμας κύκλῳ, διδάσκων.	& circuibat vicos in orbem, docens.
28 Δεῦτε πρός με πάντες οἱ κοπιῶντες ᾗ πεφορτισμένοι, κἀγὼ ἀναπαύσω ὑμᾶς.	28 Venite ad me omnes laborantes, & onerati, & ego recreabo vos.
* 29 ‡ Ἄρατε τὸν ‡ ζυγόν μου ἐφ᾽ ὑμᾶς, ᾗ ‡ μάθετε ἀπ᾽ ἐμοῦ, ὅτι † πρᾷός ‡ εἰμι, ᾗ ‡ ταπεινὸς τῇ καρδίᾳ ᾗ εὑρήσετε ‡ ἀνάπαυσιν ταῖς ‡ ψυχαῖς ὑμῶν.	29 Tollite jugum meum fuper vos, & difcite à me, quia mitis fum, & humilis corde : & invenietis requiem animabus veftris.
30 Ὁ γὰρ ζυγός μου χρηστός, ᾗ τὸ φορτίον μου ἐλαφρόν ἐστιν. 20. † 2.	30 Nam jugum meum blandum, & onus meum leve eft.
36 Ἠρώτα δὲ τις αὐτὸν τῶν Φαρισαίων ἵνα φάγῃ μετ᾽ αὐτοῦ· ᾗ εἰσελθὼν εἰς τὸν οἶκιαν τοῦ Φαρισαίου, ἀνεκλίθη.	36 Rogabat autem quidam illum Pharifæorum, ut manducaret cum illo : Et ingreffus in domum Pharifæi, difcubuit.
37 Καὶ ἰδοῦ, γυνὴ ἐν τῇ πόλει, ἥτις ἦν ἁμαρτωλὸς, ἐπιγνοῦσα ὅτι ἀνάκειται ἐν τῇ οἰκίᾳ τοῦ Φαρισαίου, κομίσασα ἀλάβαστρον μύρου.	37 Et ecce mulier in civitate, quæ erat peccatrix, cognofcens quod accubuit in domo Pharifæi, afferens alabaftrum unguenti :
38 Καὶ στᾶσα παρὰ τοὺς πόδας αὐτοῦ ὀπίσω, κλαίουσα, ἤρξατο βρέχειν τοὺς πόδας αὐτοῦ τοῖς δάκρυσιν ᾗ ταῖς θριξὶ τῆς κεφαλῆς αὐτῆς ἐξέμασσε, ᾗ κατεφίλει τοὺς πόδας αὐτοῦ, ᾗ ἤλειφε τῷ μύρῳ.	38 Et ftans fecus pedes ejus retro, flens, cœpit rigare pedes ejus lachrymis, & capillis capitis fui extergebat. & ofculabatur pedes ejus, & ungebat unguento.

26. Mais quiconque entend ces paroles que je dis, et ne les met pas en pratique, sera comparé à un homme insensé, qui a bâti sa maison sur le sable.

27. Et la pluie est tombée, les torrens se sont débordés, et les vents ont soufflé, et sont venus fondre sur cette maison-là; elle *est* tombée, et sa ruine a été grande.

28. Et quand JESUS eut achevé ces discours, le peuple fut étonné de sa doctrine.

29. Car il les enseignoit comme ayant autorité, et non pas comme les Scribes.

QUAND *Jésus* fut descendu de la montagne; une grande multitude de peuple le suivit,

..... et il parcourut les bourgades des environs, en enseignant.

28. Venez à moi, vous tous qui êtes travaillés et chargés, et je vous soulagerai.

29. Chargez-vous de mon joug, et apprenez de moi, que je suis doux et humble de cœur, et vous trouverez le repos de vos âmes;

30. Car mon joug est aisé, et mon fardeau est léger.

36. Un Pharisien ayant prié *Jésus* de manger chez lui, il entra dans la maison du Pharisien, et il se mit à table.

37. Et une femme de la ville, qui avoit été de mauvaise vie, ayant su qu'il étoit à table dans la maison du Pharisien, elle y apporta un vase d'albâtre plein d'une huile odoriférante.

38. Et se tenant derrière, aux pieds de *Jésus*, elle se mit à pleurer; elle lui arrosoit les pieds de ses larmes, et les essuyoit avec ses cheveux; elle lui baisoit les pieds, et elle les oignoit avec cette huile.

26 And every one that heareth *M. 7.* these sayings of mine, and doeth them not, shall be likened unto a foolish man, which built his house upon the sand:

27 And the rain descended, and the floods came, and the winds blew, and beat upon that house; and it fell, and great was the fall of it.

28 And it came to pass when Jesus had ended these sayings, the people were astonished at his doctrine:

29 For he taught them as *one* having authority, and not as the scribes.

WHEN he was come down *M. 8* from the mountain, great multitudes followed him.

6. And he went round *Mc. 6.* about the villages, teaching.

28 Come unto me, all *ye* that la-*M. 11.* bour and are heavy laden, and I will give you rest.

29 Take my yoke upon you, and learn of me; for I am meek and lowly in heart: and ye shall find rest unto your souls.

30 For my yoke *is* easy, and my burden is light.

36 And one of the Pharisees de-*L. 7.* sired him that he would eat with him. And he went into the Pharisee's house, and sat down to meat.

37 And, behold, a woman in the city, which was a sinner, when she knew that *Jesus* sat at meat in the Pharisee's house, brought an alabaster box of ointment,

38 And stood at his feet behind *him* weeping, and began to wash his feet with tears, and did wipe *them* with the hairs of her head, and kissed his feet, and anointed *them* with the ointment.

<table>
<tr><td>

39 Ἰδὼν δὲ ὁ Φαρισαῖος ὁ καλέσας αὐτὸν, εἶπεν ἐν ἑαυτῷ, λέγων· Οὗτ⊙, εἰ ἦν προφήτης, ἐγίνωσκεν ἂν τίς κ̀ ποταπὴ ἡ γυνὴ ἥτις ἅπθεlαι αὐτῆ ὅτι ἁμαρθωλός ἐςι.

40 Καὶ ἀποκριθεὶς ὁ Ἰησῦς, εἶπε πρὸς αὐτόν· Σίμων, ἔχω σοι τὶ εἰπεῖν. Ὁ δὲ φησι Διδάσκαλε, εἰπέ.

* 41 Δύο ‡ χρεωφειλέται ἦσαν † δανειςῇ τινὶ· ὁ εἷς ‡ ὤφειλε δηνάρια ‡ πενlακόσια, ὁ δὲ ‡ ἕτερ⊙· ‡ πεντήκονlα.

42 Μὴ ἐχόνlων δὲ αὐτῶν ἀποδῦναι, ἀμφοτέροις ἐχαρίσαlο· Τίς ἂν αὐτῶν, εἰπὲ, πλεῖον αὐτὸν ἀγαπήσει;

43 Ἀποκριθεὶς δὲ ὁ Σίμων, εἶπεν· Ὑπολαμβάνω ὅτι ᾧ τὸ πλεῖον ἐχαρίσαlο. Ὁ δὲ εἶπεν αὐτῷ· Ὀρθῶς ἔκρινας.

44 Καὶ ςραφεὶς πρὸς τὴν γυναῖκα, τῷ Σίμωνι ἔφη· Βλέπεις ταύτην τὴν γυναῖκα; εἰσῆλθόν σε εἰς τὴν οἰκίαν, ὕδωρ ἐπὶ τὰς πόδας μου οὐκ ἔδωκας· αὕτη δὲ τοῖς δάκρυσιν ἔβρεξέ μου τὰς πόδας, κ̀ ταῖς θριξὶ τῆς κεφαλῆς αὐτῆς ἐξέμαξε.

* 45 ‡ Φίλημά μοι οὐκ ἔδωκας· αὕτη δὲ ἀφ' ἧς εἰσῆλθον, ὀ † διέλιπε ‡ καlαφιλῦσά μου τὰς ‡ πόδας.

46 Ἐλαίῳ τὴν κεφαλήν μου οὐκ ἤλειψας· αὕτη δὲ μύρῳ ἤλειψέ μου τοὺς πόδας.

31 Ἔρχονlαι ἂν οἱ ἀδελφοὶ κ̀ ἡ μήτηρ αὐτῆ κ̀ ἔξω ἑςῶτες ἀπέςειλαν πρὸς αὐτὸν, φωνοῦνlες αὐτόν.

32 Καὶ ἐκάθηlο ὄχλ⊙ περὶ αὐτόν· εἶπον δὲ αὐτῷ· Ἰδὺ, ἡ μήτηρ σου κ̀ οἱ ἀδελφοί σου ἔξω ζηlῦσί σε.

33 Καὶ ἀπεκρίθη αὐτοῖς, λέγων· Τίς ἐςιν ἡ μήτηρ μου, ἢ οἱ ἀδελφοί μου;

34 Καὶ περιειλεψάμεν⊙ κύκλῳ τὰς περὶ αὐτὸν καθημένους, λέγει· Ἴδε ἡ μήτηρ μου κ̀ οἱ ἀδελφοί μου.

35 Ὃς γὰρ ἂν ποιήσῃ τὸ θέλημα τῦ Θεῦ, ὗτος ἀδελφός μου κ̀ ἀδελφή μου κ̀ μήτηρ ἐςί. 4. †. 1.

</td><td>

39 Videns autem Pharisæus vocans eum, ait in seipso, dicens: Hic si esset Propheta, sciret utique quæ & qualis mulier, quæ tangit eum, quia peccatrix est.

40 Et respondens Jesus, dixit ad illum: Simon, habeo tibi aliquid dicere. Is vero ait: Magister, dic.

41 Duo debitores erant fœneratori cuidam: unus debebat denarios quingentos, at alter quinquaginta.

42 Non habentibus autem illis reddere, ambobus donavit: Quis ergo eorum, dic, plus eum diliget?

43 Respondens autem Simon, ait: Subsumo quod cui plus donavit. Ille autem dixit ei: Recte judicasti.

44 Et conversus ad mulierem, Simoni dixit: Vides hanc mulierem? Intravi tuam in domum, aquam ad pedes meos non dedisti: hæc autem lacrymis rigavit meos pedes, & capillis capitis sui extersit.

45 Osculum mihi non dedisti: hæc autem, ex quo intravi, non cessavit osculans meos pedes.

46 Oleo caput meum non unxisti: hæc autem unguento unxit meos pedes.

31 Veniunt igitur fratres & mater ejus: & foris stantes, miserunt ad eum, vocantes eum.

32 Et sedebat turba circum eum: dicebant verò ei: Ecce mater tua, & fratres tui, foris quærunt te.

33 Et respondit eis, dicens: Quæ est mater mea, aut fratres mei?

34 Et circumspiciens circulo circa se sedentes, ait: Ecce mater mea, & fratres mei.

35 Qui enim fecerit voluntatem Dei, hic frater meus, & soror mea, & mater est.

</td></tr>
</table>

39. Le Pharisien qui l'avoit convié, voyant cela, dit en lui-même : Si cet homme étoit Prophète, il sauroit sans doute qui est cette femme qui le touche, et qu'elle est de mauvaise vie.

40. Alors Jésus prenant la parole, lui dit : Simon, j'ai quelque chose à te dire : et il dit : Maître, dis-la.

41. Un créancier avoit deux débiteurs, *dont* l'un lui devoit cinq cents deniers, et l'autre cinquante.

42. Et comme ils n'avoient pas de quoi payer, il leur quitta à tous deux leur dette. Dis-moi donc lequel des deux l'aimera le plus ?

43. Simon lui répondit : J'estime que c'est celui à qui il a le plus quitté. *Jésus* lui dit : Tu as fort bien jugé.

44. Alors se tournant vers la femme, il dit à Simon : Vois-tu cette femme ? Je suis entré dans ta maison, et tu ne m'as point donné d'eau pour *me laver* les pieds ; mais elle a arrosé mes pieds de larmes, et les a essuyés avec ses cheveux.

45. Tu ne m'as point donné de baiser ; mais elle, depuis qu'elle est entrée, n'a cessé de me baiser les pieds.

46. Tu n'as point oint ma tête d'huile ; mais elle a oint mes pieds d'une huile odoriférante.

31. Ses frères et sa mère arrivèrent donc ; et se tenant dehors, ils l'envoyèrent appeler ; et la multitude étoit assise autour de lui.

32. Et on lui dit : Voilà ta mère et tes frères sont là dehors *qui* te demandent.

33. Mais il répondit : Qui est ma mère, ou qui sont mes frères ?

34. En jetant les yeux sur ceux qui étoient autour de lui, il dit : Voilà ma mère et mes frères.

35. Car, quiconque fera la volonté de Dieu, celui-là est mon frère, et ma sœur, et ma mère.

39 Now, when the Pharisee which had bidden him saw *it*, he spake within himself, saying, This man, if he were a prophet, would have known who and what manner of woman *this is* that toucheth him; for she is a sinner.

40 And Jesus, answering, said unto him, Simon, I have somewhat to say unto thee. And he saith, Master, say on.

41 There was a certain creditor, which had two debtors : the one owed five hundred pence, and the other fifty.

42 And when they had nothing to pay, he frankly forgave them both. Tell me, therefore, which of them will love him most ?

43 Simon answered, and said, I suppose that *he* to whom he forgave most. And he said unto him, Thou hast rightly judged.

44 And he turned to the woman, and said unto Simon, Seest thou this woman ? I entered into thine house, thou gavest me no water for my feet : but she hath washed my feet with tears, and wiped *them* with the hairs of her head.

45 Thou gavest me no kiss : but this woman, since the time I came in, hath not ceased to kiss my feet.

46 My head with oil thou didst not anoint : but this woman hath anointed my feet with ointment.

31 There came then his brethren and his mother, and, standing without, sent unto him, calling him.

32 And the multitude sat about him, and they said unto him, Behold, thy mother and thy brethren without seek for thee.

33 And he answered them, saying, Who is my mother, or my brethren ?

34 And he looked round about on them which sat about him, and said, Behold my mother and my brethren !

35 For whosoever shall do the will of God, the same is my brother, and my sister, and mother.

Κεφ. ιβ´. ιβ.

CAPUT XII.

1 ἘΝ οἷς ἐπισυναχθεισῶν τῶν μυριάδων τῦ ὄχλυ, ὥςε καταπατεῖν ἀλλήλυς, ἤρξατο λέγειν πρὸς τὸς μαθητὰς αὐτῦ· Πρῶτον προσέχετε ἑαυτοῖς ἀπὸ τῆς ζύμης τῶν φαρισαίων, ἥτις ἐςὶν ὑπόκρισις.

* 2 Οὐδὲν δὲ † συγκεκαλυμμένον ἐςὶν ὃ οὐκ ἀποκαλυφθήσεται· ἠ κρυπτὸν, ὃ οὐ γνωσθήσεται.

3 Ἀνθ' ὧν ὅσα ἐν τῇ σκοτίᾳ εἴπατε, ἐν τῷ φωτὶ ἀκυσθήσεται· ἠ ὃ πρὸς τὸ ὖς ἐλαλήσατε ἐν τοῖς ταμείοις, κηρυχθήσεται ἐπὶ τῶν δωμάτων.

4 Λέγω δὲ ὑμῖν τοῖς φίλοις μυ· Μὴ φοβηθῆτε ἀπὸ τῶν ἀποκτεινόντων τὸ σῶμα, ἠ μετὰ ταῦτα μὴ ἐχόντων περισσότερόν τι ποιῆσαι.

* 5 ‡ Ὑποδείξω δὲ ὑμῖν τίνα ‡ φοβηθῆτε· φοβήθητε τὸν μετὰ τὸ ‡ ἀποκτεῖναι, ‡ ἐξυσίαν ἔχοντα † ἐμβαλεῖν εἰς τὴν γέενναν· ναὶ λέγω ὑμῖν, τῦτον φοβήθητε.

6 Οὐχὶ πέντε ςρυθία πωλεῖται ἀσσαρίων δύο, ἠ ἓν ἐξ αὐτῶν οὐκ ἔςιν ἐπιλελησμένον ἐνώπιον τῦ Θεῦ;

* 7 Ἀλλὰ ἠ αἱ ‡ τρίχες τῆς κεφαλῆς ὑμῶν πᾶσαι ‡ ἠρίθμηνται· μὴ ὖν φοβεῖσθε· πολλῶν ςρυθίων ‡ διαφέρετε.

13 Εἶπε δὲ τις αὐτῷ ἐκ τῦ ὄχλυ· Διδάσκαλε, εἰπὲ τῷ ἀδελφῷ μυ μερίσασθαι μετ' ἐμῦ τὴν κληρονομίαν.

* 14 Ὁ δὲ εἶπεν αὐτῷ· Ἄνθρωπε, τίς με ‡ κατέςησε ‡ δικαςὴν ἢ † μεριςὴν ἐφ' ὑμᾶς;

15 Εἶπε δὲ πρὸς αὐτύς· Ὁρᾶτε ἠ φυλάσσεσθε ἀπὸ τῆς πλεονεξίας· ὅτι οὐκ ἐν τῷ περισσεύειν τινὶ ἡ ζωὴ αὐτῦ ἐςιν ἐκ τῶν ὑπαρχόντων αὐτῦ.

* 16 Εἶπε δὲ παραβολὴν πρὸς αὐτύς, λέγων· Ἀνθρώπυ τινὸς πλυσίυ † εὐφόρησεν ἡ χώρα·

---

1 IN quibus adcongregatis myriadibus turbæ, ut conculcarent alii alios, cœpit dicere ad discipulos suos primum: Attendite vobis-ipsis à fermento Pharisæorum, quod est hypocrisis.

2 Nihil enim coopertum est, quod non reveletur: & absconditum, quod non sciatur.

3 Propter quæ quæ in tenebris dixistis, in lumine audientur: & quod ad aurem loquuti estis in cubiculis, prædicabitur supra domos.

4 Dico autem vobis amicis meis: Ne timeatis ab occidentibus corpus, & post hæc non habentibus abundantiùs quid facere.

5 Ostendam autem vobis quem timeatis: timete illum post occidere, auctoritatem habentem injicere in gehennam: ita dico vobis, hunc timete.

6 Nonne quinque passeres væneunt assariis duobus, & unus ex illis non est in oblivione coram Deo.

7 Sed & capilli capitis vestri omnes numerati sunt, ne ergo timete; multis passeribus præstatis vos.

13 Ait autem quidam ei de turba: Magister, dic fratri meo partiri cum me hæreditatem.

14 Ille autem dixit ei: Homo, Quis me constituit judicem aut divisorem super vos?

15 Dixit autem ad illos: Videte & cavete ab avaritia: quia non in redundare cuiquam vita ejus est ex substantia ipsius.

16 Dixit autem similitudinem ad illos, dicens: Hominis cujusdam divitis bene tulit regio.

CHAPITRE XII.

Jésus-Christ instruit ses Disciples de se garder d'hypocrisie, de l'avarice; de veiller et d'être prêts à la réconciliation.

CEPENDANT le peuple s'étant assemblé par milliers; en sorte qu'ils se pressoient les uns les autres, il se mit à dire à ses Disciples: Gardez-vous sur toutes choses du levain des Pharisiens, qui est l'hypocrisie.

2. Car il n'y a rien de caché qui ne doive être découvert; ni rien de secret qui ne doive être connu.

3. Les choses donc que vous aurez dites dans les ténèbres, seront entendues dans la lumière; et ce que vous aurez dit à l'oreille dans les chambres, sera prêché sur les maisons.

4. Je vous dis donc, à vous qui êtes mes amis: Ne craignez point ceux qui tuent le corps, et qui après cela ne peuvent rien faire de plus.

5. Mais je vous montrerai qui vous devez craindre; craignez celui qui, après avoir ôté la vie, a le pouvoir d'envoyer dans la géhenne; oui, je vous le dis; c'est celui-là que vous devez craindre!

6. Ne vend-on pas cinq petits passeraux deux pites? Cependant Dieu n'en oublie pas un seul.

7. Et même tous les cheveux de votre tête sont comptés, ne craignez donc point, vous valez plus que beaucoup de passeraux.

13. Alors quelqu'un de la troupe lui dit: Maître, dis à mon frere qu'il partage avec moi notre héritage.

14. Mais *Jésus* lui *répondit:* O homme! qui est-ce qui m'a établi pour être votre Juge, ou pour faire vos partages?

15. Puis il leur dit: Gardez-vous avec soin de l'avarice; car quoique *les biens* abondent à quelqu'un, il n'a pas la vie par ses biens.

16. Il leur proposa *là-dessus* cette parabole: Les terres d'un homme riche avoient rapporté avec abondance;

IN the mean time, when there were gathered together an innumerable multitude of people, insomuch that they trode one upon another, he began to say unto his disciples first of all, Beware ye of the leaven of the Pharisees, which is hypocrisy.

2 For there is nothing covered, that shall not be revealed; neither hid, that shall not be known.

3 Therefore whatsoever ye have spoken in darkness, shall be heard in the light; and that which ye have spoken in the ear in closets, shall be proclaimed upon the house-tops.

4 And I say unto you, my friends, Be not afraid of them that kill the body, and after that have no more that they can do.

5 But I will forewarn you whom ye shall fear: Fear him, which, after he hath killed, hath power to cast into hell; yea, I say unto you, Fear him.

6 Are not five sparrows sold for two farthings? and not one of them is forgotten before God.

7 But even the very hairs of your head are all numbered. Fear not, therefore; ye are of more value than many sparrows.

13 And one of the company said unto him, Master, speak to my brother, that he divide the inheritance with me.

14 And he said unto him, Man, who made me a judge, or a divider over you?

15 And he said unto them, Take heed, and beware of covetousness; for a man's life consisteth not in the abundance of the things which he possesseth.

16 And he spake a parable unto them, saying, The ground of a certain rich man brought forth plentifully.

17 Καὶ διελογίζετο ἐν ἑαυτῷ, λέγων· Τί ποιήσω; ὅτι οὐκ ἔχω ποῦ συνάξω τοὺς καρπούς μου.

18 Καὶ εἶπε· Τοῦτο ποιήσω· καθελῶ μου τὰς ἀποθήκας, καὶ μείζονας οἰκοδομήσω· καὶ συνάξω ἐκεῖ πάντα τὰ γενήματά μου, καὶ τὰ ἀγαθά μου.

19 Καὶ ἐρῶ τῇ ψυχῇ μου· Ψυχή, ἔχεις πολλὰ ἀγαθὰ κείμενα εἰς ἔτη πολλά· ἀναπαύου, φάγε, πίε, εὐφραίνου.

* 20 Εἶπε δὲ αὐτῷ ὁ Θεός· ‡ Ἄφρον, ταύτῃ τῇ νυκτὶ τὴν ψυχήν σου ‡ ἀπαιτοῦσιν ἀπὸ σοῦ· ἃ δὲ ἡτοίμασας, τίνι ἔσται;

21 Οὕτως ὁ θησαυρίζων ἑαυτῷ, καὶ μὴ εἰς Θεὸν πλουτῶν.

22 Εἶπε δὲ πρὸς τοὺς μαθητὰς αὐτοῦ· Διὰ τοῦτο ὑμῖν λέγω, μὴ μεριμνᾶτε τῇ ψυχῇ ὑμῶν, τί φάγητε· μηδὲ τῷ σώματι, τί ἐνδύσησθε.

23 Ἡ ψυχὴ πλεῖόν ἐστι τῆς τροφῆς, καὶ τὸ σῶμα τοῦ ἐνδύματος.

* 24 ‡ Κατανοήσατε τοὺς † κόρακας, ὅτι οὐ ‡ σπείρουσιν, οὐδὲ ‡ θερίζουσιν· οἷς οὐκ ἔστι ‡ ταμεῖον, οὐδὲ ἀποθήκη, καὶ ὁ Θεὸς τρέφει αὐτούς· πόσῳ μᾶλλον ὑμεῖς διαφέρετε τῶν πετεινῶν;

25 Τίς δὲ ἐξ ὑμῶν μεριμνῶν δύναται προσθεῖναι ἐπὶ τὴν ἡλικίαν αὐτοῦ πῆχυν ἕνα;

26 Εἰ οὖν οὔτε ἐλάχιστον δύνασθε, τί περὶ τῶν λοιπῶν μεριμνᾶτε;

27 Κατανοήσατε τὰ κρίνα, πῶς αὐξάνει· οὐ κοπιᾷ, οὐδὲ νήθει· λέγω δὲ ὑμῖν, οὐδὲ Σολομὼν ἐν πάσῃ τῇ δόξῃ αὐτοῦ περιεβάλετο ὡς ἓν τούτων.

28 Εἰ δὲ τὸν χόρτον ἐν τῷ ἀγρῷ σήμερον ὄντα, καὶ αὔριον εἰς κλίβανον βαλλόμενον, ὁ Θεὸς οὕτως ἀμφιέννυσι, πόσῳ μᾶλλον ὑμᾶς, ὀλιγόπιστοι;

* 29 Καὶ ὑμεῖς μὴ ζητεῖτε τί φάγητε, ἢ τί πίητε, καὶ μὴ † μετεωρίζεσθε.

30 Ταῦτα γὰρ πάντα, τὰ ἔθνη τοῦ κόσμου ἐπιζητεῖ· ὑμῶν δὲ ὁ πατὴρ οἶδεν ὅτι χρῄζετε τούτων.

---

17 Et ratiocinabatur in seipso, dicens: Quid faciam? quia non habeo quo congregabo fructus meos?

18 Et dixit: Hoc faciam: Destruam mea horrea, & majora ædificabo, & congregabo illuc omnia nata mea, & bona mea.

19 Et dicam animæ meæ: Anima, habes multa bona posita in annos plurimos, requiesce, comede, bibe, oblectare.

20 Dixit autem illi Deus: Stulte, hac nocte animam tuam repetunt à te: quæ autem parasti, cui erunt?

21 Sic thesaurizans sibi ipsi, & non in Deum ditescens.

22 Dixit autem ad discipulos suos: Propter hoc vobis dico: Ne soliciti sitis animæ vestræ, quid manducetis, neque corpori, quid induamini.

23 Anima plus est alimento, & corpus vestimento.

24 Considerate corvos, quia non seminant, neque metunt, quibus non est cellarium, neque horreum, & Deus alit illos: quanto magis vos præstatis volucribus?

25 Quis autem ex vobis cogitans solicitè potest apponere ad ætatem suam cubitum unum?

26 Si ergo neque minimum potestis, quid de cæteris soliciti estis.

27 Considerate lilia, quomodo crescunt: non laborant, neque nent: Dico autem vobis, Neque Solomon in omni gloria sua circumamiciebatur sicut unum istorum.

28 Si autem fœnum in agro hodie existens, & cras in clibanum missum, Deus sic circumamicit, quanto magis vos exiguæ fidei?

29 Et vos ne quærite quid manducetis, aut quid bibatis, & ne suspendamini ex sublimi.

30 Hæc enim omnia gentes mundi quærunt: vester autem pater scit quoniam indigetis his.

17. Et il disoit en lui-même : Que ferai-je ? Car je n'ai pas assez de place pour serrer toute ma récolte.

18. Voici, dit-il, ce que je ferai ; j'abattrai mes greniers, et j'en bâtirai de plus grands, et j'y amasserai toute ma récolte et tous mes biens.

19. Puis je dirai à mon ame : Mon ame, tu as beaucoup de biens en réserve pour plusieurs années ; repose-toi, mange, bois, et te réjouis.

20. Mais Dieu lui dit : Insensé, cette même nuit ton ame te sera redemandée ; et ce que tu as amassé, pour qui sera-t-il ?

21. Il en est ainsi de celui qui amasse des biens pour soi-même, et qui n'est point riche en Dieu.

22. Alors il dit à ses Disciples : C'est pourquoi je vous dis, ne soyez point en souci pour votre vie, de ce que vous mangerez ; ni pour votre corps, de quoi vous serez vêtus.

23. La vie est plus que la nourriture, et le corps plus que le vêtement.

24. Considérez les corbeaux ; ils ne sèment ni ne moissonnent, et ils n'ont point de cellier ni de grenier, et *toutefois* Dieu les nourrit ; combien ne valez-vous pas plus que des oiseaux ?

25. Et qui de vous peut par ses inquiétudes ajouter une coudée à sa taille ?

26. Si donc vous ne pouvez pas même faire les plus petites choses, pourquoi vous inquiétez-vous du reste ?

27. Considérez comment les lis croissent ; ils ne travaillent ni ne filent ; cependant je vous dis, que Salomon même, dans toute sa gloire, n'a point été vêtu comme l'un d'eux.

28. Que si Dieu revêt ainsi une herbe qui est aujourd'hui dans les champs, et qui sera demain jetée dans le four, combien plus vous *revêtira t-il*, gens de petite foi ?

29. Ne vous mettez donc point en peine de ce que vous mangerez, ou de ce que vous boirez, et n'ayez point l'esprit inquiet.

30. Car ce sont les nations du monde qui recherchent toutes ces choses ; mais votre Père sait que vous en avez besoin.

17 And he thought within himself, saying, What shall I do, because I have no room where to bestow my fruits?

18 And he said, This will I do : I will pull down my barns, and build greater ; and there will I bestow all my fruits and my goods.

19 And I will say to my soul, Soul, thou hast much goods laid up for many years : take thine ease, eat, drink, *and* be merry.

20 But God said unto him, *Thou fool* ! this night thy soul shall be required of thee ; then whose shall those things be, which thou hast provided?

21 So *is* he that layeth up treasure for himself, and is not rich toward God.

22 And he said unto his disciples, Therefore I say unto you, Take no thought for your life, what ye shall eat ; neither for the body, what ye shall put on.

23 The life is more than meat, and the body *is more* than raiment.

24 Consider the ravens : for they neither sow nor reap ; which neither have storehouse nor barn ; and God feedeth them : How much more are ye better than the fowls?

25 And which of you, with taking thought, can add to his stature one cubit?

26 If ye then be not able to do that thing which is least, why take ye thought for the rest?

27 Consider the lilies how they grow : they toil not, they spin not ; and yet I say unto you, That Solomon, in all his glory, was not arrayed like one of these.

28 If then God so clothe the grass, which is to-day in the field, and to-morrow is cast into the oven ; how much more *will he clothe* you? O ye of little faith !

29 And seek not ye what ye shall eat, or what ye shall drink ; neither be ye of doubtful mind.

30 For all these things do the nations of the world seek after : and your Father knoweth that ye have need of these things.

31 Πλὴν ζητεῖτε τὴν βασιλείαν τῦ Θεῦ, ᾧ ταῦτα πάντα προστεθήσεται ὑμῖν.

32 Μὴ φοβῦ, τὸ μικρὸν ποίμνιον· ὅτι εὐδόκησεν ὁ πατὴρ ὑμῶν δῦναι ὑμῖν τὴν βασιλείαν.

* 33 Πωλήσατε τὰ ὑπάρχοντα ὑμῶν, ᾧ δότε ἐλεημοσύνην. Ποιήσατε ἑαυτοῖς ‡ βαλάντια μὴ ‡ παλαιούμενα, θησαυρὸν † ἀνέκλειπτον ἐν τοῖς οὐρανοῖς ὅπε κλέπτης οὐκ ἐγγίζει, οὐδὲ σὴς διαφθείρει.

34 Ὅπε γάρ ἐστιν ὁ θησαυρὸς ὑμῶν, ἐκεῖ ᾧ ἡ καρδία ὑμῶν ἔσται.

35 Ἔστωσαν ὑμῶν αἱ ὀσφύες περιεζωσμέναι, ᾧ οἱ λύχνοι καιόμενοι.

36 Καὶ ὑμεῖς ὅμοιοι ἀνθρώποις προσδεχομένοις τὸν κύριον ἑαυτῶν, πότε ἀναλύσει ἐκ τῶν γάμων· ἵνα ἐλθόντος ᾧ κρούσαντος, εὐθέως ἀνοίξωσιν αὐτῷ.

37 Μακάριοι οἱ δῦλοι ἐκεῖνοι, ὃς ἐλθὼν ὁ κύριος εὑρήσει γρηγορῦντας. ἀμὴν λέγω ὑμῖν, ὅτι περιζώσεται, ᾧ ἀνακλινεῖ αὐτούς, ᾧ παρελθὼν διακονήσει αὐτοῖς.

38 Καὶ ἐὰν ἔλθῃ ἐν τῇ δευτέρᾳ φυλακῇ, ᾧ ἐν τῇ τρίτῃ φυλακῇ ἔλθῃ, ᾧ εὕρῃ ὅτω, μακάριοί εἰσιν οἱ δῦλοι ἐκεῖνοι.

39 Τῦτο δὲ γινώσκετε, ὅτι εἰ ᾔδει ὁ οἰκοδεσπότης ποίᾳ ὥρᾳ ὁ κλέπτης ἔρχεται, ἐγρηγόρησεν ἄν, ᾧ οὐκ ἂν ἀφῆκε διορυγῆναι τὸν οἶκον αὐτῦ.

40 Καὶ ὑμεῖς οὖν γίνεσθε ἕτοιμοι· ὅτι ᾗ ὥρᾳ οὐ δοκεῖτε, ὁ υἱὸς τῦ ἀνθρώπε ἔρχεται.

41 Εἶπε δὲ αὐτῷ ὁ Πέτρος· Κύριε, πρὸς ἡμᾶς τὴν παραβολὴν ταύτην λέγεις, ἢ ᾧ πρὸς πάντας;

* 42 Εἶπε δὲ ὁ Κύριος· Τίς ἄρα ἐστὶν ὁ ‡ πιστὸς ᾧ ‡ οἰκονόμος ᾧ ‡ φρόνιμος, ὃν καταστήσει ὁ κύριος ἐπὶ τῆς ‡ θεραπείας αὐτῦ, τῦ διδόναι ἐν ‡ καιρῷ τὸ ‡ σιτομέτριον;

43 Μακάριος ὁ δῦλος ἐκεῖνος, ὃν ἐλθὼν ὁ κύριος αὐτῦ εὑρήσει ποιῦντα ὅτως.

31 Verumtamen quærite regnum Dei, & hæc omnia adjicientur vobis.

32 Ne time, pusillus grex, quia bene visum est Patri vestro dare vobis regnum.

33 Vendite substantias vestras, & date eleemosynam, facite vobis crumenas non veterascentes, thesaurum non deficientem in cælis, quo fur e appropriat, neque tinea corrumpit.

34 Ubi enim est thesaurus vester, ibi & c r vestrum erit.

35 Sint vestri lumbi præcincti, & lucernæ accensæ:

36 Et vos similes hominibus expectantibus dominum suum, quando revertatur à nuptiis: ut veniente & pulsante, confestim aperiant ei.

37 Beati servi illi, quos veniens dominus invenerit vigilantes. Amen dico vobis, quod succingetur, & faciet discumbere illos, & prodiens ministrabit illis.

38 Et si venerit in secunda vigilia, & in tertia vigilia venerit, & invenerit ita, beati sunt servi illi.

39 Hoc autem scitote, quoniam si sciret paterfamilias qua hora fur veniret, vigilaret utique, & non utique sineret perfodi domum suam.

40 Et vos igitur estote parati: quia qua hora non putatis, filius hominis venit.

41 Ait autem ei Petrus: Domine, ad nos parabolam hanc dicis, an & ad omnes?

42 Dixit autem Dominus: Quisnam est fidelis dispensator & prudens, quem constituit dominus super famulitio suo, ad dandum in tempore tritici mensuram?

43 Beatus servus ille, quem veniens dominus ejus invenerit facientem ita.

31. Mais cherchez plutôt le royaume de Dieu, et toutes ces choses vous seront données par-dessus.

32. Ne crains point, petit troupeau; car il a plu à votre Père de vous donner le Royaume.

33. Vendez ce que vous avez, et *le* donnez *en* aumônes; faites-vous des bourses qui ne s'usent point, un trésor dans les cieux qui ne manque jamais, d'où les voleurs n'approchent point, *et* où la tigne ne gâte rien.

34. Car où est votre trésor, là aussi sera votre cœur.

35. Que vos reins soient ceints, et vos chandelles allumées;

36. Et *soyez* comme ceux qui attendent que leur maître revienne des nôces; afin que quand il viendra et qu'il heurtera *à la porte*, ils lui ouvrent incontinent.

37. Heureux ces serviteurs, que le maître trouvera veillans quand il arrivera! Je vous dis en vérité, qu'il se ceindra, qu'il les fera mettre à table, et qu'il viendra les servir.

38. Que s'il arrive à la seconde, ou à la troisième veille, et qu'il les trouve dans cet état, heureux ces serviteurs-là!

39. Vous savez, que si un père de famille étoit averti à quelle heure un larron doit venir, il veilleroit, et ne laisseroit pas percer sa maison.

40. Vous donc aussi soyez prêts; car le Fils de l'homme viendra à l'heure que vous ne penserez point.

41. Alors Pierre lui dit: Seigneur, est-ce seulement pour nous que tu dis cette parabole, ou est-ce aussi pour tous?

42. Et le Seigneur lui dit: Mais qui est le dispensateur fidèle et prudent, que le maître a établi sur ses domestiques, pour leur donner dans le tems la mesure ordinaire de bled?

43. Heureux *est* ce serviteur-là que son maître trouvera faisant ainsi *son devoir*, quand il arrivera!

31 But rather seek ye the kingdom of God; and all these things shall be added unto you.

32 Fear not, little flock; for it is your Father's good pleasure to give you the kingdom.

33 Sell that ye have, and give alms; provide yourselves bags which wax not old, a treasure in the heavens that faileth not, where no thief approacheth, neither moth corrupteth.

34 For where your treasure is, there will your heart be also.

35 Let your loins be girded about, and your lights burning:

36 And ye yourselves like unto men that wait for their lord, when he will return from the wedding; that when he cometh and knocketh, they may open unto him immediately.

37 Blessed *are* those servants, whom the lord, when he cometh, shall find watching: verily I say unto you, That he shall gird himself, and make them to sit down to meat, and will come forth and serve them.

38 And if he shall come in the second watch, or come in the third watch, and find *them* so, blessed are those servants.

39 And this know, that if the good man of the house had known what hour the thief would come, he would have watched, and not have suffered his house to be broken through.

40 Be ye, therefore, ready also: for the Son of Man cometh at an hour when ye think not.

41 Then Peter said unto him, Lord, speakest thou this parable unto us, or even to all?

42 And the Lord said, Who then is that faithful and wise steward, whom *his* lord shall make ruler over his household, to give *them their* portion of meat in due season?

43 Blessed *is* that servant, whom his lord, when he cometh, shall find so doing.

44 Ἀληθῶς λέγω ὑμῖν, ὅτι ἐπὶ πᾶσι τοῖς ὑπάρχουσιν αὐτοῦ καταςήσει αὐτόν.

45 Ἐὰν δὲ εἴπῃ ὁ δοῦλ۪۬Ꙩ ἐχεῖٷ· ἐν τῇ καρδίᾳ αὐτοῦ ‡ Χρονίζει ὁ κύριός μου ἔρχεσθαι· ᛕ ἄρξηται τύπἸειν τοὺς παῖδας, ᛕ τὰς ‡ παιδίϛκας, ἐσθίειν τε ᛕ πίνειν ᛕ ‡ μεθύσκεσθαι·

* 46 ἥξει ὁ κύρι۪۬Ꙩ τῷ δούλῳ ἐκείνῳ ἐν ἡμέρα ᾗ ᚕ προσδοκᾷ, ᛕ ἐν ὥρᾳ ᾗ ᚕ γινώσκει· ᛕ ‡ διχοτομήσει αὐτὸν, ᛕ τὸ μέ,Ꙩ αὐτοῦ μετὰ τῶν ἀπίϛων θήσει.

47 Ἐκεῖ۪۬Ꙩ δὲ ὁ δῦλ۪۬Ꙩ ὁ γνοὺς τὸ θέλημα τοῦ κυρίου ἑαυτῦ, ᛕ μὴ ἑτοιμάσας, μηδὲ ποιήσας πρὸς τὸ θέλημα αὐτῦ, δαρήσεῖαι πολλάς·

48 Ὁ δὲ μὴ γνοὺς, ποιήσας δὲ ἄξια πληγῶν, δαρήσεται ὀλίγας· παντὶ δὲ ᾧ ἐδόθη πολὺ, πολὺ ζητηθήσεῖαι παρ᾽ αὐτῦ· ᛕ ᾧ παρέθεντο πολὺ, περισσότερον αἰτήσουσιν αὐτόν.

* 54 Ἔλεγε δὲ ᛕ τοῖς ὄχλοις· Ὅταν ἴδητε τὴν νεφέλην ἀνατέλλουσαν ἀπὸ δυσμῶν, εὐθέως λέγετε· † Ὄμβρ۪۬Ꙩ ἔρχεῖαι· ᛕ γίνεῖαι ὕτω.

55 Καὶ ὅταν νότον πνέοντα, λέγεῖε· Ὅτι καύσων ἔςαι· ᛕ γίνεται.

56 ὙποκριΤαὶ, τὸ πρόσωπον τῆς γῆς ᛕ τοῦ ὀρανῦ οἴδαὲ δοκιμάζειν· τὸν δὲ καιρὸν τῦτον πῶς ᚕ δοκιμάζεῖε;

57 Τί δὲ ᛕ ἀφ᾽ ἑαυτῶν ᚕ κρίνεῖε τὸ δίκαιον;

* 58 Ὡς γὰρ ὑπάγεις μετὰ τῦ ἀντιδίκου σου ἐπ᾽ ἄρχοντα, ἐν τῇ ὁδῷ δὸς ἐργασίαν ἀπηλλάχθαι ἀπ᾽ αὐτῦ· ‡ μήποτε ‡ κατασύρῃ σε πρὸς τὸν κριτὴν, ᛕ ὁ κριτής σε παραδῷ τῷ ‡ πράκτορι, ᛕ ὁ πράκτωρ σε βάλλῃ εἰς φυλακήν.

᾽9 Λέγω σοι, οὐ μὴ ἐξέλθῃς ἐκεῖθεν, ἕως ᚕ ᛕ τὸ ἔσχαῖον λεπτὸν ἀποδῷς. 39. † 12.

---

44 Vere dico vobis, quoniam super omnibus subſtantiis ipſius conſtituet illum.

45 Si autem dixerit ſervus ille in corde ſuo : Tardat Dominus meus venire, & cœperit percutere pueros, & ancillas, edereque & bibere & inebriari :

46 Veniet dominus ſervi illius in die qua non exſpectat, & in hora qua non cognoſcit : & diſſecabit eum, & partem ejus cum infidelibus ponet.

47 Ille autem ſervus noſcens voluntatem domini ſui, & non apparans, neque faciens ad voluntatem ejus, cædetur multis.

48 Qui autem non noſcens, faciens autem digna plagis, cædetur paucis : omni autem cui datum eſt multum, multum quæretur ab eo : & cui depoſuerunt multum, abundantiùs repoſcent eum.

54 Dicebat autem & turbis : Quum videritis nubem orientem ab occaſibus, ſtatim dicitis : Imber venit, & fit ita.

55 Et quum Auſtrum flantem, dicitis : quia æſtus erit : & fit.

56 Hypocritæ, faciem cæli & terræ noſtis probare, at tempus hoc quomodo non probatis?

57 Quid autem & à vobis ipſis non judicatis quod juſtum?

58 Quum enim vadis cum adverſario tuo ad principem, in via da operam liberari ab illo : ne forte trahat te ad judicem, & judex te tradat exactori, & exactor jaciat te in carcerem.

59 Dico tibi : Non egredieris illinc, uſquequo etiam noviſſimum minutum reddas.

44. Je vous dis en vérité, qu'il l'établira sur tout ce qu'il a.

45. Mais si ce serviteur dit en lui-même : Mon maître ne viendra pas sitôt ; et qu'il se mette à battre les serviteurs et les servantes, à manger, à boire, et à s'enivrer ;

46. Le maître de ce serviteur viendra au jour qu'il ne s'y attend pas, et à l'heure qu'il ne sait pas ; et il le séparera, et lui donnera sa portion avec les infidèles.

47. Le serviteur qui a connu la volonté de son maître, et qui ne se sera pas tenu prêt, et n'aura pas fait cette volonté, sera battu de plus de coups.

48. Mais celui qui ne l'a point connue, et qui a fait des choses dignes de châtiment, sera battu de moins de coups. Et il sera beaucoup redemandé à quiconque il aura été beaucoup donné ; et on exigera plus de celui à qui on aura beaucoup confié.

54. Puis il disoit au peuple : Quand vous voyez une nuée qui se lève du côté d'Occident, vous dites d'abord, il va pleuvoir ; et cela arrive ainsi.

55. Et quand le vent de Midi souffle, vous dites qu'il fera chaud et cela arrive.

56. Hypocrites, vous savez bien discerner ce qui paroit au ciel et sur la terre ; et comment ne discernez-vous pas ce tems-ci ?

57. Et pourquoi ne discernez-vous pas aussi vous-mêmes ce qui est juste ?

58. Or quand tu vas devant le Magistrat, avec ton adverse partie, tâche en chemin de sortir d'affaire avec elle ; de peur qu'elle ne te tire devant le Juge, que le Juge ne te livre au Sergent, et que le Sergent ne te mette en prison.

59. Je te dis que tu ne sortiras point de là, que tu n'aies payé jusqu'à la dernière obole.

44 Of a truth I say unto you, That he will make him ruler over all that he hath.

45 But, and if that servant say in his heart, My lord delayeth his coming ; and shall begin to beat the men-servants, and maidens, and to eat and drink, and to be drunken ;

46 The lord of that servant will come in a day when he looketh not for *him*, and at an hour when he is not aware, and will cut him in sunder,

47 And that servant, which knew his lord's will, and prepared not *himself*, neither did according to his will, shall be beaten with many *stripes*.

48 But he that knew not, and did commit things worthy of stripes, shall be beaten with few *stripes*. For unto whomsoever much is given, of him shall be much required : and to whom men have committed much, of him they will ask the more.

54 And he said also to the people, When ye see a cloud rise out of the west, straightway ye say, There cometh a shower ; and so it is.

55 And when *ye see* the south wind blow, ye say, There will be heat ; and it cometh to pass.

56 Ye hypocrites ! ye can discern the face of the sky and of the earth ; but how is it, that ye do not discern this time ?

57 Yea, and why even of yourselves judge ye not what is right ?

58 When thou goest with thine adversary to the magistrate, *as thou art* in the way, give diligence that thou mayest be delivered from him ; lest he hale thee to the judge, and the judge deliver thee to the officer, and the officer cast thee into prison.

59 I tell thee, thou shalt not depart thence, till thou hast paid the very last mite.

Κεφ. ιγ΄. 13.

CAPUT XIII.

1 Πᾶρῆσαν δέ τινες ἐν αὐτῷ τῷ καιρῷ ἀπαγγέλλοντες αὐτῷ περὶ τῶν Γαλιλαίων, ὧν τὸ αἷμα Πιλάτ⟨Θ⟩ ἔμιξε μετὰ τῶν θυσιῶν τῶν.

2 Καὶ ἀποκριθεὶς ὁ Ἰησῦς εἶπεν αὐτοῖς· Δοκεῖτε ὅτι οἱ Γαλιλαῖοι ὗτοι ἁμαρτωλοὶ παρὰ πάντας τὺς Γαλιλαίυς ἐγένονῖο, ὅτι τοιαῦτα πεπόνθασιν;

3 Οὐχὶ, λέγω ὑμῖν· ἀλλ᾽ ἐὰν μὴ μετανοῆτε, πάντες ὡσαύτως ἀπολεῖσθε.

4 Ἢ ἐκεῖνοι οἱ δέκα ἠ ὀκτὼ, ἐφ᾽ ὓς ἔπεσεν ὁ πύργ⟨Θ⟩ ἐν τῷ Σιλωὰμ, ἠ ἀπέκλεινεν αὐτὺς, δοκεῖτε ὅτι ὗτοι ὀφειλέται ἐγένονῖο παρὰ πάντας ἀνθρώπυς τὺς κατοικῦνῖας ἐν Ἰερυσαλήμ;

5 Οὐχὶ, λέγω ὑμῖν· ἀλλ᾽ ἐὰν μὴ μετανοῆτε, πάντες ὁμοίως ἀπολεῖσθε.

6 Ἔλεγε δὲ ταύτην τὴν παραβολήν· Συκῆν εἶχέ τις ἐν τῷ ἀμπελῶνι αὐτῦ πεφυῖευμένην· ἠ ἦλθε καρπὸν ζηῖῶν ἐν αὐτῇ, ἠ ὀυχ εὗρεν.

7 Εἶπε δὲ πρὸς τὴν † ἀμπελυργὸν· Ἰδού, τρία ἔτη ἔρχομαι ζηῖῶν καρπὸν ἐν τῇ συκῇ ταύτῃ, ἠ ὀυχ εὑρίσκω· ‡ ἔκκοψον αὐτήν· ‡ ἱνατί ἠ τὴν γῆν ‡ καταργεῖ;

*, 8 Ὁ δὲ ἀποκριθεὶς λέγει αὐτῷ· Κύριε, ἄφις αὐτὴν ἠ τοῦτο τὸ ἔτ⟨Θ⟩, ἕως ὅτυ σκάψω περὶ αὐτὴν, ἠ βάλω ‡ κοπρίαν·

9 Κἂν μὲν ποιήσῃ καρπόν· εἰ δὲ μήγε, εἰς τὸ μέλλον ἐκκόψεις αὐτήν.

37 Ἐν δὲ τῷ λαλῆσαι, ἠρώτα αὐτὸν φαρισαῖός τις ὅπως ἀρισῄσῃ παρ᾽ αὐτῷ· εἰσελθὼν δὲ ἀνέπεσεν.

38 Ὁ δὲ φαρισαῖ⟨Θ⟩ ἰδὼν ἐθαύμασεν, ὅτι ἀ πρῶτον ἐβαπλίσθη πρὸ τῦ ἀρίςυ.

39 Εἶπε δὲ ὁ Κύρι⟨Θ⟩ πρὸς αὐτόν· Νῦν ὑμεῖς οἱ φαρισαῖοι τὸ ἔξωθεν τῦ ποτηρίυ ἠ τῦ πίνακ⟨Θ⟩ καθαρίζεῖε· τὸ δὲ ἔσωθεν ὑμῶν γέμει ἁρπαγῆς ἠ πονηρίας.

40 Ἄφρονες, ὀυχ ὁ ποιήσας τὸ ἔξωθεν, ἠ τὸ ἔσωθεν ἐποίησε;

* 41 Πλὴν τὰ † ἐνόνῖα δότε ‡ ἐλεημοσύνην· ἠ ἰδὺ, πάνῖα καθαρὰ ὑμῖν ἐςιν.

1 ADerant autem quidam in ipso tempore, nuntiantes illi de Galilæis, quorum fanguinem Pilatus mifcuit cum facrificiis eorum.

2 Et refpondens Jefus dixit illis: Putatis quod Galilæi hi. peccatores præ omnibus Galilæis fuerint, qui talia paffi funt?

3 Non, dico vobis, fed fi non pœniteamini, omnes fimiliter peribitis.

4 Vel illi decem & octo, fupra quos cecidit turris in Siloam, & occidit eos: putatis qnia ipfi debitores fuerint præter omnes homines habitantes in Hierufalem?

5 Non dico vobis, fed fi non pœnitueritis, omnes fimiliter peribitis.

6 Dicebat autem hanc fimilitudinem: Ficum habebat quidam in vinea fua plantatam, & venit fructum quærens: in illa, & non invenit.

7 Dixit autem ad vinitorem: Ecces tres annos venio quærens fructum in ficulnea hac, & non invenio. Exfcinde illam: ut quid etiam terram occupat?

8 Is autem refpondens, dicit illi: Domine, relinque eam & hunc annum, ufquedum fodiam circa illam, & mittam ftercus.

9 Et fi quidem fecerit fructum: fi verò non, in futurum exfcindes eam.

37 In autem loqui, rogavit illum Pharifæus quidam ut pranderet apud fe: ingreffus autem recubuit.

38 At Pharifæus videns admiratus eft, quod non prius ablutus effet ante prandium.

39 Ait autem Dominus ad illum: Nunc vos Pharifæi quod deforis calicis & catini mundatis: quod autem intus veftrum plenum eft rapina & malitia.

40 Stulti, nonne faciens quod deforis, & quod deintus fecit?

41 Veruntamen inexiftentia date eleëmofynam, & ecce omnia munda vobis funt.

CHAPITRE XIII.

Jésus-Christ exhorte à la repentance, et entrer par la porte étroite.

EN ce même tems, quelques personnes, qui se trouvoient là, racontèrent à Jésus ce qui étoit arrivé à des Galiléens, dont Pilate avoit mêlé le sang avec celui de leurs sacrifices.

2. Et Jésus répondant, leur dit : Pensez-vous que ces Galiléens fussent plus grands pécheurs que tous les autres Galiléens, parce qu'ils ont souffert ces choses?

3. Non, vous dis-je; mais si vous ne vous amendez, vous périrez tous aussi bien *qu'eux*.

4. Ou, pensez-vous que ces dix-huit *personnes* sur qui la tour de Siloé est tombée, et qu'elle a tuées, fussent plus coupables que tous les habitans de Jérusalem?

5. Non, vous dis-je; mais si vous ne vous amendez, vous périrez tous aussi bien *qu'eux*.

6. Il leur dit aussi cette similitude : Un homme avoit un figuier planté dans sa vigne, et il y vint chercher du fruit, et n'y en trouva point.

7. Et il dit au vigneron : Voici, il y a déjà trois ans que je viens chercher du fruit à ce figuier, et je n'y en trouve point; coupe-le; pourquoi occupe-t-il la terre inutilement?

8. *Le vigneron* lui répondit : Seigneur, laisse-le encore cette année, jusqu'à-ce que je l'aie déchaussé, et que j'y aie mis du fumier.

9. S'il porte du fruit, *à la bonne heure*; sinon, tu le couperas ci-après.

37. Comme il parloit, un Pharisien le pria à dîner chez lui; et *Jésus* y entra, et se mit à table.

38. Mais le Pharisien s'étonna de ce qu'il vit qu'il ne s'étoit pas lavé avant le dîner.

39. Et le Seigneur lui dit : Vous autres Pharisiens, vous nettoyez le dehors de la coupe et du plat; mais au dedans, vous êtes pleins de rapine et de méchanceté.

40. Insensés! celui qui a fait le dehors n'a-t-il pas aussi fait le dedans?

41. Mais plutôt donnez en aumônes ce que vous avez, et toutes choses vous seront pures.

THERE were present at that season some that told him of the Galileans, whose blood Pilate had mingled with their sacrifices.

2 And Jesus, answering, said unto them, Suppose ye that these Galileans were sinners above all the Galileans, because they suffered such things?

3 I tell you, Nay; but, except ye repent, ye shall all likewise perish.

4 Or those eighteen upon whom the tower in Siloam fell, and slew them, think ye that they were sinners above all men that dwelt in Jerusalem?

5 I tell you, Nay; but except ye repent, ye shall all likewise perish.

6 He spake also this parable: A certain *man* had a fig-tree planted in his vineyard; and he came and sought fruit thereon, and found none.

7 Then said he unto the dresser of his vineyard, Behold, these three years I come seeking fruit on this fig-tree, and find none: cut it down; why cumbereth it the ground?

8 And he, answering, said unto him, Lord, let it alone this year also, till I shall dig about it, and dung *it*:

9 And if it bear fruit, *well*: and if not, *then* after that thou shalt cut it down.

37 And as he spake, a certain Pharisee besought him to dine with him: and he went in, and sat down to meat.

38 And when the Pharisee saw *i*, he marvelled that he had not first washed before dinner.

39 And the Lord said unto him, Now do ye Pharisees make clean the outside of the cup and the platter; but your inward part is full of ravening and wickedness.

40 *Ye* fools! did not he that made that which is without, make that which is within also?

41 But rather give alms of such things as ye have; and, behold, all things are clean unto you.

Greek	Latin

42 Ἀλλ' οὐαὶ ὑμῖν τοῖς φαρισαίοις, ὅτι ἀποδεκατῦτε τὸ ἡδύοσμον ᾗ τὸ πήγανον ᾗ πᾶν λάχανον, ᾗ παρέρχεσθε τὴν κρίσιν ᾗ τὴν ἀγάπην τῦ Θεῦ· ταῦτα ἔδει ποιῆσαι, κᾀκεῖνα μὴ ἀφιέναι.

43 Οὐαὶ ὑμῖν τοῖς φαρισαίοις, ὅτι ἀγαπᾶτε τὴν πρωτοκαθεδρίαν ἐν ταῖς συναγωγαῖς, ᾗ τὺς ἀσπασμὸς ἐν ταῖς ἀγοραῖς.

44 Οὐαὶ ὑμῖν, γραμματεῖς ᾗ φαρισαῖοι ὑποκριταὶ, ὅτι ἐστὲ ὡς τὰ μνημεῖα τὰ ἄδηλα, ᾗ οἱ ἄνθρωποι οἱ περιπατῦντες ἐπάνω ἀκ οἴδασιν.

45 Ἀποκριθεὶς δέ τις τῶν νομικῶν λέγει αὐτῷ· Διδάσκαλε, ταῦτα λέγων ᾗ ἡμᾶς ὑβρίζεις.

46 Ὁ δὲ εἶπε· Καὶ ὑμῖν τοῖς νομικοῖς οὐαὶ, ὅτι φορτίζετε τὺς ἀνθρώπυς φορτία δυσβάστακτα, ᾗ αὐτοὶ ἑνὶ τῶν δακτύλων ὑμῶν ἀ προσψαύετε τοῖς φορτίοις.

52 Οὐαὶ ὑμῖν τοῖς νομικοῖς, ὅτι ἤρατε τὴν κλεῖδα τῆς γνώσεως· αὐτοὶ ἀκ εἰσήλθετε, ᾗ τὺς εἰσερχομένυς ἐκωλύσατε.

53 Λέγοντος δὲ αὐτῷ ταῦτα πρὸς αὐτὺς, ἤρξαντο οἱ γραμματεῖς ᾗ οἱ φαρισαῖοι δεινῶς ἐνέχειν, ᾗ ἀποστοματίζειν αὐτὸν περὶ πλειόνων·

54 Ἐνεδρεύοντες αὐτὸν, ᾗ ζητῦντες θηρεῦσαί τι ἐκ τῦ στόματος αὐτῦ, ἵνα κατηγορήσωσιν αὐτῦ. 45. 12.

Κεφ. ιγ. 13.

1 Ἐν δὲ τῇ ἡμέρᾳ ἐκείνῃ ἐξελθὼν ὁ Ἰησῦς ἀπὸ τῆς οἰκίας, ἐκάθητο παρὰ τὴν θάλασσαν.

2 Καὶ συνήχθησαν πρὸς αὐτὸν ὄχλοι πολλοὶ, ὥστε αὐτὸν εἰς τὸ πλοῖον ἐμβάντα καθῆσθαι· ᾗ πᾶς ὁ ὄχλος ἐπὶ τὸν αἰγιαλὸν εἱστήκει.

3 Καὶ ἐλάλησεν αὐτοῖς πολλὰ ἐν παραβολαῖς, λέγων, ἰδὺ, ἐξῆλθεν ὁ σπείρων τῦ σπείρειν.

4 Καὶ ἐν τῷ σπείρειν αὐτὸν, ἃ μὲν ἔπεσε παρὰ τὴν ὁδὸν, ᾗ ἦλθε τὰ πετεινὰ, ᾗ κατέφαγεν αὐτά.

---

42 Sed væ vobis Pharisæis, quia decimatis mentham, & rutam, & omne olus, & præteritis judicium & charitatem Dei; hæc oportebat facere, & illa non omittere.

43 Væ vobis Pharisæis, quia diligitis primam sessionem in synagogis, & salutationes in foris.

44 Væ vobis, Scribæ & Pharisæi hypocritæ, quia estis ut monumenta non apparentia, & homines deambulantes supra non sciunt.

45 Respondens autem quidam Legisperitorum ait illi: Magister, hæc dicens & nos notas.

46 Ille autem ait: Et vobis Legisperitis væ, quia oneratis homines oneribus difficulter portabilibus, & ipsi uno digitorum vestrorum non attingitis onera.

52 Væ vobis Legisperitis, quia tulistis clavem scientiæ: ipsi non introistis, & introeuntes prohibuistis.

53 Dicente autem illo hæc ad illos, cœperunt Scribæ & Pharisæi graviter insistere, & interrogare ipsum de multis:

54 Insidiantes ei, & quærentes venari aliquid de ore ejus, ut accusarent eum.

CAPUT XIII.

1 IN verò die illo exiens Jesus de domo, sedebat secundum mare.
2 Et congregatæ sunt ad eum turbæ multæ, ita ut ipse in naviculam ascendens sederet: & omnis turba in littore stabat.
3 Et locutus est eis multa in parabolis, dicens, Ecce exiit seminator seminare.
4 Et in seminare ipsum, hæc quidem ceciderunt secus viam, & venerunt volucres & comederunt ea.

42 But woe unto you, Pharisees! for ye tithe mint, and rue, and all manner of herbs, and pass over judgment and the love of God: these ought ye to have done, and not to leave the other undone.

43 Woe unto you, Pharisees! for ye love the uppermost seats in the synagogues, and greetings in the markets.

44 Woe unto you, scribes and Pharisees, hypocrites! for ye are as graves which appear not, and the men that walk over *them* are not aware *of them*.

45 Then answered one of the lawyers, and said unto him, Master, thus saying, thou reproachest us also.

46 And he said, Woe unto you also, *ye* lawyers! for ye lade men with burdens grievous to be borne, and ye yourselves touch not the burdens with one of your fingers.

52 Woe unto you, lawyers! for ye have taken away the key of knowledge: ye entered not in yourselves, and them that were entering in ye hindered.

53 And as he said these things unto them, the scribes and the Pharisees began to urge *him* vehemently, and to provoke him to speak of many things;   I 2

54 Laying wait for him, and seeking to catch something out of his mouth, that they might accuse him

THE same day went Jesus out of the house, and sat by the sea side.

2 And great multitudes were gathered together unto him, so that he went into a ship and sat; and the whole multitude stood on the shore.

3 And he spake many things unto them in parables, saying, Behold, a sower went forth to sow;

4 And, when he sowed, some *seeds* fell by the way-side, and the fowls came and devoured them

---

42. Mais malheur à vous, Pharisiens, qui payez la dîme de la menthe, de la ruë, et de toutes sortes d'herbes, tandis que vous négligez la justice, et l'amour de Dieu ! Ce sont là les choses qu'il falloit faire sans néanmoins négliger-les autres.

43. Malheur à vous, Pharisiens, qui aimez les premiers rangs dans les Synagogues, et à être salués dans les places publiques !

44. Malheur à vous, Scribes et Pharisiens hypocrites ; parce que vous ressemblez aux sépulcres qui ne paroissent point, et les hommes qui marchent dessus n'en savent rien !

45. Alors un des docteurs de la loi prit la parole et lui dit : Maître, en disant ces choses, tu nous outrages aussi.

46. Et *Jésus* dit : Malheur aussi à vous, docteurs de la loi ; parce que vous chargez les hommes de fardeaux qu'ils ne peuvent porter, et vous mêmes n'y touchez pas du bout du doigt !

52. Malheur à vous, docteurs de la loi ; parce qu'ayant pris la clef de la connoissance, vous n'y êtes point entrés vous-mêmes, et vous avez encore empêché d'y entrer ceux qui vouloient le faire !

53. Et comme il leur disoit cela, les Scribes et les Pharisiens se mirent à le presser fortement, en le faisant parler sur plusieurs choses ;

54. Lui tendant des piéges, et tâchant de tirer quelques choses de sa bouche, pour avoir de quoi l'accuser.

CE même jour, Jésus étant sorti de la maison, s'assit au bord de la mer.

2. Et une grande foule de peuple s'assembla vers lui, en sorte qu'il monta dans une barque. Il s'y assit, et toute la multitude se tenoit sur le rivage.

3. Et il leur dit plusieurs choses par des similitudes, et il leur parla ainsi : Un semeur sortit pour semer.

4. Et comme il semoit, une partie *de la semence* tomba le long du chemin, et les oiseaux vinrent, et la mangèrent toute.

23

5 Ἄλλα δὲ ἔπεσεν ἐπὶ τὰ πετρώδη, ὅπου οὐκ εἶχε γῆν πολλήν· καὶ εὐθέως ἐξανέτειλε, διὰ τὸ μὴ ἔχειν βάθος γῆς.

6 Ἡλίου δὲ ἀνατείλαντος ἐκαυματίσθη· καὶ διὰ τὸ μὴ ἔχειν ῥίζαν, ἐξηράνθη.

7 Ἄλλα δὲ ἔπεσεν ἐπὶ τὰς ἀκάνθας, καὶ ἀνέβησαν αἱ ἄκανθαι, καὶ ἀπέπνιξαν αὐτά.

8 Ἄλλα δὲ ἔπεσεν ἐπὶ τὴν γῆν τὴν καλὴν, καὶ ἐδίδου καρπὸν, ὁ μὲν ἑκατόν, ὁ δὲ ἑξήκοντα, ὁ δὲ τριάκοντα.

9 Ὁ ἔχων ὦτα ἀκούειν, ἀκουέτω.

10 Ὅτε δὲ ἐγένετο καταμόνας, ἠρώτησαν αὐτὸν οἱ περὶ αὐτὸν σὺν τοῖς δώδεκα τὴν παραβολήν.

18 Ὑμεῖς οὖν ἀκούσατε τὴν παραβολὴν τοῦ σπείροντος.

19 Παντὸς ἀκούοντος τὸν λόγον τῆς βασιλείας, καὶ μὴ συνιέντος, ἔρχεται ὁ πονηρός, καὶ ἁρπάζει τὸ ἐσπαρμένον ἐν τῇ καρδίᾳ αὐτοῦ· οὗτός ἐστιν ὁ παρὰ τὴν ὁδὸν σπαρείς.

20 Ὁ δὲ ἐπὶ τὰ πετρώδη σπαρείς, οὗτός ἐστιν ὁ τὸν λόγον ἀκούων, καὶ εὐθὺς μετὰ χαρᾶς λαμβάνων αὐτόν.

21 Οὐκ ἔχει δὲ ῥίζαν ἐν ἑαυτῷ, ἀλλὰ πρόσκαιρός ἐστι· γενομένης δὲ θλίψεως, ἢ διωγμοῦ διὰ τὸν λόγον, εὐθὺς σκανδαλίζεται.

22 Ὁ δὲ εἰς τὰς ἀκάνθας σπαρείς, οὗτός ἐστιν ὁ τὸν λόγον ἀκούων, καὶ ἡ μέριμνα τοῦ αἰῶνος τούτου, καὶ ἡ ἀπάτη τοῦ πλούτου συμπνίγει τὸν λόγον, καὶ ἄκαρπος γίνεται.

23 Ὁ δὲ ἐπὶ τὴν γῆν τὴν καλὴν σπαρείς, οὗτός ἐστιν ὁ τὸν λόγον ἀκούων, καὶ συνιών· ὃς δὴ καρποφορεῖ, καὶ ποιεῖ, ὁ μὲν ἑκατόν, ὁ δὲ ἑξήκοντα, ὁ δὲ τριάκοντα.

5 Alia autem ceciderunt in petrosa, ubi non habebant terram multam : & continuò exorta sunt, propter non habere altitudinem terræ.

6 Sole autem orto, æstuaverunt, & propter non habere radicem, exaruerunt.

7 Alia autem ceciderunt in spinas, & insurrexerunt spinæ, & suffocaverunt ea.

8 Alia autem ceciderunt in terram bonam, & dabant fructum, hoc centum, hoc autem sexaginta, hoc autem triginta.

9 Habens aures audire, audiat.

10 Quum autem factus esset solus interrogaverunt eum qui circa eum cum duodecim parabolam.

18 Vos ergo audite parabolam seminantis.

19 Omnis audientis verbum regni, & non intelligentis, venit malus, & rapit seminatum in corde ejus : hic est qui secus viam seminatus.

20 Qui autem super petrosa seminatus, hic est qui verbum audiens, & continuò cum gaudio sumens eum :

21 Non habet autem radicem in se ipso, sed temporalis est; facta autem tribulatione aut persequutione propter verbum, statim scandalizatur.

22 Qui autem in spinas seminatus, hic est qui verbum audiens, & anxietas seculi istius, & deceptio divitiarum suffocat verbum, & infructuosum fit.

23 Qui verò in terram pulchram seminatus, hic est qui verbum audiens & intelligens : quique fructum fert, & facit, hoc quidem centum, hoc autem sexaginta, hoc verò triginta.

Mt. 13.

5. Some fell upon stony places, where they had not much earth: and forthwith they sprung up, because they had no deepness of earth :—

6 And when the sun was up, they were scorched : and, because they had not root, they withered away.

7 And some fell among thorns; and the thorns sprung up and choked them :

8 But other fell into good ground, and brought forth fruit, some an hundred-fold, some sixty-fold, some thirty-fold.

9 Who hath ears to hear, let him hear.

Mc. 4.

10 And when he was alone, they that were about him, with the twelve, asked of him the parable.

Mt. 13.

18 Hear ye, therefore, the parable of the sower.

19 When any one heareth the word of the kingdom, and understandeth *it* not, *then* cometh the wicked *one*, and catcheth away that which was sown in his heart. This is he which received seed by the way *side*.

20 But he that received the seed into stony places, the same is he that heareth the word, and anon with joy receiveth it;

21 Yet hath he not root in himself, but dureth for a while; for when tribulation or persecution ariseth because of the word, by and by he is offended.

22 He also that received seed among the thorns, is he that heareth the word; and the care of this world, and the deceitfulness of riches, choke the word, and he becometh unfruitful.

23 But he that received seed into the good ground, is he that heareth the word and understandeth *it ;* which also beareth fruit, and bringeth forth, some an hundred-fold, some sixty, some thirty.

---

5. L'autre partie tomba sur des endroits pierreux , où elle n'avoit que peu de terre , et elle leva aussitôt , parce qu'elle n'entroit pas profondément dans la terre;

6. Mais le soleil étant levé , elle fut brûlée; et parce qu'elle n'avoit point de racine, elle sécha.

7. L'autre partie tomba parmi des épines, et les épines crûrent, et l'étouffèrent.

8. Et l'autre partie tomba dans une bonne terre , et rapporta du fruit ; un grain en rapporta cent, un autre soixante , et un autre trente.

9. Que celui qui a des oreilles pour ouïr , entende.

10. Et quand il fut en particulier, ceux qui *étoient* autour de lui , avec les douze *Apôtres* , l'interrogèrent touchant le sens de cette parabole.

18. Vous donc , écoutez la similitude du semeur.

19. Lorsqu'un homme entend la parole du Royaume *de Dieu* , et qu'il ne la comprend point, le malin vient, et ravit ce qui est semé dans le cœur; c'est celui qui a reçu la semence le long du chemin.

20. Et celui qui a reçu la semence dans des endroits pierreux , c'est celui qui entend la parole , et qui la reçoit d'abord avec joie ;

21. Mais il n'a point de racine en lui-même ; c'est pourquoi il n'est que pour un tems ; et lorsque l'affliction ou la persécution survient à cause de la parole , il se scandalise aussitôt.

22. Et celui qui a reçu la semence parmi les épines, c'est celui qui entend la parole ; mais les soucis de ce monde et la séduction des richesses étouffent la parole , et elle devient infructueuse.

23. Mais celui qui a reçu la semence dans une bonne terre, c'est celui qui entend la parole et qui la comprend, et qui porte du fruit ; en sorte qu'un grain en produit cent , un autre soixante, et un autre trente.

24

21 Καὶ ἔλεγεν αὐτοῖς· Μήτι ὁ λύχνος ἔρχεται, ἵνα ὑπὸ τὸν μόδιον τεθῇ, ἢ ὑπὸ τὴν κλίνην; οὐχ ἵνα ἐπὶ τὴν λυχνίαν ἐπιτεθῇ;
* 22 Οὐ γάρ ἐστί τι κρυπτὸν ὃ ἐὰν μὴ φανερωθῇ· οὐδὲ ἐγένετο ‡ ἀπόκρυφον, ἀλλ᾽ ἵνα εἰς φανερὸν ἔλθῃ.
23 Εἴ τις ἔχει ὦτα ἀκούειν ἀκουέτω.

24 Ἄλλην παραβολὴν παρέθηκεν αὐτοῖς, λέγων· Ὡμοιώθη ἡ βασιλεία τῶν οὐρανῶν ἀνθρώπῳ σπείροντι καλὸν σπέρμα ἐν τῷ ἀγρῷ αὐτοῦ·
25 Ἐν δὲ τῷ καθεύδειν τοὺς ἀνθρώπους, ἦλθον αὐτοῦ ὁ ἐχθρὸς, καὶ ἔσπειρε ζιζάνια ἀνὰ μέσον τοῦ σίτου, καὶ ἀπῆλθεν.
26 Ὅτε δὲ ἐβλάστησεν ὁ χόρτος, καὶ καρπὸν ἐποίησε, τότε ἐφάνη καὶ τὰ ζιζάνια.

27 Προσελθόντες δὲ οἱ δοῦλοι τοῦ οἰκοδεσπότου, εἶπον αὐτῷ· Κύριε, οὐχὶ καλὸν σπέρμα ἔσπειρας ἐν τῷ σῷ ἀγρῷ; πόθεν οὖν ἔχει τὰ ζιζάνια;
28 Ὁ δὲ ἔφη αὐτοῖς· Ἐχθρὸς ἄνθρωπος τοῦτο ἐποίησεν. Οἱ δὲ δοῦλοι εἶπον αὐτῷ· Θέλεις οὖν ἀπελθόντες συλλέξωμεν αὐτά;
29 Ὁ δὲ ἔφη· Οὔ· μήποτε συλλέγοντες τὰ ζιζάνια, ἐκριζώσητε ἅμα αὐτοῖς τὸν σῖτον·
* 30 ‡ Ἄφετε † συναυξάνεσθαι ἀμφότερα ‡ μέχρι τοῦ θερισμοῦ, καὶ ἐν τῷ καιρῷ τοῦ θερισμοῦ ἐρῶ τοῖς ‡ θερισταῖς· ‡ Συλλέξατε πρῶτον τὰ ζιζάνια, καὶ ‡ δήσατε αὐτὰ ‡ εἰς † δέσμας, πρὸς τὸ κατακαῦσαι αὐτά· τὸν δὲ ‡ σῖτον ‡ συναγάγετε εἰς τὴν ‡ ἀποθήκην μου.

36 Τότε ἀφεὶς τοὺς ὄχλους, ἦλθεν εἰς τὴν οἰκίαν ὁ Ἰησοῦς· καὶ προσῆλθον αὐτῷ οἱ μαθηταὶ αὐτοῦ, λέγοντες· Φράσον ἡμῖν τὴν παραβολὴν τῶν ζιζανίων τοῦ ἀγροῦ.
37 Ὁ δὲ ἀποκριθεὶς εἶπεν αὐτοῖς· Ὁ σπείρων τὸ καλὸν σπέρμα, ἐστὶν ὁ υἱὸς τοῦ ἀνθρώπου·
38 Ὁ δὲ ἀγρός, ἐστιν ὁ κόσμος· τὸ δὲ καλὸν σπέρμα, οὗτοί εἰσιν οἱ υἱοὶ τῆς βασιλείας· τὰ δὲ ζιζάνια, εἰσὶν οἱ υἱοὶ τοῦ πονηροῦ.

21 Et dicebat illis: Nunquid lucerna venit, ut sub modio ponatur, aut sub lecto? nonne ut supra candelabrum imponatur?
22 Non enim est aliquid absconditum, quod non manifestetur: nec factum est occultum, sed ut in palam veniat.
23 Si quis habet aures audire, audiat.

24 Aliam parabolam proposuit illis, dicens: Assimilatum est regnum cælorum homini seminanti pulchrum semen in agro suo.
25 In verò dormire homines, venit ejus inimicus, & seminavit zizania in medio tritici, & abiit.
26 Quum autem crevit herba, & fructum fecit, tunc apparuerunt & zizania?

27 Accedentes autem servi patris familias dixerunt ei: Domine, nonne pulchrum semen seminasti in tuo agro? Unde ergò habet zizania?
28 Ille verò ait illis: Inimicus homo hoc fecit. At servi dixerunt ei: Vis igitur abeuntes colligamus ea?
29 Ille verò ait: Non; ne forte colligentes zizania, eradicetis simul eis triticum.
30 Sinite crescere utraque usque ad messem: & in tempore messis dicam messoribus, Colligite primum zizania & alligate ea in fasciculos, ad comburendum ea: at triticum congregate in horreum meum.

36 Tunc dimittens turbas, venit in domum Jesus: & accesserunt ad eum discipuli ejus, dicentes: Explica nobis parabolam zizaniorum agri.
37 Ille verò respondens ait illis: Seminans pulchrum semen, est Filius hominis.
38 At ager est mundus. Verum pulchrum semen, hi sunt filii regni. At zizania, sunt filii mali.

21. Il leur disoit encore : Apporte-t-on une chandelle pour la mettre sous un boisseau, ou sous un lit ? N'est ce pas pour la mettre sur un chandelier ?

22. Car il n'y a rien de secret qui ne doive être manifesté, et il n'y a rien de caché qui ne doive venir en évidence.

23. Si quelqu'un a des oreilles pour entendre, qu'il entende.

24. Jésus leur proposa une autre similitude, en disant : Le Royaume des cieux est semblable à un homme qui avoit semé de bonne semence en son champ.

25. Mais pendant que les hommes dormoient, son ennemi vint, qui sema de l'yvraie parmi le blé, et s'en alla.

26. Et après que la semence eut poussé, et qu'elle eut produit du fruit, l'yvraie parut aussi.

27. Alors les serviteurs du père de famille lui vinrent dire : Seigneur, n'as-tu pas semé de bonne semence dans ton champ ? D'où vient donc qu'il y a de l'yvraie ?

28. Et il leur dit : C'est un ennemi qui a fait cela. Et les serviteurs lui répondirent : Veux-tu donc que nous allions la cueillir ?

29. Et il leur dit : Non, de peur qu'il n'arrive qu'en cueillant l'yvraie vous n'arrachiez le froment en même tems.

30. Laissez-les croître tous deux ensemble, jusqu'à la moisson ; et au tems de la moisson, je dirai aux moissonneurs : Cueillez premièrement l'yvraie, et liez-la en faisceaux pour la brûler, mais assemblez le froment dans mon grenier.

36. Alors *Jésus* ayant renvoyé le peuple, s'en alla à la maison, et ses Disciples étant venus vers lui, lui dirent : Explique-nous la similitude de l'yvraie du champ.

37. Il leur répondit et leur dit : Celui qui sème la bonne semence, c'est le Fils de l'homme.

38. Le champ, c'est le monde. La bonne semence, ce sont les enfans du Royaume. L'yvraie, ce sont les enfans du malin.

39. L'ennemi qui l'a semée, c'est le Diable. La moisson, c'est la fin du monde ; et les moissonneurs, sont les Anges.

21 And he said unto them, Is a candle brought to be put under a bushel, or under a bed, and not to be set on a candlestick ?

22 For there is nothing hid which shall not be manifested ; neither was any thing kept secret, but that it should come abroad.

23 If any man have ears to hear, let him hear.

24 Another parable put he forth unto them, saying, The kingdom of heaven is likened unto a man which sowed good seed in his field :

25 But, while men slept, his enemy came and sowed tares among the wheat, and went his way.

26 But when the blade was sprung up, and brought forth fruit, then appeared the tares also.

27 So the servants of the householder came and said unto him, Sir, didst not thou sow good seed in thy field ? from whence then hath it tares ?

28 He said unto them, An enemy hath done this. The servants said unto him, Wilt thou then that we go and gather them up ?

29 But he said, Nay ; lest, while ye gather up the tares, ye root up also the wheat with them.

30 Let both grow together until the harvest ; and in the time of harvest I will say to the reapers, Gather ye together first the tares, and bind them in bundles to burn them : but gather the wheat into my barn.

36 Then Jesus sent the multitude away, and went into the house : and his disciples came unto him, saying, Declare unto us the parable of the tares of the field.

37 H answered and said unto them, He that soweth the good seed is the Son of Man ;

38 The field is the world ; the good seed are the children of the kingdom ; but the tares are the children of the wicked *one* ;.

25.

39 Ὁ δὲ ἐχθρὸς ὁ *σπείρας* αὐτὰ, ἐςιν ὁ διάβολ⊙· ὁ δὲ θερισμὸς, ‡ *συντέλεια* τῦ αἰῶνός ἐςιν· οἱ δὲ θερισαὶ, ἄγγελοί εἰσιν.

40 Ὥσπερ ᾶν *συλλέγεται* τὰ ζιζάνια, ᾗ πυρὶ *κατακαίεται*· οὕτως ἔςαι ἐν τῇ συντελείᾳ τῦ αἰῶν⊙ τότε.

41 Ἀποςελεῖ ὁ υἱὸς τῦ ἀνθρώπε τὸς ἀγγέλες αὐτῦ, ᾗ *συλλέξεσιν* ἐκ τῆς βασιλείας αὐτῦ πάντα τὰ *σκάνδαλα*, ᾗ τὸς ποιῦντας τὴν ἀνομίαν.

42 Καὶ βαλῦσιν αὐτὸς εἰς τὴν κάμινον τῦ πυρός· ἐκεῖ ἔςαι ὁ κλαυθμὸς ᾗ ὁ βρυγμὸς τῶν ὀδόντων.

43 Τότε οἱ ‡ δίκαιοι † *ἐκλάμ- ψεσιν* ‡ ὡς ὁ ‡ ἥλιος, ἐν τῇ βασιλείᾳ τῦ πατρὸς αὐτῶν. Ὁ ἔχων ὦτα ἀκέειν, ἀκέετω.

44 Πάλιν ὁμοία ἐςὶν ἡ βασιλεία τῶν ὀρανῶν θησαυρῷ κεκρυμμένῳ ἐν τῷ ἀγρῷ, ὃν εὑρὼν ἄνθρωπ⊙ ἔκρυψε, ᾗ ἀπὸ τῆς χαρᾶς αὐτῦ ὑπάγει, ᾗ πάν]α ὅσα ἔχει, πωλεῖ, ᾗ ἀγοράζει τὸν ἀγρὸν ἐκεῖνον.

45 Πάλιν ὁμοία ἐςὶν ἡ βασιλεία τῶν ὀρανῶν ἀνθρώπῳ ἐμπόρῳ, ζητῦν]ι καλὸς μαργαρίτας.

46 Ὃς εὑρὼν ἕνα πολύτιμον μαργαρίτην, ἀπελθὼν, πέπρακε πάν]α ὅσα εἶχε, ᾗ ἠγόρασεν αὐτόν.

47 Πάλιν ‡ ὁμοία ἐςὶν ἡ βασιλεία τῶν ‡ ὀρανῶν † σαγήνῃ βληθείσῃ εἰς τὴν θάλασσαν, ᾗ ἐκ πάντος γένες *συναγαγύσῃ*.

48 Ἥν, ‡ ὅτε ἐπληρώθη, † ἀναβιβάσαντες ‡ ἐπὶ τὸν ‡ αἰγιαλὸν, ᾗ καθίσαντες, *συνέλεξαν* τὰ καλὰ εἰς ‡ ἀγγεῖα, τὰ δὲ ‡ σαπρὰ ἔξω ἔβαλον.

49 Οὕτως ἔςαι ἐν τῇ συντελείᾳ τῦ αἰῶν⊙· ἐξελεύσονται οἱ ἄγγελοι, ᾗ ἀφοριῦσι τὸς πονηρὸς ἐκ μέσε τῶν δικαίων·

50 Καὶ βαλῦσιν αὐτὸς εἰς τὴν κάμινον τῦ πυρός· ἐκεῖ ἔςαι ὁ κλαυθμὸς ᾗ ὁ βρυγμὸς τῶν ὀδόντων.

51 Λέγει αὐτοῖς ὁ Ἰησῦς. Συνήκατε ταῦτα πάντα; Λέγυσιν αὐτῷ· Ναὶ Κύριε.

52 Ὁ δὲ εἶπεν αὐτοῖς· Διὰ τῦτο πᾶς γραμμαλεὺς μαθητευθεὶς εἰς τὴν βασιλείαν τῶν ὀρανῶν, ὅμοιός ἐςιν ἀνθρώπῳ οἰκοδεσπότῃ, ὅςις ἐκβάλλει ἐκ τῦ θησαυρῦ αὐτῦ καινὰ ᾗ παλαιά.

---

39 At inimicus seminans ea, est diabolus. At messis, consummatio seculi est. At messores, angeli sunt.

40 Sicut ergo colliguntur zizania, & igni comburuntur: sic erit in consummatione seculi.

41 Mittet Filius hominis angelos suos, & colligent de regno ejus omnia scandala, & facientes iniquitatem:

42 Et mittent eos in caminum ignis, ibi erit fletus & fremitus dentium.

43 Tunc justi fulgebunt sicut Sol in regno Patris eorum. Habens aures audire, audiat.

44 Iterum simile est regnum cælorum thesauro abscondito in agro: quem inveniens homo abscondit, & præ gaudio illius vadit, & universa quæ habet vendit, & emit agrum illum.

45 Iterum simile est regnum cælorum homini negotiatori, quærenti bonas margaritas:

46 Qui inveniens unam pretiosam margaritam, abiens vendidit omnia quæ habuit, et emit eam.

47 Iterum simile est regnum cælorum sagenæ jactæ in mare, & ex omni genere cogenti.

48 Quam, quum impleta esset, producentes super littus, & sedentes, collegerunt pulcra in receptacula, at vitiosa foras ejecerunt.

49 Sic erit in consummatione seculi: exibunt angeli, & segregabunt malos de medio justorum:

50 Et projicient eos in caminum ignis: ibi erit fletus & fremitus dentium.

51 Dicit illis Jesus: Intellexistis hæc omnia? Dicunt ei, utique Domine.

52 Is autem dixit illis: Propter hoc omnis Scriba doctus in regnum cælorum, similis est homini patrifamilias, qui ejicit de thesauro suo nova & vetera.

39. L'ennemi qui l'a semée, c'est le Diable. La moisson, c'est la fin du monde ; et les moissonneurs, sont les Anges.

40. Comme donc on amasse l'yvraie et qu'on la brûle dans le feu, il en sera de même à la fin du monde.

41. Le Fils de l'homme envoyera ses Anges, qui ôteront de son Royaume tous les scandales, et ceux qui font l'iniquité.

42. Et ils les jeteront dans la fournaise ardente ; c'est là qu'il y aura des pleurs et des grincemens de dents.

43. Alors les justes luiront comme le soleil, dans le Royaume de leur Père. Que celui qui a des oreilles pour ouïr, entende.

44. Le Royaume des cieux est encore semblable à un trésor caché dans un champ, qu'un homme a trouvé, et qu'il cache ; et de la joie qu'il en a, il s'en va, et vend tout ce qu'il a, et achète ce champ-là.

45. Le Royaume des cieux est encore semblable à un marchand qui cherche de belles perles ;

46. Et qui ayant trouvé une perle de grand prix, s'en va, et vend tout ce qu'il a, et l'achète.

47. Le Royaume des cieux est encore semblable à un filet, qui étant jeté dans la mer, ramasse toutes sortes de choses ;

48. Quand il est rempli, les pêcheurs le tirent sur le rivage ; et s'étant assis, ils mettent ce qu'il y a de bon à part dans *leurs* vaisseaux, et ils jettent ce qui ne vaut rien.

49. Il en sera de même à la fin du monde. Les Anges viendront, et sépareront les méchans du milieu des justes.

50. Et ils jeteront *les méchans* dans la fournaise ardente ; c'est là qu'il y aura des pleurs et des grincemens de dents.

51. Et Jésus dit à ses Disciples,

que tout Docteur qui est *bien* instruit dans *ce qui regarde* le Royaume des cieux, est semblable à un père de famille, qui tire de son trésor des choses nouvelles et des choses vieilles.

39 The enemy that sowed them is the devil ; the harvest is the end of the world : and the reapers are the angels.

40 As, therefore, the tares are gathered and burned in the fire ; so shall it be in the end of this world.

41 The Son of Man shall send forth his angels, and they shall gather out of his kingdom all things that offend, and them which do iniquity ;

42 And shall cast them into a furnace of fire : there shall be wailing and gnashing of teeth.

43 Then shall the righteous shine forth as the sun in the kingdom of their Father. Who hath ears to hear, let him hear.

44 Again, the kingdom of heaven is like unto treasure hid in a field ; the which when a man hath found he hideth, and, for joy thereof, goeth and selleth all that he hath, and buyeth that field.

45 Again, the kingdom of heaven is like unto a merchantman, seeking goodly pearls :

46 Who, when he had found one pearl of great price, went and sold all that he had, and bought it.

47 Again, the kingdom of heaven is like unto a net, that was cast into the sea, and gathered of every kind :

48 Which, when it was full, they drew to shore, and sat down, and gathered the good into vessels, but cast the bad away.

49 So shall it be at the end of the world : the angels shall come forth, and sever the wicked from among the just.

50 And, shall cast them into the furnace of fire : there shall be wailing and gnashing of teeth.

51 Jesus saith unto them, Have ye understood all these things ? They say unto him, Yea, Lord.

52 Then said he unto them, Therefore every scribe *which is* instructed unto the kingdom of heaven is like unto a man *that is* an householder, which bringeth forth out of his treasure *things* new and old.

26 Καὶ ἔλεγεν· Οὕτως ἐςὶν ἡ βασιλεία τῶ Θεῶ, ὡς ἐὰν ἄνθρω‑π۞ βάλῃ τὸν σπόρον ἐπὶ τῆς γῆς,

27 Καὶ καθεύδῃ, κ̀ ἐγείρηται νύκτα κ̀ ἡμέραν· κ̀ ὁ ‡ σπόρ۞ ‡ βλαςάνῃ, κ̀ † μηκύνηται, ὡς ἐκ οἶδεν αὐτός.

* 28 ‡ Αὐτομάτη γὰρ ἡ γῆ ‡ καρποφορεῖ, πρῶτον χόρτον, ‡ εἶτα ‡ ςάχυν, εἶτα πλήρη σῖτον ἐν τῷ ςάχυϊ.

29 Ὅταν δὲ παραδῷ ὁ καρπός, εὐθέως ἀποςέλλει τὸ δρέπανον, ὅτι παρέςηκεν ὁ θερισμός.

30 Καὶ ἔλεγε· Τίνι ὁμοιώσω‑μεν τὴν βασιλείαν τῶ Θεῶ; ἢ ἐν ποίᾳ παραβολῇ παραβάλωμεν αὐτήν;

31 Ὡς κόκκῳ σινάπεως, ὃς ὅταν σπαρῇ ἐπὶ τῆς γῆς, μικρό‑τερ۞ πάντων τῶν σπερμάτων ἐςὶ τῶν ἐπὶ τῆς γῆς,

32 Καὶ ὅταν σπαρῇ, ἀναβαί‑νει, κ̀ γίνεται πάντων τῶν λα‑χάνων μείζων, κ̀ ποιεῖ κλά‑δους μεγάλας, ὥςε δύνασθαι ὑπὸ τὴν σκιὰν αὐτῶ τὰ πετεινὰ τῶ οὐρανῶ κατασκηνοῦν.

33 Καὶ τοιαύταις παραβολαῖς πολλαῖς ἐλάλει αὐτοῖς τὸν λό‑γον, καθὼς ἠδύναντο ἀκύειν.

34 Χωρὶς δὲ παραβολῆς ἐκ ἐλάλει αὐτοῖς· κατ᾽ ἰδίαν δὲ τοῖς μαθηταῖς αὐτῶ ἐπέλυε πάντα.

57 Ἐγένετο δὲ πορευομένων αὐ‑τῶν ἐν τῇ ὁδῷ, εἶπέ τις πρὸς αὐ‑τόν· Ἀκολυθήσω σοι ὅπυ ἂν ἀ‑πέρχῃ, Κύριε.

* 58 Καὶ εἶπεν αὐτῷ ὁ Ἰησῦς· Αἱ ‡ ἀλώπεκες ‡ φωλεὺς ἔχυ‑σι, κ̀ τὰ ‡ πετεινὰ τῶ οὐρανῶ ‡ κατασκηνώσεις· ὁ δὲ υἱὸς τῶ ἀνθρώπυ ἐκ ἔχει πῶ τὴν κεφαλὴν κλίνῃ.

59 Εἶπε δὲ πρὸς ἕτερον· Ἀκο‑λούθει μοι. Ὁ δὲ εἶπε· Κύριε, ἐπίτρεψόν μοι ἀπελθόντι πρῶτον θάψαι τὸν πατέρα μυ.

60 Εἶπε δὲ αὐτῷ ὁ Ἰησῦς· Ἄφες τὰς νεκρὰς θάψαι τὰς ἑαυ‑τῶν νεκράς· σὺ δὲ ἀπελθὼν διάγ‑γελλε τὴν βασιλείαν τῶ Θεῶ.

61 Εἶπε δὲ κ̀ ἕτερ۞· Ἀκο‑λυθήσω σοι, Κύριε· πρῶτον δὲ ἐπίτρεψόν μοι ἀποτάξασθαι τοῖς εἰς τὸν οἶκόν μυ.

* 62 Εἶπε δὲ πρὸς αὐτὸν ὁ Ἰησῦς· Οὐδεὶς ἐπιβαλὼν τὴν χεῖρα αὐτῶ ἐπ᾽ † ἄροτρον, κ̀ βλέπων εἰς τὰ ὀπίσω, εὔθετός ἐςιν εἰς τὴν βασιλείαν τῶ Θεῶ.

26 Et dicebat: Sic est regnum Dei, quemadmodum si homo jaciat sementem in terram:

27 Et dormiat, & excitetur nocte & die: & semen germinet & augeatur ut nescit ille.

28 Spontanea enim terra fructum fert, primùm herbam, deinde spicam, deinde plenum frumentum in spica.

29 Quum verò ediderit fructus, statim mittit falcem, quoniam adest messis.

30 Et dicebat: Cui assimilabimus regnum Dei? aut in qua parabola comparabimus illud?

31 Sicut grano sinapis, quod, quum seminatum fuerit in terra, minus omnibus seminibus est quæ in terra:

32 Et quum seminatum fuerit, ascendit, & fit omnibus oleribus majus, & facit ramos magnos, ita ut possint sub umbrâ ejus volatilia cæli nidulari.

33 Et talibus parabolis multis loquebatur eis sermonem prout poterant audire.

34 Sine autem parabola non loquebatur eis: privatim autem discipulis suis solvebat omnia.

57 Factum est autem ambulantibus illis in via, dixit quidam ad illum: Sequar te quocumque abieris, Domine.

58 Et dixit illi Jesus: Vulpes foveas habent, & volucres cæli nidos: verum filius hominis non habet ubi caput reclinet.

59 Ait autem ad alterum: Sequere me. Ille autem dixit: Domine, permitte mihi abeunti primùm sepelire patrem meum.

60 Dixit autem ei Jesus: Sine mortuos sepelire suos mortuos: tu autem abiens annuncia regnum Dei.

61 Ait autem & alter: Sequar te, Domine: primum autem permitte mihi renuntiare his qui ad domum meam.

62 Ait autem ad illum Jesus: Nemo immittens manum suam ad aratrum, & respiciens in quæ retro, aptus est ad regnum Dei.

26. Il dit encore: Il en est du Royaume de Dieu, comme si un homme avoit jeté de la semence en terre;

27. Soit qu'il dorme ou qu'il se lève, la nuit ou le jour, la semence germe et croît sans qu'il sache comment.

28. Car la terre produit d'elle-même, premièrement, l'herbe, ensuite l'épi, et puis le grain tout formé dans l'épi.

29. Et quand le fruit est dans sa maturité, on y met aussitôt la faucille, parce que la moisson est prête.

30. Il disoit encore: A quoi comparerons-nous le Royaume de Dieu, ou par quelle similitude le représenterons-nous?

31. Il en est comme du grain de moutarde, lequel, lorsqu'on le sème, est la plus petite de toutes les semences que l'on jette en terre.

32. Mais après qu'on l'a semé, il monte et devient plus grand que tous les autres légumes, et pousse de grandes branches; de sorte que les oiseaux du ciel peuvent demeurer sous son ombre.

33. Il leur annonçoit ainsi la parole par plusieurs similitudes de cette sorte, selon qu'ils étoient capables de l'entendre.

34. Et il ne leur parloit point sans similitudes; mais lorsqu'il étoit en particulier, il expliquoit tout à ses Disciples.

57. Et comme ils étoient en chemin, un homme lui dit: Je te suivrai, Seigneur, par-tout où tu iras.

58. Mais Jésus lui répondit: Les renards ont des tanières, et les oiseaux du ciel ont des nids; mais le Fils de l'homme n'a pas où reposer sa tête.

59. Il dit à un autre: Suis-moi. Et il lui répondit: Seigneur, permets que j'aille auparavant ensevelir mon père.

60. Jésus lui dit: Laisse les morts ensevelir leurs morts; mais toi, va et annonce le Règne de Dieu.

61. Un autre lui dit: Je te suivrai, Seigneur; mais permets-moi de prendre auparavant congé de ceux qui sont dans ma maison.

62. Mais Jésus lui répondit. Celui qui met la main à la charrue, et regarde derrière lui, n'est point propre pour le Royaume de Dieu.

26 And he said, So is the kingdom of God, as if a man should cast seed into the ground;

27 And should sleep, and rise night and day, and the seed should spring and grow up, he knoweth not how.

28 For the earth bringeth forth fruit of herself; first the blade, then the ear, after that the full corn in the ear.

29 But when the fruit is brought forth, immediately he putteth in the sickle, because the harvest is come.

30 And he said, Whereunto shall we liken the kingdom of God? or with what comparison shall we compare it?

31 It is like a grain of mustard-seed, which, when it is sown in the earth, is less than all the seeds that be in the earth:

32 But when it is sown, it groweth up, and becometh greater than all herbs, and shooteth out great branches; so that the fowls of the air may lodge under the shadow of it.

33 And with many such parables spake he the word unto them, as they were able to hear it.

34 But without a parable spake he not unto them: and when they were alone, he expounded all things to his disciples.

57 And it came to pass, that, as they went in the way, a certain man said unto him, Lord, I will follow thee whithersoever thou goest.

58 And Jesus said unto him, Foxes have holes, and birds of the air have nests; but the Son of Man hath not where to lay his head.

59 And he said unto another, Follow me. But he said, Lord, suffer me first to go and bury my father.

60 Jesus said unto him, Let the dead bury their dead: but go thou and preach the kingdom of God.

61 And another also said, Lord, I will follow thee: but let me first go bid them farewell, which are at home at my house.

62 And Jesus said unto him, No man having put his hand to the plough, and looking back, is fit for the kingdom of God.

27 Καὶ μετὰ ταῦτα ἐξῆλθε, ἢ ἐθεάσαῖο τελώνην ὀνόμαῖι Λευὶν, καθήμενον ἐπὶ τὸ τελώνιον, ἢ εἶπεν αὐτῷ· Ἀκολύθει μοι.

28 Καὶ καῖαλιπὼν ἅπαντα, ἀναςὰς ἠκολύθησεν αὐτῷ.

29 Καὶ ἐποίησε δοχὴν μεγάλην ὁ Λευὶς αὐτῷ ἐν τῇ οἰκίᾳ αὐτῦ· ἢ πολλοὶ τελῶναι ἢ ἁμαρτωλοὶ συνανέκειῆ]ο τῷ Ἰησῦ ἢ τοῖς μαθηῖαῖς αὐτῦ· ἦσαν γὰρ πολλοὶ, ἢ ἠκολύθησαν αὐτῷ.

16 Καὶ οἱ γραμμαῖεῖς ἢ οἱ φαρισαῖοι ἰδόνῖες αὐτὸν ἐσθίονῖα μετὰ τῶν τελωνῶν ἢ ἁμαρτωλῶν, ἔλεγον τοῖς μαθηῖαῖς αὐτῦ· Τί ὅτι μετὰ τῶν τελωνῶν ἢ ἁμαρτωλῶν ἐσθίει ἢ πίνει;

17 Καὶ ἀκύσας ὁ Ἰησῦς, λέγει αὐτοῖς· Οὐ χρείαν ἔχυσιν οἱ ἰσχύονῖες ἰαῖρῦ, ἀλλ᾽ οἱ κακῶς ἔχονῖες· ὐκ ἦλθον καλέσαι δικαίυς, ἀλλὰ ἁμαρτωλὺς εἰς μετάνοιαν.

36 Ἔλεγε δὲ ἢ παραβολὴν πρὸς αὐτύς· Ὅτι ὐδεὶς ἐπίβλημα ἱμαῖίυ καινῦ ἐπιβάλλει ἐπὶ ἱμάῖιον παλαιόν· εἰ δὲ μήγε, ἢ τὸ καινὸν σχίζει, ἢ τῷ παλαιῷ ὐ συμφωνεῖ ἐπίβλημα τὸ ἀπὸ τῦ καινῦ.

37 Καὶ ὐδεὶς βάλλει οἶνον νέον εἰς ἀσκὺς παλαιύς· εἰ δὲ μήγε, ῥήξει ὁ νέῷ εἶῷ τὰς ἀσκὺς, ἢ αὐτὸς ἐκχυθήσεῖαι, ἢ οἱ ἀσκοὶ ἀπολῦνῖαι.

38 Ἀλλὰ οἶνον νέον εἰς ἀσκὺς καινὺς βληῖέον· ἢ ἀμφότεροι συνῖηρῦνῖαι.

53 Καὶ ἐγένεῖο, ὅτε ἐτέλεσέν ὁ Ἰησῦς τὰς παραβολὰς ταύτας, μετῆρεν ἐκεῖθεν.

* 54 Καὶ ἐλθὼν εἰς τὴν ‡ παῖρίδα αὐτῦ, ἐδίδασκεν αὐτὺς ἐν τῇ συναγωγῇ αὐτῶν· ὥςε ἐκπλήῖτεσθαι αὐτὺς, ἢ λέγειν· Πόθεν τύτῳ ἡ σοφία αὕτη, ἢ αἱ δυνάμεις;

55 Οὐχ ὗτός ἐςιν ὁ τῦ τέκτονῷ υἱός; ὐχὶ ἡ μήτηρ αὐτῦ λέγεῖαι Μαριὰμ, ἢ οἱ ἀδελφοὶ αὐτῦ Ἰάκωβῷ, ἢ Ἰωσῆς, ἢ Σίμων, ἢ Ἰύδας;

56 Καὶ αἱ ἀδελφαὶ αὐτῦ ὐχὶ πᾶσαι πρὸς ἡμᾶς εἰσι; πόθεν ὖν

---

27 Et poſt hæc exiit, & conſpexit publicanum nomine, Levin, ſedentem ad telonium, & ait illi : Sequere me.

28 Et relinquens omnia, ſurgens ſequutus eſt eum.

29 Et fecit convivium magnum Levis ei in domo ſua : & multi publicani & peccatores ſimul diſcumbebant Jeſu, & diſcipulis ejus : erant enim multi, & ſequebantur eum.

16 Et Scribæ & Phariſæi videntes eum edentem cum publicanis & peccatoribus, dicebant diſcipulis ejus : Quid, quod cum publicanis & peccatoribus manducat & bibit ?

17 Et audiens Jeſus, ait illis : Non uſum habent valentes medico, ſed male habentes, non veni vocare juſtos, ſed peccatores ad pœnitentiam.

36 Dicebat autem & ſimilitudinem ad illos : Quia nemo adjectionem veſtimenti novi adjicit ad veſtimentum vetus : ſi vero non, & novum ſcindit, & veteri non convenit commiſſura à novo.

37 Et nemo conjicit vinum novum in utres veteres : ſi autem non, rumpet novum vinum utres, & ipſum effundetur, & utres peribunt.

38 Sed vinum novum in utres novos injiciendum, & utraque conſervantur.

53 Et factum eſt, quum conſummaſſet Jeſus parabolas iſtas, tranſiit inde.

54 Et veniens in patriam ſuam docebat eos in ſynagoga eorum, ita ut obſtupefieri ipſos, & dicere : Unde huic ſapientia hæc, & efficacitates ?

55 Nonne hic eſt fabri filius ? Nonne mater ejus dicitur Maria, & fratres ejus Jacobus, & Joſes, & Simon, & Judas ?

56 Et ſorores ejus, nonne omnes apud nos ſunt ? unde ergo

27. Après cela il sortit, et il vit un péager nommé Lévi, assis au bureau des impôts, et il lui dit: Suis-moi.

28. Et lui, quittant tout, se leva et le suivit.

29. Et Lévi lui fit un grand festin dans sa maison, où il se trouva plusieurs péagers et gens de mauvaise vie se mirent aussi à table avec Jésus et ses Disciples; car il y en avoit beaucoup qui l'avoient suivi.

16. Et les Scribes et les Pharisiens, voyant qu'il mangeoit avec des péagers et des gens de mauvaise vie, disoient à ses Disciples: Pourquoi votre Maître mange-t-il et boit-il avec les péagers, et les gens de mauvaise vie?

17. Et Jésus ayant ouï cela, leur dit: Ce ne sont pas ceux qui sont en santé qui ont besoin de Médecin, mais ce sont ceux qui se portent mal: Je suis venu appeler à la repentance, non les justes, mais les pécheurs.

36. Il leur dit aussi une similitude: Personne ne met une pièce d'un habit neuf à un vieux habit; autrement ce qui est neuf déchireroit, et la pièce du drap neuf ne convient point au vieux.

37. Personne aussi ne met le vin nouveau dans de vieux vaisseaux; autrement le vin nouveau romproit les vaisseaux, et se répandroit, et les vaisseaux seroient perdus.

38. Mais le vin nouveau doit être mis dans des vaisseaux neufs, et ainsi tous les deux se conservent.

53. Et il arriva que quand Jésus eut achevé ces similitudes, il se retira de ce lieu-là.

54. Et étant venu en sa patrie, il les enseignoit dans leur synagogue; de sorte qu'ils étoient étonnés, et qu'ils disoient: D'où viennent à cet homme cette sagesse et ces miracles?

55. N'est-ce pas le fils du charpentier? sa mère ne s'appelle-t-elle pas Marie, et ses frères, Jaques, Joses, Simon et Jude?

56. Et ses sœurs ne sont-elles pas toutes parmi nous? D'où lui

L. 5.

27 And after these things, he went forth, and saw a publican, named Levi, sitting at the receipt of custom: and he said unto him, Follow me.

28 And he left all, rose up, and followed him.

29 And Levi made him a great feast in his own house: and

15.
Mc. 2.

many publicans and sinners sat also together with Jesus and his disciples: for there were many, and they followed him.

16 And when the scribes and Pharisees saw him eat with publicans and sinners, they said unto his disciples, How is it that he eateth and drinketh with publicans and sinners?

17 When Jesus heard it, he saith unto them, They that are whole have no need of the physician, but they that are sick: I came not to call the righteous, but sinners to repentance.

L. 5.

36 And he spake also a parable unto them; No man putteth a piece of a new garment upon an old; if otherwise, then both the new maketh a rent, and the piece that was taken out of the new agreeth not with the old.

37 And no man putteth new wine into old bottles; else the new wine will burst the bottles, and be spilled, and the bottles shall perish.

38 But new wine must be put into new bottles: and both are preserved.

Mt. 13.

53 And it came to pass, that when Jesus had finished these parables, he departed thence.

54 And when he was come into his own country, he taught them in their synagogue, insomuch that they were astonished, and said, Whence hath this man this wisdom, and these mighty works?

55 Is not this the carpenter's son? is not his mother called Mary? and his brethren, James, and Joses, and Simon, and Judas?

56 And his sisters, are they not all with us? Whence then hath

ότω ταῦτα πάντα;

57 Καὶ ἐσκανδαλίζοντο ἐν αὐτῷ. Ὁ δὲ Ἰησῦς εἶπεν αὐτοῖς.
Οὐκ ἔςι προφήτης ἄτιμ⊙, εἰ μὴ
ἐν τῇ πατρίδι αὐτῦ, ἢ ἐν τῇ οἰκίᾳ
αὐτῦ.

36 Ἰδὼν δὲ τοὺς ὄχλους, ἐ-
σπλαγχνίσθη περὶ αὐτῶν, ὅτι ἦσαν
ἐκλελυμένοι ἢ ἐῤῥιμμένοι ὡσεὶ πρόβατα μὴ ἔχοντα ποιμένα.

7 Καὶ προσκαλεῖται τοὺς δώδεκα, ἢ ἤρξατο αὐτοὺς ἀποςέλ-
λειν δύο δύο· ἢ
παραγγείλας αὐτοῖς,
λέγων· Εἰς ὁδὸν ἐθνῶν μὴ ἀπέλθη-
τε, ἢ εἰς πόλιν Σαμαρειτῶν μὴ
εἰσέλθητε.

6 Πορεύεσθε δὲ μᾶλλον πρὸς τὰ
πρόβατα τὰ ἀπολωλότα οἴκου
Ἰσραήλ.

9 Μὴ κτήσησθε χρυσὸν, μηδὲ
ἄργυρον, μηδὲ χαλκὸν εἰς τὰς ζώ-
νας ὑμῶν.

*10 Μὴ ‡ πήραν εἰς ὁδὸν, μηδὲ
δύο χιτῶνας, μηδὲ ὑποδήματα,
μηδὲ ῥάβδον· ἄξι⊙· γὰρ ὁ ἐργάτης τῆς τροφῆς αὐτοῦ ἐςιν.

11 Εἰς ἣν δ᾽ ἂν πόλιν ἢ κώμην
εἰσέλθητε, ἐξετάσατε τίς ἐν αὐτῇ
ἄξιός ἐςι· κἀκεῖ μείνατε ἕως ἂν
ἐξέλθητε.

12 Εἰσερχόμενοι δὲ εἰς τὴν οἰκίαν, ἀσπάσασθη αὐτήν.

13 Καὶ ἐὰν μὲν ἢ ἡ οἰκία ἀξία,
ἐλθέτω ἡ εἰρήνη ὑμῶν ἐπ᾽ αὐτήν·
ἐὰν δὲ μὴ ἢ ἀξία, ἡ εἰρήνη ὑμῶν
πρὸς ὑμᾶς ἐπιςραφήτω.

14 Καὶ ὃς ἐὰν μὴ δέξηται ὑμᾶς,
μηδὲ ἀκούσῃ τοὺς λόγους ὑμῶν,
ἐξερχόμενοι τῆς οἰκίας ἢ τῆς πόλεως ἐκείνης, ἐκτινάξατε τὸν κο-
νιορτὸν τῶν ποδῶν ὑμῶν.

15 Ἀμὴν λέγω ὑμῖν, ἀνεκτότε-
ρον ἔςαι γῇ Σοδόμων ἢ Γομόῤῥων
ἐν ἡμέρᾳ κρίσεως, ἢ τῇ πόλει ἐ-
κείνῃ.

16 Ἰδοὺ, ἐγὼ ἀποςέλλω ὑμᾶς
ὡς πρόβατα ἐν μέσῳ λύκων· γίνεσθε οὖν φρόνιμοι ὡς οἱ ὄφεις, ἢ
ἀκέραιοι ὡς αἱ περιςεραί.

17 Προσέχετε δὲ ἀπὸ τῶν ἀν-
θρώπων· παραδώσουσι γὰρ ὑμᾶς
εἰς συνέδρια, ἢ ἐν ταῖς συναγωγαῖς
αὐτῶν μαςιγώσουσιν ὑμᾶς.

huic illa omnia?

57 Et ſcandalizabantur in eo.
At Jeſus dixit eis: non eſt Propheta inhonoratus, ſi non in pa-
tria ſua, & in domo ſua.

36 Videns autem turbas, mi-
ſertus eſt de eis, quia erant vex-
ati, & diſperſi ſicut oves non
habentes paſtorem.

7 Et advocat duodecim : &
cœpit eos mittere duos duos, &
denuncians eis, dicens: In viam
gentium ne abieritis, & in civitatem Samaritanorum ne intraveritis.

6 Ite autem magis ad oves
perditas domus Iſraël.

9 Ne poſſideatis aurum, neque argentum, neque æs in zo-
nis veſtris :

10 Non peram in viam, neque
duas tunicas, neque calceamenta, neque virgam: dignus enim
operarius alimento ſuo eſt.

11 In quamcunque autem civitatem aut caſtellum intraveritis, interrogate quis in ea dignus
ſit : & ibi manete donec exeatis.

12 Intrantes autem in do-
mum, ſalutate eam.

13 Et ſi quidem fuerit domus
digna, ingrediatur pax veſtra
ſuper eam : ſi autem non fuerit
digna, pax veſtra ad vos conver-
tatur.

14 Et qui non receperit vos
neque audierit ſermones veſtros,
exeuntes domo vel civitate illâ,
excutite pulverem pedum veſ-
trorum.

15 Amen dico vobis, Tolera-
bilius erit terræ Sodomorum &
Gomorrhæorum in die judicii,
quam civitati illi.

16 Ecce ego mitto vos ſicut o-
ves in medio luporum. Eſtote
ergo prudentes ſicut ſerpentes,
& ſimplices ſicut columbæ.

17 Cavete autem ab hominibus :
Tradent enim vos in conſeſſus, &
in ſynagogis ſuis flagellabunt vos.

viennent donc toutes ces choses?
57. De sorte qu'ils se scandali-
soient de lui. Mais Jésus leur dit:
Un Prophète n'est méprisé que
dans son pays et dans sa maison.
58. Et il ne fit là que peu de
miracles, à cause de leur incrédulité.

36. Et voyant la multitude de
peuple, il fut ému de compassion
envers eux, de ce qu'ils étoient
dispersés et errans, comme des
brebis qui n'ont point de berger.

7. Alors il appela les douze, et
il commença à les envoyer deux à
deux
                  et
il leur donna ses ordres, en disant: N'allez point vers les Gen-
tils; et n'entrez dans aucune ville
des Samaritains.
6. Mais allez plutôt aux brebis de
la Maison d'Israël, qui sont per-
dues.
9. Ne prenez ni or, ni argent, ni
monnoie dans vos ceintures;

10. Ni sac pour le voyage, ni deux
habits, ni souliers, ni bâton; càr
l'ouvrier est digne de sa nourriture.
11. Et dans quelque ville ou dans
quelque bourgade que vous entriez, informez-vous qui est digne
de vous recevoir; et demeurez-y,
jusqu'à-ce que vous partiez de ce
lieu-là.
12. Et quand vous entrerez dans
quelque maison, saluez-la.
13. Et si la maison en est digne,
que votre paix vienne sur elle;
mais si elle n'en est pas digne, que
votre paix retourne à vous.
14. Et par-tout où l'on ne vous
recevra pas, et où l'on n'écoutera
pas vos paroles, en sortant de cette
maison ou de cette ville, secouez
la poussière de vos pieds.
15. Je vous dis en vérité, que Sodome et Gomorrhe seront traitées
moins rigoureusement au jour du
Jugement, que cette ville-là.
16. Voici, je vous envoie comme
des brebis au milieu des loups;
soyez donc prudens comme des serpens, et simples comme des co-
lombes.
17. Mais donnez-vous garde des
hommes; car ils vous livreront
aux Tribunaux, et ils vous feront
fouetter dans les synagogues;

this man all these things?
57 And they were offended in
him. But Jesus said unto them,
A prophet is not without honour,
save in his own country, and in
his own house.

36 But when he saw the multitudes, he was moved with compassion on them, because they faint-
ed, and were scattered abroad, as
sheep having no shepherd.

And he calleth unto him the
twelve, and began to send them
forth by two and two;

and commanded them, saying,
Go not into the way of the Gentiles, and into any city of the Samaritans enter ye not:
6 But go rather to the lost sheep
of the house of Israel.
9 Provide neither gold, nor silver, nor brass in your purses;
10 Nor scrip for your journey,
neither two coats, neither shoes,
nor yet staves: for the workman
is worthy of his meat.
11 And into whatsoever city or
town ye shall enter, enquire who
in it is worthy; and there abide
till ye go thence.
12 And when ye come into an
house, salute it.
13 And if the house be worthy,
let your peace come upon it: but
if it be not worthy, let your peace
return to you.
14 And whosoever shall not receive you, nor hear your words,
when ye depart out of that house,
or city, shake off the dust of your
feet.
15 Verily I say unto you, It
shall be more tolerable for the
land of Sodom and Gomorrha, in
the day of judgment, than for
that city.
16 Behold, I send you forth as
sheep in the midst of wolves: be
ye, therefore, wise as serpents,
and harmless as doves.
17 But beware of men: for they
will deliver you up to the councils, and they will scourge you

29

18 Καὶ ἐπὶ ἡγεμόνας δὲ ᾳ βασιλεῖς ἀχθήσεσθε ἕνεκεν ἐμᾶ, εἰς
μαρτύριον αὐτοῖς ᾳ τοῖς ἔθνεσιν.

18 Et ad præsides autem & reges agemini propter me, in tef-
timonium illis, & gentibus.

23 Ὅταν δὲ διώκωσιν ὑμᾶς ἐν
τῇ πόλει ταύτῃ, φεύγετε εἰς τὴν
ἄλλην·

23 Quum autem insequentur
vos in civitate istâ, fugite in a-
liam.

26 Μὴ οὖν φοβηθῆτε αὐτούς·
οὐδὲν γάρ ἐςι κεκαλυμμένον, ὃ οὐκ
ἀποκαλυφθήσεται, ᾳ κρυπτὸν, ὃ
οὐ γνωσθήσεται.

26 Ne ergo timueritis eos.
Nihil enim est occultum, quod
non revelabitur, & abditum,
quod non scietur.

27 Ὁ λέγω ὑμῖν ἐν τῇ σκοτίᾳ,
εἴπατε ἐν τῷ φωτί· ᾳ ὃ εἰς τὸ ἦς
ἀκούετε, κηρύξατε ἐπὶ τῶν δωμάτων.

27 Quod dico vobis in tenebris, dicite in lumine: & quod
in aurem auditis, prædicate super domos.

28 Καὶ μὴ φοβεῖσθε ἀπὸ τῶν
ἀποκτεινόντων τὸ σῶμα, τὴν δὲ
ψυχὴν μὴ δυναμένων ἀποκτεῖναι·
φοβήθητε δὲ μᾶλλον τὸν δυνάμε-
νον ᾳ ψυχὴν ᾳ σῶμα ἀπολέσαι ἐν
γεέννῃ.

28 Et ne timeatis ab occidentibus corpus, at animam non
valentibus occidere: timete autem magis potentem & animam
& corpus perdere in gehenna.

* 29 Οὐ χὶ δύο ‡ ςρουθία ‡ ἀσσα-
ρίου ‡ πωλεῖται, ᾳ ἓν ἐξ αὐτῶν οὐ
πεσεῖται ἐπὶ τὴν γῆν, ‡ ἄνευ τοῦ
πατρὸς ὑμῶν;

29 Nonne duo passeres asse
væneunt? & unus ex illis non
cadet super terram, sine Patre
vestro.

30 Ὑμῶν δὲ ᾳ αἱ τρίχες τῆς
κεφαλῆς πᾶσαι ἐριθμημέναι εἰσί.

30 Vestri autem & capill'
capitis omnes numerati sunt.

31 Μή οὖν φοβηθῆτε· πολλῶν
ςρουθίων διαφέρετε ὑμεῖς.

31 Ne ergo timeatis: multis
passeribus præstatis vos.

12 Καὶ ἐξελθόντες ἐκήρυσσον,
ἵνα μετανοήσωσι·

12 Et exeuntes prædicabant
ut pœniterent.

30 Καὶ συνάγονίαι οἱ ἀπίςο-
λοι πρὸς τὸν Ἰησῦν, ᾳ ἀπήγ-
γειλαν αὐτῷ πάνία, ᾳ ὅσα ἐποίησαν, ᾳ ὅσα ἐδίδαξαν.

30 Et coguntur Apostoli ad
Jesum, & renuntiaverunt ei omnia, & quanta egerant & quanta
docuerant.

Κεφ. ζ. 7.

1 ΚΑΙ' περιεπάτει ὁ Ἰησῦς μετὰ ταῦτα ἐν τῇ Γαλιλαίᾳ·
ἀ γὰρ ἤθελεν ἐν τῇ Ἰυδαίᾳ περι-
πατεῖν, ὅτι ἐζήτων αὐτὸν οἱ Ἰε-
δαῖοι ἀποκλεῖναι.

CAPUT VII.

1 ET ambulabat Jesus post
hæc in Galilæa: non e-
nim volebat in Judæa ambulare,
quia quærebant eum Judæi interficere.

Κεφ. ζ'. 7.

1 ΚΑΙ' συνάγονίαι πρὸς αὐτὸν
οἱ Φαρισαῖοι, καί τινες τῶν
Γραμματέων, ἐλθόντες ἀπὸ Ἱερο-
σολύμων.

CAPUT VII.

1 ET conveniunt ad eum
Pharisæi, & qnidam Scri-
barum venientes ab Hierosolymis.

* 2 Καὶ ἰδόντες τινὰς τῶν
μαθητῶν αὐτᾶ ‡ κοιναῖς χερσὶ
(τῦτ᾽ ἔςιν ‡ ἀνίπίοις) ἐσθίονίας
ἄρτυς, ‡ ἐμέμψανίο.

2 Et videntes quosdam discipulorum ejus communibus
manibus (hoc est, illotis) edentes panes, incusarunt.

* 3 (Οἱ γὰρ Φαρισαῖοι ᾳ
πάνίες οἱ Ἰυδαῖοι, ‡ ἐὰν μὴ ‡
πυγμῇ ‡ νίψωνίαι τὰς χεῖρ᾽ς ἠκ
ἐσθίεσι, κρατῦνίες τὴν παράδοσιν
τῶν πρεσβυτέρων.

3 Nam Pharisæi & omnes
Judæi, si non pugillatim lave-
rint manus, non manducant,
tenentes traditionem seniorum:

18. Et vous serez menés devant les Gouverneurs, et devant les Rois, à cause de moi, pour me rendre témoignage devant eux et devant les nations.

18 And ye shall be brought before governors and kings for my sake, for a testimony against them and the Gentiles.

23. Or, quand ils vous persécuteront dans une ville, fuyez dans une autre:

23 But when they persecute you in this city, flee ye into another:

26. Ne les craignez donc point; car il n'y a rien de caché qui ne doive être découvert; ni rien de secret qui ne doive être connu.

26 Fear them not, therefore: for there is nothing covered, that shall not be revealed; and hid, that shall not be known.

27. Ce que je vous dis dans les ténèbres, dites-le dans la lumière; et ce que je vous dis à l'oreille, prêchez-le sur le haut des maisons.

27 What I tell you in darkness, *that* speak ye in light: and what ye hear in the ear, *that* preach ye upon the housetops.

28. Et ne craignez point ceux qui ôtent la vie du corps, et qui ne peuvent faire mourir l'âme; mais craignez plutôt celui qui peut perdre et l'âme et le corps dans la géhenne.

28 And fear not them which kill the body, but are not able to kill the soul: but rather fear him which is able to destroy both soul and body in hell.

29. Deux passeraux ne se vendent-ils pas une pite? Et néanmoins il n'en tombera pas un seul à terre sans *la permission de* votre Père.

29 Are not two sparrows sold for a farthing? and one of them shall not fall on the ground without your Father.

30. Les cheveux même de vôtre tête sont tous comptés.

30 But the very hairs of your head are all numbered.

31. Ne craignez donc rien; vous valez mieux que beaucoup de passeraux.

31 Fear ye not, therefore, ye are of more value than many spar.

12. Etant donc partis, ils prêchèrent qu'on s'amendât.

Mc. 6.

12 And they went out, and preached that men should repent.

30. Et les Apôtres se rassemblèrent auprès de Jésus, et lui racontèrent tout ce qu'ils avoient fait, et tout ce qu'ils avoient enseigné.

30 And the apostles gathered themselves together unto Jesus, and told him all things, both what they had done, and what they had taught.

5. 7.

APRÈS ces choses, Jésus se tenoit en Galilée; car il ne vouloit pas demeurer dans la Judée, parce que les Juifs cherchoient à le faire mourir.

AFTER these things Jesus walked in Galilee: for he would not walk in Jewry, because the Jews sought to kill him.

Mc. 7.

ALors des Pharisiens et quelques Scribes, qui étoient venus de Jérusalem, s'assemblèrent vers Jésus.

THEN came together unto him, the Pharisees, and certain of the scribes, which came from Jerusalem.

2. Et voyant que quelques-uns de ses Disciples prenoient leur repas avec des mains souillées, c'est-à-dire, qui n'avoient pas été lavées, ils les en blâmoient.

2 And when they saw some of his disciples eat bread with defiled (that is to say, with unwashen) hands, they found fault.

3. Car les Pharisiens et tous les Juifs ne mangent point sans se laver les mains jusqu'au coude, gardant en cela la tradition des anciens;

3 For the Pharisees, and all the Jews, except they wash *their* hands oft, eat not, holding the tradition of the elders.

30

* 4 Καὶ ἀπὸ ἀγοϱᾶς, ἐὰν μὴ βαπτίσωνlαι, ἐκ ἐσθίυσι· κ̇ ἄλλα πολλά ἐςι, ἃ ‡ παϱέλαβον κϱατεῖν, ‡ βαπλισμὲς ‡ ποlηϱίων κ̇ ‡ ξεςῶν κ̇ ‡ χαλκίων κ̇ ‡ κλινῶν.)

5 Ἔπειlα ἐπεϱωτῶσιν αὐτὸν οἱ Φαϱισαῖοι κ̇ οἱ Γϱαμμαlεῖς· Διατί οἱ μαθηlαί σε ἐ πεϱιπαlᾶσι κατὰ τὴν παϱάδοσιν τῶν πϱεσβυτέϱων, ἀλλὰ ἀνίπlοις χεϱσὶν ἐσθίυσι τὸν ἄϱlον;

14 Καὶ πϱοσκαλεσάμενος πάνlα τὸν ὄχλον, ἔλεγεν αὐτοῖς· Ἀκ̇ετέ μυ πάνlες, κ̇ συνίεlε.

15 Οὐδὲν ἐςιν ἔξωθεν τῦ ἀνθϱώπυ εἰσποϱευόμενον εἰς αὐτὸν, ὃ δύναlαι αὐτὸν κοινῶσαι ἀλλὰ τὰ ἐκποϱευόμενα ἀπ' αὐτῦ, ἐκεῖνά ἐςι τὰ κοινῦνlα τὸν ἄνθϱωπον.

16 Εἴ τις ἔχει ὦlα ἀκ̇ειν, ἀκ̇ειτω.

17 Καὶ ὅτε εἰσῆλθεν εἰς οἶκον ἀπὸ τῦ ὄχλυ, ἐπηϱώτων αὐτὸν οἱ μαθηlαὶ αὐτῦ πεϱὶ τῆς παϱαβοlῆς;

18 Καὶ λέγει αὐτοῖς· Οὕτω κ̇ ὑμεῖς ἀσύνεlοί ἐςε; ἐ νοεῖτε ὅτι πᾶν τὸ ἔξαθεν εἰσποϱευόμενον εἰς τὸν ἄνθϱωπον, ἐ δύναlαι αὐτὸν κοινῶσαι;

* 19 Ὅτι ἐκ εἰσποϱεύεlαι αὐτῦ εἰς τὴν καϱδίαν, ἀλλ' εἰς τὴν κοιλίαν κ̇ εἰς τὸν ‡ ἀφεδϱῶνα ‡ ἐκποϱεύεlαι, καθαϱίζον πάνlα τὰ βϱώμαlα.

20 Ἔλεγε δὲ, ὅτι τὸ ἐκ τῦ ἀνθϱώπυ ἐκποϱευόμενον, ἐκεῖνο κοινοῖ τὸν ἄνθϱωπον.

21 Ἔσωθεν γὰϱ ἐκ τῆς καϱδίας τῶν ἀνθϱώπων οἱ διαλογισμοὶ οἱ κακοὶ ἐκποϱεύονlαι, μοιχεῖαι, ποϱνεῖαι, φόνοι,

22 ‡ Κλοπαὶ, ‡ πλεονεξίαι, ‡ πονηϱίαι, ‡ δόλ⊙, ‡ ἀσέλγεια, ὀφθαλμὸς πονηϱὸς, ‡ βλασφημία, † ὑπεϱηφανία, ‡ ἀφϱοσύνη.

23 Πάνlα ταῦτα τὰ πονηϱὰ ἔσωθεν ἐκποϱεύεlαι, κ̇ κοινοῖ τὸν ἄνθϱωπον.

* 24 Καὶ ἐκεῖθεν ἀναςὰς ἀπῆλθεν εἰς τὰ † μεθόϱια Τύϱυ κ̇ Σιδῶν⊙· κ̇ εἰσελθὼν εἰς τὴν οἰκίαν, ἐδένα ἤθελε γνῶναι· κ̇ ἐκ ἠδυνήθη ‡ λαθεῖν.

4 Et à foro, si non baptizentur, non comedunt : & alia multa sunt, quæ assumpserunt tenere, lotiones poculorum & sextariorum, & æramentorum & lectorum.

5 Deinde interrogant eum Pharisæi & Scribæ : Quare discipuli tui non ambulant juxta traditionem seniorum, sed illotis manibus manducant panem?

14 Et advocans omnem turbam, dicebat illis : Audite me omnes, & intelligite :

15 Nihil est extra hominem introiens in cum, quod potest eum communicare : sed exeuntia ab eo, illa sunt comunicantia hominem.

16 Si quis habet aures ad audiendum, audiat,

17 Et quum introisset in domum à turba, interrogabant eum discipuli ejus de parabola.

18 Et ait illis : Sic & vos imprudentes estis? Non consideratis, quia omne extrinsecus introiens in hominem, non potest eum communicare?

19 Quia non intrat ejus in cor, sed in ventrem, & in secessum exit : purgans omnes escas.

20 Dicebat autem, quod ex homine egressum, illud communicat hominem.

21 Intus enim, de corde hominum ratiocinationes malæ egrediuntur, adulteria, fornicationes, cædes,

22 Furta, avaritiæ, malitiæ, dolus, lascivia, oculus malus, blasphemia, superbia, amentia.

23 Omnia hæc mala ab intus egrediuntur, & communicant hominem.

24 Et inde surgens, abiit in confinia Tyri & Sidonis : & ingressus in domum, neminem voluit scire, & non potuit latere.

4. Et lorsqu'ils reviennent des places publiques, ils ne mangent point non plus sans s'être lavés. Il y a aussi beaucoup d'autres choses qu'ils ont reçues pour les observer, comme de laver les coupes, les pots, les vaisseaux d'airain, et les lits.

5. Là-dessus les Pharisiens et les Scribes lui demandèrent : D'où vient que tes Disciples ne suivent pas la tradition des anciens, et qu'ils prennent leur repas sans se laver les mains ?

14. Alors ayant appelé toute la multitude, il leur dit : Ecoutez-moi tous, et comprenez-ceci :

15. Rien de ce qui est hors de l'homme, et qui entre dans lui, ne le peut souiller ; mais ce qui sort de lui, voilà ce qui souille l'homme.

16. Si quelqu'un a des oreilles pour entendre, qu'il entende.

17. Quand il fut entré dans la maison, *après s'être retiré* d'avec la multitude, ses Disciples l'interrogèrent sur cette parabole.

18. Et il leur dit : Etes-vous aussi sans intelligence ? Ne comprenez-vous pas, que rien de ce qui entre de dehors dans l'homme ne le peut souiller ?

19. Parce que cela n'entre pas dans son cœur, mais qu'il va au ventre ; et qu'il sort aux lieux secrets, avec tout ce que les alimens ont d'impur ?

20. Il leur disoit donc : Ce qui sort de l'homme, c'est ce qui souille l'homme.

21. Car du dedans du cœur des hommes, sortent les mauvaises pensées, les adultères, les fornications, les meurtres.

22. Les larcins, les mauvais moyens, pour avoir le bien d'autrui, les méchancetés, la fraude, l'impudicité, l'œil envieux, la médisance, la fierté, la folie.

23. Tous ces vices sortent du dedans, et souillent l'homme.

24. Puis étant parti de là, il s'en alla aux frontières de Tyr et de Sidon ; et étant entré dans une maison, il ne vouloit pas que personne le sût ; mais il ne put être caché.

4 And *when they come* from the market, except they wash, they eat not. And many other things there be, which they have received to hold, *as* the washing of cups, and pots, and of brasen vessels, and tables.

5 Then the Pharisees and scribes asked him, Why walk not thy disciples according to the tradition of the elders, but eat bread with unwashen hands?

14 And, when he had called all the people *unto him*, he said unto them, Hearken unto me every one *of you*, and understand:

15 There is nothing from without a man, that entering into him can defile him : but the things which come out of him, those are they that defile the man.

16 If any man have ears to hear, let him hear.

17 And, when he was entered into the house from the people, his disciples asked him concerning the parable.

18 And he saith unto them, Are ye so without understanding also ? Do ye not perceive, that whatsoever thing from without entereth into the man, *it* cannot defile him ;

19 Because it entereth not into his heart, but into the belly, and goeth out into the draught, purging all meats?

20 And he said, That which cometh out of the man, that defileth the man.

21 For from within, out of the heart of men, proceed evil thoughts, adulteries, fornications, murders,

22 Thefts, covetousness, wickedness, deceit, lasciviousness, an evil eye, blasphemy, pride, foolishness:

23 All these evil things come from within, and defile the man.

24 And from thence he arose, and went into the borders of Tyre and Sidon, and entered into an house, and would have no man know *it* : but he could not be hid.

31

Κεφ. ιη'. 18.

CAPUT XVIII.

1 ΕΝ ἐκείνῃ τῇ ὥρᾳ προσῆλθον οἱ μαθηταὶ τῷ Ἰησῷ, λέγοντες· Τίς ἄρα μείζων ἐςὶν ἐν τῇ βασιλείᾳ τῶν οὐρανῶν;

2 Καὶ προσκαλεσάμενος ὁ Ἰησῦς παιδίον, ἔςησεν αὐτὸ ἐν μέσῳ αὐτῶν,

3 Καὶ εἶπεν· Ἀμὴν λέγω ὑμῖν, ἐὰν μὴ ςραφῆτε, κ̣ γένησθε ὡς τὰ παιδία, ὐ μὴ εἰσέλθητε εἰς τὴν βασιλείαν τῶν ὐρανῶν.

4 Ὅςις ἒν ταπεινώσῃ ἑαυτὸν ὡς τὸ παιδίον τῦτο, ὖτός ἐςιν ὁ μείζων ἐν τῇ βασιλείᾳ τῶν ὐρανῶν.

7 Οὐαὶ τῷ κόσμῳ ἀπὸ τῶν σκανδάλων· ἀνάγκη γάρ ἐςιν ἐλθεῖν τὰ σκάνδαλα· πλὴν ὐαὶ τῷ ἀνθρώπῳ ἐκείνῳ, δι' ὖ τὸ σκάνδαλον ἔρχεται.

8 Εἰ δὲ ἡ χείρ σȣ, ἢ ὁ πȣς σȣ σκανδαλίζει σε, ἔκκοψον αὐτὰ, κ̣ βάλε ἀπὸ σȣ· καλόν σοι ἐςὶν εἰσελθεῖν εἰς τὴν ζωὴν χωλὸν, ἢ κυλλὸν, ἢ δύο χεῖρας ἢ δύο πόδας ἔχοντα, βληθῆναι εἰς τὸ πῦρ τὸ αἰώνιον.

9 Καὶ εἰ ὁ ὀφθαλμός σȣ σκανδαλίζει σε, ἔξελε αὐτὸν, κ̣ βάλε ἀπὸ σȣ· καλόν σοι ἐςὶ μονόφθαλμον εἰς τὴν ζωὴν εἰσελθεῖν, ἢ δύο ὀφθαλμὲς ἔχοντα βληθῆναι εἰς τὴν γέενναν τȣ πυρός.

12 Τί ὑμῖν δοκεῖ; ἐὰν γένηται τινι ἀνθρώπῳ ἑκατὸν πρόβατα, κ̣ πλανηθῇ ἓν ἐξ αὐτῶν· ὐχὶ ἀφεὶς τὰ ἐννενηκονταεννέα, ἐπὶ τὰ ὄρη πορευθεὶς, ζητεῖ τὸ πλανώμενον;

13 Καὶ ἐὰν γένηται εὑρεῖν αὐτὸ, ἀμὴν λέγω ὑμῖν, ὅτι χαίρει ἐπ' αὐτῷ μᾶλλον, ἢ ἐπὶ τοῖς ἐννενηκονταεννέα, τοῖς μὴ πεπλανημένοις.

14 Οὕτως ὐκ ἔςι θέλημα ἔμπροσθεν τȣ πατρὸς ὑμῶν, τȣ ἐν ὐρανοῖς, ἵνα ἀπόληται εἷς τῶν μικρῶν τȣτων.

15 Ἐὰν δὲ ἁμαρτήσῃ εἰς σὲ ὁ ἀδελφός σȣ, ὕπαγε, κ̣ ἔλεγξον αὐτὸν μεταξὺ σȣ κ̣ αὐτȣ μόνȣ· ἐάν σȣ ἀκȣσῃ, ἐκέρδησας τὸν ἀδελφόν σȣ.

1 IN illa hora accesserunt discipuli Jesu; dicentes: Quisnam major est in regno cælorum?

2 Et advocans Jesus puerulum, statuit eum in medio eorum.

3 Et dixit: Amen dico vobis, si non conversi fueritis, & efficiamini sicut pueruli, nequaquam intrabitis in regnum cælorum.

4 Quicumque ergo humiliaverit seipsum ut puerulus iste, hic est major in regno cælorum.

7 Væ mundo à scandalis: Necesse enim est venire scandala: verumtamen væ homini illi, per quem scandalum venit.

8 Si autem manus tua, vel pes tuus scandalizat te, abscinde ea, & jace abs te: pulchrum tibi est ingredi ad vitam claudum vel mancum, quam duas manus vel duos pedes habentem, jaci in ignem æternum.

9 Et si oculus tuus scandalizat te, erue eum, & jace abs te; pulchrum tibi est unoculum in vitam intrare, quam duos oculos habentem jaci in gehennam ignis.

12 Quid vobis videtur? fuerint alicui homini centum oves, & erraverit una ex eis: nonne relinquens nonaginta novem, in montes vadens quærit errantem?

13 Et si fiat invenire eam, amen dico vobis, quia gaudet super ea magis, quam super nonaginta novem non aberrantibus.

14 Sic non est voluntas ante Patrem vestrum qui in cælis, ut pereat unus parvulorum horum.

15 Si autem peccaverit in te frater tuus, vade, & corripe eum inter te & ipsum solum: Si te audierit, lucratus es fratrem tuum.

EN cette même heure-là, les Disciples vinrent à Jésus, et lui dirent : Qui est le plus grand dans le Royaume des cieux ?

2. Et Jésus ayant fait venir un enfant, le mit au milieu d'eux,

3. Et dit : Je vous le dis en vérité, que si vous n'êtes changés, et si vous ne devenez comme des enfans, vous n'entrerez point dans le Royaume des cieux.

4. C'est pourquoi, quiconque s'humiliera soi-même, comme cet enfant, celui-là est le plus grand dans le Royaume des cieux.

7. Malheur au monde à cause des scandales ; car il est nécessaire qu'il arrive des scandales ; mais malheur à l'homme par qui le scandale arrive !

8. Que si ta main ou ton pied te fait tomber *dans le péché*, coupe-les, et jette-les loin de toi ; car il vaut mieux que tu entres boiteux ou manchot dans la vie, que d'avoir deux pieds ou deux mains, et d'être jeté dans le feu éternel.

9. Et si ton œil te fait tomber *dans le péché*, arrache-le, et jette-le loin de toi ; car il vaut mieux que tu entres dans la vie n'ayant qu'un œil, que d'avoir deux yeux, et d'être jeté dans la géhenne du feu.

12. Que vous en semble ? Si un homme a cent brebis, et qu'il y en ait une égarée, ne laisse-t-il pas les quatre-vingt-dix-neuf, pour s'en aller par les montagnes chercher celle qui s'est égarée ?

13. Et s'il arrive qu'il la trouve, je vous dis en verité, qu'il en a plus de joie, que des quatre-vingt-dix-neuf qui ne sont point égarées.

14. Ainsi la volonté de votre Père qui *est* aux cieux, n'est pas qu'aucun de ces petits périsse.

15. Si ton frère a péché contre toi, va, et reprends-le entre toi et lui seul ; s'il t'écoute, tu auras gagné ton frère.

AT the same time came the disciples unto Jesus, saying, Who is the greatest in the kingdom of heaven ?

2 And Jesus called a little child unto him, and set him in the midst of them,

3 And said, Verily I say unto you, Except ye be converted, and become as little children, ye shall not enter into the kingdom of heaven.

4 Whosoever, therefore, shall humble himself as this little child, the same is greatest in the kingdom of heaven.

7 Woe unto the world because of offences ! for it must needs be that offences come ; but woe to that man by whom the offence cometh !

8 Wherefore, if thy hand or thy foot offend thee, cut them off, and cast *them* from thee : it is better for thee to enter into life halt or maimed, rather than having two hands, or two feet, to be cast into everlasting fire

9 And if thine eye offend thee, pluck it out, and cast *it* from thee : it is better for thee to enter into life with one eye, rather than having two eyes to be cast into hell-fire.

12 How think ye ? if a man have an hundred sheep, and one of them be gone astray, doth he not leave the ninety and nine, and goeth into the mountains, and seeketh that which is gone astray ?

13 And if so be that he find it, verily I say unto you, He rejoiceth more of that *sheep*, than of the ninety and nine which went not astray.

14 Even so it is not the will of your Father which is in heaven, that one of these little ones should perish.

15 Moreover, if thy brother shall trespass against thee, go and tell him his fault between thee and him alone : if he shall hear thee,

32

16 Ἐὰν δὲ μὴ ἀκούσῃ, παράλαβε μετὰ σοῦ ἔτι ἕνα ἢ δύο· ἵνα ἐπὶ στόματος δύο μαρτύρων ἢ τριῶν σταθῇ πᾶν ῥῆμα.

* 17 Ἐὰν δὲ παρακούσῃ αὐτῶν, εἰπὲ τῇ ἐκκλησίᾳ· ἐὰν δὲ καὶ τῆς ‡ ἐκκλησίας ‡ παρακούσῃ, ἔστω σοι ὥσπερ ὁ ἐθνικὸς καὶ ὁ τελώνης.

21 Τότε προσελθὼν αὐτῷ ὁ Πέτρος, εἶπε· Κύριε, ποσάκις ἁμαρτήσει εἰς ἐμὲ ὁ ἀδελφός μου, καὶ ἀφήσω αὐτῷ; ἕως ἑπτάκις;

22 Λέγει αὐτῷ ὁ Ἰησοῦς· Οὐ λέγω σοι, ἕως ‡ ἑπτάκις, ἀλλ᾽ ἕως † ἑβδομηκοντάκις ‡ ἑπτά.

23 Διὰ τοῦτο ὡμοιώθη ἡ βασιλεία τῶν οὐρανῶν ἀνθρώπῳ βασιλεῖ, ὃς ἠθέλησε συνᾶραι λόγον μετὰ τῶν δούλων αὐτοῦ.

* 24 ‡ Ἀρξαμένου δὲ αὐτοῦ ‡ συναίρειν, προσηνέχθη αὐτῷ εἷς ‡ ὀφειλέτης ‡ μυρίων ‡ ταλάντων·

25 Μὴ ἔχοντος δὲ αὐτοῦ ἀποδοῦναι, ἐκέλευσεν αὐτὸν ὁ κύριος αὐτοῦ πραθῆναι, καὶ τὴν γυναῖκα αὐτοῦ, καὶ τὰ τέκνα, καὶ πάντα ὅσα εἶχε, καὶ ἀποδοθῆναι.

26 Πεσὼν οὖν ὁ δοῦλος προσεκύνει αὐτῷ, λέγων· Κύριε, μακροθύμησον ἐπ᾽ ἐμοί, καὶ πάντα σοι ἀποδώσω.

* 27 Σπλαγχνισθεὶς δὲ ὁ κύριος τοῦ δούλου ἐκείνου, ἀπέλυσεν αὐτὸν, καὶ τὸ † δάνειον ἀφῆκεν αὐτῷ.

28 Ἐξελθὼν δὲ ὁ δοῦλος ἐκεῖνος, εὗρεν ἕνα τῶν συνδούλων αὐτοῦ, ὃς ὤφειλεν αὐτῷ ἑκατὸν δηνάρια· καὶ κρατήσας αὐτὸν ἔπνιγε, λέγων· Ἀπόδος μοι, ὅ,τι ὀφείλεις.

29 Πεσὼν οὖν ὁ σύνδουλος αὐτοῦ εἰς τοὺς πόδας αὐτοῦ, παρεκάλει αὐτὸν, λέγων· Μακροθύμησον ἐπ᾽ ἐμοί, καὶ πάντα ἀποδώσω σοι.

30 Ὁ δὲ οὐκ ἤθελεν· ἀλλ᾽ ἀπελθὼν, ἔβαλεν αὐτὸν εἰς φυλακὴν, ἕως οὗ ἀποδῷ τὸ ὀφειλόμενον.

---

16 Si autem non audierit, assume cum te adhuc unum vel duos: ut in ore duorum testium vel trium stet omne verbum:

17 Si autem neglexerit eos, dic ecclesiæ: si autem & ecclesiam neglexerit, sit tibi sicut ethnicus & publicanus.

21 Tunc accedens ad eum Petrus, dixit: Domine, quoties peccabit in me frater meus, & dimittam ei? usque septies?

22 Dicit illi Jesus: Non dico tibi, usque septies, sed usque septuagies septem.

23 Propter hoc assimilatum est regnum cælorum hómini regi, qui voluit conferre rationem cum servis suis.

24 Incipiente verò ipso conferre, oblatus est ei unus debitor decies mille talentorum.

25 Non habente autem illo reddere, jussit eum dominus ejus venundari, & uxorem ejus, & filios, & omnia quæ habebat, & reddi.

26 Procidens autem servus adorabat eum, dicens: Domine, longanimis esto erga me, & omnia tibi reddam.

27 Commotus visceribus autem dominus servi illius, absolvit eum, & mutuum dimisit ei.

28 Egressus autem servus ille, invenit unum conservorum suorum, qui debebat ei centum denarios: & apprehendens eum suffocabat, dicens: Redde mihi quod debes.

29 Procidens ergo conservus ejus ad pedes ejus, rogabat eum, dicens: Longanimis esto in me, & omnia reddam tibi.

30 Ille autem noluit: sed abiens conjecit eum in custodiam, donec redderet debitum.

16. Mais s'il ne t'écoute pas, prends avec toi encore une ou deux *personnes*, afin que tout soit confirmé sur la parole de deux ou de trois témoins.

17. Que s'il ne daigne pas les écouter, dis-le à l'Eglise; et s'il ne daigne pas écouter l'Eglise, regarde-le comme un païen et un péager.

21. Alors Pierre s'étant approché, lui dit : Seigneur, combien de fois pardonnerai-je à mon frère, lorsqu'il m'aura offensé jusques à sept fois ?

22. Jésus lui *répondit* : Je ne te dis pas jusques à sept fois, mais jusques à septante fois sept fois.

23. C'est pourquoi le Royaume des cieux est comparé à un Roi, qui voulut faire compte avec ses serviteurs :

24. Quand il eut commencé à compter, on lui en présenta un qui devoit dix mille talens ;

25. Et parce qu'il n'avoit pas de quoi payer, son Maître commanda qu'il fût vendu, lui, sa femme et ses enfans, et tout ce qu'il avoit, afin que la dette fût payée.

26. Et ce serviteur se jetant à terre, le supplioit, en lui disant : Seigneur, aie patience envers moi, et je te paierai tout.

27. Alors le Maître de ce serviteur, ému de compassion, le laissa aller, et lui quitta la dette.

28. Mais ce serviteur étant sorti, rencontra un de ses compagnons de service qui lui devoit cent deniers ; et l'ayant saisi, il l'étrangloit, en lui disant : Paie-moi ce que tu me dois.

29. Et son compagnon de service se jetant à ses pieds, le supplioit, en lui disant : Aie patience envers moi, et je te paierai tout.

30. Mais il n'en voulut rien faire, et s'en étant allé, il le fit mettre en prison, jusqu'à ce qu'il eût payé la dette.

thou hast gained thy brother.

16 But if he will not hear *thee*, *then* take with thee one or two more, that in the mouth of two or three witnesses every word may be established.

17 And if he shall neglect to hear them, tell *it* unto the church: but if he neglect to hear the church, let him be unto thee as an heathen man and a publican.

21 Then came Peter to him, and said, Lord, how oft shall my brother sin against me, and I forgive him? till seven times?

22 Jesus saith unto him, I say not unto thee, Until seven times; but, Until seventy times seven.

23 Therefore is the kingdom of heaven likened unto a certain king, which would take account of his servants.

24 And when he had begun to reckon, one was brought unto him, which owed him ten thousand talents.

25 But forasmuch as he had not to pay, his lord commanded him to be sold, and his wife, and children, and all that he had, and payment to be made.

26 The servant, therefore fell down, and worshipped him, saying, lord, have patience with me, and I will pay thee all.

27 Then the lord of that servant was moved with compassion, and loosed him, and forgave him the debt.

28 But the same servant went out, and found one of his fellow-servants, which owed him an hundred pence: and he laid hands on him, and took *him* by the throat, saying, Pay me that thou owest.

29 And his fellow-servant fell down at his feet, and besought him, saying, Have patience with me, and I will pay thee all.

30 And he would not: but went and cast him into prison, till he should pay the debt.

* 31 Ἰδόντες δὲ οἱ ‡ σύνδυλοι αὐτῦ τὰ γενόμενα, ἐλυπήθησαν σφόδρα· ἢ ἐλθόντες † διεσάφησαν τῷ ‡ κυρίῳ αὐτῶν πάντα τὰ γενόμενα.

32 Τότε προσκαλεσάμενος αὐτὸν ὁ κύριος αὐτῦ, λέγει αὐτῷ· δῦλε πονηρέ, πᾶσαν τὴν ὀφειλὴν ἐκείνην ἀφῆκά σοι, ἐπεὶ παρεκάλεσάς με·

33 Οὐκ ἔδει καί σε ἐλεῆσαι τὸν σύνδυλόν σε, ὡς ἢ ἐγώ σε ἠλέησα;

* 34 Καὶ ὀργισθεὶς ὁ κύριος αὐτῦ ‡ παρέδωκεν αὐτὸν τοῖς † βασανισαῖς, ἕως ὗ ἀποδῷ πᾶν τὸ ὀφειλόμενον αὐτῷ.

35 Οὕτω ἢ ὁ πατήρ με ὁ ἐπηράνιος ποιήσει ὑμῖν, ἐὰν μὴ ἀφῆτε ἕκασος τῷ ἀδελφῷ αὐτῦ ἀπὸ τῶν καρδιῶν ὑμῶν τὰ παραπτώματα αὐτῶν. 19. † 5.

Κεφ. ί. 10.

1 ΜΕτὰ δὲ ταῦτα ἀνέδειξεν ὁ Κύριος ἢ ἑτέρες ἑβδομήκοντα, ἢ ἀπέσειλεν αὐτὸς ἀνὰ δύο πρὸ προσώπυ αὐτῦ, εἰς πᾶσαν πόλιν ἢ τόπον ὗ ἔμελλεν αὐτὸς ἔρχεσθαι.

2 Ἔλεγεν ὖν πρὸς αὐτούς· Ὁ μὲν θερισμὸς πολύς, οἱ δὲ ἐργάται ὀλίγοι· δεήθητε ὖν τῦ Κυρίῳ τῦ θερισμῦ, ὅπως ἐκβάλλη ἐργάτας εἰς τὸν θερισμὸν αὐτῦ.

* 3 Ὑπάγετε· ἰδὼ, ἐγὼ ἀποςέλλω ὑμᾶς ὡς † ἄρνας ἐν ‡ μέσῳ † λύκων.

4 Μὴ βαςάζετε βαλάντιον, μὴ πήραν, μηδὲ ὑποδήματα· ἢ μηδένα κατὰ τὴν ὁδὸν ἀσπάσησθε.

5 Εἰς ἣν δ᾿ ἂν οἰκίαν εἰσέρχησθε, πρῶτον λέγετε· Εἰρήνη τῷ οἴκῳ τούτῳ.

6 Καὶ ἐὰν μὲν ἦ ἐκεῖ ὁ υἱὸς εἰρήνης, ἐπαναπαύσεται ἐπ᾿ αὐτὸν ἡ εἰρήνη ὑμῶν· εἰ δὲ μήγε, ἐφ᾿ ὑμᾶς ἀνακάμψει.

7 Ἐν αὐτῇ δὲ τῇ οἰκίᾳ μένετε, ἐσθίοντες ἢ πίνοντες τὰ παρ᾿ αὐτῶν· ἄξιος γὰρ ὁ ἐργάτης τῦ μισθῦ αὐτῦ ἐςι. Μὴ μεταβαίνετε ἐξ οἰκίας εἰς οἰκίαν.

8 Καὶ εἰς ἣν δ᾿ ἂν πόλιν εἰσέρχησθε, ἢ δέχωνται ὑμᾶς, ἐσθίετε τὰ παρατιθέμενα ὑμῖν.

---

31 Videntes autem conservi ejus facta, contristati sunt valde: & venientes declaraverunt domino suo omnia facta.

32 Tunc advocans illum dominus suus dicit illi: Serve nequam, omne debitum illud dimisi tibi, quoniam advocasti me.

33 Nonne oportuit & te misereri conservi tui, sicut & ego tui misertus sum?

34 Et iratus dominus ejus tradidit eum tortoribus, quoad usque redderet universum debitum ei.

35 Sic & Pater meus cælestis faciet vobis, si non remiseritis unusquisque fratri suo de cordibus vestris lapsus eorum.

CAPUT X.

1 POST autem hæc designavit Dominus & alios septuaginta, & misit illos per binos ante faciem suam, in omnem civitatem & locum quo futurus erat ipse venire.

2 Dicebat igitur ad illos: Ipsa quidem messis multa, operarii pauci: rogate ergo dominum messis, ut emittat operarios in messem suam.

3 Ite, ecce ego mitto vos sicut agnos in medio luporum.

4 Ne portate marsupium, non peram, neque calceamenta: & neminem per viam salutaveritis.

5 In quamcunque domum intraveritis, primum dicite: Pax domui huic.

6 Et si quidem fuerit ibi filius pacis, requiescet super illum pax vestra: si vero non, ad vos revertetur.

7 In eadem autem domo manete, edentes & bibentes quæ apud illos: dignus enim operarius mercede sua est, ne transite de domo in domum.

8 Et in quamcumque civitatem intraveritis, & susceperint vos, manducate apposita vobis.

31. Ses autres compagnons de service voyant ce qui s'étoit passé, en furent fort indignés, et ils vinrent rapporter à leur Maître tout ce qui étoit arrivé.

32. Alors son Maître le fit venir, et lui dit : Méchant serviteur, je t'avois quitté toute cette dette, parce que tu m'en avois prié ;

33. Ne te falloit-il pas aussi avoir pitié de ton compagnon de service, comme j'avois eu pitié de toi ?

34. Et son Maître étant irrité, le livra aux sergens, jusqu'à ce qu'il lui eût payé tout ce qu'il lui devoit.

35. C'est ainsi que vous fera mon Père céleste, si vous ne pardonnez pas chacun de vous, de *tout* son cœur, à son frère ses fautes.

APRÈS cela, le Seigneur établit encore soixante et dix autres *Disciples* ; et il les envoya deux à deux devant lui, dans toutes les villes et dans tous les lieux où lui-même devoit aller.

2. Et il leur disoit : La moisson est grande, mais *il y a* peu d'ouvriers ; priez donc le Maître de la moisson d'envoyer des ouvriers dans sa moisson.

3. Allez, je vous envoie comme des agneaux au milieu des loups.

4. Ne portez ni bourse, ni sac, ni souliers ; et ne saluez personne en chemin.

5. Et dans quelque maison que vous entriez, dites en entrant : La paix *soit* sur cette maison.

6. S'il y a là quelque enfant de paix ; votre paix reposera sur lui ; sinon elle retournera à vous.

7. Et demeurez dans cette maison-là, mangeant et buvant de ce qu'on vous donnera, car l'ouvrier est digne de son salaire. Ne passez point d'une maison à une autre.

8. De même, dans quelque ville que vous entriez, si on vous y reçoit, mangez de ce qu'on vous présentera.

31 So when his fellow-servants saw what was done, they were very sorry, and came and told unto their lord all that was done.

32 Then his lord, after that he had called him, said unto him, O thou wicked servant! I forgave thee all that debt, because thou desiredst me :

33 Shouldest not thou also have had compassion on thy fellow-servant, even as I had pity on thee?

34 And his lord was wroth, and delivered him to the tormentors, till he should pay all that was due unto him.

35 So likewise shall my heavenly Father do also unto you, if ye from your hearts forgive not every one his brother their trespasses.

AFTER these things the Lord appointed other seventy also, and sent them two and two before his face into every city and place, whither he himself would come.

2 Therefore said he unto them, The harvest truly *is* great, but the labourers *are* few: pray ye therefore the lord of the harvest, that he would send forth labourers into his harvest.

3 Go your ways: behold, I send you forth as lambs among wolves.

4 Carry neither purse, nor scrip, nor shoes: and salute no man by the way.

5 And into whatsoever house ye enter, first say, Peace *be* to this house.

6 And if the Son of Peace be there, your peace shall rest upon it: if not, it shall turn to you again.

7 And in the same house remain, eating and drinking such things as they give: for the labourer is worthy of his hire. Go not from house to house.

8 And into whatsoever city ye enter, and they receive you, eat such things as are set before you;

34

10 Εἰς ἣν δ' ἂν πόλιν εἰσέρχησθε, ἢ μὴ δέχωνlαι ὑμᾶς, ἐξελθόνlες εἰς τὰς πλαlείας αὐτῆς, εἴπαlε·

‡ 11 Καὶ τὸν ‡ κονιορlὸν τὸν ‡ κολληθένlα ἡμῖν ἐκ τῆς πόλεως ὑμῶν, ‡ ἀπομασσόμεθα ὑμῖν· πλὴν τᾶτο γινώσκεlε, ὅτι ἤγίlκεν ἐφ' ὑμᾶς ἡ βασιλεία τᾶ Θεᾶ.

12 Λέγω δὲ ὑμῖν, ὅτι Σοδόμοις ἐν τῇ ἡμέρᾳ ἐκείνῃ ἀνεκlότερον ἔςαι, ἢ τῇ πόλει ἐκείνῃ.

* 2 Ἦν δὲ ἐγγὺς ἡ ἑορlὴ τῶν Ἰυδαίων, ἡ † σκηνοπηγία.

3 Εἶπον πρὸς αὐτὸν οἱ ἀδελφοὶ αὐτᾶ· Μεlάβηθι ἐνlεῦθεν, ἢ ὕπαγε εἰς τὴν Ἰυδαίαν, ἵνα ἢ οἱ μαθηlαί σε θεωρήσωσι τὰ ἔργα σε ἃ ποιεῖς·

4 Οὐδεὶς γὰρ ἐν κρυπlῷ τι ποιεῖ, ἢ ζηlεῖ αὐτὸς ἐν παρρησίᾳ εἶναι. εἰ ταῦτα ποιεῖς, φανέρωσον σεαυτὸν τῷ κόσμῳ.

5 Οὐδὲ γὰρ οἱ ἀδελφοὶ αὐτᾶ ἐπίςευον εἰς αὐτόν.

6 Λέγει ἂν αὐτοῖς ὁ Ἰησᾶς· Ὁ καιρὸς ὁ ἐμὸς ὕπω πάρεςιν· ὁ δὲ καιρὸς ὁ ὑμέτερ☉ πάντοlέ ἐςιν ἕτοιμ☉.

7 Οὐ δύναlαι ὁ κόσμ☉ μισεῖν ὑμᾶς· ἐμὲ δὲ μισεῖ, ὅτι ἐγὼ μαρlυρῶ περὶ αὐτᾶ, ὅτι τὰ ἔργα αὐτᾶ πονηρά ἐςιν.

8 Ὑμεῖς ἀνάβηlε εἰς τὴν ἑορlὴν ταύτην· ἐγὼ ὕπω ἀναβαίνω εἰς τὴν ἑορlὴν ταύτην, ὅτι ὁ καιρὸς ὁ ἐμὸς ὕπω πεπλήρωlαι.

9 Ταῦτα δὲ εἰπὼν αὐτοῖς, ἔμεινεν ἐν τῇ Γαλιλαίᾳ.

10 Ὡς δὲ ἀνέβησαν οἱ ἀδελφοὶ αὐτᾶ, τότε ἢ αὐτὸς ἀνέβη εἰς τὴν ἑορlὴν, ἢ φανερῶς, ἀλλ' ὡς ἐν κρυπlῷ.

11 Οἱ ἂν Ἰυδαῖοι ἐζήτυν αὐτὸν ἐν τῇ ἑορlῇ, ἢ ἔλεγον· Πᾶ ἐςιν ἐκεῖν☉;

12 Καὶ γογγυσμὸς πολὺς περὶ αὐτᾶ ἦν ἐν τοῖς ὄχλοις. οἱ μὲν ἔλεγον, ὅτι ἀγαθός ἐςιν. ἄλλοι δὲ ἔλεγον, Οὔ· ἀλλὰ πλανᾷ τὸν ὄχλον.

13 Οὐδεὶς μένlοι παρρησίᾳ ἐλάλει περὶ αὐτᾶ, διὰ τὸν φόβον τῶν Ἰυδαίων.

* 14 Ἤδη δὲ τῆς ‡ ἑορlῆς ‡ μεσέσης, ἀνέβη ὁ Ἰησᾶς εἰς τὸ ἱερὸν, ἢ ἐδίδασκε.

15 Καὶ ἐθαύμαζον οἱ Ἰυδαῖοι, λέγονlες· Πῶς ὅτ☉ γράμμαlα οἶδε, μὴ μεμαθηκώς;

16 Ἀπεκρίθη αὐτοῖς ὁ Ἰησᾶς

10 In quamcumque autem civitatem intraveritis, & non fusceperint vos, exeuntes in plateas ejus, dicite:

11 Etiam pulverem adhærentem nobis de civitate veſtra, abſtergimus vobis: tamen hoc ſcitote, quia appropinquavit ſuper vos regnum Dei.

12 Dico autem vobis, quia Sodomis in die illa remiſſius erit, quam civitati illi.

2 Erat autem prope feſtum Judæorum, Scenopegia.

3 Dixerunt igitur ad eum fratres ejus: Tranſi hinc, & vade in Judæam, ut & diſcipuli tui videant opera tua quæ facis.

4 Nemo quippe in occulto quid facit, & quærit ipſe in manifeſto eſſe. ſi hæc facis, manifeſta teipſum mundo.

5 Neque enim fratres ejus credebant in eum.

6 Dicit ergo eis Jeſus: Tempus meum nondum adeſt: at tempus veſtrum ſemper eſt paratum.

7 Non poteſt mundus odiſſe vos, me autem odit, quia ego teſtor de illo, quia opera ejus mala ſunt.

8 Vos aſcendite ad feſtum hoc: ego nondum aſcendo ad feſtum iſtud, quia tempus meum nondum impletum eſt.

9 Hæc autem dicens eis, manſit in Galilæa.

10 Ut autem aſcenderunt fratres ejus, tunc & ipſe aſcendit ad feſtum, non manifeſtè, ſed quaſi in occulto.

11 Ipſi ergo Judæi quærebant eum in feſto, & dicebant: Ubi eſt ille?

12 Et murmur multum de eo erat in turbis. hi quidem dicebant, Quia bonus eſt. alii dicebant, Non: ſed ſeducit turbam.

13 Nemo tamen palam loquebatur de illo, propter metum Judæorum.

14 Jam autem feſto mediante, aſcendit Jeſus in templum, & docebat.

15 Et mirabantur Judæi, dicentes: Quomodo hic litteras ſcit, non doctus?

16 Reſpondit ergo eis Jeſus.

10. Mais dans quelque ville que vous entriez, si on ne vous y reçoit pas, sortez dans les rues, et dites :

11. Nous secouons contre vous la poussière qui s'est attachée à nous dans votre ville ; sachez pourtant que le Règne de Dieu s'est approché de vous.

12. Je vous dis qu'en ce jour-là ceux de Sodome seront traités moins rigoureusement que cette ville-là.

2. Or, la fête des Juifs, *appellée* des Tabernacles, approchoit.

3. Et ses frères lui dirent : Pars d'ici, et t'en va en Judée, afin que tes Disciples voient aussi les œuvres que tu fais.

4. Car personne ne fait rien en cachette, quand il veut agir franchement. Puisque tu fais ces choses, montre-toi toi-même au monde.

5. Car ses frères même ne croyoient pas en lui.

6. Jésus leur dit : Mon tems n'est pas encore venu ; mais le tems est toujours propre pour vous.

7. Le monde ne vous peut haïr ; mais il me hait, parce que je rends ce témoignage contre lui, que ses œuvres sont mauvaises.

8. Pour vous, montez à cette fête : Pour moi, je n'y monte pas encore, parce que mon tems n'est pas encore venu.

9. Et leur ayant dit cela, il demeura en Galilée.

10. Mais lorsque ses frères furent partis, il monta aussi à la fête, non pas publiquement, mais comme en cachette.

11. Les Juifs donc le cherchoient pendant la fête, et disoient : Où est-il ?

12. Et on tenoit plusieurs discours de lui parmi le peuple. Les uns disoient : C'est un homme de bien ; et les autres disoient : Non, mais il séduit le peuple.

13. Toutefois personne ne parloit librement de lui, à cause de la crainte *qu'on avoit* des Juifs.

14. Comme on étoit déjà au milieu de la fête, Jésus monta au Temple, et il y enseignoit.

15. Et les Juifs étoient étonnés, et disoient : Comment cet homme sait-il les Ecritures, ne les ayant point apprises ?

16. Jésus leur répondit

L. 10.

10 But into whatsoever city ye enter, and they receive you not, go your ways out into the streets of the same, and say,

11 Even the very dust of your city, which cleaveth on us, we do wipe off against you : notwithstanding, be ye sure of this, that the kingdom of God is come nigh unto you.

12 But I say unto you, That it shall be more tolerable in that day for Sodom, than for that city.

J. 7.

2 Now the Jews' feast of tabernacles was at hand.

3 His brethren, therefore, said unto him, Depart hence, and go into Judea, that thy disciples also may see the works that thou doest.

4 For *there is* no man *that* doeth any thing in secret, and he himself seeketh to be known openly. If thou do these things, shew thyself to the world.

5 For neither did his brethren believe in him.

6 Then Jesus said unto them, My time is not yet come : but your time is alway ready.

7 The world cannot hate you : but me it hateth, because I testify of it, that the works thereof are evil.

8 Go ye up unto this feast : I go not up yet unto this feast ; for my time is not yet full come.

9 When he had said these words unto them, he abode *still* in Galilee.

10 But when his brethren were gone up, then went he also up unto the feast, not openly, but as it were in secret.

11 Then the Jews sought him at the feast, and said, Where is he ?

12 And there was much murmuring among the people concerning him : for some said, He is a good man : others said, Nay ; but he deceiveth the people.

13 Howbeit no man spake openly of him for fear of the Jews.

14 Now, about the midst of the feast, Jesus went up into the temple, and taught.

15 And the Jews marvelled, saying, How knoweth this man letters, having never learned ?

16 Jesus answered them, and said,

35

19 Οὐ Μωσῆς δέδωκεν ὑμῖν τὸν νόμον; καὶ οὐδεὶς ἐξ ὑμῶν ποιεῖ τὸν νόμον; τί με ζητεῖτε ἀποκτεῖναι;

20 Ἀπεκρίθη ὁ ὄχλ⊚ καὶ εἶπε Δαιμόνιον ἔχεις· τίς σε ζητεῖ ἀποκτεῖναι;

21 Ἀπεκρίθη ὁ Ἰησοῦς καὶ εἶπεν αὐτοῖς· Ἓν ἔργον ἐποίησα, καὶ πάντες θαυμάζετε.

22 Διὰ τοῦτο Μωσῆς δέδωκεν ὑμῖν τὴν περιτομὴν, (οὐχ ὅτι ἐκ τοῦ Μωσέως ἐςὶν ἀλλ᾽ ἐκ τῶν πατέρων) καὶ ἐν σαββάτῳ περιτέμνετε ἄνθρωπον.

* 23 Εἰ περιτομὴν λαμβάνει ἄνθρωπ⊚ ἐν σαββάτῳ, ἵνα μὴ λυθῇ ὁ νόμ⊚ Μωσέως, ἐμοὶ † χολᾶτε, ὅτι ὅλον ἄνθρωπον ὑγιῆ ἐποίησα ἐν σαββάτῳ;

24 Μὴ κρίνετε κατ᾽ ὄψιν, ἀλλὰ τὴν δικαίαν κρίσιν κρίνατε.

25 Ἔλεγον οὖν τινες ἐκ τῶν Ἱεροσολυμιτῶν· Οὐχ οὗτός ἐςιν, ὃν ζητοῦσιν ἀποκτεῖναι;

26 Καὶ ἴδε, παῤῥησίᾳ λαλεῖ, καὶ οὐδὲν αὐτῷ λέγουσι· μήποτε ἀληθῶς ἔγνωσαν οἱ ἄρχοντες ὅτι οὗτός ἐςιν ἀληθῶς ὁ Χριςός;

32 Ἤκουσαν οἱ φαρισαῖοι τοῦ ὄχλου γογγύζοντ⊚ περὶ αὐτοῦ ταῦτα· καὶ ἀπέςειλαν οἱ φαρισαῖοι καὶ οἱ ἀρχιερεῖς ὑπηρέτας, ἵνα πιάσωσιν αὐτόν.

43 Σχίσμα οὖν ἐν τῷ ὄχλῳ ἐγένετο δι᾽ αὐτόν.

44 Τινὲς δὲ ἤθελον ἐξ αὐτῶν πιάσαι αὐτόν· ἀλλ᾽ οὐδεὶς ἐπέβαλεν ἐπ᾽ αὐτὸν τὰς χεῖρας.

45 Ἦλθον οὖν οἱ ὑπηρέται πρὸς τοὺς ἀρχιερεῖς καὶ φαρισαίους· καὶ εἶπον αὐτοῖς ἐκεῖνοι· Διὰ τί οὐκ ἠγάγετε αὐτόν;

46 Ἀπεκρίθησαν οἱ ὑπηρέται· Οὐδέποτε οὕτως ἐλάλησεν ἄνθρωπ⊚, ὡς οὗτ⊚ ὁ ἄνθρωπ⊚.

47 Ἀπεκρίθησαν οὖν αὐτοῖς οἱ φαρισαῖοι· Μὴ καὶ ὑμεῖς πεπλάνησθε;

48 Μή τις ἐκ τῶν ἀρχόντων ἐπίςευσεν εἰς αὐτὸν, ἢ ἐκ τῶν φαρισαίων;

49 Ἀλλ᾽ ὁ ὄχλ⊚ οὗτ⊚ ὁ μὴ γινώσκων τὸν νόμον, ἐπικατάρατοί εἰσι.

19 Non Moses dedit vobis legem, & nemo ex vobis facit legem? Quid me quæritis interficere?

20 Respondit turba & dixit: Dæmonium habes: quis te quærit interficere?

21 Respondit Jesus, & dixit eis: Unum opus feci, & omnes miramini.

22 Propter hoc Moses dedit vobis circumcisionem, (non quia ex Mose est, sed ex patribus) & in sabbato circumciditis hominem.

23 Si circumcisionem accipit homo in sabbato, ut non solvatur lex Mosi, Mihi indignamini quia totum hominem sanum feci in sabbato?

24 Ne judicate secundum speciem, sed justum judicium judicate.

25 Dicebant ergo quidam ex Hierosolymitanis: Nonne hic est quem quærunt interficere?

26 Et ecce palam loquitur, & nihil ei dicunt: numquid vere cognoverunt principes, quia hic est vere Christus?

32 Audierunt Pharisæi turbam murmurantem de illo hæc: & miserunt Pharisæi & principes Sacerdotum ministros, ut apprehenderent eum.

43 Dissensio itaque in turba facta est propter eum.

44 Quidam autem volebant ex ipsis apprehendere eum: sed nemo immisit super eum manus.

45 Venerunt ergo ministri ad Pontifices & Pharisæos: & dixerunt eis illi: Quare non adduxistis illum?

46 Responderunt ministri: Nunquam sic loquutus est homo, sicut hic homo.

47 Responderunt ergo eis Pharisæi: Numquid & vos seducti estis?

48 Numquid aliquis ex principibus credidit in eum, aut ex Pharisæis?

49 Sed turba hæc non noscens legem, maledicti sunt.

19. Moyse ne vous a-t-il pas donné la Loi ? et néanmoins aucun de vous n'observe la Loi. Pourquoi cherchez - vous à me faire mourir ?

20. Le peuple lui répondit : Tu es possédé du Démon : Qui est-ce qui cherche à te faire mourir ?

21. Jésus répondit, et leur dit : J'ai fait une œuvre, et vous en êtes tous étonnés.

22. Moyse vous a ordonné la circoncision (non pas qu'elle vienne de Moyse, mais *elle vient* des Pères), et vous circoncisez un homme au jour du Sabbat.

23. Si donc un homme reçoit la circoncision au jour du Sabbat, afin que la Loi de Moyse ne soit pas violée, pourquoi vous irritez-vous contre moi, parce que j'ai guéri un homme dans tout son corps le jour du Sabbat ?

24. Ne jugez point selon l'apparence, mais jugez selon la justice.

25. Et quelques-uns de ceux de Jérusalem disoient : N'est-ce pas celui qu'ils cherchent à faire mourir ?

26. Et le voilà qui parle librement, et ils ne lui disent rien. Les Chefs auroient-ils en effet reconnu qu'il est véritablement le Christ ?

32. Les Pharisiens ayant appris ce que le peuple disoit sourdement de lui, ils envoyèrent, de concert avec les principaux Sacrificateurs, des Sergens pour se saisir de lui.

43. Le peuple étoit donc partagé sur son sujet.

44. Et quelques-uns d'entr'eux vouloient le saisir ; mais personne ne mit la main sur lui.

45. Les Sergens retournèrent donc vers les principaux Sacrificateurs et les Pharisiens, qui leur dirent : Pourquoi ne l'avez-vous pas amené ?

46. Les Sergens répondirent : Jamais homme n'a parlé comme cet homme.

47. Les Pharisiens leur dirent : Avez-vous aussi été séduits ?

48. Y a-t-il quelques-uns des Chefs ou des Pharisiens qui aient cru en lui ?

49. Mais cette populace, qui n'entend point la Loi, est exécrable.

19 Did not Moses give you the law, and *yet* none of you keepeth the law? Why go ye about to kill me?

20 The people answered, and said, Thou hast a devil : who goeth about to kill thee ?

21 Jesus answered, and said unto them, I have done one work, and ye all marvel.

22 Moses, therefore, gave unto you circumcision, (not because it is of Moses, but of the fathers,) and ye on the sabbath-day circumcise a man.

23 If a man on the sabbath-day receive circumcision, that the law of Moses should not be broken ; are ye angry at me, because I have made a man every whit whole on the sabbath-day ?

24 Judge not according to the appearance, but judge righteous judgment.

25 Then said some of them of Jerusalem, Is not this he whom they seek to kill ?

26 But, lo, he speaketh boldly, and they say nothing unto him ; Do the rulers know indeed that this is the very Christ ?

32 The Pharisees heard that the people murmured such things concerning him ; and the Pharisees, and the chief priest sent officers to take him.

43 So there was a division among the people because of him.

44 And some of them would have taken him : but no man laid hands on him.

45 Then came the officers to the chief priests and Pharisees ; and they said unto them, Why have ye not brought him ?   M 2.

46 The officers answered, Never man spake like this man.

47 Then answered them the Pharisees, Are ye also deceived ?

48 Have any of the rulers, or of the Pharisees, believed on him ?

49 But this people who knoweth not the law are cursed.

36

50 Λέγει Νικόδημ⊙ πρὸς αὐτὰς, ὁ ἐλθὼν νυκτὸς πρὸς αὐτὸν, εἷς ὢν ἐξ αὐτῶν·

51 Μὴ ὁ νόμ⊙ ἡμῶν κρίνει τὸν ἄνθρωπον, ἐὰν μὴ ἀκύσῃ παρ' αὐτῷ πρότερον, κỳ γνῷ τί ποιεῖ;

52 Ἀπεκρίθησαν, κỳ εἶπον αὐτῷ· Μὴ κỳ σὺ ἐκ τῆς Γαλιλαίας εἶ; ἐρεύνησον κỳ ἴδε ὅτι προφήτης ἐκ τῆς Γαλιλαίας ὐκ ἐγήγερλαι.

53 Καὶ ἐπορεύθη ἕκασ⊙ εἰς τὸν οἶκον αὐτῦ. 9. † 5.

Κεφ. η'. 8.

1 Ἰησῦς δὲ ἐπορεύθη εἰς τὸ ὄρ⊙ τῶν ἐλαιῶν.

2 Ὄρθρυ δὲ πάλιν παρεγένετο εἰς τὸ ἱερὸν, κỳ πᾶς ὁ λαὸς ἤρχετο πρὸς αὐτὸν κỳ καθίσας ἐδίδασκεν αὐτύς.

3 Ἄγυσι δὲ οἱ γραμματεῖς κỳ οἱ φαρισαῖοι πρὸς αὐτὸν γυναῖκα ἐν μοιχεία κατειλημμένην· κỳ ςήσαντες αὐτὴν ἐν μέσῳ,

* 4 Λέγυσιν αὐτῷ· Διδάσκαλε, αὕτη ἡ γυνὴ ‡ κατειλήφθη † ἐπαυτοφώρῳ ‖ μοιχευομένη·

5 Ἐν δὲ τῷ νόμῳ ἡμετέρῳ Μωσῆς ἡμῖν ἐνετείλατο τὰς τοιαύτας λιθοβολεῖσθαι· σὺ ὖν τί λέγεις;

6 Τῦτο δὲ ἔλεγον πειράζοντες αὐτὸν, ἵνα ἔχωσι κατηγορεῖν αὐτῦ. Ὁ δὲ Ἰησῦς κάτω κύψας, τῷ δακτύλῳ ἔγραφεν εἰς τὴν γῆν.

* 7 Ὡς δὲ ἐπέμενον ἐρωτῶντες αὐτὸν, ἀνακύψας εἶπε πρὸς αὐτύς· ‡ Ὁ † ἀναμάρτητ⊙ ὑμῶν, πρῶτ⊙ τὸν λίθον ἐπ' αὐτῇ βαλέτω.

8 Καὶ πάλιν κάτω κύψας, ἔγραφεν εἰς τὴν γῆν.

9 Οἱ δὲ, ἀκύσαντες, κỳ ὑπὸ τῆς συνειδήσεως ἐλεγχόμενοι, ἐξήρχοντο εἷς καθ' εἷς, ἀρξάμενοι ἀπὸ τῶν πρεσβυτέρων ἕως τῶν ἐσχάτων· κỳ κατελείφθη μόν⊙ ὁ Ἰησῦς, κỳ ἡ γυνὴ ἐν μέσῳ ἑςῶσα.

10 Ἀνακύψας δὲ ὁ Ἰησῦς, κỳ μηδένα θεασάμεν⊙ πλὴν τῆς γυναικὸς, εἶπεν αὐτῇ· Ἡ γυνὴ, πῦ εἰσιν ἐκεῖνοι οἱ κατήγοροί συ; ἐδείς σε κατέκρινεν;

11 Ἡ δὲ Ἶπεν· Οὐδεὶς, Κύριε. Εἶπε δὲ αὐτῇ ὁ Ἰησῦς· Οὐδὲ ἐγώ σε κατακρίνω· πορεύυ, κỳ μηκέτι ἁμάρτανε.

---

50 Dicit Nicodemus ad eos, ille profectus nocte ad eum, unus exiſtens ex ipſis:

51 Numquid lex noſtra judicat hominem, ſi non audierit ab ipſo prius, & cognoverit quid faciat?

52 Reſponderunt & dixerunt ei: Numquid & tu ex Galilæa es? ſcrutare, & vide, quia propheta in Galilæa non ſurrexit.

53 Et perrexit unuſquiſque in domum ſuam.

CAPUT VIII.

1 JEſus autem perrexit in montem olearum.

2 Diluculo autem iterum acceſſit in templum, & omnis populus venit ad eum, & ſedens docebat eos.

3 Adducunt autem Scribæ & Phariſæi ad eum mulierem in adulterio deprehenſam: & ſtatuentes in medio,

4 Dicunt ei: Magiſter, hanc invenimus in ipſo facto adulterantem.

5 In autem Lege noſtra Moſes mandavit hujuſmodi lapidari: Tu ergo quid dicis?

6 Hoc autem dicebant tentantes eum, ut haberent accuſationem adverſus eum. At Jeſus deorſùm inclinans, digito ſcribebat in terram.

7 Ut autem perſeverabant interrogantes eum, erectus ait ad eos: Qui ſine peccato eſt veſtrum, primus lapidem in illam jaciat.

8 Et iterum deorſùm inclinans ſcribebat in terram.

9 Ii autem audientes, & à conſcientia redarguti, exibant unus poſt unum, incipientes à ſenioribus uſque extremos: & relictus eſt ſolus Jeſus, & mulier in medio exiſtens.

10 Erectus autem Jeſus, & neminem ſpectans præter mulierem, dixit ei: Mulier, ubi ſunt illi accuſatores tui? nemo te condemnavit?

11 Illa autem dixit: Nemo, Domine, Dixit autem ei Jeſus: Nec ego te condemno. Vade, & non ampliùs pecca.

50. Nicodème (celui qui étoit venu de nuit vers Jésus, et qui étoit l'un d'entr'eux), leur dit :

51. Notre Loi condamne-t-elle un homme sans l'avoir ouï auparavant, et sans s'être informé de ce qu'il a fait ?

52. Ils lui répondirent : Es-tu aussi Galiléen ? Informe-toi, et tu verras qu'aucun Prophète n'a été suscité de la Galilée.

53. Et chacun s'en alla dans sa maison.

Jésus s'en alla *ensuite* sur la montagne des Oliviers,

2. Et à la pointe du jour, il retourna au Temple, et tout le peuple vint à lui ; et s'étant assis, il les enseignoit.

3. Alors les Scribes et les Pharisiens lui amenèrent une femme qui avoit été surprise en adultère, et l'ayant mise au milieu,

4. Ils lui dirent : Maître, cette femme a été surprise sur le fait, commettant adultère.

5. Or, Moyse nous a ordonné dans la Loi, de lapider ces sortes de personnes ; toi donc, qu'en dis-tu ?

6. Ils disoient cela pour l'éprouver, afin de le pouvoir accuser. Mais Jésus s'étant baissé, écrivoit avec le doigt sur la terre.

7. Et comme ils continuoient à l'interroger, s'étant redressé, il leur dit : Que celui de vous qui est sans péché jette le premier la pierre contr'elle ;

8. Et s'étant encore baissé, il écrivoit sur la terre.

9. Quand ils entendirent *cela*, se sentant repris par *leur* conscience, ils sortirent l'un après l'autre, commençant depuis les plus vieux jusqu'aux derniers ; et Jésus demeura seul avec la femme qui étoit *là* au milieu.

10. Alors Jésus s'étant redressé, et ne voyant personne que la femme, il lui dit : Femme, où sont ceux qui t'accusoient ? Personne ne t'a-t-il condamnée ?

11. Elle dit : Personne, Seigneur : Et Jésus *lui* dit : Je ne te condamne point non plus ; va-t-en, et ne péche plus à l'avenir.

---

50 Nicodemus saith unto them, he that came to Jesus by night, being one of them,)

51 Doth our law judge *any* man, before it hear him, and know what he doeth ?

52 They answered, and said unto him, Art thou also of Galilee ? search, and look : for out of Galilee ariseth no prophet.

53 And every man went unto his own house.

JESUS went unto the mount of Olives.

2 And early in the morning he came again into the temple, and all the people came unto him : and he sat down, and taught them.

3 And the scribes and Pharisees brought unto him a woman taken in adultery ; and, when they had set her in the midst,

4 They say unto him, Master, this woman was taken in adultery, in the very act.

5 Now Moses in the law commanded us, That such should be stoned : but what sayest thou ?

6 This they said, tempting him, that they might have to accuse him. But Jesus stooped down, and with *his* finger wrote on the ground, *as though he heard them not.*

7 So, when they continued asking him, he lifted up himself, and said unto them, He that is without sin among you, let him first cast a stone at her.

8 And again he stooped down, and wrote on the ground.

9 And they which heard *it*, being convicted by *their own* conscience, went out one by one, beginning at the eldest, *even* unto the last ; and Jesus was left alone, and the woman standing in the midst.

10 When Jesus had lifted up himself, and saw none but the woman, he said unto her, Woman, where are those thine accusers ? hath no man condemned thee ?

11 She said, No man, Lord. And Jesus said unto her, Neither do I condemn thee : go, and sin no more.

37

*1 Καὶ παράγων εἶδεν ἄνθρωπον τυφλὸν ἐκ † γενετῆς.
2 Καὶ ἠρώτησαν αὐτὸν οἱ μαθηταὶ αὐτοῦ, λέγοντες· Ῥαββὶ, τίς ἥμαρτεν, οὗτ(ος) ἢ οἱ γονεῖς αὐτοῦ, ἵνα τυφλὸς γεννηθῇ;
3 Ἀπεκρίθη ὁ Ἰησοῦς· Οὔτε οὗτος ἥμαρτεν, οὔτε οἱ γονεῖς αὐτοῦ· ἀλλ᾽ ἵνα φανερωθῇ τὰ ἔργα τοῦ Θεοῦ ἐν αὐτῷ.

1 Et praeteriens vidit hominem caecum ex nativitate.
2 Et interrogaverunt eum discipuli ejus, dicentes: Rabbi, quis peccavit, hic aut parentes ejus, ut caecus nasceretur?
3 Respondit Jesus: Neque hic peccavit, neque parentes ejus: sed ut manifestentur opera Dei in illo.

*1 Ἀμὴν, ἀμὴν, λέγω ὑμῖν, ὁ μὴ εἰσερχόμεν(ος) διὰ τῆς θύρας εἰς τὴν αὐλὴν τῶν προβάτων, ἀλλὰ ἀναβαίνων † ἀλλαχόθεν, ἐκεῖν(ος) κλέπτης ἐστὶ καὶ λῃστής.
2 Ὁ δὲ εἰσερχόμεν(ος) διὰ τῆς θύρας, ποιμήν ἐστι τῶν προβάτων.
3 Τούτῳ ὁ θυρωρὸς ἀνοίγει, καὶ τὰ πρόβατα τῆς φωνῆς αὐτοῦ ἀκούει· καὶ τὰ ἴδια πρόβατα καλεῖ κατ᾽ ὄνομα, καὶ ἐξάγει αὐτά.
4 Καὶ ὅταν τὰ ἴδια πρόβατα ἐκβάλῃ, ἔμπροσθεν αὐτῶν πορεύεται· καὶ τὰ πρόβατα αὐτῷ ἀκολυθεῖ, ὅτι οἴδασι τὴν φωνὴν αὐτοῦ.
5 Ἀλλοτρίῳ δὲ οὐ μὴ ἀκολυθήσωσιν, ἀλλὰ φεύξονται ἀπ᾽ αὐτοῦ· ὅτι οὐκ οἴδασι τῶν ἀλλοτρίων τὴν φωνήν.

1 Amen, amen, dico vobis, non intrans per ostium in ovile ovium, sed ascendens aliunde, ille fur est & latro.
2 Intrans verò per ostium, pastor est ovium.
3 Huic ostiarius aperit, & oves vocem ejus audiunt, & proprias oves vocat juxta nomen, & educit eas.
4 Et quum proprias oves emiserit, ante eas vadit: & oves illum sequuntur, quia sciunt vocem ejus.
5 Alienum au'em non sequuntur, sed fugient ab eo: quia non noverunt alienorum vocem.

11 Ἐγώ εἰμι ὁ ποιμὴν ὁ καλός· ὁ ποιμὴν ὁ καλὸς τὴν ψυχὴν αὐτοῦ τίθησιν ὑπὲρ τῶν προβάτων.
*12 Ὁ μισθωτὸς δὲ, καὶ οὐκ ὢν ποιμὴν, οὗ οὐκ εἰσὶ τὰ πρόβατα ἴδια, θεωρεῖ τὸν λύκον ἐρχόμενον, καὶ ἀφίησι τὰ πρόβατα, καὶ φεύγει· καὶ ὁ λύκ(ος) ἁρπάζει αὐτὰ, καὶ σκορπίζει τὰ πρόβατα.
13 Ὁ δὲ μισθωτὸς φεύγει, ὅτι μισθωτός ἐστι. καὶ οὐ μέλει αὐτῷ περὶ τῶν προβάτων.
14 Ἐγώ εἰμι ὁ ποιμὴν ὁ καλός, καὶ γινώσκω τὰ ἐμά, καὶ γινώσκομαι ὑπὸ τῶν ἐμῶν.
16 Καὶ ἄλλα πρόβατα ἔχω, ἃ οὐκ ἔστιν ἐκ τῆς αὐλῆς ταύτης· κἀκεῖνά με δεῖ ἀγαγεῖν· καὶ τῆς φωνῆς μου ἀκούσουσι· καὶ γενήσεται μία ποίμνη, εἷς ποιμήν.

11 Ego sum pastor bonus: pastor bonus animam suam ponit pro ovibus.
12 Mercenarius autem, & non existens pastor, cujus non sunt oves propriae, videt lupum venientem, & dimittit oves, & fugit: & lupus rapit eas, & dispergit oves.
13 At mercenarius fugit, quia mercenarius est, & non curae est ei de ovibus.
14 Ego sum pastor bonus, & cognosco meas, & cognoscor à meis.
16 Et alias oves habeo, quae non sunt ex caula hac: & illas me oportet adducere: & vocem meam audient: & fiet unum ovile, unus pastor.

COMME Jésus passoit, il vit un homme aveugle dès sa naissance.

2. Et ses Disciples lui demandèrent : Maître, qui est-ce qui a péché ? Est-ce cet homme, ou son père, ou sa mère, qu'il soit ainsi né aveugle ?

3. Jesus répondit : Ce n'est point qu'il ait péché, ni son père, ou sa mère, mais c'est afin que les œuvres de Dieu soient manifestées en lui.

EN vérité, en vérité je vous dis, que celui qui n'entre pas par la porte dans la bergerie des brebis, mais qui y monte par un autre endroit, est un larron et un voleur.

2. Mais celui qui entre par la porte est le Berger des brebis.

3. Le portier lui ouvre, les brebis entendent sa voix, et il appelle ses propres brebis par leur nom, et les mène dehors.

4. Et quand il a mis dehors ses propres brebis ; il marche devant elles, et les brebis le suivent, parce qu'elles connoissent sa voix.

5. Mais elles ne suivront point un étranger ; au contraire, elles le fuiront ; parce qu'elles ne connoissent point la voix des étrangers.

11. Je suis le bon Berger : Le bon Berger donne sa vie pour ses brebis.

12. Mais le mercenaire, celui qui n'est point le berger, et à qui les brebis n'appartiennent pas, voit venir le loup, et il abandonne les brebis, et s'enfuit ; et le loup ravit les brebis et les disperse.

13. Le mercenaire s'enfuit, parce qu'il est mercenaire, et qu'il ne se soucie point des brebis.

14. Je suis le bon Berger, et je connois mes brebis, et mes brebis me connoissent.

16. J'ai encore d'autres brebis qui ne sont pas de cette bergerie ; il faut aussi que je les amène, et elles entendront ma voix, et il n'y aura qu'un seul troupeau et qu'un seul Berger.

---

5. 9.

AND as Jesus passed by, he saw a man which was blind from his birth.

2 And his disciples asked him, saying, Master, who did sin, this man, or his parents, that he was born blind?

3 Jesus answered, Neither hath this man sinned, nor his parents: but that the works of God should be made manifest in him.

5. 10.

VERILY, verily, I say unto you, He that entereth not by the door into the sheep-fold, but climbeth up some other way, the same is a thief and a robber.

2 But he that entereth in by the door, is the shepherd of the sheep.

3 To him the porter openeth; and the sheep hear his voice: and he calleth his own sheep by name, and leadeth them out.

4 And when he putteth forth his own sheep, he goeth before them, and the sheep follow him: for they know his voice.

5 And a stranger will they not follow, but will flee from him: for they know not the voice of strangers.

11 I am the good shepherd: the good shepherd giveth his life for the sheep.

12 But he that is an hireling, and not the shepherd, whose own the sheep are not, seeth the wolf coming, and leaveth the sheep, and fleeth: and the wolf catcheth them, and scattereth the sheep.

13 The hireling fleeth, because he is an hireling, and careth not for the sheep.

14 I am the good shepherd, and know my sheep, and am known of mine.

16 And other sheep I have, which are not of this fold: them also I must bring, and they shall hear my voice; and there shall be one fold, and one shepherd.

25 Καὶ ἰδȣ̀, νομικός τις ἀνέςη, ἐκπειράζων αὐτὸν, κỳ λέγων· Διδάσκαλε, τί ποιήσας ζωὴν αἰώνιον κληρονομήσω;

26 Ὁ δὲ εἶπε πρὸς αὐτόν· Ἐν τῷ νόμῳ τί γέγραπλαι; πῶς ἀναγινώσκεις;

27 Ὁ δὲ ἀποκριθεὶς, εἶπεν· Ἀγαπήσεις Κύριον τὸν Θεόν σȣ ἐξ ὅλης τῆς καρδίας σȣ, κỳ ἐξ ὅλης τῆς ψυχῆς σȣ, κỳ ἐξ ὅλης τῆς ἰσχȣ͂Θ σȣ, κỳ ἐξ ὅλης τῆς διανοίας σȣ· κỳ τὸν πλησίον σȣ ὡς σεαυτὸν.

28 Εἶπε δὲ αὐτῷ· ‡ Ὀρθῶς ἀπεκρίθης· τȣ͂το ποίει, κỳ ζήσῃ.

29 Ὁ δὲ, θέλων δικαιȣ͂ν ἑαυτὸν, εἶπε πρὸς τὸν Ἰησȣ͂ν· Καὶ τίς ἐςί μȣ πλησίον;

30 ‡ Ὑπολαβὼν δὲ ὁ Ἰησȣ͂ς, εἶπεν· Ἄνθρωπός τις κατέβαινεν ἀπὸ Ἱερȣσαλὴμ εἰς Ἱεριχὼ, κỳ ‡ λῃςαῖς ‡ περιέπεσεν· οἳ κỳ ἐκδύσανλες αὐτὸν, κỳ πληγὰς ἐπιθένλες, ἀπῆλθοι, ἀφένλες † ἡμιθανῆ ‡ τυγχάνονλα.

31 Καλὰ † συγκυρίαν δὲ ‡ ἱερεύς τις κατέβαινεν ἐν τῇ ὁδῷ ἐκείνῃ· κỳ ἰδὼν αὐτὸν, ‡ ἀνλιπαρῆλθεν.

32 Ὁμοίως δὲ κỳ Λευΐτης, γενόμενΘ καλὰ τὸν τόπον, ἐλθὼν κỳ ἰδὼν, ἀνλιπαρῆλθεν.

33 Σαμαρείτης δέ τις † ὁδεύων, ἦλθε κατ᾽ αὐτὸν, κỳ ἰδὼν αὐτὸν, † ἐσπλαγχνίσθη.

34 Καὶ προσελθὼν † καλέδησε τὰ † τραύμαλα αὐτȣ͂, † ἐπιχέων ‡ ἔλαιον κỳ οἶνον· ‡ ἐπιβιβάσας δὲ αὐτὸν ἐπὶ τὸ ‡ ἴδιον ‡ κλῆνΘ, ἤγαγεν αὐτὸν εἰς † πανδοχεῖον, κỳ ἐπεμελήθη αὐτȣ͂.

35 Καὶ ἐπὶ τὴν αὔριον ἐξελθὼν, ἐκβαλὼν δύο δηνάρια ἔδωκε τῷ † πανδοχεῖ, κỳ εἶπεν αὐτῷ· Ἐπιμελήθηλι αὐτȣ͂· κỳ ὅ,τι ἂν † προσδαπανήσῃς, ἐγώ ἐν τῷ ‡ ἐπανέρχεσθαί με ἀποδώσω σοι.

36 Τίς ȣ̓͂ν τȣ́των τῶν τριῶν δοκεῖ σοι πλησίον γεγονέναι τȣ͂ ἐμπεσόνλΘ εἰς τοὺς λῃςάς;

37 Ὁ δὲ εἶπεν· Ὁ ποιήσας τὸ ἔλεΘ μετ᾽ αὐτȣ͂. Εἶπεν ȣ̓͂ν αὐτῷ ὁ Ἰησȣ͂ς· Πορεύȣ, κỳ σὺ ποίει ὁμοίως.

---

25 Et ecce Legisperitus quidam surrexit, tentans illum, & dicens: Magister, quid faciens vitam æternam possidebo?

26. Ille autem dixit ad eum; in Lege quid scriptum est? quomodo legis?

27 Ille autem respondens dixit: Diliges Dominum Deum tuum ex toto corde tuo, & ex tota anima tua, & ex tota fortitudine tua, & ex omni cogitatione tua, & proximum tuum sicut teipsum.

28 Dixit autem illi: Rectè respondisti: hoc fac, & vives.

29 Ille autem volens justificare seipsum, dixit ad Jesum: Et quis est meus proximus?

30 Suscipiens autem Jesus, dixit: Homo quidam descendebat ab Hierusalem in Jericho, & in latrones incidit: qui etiam exuentes eum, & plagas imponentes, abierunt, relinquentes semivivum existentem.

31 Secundum sortem autem sacerdos quidam descendit in via illa, & videns illum, præterivit.

32 Similiter autem & Levita, factus secundum locum, veniens & videns, pertransiit.

33 Samaritanus autem quidam iter faciens, venit secus eum, & videns eum, visceribus commotus est.

34 Et accedens alligavit vulnera ejus, infundens oleum & vinum: ascendere faciens autem illum in proprium jumentum, duxit in diversorium, & curam egit ejus.

35 Et in crastinum exiens, ejiciens duos denarios dedit tabernario, & ait illi: Curam habe illius; & quodcumque adinsumpseris, ego in redire me reddam tibi.

36 Quis igitur horum trium videtur tibi proximus fuisse incidentis in latrones?

37 Ille autem dixit: Faciens misericordiam cum illo, ait ergo illi Jesus: Vade, & tu fac similiter.

25. Alors un Docteur de la loi se leva, et dit à *Jésus* pour l'éprouver : Maître, que faut-il que je fasse pour hériter la vie éternelle ?

26. *Jésus* lui dit : Q'est-ce qui est écrit dans la loi ; et qu'y lis-tu ?

27. Il répondit : Tu aimeras le Seigneur ton Dieu de tout ton cœur, de toute ton ame, de toute ta force et de toute ta pensée ; et ton prochain comme toi-même.

28. Et *Jésus* lui dit : Tu as bien répondu ; fais cela, et tu vivras.

29. Mais *cet homme* voulant paroître juste, dit à Jésus : Et qui est mon prochain ?

30. Et Jésus prenant la parole, lui dit : Un homme descendoit de Jérusalem à Jérico, et tomba entre les mains des voleurs, qui le dépouillèrent ; et après l'avoir blessé de plusieurs coups, ils s'en allèrent, le laissant à demi-mort.

31. Or, Il se rencontra qu'un Sacrificateur descendoit par ce chemin-là, et ayant vu *cet homme*, il passa outre.

32. Un Lévite étant aussi venu dans le même endroit, et le voyant, passa outre.

33. Mais un Samaritain passant son chemin, vint vers cet homme, et le voyant ; il fut touché de compassion.

34. Et s'approchant, il banda ses plaies, et il y versa de l'huile et du vin ; puis il le mit sur sa monture, et le mena à une hôtellerie, et prit soin de lui.

35. Le lendemain, en partant, il tira deux deniers *d'argent*, et les donna à l'hôte, et lui dit : Aie soin de lui ; et tout ce que tu dépenseras de plus, je te le rendrai à mon retour.

36. Lequel donc de ces trois te semble avoir été le prochain de celui qui étoit tombé entre les mains des voleurs ?

37. *Le Docteur* dit : C'est celui qui a exercé la miséricorde envers lui. Jésus lui dit : Va, et fais la même chose.

38. Comme ils étoient en che-

25 And, behold, a certain lawyer stood up, and tempted him, saying, Master, what shall I do to inherit eternal life ?

26 He said unto him, What is written in the law ? how readest thou ?

27 And he answering, said, Thou shalt love the Lord thy God with all thy heart, and with all thy soul, and with all thy strength, and with all thy mind ; and thy neighbour as thyself.

28 And he said unto him, Thou hast answered right : this do, and thou shalt live.

29 But he, willing to justify himself, said unto Jesus, And who is my neighbour ?

30 And Jesus, answering, said, A certain *man* went down from Jerusalem to Jericho, and fell among thieves, which stripped him of his raiment, and wounded *him*, and departed, leaving *him* half dead.

31 And, by chance, there came down a certain priest that way ; and when he saw him, he passed by on the other side.

32 And likewise a Levite, when he was at the place, came and looked *on him*, and passed by on the other side.

33 But a certain Samaritan, as he journeyed, came where he was : and when he saw him, he had compassion *on him*.

34 And went to *him*, and bound up his wounds, pouring in oil and wine, and set him on his own beast, and brought him to an inn, and took care of him.

35 And on the morrow, when he departed, he took out two pence, and gave *them* to the host, and said unto him, Take care of him : and whatsoever thou spendest more, when I come again, I will repay thee.

36 Which now of these three, thinkest thou was neighbour unto him that fell among the thieves ?

37 And he said, He that shewed mercy on him. Then said Jesus unto him, Go, and do thou likewise.

Κεφ. ια΄. 11.

1 ΚΑΙ ἐγένετο ἐν τῷ εἶναι αὐτὸν ἐν τόπῳ τινὶ προσευχόμενον, ὡς ἐπαύσατο, εἶπέ τις τῶν μαθητῶν αὐτῷ πρὸς αὐτόν· Κύριε, δίδαξον ἡμᾶς προσεύχεσθαι, καθὼς ἢ Ἰωάννης ἐδίδαξε τοὺς μαθητὰς αὐτῦ.

2 Εἶπε δὲ αὐτοῖς· Ὅταν προσεύχησθε, λέγετε· ΠΑΤΕΡ ἡμῶν ὁ ἐν τοῖς ὐρανοῖς, ἁγιασθήτω τὸ ὄνομά σου· ἐλθέτω ἡ βασιλεία σου· γενηθήτω τὸ θέλημά σου, ὡς ἐν ὐρανῷ, ἢ ἐπὶ τῆς γῆς·

* 3 Τὸν ἄρτον ἡμῶν τὸν ‡ ἐπιύσιον δίδου ἡμῖν τὸ καθ᾽ ἡμέραν·

4 Καὶ ἄφες ἡμῖν τὰς ἁμαρτίας ἡμῶν· ἢ γὰρ αὐτοὶ ἀφίεμεν παντὶ ὀφείλοντι ἡμῖν· ἢ μὴ εἰσενέγκῃς ἡμᾶς εἰς πειρασμὸν, ἀλλὰ ῥῦσαι ἡμᾶς ἀπὸ τῦ πονηρῦ.

* 5 Καὶ εἶπε πρὸς αὐτούς· Τίς ἐξ ὑμῶν ἕξει φίλον, ἢ πορεύσεται πρὸς αὐτὸν μεσονυκτίυ, ἢ εἴπῃ αὐτῷ· Φίλε, † χρῆσόν μοι ‡ τρεῖς ‡ ἄρτυς·

6 Ἐπειδὴ φίλ☉· μὴ παραγένετο ἐξ ὁδῦ πρός με, ἢ ἐκ ἔχω ὃ παραθήσω αὐτῷ·

7 Κἀκεῖν☉· ἔσωθεν ἀποκριθεὶς εἴπῃ· Μή μοι κόπυς πάρεχε· ἤδη ἡ θύρα κέκλεισαι, ἢ τὰ παιδία μυ μετ᾽ ἐμῦ εἰς τὴν κοίτην εἰσίν· ὐ δύναμαι ἀναςὰς δῦναί σοι.

* 8 Λέγω ὑμῖν, εἰ ἢ ὐ δώσει αὐτῷ ἀναςὰς, διὰ τὸ εἶναι αὐτῦ φίλον· διά ‡ γε τὴν ‡ ἀναίδειαν αὐτῦ ἐγερθεὶς δώσει αὐτῷ ὅσων χρῇζει.

9 Κἀγὼ ὑμῖν λέγω· Αἰτεῖτε, ἢ δοθήσεται ὑμῖν· ζητεῖτε, ἢ εὑρήσετε· κρύετε, ἢ ἀνοιγήσεται ὑμῖν.

10 Πᾶς γὰρ ὁ αἰτῶν λαμβάνει· ἢ ὁ ζητῶν εὑρίσκει· ἢ τῷ κρύοντι ἀνοιγήσεται.

11 Τίνα δὲ ὑμῶν τὸν πατέρα, αἰτήσει ὁ υἱὸς ἄρτον, μὴ λίθον ἐπιδώσει αὐτῷ; εἰ ἢ ἰχθῦν, μὴ ἀντὶ ἰχθύ☉· ὄφιν ἐπιδώσει αὐτῷ;

* 12 Ἢ ἢ ἐὰν αἰτήσῃ † ᾠὸν, μὴ ἐπιδώσει αὐτῷ σκορπίον;

CAPUT XI.

1 ET factum est in esse ipsum in loco quodàm orantem, ut cessavit, dixit quidam discipulorum ejus ad eum : Domine, doce nos orare, sicut & Joannes docuit discipulos suos.

2 Ait autem illis : Quum oratis, dicite : Pater noster qui in cælis, sanctificetur nomen tuum : adveniat regnum tuum : fiat voluntas tua, sicut in cælo, & in terra.

3 Panem nostrum quotidianum da nobis juxta diem.

4 Et dimitte nobis peccata nostra, & enim ipsi dimittimus omni debenti nobis : & ne inducas nos in tentationem, sed libera nos à malo.

5 Et ait ad illos : Quis ex vobis habebit amicum, & ibit ad illum media nocte, & dicet illi : Amice, commoda mihi tres panes :

6 Quoniam amicus meus venit de via ad me, & non habeo quod apponam ei.

7 Et ille deintus respondens dicat : Ne mihi molestias exhibe : jam ostium clausum est, & pueri mei mecum in cubili sunt : non possum surgens dare tibi.

8 Dico vobis, si & non dederit ei surgens propter esse illius amicum, propter improbitatem ejus excitatus dabit illi quotquot habet opus.

9 Et ego vobis dico : Petite, & dabitur vobis : quærite, & invenietis : pulsate, & aperietur vobis.

10 Omnis enim petens accipit, & quærens invenit, & pulsanti aperietur.

11 Quem autem vestrum patrem petet filius panem, num lapidem dabit illi ? si & piscem, num pro pisce serpentem dabit illi ?

12 Aut & si petierit ovum, num dabit illi scorpionem ?

Un jour que Jésus étoit en prière en un certain lieu, après qu'il eut achevé sa prière, un de ses Disciples lui dit : Seigneur, enseigne-nous à prier, comme Jean l'a aussi enseigné à ses Disciples.

2. Et il leur dit : Quand vous priez, dites : Notre Père qui es aux cieux : Ton nom soit sanctifié. Ton règne vienne. Ta volonté soit faite sur la terre comme au ciel.

3. Donne-nous chaque jour notre pain quotidien.

4. Pardonne-nous nos péchés, car nous pardonnons aussi à tous ceux qui nous ont offensés. Et ne nous abandonne point à la tentation, mais délivre-nous du mal.

5. Puis il leur dit : Si quelqu'un de vous avoit un ami, qui vînt le trouver à minuit, et qui lui dît : Mon ami, prête-moi trois pains.

6. Car un de mes amis est venu me voir en passant; et je n'ai rien à lui présenter.

7. Et que cet homme qui est dans sa maison lui répondît : Ne m'importune pas; ma porte est fermée, et mes enfans sont avec moi au lit ; je ne saurois me lever pour t'en donner.

8. Je vous dis que quand même il ne se leveroit pas pour lui en donner, parce qu'il est son ami; il se leveroit à cause de son importunité, et lui en donneroit autant qu'il en auroit besoin.

9. Et moi je vous dis : Demandez, et il vous sera donné ; cherchez, et vous trouverez ; heurtez, et il vous sera ouvert.

10. Car quiconque demande, reçoit ; et qui cherche, trouve ; et il sera ouvert à celui qui heurte.

11. Qui est le père d'entre vous, qui donne à son fils une pierre, lorsqu'il lui demande du pain ? Ou s'il lui demande du poisson, lui donnera-t-il un serpent au lieu d'un poisson ?

12. Ou s'il lui demande un œuf, lui donnera-t-il un scorpion ?

AND it came to pass, that, as he was praying in a certain place, when he ceased, one of his disciples said unto him, Lord, teach us to pray, as John also taught his disciples.

2 And he said unto them, When ye pray, say, Our Father, which art in heaven: Hallowed be thy name. Thy kingdom come. Thy will be done, as in heaven, so in earth.

3 Give us day by day our daily bread.

4 And forgive us our sins; for we also forgive every one that is indebted to us. And lead us not into temptation; but deliver us from evil.

5 And he said unto them, Which of you shall have a friend, and shall go unto him at midnight, and say unto him, Friend, lend me three loaves;

6 For a friend of mine in his journey is come to me, and I have nothing to set before him?

7 And he from within shall answer, and say, Trouble me not: the door is now shut, and my children are with me in bed; I cannot rise and give thee.

8 I say unto you, Though he will not rise and give him, because he is his friend; yet because of his importunity he will rise and give him as many as he needeth.

9 And I say unto you, Ask, and it shall be given you; seek, and ye shall find: knock, and it shall be opened unto you.

10 For every one that asketh, receiveth; and he that seeketh, findeth; and to him that knocketh, it shall be opened.

11 If a son shall ask bread of any of you that is a father, will he give him a stone? or, if he ask a fish, will he for a fish give him a serpent?

12 Or, if he shall ask an egg, will he offer him a scorpion?

40.

13 Εἰ ἂν ὑμεῖς πονηροὶ ὑπάρχοντες, οἴδατε ἀγαθὰ δόματα διδόναι τοῖς τέκνοις ὑμῶν, πόσῳ μᾶλλον ὁ πατὴρ ὁ ἐξ οὐρανῦ, δώσει πνεῦμα ἅγιον τοῖς αἰτῦσιν αὐτόν;

Κεφ. ιδ΄. 14.

1 ΚΑΙ ἐγένετο ἐν τῷ ἐλθεῖν αὐτὸν εἰς οἶκόν τινΘ- τῶν ἀρχόντων τῶν φαρισαίων σαββάτῳ φαγεῖν ἄρτον, ἢ αὐτοὶ ἦσαν παρατηρούμενοι αὐτόν.

2 Καὶ ἰδὲ, ἄνθρωπός τις ἦν † ὑδρωπικὸς ἔμπροσθεν αὐτῦ.

3 Καὶ ἀποκριθεὶς ὁ Ἰησῦς εἶπε πρὸς τοὺς νομικοὺς ἢ φαρισαίους, λέγων· Εἰ ἔξεςι τῷ σαββάτῳ θεραπεύειν;

* 4 Οἱ δὲ ‡ ἡσύχασαν.

Τινθ- ὑμῶν ὄνΘ- ἢ βῦς εἰς φρέαρ ἐμπεσεῖται, ἢ οὐκ εὐθέως ‡ ἀνασπάσει αὐτὸν ἐν τῇ ἡμέρᾳ τοῦ σαββάτῳ;

6 Καὶ οὐκ ἴσχυσαν ἀνταποκριθῆναι αὐτῷ πρὸς ταῦτα.

7 Ἔλεγε δὲ πρὸς τοὺς κεκλημένους παραβολὴν, ἐπέχων πῶς τὰς πρωτοκλισίας ἐξελέγοντο, λέγων πρὸς αὐτοὺς·

8 Ὅταν κληθῇς ὑπό τ.νΘ- εἰς γάμους, μὴ κατακλιθῇς εἰς τὴν πρωτοκλισίαν· μήποτε ἐντιμότερός σε ἦ κεκλημένΘ- ὑπ᾿ αὐτῦ.

9 Καὶ ἐλθὼν ὁ σὲ ἢ αὐτὸν καλέσας, ἐρεῖ σοι· Δὸς τούτῳ τόπον· ἢ τότε ἄρξῃ μετ᾿ αἰσχύνης τὸν ἔσχατον τόπον κατέχειν.

10 Ἀλλ᾿ ὅταν κληθῇς, πορευθεὶς ἀνάπεσον εἰς τὸν ἔσχατον τόπον· ἵνα ὅταν ἔλθῃ ὁ κεκληκώς σε, εἴπῃ σοι· Φίλε, † προσανάβηθι ἀνώτερον· τότε ἔςαι σοι δόξα ἐνώπιον τῶν ‡ συνανακειμένων σοι.

11 Ὅτι πᾶς ὁ ὑψῶν ἑαυτὸν ταπεινωθήσεται· ἢ ὁ ταπεινῶν ἑαυτὸν, ὑψωθήσεται.

12 Ἔλεγε δὲ ἢ τῷ κεκληκότι αὐτόν· Ὅταν ποιῇς ἄριστον ἢ δεῖπνον, μὴ ‡ φώνει τοὺς ‡ φίλους σε, μηδὲ τοὺς ἀδελφούς σε, μηδὲ τοὺς ζυγγενεῖς σε, μηδὲ ‡ γείτονας ‡ πλουσίους· μήποτε ἢ αὐτοί σε † ἀντικαλέσωσι, ἢ γένηταί σοι ‡ ἀνταπόδομα.

---

13 Si ergo vos mali subsistentes, nostis bona dona dare filiis vestris, quanto magis Pater de cælo dabit Spiritum sanctum petentibus se?

CAPUT XIV.

1 ET factum est in venire eum in domum cujusdam principum Pharisæorum Sabbato manducare panem, & ipsi erat observantes eum.

2 Et ecce homo quidam erat hydropicus ante illum.

3 Et respondens Jesus dixit ad Legisperitos & Pharisæos, dicens: Si licet Sabbato curare?

4 Illi autem tacuerunt.

Cujus vestrum asinus aut bos in puteum cadet, & non continuo extrahet illum in die Sabbati?

6 Et non poterant respondere illi ad hæc.

7 Dicebat autem ad vocatos parabolam, attendens quomodo primos accubitus eligerent, dicens ad illos:

8 Quum vocatus fueris ab aliquo ad nuptias, ne discumbas in primo accubitu, ne quando honoratior te sit vocatus ab illo.

9 Et veniens te & illum vocans, dicat tibi: Da huic locum: & tunc incipias cum pudore ultimum locum obtinere.

10 Sed quum vocatus fueris, vadens recumbe in novissimum locum, ut quum venerit qui te vocavit, dicat tibi: Amice, ascende superius, tunc erit tibi gloria coram simul discumbentibus tibi.

11 Quia omnis extollens seipsum humiliabitur, & humilians seipsum exaltabitur.

12 Dicebat autem & vocanti ipsum: Quum facis prandium aut cœnam, ne voca amicos tuos, neque fratres tuos, neque cognatos tuos, neque vicinos divites, ne quando et ipsi te vicissim vocent, & fiat tibi retributio.

13. Si donc vous, qui êtes mauvais, savez donner de bonnes choses à vos enfans, combien plus votre Père céleste, donnera-t-il le St. Esprit à ceux qui le lui demandent?

Un jour de Sabbat, *Jésus* étant entré dans la maison d'un des principaux Pharisiens pour y manger, ceux qui étoient là l'observoient,

2. Et un homme hydropique se trouva devant lui.

3. Et Jésus prenant la parole, dit aux Docteurs de la loi et aux Pharisiens : Est-il permis de guérir au jour du Sabbat?

4. Et ils demeurèrent dans le silence. Alors prenant *le malade*, il le guérit et le renvoya.

5. Puis il leur dit : Qui est celui d'entre vous qui, voyant son âne ou son bœuf tombé dans un puits, ne l'en retire aussitôt le jour du Sabbat?

6. Et ils ne pouvoient rien répondre à cela.

7. Il proposoit aussi aux conviés une parabole ; remarquant qu'ils choisissoient les premières places ; et il leur disoit :

8. Quand quelqu'un t'invitera à des nôces, ne te mets pas à la première place, de peur qu'il ne se trouve parmi les conviés une personne plus considérable que toi.

9. Et que celui qui vous aura invité, et toi et lui, ne vienne et ne te dise : Cède la place à celui-ci ; et qu'alors tu n'aies la honte d'être mis à la dernière place.

10. Mais quand tu seras invité, va te mettre à la dernière place, afin que quand celui qui t'a invité viendra, il te dise : *Mon ami*, monte plus haut. Alors cela te fera honneur devant ceux qui seront à table avec toi.

11. Car quiconque s'élève sera abaissé ; et quiconque s'abaisse sera élevé.

12. Il disoit aussi à celui qui l'avoit invité : Quand tu fais un dîner ou un souper, n'invite pas tes amis, ni tes frères, ni tes parens, ni tes voisins qui sont riches, de peur qu'ils ne t'invitent à leur tour, et qu'on ne te rende la pareille.

L. 11.

13 If ye then, being evil, know how to give good gifts unto your children ; how much more shall *your* heavenly Father give the Holy Spirit to them that ask him ?

L. 14.

AND it came to pass, as he went into the house of one of the chief Pharisees to eat bread on the sabbath-day, that they watched him.

2 And, behold, there was a certain man before him, which had the dropsy.

3 And Jesus, answering, spake unto the lawyers and Pharisees, saying, Is it lawful to heal on the sabbath-day ?

4 And they held their peace.

5 Which of you shall have an ass or an ox fallen into a pit, and will not straightway pull him out on the sabbath-day ?

6 And they could not answer him again to these things.

7 And he put forth a parable to those which were bidden, when he marked how they chose out the chief rooms ; saying unto them,

8 When thou art bidden of any *man* to a wedding, sit not down in the highest room ; lest a more honourable man than thou be bidden of him ;

9 And he that bade thee and him, come and say to thee, Give this man place ; and thou begin with shame to take the lowest room.

10 But when thou art bidden, go and sit down in the lowest room ; that when he that bade thee cometh, he may say unto thee, Friend, go up higher : then shalt thou have worship in the presence of them that sit at meat with thee.

11 For whosoever exalteth himself shall be abased ; and he that humbleth himself shall be exalted.

12 Then said he also to him that bade him, When thou makest a dinner or a supper, call not thy friends, nor thy brethren, neither thy kinsmen, nor thy rich neighbours ; lest they also bid thee again, and a recompense be made thee.

And he saith unto them.

13 Ἀλλ᾽ ὅταν ποιῇς † δο-
χὴν, κάλει πίωχοὺς, ‡ ἀναπήρως,
χωλὺς, τυφλύς·

14 Καὶ μακάρι۞ ἔσῃ· ὅτι οὐκ
ἔχωσιν ἀνταποδῆναί σοι· ἀντα-
ποδοθήσεται γάρ σοι ἐν τῇ ἀναςά-
σει τῶν δικαίων.

16 Ὁ δὲ εἶπεν αὐτῷ· Ἄνθρωπός τις ἐποίησε δεῖπνον μέγα, ὦ
ἐκάλεσε πολλοὺς·

17 Καὶ ἀπέςειλε τὸν δῦλον αὐτοῦ τῇ ὥρᾳ τοῦ δείπνυ εἰπεῖν τοῖς
κεκλημένοις Ἔρχεσθε, ὅτι ἤδη
ἕτοιμα ἐςι πάντα.

18 Καὶ ἤρξαντο ἀπὸ μιᾶς παρ-
αιτεῖσθαι πάντες· Ὁ πρῶτ۞
εἶπεν αὐτῷ· Ἀγρὸν ἠγόρασα, ὦ
ἔχω ἀνάγκην ἐξελθεῖν, ὦ ἰδεῖν
αὐτὸν ἐρωτῶ σε, ἔχε με παρῃτημένον.

19 Καὶ ἕτερ۞ εἶπε· Ζεύγη
βοῶν ἠγόρασα πέντε, ὦ πορεύομαι
δοκιμάσαι αὐτά· ἐρωτῶ σε, ἔχε
με παρῃτημένον.

20 Καὶ ἕτερ۞ εἶπε· Γυναῖκα
ἔγημα, ὦ διὰ τοῦτο οὐ δύναμαι
ἐλθεῖν.

21 Καὶ παραγενόμεν۞ ὁ δῦ-
λ۞ ἐκεῖν۞ ἀπήγγειλε τῷ κυρίῳ
αὐτῷ ταῦτα· Τότε ὀργισθεὶς ὁ
οἰκοδεσπότης εἶπε τῷ δύλῳ αὐτῷ·
Ἔξελθε ταχέως εἰς τὰς πλατείας
ὦ ῥύμας τῆς πόλεως, ὦ τοὺς πίωχοὺς ὦ ἀναπήρως ὦ χωλοὺς ὦ τυ-
φλοὺς εἰσάγαγε ὧδε.

22 Καὶ εἶπεν ὁ δῦλ۞· Κύριε,
γέγονεν ὡς ἐπέταξας, ὦ ἔτι τόπ۞
ἐςί.

23 Καὶ εἶπεν ὁ κύρι۞ πρὸς τὸν
δῦλον· Ἔξελθε εἰς τὰς ὁδοὺς ὦ
φραγμὺς, ὦ ἀνάγκασον εἰσελθεῖν,
ἵνα γεμισθῇ ὁ οἶκός μυ.

24 Λέγω γὰρ ὑμῖν, ὅτι οὐδεὶς
τῶν ἀνδρῶν ἐκείνων τῶν κεκλημέ-
νων γεύσεταί μυ τοῦ δείπνυ.

● 28 Τίς γὰρ ἐξ ὑμῶν, θέλων
πύργον οἰκοδομῆσαι, οὐχὶ πρῶτον
καθίσας † ψηφίζει τὴν † δαπάνην,
εἰ ἔχει τὰ πρὸς † ἀπαρτισμόν;

29 Ἵνα μήποτε, θέντ۞ αὐτοῦ
θεμέλιον, ὦ μὴ ἰσχύοντ۞ ἐκτελέσαι, πάντες οἱ θεωρῦντες ἄρ-
ξωνται ἐμπαίζειν αὐτῷ,

13 Sed quum facis epulum,
voca pauperes, mancos, claudos,
cæcos.

14 Et beatus eris, quia non
habent retribuere tibi: retribue-
tur enim tibi in refurrectione
juftorum.

16 Ipfe autem dixit ei. Homo quidam fecit cœnam ma-
gnam, & vocavit multos.

17 Et mifit fervum fuum hora cœnæ dicere vocatis: venite,
quia jam parata funt omnia.

18 Et cœperunt ab una excu-
fare omnes. Primus dixit ei:
Agrum emi, & habeo neceffe
exire, & videre illum: rogo te,
habe me excufatum.

19 Et alter dixit: Juga boum
emi quinque, & eo probare illa:
rogo te, habe me excufatum.

20 Et alius dixit: Uxorem
duxi, & propter hoc non poffum
venire.

21 Et adveniens fervus ille
nuntiavit domino fuo hæc.
Tunc iratus paterfamilias dixit
fervo fuo; Exi cito in plateas &
vicos civitatis, & pauperes, &
mancos, & claudos, & cæcos in-
troduc huc.

22 Et ait fervus: Domine,
factum eft ut imperafti, & adhuc locus eft.

23 Et ait dominus ad fer-
vum: Exi in vias & fepes, &
coge intrare, ut impleatur domus
mea.

24 Dico enim vobis, quia
nemo virorum illorum vocato-
rum guftabit meam cœnam.

25 Quis enim ex vobis volens
turrim ædificare, nonne prius
fedens computat fumptum, fi
habeat ea quæ ad perfectionem?

29 Ut ne quando ponente ipfo
fundamentum, & non potente
perficere, omnes videntes inci-
piant illudere ei,

13. Mais quand tu seras un festin, convie les pauvres, les impotens, les boiteux et les aveugles ;

14. Et tu seras heureux, de ce qu'ils ne peuvent pas te le rendre ;

16. Mais Jésus lui dit : Un homme fit un grand souper, et il y convia beaucoup de gens ;

17. Et il envoya son serviteur, à l'heure du souper, dire aux convies : Venez, car tout est prêt.

18. Mais ils se mirent tous *comme* de concert, à s'excuser. Le premier lui dit : J'ai acheté une terre, et il me faut nécessairement partir pour aller la voir ; je te prie de m'excuser.

19. Un autre dit : J'ai acheté cinq couples de bœufs, et je m'en vais les éprouver ; je te prie de m'excuser.

20. Un autre dit : J'ai épousé une femme, ainsi je n'y puis aller.

21. Le serviteur étant donc de retour, rapporta cela à son maître. Alors le père de famille, en colère, dit à son serviteur : Va-t-en promptement par les places, et par les rues de la ville, et amène ici les pauvres, les impotens, les boiteux et les aveugles.

22. Ensuite le serviteur dit : Seigneur, on a fait ce que tu as commandé, et il y a encore de la place.

23. Et le maître dit au serviteur : Va dans les chemins et le long des haies, et presse d'entrer ceux que tu trouveras, afin que ma maison soit remplie.

24. Car je vous dis, qu'aucun de ceux qui avoient été conviés, ne goûtera de mon souper.

28. Car qui est celui d'entre vous, qui, voulant bâtir une tour, ne s'asseye premièrement, et ne suppute la dépense, *pour voir* s'il a de quoi l'achever ?

29. De peur qu'après qu'il en aura posé les fondemens, et qu'il n'aura pu achever, tous ceux qui le verront ne viennent à se moquer de lui ;

13 But when thou makest a feast, call the poor, the maimed, the lame, the blind :

14 And thou shalt be blessed ; for they cannot recompense thee : for thou shalt be recompensed at the resurrection of the just.

15 Then said he unto him, A certain man made a great supper, and bade many :

17 And sent his servant at supper-time to say to them that were bidden, Come, for all things are now ready.

18 And they all with one *consent* began to make excuse. The first said unto him, I have bought a piece of ground, and I must needs go and see it : I pray thee have me excused.

19 And another said, I have bought five yoke of oxen, and I go to prove them : I pray thee have me excused.

20 And another said, I have married a wife ; and therefore I cannot come.

21 So that servant came, and shewed his lord these things. Then the master of the house, being angry, said to his servant, Go out quickly into the streets and lanes of the city, and bring in hither the poor, and the maimed, and the halt, and the blind.

22 And the servant said, Lord, it is done as thou hast commanded, and yet there is room.

23 And the lord said unto the servant, Go out into the highways and hedges, and compel *them* to come in, that my house may be filled.

24 For I say unto you, That none of those men which were bidden, shall taste of my supper.

28 For which of you, intending to build a tower, sitteth not down first, and counteth the cost, whether he have *sufficient* to finish *it* ?

29 Lest haply, after he hath laid the foundation, and is not able to finish *it*, all that behold *it* begin to mock him,

42

30 Λέγοντες· Ότι ούτ۟۟ ὁ
ἄνθρωπ۟۟ ἤρξατο οἰκοδομεῖν, κ̃
οὐκ ‡ ἴσχυσεν ‡ ἐκτελέσαι.

31 Ἤ τίς βασιλεὺς πορευόμε-
νۤ۟۟ συμϐαλεῖν ἑτέρῳ βασιλεῖ
εἰς πόλεμον, οὐχὶ καθίσας πρῶτον ϐυλεύεται εἰ δυνατός ἐςιν ἐν
δέκα χιλιάσιν ἀπαντῆσαι τῷ μετὰ
εἴκοσι χιλιάδων ἐρχομένῳ ἐπ᾽
αὐτόν;

32 Εἰ δὲ μήγε, ἔτι αὐτοῦ πόρ-
ρω ὄντۤ۟۟, πρεσϐείαν ἀποςείλας,
ἐρωτᾷ τὰ πρὸς εἰρήνην.

Κεφ. ιε᾽. 15.

1 Ἦσαν δὲ ἐγγίζοντες αὐτῷ
πάντες οἱ τελῶναι κ̃ οἱ ἁ-
μαρτωλοὶ, ἀκούειν αὐτοῦ·

2 Καὶ διεγόγγυζον οἱ φαρισαῖοι,
κ̃ οἱ γραμματεῖς, λέγοντες· Ὅτι
οὗτۤ۟۟ ἁμαρτωλοὺς προσδέχεται, κ̃
συνεσθίει αὐτοῖς.

3 Εἶπε δὲ πρὸς αὐτοὺς τὴν παραϐολὴν ταύτην, λέγων·

4 Τίς ἄνθρωπۤ۟۟ ἐξ ὑμῶν ἔχων
ἑκατὸν πρόϐατα, κ̃ ἀπολέσας ἓν
ἐξ αὐτῶν, οὐ καταλείπει τὰ ἐννενηκονταεννέα ἐν τῇ ἐρήμῳ, κ̃

πορεύεται ἐπὶ τὸ ἀπολωλός, ἕως
εὕρῃ αὐτό;

5 Καὶ εὑρὼν ἐπιτίθησιν ἐπὶ
τοὺς ὤμους ἑαυτοῦ χαίρων·

6 Καὶ ἐλθὼν εἰς τὸν οἶκον, συγ-
καλεῖ τοὺς φίλους κ̃ τοὺς γείτονας,
λέγων αὐτοῖς· Συγχάρητέ μοι,
ὅτι εὗρον τὸ πρόϐατόν μου τὸ ἀ-
πολωλός.

7 Λέγω ὑμῖν, ὅτι οὕτω χαρὰ
ἔςαι ἐν τῷ οὐρανῷ ἐπὶ ἑνὶ ἁμαρτωλῷ μετανοοῦντι, ἢ ἐπὶ ἐννενηκονταεννέα δικαίοις, οἵτινες οὐ χρείαν ἔ-
χουσι μετανοίας.

8 Ἤ τίς γυνὴ, δραχμὰς
ἔχουσα δέκα, ἐὰν ἀπολέσῃ ‡ δραχμὴν μίαν, ‡ οὐχὶ ‡ ἅπτει ‡ λύχνον,
κ̃ ‡ σαροῖ τὴν οἰκίαν, κ̃ ζητεῖ
‡ ἐπιμελῶς, ἕως ‡ ὅτου εὕρῃ;

9 Καὶ εὑροῦσα συγκαλεῖται τὰς
φίλας κ̃ τὰς γείτονας, λέγουσα·
Συγχάρητέ μοι, ὅτι εὗρον τὴν
δραχμὴν, ἣν ἀπώλεσα.

10 Οὕτω, λέγω ὑμῖν, χαρὰ
γίνεται ἐνώπιον τῶν ἀγγέλων τοῦ
Θεοῦ ἐπὶ ἑνὶ ἁμαρτωλῷ μετανοοῦντι.

---

30 Dicentes: Quia hic homo
cœpit ædificare, & non potuit
consummare.

31 Aut quis, rex iturus com-
mittere alteri regi in bellum,
non sedens prius consultat si
potens est in decem millibus pec-
cultore cum viginti millibus ve-
nienti ad se?

32 Si autem non, adhuc longe illo existente, legationem mittens rogat quæ ad pacem.

CAPUT XV.

1 Erant autem appropin-
quantes ei omnes publi-
cani & peccatores audire illum.

2 Et murmurabant Pharisæi
& Scribæ, dicentes: Quia hic
peccatores recipit, & manducat
cum illis.

3 Ait autem ad illos parabolam istam, dicens:

4 Quis homo ex vobis habens
centum oves, & perdens unam
ex illis, nonne dimittit nonaginta novem in deserto, & vadit ad perditam, donec inveniat
eam?

5 Et inveniens imponit in
humeros suos gaudens.

6 Et veniens in domum, convocat amicos & vicinos, dicens
illis: Congratulamini mihi,
quia inveni ovem meam perditam.

7 Dico vobis, quod ita gaudium erit in cœlo super uno
peccatore pœnitente, quam super
nonaginta novem justis, qui non
opus habent pœnitentia.

8 Aut quæ mulier drachmas
habens decem, si perdiderit
drachmam unam, nonne accen-
dit lucernam, & everrit domum,
& quærit diligenter, usquequo
inveniat?

9 Et inveniens convocat ami-
cas & vicinas, dicens: Congratulamini mihi, quia inveni
drachmam quam perdideram.

10 Ita, dico vobis gaudium
fit coram angelis Dei super uno
peccatore pœnitente.

30. Et ne disent : Cet homme a commencé à bâtir, et n'a pu achever.

31. Ou, qui est le Roi, qui, marchant pour livrer bataille à un autre Roi, ne s'asseye premièrement, et ne consulte s'il pourra, avec dix mille *hommes*, aller à la rencontre de celui qui vient contre lui avec vingt mille ?

32. Autrement, pendant que celui-ci est encore loin, il lui envoie une ambassade pour lui demander la paix.

Tous les péagers et les gens de mauvaise vie s'approchoient de *Jésus* pour l'entendre.

2. Et les Pharisiens et les Scribes en murmuroient, et disoient : Cet homme reçoit les gens de mauvaise vie, et mange avec eux.

3. Mais il leur proposa cette parabole :

4. Qui est l'homme d'entre vous, qui, ayant cent brebis, s'il en perd une, ne laisse les quatre-vingt-neuf au désert, et n'aille après celle qui est perdue, jusqu'à ce qu'il l'ait trouvée ;

5. Et qui, l'ayant trouvée, ne la mette sur ses épaules avec joie ;

6. Et étant arrivé dans la maison, n'appelle ses amis et ses voisins, et ne leur dise : Réjouissez-vous avec moi, car j'ai trouvé ma brebis qui étoit perdue ?

7. Je vous dis, qu'il y aura de même plus de joie dans le ciel pour un seul pécheur qui s'amende, que pour quatre-vingt-dix-neuf justes, qui n'ont pas besoin de repentance.

8. Ou, qui est la femme qui, ayant dix drachmes, si elle en perd une, n'allume une chandelle, ne balaie la maison, et ne cherche avec soin, jusqu'à ce qu'elle ait trouvé *sa drachme* ;

9. Et qui, l'ayant trouvée, n'appelle ses amies et ses voisins, et ne leur dise : Réjouissez-vous avec moi, car j'ai trouvé la drachme que j'avois perdue ?

10. Je vous dis, qu'il y a de même de la joie devant les Anges de Dieu, pour un seul pécheur qui s'amende.

30 Saying, This man began to build, and was not able to finish.

31 Or what king, going to make war against another king, sitteth not down first, and consulteth whether he be able with ten thousand to meet him that cometh against him with twenty thousand ?

32 Or else, while the other is yet a great way off, he sendeth an ambassage, and desireth conditions of peace.

THEN drew near unto him all the publicans and sinners for to hear him.

2 And the Pharisees and scribes murmured, saying, This man receiveth sinners, and eateth with them.

3 And he spake this parable unto them, saying,

4 What man of you, having an hundred sheep, if he lose one of them, doth not leave the ninety and nine in the wilderness, and go after that which is lost, until he find it ?

5 And when he hath found *it*, he layeth *it* on his shoulders, rejoicing.

6 And when he cometh home, he calleth together *his* friends and neighbours, saying unto them, Rejoice with me; for I have found my sheep which was lost.

7 I say unto you, That likewise joy shall be in heaven over one sinner that repenteth, more than over ninety and nine just persons, which need no repentance.

8 Either what woman, having ten pieces of silver, if she lose one piece, doth not light a candle, and sweep the house, and seek diligently till she find *it*?

9 And when she hath found *it*, she calleth *her* friends and *her* neighbours together, saying, Rejoice with me; for I have found the piece which I had lost.

10 Likewise, I say unto you, There is joy in the presence of the angels of God, over one sinner that repenteth.

43

11 Εἶπε δέ· Ἄνθρωπός τις εἶχε δύο υἱούς.

12 Καὶ εἶπεν ὁ νεώτερος αὐτῶν τῷ πατρί· Πάτερ, δός μοι τὸ ἐπιβάλλον μέρος τῆς οὐσίας. Καὶ διεῖλεν αὐτοῖς τὸν βίον.

13 Καὶ μετ᾽ οὐ πολλὰς ἡμέρας συναγαγὼν ἅπαντα ὁ νεώτερος υἱός, ἀπεδήμησεν εἰς χώραν μακράν, καὶ ἐκεῖ διεσκόρπισε τὴν οὐσίαν αὐτοῦ, ζῶν ἀσώτως.

14 Δαπανήσαντος δὲ αὐτοῦ πάντα, ἐγένετο λιμὸς ἰσχυρὸς κατὰ τὴν χώραν ἐκείνην· καὶ αὐτὸς ἤρξατο ὑστερεῖσθαι.

15 Καὶ πορευθεὶς ἐκολλήθη ἑνὶ τῶν πολιτῶν τῆς χώρας ἐκείνης· καὶ ἔπεμψεν αὐτὸν εἰς τοὺς ἀγροὺς αὐτοῦ βόσκειν χοίρους.

16 Καὶ ἐπεθύμει γεμίσαι τὴν κοιλίαν αὐτοῦ ἀπὸ τῶν κερατίων, ὧν ἤσθιον οἱ χοῖροι· καὶ οὐδεὶς ἐδίδου αὐτῷ.

17 Εἰς ἑαυτὸν δὲ ἐλθὼν, εἶπε· Πόσοι μίσθιοι τοῦ πατρός μου περισσεύουσιν ἄρτων, ἐγὼ δὲ λιμῷ ἀπόλλυμαι;

18 Ἀναστὰς πορεύσομαι πρὸς τὸν πατέρα μου, καὶ ἐρῶ αὐτῷ· Πάτερ, ἥμαρτον εἰς τὸν οὐρανὸν, καὶ ἐνώπιόν σου.

19 Καὶ οὐκέτι εἰμὶ ἄξιος κληθῆναι υἱός σου· ποίησόν με ὡς ἕνα τῶν μισθίων σου.

20 Καὶ ἀναστὰς ἦλθε πρὸς τὸν πατέρα ἑαυτοῦ. Ἔτι δὲ αὐτοῦ μακρὰν ἀπέχοντος, εἶδεν αὐτὸν ὁ πατὴρ αὐτοῦ, καὶ ἐσπλαγχνίσθη, καὶ δραμὼν ἐπέπεσεν ἐπὶ τὸν τράχηλον αὐτοῦ, καὶ κατεφίλησεν αὐτόν.

21 Εἶπε δὲ αὐτῷ ὁ υἱός· Πάτερ, ἥμαρτον εἰς τὸν οὐρανὸν καὶ ἐνώπιόν σου, καὶ οὐκέτι εἰμὶ ἄξιος κληθῆναι υἱός σου.

22 Εἶπε δὲ ὁ πατὴρ πρὸς τοὺς δούλους αὐτοῦ· Ἐξενέγκατε τὴν στολὴν τὴν πρώτην, καὶ ἐνδύσατε αὐτὸν, καὶ δότε δακτύλιον εἰς τὴν χεῖρα αὐτοῦ, καὶ ὑποδήματα εἰς τοὺς πόδας·

23 Καὶ ἐνέγκαντες τὸν μόσχον τὸν σιτευτὸν θύσατε· καὶ φαγόντες εὐφρανθῶμεν·

peccatore pœnitente.

11 Ait autem: Homo quidam habuit duos filios

12 Et dixit junior eorum patri: Pater, da mihi competentem partem substantiæ, & divisit illis vitam.

13 Et post non multos dies congregans omnia junior filius peregrè profectus est in regionem longinquam, & ibi dissipavit substantiam suam vivens profusè.

14 Consumente autem ipso omnia, facta est fames valida per regionem illam; & ipse cœpit defici.

15 Et abiens adhæsit uni civium regionis illius: & misit illum in agros suos pascere porcos.

16 Et desiderabat implere ventrem suum de siliquis quas manducabant porci: & nemo dabat illi.

17 In se autem veniens, dixit; Quot mercenarii patris mei abundant panibus, ego autem fame pereo?

18 Surgens ibo ad patrem meum, & dicam ei: Pater, peccavi in cælum, & coràm te:

19 Et non amplius sum dignus vocari filius tuus, fac me sicut unum mercenariorum tuorum.

20 Et surgens venit ad patrem suum. Adhuc autem eo longè absente, vidit illum pater ipsius, & misericordia motus est, & currens cecidit super collum ejus, & osculatus est eum.

21 Dixit autem ei filius: Pater peccavi in cælum & coram te, & non amplius sum dignus vocari filius tuus.

22 Dixit autem pater ad servos suos: Afferte stolam primam, & induite illum, & date annulum in manum ejus, & calceamenta in pedes.

23 Et afferentes vitulum saginatum occidite, & comedentes oblectemur.

11. Il leur dit encore : Un homme avoit deux fils ;

12. Dont le plus jeune dit à *son* père : Mon père, donne-moi la part du bien qui me doit échoir. Ainsi *le père* leur partagea son bien.

13. Et peu de jours après, ce plus jeune fils ayant amassé, s'en alla dehors dans un pays éloigné, et il y dissipa son bien en vivant dans la débauche.

14. Après qu'il eut tout dépensé, il survint une grande famine en ce pays-là ; et il commença à être dans l'indigence.

15. Alors il s'en alla, et se mit au service d'un des habitans de ce pays-là, qui l'envoya dans ses possessions, pour paître les pourceaux.

16. Et il eût bien voulu se rassasier des carrouges que les pourceaux mangeoient ; mais personne ne lui en donnoit.

17. Etant donc rentré en lui-même, il dit : Combien y a-t-il de gens aux gages de mon père, qui ont du pain en abondance, et moi je meurs de faim ?

18. Je me leverai, et m'en irai vers mon père, et je lui dirai : *Mon* père, j'ai péché contre le ciel, et contre toi ;

19. Et je ne suis plus digne d'être appelé ton fils : Traite-moi comme l'un de tes domestiques.

20. Il partit donc, et vint vers son père. Et comme il étoit encore loin, son père le vit, et fut touché de compassion ; et courant à lui, il se jeta à son cou et le baisa.

21. Et son fils lui dit : *Mon* père, j'ai péché contre le ciel et contre toi ; et je ne suis plus digne d'être appelé ton fils.

22. Mais le père dit à ses serviteurs : Apportez la plus belle robe, et l'en revêtez, et mettez-lui un anneau au doigt, et des souliers aux pieds ;

23. Et amenez un veau gras, et le tuez ; mangeons, et réjouissons-nous ;

11 And he said, A certain man had two sons:

12 And the younger of them said to *his* father, Father, give me the portion of goods that falleth *to me*. And he divided unto them *his* living.

13 And not many days after the younger son gathered all together, and took his journey into a far country, and there wasted his substance with riotous living.

14 And when he had spent all, there arose a mighty famine in that land ; and he began to be in want.

15 And he went and joined himself to a citizen of that country ; and he sent him into his fields to feed swine.

16 And he would fain have filled his belly with the husks that the swine did eat : and no man gave unto him.

17 And when he came to himself, he said, How many hired servants of my father's have bread enough, and to spare, and I perish with hunger !

18 I will arise, and go to my father, and will say unto him, Father, I have sinned against heaven, and before thee,

19 And am no more worthy to be called thy son : make me as one of thy hired servants.

20 And he arose, and came to his father. But, when he was yet a great way off, his father saw him, and had compassion, and ran, and fell on his neck, and kissed him.

21 And the son said unto him, Father, I have sinned against heaven, and in thy sight, and am no more worthy to be called thy son.

22 But the father said to his servants, Bring forth the best robe, and put *it* on him ; and put a ring on his hand, and shoes on *his* feet:

23 And bring hither the fatted calf, and kill *it* ; and let us eat, and be merry:

44

24 Ὅτι οὗτος ὁ υἱός μου νεκρὸς ἦν, καὶ ἀνέζησε· καὶ ἀπολωλὼς ἦν, καὶ εὑρέθη. Καὶ ἤρξαντο εὐφραίνεσθαι.

25 Ἦν δὲ ὁ υἱὸς αὐτοῦ ὁ πρεσβύτερος ἐν ἀγρῷ· καὶ ὡς ἐρχόμενος ἤγγισε τῇ οἰκίᾳ, ἤκουσε † συμφωνίας καὶ χορῶν·

26 Καὶ προσκαλεσάμενος ἕνα τῶν παίδων ἐπυνθάνετο τί εἴη ταῦτα.

27 Ὁ δὲ εἶπεν αὐτῷ Ὅτι ὁ ἀδελφός σου ἥκει· καὶ ἔθυσεν ὁ πατήρ σου τὸν μόσχον τὸν σιτευτόν, ὅτι ὑγιαίνοντα αὐτὸν ἀπέλαβεν.

28 Ὠργίσθη δὲ, καὶ οὐκ ἤθελεν εἰσελθεῖν. Ὁ οὖν πατὴρ αὐτοῦ ἐξελθὼν παρεκάλει αὐτόν·

* 29 Ὁ δὲ ἀποκριθεὶς εἶπε τῷ πατρί. Ἰδού, τοσαῦτα ἔτη δουλεύω σοι, καὶ οὐδέποτε ἐντολήν σου παρῆλθον, καὶ ἐμοὶ οὐδέποτε ἔδωκας ‡ ἔριφον, ἵνα μετὰ τῶν φίλων μου εὐφρανθῶ·

30 Ὅτε δὲ ὁ υἱός σου οὗτος, ὁ καταφαγών σου τὸν βίον μετὰ πορνῶν, ἦλθεν, ἔθυσας αὐτῷ τὸν μόσχον τὸν σιτευτόν.

31 Ὁ δὲ εἶπεν αὐτῷ· Τέκνον, σὺ πάντοτε μετ' ἐμοῦ εἶ, καὶ πάντα τὰ ἐμὰ σά ἐστιν.

32 Εὐφρανθῆναι δὲ καὶ χαρῆναι ἔδει, ὅτι ὁ ἀδελφός σου οὗτος νεκρὸς ἦν, καὶ ἀνέζησε· καὶ ἀπολωλὼς ἦν, καὶ εὑρέθη. 27. † 6.

Κεφ. ιε'. 16.

* 1 Ἔλεγε δὲ καὶ πρὸς τοὺς μαθητὰς αὐτοῦ· Ἄνθρωπός τις ἦν πλούσιος, ὃς εἶχεν οἰκονόμον· καὶ οὗτος † διεβλήθη αὐτῷ ὡς διασκορπίζων τὰ ὑπάρχοντα αὐτοῦ.

* 2 Καὶ φωνήσας αὐτόν, εἶπεν αὐτῷ· Τί τοῦτο ἀκούω περὶ σοῦ; ‡ ἀπόδος τὸν λόγον τῆς ‡ οἰκονομίας σου· οὐ γὰρ δυνήσῃ ἔτι † οἰκονομεῖν.

* 3 Εἶπε δὲ ἐν ἑαυτῷ ὁ οἰκονόμος· Τί ποιήσω, ὅτι ὁ κύριός μου ἀφαιρεῖται τὴν οἰκονομίαν ἀπ' ἐμοῦ; σκάπτειν οὐκ ἰσχύω, † ἐπαιτεῖν ‡ αἰσχύνομαι.

---

24 Quia hic filius meus mortuus erat, & revixit: & perditus fuerat, & inventus est: & cœperunt oblectari.

25 Erat autem filius ejus senior in agro: & ut veniens appropinquavit domui, audivit symphoniam & choros.

26 Et advocans unum puerorum, interrogavit quid essent hæc.

27 Is autem dixit illi: Quia frater tuus venit: & occidit pater tuus vitulum saginatum: quia valentem illum recepit.

28 Indignatus est autem, & non volebat introire, ergo pater illius egressus advocabat illum.

29 Is autem respondens dixit patri: Ecce tot annos servio tibi, & nunquam mandatum tuum prætervi, & mihi nunquam dedisti hœdum, ut cum amicis meis oblectarer.

30 Quum autem filius tuus hic, devorans tuam vitam cum meretricibus, venit, occidisti illi vitulum saginatum.

31 Is autem dixit illi: Fili, tu semper cum me es, & omnia mea tua sunt.

32 Oblectari autem & gaudere oportebat, quia frater tuus hic mortuus erat, & revixit: & perditus erat, & inventus est.

CAPUT XVI.

1 DIcebat autem & ad discipulos suos: Homo quidam erat dives, qui habebat dispensatorem, & hic delatus est ei, ut dissipans substantias illius.

2 Et vocans illum, ait illi: Quid hoc audio de te? Redde rationem dispensationis tuæ, non enim poteris adhuc dispensare.

3 Ait autem in seipso dispensator: Quid faciam, quia dominus meus aufert dispensationem à me? fodere non valeo, mendicare erubesco.

24. Parce que mon fils, que voici étoit mort, et il est revenu à la vie ; il étoit perdu, mais il est retrouvé. Et ils commencèrent à se réjouir.

25. Cependant son fils aîné, qui étoit à la campagne, revint ; et comme il approchait de la maison, il entendit les chants et les danses.

26. Et il appela un des serviteurs, à qui il demanda ce que c'étoit.

27. Et *le serviteur* lui dit : Ton frère est de retour, et ton père a tué un veau gras, parce qu'il l'a recouvré en *bonne* santé.

28. Mais il se mit en colère, et ne voulut point entrer. Son père donc sortit, et le pria *d'entrer*.

29. Mais il répondit à son père : Voici, il y a tant d'années que je te sers, sans avoir jamais contrevenu à ton commandement, et tu ne m'as jamais donné un chevreau pour me réjouir avec mes amis.

30. Mais quand ton fils que voilà, qui a mangé tout son bien avec des femmes débauchées, est revenu, tu as fait tuer un veau gras pour lui.

31. Et *son père* lui dit : Mon fils, tu es toujours avec moi, et tout ce que j'ai est à toi.

32. Mais il falloit bien faire un festin et se réjouir, parce que ton frère que voilà est mort, et il est revenu à la vie ; il étoit perdu, et il est retrouvé.

CHAPITRE XVI.

Les paraboles de l'Econome injuste, du Riche et de Lazare.

Jésus disoit aussi à ses Disciples : Un homme riche avoit un économe qui fut accusé devant lui de dissiper son bien.

2. Et l'ayant fait venir, il lui dit : Qu'est-ce que j'entends dire de toi ? Rends compte de ton administration ; car tu ne pourras plus désormais administrer *mon bien*.

3. Alors cet économe dit en lui-même : Que ferai-je, puisque mon maître m'ôte l'administration *de son bien* ? Je ne saurois travailler à la terre, et j'aurois honte de mendier.

---

24 For this my son was dead, and is alive again ; he was lost, and is found. And they began to be merry.

25 Now, his elder son was in the field : and as he came and drew nigh to the house, he heard music and dancing.

26 And he called one of the servants, and asked what these things meant.

27 And he said unto him, Thy brother is come ; and thy father hath killed the fatted calf, because he hath received him safe and sound.

28 And he was angry, and would not go in : therefore came his father out, and entreated him.

29 And he, answering, said to *his* father, Lo, these many years do I serve thee, neither transgressed I at any time thy commandment ; and yet thou never gavest me a kid, that I might make merry with my friends :

30 But as soon as this thy son was come, which hath devoured thy living with harlots, thou hast killed for him the fatted calf.

31 And he said unto him, Son, thou art ever with me, and all that I have is thine.

32 It was meet that we should make merry, and be glad : for this thy brother was dead, and is alive again ; and was lost, and is found.

CHAP. XVI.

Of the unjust steward.

AND he said also unto his disciples, There was a certain rich man, which had a steward ; and the same was accused unto him that he had wasted his goods.

2 And he called him, and said unto him, How is it that I hear this of thee ? give an account of thy stewardship ; for thou mayest be no longer steward.

3 Then the steward said within himself, What shall I do, for my lord taketh away from me the stewardship ? I cannot dig ; to beg I am ashamed.

4 Ἔγνων τί ποιήσω, ἵνα ὅταν μετασταθῶ τῆς οἰκονομίας, δέξωνταί με εἰς τοὺς οἴκους αὐτῶν.

5 Καὶ προσκαλεσάμενος ἕνα ἕκαστον τῶν χρεωφειλετῶν τοῦ κυρίου ἑαυτοῦ, ἔλεγε τῷ πρώτῳ· Πόσον ὀφείλεις τῷ κυρίῳ μου;

6 Ὁ δὲ εἶπεν· Ἑκατὸν βάτους ἐλαίου. Καὶ εἶπεν αὐτῷ· Δέξαι σου τὸ γράμμα, καὶ καθίσας ταχέως γράψον πεντήκοντα.

7 Ἔπειτα ἑτέρῳ εἶπε· Σὺ δὲ πόσον ὀφείλεις; Ὁ δὲ εἶπεν· Ἑκατὸν κόρους σίτου. Καὶ λέγει αὐτῷ· Δέξαι σου τὸ γράμμα, καὶ γράψον ὀγδοήκοντα.

8 Καὶ ἐπῄνεσεν ὁ κύριος τὸν οἰκονόμον τῆς ἀδικίας, ὅτι φρονίμως ἐποίησεν, ὅτι οἱ υἱοὶ τοῦ αἰῶνος τούτου φρονιμώτεροι ὑπὲρ τοὺς υἱοὺς τοῦ φωτὸς εἰς τὴν γενεὰν τὴν ἑαυτῶν εἰσι.

9 Κἀγὼ ὑμῖν λέγω· Ποιήσατε ἑαυτοῖς φίλους ἐκ τοῦ μαμωνᾶ τῆς ἀδικίας· ἵνα ὅταν ἐκλίπητε, δέξωνται ὑμᾶς εἰς τὰς αἰωνίους σκηνάς.

10 Ὁ πιστὸς ἐν ἐλαχίστῳ, καὶ ἐν πολλῷ πιστός ἐστι· ὁ ἐν ἐλαχίστῳ ἄδικος, καὶ ἐν πολλῷ ἄδικός ἐστιν.

11 Εἰ οὖν ἐν τῷ ἀδίκῳ μαμωνᾷ πιστοὶ οὐκ ἐγένεσθε, τὸ ἀληθινὸν τίς ὑμῖν πιστεύσει;

12 Καὶ εἰ ἐν τῷ ἀλλοτρίῳ πιστοὶ οὐκ ἐγένεσθε, τὸ ὑμέτερον τίς ὑμῖν δώσει;

13 Οὐδεὶς οἰκέτης δύναται δυσὶ κυρίοις δουλεύειν· ἢ γὰρ τὸν ἕνα μισήσει, καὶ τὸν ἕτερον ἀγαπήσει· ἢ ἑνὸς ἀνθέξεται, καὶ τοῦ ἑτέρου καταφρονήσει· οὐ δύνασθε Θεῷ δουλεύειν καὶ μαμωνᾷ.

14 Ἤκουον δὲ ταῦτα πάντα καὶ οἱ Φαρισαῖοι, φιλάργυροι ὑπάρχοντες· καὶ ἐξεμυκτήριζον αὐτόν.

15 Καὶ εἶπεν αὐτοῖς· Ὑμεῖς ἐστε οἱ δικαιοῦντες ἑαυτοὺς ἐνώπιον τῶν ἀνθρώπων· ὁ δὲ Θεὸς γινώσκει τὰς καρδίας ὑμῶν· ὅτι τὸ ἐν ἀνθρώποις ὑψηλὸν, βδέλυγμα ἐνώπιον τοῦ Θεοῦ ἐστιν.

4 Scio quid faciam, ut quum amotus fuero dispensatione, recipiant me in domos suas.

5 Et convocans unumquemque debitorum Domini sui, dicebat primo: Quantum debes domino meo?

6 Is autem dixit: Centum batos olei, & dixit illi: Accipe tuum scriptum, & sedens cito scribe quinquaginta.

Deinde alii dixit: Tu vero quantum debes? is autem ait: Centum coros tritici, & ait illi: Accipe tuas literas, & scribe octoginta.

8 Et laudavit dominus dispensatorem injustitiae, quia prudenter fecisset: quia filii seculi hujus prudentiores super filios lucis in generationem suam sunt.

9 Et ego vobis dico: Facite vobis ipsis amicos de mamona injustitiae, ut quum defeceritis, recipiant vos in aeterna tabernacula.

10 Fidelis in minimo, & in multo fidelis est: & in modico injustus, etiam in multo injustus est.

11 Si ergo in injusto mamona fideles non fuistis, verum quis vobis credet?

12 Et si in alieno fideles non fuistis, vestrum quis vobis dabit?

13 Nemo servus potest duobus dominis servire: aut enim unum odiet, & alterum diliget: aut uni adhaerebit, & alterum contemnet; non potestis Deo servire & mamonae.

14 Audiebant autem haec omnia & Pharisaei avari subsistentes, & deridebant illum.

15 Et ait illis: Vos estis justificantes vos ipsos coram hominibus: at Deus novit corda vestra, quia quod in hominibus altum, abominatio ante Deum est.

4. Je sais ce que je ferai, afin que quand on m'aura ôté mon administration, il y ait des gens qui me reçoivent dans leurs maisons.

5. Alors il fit venir séparément chacun des débiteurs de son maître; et il dit au premier : Combien dois-tu à mon maître ?

6. Il répondit : Cent mesures d'huile. Et l'*économe* lui dit : Reprends ton billet; assieds-toi là, et écris-en promptement *un autre* de cinquante.

7. Il dit ensuite à un autre : Et toi, Combien dois-tu ? Il dit : Cent mesures de froment. Et l'*économe* lui dit : Reprends ton billet, et écris-en un *autre* de quatre-vingts.

8. Et le maître loua cet économe infidèle de ce qu'il avoit agi avec habileté ; car les enfans de ce siècle sont plus prudens dans leur génération, que les enfans de lumière.

9. Et moi, je vous dis aussi : Faites-vous des amis avec les richesses injustes, afin que quand vous viendrez à manquer, ils vous reçoivent dans les tabernacles éternels.

10. Celui qui est fidèle dans les petites choses, sera aussi fidèle dans les grandes ; et celui qui est injuste dans les petites choses, sera aussi injuste dans les grandes.

11. Si donc vous n'avez pas été fidèle dans les richesses injustes, qui vous confiera les véritables *richesses?*

12. Et si vous n'avez pas été fidèles dans ce qui est à autrui : qui vous donnera ce qui est à vous ?

13. Nul serviteur ne peut servir deux maîtres ; car ou il haïra l'un, et aimera l'autre ; ou il s'attachera à l'un, et méprisera l'autre. Vous ne pouvez servir Dieu et Mammon.

14. Les Pharisiens, qui étoient avares, écoutoient tout cela, et se moquoient de lui.

15. Et il leur dit : Pour vous, vous voulez passer pour justes devant les hommes, mais Dieu connoît vos cœurs ; car ce qui est élevé devant les hommes est une abomination devant Dieu.

L. 16.

4 I am resolved what to do, that when I am put out of the stewardship, they may receive me into their houses.

5 So he called every one of his lord's debtors *unto him*, and said unto the first, How much owest thou unto my lord?

6 And he said, An hundred measures of oil. And he said unto him, Take thy bill, and sit down quickly, and write fifty.

7 Then said he to another, And how much owest thou? And he said, An hundred measures of wheat. And he said unto him, Take thy bill, and write fourscore.

8 And the lord commended the unjust steward, because he had done wisely: for the children of this world are in their generation wiser than the children of light.

9 And I say unto you, Make to yourselves friends of the mammon of unrighteousness; that, when ye fail, they may receive you into everlasting habitations.

10 He that is faithful in that which is least, is faithful also in much; and he that is unjust in the least, is unjust also in much.

11 If, therefore, ye have not been faithful in the unrighteous mammon, who will commit to your trust the true *riches?*

12 And if ye have not been faithful in that which is another man's, who shall give you that which is your own?

13 No servant can serve two masters: for either he will hate the one, and love the other; or else he will hold to the one, and despise the other. Ye cannot serve God and mammon.

14 And the Pharisees also, who were covetous, heard all these things: and they derided him.

15 And he said unto them, Ye are they which justify yourselves before men; but God knoweth your hearts: for that which is highly esteemed among men is abomination in the sight of God.

18 Πᾶς ὁ ἀπολύων τὴν γυναῖκα | 18 Omnis repudians uxorem

αὐτῦ, ℵ γαμῶν ἑτέραν, μοιχεύει·
ℵ πᾶς ὁ ἀπολελυμένην ἀπὸ ἀνδρὸς
γαμῶν, μοιχεύει.

* 19 Ἄνθρωπ⊙ δέ τις ἦν πλύ-
σι⊙, ℵ ‡ ἐνεδιδύσκετο ‡ πορφύ-
ραν ℵ βύσσον, ‡ εὐφραινόμεν⊙
καθ᾽ ἡμέραν † λαμπρῶς.

* 20 Πτωχὸς δέ τις, ἦν ὀνόματι Λάζαρ⊙, ὃς ἐβέβλητο πρὸς
τὸν πυλῶνα αὐτῦ ἡλκωμέν⊙.

* 21 Καὶ ‡ ἐπιθυμῶν χορτα-
σθῆναι ἀπὸ τῶν ‡ ψιχίων τῶν
πιπτόντων ἀπὸ τῆς τραπέζης τῦ
πλυσίυ· ἀλλὰ ℵ οἱ ‡ κύνες ἐρ-
χόμενοι † ἀπέλειχον τὰ ‡ ἕλκη
αὐτῦ.

* 22 Ἐγένετο δὲ ἀποθανεῖν τὸν
πτωχὸν, ℵ ‡ ἀπενεχθῆναι αὐτὸν
ὑπὸ τῶν ἀγγέλων εἰς τὸν κόλπον
τῦ Ἀβραάμ· ἀπέθανε δὲ ℵ ὁ
πλύσι⊙, ℵ ‡ ἐτάφη.

* 23 Καὶ ἐν τῷ ᾅδῃ ἐπάρας τοὺς
ὀφθαλμὺς αὐτῦ, ὑπάρχων ἐν βα-
σάνοις, ὁρᾷ τὸν Ἀβραὰμ ἀπὸ μακρόθεν, ℵ Λάζαρον ἐν τοῖς κόλ-
ποις αὐτῦ.

* 24 Καὶ αὐτὸς φωνήσας εἶπε·
Πάτερ Ἀβραὰμ ἐλέησόν με, ℵ
πέμψον Λάζαρον, ἵνα ‡ βάψῃ τὸ
ἄκρον τοῦ ‡ δακτύλυ αὐτῦ ‡ ὕ-
δατ⊙, ℵ † καταψύξῃ τὴν γλῶσ-
σάν μυ· ὅτι ‡ ὀδυνῶμαι ἐν τῇ
‡ φλογὶ ταύτῃ.

25 Εἶπε δὲ Ἀβραάμ· Τέκνον,
μνήσθητι ὅτι ἀπέλαβες σὺ τὰ ἀ-
γαθά συ ἐν τῇ ζωῇ συ, ℵ Λάζα-
ρ⊙ ὁμοίως τὰ κακά· νῦν δὲ ὅδε
παρακαλεῖται, σὺ δὲ ὀδυνᾶσαι.

* 26 Καὶ ἐπὶ πᾶσι τούτοις,
μεταξὺ ἡμῶν ℵ ὑμῶν † χάσμα
μέγα ‡ ἐςήρικται, ὅπως οἱ θέλον-
τες ‡ διαβῆναι ‡ ἐντεῦθεν πρὸς
ὑμᾶς, μὴ δύνωνται, μηδὲ οἱ ἐκεῖθεν πρὸς ἡμᾶς διαπερῶσιν.

27 Εἶπε δὲ· ἐρωτῶ οὖν σε
πάτερ, ἵνα πέμψῃς αὐτὸν εἰς τὸν
οἶκον τῦ πατρός μυ.

28 Ἔχω γὰρ πέντε ἀδελφὺς,
ὅπως διαμαρτύρηται αὐτοῖς, ἵνα
μὴ ℵ αὐτοὶ ἔλθωσιν εἰς τὸν τόπον
τοῦτον τῆς βασάνε.

29 Λέγει αὐτῷ Ἀβραάμ· Ἔ-
χυσι Μωσέα ℵ τοὺς προφήτας·
ἀκυσάτωσαν αὐτῶν.

suam, & ducens alteram, mœchatur: & omnis repudiatam à
viro ducens, mœchatur.

19 Homo autem quidem erat
dives, & induebatur purpuram
& byssum, oblectatus quotidie
splendide.

20 Pauper autem qui am
erat nomine Lazarus, qui ejectus
erat ad januam ejus ulcerosus.

21 Et cupiens saturari de
micis cadentibus de mensa divitis: sed & canes venientes lin-
gebant ulcera ejus.

22 Factum est autem mori
pauperem, & asportari eum ab
angelis in sinum Abrahæ: Mortuus est autem & dives, & se-
pultus est.

23 Et in inferno elevans oculos suos, existens in tormentis,
vidit Abraham à longè, & Lazarum in gremiis ejus.

24 Et ipse clamans dixit:
Pater Abraham miserere mei,
& mitte Lazarum, ut intingat
extremium digiti sui aqua, &
refrigeret linguam meam: quia
crucior in flamma hac.

25 Dixit autem Abraham:
Fili, recordare quia recepisti tu
bona tua in vita tua, & Lazarus
similiter mala: nunc autem hic
consolatur, tu verò cruciaris.

26 Et omnibus his, inter
nos & vos hiatus magnus fir-
matus est, ut volentes transire
hinc ad vos, non possint: neque
qui inde ad nos transmeent.

27 Ait autem: Rogo ergo te,
pater, ut mittas eum in domum
patris mei.

28 Habeo enim quinque fratres; ut testetur illis, ut non
& ipsi veniant in locum hunc
tormenti.

29 Ait illi Abraham: Ha-
bent Mosen, & Prophetas: au-
diant illos.

18. Quiconque répudie sa femme et en épouse une autre , commet adultère ; et quiconque épouse celle que son mari a répudiée , commet adultère.

19. Il y avoit un homme riche qui se vêtoit de pourpre et de fin lin , et qui se traitoit bien et magnifiquement tous les jours.

20. Il y avoit aussi un pauvre , nommé Lazare , qui étoit couché à la porte de ce riche , et qui étoit couvert d'ulcères.

21. Il désiroit de se rassasier des miettes qui tomboient de la table du riche ; et même les chiens venoient lécher ses ulcères.

22. Or , il arriva que le pauvre mourut , et il fut porté par les Anges dans le sein d'Abraham ; le riche mourut aussi , et fut enseveli.

23. Et étant en enfer et dans les tourmens, il leva les yeux, et vit de loin Abraham , et Lazare dans son sein.

24. Et s'écriant , il dit : Père Abraham , aie pitié de moi , et envoie Lazare , afin qu'il trempe dans l'eau le bout de son doigt , pour me rafraîchir la langue ; car je suis extrêmement tourmenté dans cette flamme.

25. Mais Abraham lui répondit : Mon fils , souviens-toi que tu as eu tes biens pendant ta vie , et Lazare y a eu des maux ; et maintenant il est consolé , et tu es dans les tourmens.

26. Outre cela , il y a un grand abyme entre vous et nous ; de sorte que ceux qui voudront passer d'ici vers vous ne le peuvent ; non plus que ceux qui voudroient passer de là ici.

27. Et le riche dit : Je te prie donc , Père Abraham , d'envoyer Lazare dans la maison de mon Père ;

28. Car j'ai cinq frères , afin qu'il les avertisse , de peur qu'ils ne viennent aussi eux-mêmes dans ce lieu de tourmens.

29. Abraham lui répondit : Ils ont Moyse et les Prophètes; qu'ils les écoutent.

18 Whosoever putteth away his wife, and marrieth another, committeth adultery : and whosoever marrieth her that is put away from her husband, committeth adultery.

19 There was a certain rich man, which was clothed in purple and fine linen, and fared sumptuously every day :

20 And there was a certain beggar, named Lazarus, which was laid at his gate full of sores,

21 And desiring to be fed with the crumbs which fell from the rich man's table : moreover, the dogs came and licked his sores.

22 And it came to pass, that the beggar died, and was carried by the angels into Abraham's bosom : the rich man also died, and was buried ;

23 And in hell he lifted up his eyes, being in torments, and seeth Abraham afar off, and Lazarus in his bosom.

24 And he cried, and said, Father Abraham, have mercy on me ; and send Lazarus, that he may dip the tip of his finger in water, and cool my tongue ; for I am tormented in this flame.

25 But Abraham said, Son, remember that thou in thy life time receivedst thy good things, and likewise Lazarus evil things : but now he is comforted, and thou art tormented.

26 And, besides all this, between us and you there is a great gulf fixed : so that they which would pass from hence to you cannot ; neither can they pass to us, that would come from thence.

27 Then he said, I pray thee, therefore, father, that thou wouldest send him to my father's house :

28 For I have five brethren ; that he may testify unto them, lest they also come into this place of torment.

29 Abraham saith unto him, They have Moses and the prophets ; let them hear them.

47

30 Ὁ δὲ εἶπεν Οὐχὶ, πάτερ Ἀβραάμ· ἀλλ᾽ ἐάν τις ἀπὸ νεκρῶν πορευθῇ πρὸς αὐτὰς, μετανοήσουσι.

31 Εἶπε δὲ αὐτῷ. Εἰ Μωσέως καὶ τῶν προφητῶν οὐκ ἀκούουσιν, οὐδὲ ἐάν τις ἐκ νεκρῶν ἀναστῇ, πεισθήσονται. 39. †11.

Κεφ. ιζ΄. 17.

* 1 Εἶπε δὲ πρὸς τοὺς μαθητάς· †Ἀνένδεκτόν ἐστι μὴ ἐλθεῖν τὰ σκάνδαλα· οὐαὶ δὲ δι᾽ οὗ ἔρχεται.

* 2 †Λυσιτελεῖ αὐτῷ, εἰ ‡μύλος ‡ὀνικὸς περίκειται περὶ τὸν τράχηλον αὐτοῦ, καὶ ἔρριπται εἰς τὴν θάλασσαν, ἢ ἵνα σκανδαλίσῃ ἕνα τῶν μικρῶν τούτων.

3 Προσέχετε ἑαυτοῖς. Ἐὰν δὲ ἁμάρτῃ εἰς σὲ ὁ ἀδελφός σου, ἐπιτίμησον αὐτῷ· καὶ ἐὰν μετανοήσῃ, ἄφες αὐτῷ.

4 Καὶ ἐὰν ἑπτάκις τῆς ἡμέρας ἁμάρτῃ εἰς σὲ, καὶ ἑπτάκις τῆς ἡμέρας ἐπιστρέψῃ ἐπὶ σὲ, λέγων Μετανοῶ· ἀφήσεις αὐτῷ.

7 Τίς δὲ ἐξ ὑμῶν δοῦλον ἔχων ἀροτριῶντα, ἢ ποιμαίνοντα, ὃς εἰσελθόντι ἐκ τοῦ ἀγροῦ ἐρεῖ εὐθέως· Παρελθὼν ἀνάπεσαι·

8 Ἀλλ᾽ οὐχὶ ἐρεῖ αὐτῷ, Ἑτοίμασον τί δειπνήσω, καὶ περιζωσάμενος διακόνει μοι, ἕως φάγω καὶ πίω· καὶ μετὰ ταῦτα φάγεσαι καὶ πίεσαι σύ;

9 Μὴ χάριν ἔχει τῷ δούλῳ ἐκείνῳ ὅτι ἐποίησε τὰ διαταχθέντα αὐτῷ; οὐ δοκῶ.

* 10 Οὕτω καὶ ὑμεῖς, ὅταν ποιήσητε πάντα τὰ διαταχθέντα ὑμῖν, λέγετε· Ὅτι δοῦλοι ἀχρεῖοί ἐσμεν· ὅτι ὃ ὠφείλομεν ποιῆσαι, πεποιήκαμεν.

* 20 Ἐπερωτηθεὶς δὲ ὑπὸ τῶν Φαρισαίων πότε ἔρχεται ἡ βασιλεία τοῦ Θεοῦ, ἀπεκρίθη αὐτοῖς, καὶ εἶπεν· Οὐκ ἔρχεται ἡ βασιλεία τοῦ Θεοῦ μετὰ †παρατηρήσεως.

30 Is autem dixit: Non pater Abraham: sed si quis ex mortuis ierit ad eos, pœnitebunt.

31 Ait autem illi: Si Mosen & Prophetas non audiunt, neque si quis ex mortuis resurrexerit, credent.

CAPUT XVII.

1 AIT autem ad discipulos: Impossibile est non venire scandala: væ autem per quem veniunt.

2 Expedit illi, si mola asinaria circumponatur circa collum ejus, & projiciatur in mare, quam ut scandalizet unum parvorum istorum.

3 Attendite vobis ipsis: si verò peccaverit in te frater tuus, increpa illum. Et si pœnituerit, dimitte illi:

4 Et si septies die peccaverit in te, & septies die conversus fuerit ad te, dicens: Pœniteo, dimittes illi.

7 Quis autem ex vobis servum habens arantem aut pascentem, qui regresso de agro dicat statim: Adveniens recumbe.

8 Imo nonne dicet ei: Para quod cœnem, & circumcinctus ministra mihi, donec manducem & bibam, & post hæc manducabis & bibes tu?

9 Num gratiam habet servo illi, quia fecit præcepta ei? non puto.

10 Sic & vos quum feceritis omnia præcepta vobis, dicite, quod servi inutiles sumus, quia quod debuimus facere, fecimus.

20 Interrogatus autem à Pharisæis, quando venit regnum Dei, respondit eis & dixit: Non venit regnum Dei cum observatione:

30. *Le riche* dit : Non , Père Abraham ; mais si quelqu'un des morts va vers eux, ils s'amenderont.

31. Et *Abraham* lui dit : S'ils n'écoutent pas Moyse et les Prophètes, ils ne seroient pas non plus persuadés, quand même quelqu'un des morts ressusciteroit.

CHAPITRE XVII.

Jésus-Christ entretient du scandale , du pardon, des serviteurs inutiles ; guérit dix lépreux , et parle du jour du fils de l'homme.

Jésus dit *aussi* à ses Disciples : Il ne se peut faire qu'il n'arrive des scandales ; toutefois malheur à celui par qui ils arrivent !

2. Il vaudroit mieux pour lui qu'on lui mît au cou une meule de moulin, et qu'on le jetât dans la mer , que de scandaliser un de ces petits.

3. Prenez *donc* garde à vous. Si ton frère t'a offensé , reprends-le ; et s'il se répent , pardonne-lui.

4. Et s'il t'a offensé sept fois le jour , et que sept fois le jour il revienne vers toi , et te dise : Je me repens ; pardonne-lui.

7. Qui de vous ayant un serviteur qui laboure ou qui paisse *les troupeaux* , et le *voyant* revenir des champs , lui dise aussitôt : Avance-toi , et te mets à table ?

8. Ne lui dira-t-il pas plutôt : Prépare-moi à souper . et ceins-toi et me sers, jusqu'à ce que j'aie mangé et bu ; et après cela tu mangeras et tu boiras.

9. Sera-t-il redevable à ce serviteur , parce qu'il aura fait ce qui lui avoit été commandé ? Je ne le pense pas.

10. Vous aussi de même , quand vous aurez fait tout ce qui vous est commandé , dites : Nous sommes des serviteurs inutiles ; parce que nous n'avons fait que ce que nous étions obligés de faire.

20. Les Pharisiens lui ayant demandé quand le Règne de Dieu viendroit ; il leur répondit : Le Règne de Dieu ne viendra point avec éclat.

---

30 And he said, Nay, father Abraham : but if one went unto them from the dead, they will repent.

31 And he said unto him, If they hear not Moses and the prophets, neither will they be persuaded though one rose from the dead.

CHAP. XVII.
To avoid giving offence.

THEN said he unto the disciples, It is impossible but that offences will come : but woe *unto him* through whom they come?

2 It were better for him that a mill-stone were hanged about his neck, and he cast into the sea, than that he should offend one of these little ones.

3 Take heed to yourselves : If thy brother trespass against thee, rebuke him ; and if he repent, forgive him.

4 And if he trespass against thee seven times in a day, and seven times in a day turn again to thee, saying, I repent ; thou shalt forgive him.

7 But which of you having a servant plowing, or feeding cattle, will say unto him by and by, when he is come from the field, Go and sit down to meat?

8 And will not rather say unto him, Make ready wherewith I may sup, and gird thyself, and serve me, till I have eaten and drunken ; and afterward thou shalt eat and drink?

9 Doth he thank that servant because he did the things that were commanded him? I trow not.

10 So likewise ye, when ye shall have done all those things which are commanded you, say, We are unprofitable servants: we have done that which was our duty to do.

20 And when he was demanded of the Pharisees, when the kingdom of God should come, he answered them, and said, The kingdom of God cometh not with observation.

48

20 Καὶ καθὼς ἐγένετο ἐν ταῖς ἡμέραις τοῦ Νῶε, ὕτως ἔςαι ἢ ἐν ταῖς ἡμέραις τοῦ υἱοῦ τοῦ ἀνθρώπȣ.

27 Ἤσθιον, ἔπινον, ἐγάμȣν, ἐξεγαμίζοντο, ἄχρι ἧς ἡμέρας εἰσῆλθε Νῶε εἰς τὴν κιϐωτόν· ἢ ἦλθεν ὁ κατακλυσμὸς, ἢ ἀπώλεσεν ἅπαντας.

28 Ὁμοίως ἢ ὡς ἐγένετο ἐν ταῖς ἡμέραις Λώτ· ἤσθιον, ἔπινον, ἠγόραζον, ἐπώλȣν, ἐφύτευον, ᾠκοδόμȣν·

29 Ἧι δὲ ἡμέρα ἐξῆλθε Λὼτ ἀπὸ Σοδόμων, ἔϐρεξε πῦρ ἢ θεῖον ἀπ᾽ ȣ᾽ρανȣ, ἢ ἀπώλεσεν ἅπαντας.

30 Κατὰ ταῦτα ἔςαι ᾗ ἡμέρα ὁ υἱὸς τοῦ ἀνθρώπȣ ἀποκαλύπτεται.

31 Ἐν ἐκείνῃ τῇ ἡμέρᾳ, ὃς ἔςαι ἐπὶ τȣ δώματ⸦, ἢ τὰ σκεύη αὐτȣ ἐν τῇ οἰκίᾳ, μὴ καταϐάτω ἆραι αὐτά· ἢ ὁ ἐν τῷ ἀγρῷ, ὁμοίως μὴ ἐπιςρεψάτω εἰς τὰ ὀπίσω.

32 Μνημονεύετε τῆς γυναικὸς Λώτ.

33 Ὃς ἐὰν ζητήσῃ τὴν ψυχὴν αὐτȣ σῶσαι, ἀπολέσει αὐτήν· ἢ ὃς ἐὰν ἀπ᾽λέσῃ αὐτὴν, ζωογονήσει αὐτήν.

34 Λέγω ὑμῖν, ταύτῃ τῇ νυκ-

τὶ ἔσονται δύο ἐπὶ κλίνης μιᾶς· ὁ εἷς παραληφθήσεται, ἢ ὁ ἕτερ⸦ ἀφεθήσεται.

35 Δύο ἔσονται ἀλήθȣσαι ἐπὶ τὸ αὐτό· ἡ μία παραληφθήσεται, ἢ ἡ ἑτέρα ἀφεθήσεται.

36 Δύο ἔσονται ἐν τῷ ἀγρῷ· ὁ εἷς παραληφθήσεται, ἢ ὁ ἕτερ⸦ ἀφεθήσεται.

Κεφ. ιή. 18.

1 Ἔλεγε δὲ ἢ παραϐολὴν αὐτοῖς πρὸς τὸ δεῖν πάντοτε προσεύχεσθαι, ἢ μὴ ἐκκακεῖν,

2 Λέγων· Κριτής τις ἦν ἔν τινι πόλει τὸν Θεὸν μὴ φοϐȣ́μεν⸦, ἢ ἄνθρωπον μὴ ἐντρεπόμεν⸦·

3 Χήρα δέ τις ἦν ἐν τῇ πόλει ἐκείνῃ· ἢ ἤρχετο πρὸς αὐτὸν, λέγȣσα· Ἐκδίκησόν με ἀπὸ τȣ ἀντιδίκȣ μȣ.

---

26 Et sicut factum est in diebus Noë, ita & erit in diebus filii hominis.

27 Edebant, bibebant, uxores ducebant, nubebant, usque quâ die intravit Noë in arcam, & venit diluvium, & perdidit omnes.

28 Similiter & sicut factum est in diebus Lot: edebant, bibebant, emebant, vendebant, plantabant, ædificabant.

29 Quâ autem die exiit Lot à Sodomis, pluit ignem & sulphur de cælo, & perdidit omnes.

30 Secundum hæc erit quâ die filius hominis revelatur.

31 In illa die, qui fuerit super domum, & vasa ejus in domo, ne descendat tollere illa: & qui in agro, similiter non redeat in quæ retrò:

32 Memores estote uxoris Lot.

33 Quicumque quæsierit animam suam servare, perdet illam: & quicumque perdiderit illam, vivificabit eam.

34 Dico vobis, illâ nocte erunt duo in lecto uno: unus assumetur, & alter relinquetur.

35 Duæ erunt molentes in idem: una assumetur, & altera relinquetur.

36 Duo erunt in agro, unus assumetur, & alter relinquetur.

1 Dicebat autem & parabolam illis, oportere semper orare, & non segnescere:

2 Dicens: Judex quidam erat in quadam civitate, Deum non timens, & hominem non reveritus.

3 Vidua autem erat in civitate illa, & veniebat ad eum, dicens: Vindica me de adversario meo.

26. Et ce qui arriva du tems de Noé, arrivera de même au tems du Fils de l'homme :

27. On mangeoit, on buvoit, on prenoit et on donnoit en mariage, jusqu'au jour que Noé entra dans l'arche ; et le Déluge vint qui les fit tous périr.

28. De même aussi, comme du tems de Lot, on mangeoit, on buvoit, on achetoit, on vendoit, on plantoit et on bâtissoit ;

29. Mais le jour que Lot sortit de Sodome, il plut du ciel du feu et du soufre, qui les fit tous périr.

30. Il en sera de même au jour que le Fils de l'homme paroîtra.

31. En ce jour-là, que celui qui sera au haut de la maison, et qui aura ses meubles dans la maison, ne descende pas pour les emporter ; et que celui qui sera aux champs ne revienne pas sur ses pas.

32. Souvenez-vous de la femme de Lot.

33. Quiconque cherchera à sauver sa vie la perdra ; et quiconque l'aura perdue la retrouvera.

34. Je vous dis qu'en cette nuit-là, de deux *hommes* qui seront dans un même lit, l'un sera pris, et l'autre laissé.

35. De deux *femmes* qui moudront ensemble, l'une sera prise, et l'autre laissée.

36. De deux *hommes* qui seront aux champs, l'un sera pris, et l'autre laissé.

CHAPITRE XVIII.

Notre Seigneur propose la parabole du Juge inique ; celle du Pharisien et du Péager ; et il impose les mains à de petits enfans qu'on lui présente.

Jésus leur dit aussi cette parabole, *pour montrer* qu'il faut toujours prier, et ne se relâcher point :

2. Il y avoit dans une ville un Juge qui ne craignoit point Dieu, et qui n'avoit aucun égard pour personne.

3. Il y avoit aussi dans cette ville-là une veuve qui venoit *souvent* à lui, et qui lui disoit : Fais-moi justice de ma partie adverse.

26 And as it was in the days of Noe, so shall it be also in the days of the Son of Man :

27 They did eat, they drank, they married wives, they were given in marriage, until the day that Noe entered into the ark ; and the flood came, and destroyed them all.

28 Likewise also, as it was in the days of Lot, they did eat, they drank, they bought, they sold, they planted, they builded :

29 But the same day that Lot went out of Sodom, it rained fire and brimstone from heaven, and destroyed *them* all.

30 Even thus shall it be in the day when the Son of Man is revealed.

31 In that day, he which shall be upon the house-top, and his stuff in the house, let him not come down to take it away : and he that is in the field, let him likewise not return back.

32 Remember Lot's wife.

33 Whosoever shall seek to save his life shall lose it ; and whosoever shall lose his life shall preserve it.

34 I tell you, in that night there shall be two *men* in one bed ; the one shall be taken, and the other shall be left.

35 Two *women* shall be grinding together ; the one shall be taken, and the other left.

36 Two *men* shall be in the field ; the one shall be taken, and the other left.

CHAP. XVIII.

The importunate widow.

AND he spake a parable unto them, *to this end*, that men ought always *to* pray, and not to faint ;

2 Saying, There was in a city a judge, which feared not God, neither regarded man :

3 And there was a widow in that city ; and she came unto him, saying, Avenge me of mine adversary.

49

4 Καὶ ἀκ ἠθέλησεν.ἐπὶ χρόνον·
μετὰ δὲ ταῦτα εἶπεν ἐν ἑαυτῷ·
Εἰ ἢ τὸν Θεὸν ἧ φοβῦμαι, ἢ ἄνθρωπον οὐκ ἐντρέπομαι,

5 Διά γε τὸ παρέχειν μοι κό-
πον τὴν χήραν, ταύτην, ἐκδικήσω
αὐτήν ἵνα μὴ εἰς τέλΘ· ἐρχομέ-
νη ὑπωπιάζη με.

6 Εἶπε δὲ ὁ ΚύριΘ· Ἀκύσατε
τί ὁ κρίτης τῆς ἀδικίας λέγει·

7 Ὁ δὲ Θεὸς ἃ μὴ ποιήσει τὴν
ἐκδίκησιν τῶν ἐκλεκτῶν αὐτῦ
τῶν βοώντων πρὸς αὐτὸν ἡμέρας
ἢ νυκτός, ἢ μακροθυμῶν ἐπ᾽ αὐτοῖς;

8 Λέγω ὑμῖν, ὅτι ποιήσει τὴν
ἐκδίκησιν αὐτῶν ἐν τάχει· πλὴν
ὁ υἱὸς τῦ ἀνθρώπυ ἐλθὼν ἆρα εὑρήσει τὴν πίςιν ἐπὶ τῆς γῆς;

9 Εἶπε δὲ ἢ πρὸς τινας τὲς
πεποιθότας ἐφ᾽ ἑαυτοῖς ὅτι εἰσὶ
δίκαιοι, ἢ ἐξεθενῦντας τὸς λοιπὸς,
τὴν παραβολὴν ταύτην·

10 Ἄνθρωποι δύο ἀνέβησαν εἰς
τὸ ἱερὸν προσεύξασθαι· ὁ εἷς φαρισαῖος, ἢ ὁ ἕτερΘ· τελώνης·

11 Ὁ φαρισαῖος σταθεὶς πρὸς
ἑαυτὸν ταῦτα προσηύχετο. Ὁ
Θεὸς, εὐχαριςῶ σοι, ὅτι οὐκ εἰμὶ
ὥσπερ οἱ λοιποὶ τῶν ἀνθρώπων,
ἅρπαγες, ἄδικοι, μοιχοί, ἢ ἢ ὡς
ἕτΘ· ὁ τελώνης·

12 Νηςεύω δὶς τῦ σαββάτυ,
ἀποδεκατῶ πάνλα ὅσα κτῶμαι.

13 Καὶ ὁ τελώνης μακρόθεν ἑ-
ςὼς οὐκ ἤθελεν οὐδὲ τὸς ὀφθαλμὸς
εἰς τὸν οὐρανὸν ἐπᾶραι· ἀλλ᾽ ἔ-
τυπλεν εἰς τὸ ςῆθΘ· αὐτῦ, λέγων·
Ὁ Θεὸς ἱλάσθητί μοι τῷ ἁμαρτωλῷ.

14 Λέγω ὑμῖν, κατέβη οὗτΘ·
δεδικαιωμένΘ· εἰς τὸν οἶκον αὐτῦ, ἢ ἐκεῖνΘ· ὅτι πᾶς ὁ ὑψῶν
ἑαυτὸν, ταπεινωθήσεται· ὁ δὲ ταπεινῶν ἑαυτὸν, ὑψαθήσεται·

38 Ἐγένελο δὲ ἐν τῷ πορεύεσθαι αὐτὼς, ἢ αὐτὸς εἰσῆλθεν εἰς
κώμην τινά· γυνὴ δὲ τις ὀνόμαλι

Μάρθα ὑπεδέξαλο αὐτὸν εἰς τὸν οἶκον αὑτῆς.

* 39 Καὶ ‡ τῆδε ἦν ἀδελφὴ κα-
λυμένη Μαρία, ἣ ἢ παρακαθί-
σασα παρὰ τὲς πόδας τῦ Ἰησῦ,
ἤκυε τὸν λόγον αὐτῦ·

* 40 Ἡ δὲ Μάρθα † περιεσπᾶ-

4 Et non volebat ad tempus:
post autem hæc dixit in seipso:
Si & Deum non timeo, & hominem non revereor:

5 Propter præbere mihi mo-
lestiam viduam hanc, vindi-
cabo istam, ne in finem veniens
sugillet me.

6 Ait autem Dominus: Au-
dite quid judex iniquus dicit:

7 At Deus non faciet vindictam electorum suorum claman-
tium ad se die & nocte, & longanimis super illos?

8 Etiam dico vobis, quia faciet vindictam illorum in cele-
ritate, veruntamen filius hominis veniens num inveniet fidem
in terra?

9 Dixit autem ad quosdam
persuasos in seipsis, quod essent
justi, & nihilifacientes cæteros,
parabolam istam:

10 Homines duo ascendebant
in templum orare, unus Pharisæus, & alter publicanus.

11 Pharisæus stans apud se
hæc orabat: Deus gratias ago
tibi: quia non sum sicut cæteri
hominum, raptores, injusti, a-
dulteri, aut & ut hic publicanus.

12 Jejuno bis sabbato, decimo omnia quæ possideo.

13 Et publicanus à longe
stans non volebat nec oculos ad
cælum levare, sed percutiebat in
pectus suum, dicens: Deus pro-
pitius esto mihi peccatori.

14 Dico vobis, descendit hic
justificatus in domum suam,
quam ille: quia omnis exaltans
seipsum humiliabitur: at humilians seipsum, exaltabitur.

38 Factum est autem in ire
eos, & ipse intravit in vicum
quendam: mulier autem quæ-

dam homine Martha excepit
illum in domum suam.

39 Et huic erat soror vocata
Maria, quæ etiam sedens secus
pedes Jesu, audiebat verbum illius.

40 At Martha distrahebatur

4. Pendant long - tems il n'en voulut rien faire. Cependant il dit enfin en lui-même : Quoique je ne craigne point Dieu, et que je n'aie nul égard pour aucun homme,

5. Néanmoins, parce que cette veuve m'importune, je lui ferai justice, afin qu'elle ne vienne pas toujours me rompre la tête.

6. Et le Seigneur dit : Ecoutez ce que dit ce Juge injuste.

7. Et Dieu ne vengera-t-il point ses élus, qui crient à lui jour et nuit, quoiqu'il diffère sa vengeance ?

8. Je vous dis qu'il les vengera bientôt. Mais quand le Fils de l'homme viendra, pensez-vous qu'il trouve de la foi sur la terre?

9. Il dit aussi cette parabole, au sujet de quelques-uns, qui présumoient d'eux-mêmes, comme s'ils étoient justes, et méprisoient les autres.

10. Deux hommes montèrent au Temple pour prier ; l'un étoit Pharisien, et l'autre Péager.

11. Le Pharisien se tenant debout, prioit ainsi en lui-même : O Dieu ! je te rends graces de ce que je ne suis pas comme le reste des hommes, *qui sont* ravisseurs, injustes, adultères ; ni même aussi comme ce péager.

12. Je jeûne deux fois la semaine, je donne la dîme de tout ce que je possède.

13. Mais le péager se tenant éloigné, n'osoit pas même lever les yeux au ciel ; mais il se frappoit la poitrine, en disant : O Dieu ! sois appaisé envers moi qui suis pécheur.

14. Je vous déclare que celui-ci s'en retournera justifié dans sa maison, préférablement à l'autre; car quiconque s'élève sera abaissé; et quiconque s'abaisse sera élevé.

min, il entra dans un bourg, et une femme nommée Marthe le reçut dans sa maison.

39. Elle avoit une sœur nommée Marie, qui se tenant assise aux pieds de Jésus, écoutoit sa parole.

40. Mais comme Marthe étoit

4 And he would not for a while: but afterward he said within himself, Though I fear not God, nor regard man ;

5 Yet, because this widow troubleth me, I will avenge her, lest by her continual coming she weary me.

6 And the Lord said, Hear what the unjust judge saith.

7 And shall not God avenge his own elect, which cry day and night unto him, though he bear long with them?

8 I tell you, that he will avenge them speedily. Nevertheless, when the Son of Man cometh, shall he find faith on the earth ?

9 And he spake this parable unto certain which trusted in themselves, that they were righteous, and despised others :

10 Two men went up into the temple to pray; the one a Pharisee, and the other a publican.

11 The Pharisee stood and prayed thus with himself, God, I thank thee, that I am not as other men *are*, extortioners, unjust, adulterers, or even as this publican.

12 I fast twice in the week, I give tithes of all that I possess.

13 And the publican, standing afar off, would not lift up so much as *his* eyes unto heaven, but smote upon his breast, saying, God be merciful to me a sinner.

14 I tell you, this man went down to his house justified *rather* than the other: for every one that exalteth himself shall be abased; and he that humbleth himself shall be exalted.

38 Now it came to pass, as they went, that he entered into a certain village: and a certain woman, named Martha, received him into her house.

39 And she had a sister called Mary, which also sat at Jesus' feet, and heard his word.

40 But Martha was cumbered

το περὶ πολλὴν ‡ διακονίαν· ‡ ἐπι-
ϛᾶσα δὲ εἶπε Κύριε, ἐ ‡ ‡ μέλει
σοι ὅτι ἡ ‡ ἀδελφή μυ ‡ μό᾽ην
με ‡ κατέλιπε ‡ διακονεῖν· εἶπὲ
ἂν αὐτῇ ἵνα μοι ‡ συναντιλάβηʹαι.

* 41 Ἀποκριθεὶς δὲ εἶπεν αὐτῇ ὁ Ἰησῦς Μάρθα, Μάρθα,
‡ μεριμνᾷς κ᾽ τυρβάζη περὶ
πολλά·

42 Ἑνὸς δέ ἐϛι χρεία. Μαρία
δὲ τὴν ἀγαθὴν μεςίδα ἐξελέξατο,
ἥτις ὐκ ἀφαιρεθήσεʹαι ἀπ᾽ αὐτῆς.
45: ‡ 14.

Κεφ. ιθʹ. 19.

* 1 ΚΑΙ ἐγένετο, ὅτε ἐτέλεσεν
ὁ Ἰησῦς τὸς λόγυς τύ-
τυς, ‡ μετῆρεν ἀπὸ τῆς Γαλιλαίας,
κ᾽ ἦλθεν εἰς τὰ ὅρια τῆς Ἰυδαίας,
πέραν τῦ Ἰορδάνυ.

2 Καὶ ἠκιλύθησαν αὐτῷ ὄχλοι
πολλοί·

3 Καὶ προσῆλθον αὐτῷ οἱ Φαρισαῖοι, πειράζοντες αὐτὸν, κ᾽ λέγοντες αὐτῷ· Εἰ ἔξεϛιν ἀνθρώπῳ
ἀπολῦσαι τὴν γυναῖκα αὐτῦ κατὰ
πᾶσαν αἰτίαν;

* 4 Ὁ δὲ ἀποκριθεὶς, εἶπεν αὐ-
τοῖς· Οὐκ ἀνέγνωτε, ὅτι ὁ ποιήσας ἀπ᾽ ἀρχῆς, ‡ ἄρσεν κ᾽ θῆλυ
ἐποίησεν αὐτές;

5 Καὶ εἶπεν· Ἕνεκεν τύτυ κα-
ταλείψει ἄνθρωπⓈ τὸν πατέρα κ᾽
τὴν μητέρα, κ᾽ προσκολληθήσεται
τῇ γυναικὶ αὐτῦ· κ᾽ ἔσονται οἱ δύο
εἰς σάρκα μίαν.

6 Ὥϛε ὐκ ἔτι εἰσὶ δύο, ἀλλὰ
σὰρξ μία, ὃ ἒν ὁ Θεὸς συνέζευξεν,
ἄνθρωπⓈ μὴ χωριζέτω.

7 Λέγυσιν αὐτῷ· Τί ἒν Μωσῆς
ἐνετείλατο δῦναι βιβλίον ἀποϛα-
σίυ, κ᾽ ἀπολῦσαι αὐτήν;

* 8 Λέγει αὐτοῖς· Ὅτι Μωσῆς
πρὸς τὴν ‡ σκληροκαρδίαν ὑμῶν
‡ ἐπέτρεψεν ὑμῖν ἀπολῦσαι τὰς
γυναῖκας ὑμῶν· ἀπ᾽ ἀρχῆς δὲ ὐ
γέγονεν ὕτω.

9 Λέγω δὲ ὑμῖν, ὅτι ὃς ἂν ἀ-
πολύσῃ τὴν γυναῖκα αὐτῦ, εἰ μὴ
ἐπὶ πορνείᾳ, κ᾽ γαμήσῃ ἄλλην,
μοιχᾶται· κ᾽ ὁ ἀπολελυμένην γαμήσας, μοιχᾶται.

10 Λέγυσιν αὐτῷ οἱ μαθηταὶ
αὐτῦ· Εἰ ὕτως ἐϛὶν ἡ αἰτία τῦ
ἀνθρώπυ μετὰ τῆς γυναικὸς, ὐ
συμφέρει γαμῆσαι.

circa multum ministerium:
stans autem ait: Domine, non
curæ est tibi quod soror mea so-
lam me reliquit ministrare? dic
ergo illi mihi ut simul suscipiat.

41 Respondens autem dixit
illi Jesus: Martha, Martha, so-
licita es, & turbaris circa multa.

42 Unius vero est usus. Maria autem bonam partem elegit,
quæ non auferetur ab ea.

CAPUT XIX.

1 ET factum est quum con-
summasset Jesus sermones
istos, transtulit se à Galilæâ, &
venit in fines Judææ trans Jordanem.

2 Et sequutæ sunt eum turbæ
multæ:

3 Et accesserunt ad eum Pharisæi tentantes eum, & dicentes
ei: Si licet homini absolvere
uxorem suam juxta omnem
causam?

4 Qui verò respondens ait
eis: Non legistis, quia faciens
ab initio, masculum & fœmi-
nam fecit eos?

5 Et dixit: Propter hoc dimittet homo patrem, & ma-
trem, & adhærebit uxori suæ:
& erunt duo in carnem unam.

6 Itaque non amplius sunt duo,
sed caro una. Quod ergo Deus
conjunxit, homo non separet.

7 Dicunt illi: Quid ergo Moses mandavit dare libellum dis-
cessionis, & absolvere eam?

8 Ait illis: Quòd Moses ad
duritiem cordis vestri permisit
vobis absolvere uxores vestras:
ab initio autem non factum est
itâ.

9 Dico autem vobis, Quia
quicumque absolverit uxorem
suam, nisi super fornicatione, &
duxerit aliam, mœchatur: &
dimissam ducens, mœchatur.

10 Dicunt ei discipuli ejus:
Si ita est causa hominis cum
uxore, non confert nubere.

distraite par divers soins, elle vint et dit à *Jésus :* Seigneur, ne considères-tu point que ma sœur me laisse servir toute seule? Dis-lui donc qu'elle m'aide aussi.

41. Et Jésus lui répondit : Marthe, Marthe, tu te mets en peine et tu t'embarrasses de plusieurs choses;

42. Mais une seule chose est nécessaire ; or, Marie à choisi la bonne part qui ne lui sera point ôtée.

CHAPITRE XIX.

Doctrine de *Jésus-Christ. Du Divorce et des Richesses.*

QUAND Jésus eut achevé ces discours, il partit de Galilée, et s'en alla dans les quartiers de la Judée, au-delà du Jourdain.

2. Et beaucoup de peuple l'y suivit,

3. Des Pharisiens y vinrent aussi pour le tenter, et ils lui dirent : Est-il permis à un homme de répudier sa femme, pour quelque sujet que ce soit ?

4. Et il leur répondit : N'avez-vous pas lu que celui qui créa *l'homme*, au commencement, fit un homme et une femme ;

5. Et qu'il est dit : C'est à cause de cela que l'homme quittera *son* père et *sa* mère, et qu'il s'attachera à sa femme, et les deux ne seront qu'une seule chair ?

6. Ainsi ils ne sont plus deux, mais *ils sont* une seule chair. Que l'homme ne sépare donc point ce que Dieu a uni.

7. Ils lui dirent : Pourquoi donc Moyse a-t-il commandé de donner la lettre de divorce, quand on veut répudier sa femme ?

8. Il leur dit : C'est à cause de la dureté de votre cœur, que Moyse vous a permis de répudier vos femmes ; mais il n'en étoit pas ainsi au commencement.

9. Mais moi je vous dis, que quiconque répudiera sa femme, si ce n'est pour cause d'adultère, et en épousera une autre, commet un adultère ; et celui qui épousera celle qui a été répudiée, commet aussi un adultère.

10. Ses Disciples lui dirent : Si telle est la condition de l'homme avec la femme, il ne convient pas de se marier.

---

about much serving, and came to him, and said, Lord, dost thou not care that my sister hath left me to serve alone? bid her, therefore, that she help me.

41 And Jesus, answered, and said unto her, Martha, Martha, thou art careful, and troubled about many things :

42 But one thing is needful: and Mary hath chosen that good part, which shall not be taken away from her.

AND it came to pass, *that,* when Jesus had finished these sayings, he departed from Galilee, and came into the coasts of Judea beyond Jordan :

2 And great multitudes followed him,

3 The Pharisees also came unto him, tempting him, and saying unto him, Is it lawful for a man to put away his wife for every cause?

4 And he answered and said unto them, Have ye not read, that he which made *them* at the beginning, made them male and female?

5 And said, For this cause shall a man leave father and mother, and shall cleave to his wife ; and they twain shall be one flesh.

6 Wherefore they are no more twain, but one flesh. What, therefore, God hath joined together, let no man put asunder.

7 They say unto him, Why did Moses then command to give a writing of divorcement, and to put her away?

8 He saith unto them, Moses, because of the hardness of your hearts, suffered you to put away your wives : but from the beginning it was not so.

9 And I say unto you, Whosoever shall put away his wife, except it be for fornication, and shall marry another, committeth adultery : and whoso marrieth her which is put away doth commit adultery.

10 His disciples say unto him, If the case of the man be so with his wife, it is not good to marry.

51

11 Ὁ δὲ εἶπεν αὐτοῖς· Οὐ πάντες χωρᾶσι τὸν λόγον τᾶτον, ἀλλ'
οἷς δέδοται.

* 12 Εἰσὶ γὰρ εὐνᾶχοι, οἵτινες
ἐκ κοιλίας μητρὸς ἐγεννήθησαν ὅ-
τω· καί εἰσιν εὐνᾶχοι, οἵτινες † εὐ-
νυχίσθησαν ὑπὸ τῶν ἀνθρώπων· ᶜ
εἰσὶν εὐνᾶχοι, οἵτινες εὐνύχισαν
ἑαυτὲς διὰ τὴν βασιλείαν τῶν ἐ-
ρανῶν. Ὁ δυνάμενῷ χωρεῖν, χω-
ρείτω.

13 Τότε προσηνέχθη αὐτῷ
παιδία, ἵνα τὰς χεῖρας ἐπιθῇ αὐτοῖς, ᶜ προσεύξηται· οἱ δὲ μαθηταὶ ἐπετίμησαν αὐτοῖς.

14 Ὁ δὲ Ἰησᾶς εἶπεν· Ἄφετε
τὰ παιδία, ᶜ μὴ κωλύετε αὐτὰ
ἐλθεῖν πρός με· τῶν γὰρ τοιότων
ἐςὶν ἡ βασιλεία τῶν ἐρανῶν.

15 Καὶ ἐπιθεὶς αὐτοῖς τὰς χεῖρας, ἐπορεύθη ἐκεῖθεν.

16 Καὶ ἰδὲ, εἷς προσελθὼν, εἶπεν αὐτῷ· Διδάσκαλε ἀγαθὲ, τί
ἀγαθὸν ποιήσω, ἵνα ἔχω ζωὴν
αἰώνιον;

17 Ὁ δὲ εἶπεν αὐτῷ· Τί με
λέγεις ἀγαθόν; ὐδεὶς ἀγαθὸς, εἰ
μὴ εἷς, ὁ Θεός· εἰ δὲ θέλεις εἰσελθεῖν εἰς τὴν ζωὴν, τήρησον τὰς
ἐντολάς.

18 Λέγει αὐτῷ· Ποίας; Ὁ δὲ
Ἰησᾶς εἶπε· Τό· Οὐ φονεύσεις·
Οὐ μοιχεύσεις· Οὐ κλέψεις· Οὐ
ψευδομαρτυρήσεις·

19 Τίμα τὸν πατέρα σε, ᶜ τὴν
μητέρα· καὶ· Ἀγαπήσεις τὸν
πλησίον σε ὡς σεαυτόν.

20 Λέγει αὐτῷ ὁ νεανίσκῷ·
Πάντα ταῦτα ἐφυλαξάμην ἐκ νεό-
τητός μᾶ· τί ἔτι ὑςερῷ;

21 Ἔφη αὐτῷ ὁ Ἰησᾶς· Εἰ θέλεις τέλειῷ εἶναι, ὕπαγε, πώλη-
σόν σε τὰ ὑπάρχοντα, ᶜ δὸς
πτωχοῖς· ᶜ ἕξεις θησαυρὸν ἐν
ὐρανῷ· ᶜ δεῦρο, ἀκολύθει μοι.

22 Ἀκόσας δὲ ὁ νεανίσκῷ τὸν
λόγον, ἀπῆλθε λυπόμενῷ· ἦν
γὰρ ἔχων κτήματα πολλά.

23 Ὁ δὲ Ἰησᾶς εἶπε τοῖς μαθηταῖς αὐτᾶ· Ἀμὴν λέγω ὑμῖν,
ὅτι δυσκόλως πλᾶσιῷ εἰσελεύσε-
ται εἰς τὴν βασιλείαν τῶν ἐρανῶν.

* 24 Πάλιν δὲ λέγω ὑμῖν, ‡ εὐ-
κοπώτερόν ἐςι ‡ κάμηλον ‡ διὰ
† τρυπήματῷ ‡ ῥαφίδῷ ‡ διελ-
θεῖν, ἢ πλόσιον εἰς τὴν βασιλείαν
τᾶ Θεᾶ εἰσελθεῖν.

25 Ἀκόσαντες δὲ οἱ μαθηταὶ

---

11 Ille verò dixit illis : Non
omnes capiunt verbum illud,
sed quibus datum est.

12 Sunt enim eunuchi, qui
de utero matris nati sunt sic : &
sunt eunuchi, qui castrati sunt
ab hominibus : & sunt eunuchi,
qui castraverunt seipsos propter
regnum cælorum, potens ca-
pere, capiat.

13 Tunc oblati sunt ei pueruli, ut manus imponeret eis, &
oraret : At Discipuli increpa-
bant eos.

14 At Jesus ait : Sinite pue-
rulos, & ne prohibete eos venire ad me : nam talium est
regnum cælorum.

15 Et imponens eis manus,
abiit inde.

16 Et ecce unus accedens, ait
illi : Magister bone, quid boni
faciam, ut habeam vitam æternam?

17 Ipse verò dixit ei : Quid
me dicis bonum? nemo bonus si
non unus, Deus. Si autem vis
ingredi ad vitam, serva man-
data.

18 Dicit illi : Quæ? At Jesus dixit : hoc, Non occides :
Non adulterabis : Non furabe-
ris : Non falsò testaberis :

19 Honora patrem tuum &
matrem : & : Diliges proximum
tuum sicut teipsum.

20 Dicit illi adolescens : Omnia hæc custodivi à juventu-
te mea : quid adhuc deficio?

21 Ait illi Jesus : Si vis per-
fectus esse, vade, vende tuam
substantiam, & da pauperibus :
& habebis thesaurum in cælo :
& veni, sequere me.

22 Audiens autem adolescens
verbum, abiit tristis : erat enim
habens possessiones multas.

23 At Jesus dixit discipulis
suis : Amen dico vobis, quia
difficile dives intrabit in regnum
cælorum.

24 Iterum autem dico vobis,
facilius est camelum per fora-
men acus transire, quam divi-
tem in regnum Dei intrare.

25 Audientes autem discipuli

11. Mais il leur dit : Tous ne sont pas capables de cela, mais ceux-là seulement à qui il a été donné.

12. Car il y a des eunuques, qui sont nés tels dès le ventre de leur mère ; il y en a qui ont été faits eunuques par les hommes ; et il y en a qui se sont faits eunuques eux-mêmes pour le Royaume des cieux. Que celui qui peut comprendre ceci, le comprenne.

13. Alors on lui présenta de petits enfans, afin qu'il leur imposât les mains, et qu'il priât pour eux ; mais les Disciples repre-noient ceux qui les présentoient.

14. Mais Jésus leur dit : Laissez ces petits enfans, et ne les empêchez point de venir à moi ; car le Royaume des cieux est pour ceux qui leur ressemblent.

15. Et leur ayant imposé les mains, il partit de là.

16. Et voici, quelqu'un s'approchant, lui dit : Mon bon Maître, que dois-je faire pour avoir la Vie éternelle ?

17. Il lui répondit : Pourquoi m'appelles-tu bon ? Il n'y a qu'un seul bon ; c'est Dieu. Que si tu veux entrer dans la vie, garde les commandemens.

18: Il leur dit : Quels commandemens ? Et Jésus lui répondit : Tu ne tueras point ; Tu ne commettras point adultère : Tu ne déroberas point : Tu ne diras point de faux témoignage :

19. Honore ton père et ta mère : Et tu aimeras ton prochain comme toi-même.

20. Le jeune homme lui dit : J'ai observé toutes ces choses-là dès ma jeunesse ; que me manque-t-il encore ?

21. Jésus lui dit : Si tu veux être parfait, vends ce que tu as, et le donne aux pauvres ; et tu auras un trésor dans le ciel ; après cela, viens, et suis-moi.

22. Mais quand le jeune homme eut entendu cette parole, il s'en alla tout triste, car il possédoit de grands biens.

23. Alors Jésus dit à ses Disciples : Je vous dis en vérité, qu'un riche entrera difficilement dans le Royaume des cieux.

24. Et je vous dis encore : Il est plus aisé qu'un chameau passe par le trou d'une aiguille, qu'il ne l'est qu'un riche entre dans le Royaume de Dieu.

25. Ses Disciples ayant entendu

11 But he said unto them, All men cannot receive this saying, save they to whom it is given.

12 For there are some eunuchs, which were so born from their mother's womb: and there are some eunuchs, which were made eunuchs of men: and there be eunuchs, which have made themselves eunuchs for the kingdom of heaven's sake. He that is able to receive it, let him receive it.

13 Then were there brought unto him little children, that he should put his hands on them and pray : and the disciples rebuked them.

14 But Jesus said, Suffer little children, and forbid them not, to come unto me : for of such is the kingdom of heaven.

15 And he laid his hands on them, and departed thence.

16 And, behold, one came and said unto him, Good Master, what good thing shall I do, that I may have eternal life ?

17 And he said unto him, Why callest thou me good ? there is none good but one, that is, God : but if thou wilt enter into life, keep the commandments.

18 He saith unto him, Which ? Jesus said, Thou shalt do no murder, Thou shalt not commit adultery, Thou shalt not steal, Thou shalt not bear false witness,

19 Honour thy father and thy mother : and, Thou shalt love thy neighbour as thyself.

20 The young man saith unto him, All these things have I kept from my youth up : what lack I yet?

21 Jesus said unto him, If thou wilt be perfect, go and sell that thou hast, and give to the poor, and thou shalt have treasure in heaven ; and come and follow me.

22 But when the young man heard that saying, he went away sorrowful : for he had great possessions.

23 Then said Jesus unto his disciples, Verily I say unto you, That a rich man shall hardly enter into the kingdom of heaven.

24 And again I say unto you, It is easier for a camel to go through the eye of a needle, than for a rich man to enter into the kingdom of God.

25 When his disciples heard it,

αὐτῷ, ἐξεπλήσσοντο σφόδρα, λέγοντες· Τίς ἄρα δύναται σωθῆναι;

26 Ἐμβλέψας δὲ ὁ Ἰησοῦς, εἶπεν αὐτοῖς· Παρὰ ἀνθρώποις τῦτο ἀδύνατόν ἐςι, παρὰ δὲ Θεῷ πάντα δυνατά ἐςι.

Κεφ. κ΄. 20.

16 Ὁμοία γάρ ἐςιν ἡ βασιλεία τῶν ὐρανῶν ἀνθρώπῳ οἰκοδεσπότῃ, ὅςις ‡ ἐξῆλθεν ἅμα πρωῒ ‡ μισθώσασθαι ‡ ἐργάτας εἰς τὸν ἀμπελῶνα αὐτῦ.

2 Συμφωνήσας δὲ μετὰ τῶν ἐργατῶν ἐκ δηναρίυ τὴν ἡμέραν, ἀπέςειλεν αὐτὲς εἰς τὸν ἀμπελῶνα αὐτῦ.

3 Καὶ ἐξελθὼν περὶ τὴν τρίτην ὥραν, εἶδεν ἄλλυς ἑςῶτας ἐν τῇ ἀγορᾷ ἀργύς·

4 Κἀκείνοις εἶπεν· Ὑπάγετε καὶ ὑμεῖς εἰς τὸν ἀμπελῶνα· καὶ ὃ ἐὰν ᾖ δίκαιον, δώσω ὑμῖν.

5 Οἱ δὲ ἀπῆλθον. Πάλιν ἐξελθὼν περὶ ἕκτην καὶ ἐνάτην ὥραν, ἐποίησεν ὡσαύτως.

6 Περὶ δὲ τὴν ἑνδεκάτην ὥραν ἐξελθὼν, εὗρεν ἄλλυς ἑςῶτας ἀργύς, καὶ λέγει αὐτοῖς· Τί ὧδε ἑςήκατε ὅλην τὴν ἡμέραν ἀργοί;

7 Λέγυσιν αὐτῷ· Ὅτι ἐδεὶς ἡμᾶς ἐμισθώσατο. Λέγει αὐτοῖς· Ὑπάγετε καὶ ὑμεῖς εἰς τὸν ἀμπελῶνα, καὶ ὃ ἐὰν ᾖ δίκαιον, λήψεσθε.

8 Ὀψίας δὲ γενομένης, λέγει ὁ κύριος τῦ ἀμπελῶνος τῷ ἐπιτρόπῳ αὐτῦ· Κάλεσον τὲς ἐργάτας, καὶ ἀπόδος αὐτοῖς τὸν μισθὸν, ἀρξάμενος ἀπὸ τῶν ἐσχάτων, ἕως τῶν πρώτων.

9 Καὶ ἐλθόντες οἱ περὶ τὴν ἑνδεκάτην ὥραν, ἔλαβον ἀνὰ δηνάριον.

10 Ἐλθόντες δὲ οἱ πρῶτοι, ἐνόμισαν ὅτι πλείονα λήψονται· καὶ ἔλαβον καὶ αὐτοὶ ἀνὰ δηνάριον.

11 Λαβόντες δὲ ἐγόγγυζον κατὰ τῦ οἰκοδεσπότυ,

12 Λέγοντες· Ὅτι ὗτοι οἱ ἔσχατοι μίαν ὥραν ἐποίησαν, καὶ ἴσυς ἡμῖν αὐτὲς ἐποίησας, τοῖς βαςάσασι τὸ βάρος τῆς ἡμέρας, καὶ τὸν καύσωνα.

ejus, mirabantur valde, dicentes: Quis ergo potest servari?

26 Aspiciens autem Jesus, dixit illis: Apud homines hoc impossibile est, apud autem Deum omnia possibilia sunt.

CAPUT. XX.

1 Simile enim est regnum cælorum homini patrifamilias, qui exiit cum diluculo conducere operarios in vineam suam.

2 Conveniens autem cum operariis ex denario diem, misit eos in vineam suam.

3 Et egressus circa tertiam horam, vidit alios stantes in foro otiosos:

4 Et illis dixit: Abite & vos in vineam: & quod fuerit justum dabo vobis.

5 Illi autem abierunt. Iterum exiens circa sextam & nonam horam, fecit similiter.

6 Circa verò undecimam horam exiens, invenit alios stantes otiosos, & dicit illis: Quid hic statis totam diem otiosi?

7 Dicunt ei: Quia nemo nos mercede conduxit. Dicit eis: Ite & vos in vineam, & quod fuerit justum, sumetis.

8 Vespere autem facto, dicit dominus vineæ procuratori suo: Voca operarios & redde illis mercedem, incipiens à novissimis usque ad primos.

9 Et venientes qui circa undecimam horam, acceperunt singuli denarium.

10 Venientes autem primi, arbitrati sunt quòd plus essent accepturi: & acceperunt & ipsi singuli denarium.

11 Accipientes autem murmurabant adversus patrem-familias,

12 Dicentes: Quòd hi novissimi unam horam fecerunt, & pares nobis illos fecisti, portantibus pondus diei, & æstum.

cela, furent fort étonnés, et ils disoient : Qui peut donc être sauvé ?

26. Et Jésus les regardant, leur dit : Quant aux hommes, cela est impossible ; mais quant à Dieu, toutes choses sont possibles.

CAR le Royaume des cieux est semblable à un père de famille, qui sortit dès la pointe du jour, afin de louer des ouvriers pour *travailler à* sa vigne.

2. Et ayant accordé avec les ouvriers à un denier par jour, il les envoya à sa vigne.

3. Il sortit encore environ la troisième heure *du jour*, et il en vit d'autres qui étoient dans la place sans rien faire ;

4. Auxquels il dit : Allez-vous-en aussi à ma vigne, et je vous donnerai ce qui sera raisonnable.

5. Et ils y allèrent. Il sortit encore environ la sixième et la neuvième heure, et il fit la même chose.

6. Et vers l'onzième heure, il sortit, et il en trouva d'autres qui étoient sans rien faire, auxquels il dit : Pourquoi vous tenez-vous ici tout le jour sans rien faire ?

7. Et ils lui répondirent : Parce que personne ne nous a loués. Et il leur dit : Allez-vous-en aussi à ma vigne, vous recevrez ce qui sera raisonnable.

8. Quand le soir fut venu, le Maître de la vigne dit à celui qui avoit le soin de ses affaires : Appelle les ouvriers, et leur paie *leur* salaire, en commençant depuis les derniers jusqu'aux premiers.

9. Et ceux *qui avoient été loués* sur l'onzième heure, étant venus, ils reçurent chacun un denier.

10. Or, quand les premiers furent venus, ils s'attendoient à recevoir davantage ; mais ils reçurent aussi chacun un denier.

11. Et l'ayant reçu, ils murmuroient contre le père de famille,

12. Disant : Ces derniers n'ont travaillé qu'une heure, et tu les égalés à nous, qui avons supporté la fatigue de *tout le* jour et la chaleur.

they were exceedingly amazed, saying, Who then can be saved?

26 But Jesus beheld *them*, and said unto them, With men this is impossible ; but with God all things are possible.

CHAP. XX.
The labourers in the vineyard.

FOR the kingdom of heaven is like unto a man *that is* an householder, which went out early in the morning to hire labourers into his vineyard.

2 And when he had agreed with the labourers for a penny a day, he sent them into his vineyard.

3 And he went out about the third hour, and saw others standing idle in the market-place,

4 And said unto them, Go ye also into the vineyard ; and whatsoever is right I will give you. And they went their way.

5 Again he went out about the sixth and ninth hour, and did likewise.

6 And about the eleventh hour he went out, and found others standing idle, and saith unto them, Why stand ye here all the day idle?

7 They say unto him, Because no man hath hired us. He saith unto them, Go ye also into the vineyard ; and whatsoever is right, *that* shall ye receive.

8 So when even was come, the lord of the vineyard saith unto his steward, Call the labourers, and give them *their* hire, beginning from the last unto the first.

9 And when they came that *were hired* about the eleventh hour, they received every man a penny.

10 But when the first came, they supposed that they should have received more ; and they likewise received every man a penny.

11 And when they had received *it*, they murmured against the good man of the house,

12 Saying, These last have wrought *but* one hour, and thou hast made them equal unto us, which have borne the burden and heat of the day.

53

13 Ὁ δὲ ἀποκριθεὶς, εἶπεν ἐνὶ αὐτῶν· † Ἑταῖρε, ἔκ † ἀδικῶ σε· ἐχὶ † δηναρίε † συνεφώνησάς μοι;

14 Ἆρον τὸ σὸν, καὶ ὕπαγε· θέλω δὲ τύτῳ τῷ ἐσχάτῳ δῶναι ὡς καὶ σοί.

15 Ἢ ἐκ ἔξεςί μοι ποιῆσαι ὃ θέλω ἐν τοῖς ἐμοῖς; ἢ ὁ ὀφθαλμός σε πονηρός ἐςιν, ὅτι ἐγὼ ἀγαθός εἰμι;

16 Οὕτως ἔσονται οἱ ἔσχατοι, πρῶτοι, καὶ οἱ πρῶτοι, ἔσχατοι. πολλοὶ γάρ εἰσι † κλητοὶ, ὀλίγοι δὲ ἐκλεκτοί.

Κεφ. ιθʹ. 19.

1 ΚΑΙ εἰσελθὼν διήρχετο τὴν Ἱεριχώ.

2 Καὶ ἰδὺ ἀνὴρ ὀνόματι καλύμεν⊙· Ζακχαῖος· καὶ αὐτὸς ἦν † ἀρχιτελώνης, καὶ ὗτος ἦν πλούσιος.

3 Καὶ ἐζήτει ἰδεῖν τὸν Ἰησῦν τίς ἐςι· καὶ ἐκ ἠδύναλο ἀπὸ τοῦ ὄχλε, ὅτι τῇ ἡλικίᾳ μικρός ἦν.

4 Καὶ † προσδραμὼν ἔμπροσθεν, ἀνέβη ἐπὶ † συκομορέαν, ἵνα ἴδῃ αὐτόν· ὅτι δι᾽ ἐκείνης ἤμελλε διέρχεσθαι.

5 Καὶ ὡς ἦλθεν ἐπὶ τὸν τόπον, ἀναβλέψας ὁ Ἰησῦς εἶδεν αὐτὸν, καὶ εἶπε πρὸς αὐτόν· Ζακχαῖε, σπεύσας κατάβηθι· σήμερον γὰρ ἐν τῷ οἴκῳ σε δεῖ με μεῖναι.

6 Καὶ σπεύσας κατέβη, καὶ ὑπεδέξατο αὐτὸν χαίρων.

7 Καὶ ἰδόντες ἅπαντες † διεγόγγυζον, λέγοντες· Ὅτι παρὰ ἁμαρτωλῷ ἀνδρὶ εἰσῆλθε καταλῦσαι.

8 Σταθεὶς δὲ Ζακχαῖος εἶπε πρὸς τὸν Κύριον· ἰδὺ, τὰ † ἡμίση τῶν † ὑπαρχόιλων μυ, Κύριε, δίδωμι τοῖς πλωχαῖς· καὶ εἴ τινός τι ἐσυκοφάνησα, ἀποδίδωμι † τετραπλῦν.

9 Εἶπε δὲ πρὸς αὐτὸν ὁ Ἰησῦς· Ὅτι σήμερον σωτηρία τῷ οἴκῳ τούτῳ ἐγένέλο, καθ᾽τι καὶ αὐτὸς υἱὸς Ἀβρααμ ἐςιν.

10 Ἦλθε γὰρ ὁ υἱὸς τῦ ἀνθρώπε ζητῆσαι καὶ σῶσαι τὸ ἀπολωλός.

11 Ἀκυόνων δὲ αὐτῶν ταῦτα προςθεὶς εἶπε παραβολὴν, διὰ τὸ ἐγγὺς αὐτὸν εἶναι Ἱερυσαλήμ, καὶ

---

13 Ille verò respondens dixit uni eorum: Amice, non facio injuriam tibi: nonne denario conve nisti mecum?

14 Tolle quod tuum, & abi, volo autem huic novissimo dare sicut & tibi.

15 Aut non licet mihi facere quod volo in meis? an oculus tuus malus est, quia ego bonus sum?

16 Sic erunt novissimi, primi: & primi, novissimi. Multi enim sunt vocati, pauci verò electi.

CAPUT XIX.

1 ET ingressus pertransibat Jericho.

2 Et ecce vir nomine vocatus Zachæus, & hic erat princeps publicanorum: & ipse erat dives.

3 Et quærebat videre Jesum quis esset, & non poterat præ turba: quia statura pusillus erat.

4 Et præcur ens coram, ascendit in sycomorum, ut videret eum: quia illàc erat transiturus.

5 Et ut venit ad locum, suspiciens Jesus vidit illum, & dixit ad eum: Zachæe, festinans defcende: hodie enim in domo tua oportet me manere.

6 Et festinans defcendit, & excepit illum gaudens.

7 Et videntes omnes murmurabant, dicentes: quod ad peccatorem hominem introivit diversari.

8 Stans autem Zachæus dixit ad Dominum: Ecce dimidia substantiarum mearum, Domine, do pauperibus, & si aliquemquid defraudavi, reddo quadruplum.

9 Ait autem ad eum Jesus: Quia hodie falus domui huic facta est, eo quod & ipse filius Abrahæ sit.

10 Venit enim filius hominis quærere & servare perditum.

11 Audientibus autem illis hæc, adjiciens dixit parabolam, propter prope eum esse Hieru-

13. Mais il répondit à l'un d'eux, et lui dit : Mon ami , je ne te fais point de tort ; n'as-tu pas accordé avec moi à un denier *par jour* ?

14. Prends ce qui est à toi, et t'en va ; mais je veux donner à ce dernier autant qu'à toi.

15. Ne m'est-il pas permis de faire ce que je veux de ce qui est à moi ? Ton œil est-il malin de ce que je suis bon ?

16. Ainsi les derniers seront les premiers , et les premiers seront les derniers ; car il y en a beaucoup d'appelés , mais peu d'élus.

CHAPITRE XIX.

La conversion de Zachée ; la parabole des dix marcs. Jésus fait son entrée à Jérusalem ; il répand des larmes sur elle , et purge le Temple.

Jésus étant entré dans Jérico , passoit par la ville.

2. Et un homme appelé Zachée , chef des péagers , qui étoit riche ,

3. Cherchoit à voir qui étoit Jésus ; mais il ne le pouvoit pas à cause de la foule, parce qu'il étoit de petite taille.

4. C'est pourquoi il courut devant , et monta sur un sycomore, pour le voir ; parce qu'il devoit passer par-là.

5. Jésus étant venu en cet endroit , et regardant en haut, le vit , et lui dit : Zachée , hâte-toi de descendre ; car il faut que je loge aujourd'hui dans ta maison.

6. Et il descendit promptement , et le reçut avec joie.

7. Et tous ceux qui virent cela , murmuroient , disant qu'il étoit entré chez un homme de mauvaise vie pour y loger.

8. Et Zachée se présentant devant le Seigneur , lui dit : Seigneur , je donne la moitié de mes biens aux pauvres , et si j'ai fait tort à quelqu'un en quelque chose, je lui en rends quatre fois autant.

9. Sur quoi Jésus lui dit : Le salut est entré aujourd'hui dans cette maison, parce que celui-ci est aussi enfant d'Abraham.

10. Car le Fils de l'homme est venu chercher et sauver ce qui étoit perdu.

11. Comme ils écoutoient ce discours , Jésus continuant, proposa une parabole , sur ce qu'il étoit près de Jérusalem , et qu'ils

13 But he answered one of them, and said, Friend, I do thee no wrong: didst not thou agree with me for a penny?

14 Take *that* thine *is*, and go thy way: I will give unto this last, even as unto thee.

15 Is it not lawful for me to do what I will with mine own? is thine eye evil because I am good?

16 So the last shall be first, and the first last : for many be called, but few chosen.

CHAP. XIX.

The publican Zaccheus.

AND *Jesus* entered and passed through Jericho.

2 And, behold, *there was* a man named Zaccheus, which was the chief among the publicans, and he was rich.

3 And he sought to see Jesus who he was ; and could not for the press, because he was little of stature.

4 And he ran before, and climbed up into a sycamore-tree to see him ; for he was to pass that *way*.

5 And, when Jesus came to the place, he looked up, and saw him, and said unto him, Zaccheus, make haste, and come down; for to-day I must abide at thy house.

6 And he made haste, and came down, and received him joyfully.

7 And when they saw *it*, they all murmured, saying, That he was gone to be guest with a man that is a sinner.

8 And Zaccheus stood, and said unto the Lord, Behold, Lord, the half of my goods I give to the poor ; and if I have taken any thing from any man by false accusation, I restore him fourfold.

9 And Jesus said unto him, This day is salvation come to this house, forasmuch as he also is a son of Abraham.

10 For the Son of Man is come to seek and to save that which was lost.

11 And, as they heard these things, he added, and spake a parable, because he was nigh to Je-

δοκεῖν αὐτοῖς ὅτι παραχρῆμα μέλλει ἡ βασιλεία τοῦ Θεῖ ἀναφαίνεσθαι.

12 Εἶπεν ἔν· Ἄνθρωπός τις εὐγενὴς ἐπορεύθη εἰς χώραν μακρὰν, λαβεῖν ἑαυτῷ βασιλείαν, ᾗ ὑποτρέψαι.

* 13 Καλέσας δὲ δέκα δούλες ἑαυτῆ, ἔδωκεν αὐτοῖς δέκα μνᾶς, ᾗ εἶπε πρὸς αὐτούς· † Πραγματεύσασθε ἕως ἔρχομαι.

* 14 Οἱ δὲ πολῖται αὐτῦ ‡ ἐμίσυν αὐτὸν, ᾗ ἀπέσειλαν ‡ πρεσβείαν ‖ ὀπίσω αὐτῦ, λέγοντες. Οὐ θέλομεν τᾶτιν βασιλεῦσαι ἐφ᾽ ἡμᾶς.

* 15 Καὶ ἐγένετο ἐν τῷ ἐπανελθεῖν αὐτὸν λαβόντα τὴν βασιλείαν, ᾗ εἶπε φωνηθῆναι αὐτῷ τὺς δούλας τούτυς, οἷς ἔδωκε τὸ ἀργύριον ἵνα γνῷ τίς τί † διεπραγματεύσατο.

* 16 Παρεγένετο δὲ ὁ πρῶτος, λέγων· Κύριε, ἡ ‡ μνᾶ σε † προσειργάσατο δέκα μνᾶς.

17 Καὶ εἶπεν αὐτῷ Εὖ ἀγαθὲ δᾶλε· ὅτι ἐν ἐλαχίςῳ πιςὸς ἐγένυ, ἴσθι ἐξυσίαν ἔχων ἐπάνω δέκα πόλεων.

18 Καὶ ἦλθεν ὁ δεύτερος, λέγων· Κύριε, ἡ μνᾶ σε ἐποίησε πέντε μνᾶς.

19 Εἶπε δὲ ᾗ τύτῳ· Καὶ σὺ γίνυ ἐπάνω πέντε πόλεων.

20 Καὶ ἕτερος ἦλθε, λέγων· Κύριε, ἰδὺ, ἡ μνᾶ σε, ἣν εἶχον ἀποκειμένην ἐν συδαρίῳ.

21 Ἐφοβύμην γάρ σε, ὅτι ἄνθρωπος αὐςηρὸς εἶ· αἴρεις ὃ ὐκ ἔθηκας, ᾗ θερίζεις ὃ ὐκ ἔσπειρας.

* 22 Λέγει δὲ αὐτῷ. Ἐκ τῦ ςόματός σε κρινῶ σε, πονηρὲ δᾶλε· ἤδεις ὅτι ἐγὼ † ἄνθρωπος ‡ αὐςηρός εἰμι αἴρων ὃ ὐκ ἔθηκα, ᾗ θερίζων ὃ ὐκ ἔσπειρα.

23 Καὶ διατί ὐκ ἔδωκας τὸ ἀργύριόν μυ ἐπὶ τὴν τράπεζαν, ᾗ ἐγὼ ἐλθὼν σὺν τόκῳ ἂν ἔπραξα αὐτό;

---

salem, & videri eis quod confestim esset regnum Dei appariturum.

12 Dixit ergo: Homo quidam nobilis abiit in regionem longinquam accipere sibi ipsi regnum, & reverti.

13 Vocans autem decem servos suos, dedit eis decem minas, & ait ad illos: Negotiamini dum venio.

14 At cives ejus oderant eum, & miserunt legationem post illum, dicentes: Non volumus hunc regnare super nos.

15 Et factum est in redire ipsum accipientem regnum, ait vocari sibi servos hos, quibus dedit argentum, ut sciret quisquid negotiatus esset.

16 Adfuit autem primus, dicens: Domine, mina tua acquisivit decem minas.

17 Et ait illi: Euge bone serve: quia in modico fidelis fuisti, esto potestatem habens super decem civitates.

18 Et venit secundus, dicens: Domine, mina tua fecit quinque minas.

19 Ait autem & huic: Et tu esto super quinque civitates.

20 Et alter venit, dicens: Domine, ecce mina tua, quam habui repositam in sudario.

21 Timui enim te, quia homo austerus es: tollis quod non posuisti, & metis quod non seminasti.

22 Dicit autem ei: Ex ore tuo judico te, scelerate serve: sciebas quod ego homo austerus sum, tollens quod non posui, & metens quod non seminavi.

23 Et quare non dedisti argentum meum mensariis, & veniens ego cum usura utique exegissem illud?

croyoient que le règne de Dieu alloit paroître bientôt.

12. Il dit donc : Un homme de grande naissance s'en alla dans un pays éloigné , pour prendre possession d'un royaume , et s'en revenir ensuite.

13. Et ayant appelé dix de ses serviteurs, il leur donna dix marcs d'argent , et leur dit : Faites-les valoir jusqu'à-ce que je revienne.

14. Mais les gens de son pays le haïssoient ; et ils envoyèrent une ambassade après lui , pour dire : Nous ne voulons point que celui-ci règne sur nous.

15. Il arriva donc , lorsqu'il fut de retour , après avoir pris possession du royaume , qu'il commanda qu'on fît venir ces serviteurs auxquels il avoit donné l'argent , pour savoir combien chacun l'avoit fait valoir.

16. Et le premier se présenta , et dit : Seigneur , ton marc a produit dix autres marcs.

17. Et il lui dit : Cela est bien , bon serviteur ; parce que tu as été fidèle dans peu de chose , tu auras le gouvernement de dix villes.

18. Et le second vint , et dit : Seigneur , ton marc a produit cinq autres marcs.

19. Et il dit aussi à celui-ci : Et toi , commande à cinq villes.

20. Et un autre vint , et dit : Seigneur , voici ton marc que j'ai gardé enveloppé dans un linge;

21. Car je te craignois , parce que tu es un homme sévère ; tu prends où tu n'as rien mis , et tu moissonnes où tu n'as point semé.

22. Et son maître lui dit : Méchant serviteur , je te jugerai par tes propres paroles : Tu savois que je suis un homme sévère , qui prends où je n'ai rien mis , et qui moissonne où je n'ai point semé ;

23. Et pourquoi n'as-tu pas mis mon argent à la banque ; et à mon retour je l'eusse retiré avec les intérêts ?

rusalem, and because they thought that the kingdom of God should immediately appear.

12 He said, therefore, A certain nobleman went into a far country to receive for himself a kingdom, and to return.

13 And he called his ten servants, and delivered them ten pounds, and said unto them, Occupy till I come.

14 But his citizens hated him, and sent a message after him, saying, We will not have this *man* to reign over us.

15 And it came to pass, that when he was returned, having received the kingdom, then he commanded these servants to be called unto him, to whom he had given the money, that he might know how much every man had gained by trading.

16 Then came the first, saying, Lord, thy pound hath gained ten pounds.

17 And he said unto him, Well, thou good servant ; because thou hast been faithful in a very little, have thou authority over ten cities.

18 And the second came, saying, Lord, thy pound hath gained five pounds.

19 And he said likewise to him, Be thou also over five cities.

20 And another came, saying, Lord, behold, *here is* thy pound, which I have kept laid up in a napkin :

21 For I feared thee, because thou art an austere man ; thou takest up that thou layedst not down, and reapest that thou didst not sow.

22 And he saith unto him, Out of thine own mouth will I judge thee, *thou* wicked servant. Thou knewest that I was an austere man, taking up that I laid not down, and reaping that I did not sow: K2

23 Wherefore then gavest not thou my money into the bank, that at my coming I might have required mine own with usury ?

55

24 Καὶ τοῖς παρεςῶσιν εἶπεν· Ἄρατε ἀπ᾽ αὐτῦ τὴν μνᾶν, κỳ δότε τῷ τὰς δέκα μνᾶς ἔχοντι.

25 Καὶ εἶπον αὐτῷ· Κύριε, ἔχει δέκα μνᾶς·

26 Λέγω γὰρ ὑμῖν, ὅτι παντὶ τῷ ἔχοντι δοθήσεται· ἀπὸ δὲ τῦ μὴ ἔχοντ۰, κỳ ὃ ἔχει, ἀρθήσεται ἀπ᾽ αὐτῦ.

*27 Πλὴν τὸς ἐχθρός μυ ἐκείνυς, τὸς μὴ θελήσαντάς με βασιλεῦσαι ἐπ᾽ αὐτὸς, ἀγάγετε ὧδε, κỳ † κατασφάξατε ἔμπροσθέν μυ.

28 Καὶ εἰπὼν ταῦτα, ἐπορεύετο ἔμπροσθεν, ἀναβαίνων εἰς Ἱεροσόλυμα.

Κεφ. κα΄ 21.

1 ΚΑὶ ὅτε ἤγγισαν εἰς Ἱεροσόλυμα, κỳ ἦλθον εἰς Βηθφαγῆ πρὸς τὸ ὄρος τῶν ἐλαιῶν, τότε ὁ Ἰησῦς ἀπέςειλε δύο μαθητὰς, λέγων αὐτοῖς·

2 Πορεύθητε εἰς τὴν κώμην, τὴν ἀπέναντι ὑμῶν· κỳ εὐθέως εὑρήσετε ὄνον δεδεμένην, κỳ πῶλον μετ᾽ αὐτῆς· λύσαντες ἀγάγετέ μοι.

3 Καὶ ἐάν τι ὑμῖν εἴπῃ τι, ἐρεῖτε ὅτι ὁ Κύρι۰ αὐτῶν χρείαν ἔχει· εὐθέως δὲ ἀποςελεῖ αὐτός.

6 Πορευθέντες δὲ οἱ μαθηταὶ, κỳ ποιήσαντες καθὼς προσέταξεν αὐτοῖς ὁ Ἰησῦς,

*7 Ἤγαγον τὴν ὄνον κỳ τὸν πῶλον, κỳ ἐπέθηκαν ἐπάνω αὐτῶν τὰ ἱμάτια αὐτῶν, κỳ † ἐπεκάθισαν ‡ ἐπάνω αὐτῶν.

8 Ὁ δὲ πλεῖςος ὄχλος ἔςρωσαν ἑαυτῶν τὰ ἱμάτια ἐν τῇ ὁδῷ· ἄλλοι δὲ ἔκοπτον κλάδυς ἀπὸ τῶν δένδρων, κỳ ἐςρώννυον ἐν τῇ ὁδῷ.

10 Καὶ εἰσελθόντ۰ αὐτῦ εἰς Ἱεροσόλυμα, ἐσείσθη πᾶσα ἡ πόλις, λέγυσα· Τίς ἐςιν ὅτ۰;

19 Οἱ ἂν Φαρισαῖοι εἶπον πρὸς ἑαυτός· Θεωρεῖτε ὅτι ὐκ ὠφελεῖτε ὐδέν; ἴδε, ὁ κόσμ۰ ὀπίσω αὐτῦ ἀπῆλθεν.

20 Ἦσον δέ τινες Ἕλληνες ἐκ τῶν ἀναβαινόντων ἵνα προσκυνήσωσιν ἐν τῇ ἑορτῇ.

---

24 Et aſtantibus dixit: Auferte ab illo minam: & date decem minas habenti.

25 Et dixerunt ei: Domine, habet decem minas.

26 Dico enim vobis, quia omni habenti dabitur: ab autem non habente, & quod habet, auferetur ab eo.

27 Veruntamen inimicos meos illos, non volentes me regnare ſuper ſe, adducite huc, & jugulate ante me.

28 Et dicens hæc, ibat ante aſcendens in Hieroſolyma.

1 ET quum appropinquaſſent in Hieroſolyma, & veniſſent in Bethphage ad montem Olivarum, tunc Jeſus miſit duos diſcipulos, dicens eis:

2 Ite in vicum qui adverſum vos: & ſtatim invenietis aſinam alligatam, & pullum cum ea: ſolventes adducite mihi.

3 Et ſi quis vobis dixerit aliquid, dicite, quia Dominus eorum uſum habet: ſtatim autem dimittet eos.

6 Euntes autem diſcipuli & facientes ſicut mandavit illis Jeſus,

7 Adduxerunt aſinam, & pullum, & impoſuerunt ſuper eos veſtimenta ſua, & collocarunt eum deſuper eos.

8 At plurima turba ſtraverunt ſua veſtimenta in via: alii autem cædebant ramos de arboribus, & ſternebant eis, via.

10 Et intrante eo in Hieroſolyma, commota eſt univerſa civitas, dicens: Quis eſt hic?

19 Ergo Phariſæi dixerunt ad ſemetipſos: Videtis quia non proficitis quicquam? ecce mundus poſt eum abiit.

20 Erant autem quidam Græci ex aſcendentibus, ut adorarent in die feſto.

24. Et il dit à ceux qui étoient présens : Otez-lui le marc, et le donnez à celui qui a les dix marcs.

25. Et ils lui dirent : Seigneur, il a déjà dix marcs.

26. Aussi vous dis-je, qu'on donnera à quiconque a déjà ; et que pour celui qui n'a pas, cela même qu'il a lui sera ôté.

27. Quant à mes ennemis, qui n'ont pas voulu que je regnasse sur eux, amenez-les ici, et faites-les mourir en ma présence.

28. Et après avoir dit cela, il marchoit devant eux, montant à Jérusalem.

CHAPITRE XXI.

Jésus-Christ entre dans Jérusalem, chasse les marchands du Temple, et répond aux Pharisiens.

COMME ils approchoient de Jérusalem, et qu'ils étoient déjà à Bethphagé, près du mont des Oliviers, Jésus envoya deux Disciples ;

2. Leur disant : Allez à la bourgade qui est devant vous ; vous y trouverez d'abord une ânesse attachée, et *son* ânon avec elle ; détachez-les et amenez-les-moi.

3. Et si quelqu'un vous dit quelque chose, vous direz que le Seigneur en a besoin ; et aussitôt il les envoiera.

6. Les Disciples s'en allèrent donc, et firent comme Jésus leur avoit ordonné.

7. Et ils amenèrent l'ânesse et l'ânon, et ayant mis leurs vêtemens dessus, ils l'y firent asseoir.

8. Alors des gens en grand nombre étendoient leurs vêtemens par le chemin ; et d'autres coupoient des branches d'arbres, et les étendoient par le chemin.

10. Et quand il fut entré dans Jérusalem, toute la ville fut émue, et on disoit : Qui est celui-ci ?

19. De sorte que les Pharisiens disoient entr'eux : Vous voyez que vous ne gagnez rien ; voilà que tout le monde va après lui.

20. Or quelques Grecs, de ceux qui étoient montés pour adorer pendant la fête,

L. 19.

24 And he said unto them that stood by, Take from him the pound, and give *it* to him that hath ten pounds.

25 (And they said unto him, Lord, he hath ten pounds.)

26 For I say unto you, That unto every one which hath, shall be given ; and from him that hath not, even that he hath, shall be taken away from him.

27 But those mine enemies, which would not that I should reign over them, bring hither, and slay *them* before me.

28 And when he had thus spoken, he went before, ascending up to Jerusalem.

M. 21.

AND when they drew nigh unto Jerusalem, and were come to Bethpage, unto the mount of Olives, then sent Jesus two disciples,

2 Saying unto them, Go into the village over against you, and straightway ye shall find an ass tied, and a colt with her : loose *them*, and bring *them* unto me.

3 And if any *man* say aught unto you, ye shall say, The Lord hath need of them ; and straightway he will send them.

6 And the disciples went, and did as Jesus commanded them,

7 And brought the ass, and the colt, and put on them their clothes, and they set *him* thereon.

8 And a very great multitude spread their garments in the way ; others cut down branches from the trees, and strawed them in the way.

10 And when he was come into Jerusalem, all the city was moved, saying, Who is this ?

J. 12.

19 The Pharisees, therefore, said among themselves, Perceive ye how ye prevail nothing ? behold, the world is gone after him.

20 And there were certain Greeks among them, that came up to worship at the feast :

56

21 Οὗτοι ἂν προσῆλθον Φιλίππῳ τῷ ἀπὸ Βηθσαϊδὰ τῆς Γαλιλαίας, καὶ ἠρώτων αὐτὸν, λέγοντες· Κύριε, θέλομεν τὸν Ἰησοῦν ἰδεῖν.

22 Ἔρχεται Φίλιππος καὶ λέγει τῷ Ἀνδρέᾳ· καὶ πάλιν Ἀνδρέας καὶ Φίλιππος λέγουσι τῷ Ἰησοῦ.

23 Ὁ δὲ Ἰησοῦς, ἀπεκρίνατο αὐτοῖς, λέγων· Ἐλήλυθεν ἡ ὥρα ἵνα δοξασθῇ ὁ υἱὸς τοῦ ἀνθρώπου.

24 Ἀμὴν, ἀμὴν, λέγω ὑμῖν, ἐὰν μὴ ὁ κόκκος τοῦ σίτου πεσὼν εἰς τὴν γῆν ἀποθάνῃ, αὐτὸς μόνος μένει· ἐὰν δὲ ἀποθάνῃ, πολὺν καρπὸν φέρει.

17 Καὶ καταλιπὼν αὐτοὺς, ἐξῆλθεν ἔξω τῆς πόλεως εἰς Βηθανίαν· καὶ ηὐλίσθη ἐκεῖ.

12 Καὶ τῇ ἐπαύριον ἐξελθόντων αὐτῶν ἀπὸ Βηθανίας,

εἰσελθὼν ὁ Ἰησοῦς εἰς τὸ ἱερόν, ἤρξατο ἐκβάλλειν τοὺς πωλοῦντας καὶ ἀγοράζοντας ἐν τῷ ἱερῷ· καὶ τὰς τραπέζας τῶν κολλυβιστῶν, καὶ τὰς καθέδρας τῶν πωλούντων τὰς περιστερὰς κατέστρεψε.

16 Καὶ οὐκ ἤφιεν ἵνα τὶς διενέγκῃ σκεῦος διὰ τοῦ ἱεροῦ.

17 Καὶ ἐδίδασκε, λέγων αὐτοῖς· Οὐ γέγραπται· Ὅτι ὁ οἶκός μου, οἶκος προσευχῆς κληθήσεται πᾶσι τοῖς ἔθνεσιν; ὑμεῖς δὲ ἐποιήσατε αὐτὸν σπήλαιον λῃστῶν.

18 Καὶ ἤκουσαν οἱ γραμματεῖς καὶ οἱ ἀρχιερεῖς, καὶ ἐζήτουν πῶς αὐτὸν ἀπολέσωσιν· ἐφοβοῦντο γὰρ αὐτὸν, ὅτι πᾶς ὁ ὄχλος ἐξεπλήσσετο ἐπὶ τῇ διδαχῇ αὐτοῦ.

19 Καὶ ὅτε ὀψὲ ἐγένετο, ἐξεπορεύετο ἔξω τῆς πόλεως.

27 Καὶ ἔρχονται πάλιν εἰς Ἱεροσόλυμα· καὶ ἐν τῷ ἱερῷ περιπατοῦντος αὐτοῦ, ἔρχονται πρὸς αὐτὸν οἱ ἀρχιερεῖς καὶ οἱ γραμματεῖς καὶ οἱ πρεσβύτεροι.

Καὶ λέγει αὐτοῖς·

28 Τί δὲ ὑμῖν δοκεῖ; Ἄνθρωπος εἶχε τέκνα δύο, καὶ προσελθὼν τῷ πρώτῳ, εἶπε· Τέκνον ὕπαγε, σήμερον ἐργάζου ἐν τῷ ἀμπελῶνί μου.

29 Ὁ δὲ ἀποκριθεὶς, εἶπεν· Οὐ θέλω. Ὕστερον δὲ μεταμεληθεὶς, ἀπῆλθε.

30 Καὶ προσελθὼν τῷ δευτέρῳ, εἶπεν ὡσαύτως. Ὁ δὲ ἀποκριθεὶς, εἶπεν· Ἐγὼ κύριε· καὶ οὐκ ἀπῆλθε.

31 Τίς ἐκ τῶν δύο ἐποίησε τὸ θέλημα τοῦ πατρός; Λέγουσιν αὐτῷ· Ὁ πρῶτος. Λέγει αὐτοῖς ὁ Ἰησοῦς· Ἀμὴν λέγω ὑμῖν, ὅτι οἱ τελῶναι καὶ αἱ πόρναι προάγουσιν ὑμᾶς εἰς τὴν βασιλείαν τοῦ Θεοῦ.

21 Hi ergo accesserunt Philippo illi à Bethsaida Galilææ: & rogabant eum, dicentes: Domine, volumus Jesum videre.

22 Venit Philippus, & dicit Andreæ: & rursum Andreas & Philippus dicunt Jesu.

23 At Jesus respondit eis, dicens: Venit hora ut glorificetur filius hominis.

24 Amen, amen, dico vobis, si non granum frumenti cadens in terram mortuum fuerit, ipsum solum manet: si autem mortuum fuerit, multum fructum affert.

17 Et relinquens ipsos, abiit extra civitatem in Bethaniam, & diversatus est ibi.

12 Et postera die exeuntibus illis de Bethania,

ingressus Jesus in templum, cœpit ejicere vendentes & ementes in templo: & mensas nummulariorum, & cathedras vendentium columbas evertit.

16 Et non sinebat ut quisquam transferret vas per templum.

17 Et docebat, dicens eis: Nonne scriptum est, Quia domus mea, domus orationis vocatur omnibus gentibus? vos autem fecistis eam speluncam latronum.

18 Et audierunt Scribæ, & principes Sacerdotum, & quærebant quomodo eum perderent: timebant enim eum, quia omnis turba admirabatur super doctrina ejus.

19 Et quum vespera facta esset, egrediebatur ex civitate.

27 Et veniunt rursus in Hierosolymam: Et in templo deambulante ipso, accedunt ad eum summi sacerdotes, & Scribæ, & seniores.

Et dicit eis:

28 Quid autem vobis videtur? Homo quidam habebat natos duos: & accedens primo, dixit: Fili, vade, hodie operare in vinea mea.

29 Ille autem respondens, ait: Nolo. Postea autem pœnitentiâ affectus, abiit.

30 Et accedens alteri, dixit similiter. Ille verò respondens, ait: Ego Domine, & non abiit.

31 Quis ex duobus fecit voluntatem patris? Dicunt ei: Primus. Dicit illis Jesus: Amen dico vobis, quod publicani & meretrices præeunt vobis in regnum Dei.

21. Vinrent vers Philippe, qui étoit de Bethsaïde en Galilée, et ils lui dirent en le priant: Seigneur, nous voudrions bien voir Jésus.

22. Philippe vint et le dit à André, et André et Philippe le dirent à Jésus.

23. Et Jésus leur répondit: L'heure est venue que le Fils de l'homme doit être glorifié.

24. En vérité, en vérité je vous le dis: Si le grain de froment ne meurt après qu'on l'a jeté dans la terre, il demeure seul; mais s'il meurt, il porte beaucoup de fruit.

17. Et les ayant laissés, il sortit de la ville, et s'en alla à Béthanie, où il passa la nuit.

12. Le lendemain, comme ils sortoient de Béthanie.

Jésus étant entré dans le Temple, se mit à chasser ceux qui vendoient et qui achetoient dans le Temple, et il renversa les tables des changeurs, et les siéges de ceux qui vendoient des pigeons.

16. Et il ne permettoit pas que personne portât *aucun* vaisseau par le Temple.

17. Et il les instruisoit, en leur disant: N'est-il pas écrit: Ma maison sera appelée, par toutes les nations, une maison de prière; mais vous en avez fait une caverne de voleurs?

18. Ce que les Scribes et les principaux Sacrificateurs ayant entendu, ils cherchoient les moyens de le faire périr; car ils le craignoient, parce que tout le peuple étoit ravi de sa doctrine.

19. Le soir étant venu, Jésus sortit de la ville.

27. Puis ils revinrent à Jérusalem; et comme il alloit par le Temple, les principaux Sacrificateurs, les Scribes, et les Sénateurs, s'approchèrent de lui;

Et il leur dit

28. Mais que vous semble-t-il de ceci? Un homme avoit deux fils; et s'adressant au premier, il *lui* dit: *Mon* fils, va, et travaille aujourd'hui dans ma vigne.

29. Mais il répondit: Je n'y veux point *aller*; cependant s'étant repenti ensuite, il y alla.

30. Puis il vint à l'autre, et lui dit la même chose. Celui-ci répondit: J'y *vais*, Seigneur; mais il n'y alla pas.

51. Lequel des deux fit la volonté de *son* père? Ils lui dirent: C'est le premier. Jésus leur dit: Je vous dis en vérité, que les péagers et les femmes de mauvaise vie, vous devancent au Royaume de Dieu.

21 The same came, therefore, to Philip, which was of Bethsaida of Galilee, and desired him, saying, Sir, we would see Jesus.

22 Philip cometh and telleth Andrew; and again, Andrew and Philip tell Jesus.

23 And Jesus answered them, saying,

24 Verily, verily, I say unto you, Except a corn of wheat fall into the ground and die, it abideth alone: but if it die, it bringeth forth much fruit.

17 And he left them, and went out of the city into Bethany; and he lodged there.

12 And on the morrow, when they were come from Bethany,

15. Jesus went into the temple, and began to cast out them that sold and bought in the temple, and overthrew the tables of the moneychangers, and the seats of them that sold doves;

16 And would not suffer that any man should carry *any* vessel through the temple.

17 And he taught, saying unto them, Is it not written, My house shall be called of all nations the house of prayer? but ye have made it a den of thieves.

18 And the scribes and chief priests heard *it*, and sought how they might destroy him: for they feared him, because all the people was astonished at his doctrine.

19 And when even was come, he went out of the city. +27

28 But what think ye? A *certain* man had two sons; and he came to the first, and said, Son, go work to-day in my vineyard.

29 He answered and said, I will not: but afterward he repented, and went.

30 And he came to the second, and said likewise. And he answered and said, I *go*, sir: and went not.

31 Whether of them twain did the will of *his* father? They say unto him, The first. Jesus saith unto them, Verily I say unto you, That the publicans and the harlots go into the kingdom of God before you.

27 And they come again to Jerusalem: and, as he was walking in the temple, there come to him the chief priests, and the scribes, and the elders:

And he saith unto them

57

* 4 Πάλιν ἀπέςειλεν ἄλλες δέλης, λέγων· Εἴπατε τοῖς κεκλημένοις· Ἰδοὺ, τὸ ἄριςόν μου ἡτοίμασα, οἱ ταῦροί μου καὶ τὰ σιτιςὰ τεθυμένα, καὶ πάντα ἕτοιμα· δεῦτε εἰς τοὺς γάμους.

* 5 Οἱ δὲ ἀμελήσαντες, ἀπῆλθον ὁ μὲν εἰς τὸν ἴδιον ἀγρὸν, ὁ δὲ εἰς τὴν ἐμπορίαν αὐτοῦ.

6 Οἱ δὲ λοιποὶ, κρατήσαντες τοὺς δέλους αὐτοῦ, ὕβρισαν καὶ ἀπέκτειναν.

* 7 Ἀκούσας δὲ ὁ βασιλεὺς ὠργίσθη· καὶ πέμψας τὰ ςρατεύματα αὐτοῦ, ἀπώλεσε τοὺς φονεῖς ἐκείνους, καὶ τὴν πόλιν αὐτῶν ἐνέπρησεν.

8 Τότε λέγει τοῖς δέλοις αὐτοῦ· Ὁ μὲν γάμος ἕτοιμός ἐςιν, οἱ δὲ κεκλημένοι οὐκ ἦσαν ἄξιοι.

* 9 Πορεύεσθε οὖν ἐπὶ τὰς διεξόδους τῶν ὁδῶν, καὶ ὅσους ἂν εὕρητε, καλέσατε εἰς τοὺς γάμους.

10 Καὶ ἐξελθόντες οἱ δοῦλοι ἐκεῖνοι εἰς τὰς ὁδοὺς, συνήγαγον πάντας ὅσους εὗρον, πονηρούς τε καὶ ἀγαθούς· καὶ ἐπλήσθη ὁ γάμος ἀνακειμένων.

11 Εἰσελθὼν δὲ ὁ βασιλεὺς θεάσασθαι τοὺς ἀνακειμένους εἶδεν ἐκεῖ ἄνθρωπον οὐκ ἐνδεδυμένον ἔνδυμα γάμου.

12 Καὶ λέγει αὐτῷ· Ἑταῖρε, πῶς εἰσῆλθες ὧδε μὴ ἔχων ἔνδυμα γάμου; Ὁ δὲ ἐφιμώθη.

13 Τότε εἶπεν ὁ βασιλεὺς τοῖς διακόνοις· Δήσαντες αὐτοῦ πόδας καὶ χεῖρας, ἄρατε αὐτὸν, καὶ ἐκβάλετε εἰς τὸ σκότος τὸ ἐξώτερον· ἐκεῖ ἔςαι ὁ κλαυθμὸς καὶ ὁ βρυγμὸς τῶν ὀδόντων.

14 Πολλοὶ γάρ εἰσι κλητοὶ, ὀλίγοι δὲ ἐκλεκτοί.

15 Τότε πορευθέντες οἱ Φαρισαῖοι, συμβούλιον ἔλαβον ὅπως αὐτὸν παγιδεύσωσιν ἐν λόγῳ.

16 Καὶ ἀποςέλλουσιν αὐτῷ τοὺς μαθητὰς αὐτῶν μετὰ τῶν Ἡρωδιανῶν, λέγοντες· Διδάσκαλε, οἴδαμεν ὅτι ἀληθὴς εἶ, καὶ τὴν ὁδὸν τοῦ Θεοῦ ἐν ἀληθείᾳ διδάσκεις, καὶ οὐ μέλει σοι περὶ οὐδενός· οὐ γὰρ βλέπεις εἰς πρόσωπον ἀνθρώπων.

17 Εἰπὲ οὖν ἡμῖν, τί σοι δοκεῖ; ἔξεςι δοῦναι κῆνσον Καίσαρι, ἢ οὔ;

18 Γνοὺς δὲ ὁ Ἰησοῦς τὴν πονη-

for the Fr. and Eng. text see pa. 58. c. d.

---

4 Iterum misit alios servos, dicens: Dicite vocatis: Ecce praudium meum paravi, tauri mei & altilia occisa, & omnia expedita: venite ad nuptias.

5 Illi autem negligentes abierunt: ille quidem in proprium agrum, ille verò ad mercaturam suam.

6 At reliqui prehendentes servos ejus, contumeliis affecerunt, & occiderunt.

7 Audiens autem rex ille, iratus est: & mittens exercitus suos, perdidit homicidas illos, & civitatem illorum incendit.

8 Tunc ait servis suis: Quidem nuptiæ expeditæ sunt: qui autem vocati non fuerunt digni.

9 Ite ergo ad compita viarum, & quascumque inveneritis, vocate ad nuptias.

10 Et egressi servi illi in vias congregaverunt omnes quos invenerunt, malosque & bonos: & impletæ sunt nuptiæ discumbentium.

11 Ingressus autem rex spectare discumbentes, vidit ibi hominem non vestitum indumentum nuptiarum.

12 Et ait illi: Amice, quomodo intrasti huc, non habens vestem nuptialem? Ille verò ore occlusus est.

13 Tunc dixit rex ministris: Ligantes ejus pedes & manus, tollite eum, & ejicite in tenebras exteriores: ibi erit fletus & fremitus dentium.

14 Multi enim sunt vocati, pauci verò electi.

15 Tunc abeuntes Pharisæi, consilium sumpserunt ut eum illaquearent in sermone.

16 Et mittunt ei discipulos suos cum Herodianis, dicentes: Magister, scimus quia verax es, & viam Dei in veritate doces: & non est cura tibi de aliquo: non enim respicis in faciem hominum.

17 Dic ergo nobis, quid tibi videtur? Licet dare censum Cæsari, an non?

18 Cognoscens autem Jesus

33. Ecoutez une autre similitude.
Un homme, dit-il, planta une vigne, il l'environna d'une haie, il y fit un creux pour un pressoir, il y bâtit une tour, et il la loua à des vignerons, et s'en alla.

2. Et dans la saison, il envoya un de ses serviteurs vers les vignerons, afin de recevoir d'eux du fruit de la vigne.

3. Mais l'ayant pris, ils le battirent, et le renvoyèrent à vuide.

4. Il leur envoya encore un autre serviteur; mais ils lui jetèrent des pierres, et lui meurtrirent toute la tête, et le renvoyèrent, après l'avoir traité outrageusement.

5. Et il en envoya encore un autre qu'ils tuèrent; et plusieurs autres, dont ils battirent les uns, et tuèrent les autres.

6. Enfin, ayant un fils qu'il chérissoit, il le leur envoya encore le dernier, disant, ils auront du respect pour mon fils.

7. Mais ces vignerons dirent entr'eux: C'est ici l'héritier; venez, tuons-le, et l'héritage sera à nous.

8. Et le prenant, ils le tuèrent, et le jetèrent hors de la vigne.

9. Que fera donc le maître de la vigne? Il viendra, et fera périr ces vignerons, et il donnera la vigne à d'autres.

10. Et quand les principaux Sacrificateurs et les Pharisiens eurent entendu ces similitudes, ils reconnurent qu'il parloit d'eux.

46. Et ils cherchoient à se saisir de lui; mais ils craignirent le peuple, parce qu'il regardoit *Jésus* comme un Prophète.

Jésus, prenant la parole, continua à leur parler en paraboles, et leur dit:

2. Le Royaume des cieux est semblable à un Roi, qui fit les noces de son Fils.

3. Et il envoya ses serviteurs pour appeler ceux qui avoient été invités aux noces; mais ils n'y voulurent point venir.

---

33 Hear another parable: A *certain* *M.* 21
man planted a vineyard, and set *Mk.* 12
an hedge about *it*, and digged *a place for* the wine-fat, and built a tower, and let it out to husbandmen, and went into a far country.

2 And at the season he sent to the husbandmen a servant, that he might receive from the husbandmen of the fruit of the vineyard.

3 And they caught *him*, and beat *him*, and sent *him* away empty.

4 And again he sent unto them another servant; and at him they cast stones, and wounded *him* in the head, and sent *him* away shamefully handled.

5 And again he sent another; and him they killed, and many others; beating some, and killing some.

6 Having yet, therefore, one son, his well-beloved, he sent him also last unto them, saying, They will reverence my son.

7 But those husbandmen said among themselves, This is the heir; come, let us kill him, and the inheritance shall be ours.

8 And they took him, and killed *him*, and cast *him* out of the vineyard.

9 What shall, therefore, the lord of the vineyard do? he will come and destroy the husbandmen, and will give the vineyard unto others.

45 And when the chief priests *M.* 21
and Pharisees had heard his parables, they perceived that he spake of them.

46 But when they sought to lay hands on him, they feared the multitude, because they took him for a prophet.

And Jesus answered, and *M.* 22
spake unto them again by parables, and said,

2 The kingdom of heaven is like unto a certain king, which made a marriage for his son,

3 And sent forth his servants to call them that were bidden to the wedding; and they would not come.

for the Gr. & Lat. text see next page. col. a. b.

58

Ἀμπε-
λῶνα ἐφύτευσεν ἄνθρωπ۞, ἢ πε-
ριέθηκε ‡ φραγμὸν, ἢ ‡ ὤρυξεν
† ὑπολήνιον, ἢ ‡ ᾠκοδόμησε
† πύργον, ἢ ‡ ἐξέδοτο αὐτὸν ‡
γεωργοῖς· ἢ ἀπεδήμησε.

2 Καὶ ἀπέςειλε πρὸς τὰς
γεωργὰς τῷ καιρῷ δῦλον, ἵνα
παρὰ τῶν γεωργῶν λάβῃ ἀπὸ τῶ
καρπῶ τῶ ἀμπελῶν۞.

3 Οἱ δὲ, λαβόντες αὐτὸν, ἔ-
δειραν, ἢ ἀπέςειλαν κενόν.

4 Καὶ πάλιν ἀπέςειλε πρὸς
αὐτὲς ἄλλον δῦλον· ‡ κἀκεῖνον
λιθοβολήσαντες † ἐκεφαλαίωσαν,
ἢ ἀπέςειλαν † ἠτιμωμένον.

5 Καὶ πάλιν ἄλλον ἀπέςειλε·
κἀκεῖνον ἀπέκλειναν· ἢ πολλὰς
ἄλλυς, τὰς μὲν δέροντες, τὰς δὲ
ἀποκλείνοντες.

6 Ἔτι ἓν ἕνα υἱὸν ἔχων ἀγα-
πητὸν αὐτῶ, ἀπέςειλε ἢ αὐτὸν
πρὸς αὐτὰς ἔσχατον, λέγων· Ὅτι
ἐνθραπήσονλαι τὸν υἱόν μυ.

7 Ἐκεῖνοι δὲ οἱ γεωργοὶ εἶπον
πρὸς ἑαυτὰς· Ὅτι ὗτός ἐςιν ὁ
κληρονόμ۞· δεῦτε, ἀποκλείνω-
μεν αὐτὸν, ἢ ἡμῶν ἔςαι ἡ κλη-
ρονομία.

8 Καὶ λαβόντες αὐτὸν, ἀπ-
έκλειναν, ἢ ἐξέβαλον ἔξω τῶ ἀμ-
πελῶν۞.

9 Τί ἓν ποιήσει ὁ κύρι۞ τῶ
ἀμπελῶν۞; Ἐλεύσεται ἢ ἀπολέσει τὰς γεωργὰς, ἢ δώσει τὸν
ἀμπελῶνα ἄλλοις.

45 Καὶ ἀκέσαντες οἱ ἀρχιερεῖς
ἢ οἱ Φαρισαῖοι τὰς παραβολὰς
αὐτῶ, ἔγνωσαν ὅτι περὶ αὐτῶν
λέγει.

46 Καὶ ζητῶντες αὐτὸν κρατῆ-
σαι, ἐφοβήθησαν τὰς ὄχλυς, ἐ-
πειδὴ ὡς προφήτην αὐτὸν εἶχον.
24. † 2.

Κεφ. κβ'. 22.

1 Κ ΑΙ ἀποκριθεὶς ὁ Ἰησῦς, πάλιν εἶπεν αὐτοῖς ἐν παραβολαῖς, λέγων·

2 Ὡμοιώθη ἡ βασιλεία τῶν ὐ-
ρανῶν ἀνθρώπῳ βασιλεῖ, ὅςις ἐ-
ποίησε γάμυς τῷ υἱῷ αὐτῶ·

3 Καὶ ἀπέςειλε τὰς δῦλυς αὐτῶ καλέσαι τὰς κεκλημένυς εἰς
τὰς γάμυς· ἢ οὐκ ἤθελον ἐλθεῖν.

Vineam plan-
tavit homo, & circumposuit
sepem, & fodit lacum, & ædificavit turrim, & elocavit eam
agricolis, & peregre profectus
est.

2 Et misit ad agricolas tempore servum, ut ab agricolis
acciperet de fructu vineæ.

3 Illi autem sumentes eum
ceciderunt, & dimiserunt va-
cuum.

4 Et iterum misit ad illos
alium servum: & illum lapi-
dantes in capite vulneraverunt,
& ablegaverunt inhonoratum.

5 Et rursum alium misit: &
illum occiderunt, & pluresalios,
hos quidem cædentes, hos verò
occidentes.

6 Adhuc ergo unum filium
habens dilectum suum, misit
& illum ad eos novissimum, dicens: Quia reverebuntur filium
meum.

7 Illi verò agricolæ dixerunt
apud seipsos: Quod hic est hæ-
res: venite occidamus eum, &
nostra erit hæreditas.

8 Et apprehendentes eum,
occiderunt, & ejecerunt extra
vineam.

9 Quid ergo faciet dominus
vineæ? Veniet, & perdet co-
lonos, & dabit vineam aliis.

45 Et audientes principes Sacerdotum & Pharisæi parabolas
ejus, cognoverunt quod de ipsis
diceret.

46 Et quærentes eum pre-
hendere, timuerunt turbas quoniam sicut Prophetam eum habebant.

CAPUT XXII.

1 ET respondens Jesus, iterum dixit eis in parabo-
lis, dicens:

2 Simile factum est regnum
cælorum homini regi, qui fecit
nuptias filio suo:

3 Et misit servos suos vocare
vocatos ad nuptias: & nolebant
venire.

---

for the Gr. & Eng. text see preceding page c.d.

4. Il envoya encore d'autres serviteurs, avec cet ordre : Dites à ceux qui ont été invités : J'ai fait préparer mon dîner ; mes taureaux et mes bêtes grasses sont tuées, et tout est prêt ; venez aux noces.

5. Mais eux n'en tenant compte, s'en allèrent, l'un à sa métairie, et l'autre à son trafic.

6. Et les autres prirent ses serviteurs, et les outragèrent, et les tuèrent.

7. Le Roi l'ayant appris, se mit en colère, et y ayant envoyé ses troupes, il fit périr ces meurtriers, et brûla leur ville.

8. Alors il dit à ses serviteurs : Le festin des noces est prêt, mais ceux qui étoient invités n'en étoient pas dignes.

9. Allez donc dans les carrefours des chemins, et invitez aux noces tous ceux que vous trouverez.

10. Et ses serviteurs étant allés dans les chemins, assemblèrent tous ceux qu'ils trouvèrent, tant mauvais que bons, en sorte que la salle des noces fut remplie de gens qui étoient à table.

11. Et le Roi étant entré pour voir ceux qui étoient à table, aperçut un homme qui n'avoit pas un habit de noces.

12. Et il lui dit : Mon ami, comment es-tu entré ici sans avoir un habit de noces ? Et il eut la bouche fermée.

13. Alors le Roi dit aux serviteurs : Liez-le pieds et mains, emportez-le, et le jetez dans les ténèbres de dehors ; c'est là qu'il y aura des pleurs et des grincemens de dents.

14. Car il y en a beaucoup d'appelés, mais peu d'élus.

15. Alors les Pharisiens s'étant retirés, consultèrent pour le surprendre dans ses discours.

16. Et ils lui envoyèrent de leurs disciples, avec des Hérodiens, qui lui dirent : Maître, nous savons que tu es sincère, et que tu enseignes la voie de Dieu selon la vérité, sans avoir égard à qui que ce soit ; car tu ne regardes point l'apparence des hommes.

17. Dis-nous donc ce qui te semble de ceci : Est-il permis de payer le tribut à César, ou non ?

18. Mais Jésus connoissant leur

for the Gr. & Lat. text see pa. 57. col. a. b.

4 Again, he sent forth other servants, saying, Tell them which are bidden, Behold, I have prepared my dinner: my oxen and *my* fatlings *are* killed, and all things *are* ready: come unto the marriage.

5 But they made light of *it*, and went their ways, one to his farm, another to his merchandise:

6 And the remnant took his servants, and intreated *them* spitefully, and slew *them*.

7 But when the king heard *thereof*, he was wroth: and he sent forth his armies, and destroyed those murderers, and burnt up their city.

8 Then saith he to his servants, The wedding is ready, but they which were bidden were not worthy.

9 Go ye therefore into the highways, and, as many as ye shall find, bid to the marriage.

10 So those servants went out into the highways, and gathered together all as many as they found, both bad and good: and the wedding was furnished with guests.

11 And when the king came in to see the guests, he saw there a man which had not on a wedding garment:

12 And he saith unto him, Friend, how camest thou in hither, not having a wedding garment? And he was speechless.

13 Then saith the king to the servants, Bind him hand and foot, and take him away; and cast *him* into outer darkness; there shall be weeping and gnashing of teeth.

14 For many are called, but few *are* chosen.

15 Then went the Pharisees, and took counsel how they might entangle him in *his* talk.

16 And they sent out unto him their disciples, with the Herodians, saying, Master, we know that thou art true, and teachest the way of God in truth, neither carest thou for any *man*: for thou regardest not the person of men.

17 Tell us, therefore, What thinkest thou? Is it lawful to give tribute unto Cesar, or not?

18 But Jesus perceived their

...ξίαν αὐτῶν, εἶπε· Τί με πειράζετε ὑποκριταί;

19 ‡ Ἐπιδείξατέ μοι τὸ † νόμισμα τῦ ‡ κήνσυ. Οἱ δὲ προσήνεγκαν αὐτῷ δηνάριον.

* 20 Καὶ λέγει αὐτοῖς· Τίνος ἡ εἰκὼν αὕτη κ̀ ἡ ‡ ἐπιγραφή;

21 Λέγυσιν αὐτῷ· Καίσαρος. Τότε λέγει αὐτοῖς· Ἀπόδοτε ὖν τὰ Καίσαρος, Καίσαρι· κ̀ τὰ τῦ Θεῦ, τῷ Θεῷ.

22 Καὶ ἀκύσαντες ἐθαύμασαν· κ̀ ἀφέντες αὐτὸν ἀπῆλθον.

23 Ἐν ἐκείνῃ τῇ ἡμέρᾳ προσῆλθον αὐτῷ Σαδδυκαῖοι, οἱ λέγοντες μὴ εἶναι ἀνάστασιν· κ̀ ἐπηρώτησαν αὐτὸν,

* 24 Λέγοντες· Διδάσκαλε, Μωσῆς εἶπεν· Ἐάν τις ἀποθάνῃ μὴ ἔχων τέκνα, † ἐπιγαμβρεύσει ὁ ‡ ἀδελφὸς αὐτῦ τὴν γυναῖκα αὐτῦ, κ̀ ἀναστήσει σπέρμα τῷ ἀδελφῷ αὐτῦ.

25 Ἦσαν δὲ παρ᾽ ἡμῖν ἑπτὰ ἀδελφοί· κ̀ ὁ πρῶτος, γαμήσας, ἐτελεύτησε· κ̀ μὴ ἔχων σπέρμα, ἀφῆκε τὴν γυναῖκα αὐτῦ τῷ ἀδελφῷ αὐτῦ.

26 Ὁμοίως κ̀ ὁ δεύτερος, κ̀ ὁ τρίτος, ἕως τῶν ἑπτά.

27 Ὕστερον δὲ πάντων ἀπέθανε κ̀ ἡ γυνή.

28 Ἐν τῇ ὖν ἀναστάσει, τίνος τῶν ἑπτὰ ἔσαι γυνή; πάντες γὰρ ἔσχον αὐτήν.

29 Ἀποκριθεὶς δὲ ὁ Ἰησῦς εἶπεν αὐτοῖς· Πλανᾶσθε, μὴ εἰδότες τὰς γραφάς, μηδὲ τὴν δύναμιν τῦ Θεῦ.

30 Ἐν γὰρ τῇ ἀναστάσει ὖτε γαμῦσιν, ὖτε ἐκγαμίζονται· ἀλλ᾽ ὡς ἄγγελοι τῦ Θεῦ ἐν ἀρανῷ εἰσι.

31 Περὶ δὲ τῆς ἀναστάσεως τῶν νεκρῶν ἀκ ἀνέγνωτε τὸ ῥηθὲν ὑμῖν ὑπὸ τῦ Θεῦ, λέγοντος·

32 Ἐγώ εἰμι ὁ Θεὸς Ἀβραάμ, κ̀ ὁ Θεὸς Ἰσαὰκ, κ̀ ὁ Θεὸς Ἰακώβ; ἀκ ἔστιν ὁ Θεὸς, Θεὸς νεκρῶν, ἀλλὰ ζώντων.

33 Καὶ ἀκύσαντες οἱ ὄχλοι, ἐξεπλήσσοντο ἐπὶ τῇ διδαχῇ αὐτῦ.

---

nequitiam eorum, ait: Quid me tentatis hypocritæ?

19 Ostendite mihi numisma census. Illi verò obtulerunt ei denarium.

20 Et ait illis: Cujus imago hæc, & superscriptio?

21 Dicunt ei: Cæsaris. Tunc ait illis: Reddite ergò quæ Cæsaris, Cæsari: & quæ Dei, Deo.

22 Et audientes mirati sunt: & relinquentes eum abierunt.

23 In illo die accesserunt ad eum Sadducæi, dicentes non esse resurrectionem: & interrogaverunt eum,

24 Dicentes: Magister, Moses dixit: Si quis mortuus fuerit non habens genitos, ob affinitatem ducet frater ejus uxorem illius, &, suscitabit semen fratri suo.

25 Erant autem apud nos septem fratres: & primus uxore ductâ, obiit: & non habens semen, reliquit uxorem suam fratri suo.

26 Similiter & secundus, & tertius usque ad septem.

27 Postremum autem omnium defuncta est & mulier.

28 In ergò resurrectione, cujus septem erit uxor? omnes enim habuerunt eam.

29 Respondens autem Jesus, ait illis: Erratis, nescientes Scripturas, neque efficaciam Dei.

30 In enim resurrectione neque nubent, neque dantur nuptui, sed sicut angeli Dei in cælo sunt.

31 De autem resurrectione mortuorum, non legistis effatum vobis à Deo, dicénte:

32 Ego sum Deus Abraham, & Deus Isaac, & Deus Jacob, Non est Deus, Deus mortuorum, sed viventium.

33 Et audientes turbæ, percellebantur in doctrina ejus.

malice, leur dit : Hypocrites, pourquoi me tentez-vous ?

19. Montrez-moi la monnoie *dont on paie* le tribut. Et ils lui présentèrent un denier.

20. Et il leur dit : De qui est cette image et cette inscription ?

21. Ils lui dirent : De César. Alors il leur dit : Rendez donc à César ce qui appartient à César, et à Dieu ce qui appartient à Dieu.

22. Et ayant entendu *cette réponse*, ils l'admirèrent ; et le laissant, ils s'en allèrent.

23. Ce jour-là, les Sadducéens, qui disent qu'il n'y a point de résurrection, vinrent à *Jésus*, et lui firent cette question :

24. Maître, Moyse a dit : Si quelqu'un meurt sans enfans, son frère épousera sa veuve, et suscitera lignée à son frère.

25. Or, il y avoit parmi nous sept frères, dont le premier s'étant marié mourut ; et n'ayant point eu d'enfans, il laissa sa femme à son frère.

26. De même aussi le second, puis le troisième, jusqu'au septième.

27. Or, après eux tous, la femme mourut aussi.

28. Duquel donc des sept sera-t-elle femme dans la résurrection ; car tous *les sept* l'ont eue ?

29. Mais Jésus répondant, leur dit : Vous êtes dans l'erreur, parce que vous n'entendez pas les Ecritures, ni quelle est la puissance de Dieu.

30. Car après la résurrection, les hommes ne prendront point de femmes, ni les femmes de maris ; mais ils seront comme les Anges de Dieu, qui sont dans le ciel.

31. Et quant à la résurrection des morts, n'avez-vous point lu ce que Dieu vous a dit :

32. Je suis le Dieu d'Abraham, le Dieu d'Isaac, et le Dieu de Jacob. Dieu n'est pas le Dieu des morts, mais *il est le Dieu* des vivans.

33. Et le peuple entendant *cela*, admiroit sa doctrine.

wickedness, and said, Why tempt ye me, *ye* hypocrites?

19 Shew me the tribute-money. And they brought unto him a penny.

20 And he saith unto them, Whose *is* this image and superscription?

21 They say unto him, Cesar's. Then saith he unto them, Render, therefore, unto Cesar the things which are Cesar's ; and unto God the things that are God's.

22 When they had heard *these words*, they marvelled, and left him, and went their way.

23 The same day came to him the Sadducees, which say that there is no resurrection, and asked him,

24 Saying, Master, Moses said, If a man die, having no children, his brother shall marry his wife, and raise up seed unto his brother.

25 Now, there were with us seven brethren : and the first, when he had married a wife, deceased ; and having no issue, left his wife unto his brother :

26 Likewise the second also, and the third, unto the seventh.

27 And last of all the woman died also.

28 Therefore, in the resurrection, whose wife shall she be of the seven ? for they all had her.

29 Jesus answered, and said unto them, Ye do err, not knowing the scriptures, nor the power of God.

30 For in the resurrection they neither marry, nor are given in marriage ; but are as the angels of God in heaven.

31 But as touching the resurrection of the dead, have ye not read that which was spoken unto you by God, saying,

32 I am the God of Abraham, and the God of Isaac, and the God of Jacob ? God is not the God of the dead, but of the living.

33 And when the multitude heard *this*, they were astonished at his doctrine.

60

28 Καὶ προσελθὼν εἷς τῶν γραμματέων, ἀκύσας αὐτῶν συζητύντων, εἰδὼς ὅτι καλῶς αὐτοῖς ἐπεκρίθη, ἐπηρώτησεν αὐτόν· Ποία ἐςὶ πρώτη πασῶν ἐντολή;

29 Ὁ δὲ Ἰησοῦς ἀπεκρίθη αὐτῷ· Ὅτι πρώτη πασῶν τῶν ἐντολῶν· Ἄκυε Ἰσραὴλ, Κύρι⊙, ὁ Θεὸς ἡμῶν, Κύρι⊙ εἷς ἐςι.

30 Καὶ ἀγαπήσεις Κύριον τὸν Θεόν σε ἐξ ὅλης τῆς καρδίας σε, κ̀ ἐξ ὅλης τῆς ψυχῆς σε, κ̀ ἐξ ὅλης τῆς διανοίας σε, κ̀ ἐξ ὅλης τῆς ἰσχύ⊙ σε· αὕτη πρώτη ἐντολή.

31 Καὶ δευτέρα ὁμοία αὕτη· Ἀγαπήσεις τὸν πλησίον σε ὡς σεαυτόν· μείζων τύτων ἄλλη ἐντολὴ ἐκ ἔςι.

40 Ἐν ταύταις ταῖς δυσὶν ἐντολαῖς ὅλ⊙ ὁ νόμ⊙ κ̀ οἱ προφῆται κρέμανλαι.

32 Καὶ εἶπεν αὐτῷ ὁ γραμματεύς· Καλῶς, διδάσκαλε, ἐπ᾽ ἀληθείας εἶπας, ὅτι εἷς ἐςι Θεὸς, κ̀ ἐκ ἔςιν ἄλλ⊙ πλὴν αὐτοῦ·

33 Καὶ τὸ ἀγαπᾷν αὐτὸν ἐξ ὅλης τῆς καρδίας, κ̀ ἐξ ὅλης τῆς συνέσεως, κ̀ ἐξ ὅλης τῆς ψυχῆς, κ̀ ἐξ ὅλης τῆς ἰσχύ⊙, κ̀ τὸ ἀγαπᾷν τὸν πλησίον ὡς ἑαυτὸν, πλεῖόν ἐςι πάνλων τῶν ὁλοκαυτωμάτων κ̀ τῶν θυσιῶν.

Κεφ. κγ. 23.

1 Τότε ὁ Ἰησᾶς ἐλάλησε τοῖς ὄχλοις κ̀ τοῖς μαθηταῖς

2 Λέγων· Ἐπὶ τῆς Μωσέως καθέδρας ἐκάθισαν οἱ Γραμματεῖς κ̀ οἱ Φαρισαῖοι·

3 Πάνλα ἒν ὅσα ἂν εἴπωσιν ὑμῖν τηρεῖν, τηρεῖτε κ̀ ποιεῖτε· καλὰ δὲ τὰ ἔργα αὐτῶν μὴ ποιεῖτε· λέγυσι γὰρ, κ̀ ᾿ ποιῦσι.

4 Δεσμεύυσι γὰρ φορλία βαρέα κ̀ δυσβάςακλα, κ̀ ἐπιλιθέασιν ἐπὶ τὰς ὤμες τῶν ἀνθρώπων· τῷ δὲ δακτύλῳ αὐτῶν ᾿ θέλυσι κινῆσαι αὐτά·

* 5 Πάνλα δὲ τὰ ἔργα αὐτῶν ποιῦσι πρὸς τὸ ‡ θεαθῆναι τοῖς ἀνθρώποις· ‡ πλατύνυσι δὲ τὰ † φυλακλήρια αὐτῶν, κ̀ μεγαλύνυσι τὰ κράσπεδα τῶν ἱμαλίων αὐτῶν.

* 6 ‡ Φιλῦσί ‡ τε τὴν ‡ πρωτοκλισίαν ἐν τοῖς ‡ δείπνοις, κ̀ τὰς ‡ πρωλοκαθεδρίας ἐν ταῖς συναγωγαῖς,

28 Et accedens unus Scribarum, audiens illos conquirentes, videns quod pulchre illis responderit, interrogavit eum: quod esset primum omnium mandatum?

29 At Jesus respondit ei, quia primum omnium mandatorum: Audi Israël, Dominus Deus noster, Dominus unus est.

30 Et diliges Dominum Deum tuum ex toto corde tuo, & ex tota anima tua, & ex tota cogitatione tua, & ex tota virtute tua. Hoc primum mandatum.

31 Et secundum simile huic: Diliges proximum tuum ut teipsum. Majus horum aliud mandatum non est.

40 In his duobus mandatis universa Lex & Prophetæ pendent.

32 Et ait illi Scriba: Pulchre Magister in veritate dixisti, quia unus est Deus, & non est alius præter eum.

33 Et diligere eum ex toto corde, & ex toto intellectu, & ex tota anima, & ex tota fortitudine: & diligere proximum ut seipsum, plus est omnibus holocautomatibus, & sacrificiis.

CAPUT XXIII.

1 Tunc Jesus loquutus est turbis, & discipulis:

2 Dicens: Super Mosi cathedram sederunt Scribæ & Pharisæi:

3 Omnia ergò quæcumque dixerint vobis servare, servate & facite: secundùm verò opera eorum ne facite: dicunt enim, & non faciunt.

4 Alligant enim onera gravia & importabilia, & imponunt in humeros hominum: at digito suo non volunt movere ea.

5 Omnia verò opera sua faciunt adspectari hominibus, dilatant verò phylacteria sua, & magnificant fimbrias vestimentorum suorum.

6 Amantque primos recubitus in cœnis, & primas cathedras in synagogis.

28. Alors un des Scribes, qui les avoit ouï disputer ensemble, voyant qu'il leur avoit bien répondu, s'approcha, et lui demanda : Quel est le premier de tous les commandemens?

29. Jésus lui répondit : Le premier de tous les commandemens *est celui-ci* : Ecoute Israël, le Seigneur notre Dieu est le seul Seigneur.

30. Tu aimeras le Seigneur ton Dieu, de tout ton cœur, de toute ton ame, de toute ta pensée, et de toute ta force. C'est là le premier commandement.

31. Et voici le second, *qui lui est* semblable : Tu aimeras ton prochain comme toi-même. Il n'y a point d'autre commandement, plus grand que ceux-ci.

40. Toute la loi et les Prophètes se rapportent à ces deux commandemens.

32. Et le Scribe lui répondit : Maître, tu as bien dit, et selon la vérité, qu'il n'y a qu'un seul Dieu, et qu'il n'y en a point d'autre que lui ;

33. Et que l'aimer de tout son cœur, de toute *son* intelligence, de toute *son* ame, et de toute sa force, et aimer *son* prochain comme soi-même, c'est plus que tous les holocaustes et que tous les sacrifices.

Alors Jésus parla au peuple, et à ses Disciples,

2. Et leur dit : Les Scribes et les Pharisiens sont assis sur la chaire de Moyse.

3. Observez donc, et faites tout ce qu'ils vous diront d'observer ; mais ne faites pas comme ils font ; parce qu'ils disent et ne font pas.

4. Car ils lient des fardeaux pesans et insupportables, et les mettent sur les épaules des hommes ; mais ils ne voudroient pas les remuer du doigt.

5. Et ils font toutes leurs actions, afin que les hommes les voient ; car ils portent de larges phylactères, et ils ont de plus longues franges à leurs habits ;

6. Ils aiment à avoir les premières places dans les festins, et les premiers siéges dans les Synagogues ;

28 And one of the scribes came, and having heard them reasoning together, and perceiving that he had answered them well, asked him, Which is the first commandment of all?

29 And Jesus answered him, The first of all the commandments *is*, Hear, O Israel ; The Lord our God is one Lord :

30 And thou shalt love the Lord thy God with all thy heart, and with all thy soul, and with all thy mind, and with all thy strength. This *is* the first commandment.

31 And the second *is* like, *namely* this, Thou shalt love thy neighbour as thyself. There is none other commandment greater than these.

40 On these two commandments hang all the law and the prophets.

32 And the scribe said unto him, Well, Master, thou hast said the truth : for there is one God ; and there is none other but he :

33 And to love him with all the heart, and with all the understanding, and with all the soul, and with all the strength, and to love *his* neighbour as himself, is more than all whole burnt-offerings and sacrifices.

CHAP. XXIII.
The Pharisees exposed, &c.

THEN spake Jesus to the multitude, and to his disciples,

2 Saying, The scribes and the Pharisees sit in Moses' seat :

3 All therefore whatsoever they bid you observe, *that* observe and do ; but do not ye after their works : for they say and do not.

4 For they bind heavy burdens and grievous to be borne, and lay *them* on mens' shoulders ; but they *themselves* will not move them with one of their fingers.

5 But all their works they do for to be seen of men : they make broad their phylacteries, and enlarge the borders of their garments.

6 And love the uppermost rooms at feasts, and the chief seats in the synagogues.

61

7 Καὶ τοὺς ἀσπασμοὺς ἐν ταῖς ἀγοραῖς, κ καλεῖσθαι ὑπὸ τῶν ἀνθρώπων, ῥαββὶ, ῥαββί.

8 Ὑμεῖς δὲ μὴ κληθῆτε ῥαββί· εἷς γάρ ἐςιν ὑμῶν ὁ καθηγηλὴς, ὁ Χριςός· πάντες δὲ ὑμεῖς, ἀδελφοί ἐςε.

9 Καὶ πατέρα μὴ καλέσητε ὑμῶν ἐπὶ τῆς γῆς· εἷς γάρ ἐςιν ὁ πατὴρ ὑμῶν, ὁ ἐν τοῖς ὑρανοῖς.

* 10 Μηδὲ ‡ κληθῆτε ‡ καθηγηλαί· εἷς γὰρ ὑμῶν ἐςιν ὁ καθηγηλὴς, ὁ Χριςός.

11 Ὁ δὲ μείζων ὑμῶν, ἔςαι ὑμῶν διάκονο.

12 Ὅςις δὲ ὑψώσει ἑαυλὸν, ταπεινωθήσεlαι κ ὅςις ταπεινώσει ἑαυλὸν, ὑψωθήσεται.

13 Οὐαὶ δὲ ὑμῖν Γραμμαλεῖς κ Φαρισαῖοι ὑποκριλαὶ, ὅτι κλείετε τὴν βασιλείαν τῶν ὑρανῶν ἔμπροσθεν τῶν ἀνθρώπων· ὑμεῖς γὰρ ὐκ εἰσέρχεσθε, ὐδὲ τοὺς εἰσερχομένους ἀφίελε εἰσελθεῖν.

14 Οὐαὶ ὑμῖν Γραμμαλεῖς κ Φαρισαῖοι ὑποκριλαὶ, ὅτι καλεσθίετε τὰς οἰκίας τῶν χηρῶν, κ προφάσει μακρὰ προσευχόμενοι· διὰ τῦτο λήψεσθε περισσότερον κρίμα.

* 15 Οὐαὶ ὑμῖν Γραμμαλεῖς κ Φαρισαῖοι ὑποκριλαὶ, ὅτι ‡ περιάγελε τὴν θάλασσαν κ τὴν ξηρὰν, ποιῆσαι ἕνα ‡ προσήλυλον· κ ὅταν γένηλαι, ποιεῖτε αὐτὸν υἱὸν γεέννης διπλότερον ὑμῶν.

16 Οὐαὶ ὑμῖν ὁδηγοὶ τυφλοὶ, οἱ λέγονλες· Ὃς ἂν ὁμόσῃ ἐν τῷ ναῷ, ὐδέν ἐςιν· ὃς δ᾽ ἂν ὁμόσῃ ἐν τῷ χρυσῷ τῦ ναῦ, ὀφείλει.

17 Μωροὶ κ τυφλοί· τίς γὰρ μείζων ἐςὶν, ὁ χρυσὸς, ἢ ὁ ναὸς ὁ ἁγιάζων τὸν χρυσόν;

18 Καὶ Ὃς ἐὰν ὁμόσῃ ἐν τῷ θυσιαςηρίῳ, ὐδέν ἐςιν· ὃς δ᾽ ἂν ὁμόσῃ ἐν τῷ δώρῳ τῷ ἐπάνω αὐτῦ, ὀφείλει.

19 Μωροὶ κ τυφλοὶ, τί γὰρ μεῖζον; τὸ δῶρον, ἢ τὸ θυσιαςήριον τὸ ἁγιάζον τὸ δῶρον;

7 Et falutationes in foris, & vocari ab hominibus, Rabbi, Rabbi.

8 Vos autem ne vocemini Rabbi: unus enim eſt veſter doctor Chriſtus: omnes autem vos fratres eſtis.

9 Et patrem ne vocetis veſtrum ſuper terram: unus enim eſt Pater veſter qui in cælis.

10 Nec vocemini doctores: unus enim veſter eſt doctor, Chriſtus.

11 Qui verò major veſtrûm, erit veſter miniſter.

12 Qui autem exaltaverit ſeipſum, humiliabitur: & qui humiliaverit ſeipſum, exaltabitur.

13 Væ autem vobis Scribæ & Phariſæi hypocritæ, quia clauditis regnum cælorum ante homines: vos enim non intratis, nec introëuntes ſinitis intrare.

14 Væ vobis Scribæ & Phariſæi hypocritæ, quia comeditis domos viduarum, & prætextu prolixa orantes: propter hoc accipietis abundantius judicium.

15 Væ vobis Scribæ & Phariſæi hypocritæ, quia circuitis mare & aridam, facere unum proſelytum: & quum fuerit factus, facitis eum filium gehennæ, dupliciorem vobis.

16 Væ vobis duces cæci, dicentes: Quicumque juraverit in templo, nihil eſt: qui autem juraverit in auro templi, debet.

17 Stulti & cæci: quid enim majus eſt, aurum, aut templum ſanctificans aurum?

18 Et quicumque juraverit in altari, nihil eſt: quicumque autem juraverit in dono quod ſuper illud, debet.

19 Stulti & cæci: quid enim majus, donum, an altare ſanctificans donum?

7. Et à être salués dans les places publiques, et à être appelés par les hommes, Maître, Maître.

8. Mais vous, ne vous faites point appeler Maître ; car vous n'avez qu'un Maître, qui est le Christ ; et pour vous, vous êtes tous frères.

9. Et n'appelez personne sur la terre *votre* Père ; car vous n'avez qu'un seul Père, *savoir*, celui qui *est* dans les cieux.

10. Et ne vous faites point appeler Docteur ; car vous n'avez qu'un seul Docteur, qui est le Christ.

11. Mais que le plus grand d'entre vous soit votre serviteur.

12. Car quiconque s'élevera sera abaissé, et quiconque s'abaissera sera élevé.

13. Mais malheur à vous, Scribes et Pharisiens hypocrites ; parce que vous fermez aux hommes le Royaume des cieux ; vous n'y entrez point, et vous n'y laissez pas entrer ceux qui voudroient y entrer.

14. Malheur à vous, Scribes et Pharisiens hypocrites ; car vous dévorez les maisons des veuves, en affectant de faire de longues prières ; à cause de cela vous serez punis d'autant plus sévèrement.

15. Malheur à vous, Scribes et Pharisiens hypocrites ; car vous courez la mer et la terre, pour faire un prosélyte ; et quand il l'est devenu, vous le rendez digne de la géhenne deux fois plus que vous !

16. Malheur à vous, Conducteurs aveugles, qui dites : Si quelqu'un jure par le temple, cela n'est rien ; mais celui qui aura juré par l'or du temple, est obligé *de tenir son serment !*

17. Insensés et aveugles ! Car lequel est le plus considérable, ou l'or, ou le temple qui rend cet or sacré ?

18. Et si quelqu'un, *dites-vous,* jure par l'autel, cela n'est rien ; mais celui qui aura juré par le don qui est sur *l'autel,* est obligé *de tenir son serment.*

19. Insensés et aveugles ! Car lequel est le plus grand, le don, ou l'autel qui rend ce don sacré ?

7 And greetings in the markets, and to be called of men, Rabbi, Rabbi.

8 But be not ye called Rabbi ; for one is your Master, *even* Christ ; and all ye are brethren.

9 And call no *man* your Father upon the earth: for one is your Father, which is in heaven.

10 Neither be ye called masters: for one is your master, *even* Christ.

11 But he that is greatest among you shall be your servant.

12 And whosoever shall exalt himself shall be abased ; and he that shall humble himself shall be exalted.

13 But woe unto you, scribes and Pharisees, hypocrites! for ye shut up the kingdom of heaven against men: for ye neither go in *yourselves,* neither suffer ye them that are entering, to go in.

14 Woe unto you, scribes and Pharisees, hypocrites! for ye devour widows' houses, and for a pretence make long prayer: therefore ye shall receive the greater damnation.

15 Woe unto you, scribes and Pharisees, hypocrites! for ye compass sea and land to make one proselyte ; and when he is made, ye make him two-fold more the child of hell than yourselves.

16 Woe unto you, ye blind guides! which say, Whosoever shall swear by the temple, it is nothing ; but whosoever shall swear by the gold of the temple, he is a debtor.

17 *Ye* fools and blind! for whether *is* greater, the gold, or the temple that sanctifieth the gold?

18 And, whosoever shall swear by the altar, it is nothing ; but whosoever sweareth by the gift that is upon it, he is guilty.

19 *Ye* fools, and blind! for whether *is* greater, the gift, or the altar that sanctifieth the gift?

62

20. Ὁ ἂν ὀμόσας ἐν τῷ θυσιαςηρίῳ, ὀμνύει ἐν αὐτῷ ὴ ἐν πᾶσι τοῖς ἐπάνω αὐτῦ·

21 Καὶ ὁ ὀμόσας ἐν τῷ ναῷ, ὀμνύει ἐν αὐτῷ ὴ ἐν τῷ καlοικῦνlι αὐτόν.

22 Καὶ ὁ ὀμόσας ἐν τῷ ὀρανῷ, ὀμνύει ἐν τῷ θρόνῳ τῦ Θεῦ ὴ ἐν τῷ καθημένῳ ἐπάνω αὐτῦ.

* 23 Οὐαὶ ὑμῖν Γραμμαlεῖς ὴ Φαρισαῖοι ὑποκριlαὶ, ὅτι † ἀποδεκαlῦτε τὸ † ἡδύοσμον ὴ τὸ † ἄνηθον ὴ τὸ † κύμινον, ὴ ἀφήκαlε τὰ βαρύτερα τῦ νόμι, τὴν κρίσιν, ὴ τὸν ἔλεον ὴ τὴν πίσιν· Ταῦτα ἔδει ποιῆσαι, κἀκεῖνα μὴ ἀφιέναι.

* 24 † Ὁδηγοὶ τυφλοὶ, οἱ † διϋλίζονlες τὸν † κώνωπα, τὴν δὲ κάμηλον † καlαπίνοlες;

* 25 Οὐαὶ ὑμῖν Γραμμαlεῖς ὴ Φαρισαῖοι ὑποκριlαὶ, ὅτι καθαρίζεlε τὸ † ἔξωθεν τῦ ποληρίυ ὴ τῆς † παροψίδῷ, ἔσωθεν δὲ † γέμυσιν ἐξ † ἁρπαγῆς ὴ ἀκρησίας.

26 Φαρισαῖε τυφλὲ, καθάρισον πρῶτον τὸ ἐντὸς τῦ ποληρίυ ὴ τῆς παροψίδῷ, ἵνα γένηlαι ὴ τὸ ἐκlὸς αὐτῶν καθαρόν.

* 27 Οὐαὶ ὑμῖν Γραμμαlεῖς ὴ Φαρισαῖοι ὑποκριlαὶ, ὅτι † παρομμιάζεlε † τάφοις † κεκονιαμένοις, οἵτινες ἔξωθεν μέν φαίνοlαι † ὡραῖοι, † ἔξωθεν δὲ γέμυσιν ὀςέων νεκρῶν ὴ πάσης ἀκαθαρσίας.

28 Οὕτω ὴ ὑμεῖς ἔξωθεν μέν φαίνεσθε τοῖς ἀνθρώποις δίκαιοι, ἔσωθεν δὲ μεςοί ἐςε ὑποκρίσεως ὴ ἀνομίας.

29 Οὐαὶ ὑμῖν Γραμμαlεῖς ὴ Φαρισαῖοι ὑποκριlαὶ, ὅτι οἰκοδομεῖτε τὰς τάφας τῶν προφηλῶν, ὴ κοσμεῖτε τὰ μνημεῖα τῶν δικαίων·

30 Καὶ λέγεlε· Εἰ ἦμεν ἐν ταῖς ἡμέραις τῶν παlέρων ἡμῶν, ὀκ ἂν ἦμεν κοινωνοὶ αὐτῶν ἐν τῷ αἵμαlι τῶν προφηλῶν.

31 Ὥςε μαρlυρεῖlε ἑαυlοῖς, ὅτι υἱοί ἐςε τῶν φονευσάνlων τὰς προφήlας.

32 Καὶ ὑμεῖς πληρώσαlε τὸ μέτρον τῶν παlέρων ὑμῶν.

* 33 Ὄφεις, † γεννήμαlα † ἐχιδνῶν, πῶς † φύγηlε ἀπὸ τῆς κρίσεως τῆς γεέννης;

---

20 Ergo jurans in altari, jurat in eo, & in omnibus quæ super illud.

21 Et jurans in templo, jurat in illo, & in habitante illud.

22 Et jurans in cælo, jurat in throno Dei, & in sedente super eum.

23 Væ vobis Scribæ, & Pharisæi hypocritæ, quia decimatis mentham, & anethum, & cyminum, & reliquistis graviora Legis, judicium, & misericordiam, & fidem, hæc oportuit facere, & illa non omittere.

24 Duces cæci, excolantes culicem, at camelum glutientes.

25 Væ vobis Scribæ & Pharisæi hypocritæ, quia mundatis quod deforis poculi & patinæ, intus autem plena sunt ex rapina & intemperantia.

26 Pharisæe cæce, munda prius quod intus poculi, & patinæ, ut fiat & quod deforis ipsorum mundum.

27 Væ vobis Scribæ & Pharisæi hypocritæ, quia adsimilamini sepulchris dealbatis, quæ à foris quidem apparent speciosa, intus verò plena sunt ossibus mortuorum, & omni immunditia.

28 Sic & vos à foris quidem paretis hominibus justi: intus autem pleni estis hypocrisi & iniquitate.

29 Væ vobis Scribæ & Pharisæi hypocritæ, quia ædificatis sepulchra Prophetarum, & ornatis monumenta justorum:

30 Et dicitis: quod si fuissemus in diebus patrum nostrorum, non essemus communicatores eorum in sanguine Prophetarum.

31 Itaque testamini vobismetipsis, quia filii estis occidentium Prophetas.

32 Et vos implete mensuram patrum vestrorum.

33 Serpentes, geminina viperarum, quomodo fugietis à judicio gehennæ?

20. Celui donc qui jure par l'autel, jure par l'autel, et par ce qui est dessus.

21. Et celui qui jure par le temple, jure par le temple et par celui qui y habite.

22. Et celui qui jure par le ciel, jure par le trône de Dieu et par celui qui est assis dessus.

23. Malheur à vous, Scribes et Pharisiens hypocrites; car vous payez la dîme de la mente, de l'anet, et du cumin, et vous négligez les choses les plus importantes de la loi, la justice, la miséricorde, et la fidélité. Ce sont là les choses qu'il falloit faire, sans néanmoins omettre les autres.

24. Conducteurs aveugles, qui coulez un moucheron, et qui avalez un chameau.

25. Malheur à vous, Scribes et Pharisiens hypocrites; car vous nettoyez le dehors de la coupe et du plat, pendant qu'au-dedans vous êtes pleins de rapines et d'intempérance.

26. Pharisien aveugle, nettoie premièrement le dedans de la coupe et du plat, afin que ce qui est dehors devienne aussi net.

27. Malheur à vous, Scribes et Pharisiens hypocrites; car vous ressemblez à des sépulcres blanchis, qui paroissent beaux par dehors; mais qui, au-dedans, sont pleins d'ossemens de morts, et de toute sorte de pourriture.

28. De même aussi au-dehors, vous paroissez justes aux hommes, mais au-dedans, vous êtes remplis d'hypocrisie et d'injustice.

29. Malheur à vous, Scribes et Pharisiens hypocrites; car vous bâtissez les tombeaux des Prophètes, et vous ornez les sépulcres des justes;

30. Et vous dites : Si nous eussions été du temps de nos pères, nous ne nous serions pas joints à eux pour répandre le sang des Prophètes.

31. Ainsi vous êtes témoins contre vous-mêmes, que vous êtes les enfans de ceux qui ont tué les Prophètes.

32. Vous *donc* aussi, vous achevez de combler la mésure de vos pères.

33. Serpens, race de vipères, comment éviterez-vous le jugement de la géhenne ?

20 Whoso, therefore, shall swear by the altar, sweareth by it, and by all things thereon.

21 And whoso shall swear by the temple, sweareth by it, and by him that dwelleth therein.

22 And he that shall swear by heaven, sweareth by the throne of God, and by him that sitteth thereon.

23 Woe unto you, scribes and Pharisees, hypocrites! for ye pay tithe of mint, and anise, and cummin, and have omitted the weightier *matters* of the law, judgment, mercy, and faith : these ought ye to have done, and not to leave the other undone.

24 *Ye* blind guides! which strain at a gnat, and swallow a camel.

25 Woe unto you, scribes and Pharisees, hypocrites! for ye make clean the outside of the cup and of the platter, but within they are full of extortion and excess.

26 *Thou* blind Pharisee! cleanse first that *which* is within the cup and platter, that the outside of them may be clean also.

27 Woe unto you, scribes and Pharisees, hypocrites! for ye are like unto whited sepulchres, which indeed appear beautiful outward, but are within full of dead *mens'* bones, and of all uncleanness.

28 Even so ye also outwardly appear righteous unto men, but within ye are full of hypocrisy and iniquity.

29 Woe unto you, scribes and Pharisees, hypocrites! because ye build the tombs of the prophets, and garnish the sepulchres of the righteous,

30 And say, If we had been in the days of our fathers, we would not have been partakers with them in the blood of the prophets.

31 Wherefore ye be witnesses unto yourselves, that ye are the children of them which killed the prophets.

32 Fill ye up then the measure of your fathers.

33 *Ye* serpents, *ye* generation of vipers! how can ye escape the damnation of hell ?

63

* 41 Καὶ καθίσας ὁ Ἰησοῦς
‡ κατέναντι τῦ ‡ γαζοφυλακίυ,
ἐθεώρει πῶς ὁ ὄχλⓈ βάλλει
χαλκὸν εἰς τὸ γαζοφυλάκιον ᾧ
πολλοὶ πλύσιοι ἔϐαλλον πολλά.
* 42 Καὶ ἐλθῦσα μία ‡ χήρα
πlωχὴ ἔϐαλε ‡ λεπτὰ δύο, ὅ ἐςι
‡ κοδϱάντης.

43 Καὶ προσκαλεσάμενⓈ τὰς
μαθητὰς αὐτῦ, λέγει αὐτοῖς·
Ἀμὴν λέγω ὑμῖν, ὅτι ἡ χήρα
αὕτη ἡ πlωχὴ πλεῖον πάνίων
βέϐληκε τῶν βαλόνίων εἰς τὸ γαζοφυλάκιον.

44 Πάνίες γὰρ ἐκ τῦ περισ-
σεύονίⓈ αὐτοῖς ἔϐαλον· αὕτη δὲ
ἐκ τῆς ὑςερήσεως αὐτῆς πάνlα
ὅσα εἶχεν ἔϐαλεν, ὅλον τὸν βίον
αὐτῆς. 25. † 6.

Κεφ. κδ΄ 24.

1 ΚΑὶ ἐξελθὼν ὁ Ἰησῦς ἐπορεύετο ἀπὸ τῦ ἱερῦ· ᾧ προσ-
ῆλθον οἱ μαθηlαὶ αὐτῦ ἐπιδεῖξαι
αὐτῷ τὰς οἰκοδομιὰς τῦ ἱερῦ.

2 Ὁ δὲ Ἰησῦς εἶπεν αὐτοῖς· Οὐ
βλέπεlε πάνlα ταῦτα; ἀμὴν λέγω ὑμῖν, ᾧ μὴ ἀφεθῇ ᾧδε λίθⓈ
ἐπὶ λίθον, ὃς ᾧ μὴ καlαλυθήσεlαι.

16 Τότε οἱ ἐν τῇ Ἰυδαίᾳ φευ-
γέτωσαν ἐπὶ τὰ ὄρη.

17 Ὁ ἐπὶ τῦ δώμαlⓈ, μὴ
καlαϐαινέτω ἆραί τι ἐκ τῆς οἰκίας
αὐτῦ·

18 Καὶ ὁ ἐν τῷ ἀγρῇ, μὴ ἐπιςρεψάτω ὀπίσω ἆραι τὰ ἱμάτια
αὐτῦ·

19 Οὐαὶ δὲ ταῖς ἐν γαςρὶ ἐχύ-
σαις ᾧ ταῖς θηλαζύσαις ἐν ἐκείναις ταῖς ἡμέραις.

20 Προσεύχεσθε δὲ ἵνα μὴ γένηlαι ἡ φυγὴ ὑμῶν χειμῶνⓈ,
μηδὲ ἐν σαϐϐάτῳ.

21 Ἔςαι γὰρ τότε θλίψις μεγάλη, ἵα ᾧ γέγονεν ἀπ᾽ ἀρχῆς
κόσμυ ἕως τῦ νῦν, ᾧδ᾽ ᾧ μὴ γένηlαι.

29 Εὐθέως δὲ μεlὰ τὴν θλῖψιν
τῶν ἡμερῶν ἐκείνων ὁ ἥλιⓈ σκο-
τισθήσεlαι, ᾧ ἡ σελήνη ᾧ δώσει τὸ
φέγγⓈ αὐτῆς, ᾧ οἱ ἀςέρες πε-
συῦlαι ἀπὸ τῦ ὑρανῦ, ᾧ αἱ δυνάμεις τῶν ὑρανῶν σαλευθήσονlαι.

41 Et sedens Jesus contra gazophylacium, aspiciebat quomodo turba jactaret æs in gazophylacium : & multi divites jactabant multa.

42 Et veniens una vidua pauper, injecit minuta duo, quod est quadrans.

43 Et advocans discipulos suos, ait illis : Amen dico vobis, quoniam vidua hæc pauper plus omnibus injecit injicientibus in gazophylacium.

44 Omnes enim ex redundante sibi injecerunt : hæc verò ex penuria sua omnia quæ habuit jecit, totum victum suum.

1 ET egressus Jesus ibat de templo : & accesserunt discipuli ejus ostendere ei ædificationes templi.

2 At Jesus dixit illis : Non intuemini hæc omnia ? Amen dico vobis, non relinquetur hic lapis super lapidem, qui non dissolvetur.

16 Tunc qui in Judæa fugiant ad montes.

17 Qui super domum, non descendat tollere quid de æde sua.

18 Et qui in agro, non revertatur retrò tollere vestem suam.

19 Væ autem in utero habentibus, & lactantibus in illis diebus.

20 Orate autem ut non fiat fuga vestra hyeme, neque in Sabbato.

21 Erit enim tunc tribulatio magna, qualis non fuit ab initio mundi, usque modo, neque non fiet.

29 Statim autem post tribulationem dierum illorum Sol obscurabitur, & Luna non dabit lumen suum, & stellæ cadent de cælo, & efficaciæ cælorum concutientur.

41, Et Jésus étant assis vis-à-vis du tronc, regardoit comment le peuple mettoit de l'argent dans le tronc.

42. Et plusieurs *personnes* riches y mettoient beaucoup; et une pauvre veuve vint, qui y mit deux petites pièces, qui font un quadrin.

43. Alors ayant appelé ses Disciples, il leur dit : Je vous dis en vérité, que cette pauvre veuve a plus mis au tronc, que tous ceux qui y ont mis.

44. Car tous *les autres* y ont mis de leur superflu ; mais celle-ci y a mis de son indigence, tout ce qu'elle avoit, tout ce qui lui restoit pour vivre.

COMME Jésus sortoit du Temple et qu'il s'en alloit, ses Disciples vinrent pour lui en faire considérer les édifices.

2. Et Jésus leur dit : Voyez-vous tous ces bâtimens ? Je vous dis en vérité, qu'il ne restera ici pierre sur pierre qui ne soit renversée.

16. Alors, que ceux qui seront dans la Judée, s'enfuient aux montagnes;

17. Que celui qui sera au haut de la maison, ne descende point pour s'arrêter à emporter quoi que ce soit de sa maison ;

18. Et que celui qui est aux champs, ne retourne point en arrière, pour emporter ses habits.

19. Malheur aux femmes qui seront enceintes, et à celles qui allaiteront en ces jours-là.

20. Priez que votre fuite n'arrive pas en hiver, ni en un jour de Sabbat.

21. Car il y aura une grande affliction, telle que, depuis le commencement du monde jusqu'à présent, il n'y en a point eu, et qu'il n'y en aura jamais de semblable.

29. Et aussitôt après l'affliction de ces jours-là, le soleil s'obscurcira, la lune ne donnera point sa lumière, les étoiles tomberont du ciel, et les puissances des cieux seront ébranlées.

41 And Jesus sat over against the treasury, and beheld how the people cast money into the treasury; and many that were rich cast in much.

42 And there came a certain poor widow; and she threw in two mites, which make a farthing.

43 And he called *unto him* his disciples, and saith unto them, Verily I say unto you, That this poor widow hath cast more in than all they which have cast into the treasury :

44 For all *they* did cast in of their abundance ; but she of her want did cast in all that she had, *even* all her living.

CHAP. XXIV.

Jerusalem's destruction foretold.

AND Jesus went out, and departed from the temple; and his disciples came *to him,* for to shew him the buildings of the temple.

2 And Jesus said unto them, See ye not all these things? Verily I say unto you, There shall not be left here one stone upon another, that shall not be thrown down.

16 Then let them which be in Judea flee into the mountains :

17 Let him which is on the house-top not come down to take any thing out of his house :

18 Neither let him which is in the field return back to take his clothes

19 And woe unto them that are with child, and to them that give suck in those days !

20 But pray ye that your flight be not in the winter, neither on the sabbath-day :

21 For then shall be great tribulation, such as was not since the beginning of the world to this time, no, nor ever shall be.

29 Immediately after the tribulation of those days shall the sun be darkened, and the moon shall not give her light, and the stars shall fall from heaven, and the powers of the heavens shall be shaken:

64

32 Ἀπὸ δὲ τῆς συκῆς μάθετε τὴν παραβολήν· ὅταν ἤδη ὁ κλάδος αὐτῆς γένηται ἁπαλὸς, καὶ τὰ φύλλα ἐκφύῃ, γινώσκετε ὅτι ἐγγὺς τὸ θέρ۟۟۟.

33 Οὕτω καὶ ὑμεῖς, ὅταν ἴδητε πάντα ταῦτα, γινώσκετε ὅτι ἐγγύς ἐςιν ἐπὶ θύραις.

36 Περὶ δὲ τῆς ἡμέρας ἐκείνης καὶ τῆς ὥρας ἐδεὶς οἶδεν, ἐδὲ οἱ ἄγγελοι τῶν ἐρανῶν, εἰ μὴ ὁ πατήρ μυ μόν۟۟.

37 Ὥσπερ δὲ αἱ ἡμέραι τῦ Νῶε, ὕτως ἔςαι καὶ ἡ παρυσία τῦ υἱῦ τῦ ἀνθρώπυ.

38 Ὥσπερ γὰρ ἦσαν ἐν ταῖς ἡμέραις ταῖς πρὸ τῦ καλακλυσμῦ τρώγοντες καὶ πίνοντες, γαμῦντες καὶ ἐκγαμίζοντες, ἄχρι ἧς ἡμέρας εἰσῆλθε Νῶε εἰς τὴν κιβωτόν·

39 Καὶ ἐκ ἔγνωσαν, ἕως ἦλθεν ὁ καλακλυσμὸς, καὶ ἦρεν ἅπαντας· ὕτως ἔςαι καὶ ἡ παρυσία τῦ υἱῦ τῦ ἀνθρώπυ.

40 Τότε δύο ἔσονται ἐν τῷ ἀγρῷ· ὁ εἷς παραλαμβάνεται καὶ ὁ εἷς ἀφίεται.

* 41 Δύο ‡ ἀλήθυσαι ἐν τῷ † μύλωνι· μία παραλαμβάνεται, καὶ μία ἀφίεται.

42 Γρηγορεῖτε ἐν, ὅτι ἐκ οἴδατε ποίᾳ ὥρᾳ ὁ κύρι۟ ὑμῶν ἔρχεται.

43 Ἐκεῖνο δὲ γινώσκετε, ὅτι εἰ ἤδει ὁ οἰκοδεσπότης ποίᾳ φυλακῇ ὁ κλέπτης ἔρχεται, ἐγρηγόρησεν ἀν, καὶ ἐκ ἂν εἴασε διορυγῆναι τὴν οἰκίαν αὐτῦ.

44 Διὰ τῦτο καὶ ὑμεῖς γίνεσθε ἕτοιμοι·

45 Τίς ἄρα ἐςὶν ὁ πιςὸς δῦλ۟ καὶ φρόνιμ۟, ὃν καλέςησεν ὁ κύρι۟ αὐτῦ ἐπὶ τῆς θεραπείας αὐτῦ, τῦ διδόναι αὐτοῖς τὴν τροφὴν ἐν καιρῷ;

46 Μακάρι۟ ὁ δῦλ۟ ἐκεῖν۟, ὃν ἐλθὼν ὁ κύρι۟ αὐτῦ εὑρήσει ποιῦντα ὕτως.

47 Ἀμὴν λέγω ὑμῖν, ὅτι ἐπὶ πᾶσι τοῖς ὑπάρχουσιν αὐτοῦ καταςήσει αὐτόν.

48 Ἐὰν δὲ εἴπῃ ὁ κακὸς δῦλ۟ ἐκεῖν۟ ἐν τῇ καρδίᾳ αὐτοῦ· Χρονίζει ὁ κύριός μου ἐλθεῖν·

49 Καὶ ἄρξηται τύπτειν τοὺς συνδύλους, ἐσθίειν δὲ καὶ πίνειν μετὰ τῶν μεθυόντων·

---

32 A verò ficu difcite parabolam: quum jam ramus ejus fuerit tener, & folia germinaverint, fcitis quia propè æftas.

33 Ita & vos, quum videritis hæc omnia, fcitote quia propè eft in januis.

36 De autem die illa & hor: nemo fcit, neque angeli cælorum, fi non Pater meus folus.

37 Sicut autem dies Noë ita erit & adventus Filii hominis.

38 Sicut enim erant in diebu[s] ante diluvium, comedentes & bibentes, nubentes & nuptui tra[dentes], dentes, ufque quo die intravi[t] Noë in arcam:

39 Et non cognoverunt done[c] venit diluvium, & tulit omnes[:] ita erit & præfentia Filii hominis.

40 Tunc duo erunt in agro: unus affumitur, & unus relinquitur.

41 Duæ molentes in mola: una affumetur, & una relinquetur.

42 Vigilate ergo, quia nefcitis quâ horâ Dominus vefter venit.

43 Illud autem fcitote, quoniam fi fciret paterfamilias quâ cuftodiâ fur venit, vigilaret utique, & non fineret perfodi domum fuam.

44 Propter hoc & vos eftote parati,

45 Quis putas eft fidelis fervus & prudens, quem conftituit dominus fuus fuper familiam fuam, ad dandum illis cibum in tempore?

46 Beatus fervus ille, quem veniens dominus ejus, invenerit facientem fic.

47 Amen dico vobis, quoniam fuper omnibus fubftantiis fuis conftituet eum.

48 Si autem dixerit malus fervus ille in corde fuo: Tardat dominus meus venire.

49 Et cœperit percutere confervos, edere autem & bibere cum ebriofis:

32. Apprenez ceci par la similitude du figuier : Quand ses branches commencent à être tendres, et qu'il poussent des feuilles, vous connoissez que l'été est proche.

33. Vous aussi de même, quand vous verrez toutes ces choses, sachez que *le Fils de l'homme* est proche, et à la porte.

36. Pour ce qui est du jour et de l'heure, personne ne le sait, non pas même les Anges du ciel, mais mon Père seul.

37. Mais comme il en étoit dans les jours de Noé, il en sera de même à l'avénement du Fils de l'homme ;

38. Car comme, dans les jours avant le Déluge, *les hommes* mangeoient et buvoient, se marioient et donnoient en mariage, jusqu'au jour que Noé entra dans l'arche :

39. Et qu'ils ne pensèrent au Déluge, que lorsqu'il vint et qu'il les emporta tous ; il en sera aussi de même à l'avénement du Fils de l'homme.

40. Alors de deux *hommes* qui seront dans un champ, l'un sera pris, et l'autre laissé.

41. De deux femmes qui moudront au moulin, l'une sera prise, et l'autre laissée.

42. Veillez donc ; car vous ne savez pas à quelle heure votre Seigneur doit venir.

43. Vous savez que si un père de famille étoit averti à quelle veille *de la nuit* un larron doit venir, il veilleroit, et ne laisseroit pas percer sa maison.

44. C'est pourquoi, vous aussi tenez-vous prêts ;

45. Qui est donc le serviteur fidèle et prudent que son Maître a établi sur ses domestiques, pour leur donner la nourriture dans le tems *qu'il faut ?*

46. Heureux ce serviteur que son Maître trouvera faisant ainsi quand il arrivera !

47. Je vous dis en vérité, qu'il l'établira sur tous ses biens.

48. Mais si c'est un méchant serviteur, qui dise en lui-même, Mon Maître tarde à venir ;

49. Et qu'il se mette à battre ses compagnons de service, et à manger et à boire avec des ivrognes ;

32 Now learn a parable of the fig-tree; When his branch is yet tender, and putteth forth leaves, ye know that summer *is* nigh:

33 So likewise ye, when ye shall see all these things, know that it is near, *even* at the doors.

36 But of that day and hour knoweth no *man*; no, not the angels of heaven, but my Father only.

37 But as the days of Noe *were*, so shall also the coming of the Son of Man be.

38 For in the days that were before the flood they were eating and drinking, marrying and giving in marriage, until the day that Noe entered into the ark,

39 And knew not until the flood came, and took them all away;

40 Then shall two be in the field; the one shall be taken, and the other left.

41 Two *women shall be* grinding at the mill; the one shall be taken, and the other left.

42 Watch, therefore; for ye know not what hour your Lord doth come.

43 But know this, that if the good man of the house had known in what watch the thief would come, he would have watched, and would not have suffered his house to be broken up.

44 Therefore be ye also ready:

45 Who then is a faithful and wise servant, whom his lord hath made ruler over his household, to give them meat in due season?

46 Blessed *is* that servant, whom his lord, when he cometh, shall find so doing.

47 Verily I say unto you, That he shall make him ruler over all his goods.

48 But and if that evil servant shall say in his heart, My lord delayeth his coming;

49 And shall begin to smite *his* fellow-servants, and to eat and drink with the drunken;

65

50 Ἥξει ὁ κύριΘ· τοῦ δούλου ἐκείνου ἐν ἡμέρᾳ ᾗ οὐ προσδοκᾷ, ἢ ἐν ὥρᾳ ᾗ οὐ γινώσκει.

51 Καὶ διχοτομήσει αὐτὸν, ἢ τὸ μέρος αὐτοῦ μεὶὰ τῶν ὑποκριτῶν θήσει· ἐκεῖ ἔςαι ὁ κλαυθμὸς ἢ ὁ βρυγμὸς τῶν ὀδόντων. 14.
† 2.

Κεφ. κε΄. 25.

1 ΤΌτε ὁμοιωθήσεται ἡ βασιλεία τῶν οὐρανῶν δέκα παρθένοις, αἵτινες λαβοῦσαι τὰς λαμπάδας αὑτῶν, ἐξῆλθον εἰς ἀπάντησιν τοῦ νυμφίου.

2 Πέντε δὲ ἦσαν ἐξ αὐτῶν φρόνιμοι, ἢ πέντε μωραί.

3 Αἵτινες μωραὶ, λαβοῦσαι τὰς λαμπάδας ἑαυτῶν, οὐκ ἔλαβον μεθ᾽ ἑαυτῶν ἔλαιον.

4 Αἱ δὲ φρόνιμοι ἔλαβον ἔλαιον ἐν τοῖς ἀγγείοις αὐτῶν μεὶὰ τῶν λαμπάδων αὐτῶν.

5 ΧρονίζονΘ· δὲ τοῦ νυμφίου, ἐνύςαξαν πᾶσαι, ἢ ἐκάθευδον.

6 Μέσης δὲ νυκὶὸς κραυγὴ γέγονεν· Ἰδοὺ, ὁ νυμφίΘ· ἔρχεͅαι, ἐξέρχεσθε εἰς ἀπάντησιν αὐτοῦ.

7 Τότε ἠγέρθησαν πᾶσαι αἱ παρθένοι ἐκεῖναι, ἢ ἐκόσμησαν τὰς λαμπάδας αὐτῶν.

8 Αἱ δὲ μωραὶ ταῖς φρονίμοις εἶπον· Δότε ἡμῖν ἐκ τοῦ ἐλαίου ὑμῶν· ὅτι αἱ λαμπάδες ἡμῶν σβέννυνͰαι.

9 Ἀπεκρίθησαν δὲ αἱ φρόνιμοι, λέγουσαι· Μήποτε οὐκ ἀρκέσῃ ἡμῖν ἢ ‡ ὑμῖν· πορεύεσθε δὲ μᾶλλον πρὸς τοὺς πωλοῦνͰας, ἢ ἀγοράσαͰε ἑαυταῖς.

10 Ἀπερχομένων δὲ αὐτῶν ἀγοράσαι, ἦλθεν ὁ νυμφίΘ· ἢ αἱ ἕτοιμοι εἰσῆλθον μεͺ᾽ αὐτῦ εἰς τοὺς γάμους, ἢ ἐκλείσθη ἡ θύρα.

11 Ὕςερον δὲ ἔρχονͰαι ἢ αἱ λοιπαὶ παρθένοι, λέγουσαι· Κύριε, κύριε, ἄνοιξον ἡμῖν.

12 Ὁ δὲ ἀποκριθεὶς, εἶπεν· Ἀμὴν λέγω ὑμῖν, οὐκ οἶδα ὑμᾶς.

13 Γρηγορεῖτε οὖν,

14 Ὥσπερ γὰρ ἄνθρωπΘ· ἀποδημῶν ἐκάλεσε τοὺς ἰδίους δούλους, ἢ παρέδωκεν αὐτοῖς τὰ ὑπάρχονͰα αὐτοῦ.

15 Καὶ ᾧ μὲν ἔδωκε πέντε τάλανͰα, ᾧ δὲ δύο, ᾧ δὲ ἕν· ἑκάςῳ

50 Veniet dominus servi illius in die quâ non expectat, & in horâ quâ non scit.

51 Et dividet eum, & partem ejus cum hypocritis ponet : illic erit fletus, & stridor dentium.

CAPUT XXV.

1 TUnc similabitur regnum cælorum decem virginibus, quæ accipientes lampadas suas, exierunt in occursum sponsi.

2 Quinque autem erant ex eis prudentes, & quinque fatuæ.

3 Quæ fatuæ sumentes lampadas suas, non sumpserunt secum oleum.

4 Verùm prudentes acceperunt oleum in vasis suis cum lampadibus suis.

5 Tardante autem sponso dormitaverunt omnes, & dormierunt.

6 Mediâ autem nocte clamor factus est : Ecce sponsus venit : exite in occursum ejus.

7 Tunc surrexerunt omnes virgines illæ : & ornaverunt lampadas suas.

8 At fatuæ sapientibus dixerunt : Date nobis de oleo vestro, quia lampades nostræ extinguuntur.

9 Responderunt autem prudentes, dicentes : Ne forte non sufficiat nobis, & vobis : ite autem potiùs ad vendentes, & emite vobis ipsis.

10 Abeuntibus autem illæ mercari, venit sponsus : & expeditæ intraverunt cum eo ad nuptias, & clausa est janua.

11 Posteriùs verò veniunt & reliquæ virgines, dicentes : Domine, Domine, aperi nobis.

12 Ille verò respondens, ait : Amen dico vobis, non novi vos.

13 Vigilate itaque,

14 Sicut enim homo peregrè proficiscens, vocavit proprios servos, & tradidit illis substantias suas :

15 Et huic quidem dedit quinque talenta, illi autem duo, illi

50. Le Maître de ce serviteur-là viendra le jour qu'il ne l'attend pas, et à l'heure qu'il ne sait pas;

51. Et il le séparera, et il lui donnera sa portion avec les hypocrites; c'est là qu'il y aura des pleurs et des grincemens de dents.

CHAPITRE XXV.

La Parabole des Vierges et des Talens. La description du Jugement dernier.

ALORS le Royaume des cieux sera semblable à dix vierges, qui ayant pris leurs lampes, allèrent au-devant de l'Epoux.

2. Or, il y en avoit cinq d'entre elles *qui étoient* sages, et cinq *qui étoient* folles.

3. Celles qui *étoient* folles, en prenant leurs lampes, n'avoient point pris d'huile avec elles.

4. Mais les sages avoient pris de l'huile dans leurs vaisseaux avec leurs lampes.

5. Et comme l'époux tardoit à venir, elles s'assoupirent toutes et s'endormirent.

6. Et sur le minuit, on entendit crier : Voici l'époux qui vient, sortez au-devant de lui.

7. Alors ces vierges se levèrent toutes, et préparèrent leurs lampes.

8. Et les folles dirent aux sages : Donnez-nous de votre huile ; car nos lampes s'éteignent.

9. Mais les sages répondirent : *Nous ne le pouvons*, de peur que nous n'en ayons pas assez pour nous et pour vous ; allez plutôt vers ceux qui en vendent, et en achetez pour vous.

10. Mais pendant qu'elles en alloient acheter, l'Epoux vint ; et celles qui étoient prêtes entrèrent avec lui aux noces, et la porte fut fermée.

11. Après cela les autres vierges vinrent aussi, et dirent : Seigneur, Seigneur, ouvre-nous.

12. Mais il leur répondit : Je vous dis en vérité, que je ne vous connois point.

13. Veillez donc ;

14 Car il en *est* comme d'un homme, qui, s'en allant en voyage, appela ses serviteurs et leur remit ses biens.

15. Et il donna cinq talens à l'un, à l'autre deux, et à l'autre

50 The lord of that servant shall come in a day when he looketh not for *him*, and in an hour that he is not aware of.

51 And shall cut him asunder, and appoint *him* his portion with the hypocrites: there shall be weeping and gnashing of teeth.

CHAP. XXV.

Parable of the ten virgins.

THEN shall the kingdom of heaven be likened unto ten virgins, which took their lamps, and went forth to meet the bridegroom.

2 And five of them were wise, and five *were* foolish.

3 They that *were* foolish took their lamps, and took no oil with them:

4 But the wise took oil in their vessels with their lamps.

5 While the bridegroom tarried, they all slumbered and slept.

6 And at midnight there was a cry made, Behold, the bridegroom cometh; go ye out to meet him.

7 Then all those virgins arose, and trimmed their lamps.

8 And the foolish said unto the wise, Give us of your oil; for our lamps are gone out.

9 But the wise answered, saying, *Not so*: lest there be not enough for us and you: but go ye rather to them that sell, and buy for yourselves.

10 And while they went to buy, the bridegroom came; and they that were ready went in with him to the marriage: and the door was shut.

11 Afterward came also the other virgins, saying, Lord, Lord, open to us.

12 But he answered and said, Verily I say unto you, I know you not.

13 Watch, therefore,

14 For *the kingdom of heaven is* as a man travelling into a far country, *who* called his own servants, and delivered unto them his goods.

15 And unto one he gave five talents, to another two, and to

κατὰ τὴν ἰδίαν δύναμιν· καὶ ἀπεδή-μησεν εὐθέως.

16 Πορευθεὶς δὲ ὁ τὰ πέντε τάλαντα λαβὼν, εἰργάσατο ἐν αὐτοῖς, καὶ ἐποίησεν ἄλλα πέντε τάλαντα.

17 Ὡσαύτως καὶ ὁ τὰ δύο, ἐκέρδησε καὶ αὐτὸς ἄλλα δύο.

18 Ὁ δὲ τὸ ἓν λαβὼν, ἀπελ-θὼν ὤρυξεν ἐν τῇ γῇ, καὶ ἀπέ-κρυψε τὸ ἀργύριον τοῦ κυρίου αὐτοῦ.

19 Μετὰ δὲ χρόνον πολὺν ἔρ-χεται ὁ κύριος τῶν δούλων ἐκεί-νων, καὶ συναίρει μετ' αὐτῶν λό-γον.

20 Καὶ προσελθὼν ὁ τὰ πέντε τάλαντα λαβὼν, προσήνεγκεν ἄλ-λα πέντε τάλαντα, λέγων· Κύριε, πέντε τάλαντά μοι παρέδωκας· ἴδε, ἄλλα πέντε τάλαντα ἐκέρ-δησα ἐπ' αὐτοῖς.

21 Ἔφη δὲ αὐτῷ ὁ κύριος αὐ-τοῦ· Εὖ, δοῦλε ἀγαθὲ καὶ πιστέ· ἐπὶ ὀλίγα ἦς πιστός, ἐπὶ πολλῶν σε καταστήσω· εἴσελθε εἰς τὴν χαρὰν τοῦ κυρίου σου.

22 Προσελθὼν δὲ καὶ ὁ τὰ δύο τάλαντα λαβὼν, εἶπε· Κύριε, δύο τάλαντά μοι παρέδωκας· ἴδε, ἄλ-λα δύο τάλαντα ἐκέρδησα ἐπ' αὐ-τοῖς.

23 Ἔφη αὐτῷ ὁ κύριος αὐτοῦ· Εὖ, δοῦλε ἀγαθὲ καὶ πιστὲ· ἐπὶ ὀλίγα ἦς πιστός, ἐπὶ πολλῶν σε καταστήσω· εἴσελθε εἰς τὴν χα-ρὰν τοῦ κυρίου σου.

24 Προσελθὼν δὲ καὶ ὁ τὸ ἓν τά-λαντον εἰληφὼς, εἶπε· Κύριε, ἔγ-νων σε ὅτι σκληρὸς εἶ ἄνθρωπος, θερίζων ὅπου οὐκ ἔσπειρας, καὶ συν-άγων ὅθεν οὐ διεσκόρπισας·

25 Καὶ φοβηθεὶς, ἀπελθὼν ἔκ-ρυψα τὸ τάλαντόν σου ἐν τῇ γῇ· ἴδε ἔχεις τὸ σόν.

26 Ἀποκριθεὶς δὲ ὁ κύριος αὐ-τοῦ, εἶπεν αὐτῷ· Πονηρὲ δοῦλε καὶ ὀκνηρὲ, ᾔδεις ὅτι θερίζω ὅπου οὐκ ἔσπειρα, καὶ συνάγω ὅθεν οὐ διεσκόρπισα·

verò unum : unicuique secun-dùm propriam facultatem : & peregrè profectus est statim.

16 Profectus autem quinque talenta accipiens, operatus est in eis, & fecit alia quinque talenta.

17 Similiter & qui duo, lu-cratus est & ipse alia duo.

18 Verùm unum accipiens, abiens fodit in terra, & abscon-dit pecuniam domini sui.

19 Post verò tempus multum venit dominus servorum illo-rum, & confert rationem cum eis.

20 Et accedens quinque ta-lenta accipiens, attulit alia quin-que talenta, dicens : Domine, quinque talenta mihi tradidisti : ecce alia quinque talenta lucra-tus sum super illis.

21 Ait verò illi dominus ejus : Benè, serve bone & fide-lis, super pauca fuisti fidelis : super multa te constituam : in-gredere in gaudium domini tui.

22 Accedens autem & qui duo talenta accipiens, dixit : Do-mine, duo talenta mihi tradi-disti : ecce alia duo talenta lu-cratus sum super illis.

23 Ait illi dominus ejus : Benè, serve bone & fidelis : su-per pauca fuisti fidelis, super multa te constituam : ingredere in gaudium domini tui.

24 Accedens autem & unum talentum sumens, ait : Domine, scio te quia durus es homo, me-tens ubi non seminasti, & con-gregans unde non sparsisti :

25 Et timore perculsus, abi-ens abscondi talentum tuum in terra : ecce habes tuum.

26 Respondens autem domi-nus ejus, dixit ei : Male serve & piger, sciebas quia meto ubi non seminavi, & congrego unde non sparsi.

[un] ; à chacun selon ses forces ; et il partit aussitôt.

16. Or celui qui avoit reçu cinq talens s'en alla et en trafiqua ; et il gagna cinq autres talens.

17. De même celui qui en *avoit reçu* deux, en gagna aussi deux autres.

18. Mais celui qui n'en avoit reçu qu'un, s'en alla et creusa dans la terre, et y cacha l'argent de son Maître.

19. Long-tems après, le Maître de ces serviteurs revint, et il leur fit rendre compte.

20. Alors celui qui avoit reçu cinq talens vint, et présenta cinq autres talens, et dit : Seigneur, tu m'avois remis cinq talens ; en voici cinq autres que j'ai gagnés de plus.

21. Et son Maître lui dit : Cela va bien, bon et fidèle serviteur ; tu as été fidèle en peu de chose ; je t'établirai sur beaucoup ; entre dans la joie de ton Seigneur.

22. Et celui qui avoit reçu deux talens, vint et dit : Seigneur, tu m'avois remis deux talens ; en voici deux autres que j'ai gagnés de plus.

23. Et son Maître lui dit : Cela va bien, bon et fidèle serviteur ; tu as été fidèle en peu de chose ; je t'établirai sur beaucoup ; entre dans la joie de ton Seigneur.

24. Mais celui qui n'avoit reçu qu'un talent, vint et dit : Seigneur, je savois que tu étois un homme dur qui moissonnes où tu n'as pas semé, et qui recueilles où tu n'as pas répandu ;

25. C'est pourquoi *te* craignant, je suis allé, et j'ai caché ton talent dans la terre ; voici, tu as ce qui est à toi.

26. Et son Maître lui répondit : Méchant et paresseux serviteur, tu savois que je moissonnois où je n'ai pas semé, et que je recueillois où je n'ai pas répandu :

another one ; to every man according to his several ability ; and straightway took his journey.

16 Then he that had received the five talents went and traded with the same, and made *them* other five talents.

17 And likewise he that *had received* two, he also gained other two.

18 But he that had received one, went and digged in the earth, and hid his lord's money.

19 After a long time the lord of those servants cometh, and reckoneth with them.

20 And so he that had received five talents came, and brought other five talents, saying, Lord, thou deliveredst unto me five talents : behold, I have gained beside them five talents more.

21 His lord said unto him, Well done, *thou* good and faithful servant : thou hast been faithful over a few things, I will make thee ruler over many things : enter thou into the joy of thy lord.

22 He also that had received two talents came, and said, Lord, thou deliveredst unto me two talents : behold, I have gained two other talents beside them.

23 His lord said unto him, Well done, good and faithful servant : thou hast been faithful over a few things, I will make thee ruler over many things : enter thou into the joy of thy lord.

24 Then he which had received the one talent came, and said, Lord, I knew thee, that thou art an hard man, reaping where thou hast not sown, and gathering where thou hast not strawed :

25 And I was afraid, and went and hid thy talent in the earth : lo, *there* thou hast *that is* thine.

26 His lord answered, and said unto him, *Thou* wicked and slothful servant, thou knewest that I reap where I sowed not, and gather where I have not strawed :

67

27 ‡ Ἔδει οὖν ‡ σε βαλεῖν τὸ ‡ ἀργύριόν μου τοῖς † τραπεζί-ταις· ‡ καὶ ἐλθὼν ‡ ἐγὼ ‡ ἐκομισά-μην ‡ ἂν τὸ ‡ ἐμὸν σὺν ‡ τόκῳ.

28 Ἄρατε οὖν ἀπ᾽ αὐτοῦ τὸ τάλαντον, ‡ καὶ δότε τῷ ἔχοντι τὰ δέκα τάλαντα.

29 (Τῷ γὰρ ἔχοντι παντὶ δο-θήσεται, ‡ καὶ περισσευθήσεται· ἀπὸ δὲ τοῦ μὴ ἔχοντος, ‡ καὶ ὃ ἔχει, ἀρ-θήσεται ἀπ᾽ αὐτοῦ.)

* 30 Καὶ τὸν ἀχρεῖον δοῦλον ἐκβάλλετε εἰς τὸ ‡ σκότος τὸ ‡ ἐξώτερον· ἐκεῖ ἔσται ὁ κλαυθμὸς καὶ ὁ ‡ βρυγμὸς τῶν ‡ ὀδόντων.

* 34 Προσέχετε δὲ ἑαυτοῖς, μή-ποτε † βαρυνθῶσιν, ὑμῶν αἱ καρ-δίαι ἐν † κραιπάλῃ, ‡ καὶ μέθῃ, ‡ καὶ ‡ μερίμναις ‡ βιωτικαῖς, ‡ καὶ αἰφνίδιος ἐφ᾽ ὑμᾶς ἐπιστῇ ἡ ἡμέ-ρα ἐκείνη·

35 Ὡς παγὶς γὰρ ἐπελεύσε-ται ἐπὶ πάντας τοὺς καθημένους ἐπὶ πρόσωπον πάσης τῆς γῆς.

36 Ἀγρυπνεῖτε οὖν, ἐν παντὶ καιρῷ δεόμενοι, ἵνα καταξιωθῆτε ἐκφυγεῖν ταῦτα πάντα τὰ μέλ-

31 Ὅταν δὲ ἔλθη ὁ υἱὸς τοῦ ἀνθρώπου ἐν τῇ δόξῃ αὐτοῦ, καὶ πάντες οἱ ἅγιοι ἄγγελοι μετ᾽ αὐ-τοῦ, τότε καθίσει ἐπὶ θρόνου δόξης αὐτοῦ.

32 Καὶ συναχθήσεται ἔμπροσ-θεν αὐτοῦ πάντα τὰ ἔθνη· καὶ ἀφο-ριεῖ αὐτοὺς ἀπ᾽ ἀλλήλων, ὥσπερ ὁ ποιμὴν ἀφορίζει τὰ πρόβατα ἀπὸ τῶν ἐρίφων.

* 33 Καὶ ‡ στήσει τὰ μὲν ‡ πρόβατα ‡ ἐκ ‡ δεξιῶν ‡ αὐτοῦ, τὰ ‡ δὲ ‡ ἐρίφια ‡ ἐξ ‡ εὐωνύμων.

34 Τότε ἐρεῖ ὁ βασιλεὺς τοῖς ἐκ δεξιῶν αὐτοῦ· Δεῦτε οἱ εὐλο-γημένοι τοῦ πατρός μου, κλη-ρονομήσατε τὴν ἡτοιμασμένην ὑμῖν βασιλείαν ἀπὸ καταβολῆς κόσμου.

35 Ἐπείνασα γὰρ, ‡ καὶ ἐδώκατέ μοι φαγεῖν· ἐδίψησα, ‡ καὶ ἐποτί-σατέ με· ξένος ἤμην, ‡ καὶ συνη-γάγετέ με·

36 Γυμνὸς, ‡ καὶ περιεβάλετέ με· ἠσθένησα, ‡ καὶ ἐπεσκέψασθέ με· ἐν φυλακῇ ἤμην, ‡ καὶ ἤλθετε πρός με.

---

27 Oportuit ergo te jacere ar-gentum meum menfariis: & veniens ego recepiſſem utique meum cum ufura.

28 Tollite itaque ab eo ta-lentum, & date habenti decem talenta.

29 (Nam habenti omni dabi-tur, & augebitur: à verò non habente, & quod videtur ha-bere, auferetur ab eo.)

30 Et inutilem fervum ejicite in tenebras exteriores: illic erit fletus & fremitus dentium.

34 Attendite autem vobis ipfis, ne forte graventur veſtra corda in crapula, & ebrietate, & curis vitalibus, & repentina in vos fuperveniat dies illa.

35 Tanquam laqueus enim fuperveniet in omnes fedentes fuper faciem omnis terræ.

36 Vigilate itaque in omni tempore rogantes, ut digni ha-beamini effugere ista omnia fu-

31 Quum autem venerit Fi-lius hominis in gloria fua, & omnes fancti angeli cum eo, tunc fedebit fuper throno gloriæ fuæ:

31 Et cogentur ante eum omnes gentes, & feparabit eos ab invicem, ficut paftor fegregat oves ab hoedis.

33 Et ftatuet quidem oves à dexteris fuis, at hoedos a fi-niftris.

34 Tunc dicet rex his qui à dextris ejus: Venite benedic-ti Patris mei, poffidete paratum vobis regnum à fundamento mundi.

35 Efurivi enim, & dediftis mihi manducare: fitivi, & po-taſtis me: hofpes eram, & collegiftis me:

36 Nudus, & amiciviftis me: ægrotavi, & v fitaftis me: in carcere eram, & veniftis ad me.

27. Il te falloit donc donner mon argent aux banquiers; et à mon retour, j'aurois retiré ce qui est à moi avec l'intérêt.

28. Otez-lui donc le talent, et le donnez à celui qui a dix talens.

29. Car on donnera à celui qui a, et il aura encore davantage; mais à celui qui n'a pas, on lui ôtera même ce qu'il a.

30. Jetez donc le serviteur inutile dans les ténèbres de déhors; et là qu'il y aura des pleurs et grincemens de dents.

34. Prenez donc garde à vous-mêmes, de peur que vos cœurs ne soient appesantis par la gourmandise, par les excès du vin, et par les inquiétudes de cette vie; et que ce jour-là ne vous surprenne subitement.

35. Car il surprendra comme un filet tous ceux qui habitent sur la face de la terre.

36. Veillez donc, et priez en tout tems, afin que vous soyez trouvés dignes d'éviter toutes ces choses qui doivent arriver, et de subsister devant le Fils de l'homme.

31. Or, quand le Fils de l'homme viendra dans sa gloire, avec tous les saints Anges, alors il s'asseiera sur le trône de sa gloire.

32. Et toutes les nations seront assemblées devant lui; et il séparera les uns d'avec les autres, comme un berger sépare les brebis d'avec les boucs.

33. Et il mettra les brebis à sa droite, et les boucs à sa gauche.

34. Alors le Roi dira à ceux qui seront à sa droite : Venez, vous qui êtes bénis de mon Père, possédez en héritage le Royaume qui vous a été préparé dès la création du monde.

35. Car j'ai eu faim, et vous m'avez donné à manger; j'ai eu soif, et vous m'avez donné à boire; j'étois étranger, et vous m'avez recueilli;

36. J'étois nud, et vous m'avez vêtu; j'étois malade, et vous m'avez visité; j'étois en prison, et vous m'êtes venu voir.

27 Thou oughtest, therefore, to have put my money to the exchangers, and *then* at my coming I should have received mine own with usury.

28 Take, therefore, the talent from him, and give it unto him which hath ten talents.

29 For unto every one that hath shall be given, and he shall have abundance: but from him that hath not, shall be taken away even that which he hath.

30 And cast ye the unprofitable servant into outer darkness: there shall be weeping and gnashing of teeth.

34 And take heed to yourselves, lest at any time your hearts be overcharged with surfeiting, and drunkenness, and cares of this life, and *so* that day come upon you unawares.

35 For as a snare shall it come on all them that dwell on the face of the whole earth.

36 Watch ye, therefore, and pray always, that ye may be accounted worthy to escape all these things that shall come to pass, and to stand before the Son of Man.

31 When the Son of Man shall come in his glory, and all the holy angels with him, then shall he sit upon the throne of his glory:

32 And before him shall be gathered all nations: and he shall separate them one from another, as a shepherd divideth his sheep from the goats:

33 And he shall set the sheep on his right hand, but the goats on the left.

34 Then shall the King say unto them on his right hand, Come, ye blessed of my Father, inherit the kingdom prepared for you from the foundation of the world:

35 For I was an hungered, and ye gave me meat: I was thirsty, and ye gave me drink: I was a stranger, and ye took me in:

36 Naked, and ye clothed me: I was sick, and ye visited me: I was in prison, and ye came unto me.

68

37 Τότε ἀποκριθήσονlαι αὐτῷ οἱ δίκαιοι, λέγονlες· Κύριε, πότε σε εἴδομεν πεινῶνlα, καὶ ἐθρέψαμεν; ἢ διψῶνlα, καὶ ἐποτίσαμεν;

38 Πότε δέ σε εἴδομεν ξένον, καὶ συνηγάγομεν; ἢ γυμνὸν, καὶ περιεϐάλομεν;

39 Πότε δέ σε εἴδομεν ἀσθενῆ, ἢ ἐν φυλακῇ, καὶ ἤλθομεν πρός σε;

40 Καὶ ἀποκριθεὶς ὁ βασιλεὺς, ἐρεῖ αὐτοῖς· Ἀμὴν λέγω ὑμῖν, ἐφ᾽ ὅσον ἐποιήσαlε ἑνὶ τούτων τῶν ἀδελφῶν μου τῶν ἐλαχίσων, ἐμοὶ ἐποιήσαlε.

41 Τότε ἐρεῖ καὶ τοῖς ἐξ εὐωνύμων· Πορεύεσθε ἀπ᾽ ἐμοῦ οἱ καlηραμένοι εἰς τὸ πῦρ τὸ αἰώνιον, τὸ ἡτοιμασμένον τῷ διαϐόλῳ καὶ τοῖς ἀγγέλοις αὐτοῦ·

42 Ἐπείνασα γὰρ, καὶ οὐκ ἐδώκαlέ μοι φαγεῖν· ἐδίψησα, καὶ οὐκ ἐποτίσαlέ με·

43 Ξένος ἤμην, καὶ οὐ συνηγάγεlέ με· γυμνὸς, καὶ οὐ περιεϐάλεlέ με· ἀσθενὴς καὶ ἐν φυλακῇ, καὶ οὐκ ἐπεσκέψασθέ με.

44 Τότε ἀποκριθήσονlαι αὐτῷ καὶ αὐτοὶ, λέγονlες· Κύριε, πότε σε εἴδομεν, πεινῶνlα, ἢ διψῶνlα, ἢ ξένον, ἢ γυμνὸν, ἢ ἀσθενῆ, ἢ ἐν φυλακῇ, καὶ οὐ διηκονήσαμέν σοι;

45 Τότε ἀποκριθήσεlαι αὐτοῖς, λέγων· Ἀμὴν λέγω ὑμῖν, ἐφ᾽ ὅσον οὐκ ἐποιήσαlε ἑνὶ τούτων τῶν ἐλαχίσων, οὐδὲ ἐμοὶ ἐποιήσαlε.

46 Καὶ ἀπελεύσονlαι οὗτοι εἰς κόλασιν αἰώνιον· οἱ δὲ δίκαιοι εἰς ζωὴν αἰώνιον. 24 † 2.

Κεφ. ιδ´. 14.

1 ἩΝ δὲ τὸ πάσχα καὶ τὰ ἄζυμα μετὰ δύο ἡμέρας· καὶ ἐζήτουν οἱ ἀρχιερεῖς καὶ οἱ γραμμαlεῖς πῶς αὐτὸν ἐν δόλῳ κραlήσανlες ἀποκlείνωσιν.

2 Ἔλεγον δέ· Μὴ ἐν τῇ ἑορτῇ, μήποlε θόρυϐΘ- ἔσαι τῷ λαῷ.

* 3 Καὶ ὄνΘ- αὐτῷ ἐν Βηθανίᾳ ἐν τῇ οἰκίᾳ ΣίμωνΘ- τῷ λεπρῷ, καlακειμένο αὐτῷ, ἦλθε

37 Tunc respondebunt ei justi, dicentes: Domine, quando te vidimus esurientem, & aluimus? vel sitientem, & potavimus?

38 Quando autem te vidimus hospitem, & collegimus? aut nudum, & amicivimus?

39 Quando vero te vidimus infirmum, aut in carcere, & venimus ad te?

40 Et respondens rex dicet illis: Amen dico vobis, quatenus fecistis uni horum fratrum meorum minimorum, mihi fecistis.

41 Tunc dicet & his qui à sinistris: Ite à me maledicti in ignem æternum, præparatum diabolo & angelis ejus.

42 Esurivi enim, & non dedistis mihi manducare: sitivi, & non potastis me:

43 Hospes eram, & non collegistis me: nudus, & non amicivistis me: infirmus, & in carcere, & non visitastis me.

44 Tunc respondebunt ei & ipsi, dicentes: Domine, quando te vidimus esurientem, aut sitientem, aut hospitem, aut nudum, aut infirmum, aut in carcere, & non ministravimus tibi?

45 Tunc respondebit illis, dicens: Amen dico vobis, quatenus non fecistis uni horum minimorum, nec mihi fecistis.

46 Et ibunt hi in supplicium æternum: at justi in vitam æternam.

CAPUT XIV.

1 ERat autem Pascha, & Azyma post duos dies: & quærebant summi Sacerdotes & Scribæ quomodo eum dolo prehendentes occiderent.

2 Dicebant autem: non in festo, ne quando tumultus sit populi.

3 Et existente eo in Bethania, in domo Simonis leprosi, accumbente eo, venit mulier

37. Alors les justes lui répondront : Seigneur , quand est-ce que nous t'avons vu avoir faim , et que nous t'avons donné à manger ; *ou* avoir soif , et que nous t'avons donné à boire ?

58. Et quand est-ce que nous t'avons vu étranger , et que nous t'avons recueilli ; ou nud , et que nous t'avons vêtu.

39. Ou quand est-ce que nous t'avons vu malade , ou en prison , et que nous sommes venus te voir?

40. Et le Roi répondant , leur dira : Je vous dis en vérité , qu'en tant que vous avez fait ces choses à l'un de ces plus petits de mes frères , vous me les avez faites.

41. Ensuite il dira à ceux qui seront à sa gauche : Retirez-vous de moi, maudits , et *allez* dans le feu éternel , qui est préparé au Diable et à ses Anges.

42. Car j'ai eu faim , et vous ne m'avez pas donné à manger ; j'ai eu soif , et vous ne m'avez pas donné à boire.

43. J'étois étranger , et vous ne m'avez pas recueilli ; *j'etois* nud , et vous ne m'avez pas vêtu ; *j'étois* malade et en prison , et vous ne m'avez pas visité.

44. Alors ceux-là lui répondront aussi : Seigneur, quand est-ce que nous t'avons vu avoir faim , ou soif , ou être étranger , ou nud , ou malade , ou en prison , et que nous ne t'avons point assisté ?

45. Et il leur repondra : Je vous dis en vérité , qu'en ce que vous ne l'avez pas fait à l'un de ces plus petits , vous ne me l'avez pas fait *non plus*.

46. Et ceux-ci s'en iront aux peines éternelles ; mais les justes s'en iront à la vie éternelle.

CHAPITRE XIV.

Jésus-Christ oint d'une femme; trahi par Judas ; institue la Sainte Cène; se prépare à la mort par de très-ardentes prières. Il est saisi dans le jardin , amené au procès et renié de Pierre.

LA fête de Pâque et des pains sans levain étoit deux jours après ; et les Scribes cherchoient comment ils pourroient se saisir de Jésus par finesse , et le faire mourir.

2. Mais ils disoient : Il ne faut pas que ce soit durant la fête , de peur qu'il ne se fasse du tumulte parmi le peuple.

3. Et Jésus étant à Béthanie , dans la maison de Simon le lépreux ,

---

37 Then shall the righteous answer him, saying, Lord, when saw we thee an hungered, and fed *thee?* or thirsty, and gave *thee* drink ?

38 When saw we thee a stranger, and took *thee* in ? or naked, and clothed *thee?*

39 Or when saw we thee sick, or in prison, and came unto *thee?*

40 And the King shall answer, and say unto them, Verily I say unto you, Inasmuch as ye have done *it* unto one of the least of these my brethren, ye have done *it* unto me.

41 Then shall he say also unto them on the left hand, Depart from me, ye cursed, into everlasting fire, prepared for the devil and his angels :

42 For I was an hungered, and ye gave me no meat: I was thirsty, and ye gave me no drink :

43 I was a stranger, and ye took me not in : naked, and ye clothed me not : sick, and in prison, and ye visited me not.

44 Then shall they also answer him, saying, Lord, when saw we *thee* an hungered, or athirst, or a stranger, or naked, or sick, or in prison, and did not minister unto thee ?

45 Then shall he answer them, saying, Verily I say unto you, Inasmuch as ye did *it* not to one of the least of these, ye did *it* not to me.

46 And these shall go away into everlasting punishment: but the righteous into life eternal.

CHAP. XIV.

Conspiracy against Christ.

AFTER two days was *the feast* of the passover, and of unleavened bread : and the chief priests and the scribes sought how they might take him by craft, and put *him* to death.

2 But they said, Not on the feast-day, lest there be an uproar of the people.

3 And being in Bethany, in the house of Simon the leper, as he sat at meat, there came a woman,

γυνὴ ἔχυσα ἀλάβασρον μύρα,
‡ νάρδυ ‡ πισικῆς ‡ πολυτελῆς·
ᾗ συντρίψασα τὸ ἀλάβασρον,
κατέχεεν αὐτῆ κατὰ τῆς κεφαλῆς.

4 Ἦσαν δέ τινες ἀγανακτῦν-
τες πρὸς ἑαυτὸς, ᾗ λέγοντες·
Εἰς τί ἡ ἀπώλεια αὕτη τῦ μύρα
γέγονεν;

5 Ἠδύνατο γὰρ τῦτο πραθῆ-
ναι ἐπάνω τριακοσίων δηναρίων,
ᾗ δοθῆναι τοῖς πτωχοῖς. Καὶ
ἐνεβριμῶντο αὐτῆ.

6 Ὁ δὲ Ἰησῦς εἶπεν· Ἄφετε
αὐτήν· τί αὐτῆ κόπυς παρέχετε;
καλὸν ἔργον εἰργάσατο εἰς ἐμέ.

7 Πάντοτε γὰρ τὸς πτωχὸς
ἔχετε μεθ' ἑαυτῶν, ᾗ ὅταν θέλητε, δύνασθε αὐτὸς εὖ ποιῆσαι·
ἐμὲ δὲ ὐ πάντοτε ἔχετε.

* 8 Ὃ εἶχεν αὕτη, ἐποίησε·
‡ προέλαβε † μυρίσαι μυ τὸ
σῶμα εἰς τὸν ‡ ἐνταφιασμόν.

14 Τότε πορευθεὶς εἷς τῶν δώδεκα, ὁ λεγόμενος Ἰούδας Ἰσκα-
ριώτης, πρὸς τὸς ἀρχιερεῖς,

15 Εἶπε· Τί θέλετέ μοι δῦναι,
κἀγὼ ὑμῖν παραδώσω αὐτόν;
Οἱ δὲ ἔστησαν αὐτῷ τριάκοντα ἀργύρια.

16 Καὶ ἀπὸ τότε ἐζήτει εὐ-
καιρίαν ἵνα αὐτὸν παραδῷ.

17 Τῇ δὲ πρώτῃ τῶν ἀζύμων
προσῆλθον οἱ μαθηταὶ τῷ Ἰησῦ,
λέγοντες αὐτῷ· Ποῦ θέλεις ἑτοι-
μάσωμέν σοι φαγεῖν τὸ πάσχα;

18 Ὁ δὲ εἶπεν· ‡ Ὑπάγετε
εἰς τὴν πόλιν ‡ πρὸς τὸν † δεῖνα,
ᾗ εἴπατε αὐτῷ· Ὁ διδάσκαλος
λέγει· Ὁ καιρός μυ ἐγγύς ἐσιν,
πρός σε ποιῶ τὸ πάσχα μετὰ
τῶν μαθητῶν μυ.

19 Καὶ ἐποίησαν οἱ μαθηταὶ
ὡς συνέταξεν αὐτοῖς ὁ Ἰησῦς· ᾗ
ἡτοίμασαν τὸ πάσχα.

20 Ὀψίας δὲ γενομένης ἀνέ-
κειτο μετὰ τῶν δώδεκα.

24 Ἐγένετο δὲ ᾗ † φιλονει-
κία ἐν αὐτοῖς, τὸ τίς αὐτῶν δοκεῖ εἶναι † μείζων.

* 25 Ὁ δὲ εἶπεν αὐτοῖς· Οἱ
βασιλεῖς τῶν ἐθνῶν † κυριεύυσιν

αὐτῶν· ᾗ ‡ ἐξυσιάζοντες αὐτῶν,
† εὐεργέται καλῦνται.

---

habens alabaſtrum unguenti,
nardi probati multi pretii : &
confringens alabaſtrum, effudit
ei juxta caput.

4 Erant autem quidam in-
dignati apud ſemetipſos, & dicentes? Ad quid perditio iſta
unguenti facta eſt?

5 Poterat enim iſtud venundari ſuper trecentis denariis, &
dari pauperibus. Et fremebant
ei.

6 At Jeſus dixit : Sinite eam·
Quid illi moleſtias exhibetis?
Pulchrum opus operata eſt in me.

7 Semper enim pauperes habetis cum vobis, & quum vo-
lueritis poteſtis illis benefacere :
me autem non ſemper habetis.

8 Quod habuit hæc, fecit :
præoccupavit ungere meum
corpus in ſepulturam.

14 Tunc vadens unus duodecim, dictus Judas Iſcariotes, ad
principes Sacerdotum,

15 Ait : Quid vultis mihi
dare, & ego vobis tradam eum?
Illi verò conſtituerunt ei triginta argenteos.

16 Et exinde quærebat oppor-
tunitatem ut eum traderet.

17 At primâ Azymorum ac-
ceſſerunt diſcipuli Jeſu, dicentes
ei : Ubi vis paremus tibi come-
dere Paſcha?

18 Ille autem dixit : Ite in
civitatem ad quendam, & dicite
ei : Magiſter dicit : Tempus
meum prope eſt, apud te facio
Paſcha cum diſcipulis meis.

19 Et fecerunt diſcipuli ſicut
ordinâverat illis Jeſus, & para-
verunt Paſcha.

20 Veſpere autem facto, diſ-
cumbebat cum duodecim.

24 Facta eſt autem & con-
tentio in eis, hoc, quis eorum
videretur eſſe major.

25 Is autem dixit eis ; Reges
gentium dominantur in eos : &

poteſtatem habentes ipſorum,
benefici vocantur.

une femme vint à lui, lorsqu'il étoit à table, avec un vase d'albâtre, plein d'une huile odoriférante et de grand prix, qu'elle lui répandit sur la tête, ayant rompu le vase.

4. Et quelques-uns en furent indignés en eux-mêmes, et dirent; Pourquoi perdre ainsi ce parfum?

5. Car on pouvoit le vendre plus de trois cents deniers, et les donner aux pauvres. Ainsi ils murmuroient contr'elle.

6. Mais Jésus leur dit : Laissez-la; pourquoi lui faites-vous de la peine? Elle a fait une bonne action à mon égard.

7. Car vous aurez toujours des pauvres parmi vous; et toutes les fois que vous voudrez, vous pourrez leur faire du bien; mais vous ne m'aurez pas toujours.

8. Elle a fait tout ce qui étoit en son pouvoir; elle a embaumé par avance mon corps pour ma sépulture.

14. Alors l'un des douze, appelé Judas Iscariot, s'en alla vers les principaux Sacrificateurs,

15. Et leur dit : Que voulez-vous me donner, et je vous le livrerai? Et ils convinrent de lui donner trente pièces d'argent.

16. Et depuis ce tems-là, il cherchoit une occasion propre pour le livrer.

17. Or, le premier jour de la fête des pains sans levain, les Disciples vinrent à Jésus et lui dirent : Où veux-tu que nous préparions pour manger la Pâque?

18. Et il répondit : Allez dans le village chez un tel, et lui dites : Le Maître dit : Mon tems est proche; je ferai la Pâque chez toi avec mes Disciples.

19. Et les Disciples firent comme Jésus leur avoit ordonné, et préparèrent la Pâque.

20. Quand le soir fut venu, il se mit à table avec les douze Apôtres.

24. Il arriva aussi une contestation entr'eux, pour savoir lequel d'entr'eux devoit être regardé comme le plus grand.

25. Mais il leur dit : Les Rois des nations les maîtrisent; et ceux qui usent d'autorité sur elles sont nommés bienfaiteurs.

having an alabaster-box of ointment of spikenard, very precious; and she brake the box, and poured it on his head.

4 And there were some that had indignation within themselves, and said, Why was this waste of the ointment made?

5 For it might have been sold for more than three hundred pence, and have been given to the poor. And they murmured against her.

6 And Jesus said, Let her alone, why trouble ye her? she hath wrought a good work on me.

7 For ye have the poor with you always, and whensoever ye will, ye may do them good; but me ye have not always.

8 She hath done what she could; she is come aforehand to anoint my body to the burying.

14 Then one of the twelve called Judas Iscariot, went unto the chief priests,

15 And said unto them, What will ye give me, and I will deliver him unto you? And they covenanted with him for thirty pieces of silver.

16 And from that time he sought opportunity to betray him.

17 Now, the first day of the feast of unleavened bread, the disciples came to Jesus, saying unto him, Where wilt thou that we prepare for thee to eat the passover?

18 And he said, Go into the city to such a man, and say unto him, The Master saith, My time is at hand; I will keep the passover at thy house with my disciples.

19 And the disciples did as Jesus had appointed them; and they made ready the passover.

20 Now, when the even was come, he sat down with the twelve.

24 And there was also a strife among them, which of them should be accounted the greatest.

25 And he said unto them, The kings of the Gentiles exercise lordship over them; and they that exercise authority upon them are called benefactors.

70

26 Ὑμεῖς δὲ ἐχ ὕτως· ἀλλ᾽ ὁ μείζων ἐν ὑμῖν, γενέσθω ὡς ὁ νεώτερ⟨⟩· ⁊ ὁ ἡγούμεν⟨⟩, ὡς ὁ διακονῶν.

27 Τίς γὰρ μείζων, ὁ ἀνακείμεν⟨⟩, ἢ ὁ διακονῶν; ἐχὶ ὁ ἀνακείμεν⟨⟩; ἐγὼ δέ εἰμι ἐν μέσῳ ὑμῶν ὡς ὁ διακονῶν.

2 Καὶ δείπνυ γενομένυ

4 Ἐγείρεται ἐκ τῦ δείπνυ, ⁊ τίθησι τὰ ἱμάτια· ⁊ λαβὼν λέντιον, διέζωσεν ἑαυτόν.

* 5 Εἶτα βάλλει ὕδωρ εἰς τὸν † νιπτῆρα, ⁊ ἤρξατο νίπ⟨⟩ειν τὰς πόδας τῶν μαθητῶν, ⁊ ‡ ἐκμάσσειν τῷ ‡ λεντίῳ ᾧ ἦν διεζωσμέν⟨⟩.

6 Ἔρχεται ἔν πρὸς Σίμωνα Πέτρον· ⁊ λέγει αὐτῷ ἐκεῖν⟨⟩· Κύριε, σύ μυ νίπίεις τὰς πόδας;

7 Ἀπεκρίθη Ἰησῦς ⁊ εἶπεν αὐτῷ· Ὃ ἐγὼ ποιῶ, σὺ ἐκ οἶδας ἄρτι, γνώσῃ δὲ μετὰ ταῦτα.

8 Λέγει αὐτῷ Πέτρ⟨⟩· Οὐ μὴ νίψῃς τὰς πόδας μυ εἰς τὸν αἰῶτα. Ἀπεκρίθη αὐτῷ ὁ Ἰησῦς· Ἐὰν μὴ νίψω σε, ἐκ ἔχεις μέρ⟨⟩ μετ᾽ ἐμῦ.

9 Λέγει αὐτῷ Σίμων Πέτρ⟨⟩· Κύριε, μὴ τὰς πόδας μυ μόνον, ἀλλὰ ⁊ τὰς χεῖρας ⁊ τὴν κεφαλήν.

10 Λέγει αὐτῷ ὁ Ἰησῦς· Ὁ λελυμέν⟨⟩ ἐ χρείαν ἔχει ἢ τὰς πόδας νίψασθαι, ἀλλ᾽ ἔςι καθαρὸς ὅλ⟨⟩· ⁊ ὑμεῖς καθαροί ἐςε, ἀλλ᾽ ἐχὶ πάντες.

11 Ἤδει γὰρ τὸν παραδιδόντα αὐτόν· διὰ τῦτο εἶπεν· Οὐχὶ πάντες καθαροί ἐςε.

12 Ὅτε ἔν ἔνιψε τὰς πόδας αὐτῶν, ⁊ ἔλαβε τὰ ἱμάτια αὐτῦ, ἀναπεσὼν πάλιν, εἶπεν αὐτοῖς· Γινώσκετε τί πεποίηκα ὑμῖν;

13 Ὑμεῖς φωνεῖτέ με· Ὁ διδάσκαλ⟨⟩ ⁊ ὁ κύρι⟨⟩· ⁊ καλῶς λέγετε· εἰμὶ γάρ.

14 Εἰ ἔν ἐγὼ ἔνιψα ὑμῶν τὰς πόδας, ὁ κύρι⟨⟩ ⁊ ὁ διδάσκαλ⟨⟩, ⁊ ὑμεῖς ὀφείλετε ἀλλήλων νίπίειν τὰς πόδας.

15 Ὑπόδειγμα γὰρ ἔδωκα ὑμῖν, ἵνα καθὼς ἐγὼ ἐποίησα ὑμῖν, ⁊ ὑμεῖς ποιῆτε.

16 Ἀμὴν, ἀμὴν, λέγω ὑμῖν, ἐκ ἔςι δῦλ⟨⟩ μείζων τῦ κυρίυ αὐτῦ, ἐδὲ ἀπόςολ⟨⟩ μείζων τῦ πέμψαν⟨⟩ αὐτόν.

17 Εἰ ταῦτα οἴδατε, μακάριοί ἐςε ἐὰν ποιῆτε αὐτά.

---

26 Vos autem non sic: sed qui major in vobis, fiat sicut junior: & qui præcessor, sicut ministrat_r.

27 Quis enim major, recumbens, an ministrans? nonne recumbens? ego autem sum in medio vestrum sicut ministrans.

2 Et cœna facta,

4 Surgit à cœna, & ponit vestimenta: & accipiens linteum, præcinxit seipsum.

5 Deinde injicit aquam in pelvim, & cœpit lavare pedes discipulorum, & extergere linteo quo erat præcinctus.

6 Venit ergo ad Simonem Petrum: & dicit ei ille: Domine, tu meos lavas pedes?

7 Respondit Jesus & dixit ei: Quod ego facio, tu nescis modo, scies autem post hæc.

8 Dicit ei Petrus: Non lavabis pedes meos in æternum. Respondit ei Jesus: Si non lavero te, non habes partem cum me.

9 Dicit ei Simon Petrus: Domine, non pedes meos tantum, sed & manus & caput.

10 Dicit ei Jesus: Lotus non opus habet quam pedes lavare, sed est mundus totus: Et vos mundi estis, sed non omnes.

11 Sciebat enim tradentem se; propter hoc dixit: Non omnes mundi estis.

12 Postquam ergo lavit pedes eorum, & accepit vestimenta sua, recumbens iterum, dixit eis: Scitis quid fecerim vobis?

13 Vos vocatis me: Magister & Dominus: & pulchre dicitis: sum etenim.

14 Si ergo ego lavi vestros pedes, dominus & magister, & vos debetis alii aliorum lavare pedes.

15 Exemplum enim dedi vobis ut quemadmodum ego feci, vobis, & vos faciatis.

16 Amen, amen, dico vobis, non est servus major domino suo, neque legatus major mittente illum.

17 Si hæc scitis, beati estis si feceritis ea.

26. Il n'en doit pas être de même entre vous ; mais que celui qui est le plus grand parmi vous, soit comme le moindre ; et celui qui gouverne, comme celui qui sert.

27. Car qui est le plus grand, celui qui est à table, ou celui qui sert ? N'est-ce pas celui qui est à table ? Et cependant je suis au milieu de vous comme celui qui sert.

2. Et après le souper

4. Se leva du souper, et ôta sa robe ; et ayant pris un linge, il s'en ceignit.

5. Ensuite il mit de l'eau dans un bassin, et se mit à laver les pieds de ses Disciples, et à les essuyer avec le linge dont il étoit ceint.

6. Il vint donc à Simon Pierre, qui lui dit, Toi, Seigneur, tu me laverois les pieds !

7. Jésus répondit, et lui dit : Tu ne sais pas maintenant ce que je fais ; mais tu le sauras dans la suite.

8. Pierre lui dit : Tu ne me laveras jamais les pieds. Jésus lui répondit : Si je ne te lave, tu n'auras point de part avec moi.

9. Simon Pierre lui dit : Seigneur, non-seulement les pieds, mais aussi les mains et la tête.

10. Jesus lui dit : Celui qui est lavé, n'a besoin sinon qu'on lui lave les pieds, puis il est entièrement net. Or vous êtes nets, mais non pas tous.

11. Car il savoit qui étoit celui qui le trahiroit ; c'est pour cela qu'il dit : Vous n'êtes pas tous nets.

12. Après donc qu'il leur eut lavé les pieds, et qu'il eut repris sa robe, s'étant remis à table, il leur dit : Savez-vous ce que je vous ai fait ?

13. Vous m'appelez Maître et Seigneur, et vous dites vrai, car je le suis.

14. Si donc je vous ai lavé les pieds, moi qui suis le Seigneur et le Maître, vous devez aussi vous laver les pieds les uns aux autres.

15. Car je vous ai donné un exemple, afin que vous fassiez comme je vous ai fait.

16. En vérité, en vérité je vous dis : Que le Serviteur n'est pas plus que son Maître, ni l'Envoyé plus que celui qui l'a envoyé.

17. Si vous savez ces choses, vous êtes bienheureux, pourvu que vous les pratiquiez.

---

26 But ye *shall* not *be* so: but he that is greatest among you, let him be as the younger; and he that is chief, as he that doth serve.

27 For whether *is* greater, he that sitteth at meat, or he that serveth? *is* not he that sitteth at meat? but I am among you as he that serveth.

2 And supper being ended,

4 He riseth from supper, and laid aside his garments; and took a towel, and girded himself.

5 After that he poureth water into a bason, and began to wash the disciples' feet, and to wipe them with the towel wherewith he was girded.

6 Then cometh he to Simon Peter: and Peter saith unto him, Lord, dost thou wash my feet?

7 Jesus answered, and said unto him, What I do, thou knowest not now; but thou shalt know hereafter.

8 Peter saith unto him, Thou shalt never wash my feet. Jesus answered him, If I wash thee not, thou hast no part with me.

9 Simon Peter saith unto him, Lord, not my feet only, but also *my* hands and *my* head.

10 Jesus saith to him, He that is washed, needeth not, save to wash *his* feet, but is clean every whit: and ye are clean, but not all.

11 For he knew who should betray him; therefore said he, Ye are not all clean.

12 So, after he had washed their feet, and had taken his garments, and was set down again, he said unto them, Know ye what I have done to you?

13 Ye call me Master and Lord: and ye say well; for so I am.

14 If I then, *your* Lord and Master, have washed your feet, ye also ought to wash one another's feet.

15 For I have given you an example, that ye should do as I have done to you.

16 Verily, verily, I say unto you, The servant is not greater than his lord; neither he that is sent, greater than he that sent him.

17 If ye know these things, happy are ye if ye do them.

71

21 Ταῦτα εἰπὼν ὁ Ἰησοῦς ἐ-
ταράχθη τῷ πνεύματι, καὶ ἐμαρτύ-
ρησε, καὶ εἶπεν Ἀμὴν, ἀμὴν, λέγω
ὑμῖν, ὅτι εἷς ἐξ ὑμῶν παραδώ-
σει με.

22 Ἔβλεπον οὖν εἰς ἀλλήλους
οἱ μαθηταὶ, ἀπορούμενοι περὶ τίνος λέγει.

23 Ἦν δὲ ἀνακείμενος εἷς τῶν
μαθητῶν αὐτοῦ ἐν τῷ κόλπῳ τοῦ
Ἰησοῦ, ὃν ἠγάπα ὁ Ἰησοῦς.

24 Νεύει οὖν τούτῳ Σίμων Πέτρος πυθέσθαι τίς ἂν εἴη περὶ
οὗ λέγει.

25 Ἐπιπεσὼν δὲ ἐκεῖνος ἐπὶ
τὸ στῆθος τοῦ Ἰησοῦ, λέγει αὐτῷ·
Κύριε, τίς ἐστι;

26 Ἀποκρίνεται ὁ Ἰησοῦς· Ἐ-
κεῖνός ἐστιν ᾧ ἐγὼ βάψας τὸ ψωμίον ἐπιδώσω. Καὶ ἐμβάψας τὸ
ψωμίον, δίδωσιν Ἰούδᾳ Σίμωνος
Ἰσκαριώτῃ.

31 Ὅτε οὖν ἐξῆλθε, λέγει ὁ
Ἰησοῦς·

34 Ἐντολὴν καινὴν δίδωμι ὑμῖν,
ἵνα ἀγαπᾶτε ἀλλήλους· καθὼς ἠ-
γάπησα ὑμᾶς, ἵνα καὶ ὑμεῖς ἀγαπᾶτε ἀλλήλους.

35 Ἐν τούτῳ γνώσονται πάντες
ὅτι ἐμοὶ μαθηταί ἐστε, ἐὰν ἀγάπην
ἔχητε ἐν ἀλλήλοις.

31 Τότε λέγει αὐτοῖς ὁ Ἰησοῦς·
Πάντες ὑμεῖς σκανδαλισθήσεσθε ἐν
ἐμοὶ ἐν τῇ νυκτὶ ταύτῃ·

33 Ἀποκριθεὶς δὲ ὁ Πέτρος,
εἶπεν αὐτῷ· Εἰ καὶ πάντες σκανδα-
λισθήσονται ἐν σοὶ, ἐγὼ οὐδέποτε
σκανδαλισθήσομαι.

μετὰ σοῦ ἕτοιμός εἰμι καὶ εἰς φυλακὴν καὶ εἰς θάνατον πορεύεσθαι.

34 Ὁ δὲ εἶπε· Λέγω σοι,
Πέτρε, οὐ μὴ φωνήσει σήμερον
ἀλέκτωρ, πρὶν ἢ τρὶς ἀπαρνήσῃ
μὴ εἰδέναι με.

35 Λέγει αὐτῷ ὁ Πέτρος· Κἂν
δέῃ με σὺν σοὶ ἀποθανεῖν, οὐ μή σε
ἀπαρνήσομαι. Ὁμοίως καὶ πάντες
οἱ μαθηταὶ εἶπον.

36 Τότε ἔρχεται μετ᾽ αὐτῶν
ὁ Ἰησοῦς εἰς χωρίον λεγόμενον
Γεθσημανῆ· καὶ λέγει τοῖς μαθηταῖς·
Καθίσατε αὐτοῦ, ἕως οὗ ἀπελθὼν
προσεύξωμαι ἐκεῖ·

21 Hæc dicens Jesus turba-
tus est spiritu, & protestatus est,
& dixit: Amen amen dico vobis, unus ex vobis tradet me.

22 Aspiciebant ergo ad invicem discipuli, hæsitantes de
quo diceret.

23 Erat autem recumbens u-
nus discipulorum ejus in sinu
Jesu, quem diligebat Jesus.

24 Innuit ergo huic Simon
Petrus percontari quis esset de
quo dicit.

25 Incumbens autem ille supra pectus Jesu, dicit ei: Domine, quis est?

26 Respondit Jesus: Ille est
cui ego intingens buccellam de-
dero. Et intingens buccellam,
dat Judæ Simonis Iscariotæ.

31 Quum ergo exisset, dicit
Jesus:

34 Mandatum novum do vo-
bis, Ut diligatis invicem: sicut di-
lexi vos, ut & vos diligatis invicem.

35 In hoc cognoscent omnes
quia mei discipuli estis, si dilec-
tionem habueritis ad invicem.

31 Tunc dicit illis Jesus:
Omnes vos offendemini in me
in nocte istâ.

33 Respondens autem Petrus,
ait illi: Si & omnes scandalizati
fuerint in te, ego nunquam
scandalizabor.

tecum paratus sum & in
carcerem, & in mortem ire.

34 Ille autem dixit. Dico
tibi, Petre, non cantabit hodie
gallus, prius quàm ter abneges,
nosse me.

35 Ait illi Petrus: Etiam si
oportuerit me cum te mori, non
te negabo. Similiter & omnes
discipuli dixerunt.

36 Tunc venit cum illis Jesus in villam dictam Gethse-
mani, & dicit discipulis: Se-
dete hic, usquequò vadens orem
illic.

21. Quand Jésus eut dit cela , il fut ému en son esprit , et il dit ouvertement : En vérité, en vérité je vous dis , que l'un de vous me trahira.

22. Et les Disciples se regardoient les uns les autres , étant en peine de qui il parloit.

23. Or il y avoit un des Disciples de Jésus , celui que Jésus aimoit, qui étoit couché vers son sein.

24. Simon Pierre lui fit signe de demander qui étoit celui de qui il parloit.

25. Lui donc s'étant penché sur le sein de Jésus , lui dit : Seigneur , qui est-ce ?

26. Jésus répondit : C'est celui à qui je donnerai un morceau trempé. Et ayant trempé un morceau , il le donna à Judas Iscariot , fils de Simon.

31. Quand il fut sorti , Jésus dit :

34. Je vous donne un commandement nouveau , que vous vous aimiez les uns les autres ; que comme je vous ai aimés , vous vous aimiez aussi les uns les autres.

35. C'est à cela que tous connoîtront que vous êtes mes Disciples , si vous avez de l'amour les uns pour les autres.

31. Alors Jésus leur dit : Je vous serai cette nuit à tous une occasion de chute :

33. Et Pierre prenant la parole, lui dit : Quand même tous les autres se scandaliseroient en toi, je ne serai jamais scandalisé.
je suis tout prêt d'aller avec toi , et en prison et à la mort.

34. Mais Jésus lui dit : Pierre, je te dis que le coq ne chantera point aujourd'hui , que tu n'aies nié trois fois de me connoître.

35. Puis il leur dit : Lorsque je vous ai envoyés sans bourse , sans sac , et sans souliers , avez-vous manqué de quelque chose ? Et ils répondirent : De rien.

36. Mais maintenant , leur dit-il , que celui qui a une bourse la prenne , et de même celui qui a un sac ; et que celui qui n'a point d'épée vende sa robe , et en achète une.

J. 13

21 When Jesus had thus said, he was troubled in spirit, and testified, and said, Verily, verily, I say unto you, that one of you shall betray me.

22 Then the disciples looked one on another, doubting of whom he spake.

23 Now there was leaning on Jesus' bosom one of his disciples, whom Jesus loved.

24 Simon Peter, therefore, beckoned to him, that he should ask who it should be of whom he spake.

25 He then, lying on Jesus' breast, saith unto him, Lord, who is it?

26 Jesus answered, He it is, to whom I shall give a sop, when I have dipped it. And when he had dipped the sop, he gave it to Judas Iscariot, the son of Simon.

31 Therefore, when he was gone out, Jesus said,

34 A new commandment I give unto you, That ye love one another; as I have loved you, that ye also love one another.

35 By this shall all men know that ye are my disciples, if ye have love one to another.

M. 26

31 Then saith Jesus unto them, All ye shall be offended because of me this night:

33 Peter answered, and said unto him, Though all men shall be offended because of thee, yet will I never be offended.

L. 22

I am ready to go with thee, both into prison, and to death.

34 And he said, I tell thee, Peter, the cock shall not crow this day, before that thou shalt thrice deny that thou knowest me.

M. 26

35 Peter said unto him, Though I should die with thee, yet will I not deny thee. Likewise also said all the disciples.

36 Then cometh Jesus with them unto a place called Gethsemane, and saith unto the disciples, Sit ye here, while I go and pray yonder.

72.

* 37 Καὶ παϱαλαβὼν τὸν Πέ-
τϱον κỳ τὲς δύο υἱὲς Ζεβεδαίε ἤϱξαλο
λυπεῖσθαι κỳ ‡ ἀδημονεῖν.

38 Τότε λέγει αὐτοῖς· Πεϱί-
λυπός ἐςιν ἡ ψυχή με ἕως θανάτε·
μείναλε ὧδε, κỳ γϱηγοϱεῖτε μετ'
ἐμῶ.

39 Καὶ πϱοελθὼν μικϱὸν, ἔπεσεν ἐπὶ πϱόσωπον αὐτῶ, πϱοσευ-

χόμενΘ-, κỳ λέγων· Πάτεϱ με,
εἰ δυναλόν ἐςι, παϱελθέτω ἀπ'
ἐμῶ τὸ ποτήϱιον τῶτο. πλὴν ἐχ
ὡς ἐγὼ θέλω, ἀλλ' ὡς σύ.

40 Καὶ ἔϱχελαι πϱὸς τὲς μα-
θηλὰς, κỳ εὑϱίσκει αὐτὲς καθεύ-
δονλας· κỳ λέγει τῶ Πέτϱῳ· Οὕτως
ἐκ ἰσχύσαλε μίαν ὥϱαν γϱηγοϱῆσαι
μετ' ἐμῶ;

41 Γϱηγοϱεῖτε κỳ πϱοσεύχεσθε,
ἵνα μὴ εἰσέλθηλε εἰς πειϱασμόν·
τὸ μὲν πνεῦμα πϱόθυμον, ἡ δὲ σὰϱξ
ἀσθενής.

42 Πάλιν ἐκ δευλέϱε ἀπελθὼν
πϱοσηύξαλο, λέγων· Πάτεϱ με,
εἰ ἐ δύναλαι τῶτο τὸ ποτήϱιον πα-
ϱελθεῖν ἀπ' ἐμῶ, ἐὰν μὴ αὐτὸ πίω,
γειηθήτω τὸ θέλημά σε.

43 Καὶ ἐλθὼν εὑϱίσκει αὐτὲς
πάλιν καθεύδονλας· ἦσαν γὰϱ αὐτῶν οἱ ὀφθαλμοὶ βεβαϱημένοι.

44 Καὶ ἀφεὶς αὐτὲς, ἀπελθὼν
πάλιν, πϱοσηύξαλο ἐκ τϱίτε, τὸν
αὐτὸν λόγον εἰπών.

45 Τότε ἔϱχελαι πϱὸς τὲς μα-
θηλὰς αὐτῶ, κỳ λέγει αὐτοῖς· Κα-
θεύδελε τὸ λοιπὸν, κỳ ἀναπαύεσθε·

Κεφ. ιη'. 18.

* 1 Ταῦτα εἰπὼν ὁ Ἰησῦς, ἐξῆλθε σὺν τοῖς μαθηλαῖς
αὐτῶ ‡ πέϱαν τῶ † χειμάϱϱε τῶν
† κέδϱων, ὅπη ἦν ‡ κῆπΘ-, εἰς
ὃν εἰσῆλθεν αὐτὸς κỳ οἱ μαθηλαὶ
αὐτῶ.

2 Ἤδει δὲ κỳ Ἰέδας, ὁ παϱα-
διδὲς αὐτὸ, τὸν τόπον· ὅτι πολ-
λάκις συνήχθη ὁ Ἰησῦς ἐκεῖ μελὰ
τῶν μαθηλῶν αὐτῶ.

3 Ὁ ἒν Ἰέδας λαβὼν τὴν
σπεῖϱαν, κỳ ἐκ τῶν ἀϱχιεϱέων κỳ
φαϱισαίων ὑπηϱέτας, ἔϱχελαι ἐκεῖ
μελὰ † φανῶν κỳ ‡ λαμπάδων κỳ
ὅπλων.

37 Et assumens Petrum, &
duos filios Zebedæi, cœpit con-
tristari & gravissimè angi.

38 Tunc ait illis: Undique
tristis est anima mea usque ad
mortem. Manete hic, & vigilate cum me.

39 Et progressus pusillùm,
procidit in faciem suam, o-
rans, & dicens: Pater mi, si
possibile est, transeat à me calix
iste, veruntamen non sicut ego
volo, sed sicut tu.

40 Et venit ad discipulos, &
invenit eos dormientes: & dicit
Petro: Sic non potuistis una
hora vigilare cum me?

41 Vigilate & orate, ut non
intretis in tentationem: Quidem
spiritus promptus, verùm caro
infirma.

42 Iterum ex secundò abiens
oravit dicens: Pater mi, si non
potest hic calix transire à me,
si non illum bibam, fiat voluntas tua.

43 Et veniens invenit eos
rursus dormientes: erant enim
eorum oculi gravati.

44 Et relinquens illos, abiens
iterum, oravit ex tertio, eun-
dem sermonem dicens.

45 Tunc venit ad discipulos
suos, & dicit illis: Dormite
cæterum, & requiescite:

CAPUT XVIII.

1 Hæc dicens Jesus, egressus
est cum discipulis suis
trans torrentem Cedron, ubi
erat hortus, in quem introivit
ipse, & discipuli ejus.

2 Sciebat autem & Judas,
tradens eum, locum, quia fre-
quenter convenerat Jesus illuc
cum discipulis suis.

3 Ergo Judas accipiens cohortem, & ex principibus Sacerdotum & Pharisæis ministros,
venit illuc cum laternis & faci-
bus, & armis.

37. Et ayant pris avec lui Pierre et les deux fils de Zébédée, il commença à être fort triste, et dans une amère douleur.

38. Et il leur dit : Mon ame est saisie de tristesse jusqu'à la mort; demeurez ici, et veillez avec moi.

39. Et étant allé un peu plus avant, il se jeta le visage contre terre, priant et disant : Mon Père, que cette coupe passe loin de moi, s'il est possible! Toutefois, *qu'il en soit*, non comme je le voudrois, mais comme tu le veux.

40. Puis il vint vers ses Disciples, et les trouva endormis ; et il dit à Pierre : Est-il possible que vous n'ayez pu veiller une heure avec moi ?

41. Veillez et priez, de peur que vous ne tombiez dans la tentation; car l'esprit *est* prompt, mais la chair *est* foible.

42. Il s'en alla encore pour la seconde fois, et pria, disant : Mon Père, s'il n'est pas possible que cette coupe passe loin de moi, sans que je la boive, que ta volonté soit faite !

43. Et revenant *à eux*, il les trouva encore endormis; car leurs yeux étoient appesantis.

44. Et les ayant laissés, il s'en alla encore, et pria pour la troisième fois, disant les mêmes paroles.

45. Alors il vint vers ses disciples, et leur dit : Vous dormez encore, et vous vous reposez !

APRÈS que Jésus eut dit ces choses, il s'en alla avec ses Disciples au-delà du torrent de Cédron, où il y avoit un jardin dans lequel il entra avec ses Disciples.

2. Judas, qui le trahissoit, connoissoit aussi ce lieu-là, parce que Jésus s'y étoit souvent assemblé avec ses Disciples.

3. Judas ayant donc pris une compagnie *de soldats* et des sergens, de la part des principaux Sacrificateurs et des Pharisiens, vint là avec des lanternes, des flambeaux et des armes.

37 And he took with him Peter and the two sons of Zebedee, and began to be sorrowful and very heavy.

38 Then saith he unto them, My soul is exceeding sorrowful, even unto death : tarry ye here, and watch with me.

39 And he went a little farther, and fell on his face, and prayed, saying, O my Father, if it be possible, let this cup pass from me : nevertheless, not as I will, but as thou *wilt*.

40 And he cometh unto the disciples, and findeth them asleep, and saith unto Peter, What! could ye not watch with me one hour?

41 Watch and pray, that ye enter not into temptation : the spirit indeed *is* willing, but the flesh *is* weak.

42 He went away again the second time, and prayed, saying, O my Father, if this cup may not pass away from me, except I drink it, thy will be done.

43 And he came and found them asleep again : for their eyes were heavy.

44 And he left them, and went away again, and prayed the third time, saying the same words.

45 Then cometh he to his disciples, and saith unto them, Sleep on now, and take *your* rest :

CHAP. XVIII.
Judas betrayeth Jesus.

WHEN Jesus had spoken these words, he went forth with his disciples over the brook Cedron, where was a garden, into the which he entered, and his disciples.

2 And Judas also, which betrayed him, knew the place : for Jesus oft-times resorted thither with his disciples.

3 Judas then, having received a band *of men* and officers from the chief priests and Pharisees, cometh thither with lanterns, and torches, and weapons.

48 Ὁ δὲ παραδιδοὺς αὐτὸν, ἔδωκεν αὐτοῖς σημεῖον, λέγων· Ὃν ἂν φιλήσω, αὐτός ἐςι· κρατήσαιε αὐτόν.

49 Καὶ εὐθέως προσελθὼν τῷ Ἰησῦ, εἶπε· Χαῖρε ῥαββι. Καὶ κατεφίλησεν αὐτόν.

50 Ὁ δὲ Ἰησῦς εἶπεν αὐτῷ· Ἑταῖρε, ἐφ᾽ ᾧ πάρει; Τότε προσελθόντες ἐπέβαλον τὰς χεῖρας ἐπὶ τὸν Ἰησῦν, ἢ ἐκράτησαν αὐτόν.

4 Ἰησῦς ἐν εἰδὼς πάντα τὰ ἐρχόμενα ἐπ᾽ αὐτὸν, ἐξελθὼν εἶπεν αὐτοῖς· Τίνα ζητεῖτε;

5 Ἀπεκρίθησαν αὐτῷ· Ἰησῦν τὸν Ναζωραῖον. Λέγει αὐτοῖς ὁ

Ἰησῦς· Ἐγώ εἰμι. Εἱστήκει δὲ ἢ Ἰούδας ὁ παραδιδοὺς αὐτὸν μετ᾽ αὐτῶν.

6 Ὡς ἐν εἶπεν αὐτοῖς· Ὅτι ἐγώ εἰμι, ἀπῆλθον εἰς τὰ ὀπίσω, ἢ ἔπεσον χαμαί.

7 Πάλιν ἐν αὐτὸς ἐπηρώτησε· Τίνα ζητεῖτε; Οἱ δὲ εἶπον· Ἰησῦν τὸν Ναζωραῖον.

8 Ἀπεκρίθη ὁ Ἰησῦς· Εἶπον ὑμῖν ὅτι ἐγώ εἰμι· εἰ ἐν ἐμὲ ζητεῖτε, ἄφετε τούτους ὑπάγειν.

51 Καὶ ἰδὲ, εἷς τῶν μετὰ Ἰησῦ, ἐκτείνας τὴν χεῖρα, ἀπέσπασε τὴν μάχαιραν αὐτῦ· ἢ πατάξας τὸν δῦλον τῦ ἀρχιερέως, ἀφεῖλεν αὐτῦ τὸ ὠτίον.

52 Τότε λέγει αὐτῷ ὁ Ἰησῦς· Ἀπόςρεψόν σου τὴν μάχαιραν εἰς τὸν τόπον αὐτῆς· πάντες γὰρ οἱ λαβόντες μάχαιραν, ἐν μαχαίρᾳ ἀπολῦνται.

55 Ἐν ἐκείνῃ τῇ ὥρᾳ εἶπεν ὁ Ἰησῦς τοῖς ὄχλοις· Ὡς ἐπὶ λῃςὴν ἐξήλθετε μετὰ μαχαιρῶν ἢ ξύλων συλλαβεῖν με· καθ᾽ ἡμέραν πρὸς ὑμᾶς ἐκαθεζόμην διδάσκων ἐν τῷ ἱερῷ, ἢ ὐκ ἐκρατήσατέ με.

Τότε οἱ μαθηταὶ πάντες, ἀφέντες αὐτὸν, ἔφυγον.

51 Καὶ εἷς τις νεανίσκος ἠκολούθει αὐτῷ, περιβεβλημένος σινδόνα ἐπὶ γυμνῦ· ἢ κρατῦσιν αὐτὸν οἱ νεανίσκοι.

52 Ὁ δὲ καταλιπὼν τὴν σινδόνα, γυμνὸς ἔφυγεν ἀπ᾽ αὐτῶν.

---

48 At tradens eum, dedit illi ſignum, dicens: Quemcumque oſculatus fuero, ipſe eſt: prehendite eum.

49 Et confeſtim accedens ad Jeſum, dixit: Gaude Rabbi. Et oſculatus eſt eum.

50 At Jeſus ait illi, Amice, in quo ades? Tunc accedentes injecerunt manus in Jeſum, & prehenderunt eum.

4 Jeſus itaque ſciens omnia ventura ſuper ſe, exiens dixit eis: Quem quæritis?

5 Reſponderunt ei: Jeſum Nazarenum. Dicit eis Jeſus:

Ego ſum. Stabat autem & Judas ille tradens eum cum ipſis.

6 Ut ergo dixit eis: Ego ſum, abierunt in ea quæ poſt, & ceciderunt humi.

7 Iterum ergo eos interrogavit: Quem quæritis? At dixerunt: Jeſum Nazarenum.

8 Reſpondit Jeſus: Dixi vobis, quia ego ſum. ſi ergo me quæritis, ſinite hos abire.

51 Et ecce unus eorum qui cum Jeſu, extendens manum exemit gladium ſuum: & percutiens ſervum principis ſacerdotum, amputavit ejus auriculam.

52 Tunc ait illi Jeſus, Converte tuum gladium in locum ſuum: omnes enim accipientes gladium, in gladio peribunt.

55 In illa hora dixit Jeſus turbis: Tanquam ad latronem exiſtis cum gladiis & lignis, comprehendere me: quotidie apud vos ſedebam docens in templo, & non prehendiſtis me.

Tunc diſcipuli omnes relicto eo, fugerunt.

51 Et unus quidam juvenis ſequebatur eum amictus ſindone ſuper nudo: & tenent eum juvenes.

52 Ille autem relinquens ſindonem, nudus profugit ab eis.

48. Et celui qui le trahissoit, leur avoit donné ce signal : Celui que je baiserai, c'est lui ; saisissez-le.

49. Et aussitôt s'approchant de Jésus, il lui dit : Maître, je te salue ; et il le baisa.

50. Et Jésus lui dit : Mon ami, pour quel sujet es-tu ici ?

4. Et Jésus qui savoit tout ce qui lui devoit arriver, s'avança, et leur dit : Qui cherchez-vous ?

5. Ils lui répondirent : Jésus de Nazareth. Jésus leur dit : C'est moi. Et Judas qui le trahissoit étoit aussi avec eux.

6. Et dès qu'il leur eut dit : C'est moi, ils reculèrent, et tombèrent par terre.

7. Il leur demanda encore une fois : Qui cherchez-vous ? Et ils répondirent : Jésus de Nazareth.

8. Jésus répondit : Je vous ai dit que c'est moi ; si donc c'est moi que vous cherchez, laissez aller ceux-ci.

Alors ils s'approchèrent, et jetèrent les mains sur Jésus, et le saisirent.

51. En même-tems, un de ceux qui étoient avec Jésus, portant la main à l'épée, la tira, et en frappa un serviteur du Souverain Sacrificateur, et lui emporta une oreille.

52. Alors Jésus lui dit : Remets ton épée dans le fourreau ; car tous ceux qui prendront l'épée, périront par l'épée.

55. En même-tems Jésus dit à cette troupe : Vous êtes sortis avec des épées et des bâtons, comme après un brigand, pour me prendre ; j'étois tous les jours assis parmi vous, enseignant dans le temple, et vous ne m'avez point saisi.

Alors tous les Disciples l'abandonnèrent et s'enfuirent.

51. Et il y avoit un jeune homme qui le suivoit, ayant le corps couvert seulement d'un linceul : et quelques jeunes gens l'ayant pris,

52. Il leur laissa le linceul, et s'enfuit nud de leurs mains.

48 Now he that betrayed him gave them a sign, saying, Whomsoever I shall kiss, that same is he: hold him fast.

49 And forthwith he came to Jesus, and said, Hail, Master, and kissed him.

50 And Jesus said unto him, Friend, wherefore art thou come?

4 Jesus, therefore, knowing all things that should come upon him, went forth, and said unto them, Whom seek ye?

5 They answered him, Jesus of Nazareth. Jesus saith unto them, I am *he*. (And Judas also, which betrayed him, stood with them.)

6 As soon then as he had said unto them, I am *he*, they went backward, and fell to the ground.

7 Then asked he them again, Whom seek ye? And they said, Jesus of Nazareth.

8 Jesus answered, I have told you, that I am *he*: if, therefore, ye seek me, let these go their way;

Then came they and laid hands on Jesus, and took him.

51 And, behold, one of them, which were with Jesus, stretched out *his* hand, and drew his sword, and struck a servant of the high priest, and smote off his ear.

52 Then said Jesus unto him, Put up again thy sword into his place: for all they that take the sword shall perish with the sword.

55 In that same hour said Jesus to the multitudes, Are ye come out, as against a thief, with swords, and staves for to take me? I sat daily with you, teaching in the temple, and ye laid no hold on me.

56. Then all the disciples forsook him and fled.

51 And there followed him a certain young man, having a linen cloth cast about *his* naked *body*; and the young men laid hold on him:

52 And he left the linen cloth, and fled from them naked.

74

57 Οἱ δὲ κρατήσαντες τὸν Ἰησοῦν, ἀπήγαγον πρὸς Καϊά-φαν τὸν ἀρχιερέα, ὅπε οἱ γραμ-ματεῖς κ᾽ οἱ πρεσβύτεροι συνήχ-θησαν.

* 15 Ἠκολούθει δὲ τῷ Ἰησῦ Σίμων Πέτρος, κ᾽ ὁ ἄλλος μα-θητής. ὁ δὲ μαθητὴς ἐκεῖνος ἦν γνωςὸς τῷ ἀρχιερεῖ, κ᾽ συνεισῆλ-θε τῷ Ἰησῦ εἰς τὴν αὐλὴν τῦ ἀρχιερέως.

16 Ὁ δὲ Πέτρος εἱςήκει πρὸς τῇ θύρᾳ ἔξω· ἐξῆλθεν ὖν ὁ μα-θητὴς ὁ ἄλλος, ὃς ἦν γνωςὸς τῷ ἀρχιερεῖ, κ᾽ εἶπε τῇ θυρωρῷ, κ᾽ εἰσήγαγε τὸν Πέτρον.

18 Εἱςήκεισαν δὲ οἱ δῦλοι, κ᾽ οἱ ὑπηρέται ἀνθρακιὰν πεποιηκό-τες, ὅτι ψύχος ἦν, κ᾽ ἐθερμαί-νοντο· ἦν δὲ μετ᾽ αὐτῶν ὁ Πέ-τρος κ᾽ θερμαινόμενος.

17 Λέγει ὖν ἡ παιδίσκη ἡ θυ-ρωρὸς τῷ Πέτρῳ· Μὴ κ᾽ σὺ ἐκ τῶν μαθητῶν εἶ τῦ ἀνθρώπυ τύτυ; Λέγει ἐκεῖνος· Οὐκ εἰμί.

25 Ἦν δὲ Σίμων Πέτρος ἑςὼς κ᾽ θερμαινόμενος. εἶπον ὖν αὐτῷ· Μὴ κ᾽ σὺ ἐκ τῶν μαθητῶν αὐτῦ εἶ; Ἠρνήσατο ἐκεῖνος, κ᾽ εἶπεν· Οὐκ εἰμί.

26 Λέγει εἷς ἐκ τῶν δῦλων τῦ ἀρχιερέως, συγγενὴς ὢν ὗ ἀ-πέκοψε Πέτρος τὸ ὠτίον· Οὐκ ἐγώ σε, εἶδον ἐν τῷ κήπῳ μετ᾽ αὐτῦ;

27 Πάλιν ὖν ἠρνήσατο ὁ Πέ-τρος, κ᾽ εὐθέως ἀλέκτωρ ἐφώνησεν.

75 Καὶ ἐμνήσθη ὁ Πέτρος τῦ ῥήματος τῦ Ἰησῦ, εἰρηκότος αὐ-τῷ· Ὅτι πρὶν ἀλέκτορα φωνῆσαι, τρὶς ἀπαρνήσῃ με. Καὶ ἐξελθὼν ἔξω, ἔκλαυσε πικρῶς. 26. †

19 Ὁ ὖν ἀρχιερεὺς ἠρώτησε τὸν Ἰησῦν περὶ τῶν μαθητῶν αὐ-τῦ, κ᾽ περὶ τῆς διδαχῆς αὐτῦ.

20 Ἀπεκρίθη αὐτῷ ὁ Ἰησῦς· Ἐγὼ παρρησίᾳ ἐλάλησα τῷ κόσ-μῳ· ἐγὼ πάντοτε ἐδίδαξα ἐν τῇ συναγωγῇ κ᾽ ἐν τῷ ἱερῷ, ὅπε πάντοθεν οἱ Ἰυδαῖοι συνέρχονται, κ᾽ ἐν κρυπτῷ ἐλάλησα ἰδέν·

57 Illi verò tenentes Jesum, adduxerunt ad Caipham princi-pem Sacerdotum, ubi Scribæ, & seniores convenerant.

15 Sequebatur autem Jesum Simon Petrus, & alius discipu-lus. At discipulus ille erat no-tus principi Sacerdotum, & si-mul introivit Jesu in atrium principis Sacerdotum.

16 At Petrus stabat ad ostium foris: Exivit ergo discipulus a-lius, qui erat notus principi Sa-cerdotum, & dixit ostiariæ, & introduxit Petrum.

18 Stabant autem servi & mi-nistri prunam facientes, quia frigus erat, & calefaciebant se: erat autem cum eis Petrus stans & calefaciens se.

17 Dicit ergo ancilla ostiaria Petro: Nunquid & tu ex disci-pulis es hominis istius? Dicit ille: Non sum.

25 Erat autem Simon Petrus stans, & calefaciens se. Dixe-runt ergo ei: Num & tu ex dis-cipulis ejus es? Negavit ille, & ait: Non sum.

26 Dicit unus ex servis prin-cipis Sacerdotum, cognatus exi-stens cujus absciderat Petrus au-riculam: Non ego te vidi in horto cum illo?

27 Iterum ergo negavit Pe-trus, & statim gallus cantavit.

75 Et recordatus est Petrus verbi Jesu, dicentis ei: Quod ante gallum vociferari, ter ab-negabis me. Et egressus foras, flevit amarè.

19 Ergo princeps Sacerdotum interrogavit Jesum de discipulis suis, & de doctrina ejus.

20 Respondit ei Jesus: Ego palam loquutus sum mundo: ego semper docui in synagoga & in templo, quo undique Ju-dæi conveniunt, & in occulto loquutus sum nihil.

57. Mais ceux qui avoient saisi Jésus, l'emmenèrent chez Caïphe le Souverain Sacrificateur, où les Scribes et les Sénateurs étoient assemblés.

15. Or, Simon Pierre, avec un autre Disciple, avoit suivi Jésus; et ce Disciple étoit connu du Souverain Sacrificateur; et il entra avec Jésus dans la cour de la maison du Souverain Sacrificateur.

16. Mais Pierre étoit demeuré dehors à la porte. Et cet autre Disciple qui étoit connu du souverain Sacrificateur, sortit, et parla à la portière, qui fit entrer Pierre.

18. Et les serviteurs et les sergens étoient là, et ayant fait du feu, parce qu'il faisoit froid, ils se chauffoient. Pierre étoit aussi avec eux, et se chauffoit.

17. Et cette servante, qui étoit la portière, dit à Pierre: N'es-tu pas aussi des Disciples de cet homme? Il dit: Je n'en suis point.

25. Et Simon Pierre étoit là, et se chauffoit; et ils lui dirent:

N'es-tu pas aussi de ses Disciples? Il le nia, et dit: Je n'en suis point.

26. Et l'un des serviteurs du Souverain Sacrificateur, parent de celui à qui Pierre avoit coupé l'oreille, lui dit: Ne t'ai-je pas vu dans le jardin avec lui?

27. Pierre le nia encore une fois; et aussi le coq chanta.

75. Alors Pierre se souvint de la parabole de Jesus, qui lui avoit dit: Avant que le coq ait chanté, tu me renieras trois fois. Et étant sorti, il pleura amèrement.

19. Et le souverain Sacrificateur interrogea Jésus touchant ses Disciples, et touchant sa doctrine.

20. Jésus lui répondit: J'ai parlé ouvertement à tout le monde, j'ai toujours enseigné dans la Synagogue et dans le Temple où les Juifs s'assemblent de toutes parts, et je n'ai rien dit en cachette.

M. 26.

57 And they that had laid hold on Jesus, led, *him* away to Caiaphas the high priest, where the scribes and the elders were assembled.

J. 18.

15 And Simon Peter followed Jesus, and *so did* another disciple. That disciple was known unto the high priest, and went in with Jesus into the palace of the high priest.

16 But Peter stood at the door without. Then went out that other disciple, which was known unto the high priest, and spake unto her that kept the door, and brought in Peter.

18 And the servants and officers stood there, who had made a fire of coals, (for it was cold,) and they warmed themselves: and Peter stood with them, and warmed himself.

17 Then saith the damsel, that kept the door, unto Peter, Art not thou also *one* of this man's disciples? He saith, I am not.

25 And Simon Peter stood and warmed himself: they said, therefore, unto him, Art not thou also *one* of his disciples? He denied *it*, and said, I am not.

26 One of the servants of the high priest, (being *his* kinsman whose ear Peter cut off,) saith, Did not I see thee in the garden with him?

27 Peter then denied again; and immediately the cock crew.

M. 26.

75 And Peter remembered the words of Jesus, which said unto him, Before the cock crow, thou shalt deny me thrice. And he went out, and wept bitterly.

J. 18.

19 The high priest then asked Jesus of his disciples, and of his doctrine.

20 Jesus answered him, I spake openly to the world; I ever taught in the synagogue, and in the temple, whither the Jews always resort; and in secret have I said nothing.

75

21 Τί με ἐπερωτᾷς; ἐπερώτησον τὰς ἀκηκοότας, τί ἐλάλησα αὐτοῖς· ἴδε, ὗτοι οἴδασιν ἃ εἶπον ἐγώ.

22 Ταῦτα δὲ αὐτῷ εἰπόντ⊙, εἷς τῶν ὑπηρετῶν παρεςηκὼς ἔδωκε ῥάπισμα τῷ Ἰησῦ, εἰπών· Οὕτως ἀποκρίνῃ τῷ ἀρχιερεῖ;

23 Ἀπεκρίθη αὐτῷ ὁ Ἰησῦς· Εἰ κακῶς ἐλάλησα, μαρτύρησον περὶ τῦ κακῦ· εἰ δὲ καλῶς, τί με δέρεις;

55 Οἱ δὲ ἀρχιερεῖς κ̈ ὅλον τὸ συνέδριον ἐζήτην κατὰ τῦ Ἰησῦ μαρτυρίαν, εἰς τὸ θανατῶσαι αὐτὸν, κ̈ ἐχ εὕρισκον.

-56 Πολλοὶ γὰρ ἐψευδομαρτύρων κατ' αὐτῦ κ̈ ἴσαι αἱ μαρτυρίαι ἐκ ἦσαν.

57 Καί τινες ἀναςάντες, ἐψευδομαρτύρων κατ' αὐτῦ, λέγοντες·

* 58 Ὅτι ἡμεῖς ἠκύσαμεν αὐτῦ λέγοντ⊙· Ὅτι ἐγὼ ‡ καταλύσω τὸν ‡ ναὸν τῦτον τὸν ‡ χειροποίητον, κ̈ διὰ τριῶν ἡμερῶν ἄλλον ἀχειροποίητον οἰκοδομήσω.

59 Καὶ ἐδὲ ὕτως ἴση ἦν ἡ μαρτυρία αὐτῶν.

60 Καὶ ἀναςὰς ὁ ἀρχιερεὺς εἰς τὸ μέσον, ἐπηρώτησε τὸν Ἰησῦν, λέγων· Οὐκ ἀποκρίνῃ ἐδὲν; τί ὗτοί σε καταμαρτυρῦσιν;

61 Ὁ δὲ ἐσιώπα, κ̈ ἐδὲν ἀπεκρίνατο· Πάλιν ὁ ἀρχιερεὺς ἐπηρώτα αὐτὸν, κ̈ λέγει αὐτῷ· Σὺ εἶ ὁ Χριςὸς ὁ υἱὸς τοῦ εὐλογητῦ;

Εἶπε δὲ αὐτοῖς· Ἐὰν ὑμῖν εἴπω, ἐ μὴ πιςεύσητε·

68 Ἐὰν δὲ κ̈ ἐρωτήσω, οὐ μὴ ἀποκριθῆτέ μοι, ἢ ἀπολύσητε.

70 Εἶπον δὲ πάντες· Σὺ ἂν εἶ ὁ υἱὸς τῦ Θεῦ; Ὁ δὲ πρὸς αὐτὺς, ἔφη· Ὑμεῖς λέγετε, ὅτι ἐγώ εἰμι.

63 Ὁ δὲ ἀρχιερεὺς, διαρρήξας τὺς χιτῶνας αὐτῦ, λέγει· Τί ἔτι χρείαν ἔχομεν μαρτύρων;

64 Ἠκύσατε τῆς βλασφημίας· τί ὑμῖν φαίνεται; Οἱ δὲ

---

21 Quid me interrogas? Interroga audientes, quid loquutus sim ipsis: ecce hi sciunt quæ dixerim ego.

22 Hæc autem eo dicente, unus ministrorum assistens dedit alapam Jesu, dicens: Sic respondes principi Sacerdotum?

23 Respondit ei Jesus: Si male loquutus sum, testare de malo: si autem bene, quid me cædis?

55 At summi Sacerdotes, & omnis confessus quærebant adversus Jesum testimonium, ad morte afficiendum eum, & non inveniebant.

56 Multi enim testimonium falsum dicebant adversus eum, & paria testimonia non erant.

57 Et quidam surgentes falsum testimonium ferebant adversus eum, dicentes:

58 Quoniam nos audivimus eum dicentem: Quod ego dissolvam templum hoc manufactum, & per tres dies aliud non manufactum ædificabo.

59 Et nec sic par erat testimonium illorum.

60 Et exurgens summus Sacerdos in medium, interrogavit Jesum, dicens: Non respondes quicquam quid hi te adversum testantur?

61 Ille autem tacebat, & nihil respondit. Rursum summus Sacerdos interrogabat eum, & dicit ei: Tu es Christus filius benedicti?

Ait autem illis: Si vobis dixero non credetis.

68 Si autem & interrogavero, non respondebitis mihi, aut dimittetis.

70 Dixerunt autem omnes: Tu ergo es filius Dei? is autem ad eos ait: Vos dicitis, quia ego sum.

63 At summus Sacerdos dirumpens vestes suas, ait: Quid adhuc usum habemus testium?

64 Auditis blasphemiam: quid vobis videtur? Ii autem

21. Pourquoi m'interroges-tu? Interroge ceux qui ont entendu ce que je leur ai dit: Ces gens-là savent ce que j'ai dit.

22. Lorsqu'il eut dit cela, un des sergens qui étoit présent donna un soufflet à Jésus, en lui disant: Est-ce ainsi que tu réponds au Souverain Sacrificateur?

23. Jésus lui répondit: Si j'ai mal parlé, fais voir ce que j'ai dit de mal; et si j'ai bien parlé, pourquoi me frappes-tu?

55. Or les principaux Sacrificateurs et tout le Conseil cherchoient *quelque* témoignage contre Jésus pour le faire mourir; et ils n'en trouvoient point.

56. Car plusieurs rendoient de faux témoignages contre lui; mais leurs dépositions ne s'accordoient pas.

57. Alors quelques-uns se levèrent, qui portèrent un faux témoignage contre lui, disant:

58. Nous lui avons ouï dire: Je détruirai ce Temple, qui a été bâti par la main des hommes, et, dans trois jours, j'en rebâtirai un autre qui ne sera point fait de main d'*homme*.

59. Mais leur déposition ne s'accordoit pas non plus.

60. Alors le Souverain Sacrificateur se levant au milieu du *Conseil*, interrogea Jésus, et lui dit: Ne réponds-tu rien? Qu'est-ce que ces gens déposent contre toi?

61. Mais *Jésus* se tut et ne répondit rien. Le Souverain Sacrificateur l'interrogea encore, et lui dit: Es-tu le Christ, le Fils du *Dieu* béni?

Et il leur *répondit*: Si je vous le dis, vous ne le croirez point:

68. Et si je *vous* interroge aussi, vous ne me répondrez point, ni ne me laisserez point aller.

70. Alors ils dirent tous: Es-tu donc le Fils de Dieu? Et il leur dit: Vous le dites vous-mêmes; Je le suis.

63. Alors le Souverain Sacrificateur, déchira ses vêtemens, et dit: Qu'avons-nous plus à faire de témoins?

64. Vous avez entendu le blasphème; que vous en semble?

J. 18.

21 Why askest thou me? ask them which heard me, what I have said unto them: behold, they know what I said.

22 And, when he had thus spoken, one of the officers which stood by struck Jesus with the palm of his hand, saying, Answerest thou the high priest so?

23 Jesus answered him, If I have spoken evil, bear witness of the evil; but if well, why smitest thou me?

Mr. 14.

53 And they led Jesus away to the high priest; and with him were assembled all the chief priests, and the elders, and the scribes.

55 And the chief priests, and all the council sought for witness against Jesus to put him to death; and found none:

56 For many bare false witness against him, but their witness agreed not together.

57 And there arose certain, and bare false witness against him, saying,

58 We heard him say, I will destroy this temple that is made with hands, and within three days I will build another made without hands.

59 But neither so did their witness agree together.

60 And the high priest stood up in the midst, and asked Jesus, saying, Answerest thou nothing? what *is it* *which* these witness against thee.

61 But he held his peace, and answered nothing. Again the high priest asked him, and said unto him, Art thou the Christ, the Son of the Blessed?

L. 22.

67 And he said unto them, If I tell you, ye will not believe:

68 And if I also ask *you*, ye will not answer me, nor let *me* go.

70 Then said they all, Art thou then the Son of God? And he said unto them, Ye say that I am.

Mr. 14.

63 Then the high priest rent his clothes, and saith, What need we any further witnesses?

64 Ye have heard the blasphemy: what think ye? And they

πάντες κατέκριναν αὐτὸν εἶναι
ἔνοχον θανάτε.

* 65 Καὶ ἤρξαντό τινες ἐμπτύειν αὐτῷ, καὶ περικαλύπτειν τὸ πρόσωπον αὐτῶ, καὶ κολαφίζειν αὐτὸν, καὶ λέγειν αὐτῷ Προφήτευσον· καὶ οἱ ὑπηρέται ῥαπίσμασιν αὐτὸν ἔβαλλον.

omnes condemnaverunt eum obnoxium esse mortis.

65 Et cœperunt quidam conspuere eum, & velare faciem ejus, & colaphizare eum, & dicere ei: Prophetiza, & ministri alapis eum impetebant.

* 28 Ἄγουσιν ἐν τὸν Ἰησῦν ἀπὸ τῦ Καϊάφα εἰς τὸ πραιτώριον· ἦν δὲ πρωΐα· καὶ αὐτοὶ ἐκ εἰσῆλθον εἰς τὸ πραιτώριον, ἵνα μὴ μιανθῶσιν, ἀλλ' ἵνα φάγωσι τὸ πάσχα.

* 29 Ἐξῆλθεν ἐν ὁ Πιλᾶτος πρὸς αὐτὲς, καὶ εἶπε Τίνα κατηγορίαν φέρετε κατὰ τῦ ἀνθρώπε τέτε;

30 Ἀπεκρίθησαν καὶ εἶπον αὐτῷ Εἰ μὴ ἦν ὅτος κακοποιὸς, ἐκ ἄν σοι παρεδώκαμεν αὐτόν.

31 Εἶπεν ἐν αὐτοῖς ὁ Πιλᾶτος Λάβετε αὐτὸν ὑμεῖς, καὶ κατὰ τὸν νόμον ὑμῶν κρίνατε αὐτόν. Εἶπον ἐν αὐτῷ οἱ Ἰουδαῖοι Ἡμῖν ἐκ ἔξεστιν ἀποκτεῖναι ὐδένα.

33 Εἰσῆλθεν ἐν εἰς τὸ πραιτώριον πάλιν ὁ Πιλᾶτος, καὶ ἐφώνησε τὸν Ἰησῦν καὶ εἶπεν αὐτῷ Σὺ εἶ ὁ βασιλεὺς τῶν Ἰουδαίων;

34 Ἀπεκρίθη αὐτῷ ὁ Ἰησῦς Ἀφ' ἑαυτῦ σὺ τῦτο λέγεις, ἢ ἄλλοι σοι εἶπον περὶ ἐμῦ;

35 Ἀπεκρίθη ὁ Πιλᾶτος Μήτι ἐγὼ Ἰουδαῖός εἰμι; τὸ ἔθνος τὸ σὸν καὶ οἱ ἀρχιερεῖς παρέδωκάν σε ἐμοί· τί ἐποίησας;

36 Ἀπεκρίθη ὁ Ἰησῦς Ἡ βασιλεία ἡ ἐμὴ ἐκ ἔστιν ἐκ τῦ κόσμε τότε· εἰ ἐκ τῦ κόσμε τότε ἦν ἡ βασιλεία ἡ ἐμὴ, οἱ ὑπηρέται ἄν οἱ ἐμοὶ ἠγωνίζοντο, ἵνα μὴ παραδοθῶ τοῖς Ἰουδαίοις· νῦν δὲ ἡ βασιλεία ἡ ἐμὴ ἐκ ἔστιν ἐντεῦθεν.

* 37 Εἶπεν ἐν αὐτῷ ὁ Πιλᾶτος Ὀκῦν βασιλεὺς εἶ σύ; Ἀπεκρίθη ὁ Ἰησῦς Σὺ λέγεις ὅτι βασιλεύς εἰμι ἐγώ· ἐγὼ εἰς τῦτο γεγέννημαι, καὶ εἰς τῦτο ἐλήλυθα εἰς τὸν κόσμον, ἵνα μαρτυρήσω τῇ ἀληθείᾳ. Πᾶς ὁ ὢν ἐκ τῆς ἀληθείας, ἀκούει μου τῆς φωνῆς.

38 Λέγει αὐτῷ ὁ Πιλᾶτος Τί ἐστιν ἀλήθεια; Καὶ τῦτο εἰπὼν, πάλιν ἐξῆλθε πρὸς τὰς Ἰουδαίους, καὶ λέγει αὐτοῖς Ἐγὼ ἐδεμίαν αἰτίαν εὑρίσκω ἐν αὐτῷ.

28 Adducunt ergo Jesum à Cajapha in prætorium; erat autem manè; & ipsi non introierunt in prætorium, ut non contaminarentur, sed ut manducarent Pascha.

29 Exivit ergo Pilatus ad eos, & dixit: Quam accusationem asfertis adversus hominem hunc?

30 Responderunt & dixerunt ei: Si non esset hic malefactor, non utique tibi tradidissemus eum.

31 Dixit ergo eis Pilatus: Accipite eum vos, & secundum legem vestram judicate eum. Dixerunt ergo ei Judæi: Nobis non licet interficere quemquam.

33 Introivit ergo in prætorium iterum Pilatus, & vocavit Jesum, & dixit ei: Tu es rex Judæorum?

34 Respondit ei Jesus: A temetipso tu hoc dicis, an alii tibi dixerunt de me?

35 Respondit Pilatus: Numquid ego Judæus sum? Gens tua & principes Sacerdotum tradiderunt te mihi: quid fecisti?

36 Respondit Jesus: Regnum meum non est de mundo hoc: si ex mundo hoc esset regnum meum, ministri utique mei decertarent, ut non traderer Judæis: nunc autem regnum meum non est hinc.

37 Dixit itaque ei Pilatus: Num ergo rex es tu? Respondit Jesus: Tu dicis, quia rex sum ego: Ego in hoc natus sum, & ad hoc veni in mundum, ut tester veritati: omnis existens ex veritate, audit meam vocem.

38 Dicit ei Pilatus: Quid est veritas? Et hoc dicens, iterum exivit ad Judæos, & dicit eis: Ego nullam causam invenio in eo.

Alors tous le condamnèrent comme étant digne de mort.

65. Et quelques-uns se mirent à cracher contre lui , à lui couvrir le visage , et à lui donner des coups de poing , et ils lui disoient: Devine , *qui t'a frappé.* Et les Sergens lui donnoient des coups de leurs bâtons.

28. Ils menèrent ensuite Jésus , de Caïphe au Prétoire ; c'étoit le matin ; et ils n'entrèrent point dans le Prétoire , de peur de se souiller , et afin de pouvoir manger la Pâque.

29. Pilate donc sortit vers eux , et leur dit : Quelle accusation portez-vous contre cet homme ?

30. Ils lui répondirent : Si cet homme n'étoit pas un malfaiteur, nous ne te l'aurions pas livré.

31. Sur quoi Pilate leur dit : Prenez-le vous-mêmes, et le jugez selon votre Loi. Les Juifs lui dirent : Nous n'avons pas le pouvoir de faire mourir personne.

33. Pilate rentra dans le Prétoire et ayant fait venir Jésus , il lui dit : Es-tu le Roi des Juifs ?

34. Jésus lui répondit : Dis - tu ceci de ton propre mouvement , ou si d'autres te l'ont dit de moi ?

35. Pilate répondit : Suis-je Juif ? Ta nation et les principaux Sacrificateurs t'ont livré à moi ; qu'as-tu fait ?

36. Jésus répondit : Mon règne n'est pas de ce monde ; si mon règne étoit de ce monde, mes gens combattroient, afin que je ne fusse pas livré aux Juifs ; mais maintenant mon règne n'est point d'ici-bas.

37. Alors Pilate lui dit : tu es donc Roi ? Jésus répondit : Tu le dis ; je suis Roi , je suis né pour cela , et je suis venu dans le monde , pour rendre témoignage à la vérité. Quiconque est pour la vérité écoute ma voix.

38. Pilate lui dit : Qu'est-ce que cette vérité ? Et quand il eut dit cela , il sortit encore pour aller vers les Juifs , et leur dit : Je ne trouve aucun crime en lui.

all condemned him to be guilty of death.

65 And some began to spit on him, and to cover his face, and to buffet him, and to say unto him, Prophesy : and the servants did strike him with the palms of their hands, and it was early ; and they themselves went not into the judgment-hall, lest they should be defiled ; but that they might eat the passover.

29 Pilate then went out unto them, and said, What accusation bring ye against this man ?

30 They answered, and said unto him, If he were not a malefactor, we would not have delivered him up unto thee.

31 Then said Pilate unto them, Take ye him, and judge him according to your law. The Jews, therefore, said unto him, It is not lawful for us to put any man to death :

33 Then Pilate entered into the judgment-hall again, and called Jesus, and said unto him, Art thou the King of the Jews ?

34 Jesus answered him, Sayest thou this thing of thyself, or did others tell it thee of me ?

35 Pilate answered, Am I a Jew ? Thine own nation and the chief priests have delivered thee unto me. What hast thou done ?

36 Jesus answered, My kingdom is not of this world. If my kingdom were of this world, then would my servants fight, that I should not be delivered to the Jews : but now is my kingdom not from hence.

37 Pilate, therefore, said unto him, Art thou a King then ? Jesus answered, thou sayest that I am a king. To this end was I born, and for this cause came I into the world, that I should bear witness unto the truth. Every one that is of the truth heareth my voice.

38 Pilate saith unto him, What is truth ? And when he had said this, he went out again unto the Jews, and saith unto them, I find in him no fault *at all.*

28 Then led they Jesus from Caiaphas unto the hall of judgment

77

*5 Οἱ δὲ † ἐπίσχυον, λέ-
γοντες· Ὅτι ‡ ἀνασείει τὸν λαὸν,
διδάσκων καθ᾽ ὅλης τῆς Ἰουδαίας,
ἀρξάμενος ⊙ ἀπὸ τῆς Γαλιλαίας
ἕως ὧδε.

5 Illi autem invalescebant,
dicentes: Quia commovet populum, docens per universam
Judæam, incipiens à Galilæa
usque huc.

13 Τότε λέγει αὐτῷ ὁ Πιλά-
τος· Οὐκ ἀκούεις πόσα σου κα-
τημαρτυροῦσι.

13 Tunc dicit illi Pilatus:
Non audis quanta te contra testantur?

6 Πιλάτος δὲ ἀκούσας Γαλιλαίαν, ἐπηρώτησεν, εἰ ὁ ἄνθρωπος Γαλιλαῖός ἐςι.

6 Pilatus autem audiens Galilæam, interrogavit si homo
Galilæus esset.

7 Καὶ ἐπιγνοὺς ὅτι ἐκ τῆς
ἐξουσίας Ἡρώδου ἐςιν, ἀνέπεμψεν
αὐτὸν πρὸς Ἡρώδην, ὄντα καὶ αὐτὸν
ἐν Ἱεροσολύμοις ἐν ταύταις ταῖς
ἡμέραις.

7 Et cognoscens quod de po-
testate Herodis esset, remisit
eum ad Herodem, existentem
& ipsum in Hierosolymis, in
illis diebus.

8 Ὁ δὲ Ἡρώδης, ἰδὼν τὸν Ἰησοῦν, ἐχάρη λίαν· ἦν γὰρ θέλων
ἐξ ἱκανοῦ ἰδεῖν αὐτὸν, διὰ τὸ ἀ-
κούειν πολλὰ περὶ αὐτοῦ· καὶ ἤλ-
πιζέ τι σημεῖον ἰδεῖν ὑπ᾽ αὐτοῦ
γινόμενον.

8 At Herodes videns Jesum
gavisus est valde: erat enim
volens ex multo videre eum,
propterea quod audiret multa
de eo: & sperabat aliquod signum videre ab eo factum.

9 Ἐπηρώτα δὲ αὐτὸν ἐν λό-
γοις ἱκανοῖς· αὐτὸς δὲ οὐδὲν ἀ-
πεκρίνατο αὐτῷ.

9 Interrogabat autem eum in
sermonibus multis: ipse autem
nihil respondebat illi.

10 Εἱστήκεισαν δὲ οἱ ἀρχιερεῖς
καὶ οἱ γραμματεῖς εὐτόνως κατη-
γοροῦντες αὐτοῦ.

10 Stabant autem principes
Sacerdotum & Scribæ constan-
ter accusantes eum.

11 Ἐξουθενήσας δὲ αὐτὸν ὁ Ἡ-
ρώδης σὺν τοῖς στρατεύμασιν αὐτοῦ,
καὶ ἐμπαίξας, περιβαλὼν αὐτὸν
ἐσθῆτα λαμπρὰν, ἀνέπεμψεν αὐτὸν
τῷ Πιλάτῳ.

11 Nihil faciens autem illum
Herodes cum exercitibus suis,
&illudens, amiciens eum vestem
splendidam, remisit eum Pilato.

12 Ἐγένοντο δὲ φίλοι ὅ, τε
Πιλάτος καὶ ὁ Ἡρώδης ἐν αὐτῇ τῇ
ἡμέρᾳ μετ᾽ ἀλλήλων· προϋπῆρ-
χον γὰρ ἐν ἔχθρᾳ ὄντες πρὸς ἑαυ-
τούς.

12 Facti sunt autem amici
hicque Pilatus & Herodes hac
ipsa die cum invicem: præex-
titerant enim in inimicitia ex-
istentes ad seipsos.

13 Πιλάτος δὲ, συγκαλεσά-
μενος τοὺς ἀρχιερεῖς, καὶ τοὺς ἄρ-
χοντας, καὶ τὸν λαὸν,

13 Pilatus autem convocans
principes sacerdotum, & magi-
stratus & populum,

14 Εἶπε πρὸς αὐτούς· Προσ-
ηνέγκατέ μοι τὸν ἄνθρωπον τοῦτον,
ὡς ἀποστρέφοντα τὸν λαόν· καὶ ἰδοὺ,
ἐγὼ ἐνώπιον ὑμῶν ἀνακρίνας, οὐδὲν
εὗρον ἐν τῷ ἀνθρώπῳ τούτῳ αἴτιον,
ὧν κατηγορεῖτε κατ᾽ αὐτοῦ.

14 Dixit ad illos: Obtulistis
mihi hominem hunc, quasi a-
vertentem populum, & ecce ego
coramvobis interrogans, nullam
inveni in homine isto causam,
quorum accusatis adversus eum.

15 Ἀλλ᾽ οὐδὲ Ἡρώδης· ἀνέ-
πεμψα γὰρ ὑμᾶς πρὸς αὐτὸν, καὶ
ἰδού, οὐδὲν ἄξιον θανάτου ἐςι πε-
πραγμένον αὐτῷ.

15 Sed neque Herodes: re-
misi enim vos ad illum, & ecce
nihil dignum morte est factum
ei.

16 Παιδεύσας οὖν αὐτὸν ἀπολύσω.

16 Castigans ergo illum dimittam.

5. Mais ils insistoient encore plus fortement, en disant : Il soulève le peuple, enseignant par toute la Judée, ayant commencé depuis la Galilée jusqu'ici.

5 And they were the more fierce, saying, He stirreth up the people, teaching throughout all Jewry, beginning from Galilee to this place.

13. Alors Pilate lui dit : N'entends-tu pas combien de choses ils déposent contre toi ?

13 Then said Pilate unto him, Hearest thou not how many things they witness against thee?

6. Quand Pilate entendit parler de la Galilée, il demanda si Jésus étoit Galiléen.

6 When Pilate heard of Galilee, he asked whether the man were a Galilean.

7. Ayant appris qu'il étoit de la juridiction d'Hérode, il le renvoya à Hérode, qui étoit aussi alors à Jérusalem.

7 And as soon as he knew that he belonged unto Herod's jurisdiction, he sent him to Herod, who himself also was at Jerusalem at that time.

8. Quand Hérode vit Jésus, il en eut une grande joie ; car il y avoit long-tems qu'il souhaitoit de le voir, parce qu'il avoit ouï-dire beaucoup de choses de lui ; et il espéroit qu'il lui verroit faire quelque miracle.

8 And when Herod saw Jesus, he was exceeding glad: for he was desirous to see him of a long *season*, because he had heard many things of him; and he hoped to have seen some miracle done by him.

9. Il lui fit donc plusieurs questions, mais Jésus-Christ ne lui répondit rien,

9 Then he questioned with him in many words; but he answered him nothing.

10. Et les principaux Sacrificateurs et les Scribes étoient-là, qui l'accusoient avec la plus grande véhémence.

10 And the chief priests and scribes stood, and vehemently accused him.

11. Mais Hérode, avec les gens de la garde, le traita avec mépris ; et pour se moquer de lui, il le fit vêtir d'un habit éclatant, et le renvoya à Pilate.

11 And Herod, with his men of war, set him at nought, and mocked *him*, and arrayed him in a gorgeous robe, and sent him again to Pilate.

12. En ce même jour, Pilate et Hérode devinrent amis, car auparavant ils étoient ennemis.

12 And the same day Pilate and Herod were made friends together: for before they were at enmity between themselves.

13. Alors Pilate ayant assemblé les principaux Sacrificateurs, et les Magistrats, et le peuple, leur dit :

13 And Pilate, when he had called together the chief priests, and the rulers, and the people,

14. Vous m'avez présenté cet homme comme soulevant le peuple ; et cependant l'ayant interrogé en votre présence, je ne l'ai trouvé coupable d'aucun des crimes dont vous l'accusez ;

14 Said unto them, Ye have brought this man unto me, as one that perverteth the people: and, behold, I, having examined *him* before you, have found no fault in this man, touching those things whereof ye accuse him:

15. Ni Hérode non plus ; car je vous ai renvoyés à lui, et on ne lui a rien fait *qui marque qu'il soit* digne de mort.

15 No, nor yet Herod: for I sent you to him; and, lo, nothing worthy of death is done unto him:

16. Ainsi, après l'avoir fait châtier, je le relâcherai.

16 I will, therefore, chastise him, and release *him*.

* under the Roman law de seditionis in cruce cum tollendis: Digest de poenis L. 48. tit. 19. 6. 28.3 'capite
plectendi cum saepius seditiose et turbulente
se gesserint, et aliquoties apprehensi clementius in
eandem temeritate propositi perseveraverint?'

78

15 Κατὰ δὲ ἑορτὴν εἰώθει ὁ ἡγεμὼν ἀπολύειν ἕνα τῷ ὄχλῳ δέσμιον, ὃν ἤθελον.

16 Εἶχον δὲ τότε δέσμιον ἐπίσημον λεγόμενον Βαραββᾶν.

17 Συνηγμένων ἦν αὐτῶν, εἶπεν αὐτοῖς ὁ Πιλάτ⊙· Τίνα θέλετε ἀπολύσω ὑμῖν; Βαραββᾶν, ἢ Ἰησᾶν τὸν λεγόμενον Χριςόν;

18 Ἤδει γὰρ ὅτι διὰ φθόνον παρέδωκαν αὐτόν.

19 Καθημένε δὲ αὐτῶ ἐπὶ τῶ βήμα⊙, ἀπέςειλε πρὸς αὐτῶ ἡ γυνὴ αὐτῶ, λέγεσα· Μηδέν σοι κ̣ τῷ δικαίῳ ἐκείνῳ· πολλὰ γὰρ ἔπαθον σήμερον κατ᾽ ὄναρ δι᾽ αὐτόν.

20 Οἱ δὲ ἀρχιερεῖς κ̣ οἱ πρεσβύτεροι ἔπεισαν τὰς ὄχλες, ἵνα αἰτήσωνίαι τὸν Βαραββᾶν, τὸν δὲ Ἰησᾶν ἀπολέσωσιν.

21 Ἀποκριθεὶς δὲ ὁ ἡγεμὼν, εἶπεν αὐτοῖς· Τίνα θέλετε ἀπὸ τῶν δύο ἀπολύσω ὑμῖν; Οἱ δὲ εἶπον, Βαραββᾶν.

22 Λέγει αὐτοῖς ὁ Πιλάτ⊙· Τί ἂν ποιήσω Ἰησᾶν, τὸν λεγόμενον Χριςόν; Λέγεσιν αὐτῷ πάντες· Σταυρωθήτω.

23 Ὁ δὲ ἡγεμὼν ἔφη· Τί γὰρ κακὸν ἐποίησεν; Οἱ δὲ περισσῶς ἔκραζον, λέγονίες· Σταυρωθήτω.

26 Τότε ἀπέλυσεν αὐτοῖς· τὸν Βαραββᾶν· τὸν δὲ Ἰησᾶν φραγελλώσας παρέδωκεν ἵνα ςαυρωθῇ.

27 Τότε οἱ ςραλιῶται τῶ ἡγεμόν⊙, παραλαβόνίες τὸν Ἰησᾶν εἰς τὸ πραιτώριον, συνήγαγον ἐπ᾽ αὐτὸν ὅλην τὴν σπεῖραν.

* 29 Καὶ ‡ πλέξανίες ‡ ςέφανον ἐξ ἀκανθῶν, ἐπέθηκαν ἐπὶ τὴν κεφαλὴν αὐτῶ· κ̣ κάλαμον ἐπὶ τὴν δεξιὰν αὐτῶ· κ̣ ‡ γονυπετήσανίες ἔμπροσθεν αὐτῶ, ‡ ἐνέπαιζον αὐτῷ, λέγονίες· Χαῖρε ὁ βασιλεὺς τῶν Ἰεδαίων.

30 Καὶ ἐμπλύσανίες εἰς αὐτὸν, ἔλαβον τὸν κάλαμον, κ̣ ἔτυπτον εἰς τὴν κεφαλὴν αὐτῶ.

* 31 Καὶ ὅτε ἐνέπαιξαν αὐτῷ, ‡ ἐξέδυσαν αὐτὸν τὴν ‡ χλαμύδα, κ̣ ἐνέδυσαν αὐτὸν τὰ ἱμάτια αὐτῶ· κ̣ ἀπήγαγον αὐτὸν εἰς τὸ ςαυρῶσαι.

15 Per autem feſtum conſueverat præſes abſolvere unum vinctum turbæ, quem voluiſſet.

16 Habebant autem tunc vinctum inſignem, dictum Barabbam.

17 Coactis ergo illis, dixit illis Pilatus: Quem vultis abſolvam vobis? Barabbam, an Jeſum dictum Chriſtum?

18 Sciebat enim quod per invidiam tradidiſſent eum.

19 Sedente autem illo ſuper tribunali, miſit ad eum uxor ejus, dicens: Nihil tibi & juſto illi: multa enim paſſa ſum hodie per ſomnium propter eum.

20 At principes Sacerdotum & ſeniores perſuaſerunt turbis, ut peterent Barabbam, at Jeſum perderent.

21 Reſpondens autem præſes, ait illis: Quem vultis de duobus abſolvam vobis? Illi verò dixerunt: Barabbam.

22 Dicit ergo illis Pilatus: Quid igitur faciam Jeſum dictum Chriſtum? dicunt ei omnes: Crucifigatur.

23 At præſes ait : Quid enim mali fecit? Illi autem magis clamabant, dicentes: Crucifigatur.

26 Tunc abſolvit illis Barabbam: At Jeſum flagellans, tradidit ut crucifigeretur.

27 Tunc milites præſidis aſſumentes Jeſum in prætorium, coëgerunt ad eum univerſam cohortem.

29 Et plectentes coronam de ſpinis, impoſuerunt ſuper caput ejus, & arundinem in dextera ejus: & genu flectentes ante eum, illudebant ei, dicentes: Gaude rex Judæorum.

30 Et inſpuentes in eum, acceperunt arundinem, & percutiebant in caput ejus.

31 Et poſtquam illuſerunt ei, exuerunt eum chlamydem, & induerunt eum veſtimentis ejus: & abduxerunt eum ad crucifigendum.

15. Or le Gouverneur avoit accoutumé, à chaque fête *de Pâques*, de relâcher au peuple celui des prisonniers qu'ils vouloient.

16. Et il y avoit alors un prisonnier insigne, nommé Barabbas.

17. Comme ils étoient donc assemblés, Pilate leur dit : Lequel voulez-vous que je vous relâche; Barabbas, ou Jésus qu'on appelle Christ?

18. Car il savoit bien que c'étoit par envie qu'ils l'avoient livré.

19. Et pendant qu'il étoit assis sur le tribunal, sa femme lui envoya dire : N'aie rien à faire avec cet homme de bien ; car j'ai beaucoup souffert aujourd'hui en songe à son sujet.

20. Alors les principaux Sacrificateurs et les Sénateurs persuadèrent au peuple de demander Barabbas, et de faire périr Jésus.

21. Et le Gouverneur prenant la parole, leur dit : Lequel des deux voulez-vous que je vous relâche? Et ils dirent : Barabbas.

22. Pilate leur dit : Que ferai-je donc de Jésus qu'on appelle Christ?

Tous lui dirent : Qu'il soit crucifié.

23. Et le Gouverneur *leur* dit : Mais quel mal-a-t-il fait? Alors ils crièrent encore plus fort : Qu'il soit crucifié.

26. Alors il leur relâcha Barabbas, et après avoir fait fouetter Jésus, il le leur livra pour être crucifié.

27. Et les soldats du Gouverneur amenèrent Jésus au Prétoire, et ils assemblèrent autour de lui toute la compagnie *des soldats.*

29. Puis ayant fait une couronne d'épines, ils la lui mirent sur la tête, et lui mirent un roseau à la *main* droite, et s'agenouillant devant lui, ils se moquoient de lui, en lui disant : Je te salue, Roi des Juifs.

30. Et crachant contre lui, ils prenoient le roseau, et ils lui en donnoient des coups sur la tête.

31. Après s'être ainsi moqués de lui, ils lui ôtèrent le manteau, et lui remirent ses habits, et ils l'emmenèrent pour le crucifier.

15 Now at *that* feast the governor was wont to release unto the people a prisoner, whom they would.

16 And they had then a notable prisoner, called Barabbas.

17 Therefore, when they were gathered together, Pilate said unto them, Whom will ye that I release unto you? Barabbas, or Jesus, which is called Christ?

18 For he knew that for envy they had delivered him.

19 When he was set down on the judgment-seat, his wife sent unto him, saying, Have thou nothing to do with that just man: for I have suffered many things this day in a dream because of him.

20 But the chief priests and elders persuaded the multitude that they should ask Barabbas, and destroy Jesus.

21 The governor answered, and said unto them, Whether of the twain will ye that I release unto you? They said, Barabbas.

22 Pilate saith unto them, What shall I do then with Jesus, which is called Christ? *They* all say unto him, Let him be crucified.

23 And the governor said, Why, what evil hath he done? But they cried out the more, saying, Let him be crucified.

26 Then released he Barabbas unto them; and when he had scourged Jesus, he delivered *him* to be crucified.

27 Then the soldiers of the governor took Jesus into the common hall, and gathered unto him the whole band *of soldiers.*

29 And when they had platted a crown of thorns, they put *it* upon his head, and a reed in his right hand; and they bowed the knee before him, and mocked him, saying, Hail, king of the Jews!

30 And they spit upon him, and took the reed, and smote him on the head.

31 And after that they had mocked him, they took the robe off from him, and put his own raiment on him, and led him away to crucify *him.*

79

3 Τότε ἰδὼν Ἰούδας ὁ παραδιδοὺς αὐτὸν, ὅτι κατεκρίθη, μεταμεληθεὶς, ἀπέςρεψε τὰ τριάκοντα ἀργύρια τοῖς ἀρχιερεῦσι ἢ τοῖς πρεσβυτέροις,

4 Λέγων· Ἥμαρτον, παραδοὺς αἷμα ἀθῶον. Οἱ δὲ εἶπον· Τί πρὸς ἡμᾶς; σὺ ὄψει.

* 5. Καὶ ῥίψας τὰ ἀργύρια ἐν τῷ ναῷ, ‡ ἀνεχώρησε ἢ ἀπελθὼν, † ἀπήγξατο.

6 Οἱ δὲ ἀρχιερεῖς λαβόντες τὰ ἀργύρια, εἶπον· Οὐκ ἔξεςι βαλεῖν αὐτὰ εἰς τὸν κορβανᾶν· ἐπεὶ τιμὴ αἵματός ἐςι.

* 7 Συμβέλιον δὲ λαβόντες, ‡ ἠγόρασαν ἐξ αὐτῶν τὸν ἀγρὸν τᾶ ‡ κεραμέως, εἰς † ταφὴν τοῖς ‡ ξένοις.

* 8 Διὸ ἐκλήθη ὁ ἀγρὸς ἐκεῖνος, ἀγρὸς αἵματος, ἕως τῆς σήμερον.

---

26 Καὶ ὡς ἀπήγαγον αὐτὸν, ἐπιλαβόμενοι Σίμωνός τιν۞ Κυρηναίε τᾶ ἐρχομένε ἀπ᾽ ἀγρᾶ, ἐπέθηκαν αὐτῷ τὸν ςαυρὸν, φέρειν ὄπισθεν τᾶ Ἰησᾶ.

27 Ἠκολούθει δὲ αὐτῷ πολὺ πλῆθ۞ τᾶ λαᾶ ἢ γυναικῶν· αἱ ἢ ἐκόπτοντο ἢ ἐθρήνουν αὐτόν.

28 Στραφεὶς δὲ πρὸς αὐτὰς ὁ Ἰησᾶς, εἶπε· Θυγατέρες Ἱερουσαλὴμ, μὴ κλαίετε ἐπ᾽ ἐμὲ, πλὴν ἐφ᾽ ἑαυτὰς κλαίετε, ἢ ἐπὶ τὰ τέκνα ὑμῶν.

29 Ὅτι ἰδὺ, ἔρχονται ἡμέραι ἐν αἷς ἐρᾶσι· Μακάριαι αἱ ςεῖραι,

ἢ κοιλίαι αἱ ὐκ ἐγέννησαν, ἢ μαςοὶ οἳ ὐκ ἐθήλασαν.

30 Τότε ἄρξονται λέγειν τοῖς ὄρεσι· Πέσετε ἐφ᾽ ἡμᾶ· ἢ τοῖς βουνοῖς· Καλύψετε ἡμᾶς.

* 31 Ὅτι εἰ ἐν τῷ † ὑγρῷ ξύλῳ ταῦτα ποιᾶσιν, ἐν τῷ ξηρῷ τί γένηται;

32 Ἤγοντο δὲ ἢ ἕτεροι δύο κακᾶργοι σὺν αὐτῷ ἀναιρεθῆναι.

---

3 Tunc videns Judas qui tradens [fuit] eum, quod damnatus esset, pœnitens, retulit triginta argenteos principibus Sacerdotum, & senioribus,

4 Dicens, Peccavi, tradens sanguinem innoxium. Illi verò dixerunt, Quid ad nos? tu videris.

5 Et projiciens argenteos in templo, recessit: & abiens se strangulavit.

6 At principes Sacerdotum accipientes argenteos, dixerunt: Non licet injicere eos in corbanam: quia pretium sanguinis est.

7 Consilium autem sumentes mercati sunt ex illis agrum figuli in sepulturam peregrinis.

8 Quapropter vocatus est ager ille, Ager sanguinis, usque hodie.

---

26 Et quum abducerent eum, apprehendentes Simonem quendam Cyrenæum venientem ab agro, imposuerunt illi crucem, ut ferret post Jesum.

27 Sequebatur autem illum multa turba populi, & mulierum, quæ & plangebant, & lamentabantur eum.

28 Conversus autem ad illas Jesus, dixit: Filiæ Hierusalem, ne flete super me, sed super vos ipsas flete, & super filios vestros.

29 Quoniam ecce venient dies, in quibus dicent: Beatæ steriles, & ventres qui non genuerunt, & ubera quæ non lactaverunt.

30 Tunc incipient dicere montibus: Cadite super nos: & collibus: Operite nos.

31 Quia si in viridi ligno hæc faciunt, in arido quid fiet?

32 Ducebantur autem & alii duo malefici ut cum eo tollerentur.

5. Alors Judas, qui l'avoit trahi, voyant qu'il étoit condamné, se repentit, et reporta les trente pièces d'argent aux principaux Sacrificateurs et aux Sénateurs;

4. Disant : J'ai péché en trahissant le sang innocent. Mais ils dirent · Que nous importe? tu y pourvoiras.

5. Alors après avoir jeté les pièces d'argent dans le temple, il se retira, et s'en alla, et s'étrangla.

6. Et les principaux Sacrificateurs ayant pris les pièces d'argent, dirent : Il n'est pas permis de les mettre dans le trésor *sacré*; car c'est le prix du sang.

7. Et ayant délibéré, ils en achetèrent le champ d'un potier, pour la sépulture des étrangers.

8. C'est pourquoi ce champ-là a été appelé jusqu'à aujourd'hui : Le champ du sang.

26. Et comme ils le menoient *au supplice*, ils prirent un homme de Cyrène, nommé Simon, qui revenoit des champs, et le chargèrent de la croix, pour la porter après Jésus.

27. Et une grande multitude de peuple et de femmes le suivoient, qui se frappoient la poitrine, et se lamentoient.

28. Mais Jésus se tournant vers elles, leur dit : Filles de Jérusalem, ne pleurez point sur moi, mais pleurez sur vous-mêmes et sur vos enfans.

29. Car les jours viendront auxquels on dira : Heureuses les stériles, les femmes qui n'ont point enfanté, les mamelles qui n'ont point allaité!

30. Alors ils se mettront à dire aux montagnes : Tombez sur nous, et aux côteaux, couvrez-nous.

31. Car si l'on fait ces choses au bois vert, que fera-t-on au bois sec.

32. On menoit aussi deux autres *hommes* qui étoient des malfaiteurs, pour les faire mourir avec lui.

3 Then Judas which had betrayed him, when he saw that he was condemned, repented himself, and brought again the thirty pieces of silver to the chief priests and elders,

4 Saying, I have sinned, in that I have betrayed the innocent blood. And they said, What *is that* to us? see thou *to that.*

5 And he cast down the pieces of silver in the temple, and departed, and went and hanged himself.

6 And the chief priests took the silver pieces, and said, It is not lawful for to put them into the treasury, because it is the price of blood.

7 And they took counsel, and bought with them the potter's field, to bury strangers in.

8 Wherefore that field was called, The field of blood, unto this day.

26 And, as they led him away, they laid hold upon one Simon, a

Cyrenian, coming out of the country, and on him they laid the cross, that he might bear *it* after Jesus.

27 And there followed him a great company of people, and of women, which also bewailed and lamented him.

28 But Jesus, turning unto them, said, Daughters of Jerusalem, weep not for me, but weep for yourselves, and for your children.

29 For, behold, the days are coming, in the which they shall say, Blessed *are* the barren, and the wombs that never bare, and the paps which never gave suck.

30 Then shall they begin to say to the mountains, Fall on us; and to the hills, Cover us.

31 For if they do these things in a green tree, what shall be done in the dry?

32 And there were also two others, malefactors, led with him to be put to death.

80

17. Καὶ βαςάζων τὸν ςαυρὸν αὑτῦ ἐξῆλθεν εἰς τὸν λεγόμενον Κρανίυ τόπον, ὃς λέγεται Ἑβραϊςὶ Γολγοθᾶ.

18. Ὅπυ αὐτὸν ἐςαύρωσαν, κ μετ᾽ αὐτῦ ἄλλυς δύο, ἐντεῦθεν ἐντεῦθεν, μέσον δὲ τὸν Ἰησῦν.

19. Ἔγραψε δὲ κ τίτλον ὁ Πιλᾶτ⊙, κ ἔθηκεν ἐπὶ τῦ ςαυρῦ· ἦν δὲ γεγραμμένον· ΙΗΣΟΥΣ Ο ΝΑΖΩΡΑΙΟΣ Ο ΒΑ-ΣΙΛΕΥΣ ΤΩΝ ΙΟΥΔΑΙΩΝ.

* 20 Τῦτον ἲν τὸν ‡ τίτλον πολλοὶ ἀνέγνωσαν τῶν Ἰυδαί·ν, ὅτι ἐγγὺς ἦν τῆς πόλεως ὁ τόπ⊙·

ὅπυ ἐςαυρώθη ὁ Ἰησῦς· κ ἦν γε-γραμμένον Ἑβραϊςί, ‡ Ἑλληνιςί, ‡ Ῥωμαϊςί.

21. Ἔλεγον ἲν τῷ Πιλάτῳ οἱ ἀρχιερεῖς τῶν Ἰυδαίων· Μὴ γρά-φε· Ὁ βασιλεὺς τῶν Ἰυδαίων· ἀλλ᾽ ὅτι ἐκεῖν⊙ εἶπε· Βασιλεύς εἰμι τῶν Ἰυδαίων.

22. Ἀπεκρίθη ὁ Πιλᾶτ⊙· Ὃ γέγραφα, γέγραφα.

* 23 Οἱ ἲν ςρατιῶται, ὅτε ἐςαύρωσαν τὸν Ἰησῦν, ἔλαβον τὰ ἱμάτια αὐτῦ, (κ ἐποίησαν τέσ-σαρα μέρη, ἑκάςῳ ςρατιώτῃ μέ-ρ⊙·) κ τὸν χιτῶνα· ἦν δὲ ὁ χι-τὼν † ἄρραφ⊙·, ἐκ τῶν ‡ ἄνωθεν † ὑφαντὸς δι᾽ ὅλυ.

24. Εἶπον ἲν πρὸς ἀλλήλυς· Μὴ σχίσωμεν αὐτὸν, ἀλλὰ λά-χωμεν περὶ αὐτῦ, τίν⊙ ἔςαι·

39. Οἱ δὲ παραπορευόμενοι ἐ-βλασφήμυν αὐτὸν, κινῦντες τὰς κεφαλὰς αὐτῶν,

40. Καὶ λέγοντες· Ὁ καταλύων τὸν ναὸν κ ἐν τρισὶν ἡμέραις οἰκο-δομῶν, σῶσον σεαυτόν· εἰ υἱὸς εἶ τῦ Θεῦ, κατάβηθι ἀπὸ τῦ ςαυρῦ.

41. Ὁμοίως δὲ κ οἱ ἀρχιερεῖς, ἐμπαίζοντες μετὰ τῶν γραμμα-τέων κ πρεσβυτέρων, ἔλεγον·

42. Ἄλλυς ἔσωσεν, ἑαυτὸν ὐ δύναται σῶσαι· εἰ βασιλεὺς Ἰσ-ραὴλ ἐςι, καταβάτω νῦν ἀπὸ τῦ ςαυρῦ, κ πιςεύσομεν αὐτῷ.

43. Πέποιθεν ἐπὶ τὸν Θεόν· ῥυ-σάσθω νῦν αὐτὸν, εἰ θέλει αὐτόν· εἶπε γάρ· Ὅτι Θεῦ εἰμι υἱός.

17. Et portans crucem suam, exivit in dictum Calvariæ lo-cum, qui dicitur Hebraice Gol-gotha.

18. Ubi eum crucifixerunt, & cum eo alios duos, hinc & hinc, medium autem Jesum.

19. Scripsit autem & titulum Pilatus, & posuit super crucem. Erat autem scriptum: JESUS NAZARENUS REX JU-DÆORUM.

20. Hunc ergo titulum multi legerunt Judæorum: quia prope erat locus civitatem ubi crucifi-xus est Jesus. Et erat scriptum, Hebraice, Græce, Romane.

21. Dicebant ergo Pilato prin-cipes Sacerdotum Judæorum: Ne scribe: Rex Judæorum: sed quia ipse dixit: Rex sum Ju-dæorum.

22. Respondit Pilatus: Quod scripsi, scripsi.

23. Ergo milites quum cruci-fixissent Jesum, acceperunt vesti-menta ejus, (& fecerunt quatuor partes, unicuique militi partem,) & tunicam: Erat autem tunica inconsutilis, ex iis quæ desuper contexta per totum.

24. Dixerunt ergo ad invicem: Non scindamus eam, sed sortia-mur de illa, cujus erit.

39. At prætereuntes blasphe-mabant eum, moventes capita sua,

40. Et dicentes: Dissolvens templum, & in tribus diebus ædificans, serva teipsum. Si filius es Dei, descende de cruce.

41. Similiter verò & princi-pes Sacerdotum illudentes cum Scribis, & senioribus, dicebant:

42. Alios servavit, seipsum non potest servare: Si rex Is-raël est, descendat nunc de cruce, & credemus ei.

43. Confidit in Deo, liberet nunc eum, si vult eum; dixit enim: Quia Dei sum filius.

17. Et Jésus, portant sa croix, vint au lieu appelé le Calvaire, qui se nomme en hébreu, Golgotha ;

18. Où ils le crucifièrent, et deux autres avec lui, l'un d'un côté, et l'autre de l'autre, et Jésus au milieu.

19. Pilate fit aussi faire un écriteau, et le fit mettre au-dessus de la croix ; et on y avoit écrit :

JESUS DE NAZARETH, ROI DES JUIFS.

20. Plusieurs donc des Juifs lurent cet écriteau, parce que le lieu où Jésus étoit crucifié étoit près de la ville, et il étoit écrit en Hébreu, en Grec, et en Latin.

21. Et les principaux Sacrificateurs des Juifs dirent à Pilate : N'écris pas, Le Roi des Juifs ; mais qu'il a dit : Je suis le Roi des Juifs.

22. Pilate répondit : Ce que j'ai écrit, je l'ai écrit.

23. Après que les soldats eurent crucifié Jésus, ils prirent ses habits, et ils en firent quatre parts, une part pour chaque soldat ; ils prirent aussi la robe ; mais la robe étoit sans couture, d'un seul tissu, depuis le haut jusqu'au bas.

24. Ils dirent donc entr'eux : Ne la mettons pas en pièces, mais tirons au sort à qui l'aura ;

39. Et ceux qui passoient par là, lui disoient des outrages, branlant la tête ;

40. Et disant : toi qui détruits le temple, et qui le rebâtis en trois jours, sauve-toi toi-même ; si tu es le Fils de Dieu, descends de la croix.

41. De même aussi les principaux Sacrificateurs, avec les Scribes et les Sénateurs, disoient en se moquant :

42. Il a sauvé les autres et il ne se peut sauver lui-même : s'il est le Roi d'Israël, qu'il descende maintenant de la croix et nous croirons en lui.

43. Il se confie en Dieu ; que Dieu le délivre maintenant, s'il lui est agréable ; car il a dit : Je suis le Fils de Dieu.

17 And he, bearing his cross, went forth into a place called *the place* of a skull, which is called in the Hebrew, Golgotha ;

18 Where they crucified him, and two others with him, on either side one, and Jesus in the midst.

19 And Pilate wrote a title, and put it on the cross. And the writing was, JESUS OF NAZARETH, THE KING OF THE JEWS.

20 This title then read many of the Jews : for the place where Jesus was crucified was nigh to the city : and it was written in Hebrew, *and* Greek, *and* Latin.

21 Then said the chief priests of the Jews to Pilate, Write not, The King of the Jews ; but that he said, I am King of the Jews.

22 Pilate answered, What I have written, I have written.

23 Then the soldiers, when they had crucified Jesus, took his garments, and made four parts, to every soldier a part, and also *his* coat : now the coat was without seam, woven from the top throughout.

24 They said, therefore, among themselves, Let us not rend it, but cast lots for it, whose it shall be :

39 And they that passed by reviled him, wagging their heads,

40 And saying, Thou that destroyest the temple, and buildest *it* in three days, save thyself. If thou be the Son of God, come down from the cross.

41 Likewise also the chief priests mocking *him*, with the scribes and elders, said,

42 He saved others ; himself he cannot save. If he be the King of Israel, let him now come down from the cross, and we will believe him.

43 He trusted in God ; let him deliver him now, if he will have him : for he said, I am the Son of God.

81

39 Εἷς δὲ τῶν κρεμασθέντων κακούργων ἐϐλασφήμει αὐτῷ, λέγων· Εἰ σὺ εἶ ὁ Χριϛὸς, σῶσον σεαυτὸν κ) ἡμᾶς.

40 Ἀποκριθεὶς δὲ ὁ ἕτερ) ἐπετίμα αὐτῷ, λέγων· Οὐδὲ φοϐῇ σὺ τὸν Θεὸν, ὅτι ἐν τῷ αὐτῷ κρίματί εἶ;

41 Καὶ ἡμεῖς μὲν δικαίως· ἄξια γὰρ ὧν ἐπράξαμεν ἀπολαμ-

39 Unus autem pendentium maleficorum blasphemabat e- um, dicens: Si tu es Christus, serva temetipsum & nos.

40 Respondens autem alter increpabat eum, dicens: Neque times tu Deum, quod in eadem damnatione es?

41 Et nos quidem juste: di- gua enim eorum quæ fecimus

βάνομεν· ὅτ) δὲ οὐδὲν ἄτοπον ἔπραξε.

recipimus: hic vero nihil in- folens egit.

34 Ὁ δὲ Ἰησῦς ἔλεγε· Πάτερ, ἄφες αὐτοῖς· οὐ γὰρ οἴδασι τί ποιῦσι·

34 At Jesus dicebat: Pater, dimitte illis: non enim fciunt quid faciunt.

25 Εἱστήκεισαν δὲ παρὰ τῷ ϛαυρῷ τῦ Ἰησῦ ἡ μήτηρ αὐτῦ, κ) ἡ ἀδελφὴ τῆς μητρὸς αὐτῦ, Μαρία ἡ τῦ Κλωπᾶ, κ) Μαρία ἡ Μαγδα- ληνή.

26 Ἰησῦς ὖν ἰδὼν τὴν μητέρα, κ) τὸν μαθητὴν παρεϛῶτα, ὃν ἠ- γάπα, λέγει τῇ μητρὶ αὐτῦ· Γύ- ναι, ἰδὲ ὁ υἱός σε.

27 Εἶτα λέγει τῷ μαθητῇ· Ἰδὲ ἡ μήτηρ σε. Καὶ ἀπ' ἐκείνης τῆς ὥρας ἔλαϐεν αὐτὴν ὁ μαθητὴς εἰς τὰ ἴδια.

25 Stabant autem juxta cru- cem Jesu, mater ejus & soror matris ejus, Maria Cleopæ, & Maria Magdalene.

26 Jesus ergo videns matrem & discipulum adstantem, quem diligebat, dicit matri suæ: Mu- lier, ecce filius tuus.

27 Deinde dicit discipulo: Ecce mater tua. Et ex illa hora accepit eam discipulus ille in propria.

46 Περὶ δὲ τὴν ἐννάτην ὥραν ἀνεϐόησεν ὁ Ἰησῦς φωνῇ μεγάλῃ, λέγων· Ἠλὶ, Ἠλὶ, λαμὰ σαϐαχ- θανί; τῦτ' ἔϛι, Θεέ μυ, Θεέ μυ, ἱνατί με ἐγκατέλιπες;

47 Τινὲς δὲ τῶν ἐκεῖ ἑϛώτων ἀκούσαντες, ἔλεγον· Ὅτι Ἠλίαν φωνεῖ ὖτ).

48 Καὶ εὐθέως δραμὼν εἷς ἐξ αὐτῶν, κ) λαϐὼν ϛπόγγον, πλή- σας τε ὄξυς, κ) περιθεὶς καλάμῳ, ἐπότιζεν αὐτόν.

49 Οἱ δὲ λοιποὶ ἔλεγον· Ἄφες ἴδωμεν εἰ ἔρχεται Ἠλίας σώσων αὐτόν.

50 Ὁ δὲ Ἰησῦς πάλιν κρά-

46 Circa vero nonam horam clamavit Jesus voce magna, di- cens: Eli, Eli, lama fabachtha- ni? hoc est, Deus meus, Deus meus, ut quid me dereliquisti?

47 Quidam autem illic stan- tium, audientes, dicebant, Quod Eliam vocat iste.

48 Et continuò currens unus ex eis, & accipiens spongiam, implensque aceti, & circumpo- nens arundini potabat eum.

49 Verùm cæteri dicebant: Sine, videamus an veniat Elias liberaturus eum.

50 At Jesus iterum cla-

ξας φωνῇ μεγάλῃ, ἀφῆκε τὸ πνεῦμα.

mans voce magna, emisit spiri- tum.

55 Ἦσαν δὲ ἐκεῖ γυναῖκες πολλαὶ, ἀπὸ μακρόθεν θεωρῦσαι· αἵτινες ἠκολούθησαν τῷ Ἰησῦ ἀπὸ τῆς Γαλιλαίας, διακονῦσαι αὐτῷ·

56 Ἐν αἷς ἦν Μαρία ἡ Μαγ- δαληνὴ, κ) Μαρία ἡ τῦ Ἰακώϐυ κ) Ἰωσῆ μήτηρ, κ) ἡ μήτηρ τῶν υἱῶν Ζεϐεδαίυ.

55 Erant autem ibi mulieres multæ à longè fpectantes, quæ fequutæ erant Jesum à Galilæa, ministrantes ei:

56 In quibus erat Maria Magdalene, & Maria Jacobi & Jofe mater, & mater filiorum Zebedæi.

39. L'un des malfaiteurs qui étoient crucifiés, l'outrageoit aussi, en disant : Si tu es le Christ, sauve-toi toi-même, et nous aussi.

40. Mais l'autre le prenant, lui dit : Ne crains-tu point Dieu, puisque tu es condamné au même suplice.

41. Et pour nous, *nous le sommes* avec justice; car nous souffrons ce que nos crimes méritent; mais celui-ci n'a fait aucun mal.

34. Mais Jésus disoit : Mon père, pardonne-leur : car ils ne savent ce qu'ils font.

25. Or, la Mère de Jésus, et la sœur de sa Mère, Marie, *femme* de Cléopas, et Marie Magdelaine, se tenoient près de sa croix.

26. Jésus donc voyant sa Mère, et près d'elle, le Disciple qu'il aimoit, dit à sa Mère: Femme, voilà ton Fils.

27. Puis il dit au Disciple : Voilà ta Mère : Et dès cette heure-là, ce Disciple la prit chez lui.

46. Et environ la neuvième heure, Jésus s'écria à haute voix, disant : Eli, Eli, lamma sabachthani? C'est à-dire, mon Dieu, mon Dieu, pourquoi m'as-tu abandonné!

47. Et quelques-uns de ceux qui étoient présens, ayant ouï cela, disoient : il appelle Elie.

48. Et aussitôt quelqu'un d'entr'eux courut et prit une éponge, et l'ayant remplie de vinaigre, il la mit au bout d'une canne, et lui en donna à boire.

49. Et les autres disoient : attendez, voyons si Elie viendra le délivrer.

50. Et Jésus ayant encore crié à haute voix, rendit l'esprit.

55. Il y avoit aussi là plusieurs femmes, qui regardoient de loin, et qui avoient suivi Jésus, depuis la Galilée, en le servant ;

56. Entre lesquelles étoient Marie-Magdeleine, et Marie, mère de Jacques et de Joses, et la mère des fils de Zébédée.

L. 23.

39 And one of the malefactors, which were hanged, railed on him, saying, If thou be Christ, save thyself and us.

40 But the other, answering, rebuked him, saying, Dost not thou fear God, seeing thou art in the same condemnation?

41 And we indeed justly; for we receive the due reward of our deeds: but this man hath done nothing amiss.

34 Then said Jesus, Father, forgive them; for they know not what they do.

J. 19

25 Now there stood by the cross of Jesus, his mother, and his mother's sister, Mary the *wife* of Cleophas, and Mary Magdalene.

26 When Jesus, therefore, saw his mother, and the disciple standing by whom he loved, he saith unto his mother, Woman, behold thy Son!

27 Then saith he to the disciple, Behold thy mother! And from that hour that disciple took her unto his own *home*.

M. 27.

46 And about the ninth hour, Jesus cried with a loud voice, saying, Eli, Eli, lama sabachthani? that is to say, My God, my God, why hast thou forsaken me?

47 Some of them that stood there, when they heard *that*, said, This *man* calleth for Elias.

48 And straightway one of them ran, and took a spunge, and filled *it* with vinegar, and put *it* on a reed, and gave him to drink.

49 The rest said, Let be, let us see whether Elias will come to save him.

50 Jesus, when he had cried again with a loud voice, yielded up the ghost.

55 And many women were there, beholding afar off, which followed Jesus from Galilee, ministering unto him:

56 Among which was Mary Magdalene, and Mary the mother of James and Joses, and the mother of Zebedee's children.

82

31 Οἱ οὖν Ἰουδαῖοι, ἵνα μὴ μείνῃ ἐπὶ τοῦ σταυροῦ τὰ σώματα ἐν τῷ σαββάτῳ, ἐπεὶ παρασκευὴ ἦν, (ἦν γὰρ μεγάλη ἡ ἡμέρα ἐκείνη τοῦ σαββάτου) ἠρώτησαν τὸν Πιλάτον ἵνα κατεαγῶσιν αὐτῶν τὰ σκέλη, καὶ ἀρθῶσιν.

32 Ἦλθον οὖν οἱ στρατιῶται, καὶ τοῦ μὲν πρώτου κατέαξαν τὰ σκέλη, καὶ τοῦ ἄλλου τοῦ συσταυρωθέντος αὐτῷ.

33 Ἐπὶ δὲ τὸν Ἰησοῦν ἐλθόντες, ὡς εἶδον αὐτὸν ἤδη τεθνηκότα, οὐ κατέαξαν αὐτοῦ τὰ σκέλη.

34 Ἀλλ' εἷς τῶν στρατιωτῶν † λόγχῃ αὐτοῦ τὴν ‡ πλευρὰν † ἔνυξε, καὶ ‡ εὐθὺς ἐξῆλθεν αἷμα καὶ ὕδωρ.

38 Μετὰ δὲ ταῦτα ἠρώτησε τὸν Πιλάτον ὁ Ἰωσὴφ ὁ ἀπὸ Ἀριμαθαίας, (ὢν μαθητὴς τοῦ Ἰησοῦ, κεκρυμμένος δὲ διὰ τὸν φόβον τῶν Ἰουδαίων) ἵνα ἄρῃ τὸ σῶμα τοῦ Ἰησοῦ· καὶ ἐπέτρεψεν ὁ Πιλάτος. ἦλθεν οὖν καὶ ἦρε τὸ σῶμα τοῦ Ἰησοῦ.

39 Ἦλθε δὲ καὶ Νικόδημος, (ὁ ἐλθὼν πρὸς τὸν Ἰησοῦν νυκτὸς τὸ πρῶτον) φέρων † μίγμα ‡ σμύρνης καὶ ‡ ἀλόης ὡσεὶ λίτρας ἑκατόν.

40 Ἔλαβον οὖν τὸ σῶμα τοῦ Ἰησοῦ, καὶ ἔδησαν αὐτὸ ‡ ὀθονίοις μετὰ τῶν ‡ ἀρωμάτων, καθὼς ἔθος ἐστὶ τοῖς Ἰουδαίοις ‡ ἐνταφιάζειν.

41 Ἦν δὲ ἐν τῷ τόπῳ, ὅπου ἐσταυρώθη, κῆπος, καὶ ἐν τῷ κήπῳ μνημεῖον καινόν, ἐν ᾧ οὐδέπω οὐδεὶς ἐτέθη.

42 Ἐκεῖ ... ἔθηκαν τὸν Ἰησοῦν ... καὶ προσ... κυλίσας λίθον μέγαν τῇ θύρᾳ τοῦ μνημείου, ἀπῆλθεν.

31 Ergo Judæi, ut non remanerent in cruce corpora in Sabbato, quoniam Parasceve erat, (erat enim magnus dies ille Sabbati) rogaverunt Pilatum ut frangerentur eorum crura, & tollerentur.

32 Venerunt ergo milites, & quidem primi fregerunt crura: & alterius concrucifixi ei.

33 Ad autem Jesum venientes, ut viderunt eum jam mortuum, non fregerunt ejus crura.

34 Sed unus militum lancea ejus latus fodit, & continuo exivit sanguis & aqua.

38 Post hæc rogavit Pilatum Joseph ab Arimathæa (existens discipulus Jesu, occultus autem propter metum Judæorum) ut tolleret corpus Jesu: & permisit Pilatus: Venit ergo & tulit corpus Jesu.

39 Venit autem & Nicodemus (ille veniens ad Jesum nocte primum) ferens mixturam myrrhæ & aloës, quasi libras centum.

40 Acceperunt ergo corpus Jesu, & ligaverunt illud linteis cum aromatibus, sicut mos est Judæis sepelire.

41 Erat autem in loco, ubi crucifixus est, hortus, & in horto monumentum novum, in quo nondum quisquam positus erat.

42 Ibi ergo posuerunt Je... ... solvens la... dem m... abiit.

31. Or, les Juifs, de peur que les corps ne demeurassent sur la croix le jour du Sabbat (car c'en étoit la préparation, et ce Sabbat étoit un jour fort solennel), prièrent Pilate de leur faire rompre les jambes, et qu'on les ôtât.

32. Les soldats vinrent donc, et rompirent les jambes au premier, et ensuite à l'autre qui étoit crucifié avec lui.

33. Mais lorsqu'ils vinrent à Jésus, voyant qu'il étoit déjà mort, ils ne lui rompirent point les jambes.

34. Mais un des soldats lui perça le côté avec une lance, et aussitôt il en sortit du sang et de l'eau.

38. Après cela, Joseph d'Arimathée, qui étoit Disciple de Jésus, mais en secret, parce qu'il craignoit les Juifs, pria Pilate qu'il pût ôter le corps de Jésus; et Pilate le lui permit. Il vint donc et emporta le corps de Jésus.

39. Nicodème qui, au commencement, étoit venu de nuit vers Jésus, y vint aussi, apportant environ cent livres d'une composition de myrrhe et d'aloës.

40. Ils prirent donc le corps de Jésus, et l'enveloppèrent de linges, avec des drogues aromatiques, comme les Juifs ont accoutumé d'ensevelir.

41. Or, il y avoit un jardin au lieu où il avoit été crucifié, et dans ce jardin un sépulcre neuf, où personne n'avoit été mis.

42. Ils mirent donc là Jésus, et ayant roulé une grand pierre à l'entrée du sépulcre, il s'en alla.

31 The Jews, therefore, because it was the preparation, that the bodies should not remain upon the cross on the sabbath-day, (for that sabbath-day was an high day,) besought Pilate that their legs might be broken, and *that* they might be taken away.

32 Then came the soldiers, and brake the legs of the first, and of the other which was crucified with him.

33 But when they came to Jesus, and saw that he was dead already, they brake not his legs:

34 But one of the soldiers with a spear pierced his side, and forthwith came thereout blood and water.

38 And after this, Joseph of Arimathea, (being a disciple of Jesus, but secretly for fear of the Jews,) besought Pilate that he might take away the body of Jesus: and Pilate gave *him* leave. He came therefore, and took the body of Jesus.

39 And there came also Nicodemus, (which at the first came to Jesus by night and brought a mixture of myrrh and aloes, about an hundred pound *weight*.

40 Then took they the body of Jesus, and wound it in linen clothes with the spices, as the manner of the Jews is to bury.

41 Now, in the place where he was crucified, there was a garden; and in the garden a new sepulchre, wherein was never man yet laid.

42 There laid they Jesus,

60. and he rolled a great stone to the door of the sepulchre, and departed.

NOTES TO
"THE LIFE AND MORALS
OF JESUS"

GENERAL EXPLANATION OF THE NOTES

The following notes to "The Life and Morals of Jesus" (hereafter referred to as LJ) are primarily designed to point out discrepancies in the text of LJ and to supply the remaining portions of every verse which was only partially used or which is now illegible. In every case the text supplied by the notes conforms to the one contained in the editions of the Greek-Latin, French, and English New Testaments (hereafter referred to as NT) that TJ actually used to compile LJ, except that archaic Greek ligatures have been rendered in separate letters and certain symbols in the Greek text, described below, have been eliminated. In addition to supplying correct readings for the unused portions of LJ verses, these editions of the NT often provide the best explanation for the discrepancies in the text of LJ.

The editions of the NT used by TJ to compile LJ are as follows:

(1) The English NTs were both editions of the the King James Version printed in Philadelphia in 1804 by Jacob Johnson & Co. The English NTs actually clipped by TJ are now at the Smithsonian Institution, Washington, D.C., where for purposes of identification they are designated as NT 1 and NT 2.

(2) The twin pairs of Greek-Latin and French NTs used by TJ are no longer extant. The French NT he used was *Le Nouveau Testament . . . Corrigé sur le Texte Grec* (Paris, 1802). The translation was made by Jean F. Ostervald (1663-1747), a Swiss Protestant. The only copy of this edition known to exist is held by the British and Foreign Bible Society in London.

(3) The Greek-Latin NT used by TJ was *HKAINH ΔIAΘĤKH Novum Testamentum, Cum Versione Latina*, published in London in 1794 by F. Wingrave and others. The text of this edition is unusual in several respects. The Greek text was translated by Johannes Leusden (1624-1699) and first published in 1688. There are a number of peculiar marks in that text, and hence in LJ, which are explained by the following note in Darlow and Moule, *Catalogue of the Printed Editions of Holy Scripture*, item 4717: "Leusden discovered that the vocabulary of the Greek Testament amounted to 4956 words, of which 1686 occurred only once; and that 1900 selected verses contained the whole number." These 1900 verses were marked by an asterisk at the beginning of each verse. In the edition of 1688, Leusden added special marks—a single dagger to indicate words that occurred once and a double dagger to indicate those that occurred more than once. The whole number of words so indicated is noted at the end of every chapter. These symbols have been eliminated in the notes to this edition of LJ.

The Latin text of this volume, which was the work of Benedictus Arias Montanus (1527-1598), is not the Vulgate but rather a translation that was designed to serve as an interlinear text and that paralleled the Greek text as closely as possible. Many apparent anomalies in the Greek-Latin text are readily explicable if one remembers that the NTs from which TJ clipped verses in these languages were arranged with parallel columns of text. Since these verses do not always follow each other line for line, in some cases the clipped parallel verses in LJ are uneven and in others TJ repeated or omitted part of a line in one language by cutting straight across a page on which the Greek and Latin verses were not exactly aligned.

NOTES FOR PAGE 1

L2:21: Portion of verse not used: "which was so named of the angel before he was conceived in the womb."

Greek: "τὸ κληθὲν ὑπὸ τοῦ ἀγγελου πρὸ τοῦ συλληφθῆναι αὐτὸν ἐν τῇ κοιλίᾳ."

Latin: "vocatum ab angelo ante concipi eum in utero."

French: "qui est le nom qui lui avoit été donné par l'Ange, avant qu'il fut conçu dans le sein de sa Mère."

L2:40: Portion of verse not used: "and the grace of God was upon him."

Greek: "καὶ χάρις Θεοῦ ἦν ἐπ᾿ αὐτό."

Latin: "et gratia Dei erat in illo."

French: "et la grace de Dieu étoit sur lui."

NOTES FOR PAGE 2

L2:51: Portion of verse not used: "but his mother kept all these sayings in her heart."

French: "Et sa Mère conservoit toutes ces choses dans son cœur."

Entire verse omitted in other two languages:

Greek: "Καὶ κατέβη μετ᾿ αὐτῶν, καὶ ἦλθεν εἰς Ναζαρέτ· καὶ ἦν ὑποτασσόμενος αὐτοῖς. καὶ ἡ μήτηρ αὐτοῦ διετήρει πάντα τὰ ῥήματα ταῦτα ἐν τῇ καρδίᾳ αὐτῆς."

Latin: "Et descendit cum eis, et venit in Nazaret: et erat subditus illis. Et mater ejus conservabat omnia verba hæc in corde suo."

L2:52: Portion of verse not used: "and in favour with God and man."

Greek: "καὶ χάριτι παρὰ Θεῷ καὶ ἀνθρώποις."

Latin: "et gratia apud Deum et homines."

French: "devant Dieu et devant les hommes."

L3:2: Portion of verse not used: "the word of God came unto John the son of Zacharis in the wilderness."

Greek: "ἐγένετο ῥῆμα Θεοῦ ἐπὶ Ἰωάννην τὸν τοῦ Ζαχαρίου υἱὸν ἐν τῇ ἐρήμῳ."

Latin: "factum est verbum Dei ad Joannem Zachariæ filium in deserto."

French: "la parole de Dieu fut adressée à Jean, fils de Zacharie, dans le désert."

Mk1:4: Portion of verse not used: "and preach the baptism of repentance for the remission of sins."

> Greek: "καὶ κηρύσσων βάπτισμα μετανοίας εἰς ἄφεσιν ἁμαρτιῶν."
> Latin: "et prædicans baptismum pœnitentiæ in remissionem peccatorum."
> French: "et prêchoit le Baptême de repentance, pour la rémission des péchés."

M3:6: Portion of verse not used: "confessing their sins."

> Greek: "ἐξομολογούμενοι τὰς ἁμαρτίας αὐτῶν."
> Latin: "confitentes peccata sua."
> French: "confessant leurs péchés."

L3:23: Portion of verse not used: "being (as was supposed) the son of Joseph, which was *the son* of Heli."

> Greek: "ὤν, ὡς ἐνομίζετο, υἱὸς Ἰωσήφ, τοῦ Ἡλί."
> Latin: "existens, ut existimabatur filius Joseph, Heli."
> French: "et il étoit, comme on le croyoit, *fils* de Joseph, *fils* d'Héli."

NOTE FOR PAGE 3

M6:23: The two partially obscured words in French are "donnerai, jusqu'à."

NOTE FOR PAGE 4

Mk6:28: The entry "29 Et" after this verse in Latin is the beginning of Mk6:29 and was inadvertently included by TJ because the Greek and Latin texts were not exactly parallel to each other on this page of the NT. TJ did not use Mk6:29 elsewhere in LJ or PJ.

NOTES FOR PAGE 5

M12:15: Portion of verse not used: "and he healed them all."

> French: "et il les guérit tous."

L6:12: TJ changed "out" to "up" in English.

L6:17: Portion of verse not used: "and to be healed of their diseases."

> French: "et pour être guéris de leurs maladies."
>
> TJ probably included the full Greek and Latin texts of M12:15 and L6:17 in LJ through inadvertence.

NOTES FOR PAGE 8

M5:33: The partially obscured Greek words are ἐρρέθη (lines 1-2), ἐπιορκήσεις (lines 2-3), and τοὺς (line 4).

M5:34: The partially obscured Greek words are ὀμόσαι (lines 1-2) and θρόνος (line 3).

M6:12: The partially obscured Greek word is ὀφειλήματα (lines 1-2).

M6:13: The partially obscured Greek words are τοῦ (line 3), βασιλεία (lines 3-4), and τοὺς (line 5).

M6:14: The partially obscured Greek words are ἀνθρώποις (lines 1-2), ἀφήσει (line 3), and οὐράνιος (lines 3-4).

M6:16: Portion of verse not used: "Je vous dis en vérité, qu'ils reçoivent leur récompense." This omission must have been inadvertent, inasmuch as TJ used the full verse in the other three languages.

M7:[2]: Although this verse no longer appears in the Table of Texts, it seems virtually certain that TJ entered it at the edge of the page and that it has since been worn away.

L6:38: Portion of verse not used: "For with the same measure that ye mete withal, it shall be measured to you again."

Greek: "τῷ γὰρ αὐτῷ μέτρῳ ᾧ μετρεῖτε, ἀντιμετρηθήσεται ὑμῖν."

Latin: "Quippe ea mensura qua mensi fueritis, remetietur vobis."

French: "car on vous mesurera de la mesure dont vous vous servez *envers les autres.*"

M7:21-23: TJ's use of these verses in French, as opposed to M12:35-37 in the other three languages, must have been inadvertent. With the exception of the first line of the first verse, he removed M7:18-25 in one clipping from the French NT. Although TJ did not list M7:21-23 in the Table of Texts for LJ, he did use them in PJ, p. 19. The French text of M12:35-37, the verses TJ used in the other three languages on this page of LJ, are:

35. L'homme de bien tire de bonnes choses du bon trésor de son cœur; mais le méchant tire de mauvaises choses du mauvais trésor *de son cœur.*

36. Or, je vous dis, que les hommes rendront compte au jour du Jugement de toutes les paroles impies qu'ils auront dites;

37. Car tu seras justifié par tes paroles, et par tes paroles, tu seras condamué.

Mk6:6: Portion of verse not used: "And he marvelled, because of their unbelief."

Greek: "καὶ ἐθαύμαζε διὰ τὴν ἀπιστίαν αὐτῶν."

Latin: "Et mirabatur propter incredulitatem eorum."

French: "Et il s'étonnoit de leur incrédulité."

NOTES

NOTE FOR PAGE 16

Mk3:34: The partially obscured Greek words are περιβλεψάμενος (line 1), περί (line 2), and μήτηρ (line 3).

NOTE FOR PAGE 20

L12:46: Portion of verse not used: "and will appoint him his portion with the unbelievers." TJ used the entire verse in the other three languages.

NOTE FOR PAGE 22

M13:4: Portion of verse not used: "up." TJ probably omitted this word in the English text for stylistic reasons.

NOTE FOR PAGE 24

M13:39: TJ incorrectly used the French verse here and then inserted another text of it in its proper place in LJ, p. 25.

NOTE FOR PAGE 25

M13:51-52: Portion of verses not used: "51. Et Jésus dit *à ses Disciples*: Avez-vous compris toutes ces choses? Ils lui *répondirent*: Oui, Seigneur. 52. Et il leur dit: C'est pour cela." It is virtually certain that TJ left these verses out by error. He mistakenly placed M13:39 at the bottom of LJ, p. 24, and then had to clip the same verse from the second French NT for use on LJ, p. 25. The unused portions of M13:51-52 were on the reverse side of M13:39 in the French NTs and thus could not be used by TJ in LJ.

NOTE FOR PAGE 26

Mk4:35: This is a misprint in the French text, which should read Mk4:33.

NOTES FOR PAGE 27

L5:29: Portion of verse not used: "there was a great company of publicans, and of others, that sat down with them."

Greek: "ἦν ὄχλος τελωνῶν πολύς, καὶ ἄλλων οἳ ἦσαν μετ᾽ αὐτῶν κατακείμενοι."

Latin: "erat turba publicanorum multa, et aliorum, qui erant cum illis discumbentes."

French: "une grande assemblée de péagers, et d'autres personnes qui étoient à table avec eux."

Mk2:15: Portion of verse not used: "And it came to pass, that, as Jesus sat at meat in his house."

Greek: "Καὶ ἐγένετο ἐν τῷ κατακεῖσθαι αὐτὸν ἐν τῇ οἰκίᾳ αὐτοῦ, καὶ."

Latin: "Et factum est in accumbere ipsum in domo illius, et."

French: "Jésus étant à table dans la maison *de cet homme*."

L5:36-38: Some transcriptions of the Table of Texts give this selection as L5:36-39 (Henry S. Randall, *The Life of Thomas Jefferson* [Philadelphia, 1858], III, 657). TJ seems to have first written 39 and then changed it to 38. He took all but the last word of L5:38 ("preserved") from NT 1. He had to use the "preserved" from NT 2 because he had eliminated it from NT 1 in the process of clipping verses for a previous section of LJ. This further indicates that TJ made his Table of Texts before he clipped the verses for LJ. Neither LJ nor PJ has L5:39 or any parallel to it. The text of L5:39 reads: "No man also, having drunk old *wine*, straightway desireth new: for he saith, The old is better."

M13:36: This is a misprint in the French text, which should read M13:56.

NOTES FOR PAGE 28

M13:58: The inclusion of this verse in French was obviously an error by TJ. It is not used in any of the other three languages, it is not listed in the Table of Texts, and it is not part of PJ.

Mk6:7: Portion of verse not used: "and gave them power over unclean spirits."

Greek: "καὶ ἐδίδου αὐτοῖς ἐξουσίαν τῶν πνευμάτων τῶν ἀκαθάρτων."

Latin: "et dabat illis auctoritatem spirituum immundorum."

French: "et leur donna pouvoir sur les esprits immondes."

M10:5: Portion of verse not used: "These twelve Jesus sent forth."

Greek: "Τούτους τοὺς δώδεκα ἀπέοτειλεν ὁ Ἰησοῦς."

Latin: "Hos duodecim legavit Jesus."

French: "Jésus envoya ces douze-là."

M10:17: Although the Greek, Latin, and French texts of this verse are complete on this page, the last line of the English text appears on LJ, p. 29. TJ inadvertently cut in two the first line of M10:18.

NOTE FOR PAGE 29

M10:23: Portion of verse not used: "for verily I say unto you, Ye shall not have gone over the cities of Israel, till the Son of man be come."

Greek: "ἀμὴν γὰρ λέγω ὑμῖν, Οὐ μὴ τελέσητε τὰς πόλεις τοῦ Ἰσραήλ, ἕως ἂν ἔλθῃ ὁ υἱὸς τοῦ ἀνθρώπου."

Latin: "Amen enim dico vobis, non finietis civitates Israel, donec veniat Filius hominis."

French: "Je vous dis en vérité, que vous n'aurez achevé d'aller, par toutes les villes d'Israel, que le Fils de l'homme ne soit venu."

NOTE FOR PAGE 32

M18:21-22: The entry for these verses in the Table of Texts is obscured. TJ probably first wrote 21-35 because these verses from Matthew do appear in sequence in LJ. Then, realizing that he wished to characterize M18:23-35 differently than he had characterized the passages ending with M18:21-22, he wrote 22 over the 35 in the Table of Texts. Afterwards, someone, possibly TJ, being unable to read the obscure entry, entered a 5 above the 22, leading some scholars to transcribe it incorrectly as 25 or even 35 (Randall, *Life of Jefferson*, III, 657). An inspection of the original manuscript at the Smithsonian leaves little doubt that it was intended to be 22.

NOTES FOR PAGE 34

J7:14: The partially obscured materials just above the Greek and Latin texts of this verse are clippings of a portion of the first line of this verse from the other Greek-Latin NT.

J7:16: Portion of verse not used: "My doctrine is not mine, but his that sent me."

Greek: "καὶ εἶπεν, Ἡ ἐμὴ διδαχὴ οὐκ ἔστιν ἐμή, ἀλλὰ τοῦ πέμψαντός με."

Latin: "et dixit: Mea doctrina non est mea, sed mittentis me."

French: "Ma doctrine n'est pas de moi; mais elle est de celui qui m'a envoyé."

NOTES FOR PAGE 35

J7:48: The partially missing word on the second line of this verse in English is "the."

J7:49: The partially missing word on the second line of this verse in English is "not."

NOTES FOR PAGE 36

J7:50-53: The partially obscured words and endings on the left margin of these verses in English are "(he," "being," "before," "he," "to," "Search," "-lilee," and "own."

J7:53: TJ corrected a misprinted verse number 58 in the English column.

J8:1-5: The partially obscured words and endings on the left margin of these verses in English are "came," "all," "and," "brought," "in," "set," "this," "-ry," "-manded," and "stoned."

NOTE FOR PAGE 38

L10:38: TJ accidentally placed the first line of this verse in French at this point in LJ. It actually belongs at the bottom of LJ, p. 49, where it is missing. TJ made this error by pasting on to LJ, p. 38, an entire column from the French NT, the last line of which was this part of L10:38.

NOTES FOR PAGE 40

L14:1-6: The entry in the Table of Texts originally read L14:1-4 and was changed by TJ to L14:1-6. TJ placed part of M4:19 between L14:4 and L14:5 in the English text only. The original entry in the Table of Texts may indicate that he planned to use the first line of M4:19 but forgot to list it in the Table. TJ used part of M21:27 in the same way on LJ, p. 56, and listed it in the Table of Texts. The first line of L14:5, for which TJ substituted M4:19 in the English text, is still extant as a loose clipping in NT 1.

L14:4: Portion of verse not used: "and he took *him*, and healed him, and let him go."

Greek: "Καὶ ἐπιλαβόμενος ἰάσατο αὐτὸν, καὶ ἀπέλυσε."

Latin: "Et apprehendens sanavit eum, et dimisit."

This verse is complete in French, probably because of an oversight by TJ.

M4:19: The single line of this English verse is placed in the margin, at right angles to the text, with a bracket indicating that the material belongs between L14:4 and L14:5. TJ did not list this verse in the Table of Texts. He probably preferred the phrase from M4:19 to the one in the first line of L14:5 because it provided a better transition once the reference to the supernatural healing was eliminated from L14:4. The phrase from M4:19 corresponds with the French text of L14:5, whereas the Greek and Latin texts do not.

L14:5: Portion of verse not used: "And answered them, saying."

Greek: "Καὶ ἀποκριθεὶς πρὸς αὐτοὺς εἶπε."

Latin: "Et respondens ad illos dixit."

This verse is complete in French, probably because of an oversight by TJ.

NOTES FOR PAGE 41

L14:14: Portion of verse not used: "car tu en recevras la récompense à la résurrection des Justes." TJ must have excluded this portion by accident, for the verse is complete in the other three languages.

L14:15: Neither this verse nor any parallel appears in LJ or PJ. TJ apparently listed it in the Table of Texts as part of L14:7-24 ("the bidden to a feast"), but the clipped English NTs show that he did not use it. The verse reads: "And when one of them that sat at meat with him, heard these things, he said unto him, Blessed *is* he that shall eat bread in the kingdom of God."

NOTES

NOTE FOR PAGE 43

L15:10: The full text of this verse in Latin appears on LJ, p. 42. TJ repeated the last two words here, "peccatore pœnitente," because he clipped the Greek-Latin NT straight across the page for the verses he used in LJ, p. 43, even though these two Latin words were parallel to the first line of the Greek text of L15:11.

NOTE FOR PAGE 46

L16:18: Although this verse is listed in the Table of Texts, its placement here seems inappropriate in view of the fact that TJ characterized L16:18-31 as the "parable of Lazarus." Perhaps he meant it to be understood in the context of L16:14-15 (LJ, p. 45) as a continuation of Jesus' criticism of the Pharisees, whose teachings on the durability of the marriage bond were less strict than his own.

NOTE FOR PAGE 47

L17:20: The scraps of words that appear below the Latin and French texts of this verse in the 1904 facsimile edition of LJ were the consequence of holes in this page that allowed material from the pages immediately before and after it to show through.

NOTE FOR PAGE 49

L10:38: The missing first line of this verse in French, which erroneously appears as the last line in the French column in LJ, p. 38, reads: "Comme ils étoient en che-."

NOTE FOR PAGE 50

M19:2: Portion of verse not used: "and he healed them there."

> Greek: "καὶ ἐθεράπευσεν αὐτοὺς ἐκεῖ."
> Latin: "et curavit eos ibi."
> French: "et il guérit-là *leurs malades*."

NOTES FOR PAGE 51

M19:12: TJ left out five lines of this verse in English. These lines are cut from both of the English NTs he used to compile LJ. They read: "mother's womb; and there are some eunuchs, which were made eunuchs of men; and there be eunuchs, which have made themselves eunuchs for the kingdom." The fact that the verse is complete in the other three languages sugggests that TJ made this omission through oversight.

M19:23: The partially illegible first line of this verse in Latin reads: "At Jesus dixit discipulis."

M20:8: The words partially cut off on the right margin of this verse in Latin are "dicit," "suo:," and "illis."

M20:10: The partially obscured word on the right margin of the third line of this verse in Latin is "ipsi."

J12:23: Portion of verse not used: "The hour is come, that the Son of man should be glorified." TJ used the whole verse in the other three languages.

Mk:11:12: Portion of verse not used: "he was hungry."

> Greek: "ἐπείνασε."
> Latin: "esuriit."
> French: "il eut faim."

Mk11:15: Portion of verse not used: "And they came to Jerusalem: and."

> Greek: "Καὶ ἔρχονται εἰς Ἱεροσόλυμα· καὶ."
> Latin: "Et veniunt in Hierosolyma: et."
> French: "Ils vinrent donc à Jérusalem; et."

Mk11:27: TJ placed this verse in the margin of the English column, at right angles to the text, and folded it so that it would not project beyond the boards in the closed volume. The clipping was folded in the 1904 facsimile edition of LJ, making it appear that Mk11:27 was not part of the text and covering some of the adjoining verses. TJ listed Mk11:27 in the Table of Texts and, as the 1904 facsimile edition shows, he wrote on the reverse side of it "Mark 11.27."

M21:27: TJ placed the English clipping of this partially used verse ("And he said unto them") at right angles to the text of the English column. The corresponding phrase in the other three languages is probably from M8:26. The unused portion of M21:27 reads: "And they answered Jesus, and said, We cannot tell . . . Neither tell I you by what authority I do these things."

M21:33: Portion of verse not used: "There was a certain householder, which planted a vineyard, and hedged it round about, and digged a winepress in it, and built a tower, and let it out to husbandmen, and went into a far country."

> Greek: "Ἄνθρωπός τις ἦν οἰκοδεσπότης, ὅστις ἐφύτευσεν ἀμ-πελῶνα, καὶ φραγμὸν αὐτῷ περιέθηκε, καὶ ὤρυξεν ἐν αὐτῷ ληνὸν, καὶ ᾠκοδόμησε πύργον, καὶ ἐξέδοτο αὐτὸν γεωργοῖς, καὶ ἀπε-δήμησεν."
> Latin: "Homo quidam erat paterfamilias, qui plantavit vineam, et sepem ei circumposuit, et fodit in ea torcular, et ædificavit turrim, et locavit eam agricolis, et peregre profectus est."

French: "Il y avait un père de famille, qui planta une vigne, il l'envirrona d'une haie, il y creusa un pressoir, et il y bâtit une tour, puis il la loua à des vignerons, et s'en alla faire un voyage."

Mk12:1: Portion of verse not used: "And he began to speak unto them by parables."

Greek: "Καὶ ἤρξατο αὐτοῖς ἐν παραβολαῖς λέγειν."
Latin: "Et cœpit illis in parabolis dicere."
French: "Jésus se mit ensuite à leur parler en paraboles."

M22:1: The partially obscured words on the first line of this verse in English are "And Jesus." In the Table of Texts, TJ wrote the entry for M21:45-46, the verses which partially cover these words, above the line, indicating that he decided to include those two verses while clipping passages for the English column after the Table had been prepared.

NOTE FOR PAGE 60

M23:1: Portion of verse not used in Greek: "αὐτοῦ" and in Latin: "suis." The verse is complete in the other two languages.

NOTE FOR PAGE 63

M24:29: TJ did not list this verse in the Table of Texts, which is another indication that in compiling LJ he first prepared a Table of Texts and then sometimes added new verses in the process of clipping passages from the NTs.

NOTES FOR PAGE 64

M24:33: There is no equivalent in the other three languages of the interpolated "*le Fils de l'homme*" in the French text of this verse.

M24:36: The partially clipped word on the right margin of the first line of this verse in Latin is "hora."

M24:38: The partially clipped words on the right margin of the first four lines of this verse in Latin are "diebus," "et," "tradentes," and "intravit."

TJ carefully cut out the word "as" in the first line of this verse in English.

M24:39: Portion of verse not used: "so shall also the coming of the Son of Man be." TJ used the whole verse in the other three languages.

M24:44: Portion of verse not used: "for in such an hour as ye think not, the Son of Man cometh."

Greek: "ὅτι ᾗ ὥρᾳ οὐ δοκεῖτε, ὁ υἱὸς τοῦ ἀνθρώπου ἔρχεται."
Latin: "quia quâ horâ non putatis: Filius hominis venturus est."
French: "car le Fils de l'homme viendra à l'heure que vous ne pensez pas."

NOTE FOR PAGE 65

M25:13: Portion of verse not used: "for ye know neither the day nor the hour wherein the Son of Man cometh."

Greek: "ὅτι οὐκ οἴδατε τὴν ἡμέραν οὐδὲ τὴν ὥραν, ἐν ᾗ ὁ υἱὸς τοῦ ἀνθρώπου ἔρχεται."

Latin: "quia nescitis diem neque horam, in quâ Filius hominis veniet."

French: "car vous ne savez ni le jour ni l'heure à laquelle le Fils de l'homme viendra."

NOTES FOR PAGE 67

M25:30: The words that have been obscured by the folding back of this verse in the French column are "inutile" (lines 1-2), "c'est," (line 3), and "des" (line 4).

L21:36: Portion of verse not used:

Greek: "λοντα γίνεσθαι, καὶ σταθῆναι ἔμπροσθεν τοῦ υἱοῦ τοῦ ἀνθρώπου."

Latin: "tura fieri, et stare ante filium hominis."

TJ used the whole verse in French and English. He undoubtedly used only part of it in Greek and Latin because he failed to realize that in the Greek-Latin NT the section he omitted was printed on the page immediately after the page on which appeared the section he included.

NOTE FOR PAGE 68

M25:43: The partially obscured first line of this verse in Greek and Latin reads, respectively: "ξένος ἤμην, καὶ οὐ συνηγάγ-" and "Hospes eram, et non col-."

NOTES FOR PAGE 70

J13:2: Portion of verse not used: "the devil having now put into the heart of Judas Iscariot, Simon's *son*, to betray him."

Greek: "τοῦ διαβόλου ἤδη βεβληκότος εἰς τὴν καρδίαν Ἰούδα Σίμωνος Ἰσκαριώτου ἵνα αὐτὸν παραδῷ."

Latin: "diabolo jam jaculato in cor Judæ Simonis Iscariotæ, ut eum traderet."

French: "le Diable ayant déjà mis au cœur de Judas Iscariot, fils de Simon, de le trahir."

J13:16: TJ clipped almost all of the first line of the English text of this verse from NT 2 and the rest, which was on the reverse side of the page, from NT 1.

J13:31: Portion of verse not used: "Now is the Son of Man glorified, and God is glorified in him."

Greek: "Νῦν ἐδοξάσθη ὁ υἱὸς τοῦ ἀνθρώπου, καὶ ὁ Θεὸς ἐδοξάσθη ἐν αὐτῷ."

Latin: "Nunc glorificatus est filius hominis, et Deus glorificatus est in eo."

French: "Maintenant le Fils de l'homme est glorifié et Dieu est glorifié par lui."

M26:31: Portion of verse not used: "for it is written, I will smite the shepherd, and the sheep of the flock shall be scattered abroad."

Greek: "γέγραπται γὰρ, Πατάξω τὸν ποιμένα, καὶ διασκορπισθήσεται τὰ πρόβατα τῆς ποίμνης."

Latin: "Scriptum est enim: Percutiam pastorem, et dispergentur oves gregis."

French: "car il est écrit: Je frapperai le Berger, et les brebis du troupeau seront dispersées."

L22:33: Portion of verse not used: "And he said unto him, Lord."

Greek: "Ὁ δὲ εἶπεν αὐτῷ, Κύριε."

Latin: "Is autem dixit ei: Domine."

French: "Et *Pierre* lui dit: Seigneur."

L22:35-36: Evidently TJ accidentally used these verses in French instead of M26:35-36, for he cut the last two lines of L22:33 through L22:36 in one clipping. Neither L22:35-36 nor any parallel appears elsewhere in LJ or PJ. The French text of M26:35-36 reads:

35. Pierre lui dit: Quand même il me faudroit mourir avec toi, je ne te renierai point. Et tous les Disciples dirent la même chose.

36. Alors Jésus s'en alla avec eux dans un lieu appelé Gethsémané; et il dit à ses Disciples: Asseyez-vous ici, pendant que je m'en irai là pour prier.

M26:45: Portion of verse not used: "behold, the hour is at hand, and the Son of Man is betrayed into the hands of sinners."

Greek: "ἰδοὺ, ἤγγικεν ἡ ὥρα, καὶ ὁ υἱὸς τοῦ ἀνθρώπου παραδίδοται εἰς χεῖρας ἁμαρτωλῶν."

Latin: "ecce, appropinquavit hora, et Filius hominis tradetur in manus peccatorum."

French: "Voici l'heure est venue, et le Fils de l'homme va être livré entre les mains de méchans."

M26:48: The poorly clipped second line of this verse in Latin reads: "illis signum, dicens: Quem-."

M26:50: TJ placed the entire Greek and Latin texts of this verse before J18:4, which results in an absurd order of events and is clearly an error. As in the French and English columns, the last part of this verse should follow J18:8. Except for its division into two parts, M26:50 is complete in French and English on this page of LJ.

M26:56: Portion of verse not used: "But all this was done, that the scriptures of the prophets might be fulfilled."

Greek: "Τοῦτο δὲ ὅλον γέγονεν, ἵνα πληρωθῶσιν αἱ γραφαὶ τῶν προφητῶν."

Latin: "Hoc autem totum factum est, ut adimplerentur Scripturæ Prophetarum."

French: "Mais tout ceci est arrivé, afin que ce qui est écrit dans les Prophètes fût accompli."

J18:25: The blurred word on the last line of this verse in Latin is "dixit."

J18:27: The partially obscured word on the last line of this verse in French is "aussitôt."

Mk14:53: TJ did not list this verse, which appears only in the English column, in the Table of Texts and undoubtedly lined it out after realizing that it contained another description of the same incident in M26:57, which he had already entered in LJ, p. 74.

L22:67: Portion of verse not used: "Saying, Art thou the Christ? tell us."

Greek: "Λέγοντες, Εἰ σὺ εἶ ὁ Χριστός; εἰπὲ ἡμῖν."
Latin: "Dicentes: Si tu es Christus, dic nobis."
French: "Et ils lui dirent: Si tu es le Christ, dis-le nous."

J18:28: TJ placed the first two lines of this verse in English at right angles to the main text and wrote in the last four letters of "judgment."

L23:14: TJ's marginal note to this verse reads: "under the Roman law de seditiosis in crucem tollendis? Digest de poenis L. 48, tit. 19.6.28.3. 'capite plectendi cum saepius seditiosé et turbulenté se gesserint, et aliquotiens adprehensi clementius in eâdem temeritate propositi perseveraverint'?"

TJ was clearly referring to Justinian's *Digesta*, book 48, title 19, "DE POENIS." According to his legal commonplace book, TJ took this reference to the Digesta from Johann Albert Fabricius, *Codex Apochryphus Novi Testamenti* (Hamburg, 1703), p. 258n (see E. Millicent Sowerby, comp., *Catalogue of the Library of Thomas Jefferson* [Washington, D.C., 1952-59], No. 1498). He must have meant the 6 to be §, because section 6 of book 48, title 19 of the *Digesta* is unrelated to the question of the law under which Jesus was crucified. He also used the same reference in TJ to Peter Carr, 10 Aug. 1787.

Freely translated, paragraph 28.3 of the *Digesta* reads as follows, with the part quoted by TJ in italics: "And in certain cities which are in turmoil, there are some, who call themselves young men, and who regularly conduct themselves so as to receive the acclamations of the populace. The first time these young men are brought before the judge for this offense, they should be beaten with the *fustis* and released (provided they have done nothing serious) or perhaps they ought to be forbidden to watch the spectacles. But if they are guilty of the same offense the second time, after having been corrected, they are to be punished by exile. *Even capital punishment is in order if they have continuously conducted themselves in a seditious and turbulent fashion, and having previously been treated with clemency, nonetheless persevere in the same boldness of purpose.*" According to an authoritative edition of the *Digesta*, TJ left out two words in his quotation from this work—"scilicet" after "plectendi" and "tractati" after "adprehensi" *(Corpus Iuris Civilis*, ed. Paul Krueger and others, 3 vols. [Berlin, 1900-06], I, 816).

NOTE FOR PAGE 80

J19:24: Portion of verse not used: "that the scripture might be fulfilled, which saith, They parted my raiment among them, and for my vesture they did cast lots. These things, therefore, the soldiers did."

Greek: "ἵνα ἡ γραφὴ πληρωθῇ ἡ λέγουσα, Διεμερίσαντο τὰ ἱμάτιά μου ἑαυτοῖς, καὶ ἐπὶ τὸν ἱματισμόν μου ἔβαλον κλῆρον. Οἱ μὲν οὖν στρατιῶται ταῦτα ἐποίησαν."

Latin: "Ut scriptura impleretur, dicens: Partiti sunt vestimenta mea sibi ipsis, et super vestem meam miserunt sortem. Illi quidem igitur milites hæc fecerunt."

French: "de sorte que cette parole de l'Ecriture fut accompli: ils ont partagé mes vêtemens entr'eux, et ils ont jeté le sort sur ma robe. C'est ce que firent les soldats."

NOTE FOR PAGE 81

L23:34: Portion of verse not used: "And they parted his raiment, and cast lots."

Greek: "Διαμεριζόμενοι δὲ τὰ ἱμάτια αὐτοῦ, ἔβαλον κλῆρον."

Latin: "Dividentes vero vestimenta ejus miserunt sortem."

French: "Puis faisant le partage de ses vêtemens, ils les jetèrent au sort."

J19:42: Portion of verse not used: "therefore, because of the Jews' preparation *day*; for the sepulchre was nigh at hand."

Greek: "διὰ τὴν παρασκευὴν τῶν Ἰουδαίων, ὅτι ἐγγὺς ἦν τὸ μνημεῖον."

Latin: "propter Parasceven Judæorum, quia juxta erat monumentum."

French: "à cause que c'étoit *le jour* de la preparation *du Sabbat* des Juifs, parce que le sépulcre étoit proche."

M27:60: Portion of verse not used: "And laid it in his own new tomb, which he had hewn out in the rock."

Greek: "Καὶ ἔθηκεν αὐτὸ ἐν τῷ καινῷ αὐτοῦ μνημείῳ, ὁ ἐλατόμησεν ἐν τῇ πέτρᾳ."

Latin: "Et posuit illud in novo suo monumento, quod exciderat in petra."

French: "Et le mit dans son sépulcre, qui étoit neuf, et qu'il avoit fait tailler *pour lui-même* dans un roc."

TJ deleted the word "he" in the English text of this verse to make it conform to the use of "they" in J19:42. He did not make corresponding changes in the other three languages.

APPENDIX

From Benjamin Rush

DEAR SIR   Philadelphia August 22nd: 1800

The following thoughts have lately occurred to me. To whom can they be communicated with so much propriety as to that man, who has so uniformly distinguished himself by an Attachment to republican forms of government?

In the Constitution of the United states titles are wisely forbidden, and pensions for public Services are considered as equally improper by many of our Citizens. There is a mode of honouring distinguished worth which is Cheap, and which if directed properly, would stimulate to greater exploits of patriotism, than all the high sounding titles of a German, or the expensive pensions of a British Court. It consists in calling *states*, *Counties*, *towns*, *Forts*, and *Ships of War* by the names of men who have deserved well of their Country. To prevent an improper application of those names, the power of confirming them should be exercised only by our Governments. No man should have a town, County, Fort or Ship, called by his name 'till after his death; and to prevent any Ambiguity in the names thus given, the Act of government which confers them, should mention the person's families, places of former abode, and the Services, civil, military, philosophical or humane which they rendered to their Country. From the connection between *words*, and *ideas*, much good might be done. A map of a state, and the history of travels through the united States, would fill the mind with respect for departed worth, and inspire exertions to imitate it. Some Advantage likewise would arise to the public, by preventing the Confusion in business which arises from the multiplication of the same names in different States, and sometimes in the same State, and which is the unavoidable consequence of those names being given by Individuals. An end would likewise be put by the practice which is here recommended, to those indications of Vanity which appear in the numerous names of towns given by their founders after themselves, and which too frequently suggest other ideas than those of public or even private Virtue.

The Citizens of Boston in the republican years of 1776 and 1777 rejected the royal names of several Streets, and substituted in the room of them, names that comported with the new, and republican State of their town. Why has not Virginia imitated her example? If I mistake not, most of your old Counties bear the names or titles of several successive British Royal families. They are the disgraceful remains of your former degraded State as men, and Should by all means be changed for the names of those worthies on whose characters death has placed his Seal, and thereby removed beyond the power of forfeiting thier well earned fame.

A Spirit of moderation, and mutual forbearance begins to revive among our Citizens. What the issue of the present single and double elective Attractions in our parties will be, is difficult to determin. As yet appearances are turbid. Much remains to be precipitated, before the public mind can become clear.—As a proof of the growing moderation of our Citizens I shall mention two facts. Mr Bingham lamented your supposed death in the most liberal and pathetic terms, and Judge Peters spoke of you yesterday at his table in my hearing, in the most respectful and even affectionate manner. This is between ourselves.

You promised me when we parted, to read Paley's last work, and to send me your religious Creed.[1]—I have always considered Christianity as the *strong ground* of Republicanism. Its Spirit is opposed, not only to the Splendor, but even to the very *forms* of monarchy, and many[2] of its precepts have for their Objects, republican liberty and equality, as well as simplicity, integrity and Œconomy in government.[3] It is only necessary for Republicanism to ally itself to the christian Religion, to overturn all the corrupted political and religious institutions in the world.

I have lately heard that Lord Kaims became so firm a Beleiver in Christianity some years before he died, as to dispute with his former disciples in its favor. Such a mind as Kaims' could only yeild to the strongest evidence, especially as his prejudices were on the other Side of the Question.

Sir John Pringle had lived near 60 years in a State of indifference to the truth of the Christian Religion.—He devoted himself to the Study of the Scriptures in the evening of his life, and became a christian. It was remarkable that he became a decided Republican[4] at the same time. It is said this change in his political principles exposed him to the neglect of the Royal family, to whom he was Physician, and drove him from London, to end his days in his native Country.

Our City continues to be healthy, and business is carried on with its usual Spirit. It is yet uncertain whether we shall enjoy an exemption from the yellow fever. It is in favor of this hope, that vegetation has assumed its ancient and natural appearance, that all our fruits (the peach excepted) are perfect—that we have much fewer insects than in our sickly years, and that the few diseases we have had, in general put on a milder type than they have done since the year 1793.

An ingenious work has lately arrived here by Dr Darwin,—full of original matter upon Botany and Agriculture. Dr Barton speaks of it in high terms. A translation of Sonnoni's travels into Egypt is likewise for sale in our city. They will be memorable from the information they gave to Buonparte in that Country. They contain a good deal of physical matter particularly upon the diet, diseases, and medicine of the inhabitants. A Dieu! From Dear Sir your sincere old friend of 1775,   BENJN: RUSH

RC (DLC); endorsed by TJ as received 5 Sep. [1800] and so recorded in Summary Journal of Letters (hereafter referred to as SJL).

William PALEY'S LAST WORK was *A View of the Evidences of Christianity* . . . (London, 1794); TJ owned a 1795 edition printed in Philadelphia. See E. Millicent Sowerby, comp., *Catalogue of the Library of Thomas Jefferson* (Washington, D.C., 1952-59), No. 1519. Henry Home, Lord Kames (1692-1782), a Scottish judge, was the author of numerous works on law, theology, and metaphysics, many of which TJ owned (same, *passim*). SIR JOHN PRINGLE (1707-1782), a Scottish physician and author of several influential medical treatises, had been royal physician to King George

III and his wife Queen Charlotte Sophia. Dr. Erasmus Darwin's INGENIOUS WORK was *Phytologia; or the Philosophy of Agriculture and Gardening* (London, 1800). The edition of SONNONI'S TRAVELS was C. N. S. Sonnini de Mancourt, *Travels in Upper and Lower Egypt. Undertaken by Order of the Old Government of France*, 3 vols. (London, 1797).

[1] Rush lined out the next three and a half lines of the MS, making them illegible.

[2] Rush first wrote "all."

[3] Rush first wrote "republican equality and just government" and then expanded it to read as above.

[4] At this point Rush lined out a parenthetical phrase that appears to read: "(from the [arguments?] of Dr. Franklin)."

To Benjamin Rush

DEAR SIR   Monticello Sep. 23. 1800.

I have to acknolege the reciept of your favor of Aug. 22. and to congratulate you on the healthiness of your city. Still Baltimore, Norfolk and Providence admonish us that we are not clear of our new scourge. When great evils happen, I am in the habit of looking out for what good may arise from them as consolations to us: and Providence has in fact so established the order of things as that most evils are the means of producing some good. The yellow fever will discourage the growth of great cities in our nation; and I view great cities as pestilential to the morals, the health and the liberties of man. True, they nourish some of the elegant arts; but the useful ones can thrive elsewhere, and less perfection in the others with more health virtue and freedom would be my choice.—I agree with you entirely in condemning the mania of giving names to objects of any kind after persons still living. Death alone can seal the title of any man to this honour by putting it out of his power to forfeit it. There is one other mode of rewarding merit which I have often thought might be introduced so as to gratify the living by praising the dead. In giving for instance a commission of chief justice to Bushrod Washington it should be in consideration of his integrity and science in the laws, and of the services rendered to our country by his illustrious relation &c. A commission to a descendant of Dr. Franklin, besides being in consideration of the proper qualifications of the person, should add that of the great services rendered by his illustrious ancestor B.F. by the advancement of science, and by inventions useful to man, &c. I am not sure that we ought to change all our names imposed during the regal government. Sometimes indeed they were given through adulation, but often also as the reward of the merit of the times, sometimes for services rendered the colony. Perhaps too a name when given should be deemed a sacred property.

I promised you a letter on Christianity, which I have not forgotten. On the contrary it is because I have reflected on it, that I find much more time necessary for it than I can at present dispose of. I have a view of the subject which ought to displease neither the rational Christian or Deist; and would reconcile many to a character they have too hastily rejected. I do not know however that it would reconcile the genus irritabile vatum, who are all in arms against me. Their hostility is on too interesting ground to be softened. The delusions into which the XYZ plot shewed it possible to push the people, the succesful experiment made under the prevalence of that delusion, on the clause of the constitution which while it secured the freedom of the press, covered also the freedom of religion, had given to the clergy a very favorite hope of obtaining an establishment of a particular form of Christianity thro' the US. And as every sect believes it's own form the true one, every one perhaps hoped for it's own: but especially the Episcopalians and Congregationalists. The returning good sense of our country threatens abortion to their hopes, and they believe that any portion of power confided to me will be exerted in opposition to their schemes. And they believe truly.[1] For I have sworn upon the altar of god eternal hostility against every form of tyranny over the mind of man. But this is all they have to fear from me: and enough too in their opinion; and this is the cause of their printing lying pamphlets against me, forging conversations for me with Mazzei, Bishop Madison &c which are absolute falshoods without a circumstance of truth to rest on; falshoods too of which I acquit Mazzei and Bishop Madison for they are men of truth.—But enough of this. It is more than I have before committed to paper on the subject of all the lies which have been preached or printed against me.—I have not seen the work of Sonnoni which you mention. But I have seen another work on Africa, Parke's, which I fear will throw cold water on the hopes of the friends of freedom. You will have seen[2] an account of an attempt at insurrection in this state. I am looking with anxiety to see what will be it's effect on our state. We are truly to be pitied.—I fear we have little chance to see you at the Federal city or in Virginia, and as little at Philadelphia. It would be a great treat to recieve you here. But nothing but sickness could effect that: so I do not wish it: for I wish you health and happiness, and think of you with affection. Adieu.

TH: JEFFERSON

RC (DLC); endorsed by Rush "answd Octobr. 6. 1800." Dft (DLC).

GENUS IRRITABILE VATUM: "The irritable tribe of priests." PARKE'S work was Mungo Park, *Travels in the Interior Districts of Africa . . . in the Years 1795, 1796, and 1797* (Philadelphia, 1800). The AT-

TEMPT AT INSURRECTION was Gabriel's Plot, an abortive slave conspiracy near Richmond, Va. See Herbert Aptheker, *American Negro Slave Revolts* (New York, 1943), p. 219-24.

[1] "rightly" in Dft.
[2] "You will hear of" in Dft.

From Benjamin Rush

DEAR SIR   Philadelphia October 6th 1800

I agree with you in your Opinion of Cities. Cowper the poet very happily expresses our ideas of them compared with the Country. "God made the Country—man made Cities." I consider them in the same light that I do Abscesses on the human body viz: as reservoirs of all the impurities of a Community.

I agree with you likewise in your wishes to keep religion and government independant of each Other. Were it possible for St. Paul to rise from his grave at the present juncture, he would say to the Clergy who are now so active in settling the political Affairs of the World: "Cease from your political labors—your kingdom is not of *this* World. Read my Epistles. In no part of them will you perceive me aiming to depose a pagan Emperor, or to place a Christian upon a throne. Christianity disdains to receive Support from human Governments. From this, it derives its preeminence over all the religions that ever have, or ever shall exist in the World. Human Governments may receive Support from Christianity but it must be only from the love of justice, and peace which it is calculated to produce in the minds of men. By promoting these, and all the other Christian virtues by your precepts, and example, you will much sooner over-throw errors of all kind, and establish our pure and holy religion in the World, than by aiming to produce by your preaching, or pamphlets any thing in the political State of mankind."

A certain Dr Owen an eminent minister of the Gospel among the dissenters in England, and a sincere friend to liberty, was once complained of by one of Cromwell's time serving priests, that he did not preach to the *times*. "My business and duty said the disciple of St Paul is to preach, to *Eternity*, not to the *times*." He has left many volumes of Sermons behind him that are so wholly religious, that no one from reading them, could tell, in what country, or age they were preached.

I have sometimes amused myself in forming a Scale of the different kinds of *hatreds*. They appear to me to rise in the following order. *Odium Juris-consultum, Odium medicum, Odium philalogicum, Odium politicum, and Odium theologicum.* You are now the Subject of the two last. I have felt the full force of the 2nd. and 4th. degrees of hostily from my fellow Creatures. But I do not think we shall ultimately suffer from either of them. My persecutions have averted, or delayed the usual languor of 55 in my mind. I read, write, and think with the same vigor and pleasure that I did fifteen years ago. As natural stimuli are sometimes supplied by such as are artificial in the production of human life, so Slander seems to act upon the human mind. It not only supplies the place of fame, but it is much more powerful in exciting our faculties into vigorous and successful exercises.

To persevere in benevolent exertions after ungrateful returns for former Services, it is only necessary to consider mankind as Solomon considered them several thousand years ago, viz: as labouring under madness. A few Cures, or even a few lucid intervals produced in a State, or nation, will repay the unsuccessful labors of many years. "No good effort is lost" was a favorite saying of the late Dr. Jebb.— A truth cannot perish, altho' it may sleep for Centuries. The Republics of America are the fruits of the precious truths that were disseminated in the Speeches and publications of the republican patriots in the British parliament one hundred and sixty years ago. My first american Ancestor Jno. Rush commanded a troop of horse in Cromwell's army. He afterwards became a Quaker and followed Wm. Penn in 1683 to Pennsylvania. My brother possesses his horseman's sword. General Darke of your state, who is descended from his youngest daughter, owns his watch. To the sight of his sword, I owe much of the Spirit which animated me in 1774, and to the respect and admiration which I was early taught to cherish for his Virtues and exploits, I owe a large portion of my republican temper and principles.—Similar circumstances I beleive produced a great deal of the Spirit and exertions of all those americans who are descended from Ancestors that emigrated from England between the years 1645 and 1700.

I send you herewith some musk melon seeds of a quality as much above the common melons of our country, as a pine apple is superior to a potatoe. They were brought originally from Minorca. The ground must be prepared for them at the usual time, by having some brush burnt upon it.—The fire destroys the eggs of insects in the ground, and the ashes left by it, manures the ground so as to prepare it for the Seeds. No vine of any kind should grow near them. They are, when ripe, a little larger than a child's head, round, and have a green rind. They are never mealy, but juicy, and cannot be improved by sugar, pepper, salt, or any other addition that can be made to them.

We have had a few Cases of yellow fever in our City, eno' to satisfy unprejudiced persons that we have not been defended from it by our quarantine law. They were all evidently of domestic origin.

I reciprocate your kind expressions, upon the probability of our not meeting again, and feel sincere distress upon the Account of it. I shall always recollect with pleasure the many delightful hours we have spent together from the day we first met on the banks of Skuilkill in the year 1775 to the day in which we parted. If the innocent and interesting subjects of our occasional Conversations should be a delusive one, the delusion is enchanting. But I will not admit that we have been deceived in our early, and long affection for republican forms of government. They are, I believe, not only rational, but practicable. As well might we reject the pure and simple doctrines and precepts of Christianity, because they have been dishonoured by being mixed with human follies and crimes by the corrupted churches of Europe, as renounce our republics because their name has been dishonoured by the follies and crimes of the French nation. The preference which men, depraved by false government have given to monarchy, is no more a proof of its excellency, than the preference which men whose appetites have been depraved by drinking Whiskey, is a proof that it is more wholesome than water. Thousands have derived health and long life from that wholsome beveridge of nature, while tens of thousands have perished from the use of the former liquor.

Representative and elective Government appears to be a discovery of modern times. It has met with the fate of many other discoveries which have had for their objects the melioration of the condition of man. It has been opposed, traduced, and nearly scouted from the face of the earth. The Science of medicine abounds with instances of new truths being treated in the same manner. The cool Regimen which Dr Sydenham applies with general success to the small pox, was exploded before he died by his cotemporary physicians. In the year 1767 it was revived in London by Dr Sutton, and now prevails all over the world.

Excuse the length of this letter. My pen has run away with me.— Pray throw it in the fire as soon as you have read it. Not a line of it must be communicated to a human creature with my name.

When you see Mr Madison please to tell him he is still very dear to *his*, and *your* sincere & affectionate friend,   BENJN: RUSH

PS: From the difficulty of packing up the melon seed so as to send them by the post, I have concluded to send them to you in the winter at the federal city by a private hand.

RC (DLC); endorsed by TJ as received 16 Oct. [1800] and so recorded in SJL.

To Moses Robinson

DEAR SIR   Washington Mar. 23. 1801.

I have to acknolege the reciept of your favor of the 3d. inst. and to thank you for the friendly expressions it contains. I entertain real hope that the whole body of our fellow citizens (many of whom had been carried away by the XYZ. business) will shortly be consolidated in the same sentiments. When they examine the real principles of both parties I think they will find little to differ about. I know indeed that there are some of their leaders who have so committed themselves that pride, if no other passion, will prevent their coalescing. We must be easy with them. The eastern states will be the last to come over, on account of the dominion of the clergy, who had got a smell of union between church and state, and began to indulge reveries which can never be realized in the present state of science. If indeed they could have prevailed on us to view all advances in science as dangerous innovations and to look back to the opinions and practices of our forefathers, instead of looking forward, for improvement, a promising ground work would have been laid. But I am in hopes their good sense will dictate to them that since the mountain will not come to them, they had better go to the mountain: that they will find their interest in acquiescing in the liberty and science of their country, and that the Christian religion when divested of the rags in which they have inveloped it, and brought to the original purity and simplicity of it's benevolent institutor, is a religion of all others most friendly to liberty, science, and the freest expansions of the human mind.

I sincerely wish with you we could see our government so assured as to depend less on the character of the person in whose hands it is trusted. Bad men will sometimes get in, and with such an immense patronage, may make great progress in corrupting the public mind and principles. This is a subject with which wisdom and patriotism should be occupied. I pray you to accept assurances of my high respect & esteem. TH: JEFFERSON

PrC (DLC).

YOUR FAVOR OF THE 3D.: Robinson to TJ, 3 Mar. 1801, congratulated TJ upon his election to the presidency, expressed the hope that "the time may arive when the Safety of our Civil and Religious Rights will not so much depend on the disposition of the person administering the Executive branch of Government as at present it does," and discussed political affairs in Vermont. Robinson (1742-1813), a leading Republican leader in Vermont, was a former Vermont chief justice and governor who had served in the U.S. Senate from 1791 to 1796.

To the Rev. Isaac Story

SIR   Washington Dec. 5. 1801.

Your favor of Oct. 27. was recieved some time since, and read with pleasure. It is not for me to pronounce on the hypothesis you present of a transmigration of souls from one body to another in certain cases. The laws of nature have witheld from us the means of physical knowlege of the country of spirits and revelation has, for reasons unknown to us, chosen to leave us in the dark as we were. When I was young I was fond of the speculations which seemed to promise some insight into that hidden country, but observing at length that they left me in the same ignorance in which they had found me, I have for very many years ceased to read or to think concerning them, and have reposed my head on that pillow of ignorance which a benevolent creator has made so soft for us knowing how much we should be forced to use it. I have thought it better by nourishing the good passions, and controuling the bad, to merit an inheritance in a state of being of which I can know so little, and to trust for the future to him who has been so good for the past. I percieve too that these speculations have with you been only the amusement of leisure hours; while your labours have been devoted to the education of your children, making them good members of society, to the instructing men in their duties, and performing the other offices of a large parish. I am happy in your approbation of the principles I avowed on entering on the government. Ingenious minds, availing themselves of the imperfection of language, have tortured the expressions out of their plain meaning in order to infer departures from them in practice. If revealed language has not been able to guard itself against misinterpretations, I could not expect it. But if an 'administration quadrating with the obvious import of my language can conciliate the affections of my opposers' I will merit that conciliation. I pray you to accept assurances of my respect & best wishes.   TH: JEFFERSON

PrC (DLC).

Story's FAVOR OF OCT. 27. extolled TJ as "a Gentleman of great Erudition and of a most excellent taste," described his own career as a clergyman in Marblehead, Mass., and insinuated that the inadequacy of his clerical salary made him ready to accept "a handsome public appointment." Enclosed with that letter was a nine-page manuscript entitled "The Metempsychosis-doctrine, in a limited sense, defended." In this work, originally written in 1790 for submission to the American Academy of Arts and Sciences, Story advanced the hypothesis that after death the souls of infants and "Ideots" passed into the bodies of other persons. Story was the father of the poet Isaac Story (1774-1803) and the uncle of Supreme Court Justice Joseph Story.

From Edward Dowse

SIR   Dedham, Massachusetts 5 April 1803

The extraordinary merit of this little treatise, which I now transmit to you, must be my apology, for the liberty I have taken in sending it. As its design (among other objects) is to promote the extension of civilization and christian knowledge among the Aborigines of North-America, it seem'd to me to have a claim to your attention: at any rate, the Idea, hath struck me that *you will find it of use*; and, perhaps, may see fit, to cause some copies of it to be reprinted, at your own charge, to distribute among our Indian Missionaries.—The gratification you find, in whatever is interesting to philanthropy, renders it unnecessary for me to glance at any advantage, which might result from such a measure, in silencing the voice of a calumniating opposition, on the score of your alleged indifference to the cause of religion.

You will please, Sir, to consider this as the private* communication of a private friend, one who is sincerely attach'd to your person and administration, warm in your praises, and who wants nothing in your power to bestow.—I am under the necessity, however, of making one stipulation, in regard to this pamphlet, which is, that you return it to me again, after keeping it as short a time only, as you conveniently can, it being a borrow'd book, and I do not know that there is another copy of it, on this side of the Atlantic, certainly none within my reach.

Amidst the multifarious employment, which your high station imposes, I do not presume to trouble you to write a line accompanying the return of this book; let it be simply enveloped in a blank cover, and directed to me, at this place.

The Appendix to your "Notes on Virginia," of which you did me the honour, soon after its publication, to inclose me a copy, I take this opportunity to thank you for; and beg you to accept the assurances of my profound respect.   EDWARD DOWSE

* No person whatever is acquainted with it, or ever shall be.

RC (MHi); at foot of text: "Thomas Jefferson President of the United States"; endorsed by TJ as received 14 Apr. 1803 and so recorded in SJL.

The LITTLE TREATISE enclosed by Dowse was *The Excellence of Christian Morality; a Sermon Preached before the Society in Scotland for Propagating Christian Knowledge* . . . (Edinburgh, 1800), by William Bennet, a Scottish dissenting minister. Dowse (1756-1828), a Massachusetts shipmaster engaged in the China trade who had known TJ since 1789, served in the U.S. House of Representatives, 1819-1820.

To Joseph Priestley

DEAR SIR   Washington Apr. 9. 1803.

While on a short visit lately to Monticello, I recieved from you a copy of your comparative view of Socrates and Jesus, and I avail myself of the first moment of leisure after my return to acknolege the pleasure I had in the perusal of it, and the desire it excited to see you take up the subject on a more extensive scale. In consequence of some conversation with Dr. Rush in the years 1798.99. I had promised some day to write him a letter giving him my view of the Christian system. I have reflected often on it since, and even sketched the outlines in my own mind. I should first take a general view of the moral doctrines of the most remarkeable of the antient philosophers, of whose ethics we have sufficient information to make an estimate: say of Pythagoras, Epicurus, Epictetus, Socrates, Cicero, Seneca, Antoninus. I should do justice to the branches of morality they have treated well, but point out the importance of those in which they are deficient. I should then take a view of the deism, and ethics of the Jews, and shew in what a degraded state they were, and the necessity they presented of a reformation. I should proceed to a view of the life, character, and doctrines of Jesus, who, sensible of the incorrectness of their ideas of the deity, and of morality, endeavored to bring them to the principles of a pure deism, and juster notions of the attributes of god, to reform their moral doctrines[1] to the standard of reason, justice, and philanthropy, and to inculcate the belief of a future state. This view would purposely omit the question of his divinity and even of his inspiration. To do him justice it would be necessary to remark the disadvantages his doctrines have to encounter, not having been committed to writing by himself, but by the most unlettered of men, by memory, long after they had heard them from him; when much was forgotten, much misunderstood, and presented in very paradoxical shapes. Yet such are the fragments remaining as to shew a master workman, and that his system of morality was the most benevolent and sublime probably that has been ever taught; and eminently[2] more perfect than those of any of the antient philosophers. His character and doctrines have recieved still greater injury from those who pretend to be his special disciples, and who have disfigured and sophisticated his actions and precepts, from views of personal interest, so as to induce the unthinking part of mankind to throw off the whole system in disgust, and to pass sentence as an imposter on the most innocent, the most benevolent the most eloquent and sublime character that ever has been exhibited to man.—This is the outline; but I have not the time, and still less the information which the subject needs. It will therefore rest with me in contemplation only. You are the person who of all others would do it best, and most promptly. You have all the materials at hand, and you put together with ease. I wish you could be induced to extend your late work to the whole subject.—I have not heard particularly what is the state of your health: but as it has been equal to the journey to Philadelphia, perhaps it might encourage the curiosity you must feel to see for once this place, which nature has formed on a beautiful scale, and circumstances destine for a great one. As yet we are but a cluster of villages: we cannot offer you the learned society of Philadelphia; but you will have that of a few characters whom you esteem, and a bed and hearty welcome with one who will rejoice in every opportunity of testifying to you his high veneration & affectionate attachment.

TH: JEFFERSON

PrC (DLC). Since the PrC is blurred, several word endings have been supplied from Tr (ViW), written in an unidentified nineteenth-century hand. For a discussion of the texts of this letter that appeared during TJ's lifetime, see notes below.

The COMPARATIVE VIEW OF SOCRATES AND JESUS was Priestley's pamphlet *Socrates and Jesus Compared* (Philadelphia, 1803), which TJ received near the end of a SHORT VISIT to Monticello from 11 to 31 Mch. 1803. See Sowerby, comp., *Catalogue*, No. 1661.

Much to TJ's surprise, this letter to Priestley was published twice in his lifetime, first by an English Unitarian who sought to lend an ex-president's prestige to the cause of rational religion and then by an American Calvinist who wanted to discredit his Unitarian rivals. Priestley, who had hoped TJ would be impressed by *Socrates and Jesus*, was so pleased by TJ's reaction that he sent a copy of the president's letter to the Rev. Theophilus Lindsey (1723-1808), one of the founders of English Unitarianism, together with a covering letter of 23 Apr. 1803, which stated: "In my last I promised to send you a copy of Mr. Jefferson's Letter on reading my pamphlet entitled 'Socrates and Jesus compared.' The above is that copy. He is generally considered as an unbeliever; if so, however, he cannot be far from us, and I hope in the way to be not only almost, but altogether what we are. He now attends public worship very regularly, and his moral conduct was never impeached." After Lindsey's death, Thomas Belsham, an-

other Unitarian minister in England, published both TJ's letter to Priestley and Priestley's letter to Lindsey in his *Memoirs of the Late Reverend Theophilus Lindsey . . .* (London, 1812), p. 538-40. In addition, Belsham's work also included a chapter on the subject of American Unitarianism in which he printed a number of letters to Lindsey from various American correspondents describing the prevalence of Unitarian views among the New England clergy. This chapter subsequently caught the eye of the Rev. Jedidiah Morse (1761-1826), a Massachusetts Calvinist and sometime critic of TJ, whose alarm at the spread of liberal religious ideas in New England made him eager to call public attention to what seemed to him irrefutable proof of his worst apprehensions. Accordingly, he arranged for the publication of the offending chapter, as well as a lengthy extract of TJ's letter to Priestley, in a highly abridged edition of the *Memoirs of Lindsey* entitled *American Unitarianism, or a Brief History of "The Progress and Present State of the Unitarian Churches in America"* (Boston, 1815). See H. Shelton Smith and others, *American Christianity* ([New York, 1960]), p. 483-84. Although TJ denounced the first printing of his letter as a gross "abuse of confidence," he made no recorded comment on the second (Adams to TJ, 29 May 1813; TJ to Adams, 15 June 1813; and Adams to TJ, 20 June 1815).

[1] At this point TJ first wrote and then deleted "and bring them."

[2] Tr has "consequently" for "eminently."

To Edward Dowse

DEAR SIR   Washington Apr. 19. 1803.

I now return the sermon you were so kind as to inclose me, having perused it with attention. The reprinting it by me, as you have proposed, would very readily be ascribed to hypocritical affectation, by those who, when they cannot blame our acts, have recourse to the expedient of imputing them to bad motives. This is a resource which can never fail them; because there is no act, however virtuous, for which ingenuity may not find some bad motive. I must also add that tho' I concur with the author in considering the moral precepts of Jesus, as more pure, correct, and sublime than those of the antient philosophers, yet I do not concur with him in the mode of proving it. He thinks it necessary to libel and decry the doctrines of the philosophers. But a man must be blinded indeed by prejudice, who can deny them a great degree of merit. I give them their just due, and yet maintain that the morality of Jesus, as taught by himself and freed from the corruptions of latter times, is far superior. Their philosophy went chiefly to the government of our passions, so far as respected ourselves, and the procuring our own tranquility. On our duties to others they were short and deficient. They extended their cares scarcely beyond our kindred and friends individually, and our country in the abstract. Jesus embraced, with charity and philanthropy, our neighbors, our countrymen, and the whole family of mankind. They confined themselves to actions: he pressed his scrutinies into the region of our thoughts, and called for purity at the fountain head. In a pamphlet lately published in Philadelphia by Dr. Priestly, he has treated, with more justice and skill than Mr. Bennet, a small portion of this subject. His is a comparative view of Socrates only with Jesus. I have urged him to take up the subject on a broader scale.

Every word which goes from me, whether verbally or in writing, becomes the subject of so much malignant distortion, and perverted construction, that I am obliged to caution my friends against admitting the possibility of my letters getting into the public papers, or a copy of them to be taken under any degree of confidence. The present one is perhaps of a tenor to silence some calumniators. But I never will, by any word or act, bow to the shrine of intolerance, or admit a right of enquiry into the religious opinions of others. On the contrary we are bound, you, I, and every one, to make common cause, even with error itself, to maintain the common right of freedom of conscience. We ought with one heart and one hand to hew down the daring and dangerous efforts of those who would seduce the public opinion to substitute itself into that tyranny over religious faith which the laws have so justly abdicated. For this reason, were my opinions up to standard of those who arrogate the right of questioning them, I would not countenance that arrogance by descending to an explanation. Accept my friendly salutations & high esteem.　　　　　　　　　　　　　　　　Th: Jefferson

PrC (DLC). Tr (ViW); in the same unidentified hand as the Tr of TJ to Priestley, 9 Apr. 1803; incomplete and mutilated.

To Benjamin Rush

DEAR SIR   Washington April 21, 1803.

In some of the delightful conversations with you, in the evenings of 1798.99., which[1] served as an Anodyne to the afflictions of the crisis through which our country was then labouring, the Christian religion was sometimes our topic: and I then promised you that, one day or other, I would give you my views of it. They are the result of a life of enquiry and reflection, and very different from that Anti-Christian system, imputed to me by those who know nothing of my opinions. To the corruptions of Christianity, I am indeed opposed; but not to the genuine precepts of Jesus himself. I am a Christian, in the only sense in which he wished any one to be; sincerely attached to his doctrines, in preference to all others; ascribing to himself every human[2] excellence, and believing he never claimed any other. At the short intervals, since these conversations, when I could justifiably abstract my mind from public affairs,[3] this subject has been under my contemplation. But the more I considered it, the more it expanded beyond the measure of either my time or information. In the moment of my late departure from Monticello,[4] I recieved from Doctr. Priestly his little treatise of 'Socrates and Jesus compared.' This being a section of the general view I had taken of the field, it became a subject of reflection, while on the road, and unoccupied otherwise. The result was, to arrange in my mind a Syllabus, or Outline, of such an Estimate of the comparative merits of Christianity, as I wished to see executed, by some one of more leisure and information for the task than myself. This I now send you, as the only discharge of my promise I can probably ever execute. And, in confiding it to you, I know it will not be exposed to the malignant perversions of those who make[5] every word from me a text for new misrepresentations and calumnies. I am moreover averse to the communication of my religious tenets to the public; because it would countenance the presumption of those who have endeavored to draw them before that tribunal, and to seduce public opinion to erect itself into that Inquisition over the rights of conscience, which the laws have so justly proscribed. It behoves every man, who values liberty of[6] conscience for himself, to resist invasions of it in the case of others;[7] or their case may, by change of circumstances, become his own. It behoves him too, in his own case, to give no example of concession, betraying the common right of independant opinion, by answering questions of faith, which the laws have left between god and himself. Accept my affectionate salutations.   TH: JEFFERSON

Syllabus of an Estimate of the merit[8] of the doctrines of Jesus, compared with those of others.

In a comparative view of the Ethics of the enlightened nations of antiquity, of the Jews, and of Jesus, no notice should be taken of the corruptions of reason, among the antients, to wit, the idolatry and superstition of their vulgar, Nor of the corruptions of Christianity by the over learned[9] among it's professors.

Let a just view be taken of the moral principles inculcated by the most esteemed of the sects of antt. philosophy, or of their individuals; particularly Pythagoras, Socrates, Epicurus, Cicero, Epictetus, Seneca, Antoninus.

I. Philosophers. 1. Their precepts related chiefly to ourselves, and the government of those passions which, unrestrained, would disturb our tranquility of mind.* In this branch of Philosophy they were really great.

2. In developing our duties to others, they were short and defective. They embraced indeed the circles of kindred and friends: and inculcated patriotism, or the love of our country in the aggregate, as a primary obligation: towards our neighbors and countrymen, they taught justice, but scarcely viewed them as within the circle of benevolence. Still less have they inculcated peace, charity, and love to our fellow men, or embraced with benevolence, the whole family of[10] mankind.

II. Jews. 1. Their system was Deism, that is, the belief of one only god. But their ideas of him, and of his attributes, were degrading and injurious.

2. Their Ethics were not only imperfect, but often irreconcileable with the sound dictates of reason and morality, as they respect intercourse with those around us: and repulsive, and anti-social, as respecting other nations. They needed reformation therefore in an eminent degree.

III. Jesus. In this state of things among the Jews, Jesus appeared. His parentage was obscure, his condition poor, his education null, his natural endowments great, his life

---

* To explain, I will exhibit the heads of Seneca's and Cicero's philosophical works, the most extensive of any we have recieved from the antients. Of 10. heads in Seneca, 7. relate to ourselves, to wit, de irâ, Consolatio, de tranquilitate, de constantiâ sapientis, de otio sapientis, de vitâ beatâ, de brevitate vitae. 2. relate to others, de clementia, de beneficiis, and 1. relates to the government of the world, de providentiâ. Of 11. tracts of Cicero, 5 respect ourselves, viz. de finibus, Tusculana, Academica, Paradoxa, de Senectute. 1. de officiis, partly to ourselves, partly to others. 1. de amicitiâ, relates to others: and 4. are on different subjects, to wit, de naturâ deorum, de divinatione, de fato, Somnium Scipionis.

correct and innocent; he was meek, benevolent, patient, firm, disinterested, and of the sublimest eloquence.

The disadvantages under which his doctrines appear are remarkeable.

1. Like Socrates and Epictetus, he wrote nothing himself.

2. But he had not, like them, a Xenophon or an Arrian to write for him.[11]

On the contrary, all the learned of his country, entrenched in it's power and riches, were opposed to him lest his labours should undermine their advantages:

and the committing to writing his life and doctrines, fell on the most unlettered, and ignorant of men:[12]

who wrote too from memory, and not till long after the transactions had passed.

3. According to the ordinary fate of those who attempt to enlighten and reform mankind,

he fell an early victim to the jealousy and combination of the altar and the throne;

at about 33. years of age,[13] his reason having not yet attained the maximum of it's energy,

nor the course of his preaching, which was but of about 3. years,[14] presented occasions for developing a compleat system of morals.[15]

4. Hence the doctrines which he really delivered were defective as a whole.

And fragments only of what he did deliver have come to us, mutilated, mistated, and often unintelligible.

5. They have been still more disfigured by the corruptions of schismatising followers,

who have found an interest in sophisticating and perverting the simple doctrines he taught,

by engrafting on them the mysticisms of a Graecian Sophist,[16] frittering them into subtleties, and obscuring them with jargon,

until they have caused good men to reject the whole in disgust, and to view Jesus himself as an impostor.

Notwithstanding these disadvantages, a system of morals is presented to us, which,

if filled up in the true style and spirit of the rich fragments he left us,

would be the most perfect and sublime that has ever been taught by man.

The question of his being a member of the god-head, or in direct communication with it,

claimed for him by some of his followers, and denied by others,

is foreign to the present view, which is merely an estimate of the intrinsic merit of his doctrines.

1. He corrected the Deism of the Jews, confirming them
   in their belief of one only god,
     and giving them juster notions of his attributes and
       government.
2. His moral doctrines relating to kindred and friends
   were more pure and perfect, than those of the most
   correct of the philosophers, and greatly more so than
   those of the Jews.
     And they went far beyond both in inculcating universal
       philanthropy,
         not only to kindred and friends, to neighbors and
           countrymen,
         but to all mankind, gathering all into one family,
           under the bonds of love, charity, peace, common
           wants, and common aids. A developement of this
           head will evince the peculiar superiority of the
           system of Jesus over all others.
3. The precepts of Philosophy, and of the Hebrew code,
   laid hold of actions only.
     He pushed his scrutinies into the heart of man; erected
       his tribunal in the region of his thoughts, and pur-
       ified the waters at the fountain head.
4. He taught, emphatically, the doctrine of a future state:
     which was either doubted or disbelieved by the Jews:
     and wielded it with efficacy, as an important incentive,
       supplementory to the other motives to moral con-
       duct.

RC (ViU). PrC (DLC: TJ Papers, 131:22622). Jefferson actually enclosed this letter and the "Syllabus" with a second letter, which states in part: "At length I send you a letter, long due, and even now but a sketch of what I wished to make it. But your candour will find my just excuse in the indispensable occupations of my public duties. I communicate a copy of the Syllabus to Dr. Priestley in the hope he will extend his work of Socrates and Jesus compared. He views a part of the subject differently from myself: but in the main object of my syllabus we go perfectly together" (TJ to Rush, 23 Apr. 1803).

Tr 1 (DLC: TJ Papers, 131:22620-21); in TJ's hand; at foot of text: "Doctr. Benjamin Rush." Apparently this is the copy that TJ enclosed with his letters to Henry Dearborn and others of 23 Apr. 1803 and to Joseph Priestley of 24 Apr. 1803 (printed below). In an undated letter received by TJ on 4 May 1803, Dearborn suggested that the phrase "most unlettered of men" in the "Syllabus" be altered to read "men of but little litterary information" (same, 131:22667). TJ deleted part of this phrase in Tr 1, evidently in response to Dearborn's suggestion, but provided no substitute for it. In addition, TJ changed this version of the "Syllabus" to state that Jesus' ministry lasted "3. years at most," in comparison to "about 3. years" in the RC. The former may have been intended as a concession to Dr. Priestley, who believed that Jesus' public ministry lasted only a year or so.

Tr 2 (MHi); in TJ's hand; at head of text: "To Doctr. Benjamin Rush." These are the texts that TJ sent to his older daughter, Martha Jefferson Randolph, and are among the papers her descendants donated to the Massachusetts Historical Society near the end of the nineteenth century (MHS, *Procs.*, 2d ser., XII [1897-99], 264-68). The texts he sent to his younger daughter, Mary Jefferson Eppes, have not been found. TJ transmitted both documents to his daughters with separate letters, each containing the same introductory paragraph: "A promise made to a friend some years ago, but executed only lately, has placed my religious creed on paper. I have thought it just that my family, by possessing this, should be enabled to estimate the libels published against me on this, as on every other possible subject. I have written to Philadelphia for Dr. Priestley's history of the corruptions of Christianity, which I will send you, and recommend to an attentive perusal, because it establishes the groundwork of my view of this subject" (TJ to Martha Jefferson Randolph, TJ to Mary Jefferson Eppes, 25 Apr. 1803).

Tr 3 (DLC: TJ Papers, 131:22617-18); in TJ's hand; at foot of text: "Doctr. Benjamin Rush." TJ sent these texts with his letter to John Adams of 22 Aug. 1813 (printed below), and Adams returned them as requested (Adams to TJ, 14 Sep. 1813).

Tr 4 (MHi: AM); in Ellen Wayles Randolph's hand; includes only the "Syllabus." Tr 4, the text of the "Syllabus" that TJ sent to John Adams with his letter of 12 Oct. 1813 (printed below), is virtually a line-by-line copy by TJ's granddaughter of the same document in Tr 3.

Tr 5 (NBuHi: Van der Kemp Papers); in TJ's hand; lacks place line, complimentary close, and signature; at foot of text: "To Mr. _____ ." Since these are the texts of the letter to Rush and the "Syllabus" that TJ sent to Francis Adrian Van der Kemp on 25 Apr. 1816 (printed below) for publication in England, he made numerous changes in them to disguise his authorship (see the textual notes below). The two documents appeared in a Unitarian theological journal entitled *The Monthly Repository of Theology and General Literature*, XI (October 1816), 573-76. The printed version of the "Syllabus" lacks the section describing Jewish ethics as "repulsive and anti-social, as respecting other nations. They needed reformation therefore in an eminent degree." Whether this deletion was made by Van der Kemp or by the editor of the *Monthly Repository* is not known.

Tr 6 (ViW: Tucker-Coleman Papers); in Ellen Wayles Randolph's hand. TJ's granddaughter made this copy for TJ to transmit with his 13 Apr. 1820 letter to William Short (printed below).

Tr 7 (ViU: Edgehill-Randolph Papers); in an unidentified hand, perhaps that of Cornelia Jefferson Randolph; includes the letter to Rush, the "Syllabus," and the title page and table of contents for "The Philosophy of Jesus". The copyist made a conscious effort to imitate TJ's handwriting and probably copied from the letter and "Syllabus" in Tr 2, which belonged to Cornelia's mother, Martha Jefferson Randolph. The documents in Tr 7 were originally bound together inside a paper cover containing extracts by the same copyist of the purported deathbed speech of Julian the Apostate from Jean Philippe René de La Bletterie, *The Life of the Emperor Julian*, trans. Anna Williams (London, 1746). See Sowerby, comp., *Catalogue*, No. 90. Since TJ sold La Bletterie's volume to the Library of Congress in 1815, it is possible that Tr 7 was made before that year, but in the absence of more reliable evidence, its provenance and date remain a mystery.

[1] TJ first wrote "and" and then overwrote "which"; all Trs read "and which" (or "& which") except Tr 5, which lacks the entire phrase, "which served as an Anodyne to the afflictions of the crisis through which our country was then labouring."

[2] This word is underscored in Trs 1, 2, and 7.

[3] In Tr 5, TJ substituted for the preceding words in this sentence the phrase, "At intervals since these conversations, when I could justifiably abstract myself from other affairs."

[4] In Tr 5, TJ substituted for the preceding five words the phrase, "setting out on a late journey"; Tr 7 substitutes a blank line for the word "Monticello."

[5] In Tr 5, TJ substituted for the remainder of this sentence the phrase, "of every word on the subject of religion, a text for misrepresentations and calumnies."

[6] At this point in Tr 5, TJ inserted and then deleted the word "private."

[7] In Tr 5, TJ omitted the remainder of this sentence.

[8] The words "of the merit" are deleted from Trs 2 and 3 and are omitted in Trs 4, 5, 6, and 7.

[9] The word "over" is interlined in RC, PrC, and Tr 3, and omitted in Trs 4, 5, 6, and 7.

[10] The word "in" is substituted for "of" in all copies but RC and PrC.

[11] At this point in Tr 1, TJ interlined

the sentence, "I name not Plato, who only used the name of Socrates to cover the whimsies of his own brain." The same sentence is added in Trs 2 and 7.

[12] Trs 2 and 7 substitute for the preceding seven words the phrase, "unlettered and ignorant men."

[13] In the RC, TJ wrote the preceding six words over erased and illegible material.

[14] Trs 1, 2, and 7 substitute for the preceding three words the phrase "three years at most." In Tr 1, TJ made the change by deleting "about" and interlining the words "at most."

[15] Trs 3, 4, 5, and 6 substitute "moral duties" for "morals."

[16] At this point "(Plato)" is added in Trs 2 and 7.

To Henry Dearborn, Levi Lincoln, and others

[April 23, 1803]

A promise to a friend sometime ago, executed but lately, has placed my religious creed on paper. I am desirous it should be perused by three or four particular friends, with whom tho' I never desired to make a mystery of it, yet no occasion has happened to occur of explaining it to them. It is communicated for their personal satisfaction, and to enable them to judge of the truth or falsehood of the libels published on that subject. When read, the return of the paper with this cover is asked.   TH: JEFFERSON

PrC (DLC); undated, unaddressed, and not recorded in SJL. Enclosures: TJ to Benjamin Rush, 21 Apr. 1803, and the "Syllabus"; see notes to that letter.

Attorney General Levi Lincoln and Secretary of War Henry Dearborn were among the THREE OR FOUR PARTICULAR FRIENDS mentioned by TJ. Although no evidence has been found that reveals the identity of the other FRIENDS to whom TJ sent this letter and the accompanying "Syllabus," the fact that Lincoln and Dearborn were members of his cabinet suggests that Secretary of the Treasury Albert Gallatin and Postmaster General Gideon Granger also received copies of them. TJ probably showed copies to his close friend and Secretary of State, James Madison, also.

To Joseph Priestley

DEAR SIR   Washington Apr. 24. 1803.

I have heard that you have left Philadelphia, and altho' it was not said for what place, yet I presume for Northumberland, and consequently that we are not to have the pleasure of seeing you here. I am almost persuaded that were you to try the difference between 41° and 38° of latitude you would find the genial effects of the latter towards that happiness which arises from sensation, and which produces that which is moral also, so superior to what it is in the former,

as to court you to a Southern residence, and to surmount all the obstacles opposed to it. I confess I concur with my friend Mr. Rittenhouse in wondering that men should ever settle in a Northern climate, as long as there is room for them in a Southern one. But of all things, I have been the most astonished at the location our friend Mr. B. Vaughan made of himself, because I consider man not only as an animal of a warm climate, but as social also, meaning by society that which is assorted to his own mind.

In my letter of Apr. 9. I gave you the substance of a view I had taken of the morality taught by the antient philosophers and by Jesus. The subject being in my mind, I committed to writing a syllabus of it, as I would treat it had I time or information sufficient, and sent it to Dr. Rush in performance of the promise I had formerly made him. Tho' this differs no otherwise from my letter to you than in being more full and formal, yet I send you a copy of it. There is a point or two in which you and I probably differ. But the wonder would be that any two persons should see in the same point of view all the parts of an extensive subject. I did not know that any comparative view of these schemes of morality had been taken till I saw your tract on Socrates and Jesus, and learnt from that that a Mr. Toulmin had written a dissertation in the same way, but I am sure he has left enough of the field to employ your pen advantageously. Accept my sincere prayers for your health and life, and assurances of my affectionate esteem & respect.   TH: JEFFERSON

PrC (DLC). Enclosures: TJ to Benjamin Rush, 21 Apr. 1803, and the "Syllabus"; see notes to that letter.

Joshua TOULMIN (1740-1815) was an English Unitarian minister, theologian, and historian, to whom Priestley had dedicated *Socrates and Jesus Compared.*

To Levi Lincoln

Apr. 26. 1803

Th: Jefferson with his compliments to Mr. Lincoln returns him Mr. Crowninshield's letter. The appointmt. of a substitute for Mr. Story shall await further information.—He has not been at all moved to doubt the propriety of Fosdick's removal.

Mr. Lincoln is perfectly free to retain the copy of the Syllabus, and to make any use of it his discretion would approve, confident as Th: J. is that his discretion would not permit him to let it be copied lest it should get into print. In the latter case Th: J. would become the butt of every set of disquisitions which every priest would undertake to write on every tenet it expresses. Their object is not truth, but matter whereon to write against Th: J. and this Synopsis would furnish matter for repeating in new forms all the volumes of divinity which are now mouldering on the shelves from which they should never more be taken. Th: J. would thank Mr. L. not to put his name on the paper in filing it away, lest in case of accident to Mr. L. it should get out.

PrC (DLC).
This was a response to Lincoln to TJ, 24 Apr. 1803.

From Benjamin Rush

Philadelphia, 5 May 1803. Is pleased to learn "from your letter of the 23rd of April that your disease is less troublesome than formerly." He realizes that TJ has "no faith in the *principles* of our science," but is determined to combat his prejudice against physicians. Describes two recent cases which have added to his stock of facts upon the Diarrhea.—"I have read your Creed with great attention, and was much pleased to find you are by no means so heterodox as you have been supposed to be by your enemies. I do not think with you in your account of the character and mission of the author of our Religion, and my opinions are the result of a long and patient investigation of that subject. You shall receive my Creed shortly. In the mean while we will agree, to disagree. From the slender influence which Opinions in Religion have upon morals, and from the bad practices of many people who have[1] graduated themselves at the highest point in the Scale of Orthodoxy, I have long ceased to consider principles of any kind as the criterion of disposition and Conduct, and much less of our future acceptance at the bar of the supreme Judge of the World.—The prevalence of a narrow Spirit in our Country with respect to principles, to which you allude, shall induce me faithfully to comply with your request by not communicating the Contents of your Creed even to your friends.—Adieu! my Dear Sir. May the Ruler of nations direct, and prosper you in all your duties and enterprises in the present difficult and awful posture of human affairs!"

RC (DLC); endorsed by TJ as received 7 May [1803] and so recorded in SJL.

There is no evidence that Rush ever sent his religious CREED to TJ.
[1] Rush first wrote "supposed to be" and then changed it to "who have."

From Joseph Priestley

DEAR SIR   Northumberland May 7. 1803

I have now to acknowledge the receipt of two of your valuable letters, one of them directed to me at Philadelphia, and the other to this place. They give me the more pleasure as I perceive by them that you are not so much occupied by public business, but that you are at leisure for speculations of a different and higher nature, and that you do not think unfavourably of my late tract on the *comparison of Socrates and Jesus*. Your flattering invitation to enter farther into the comparison of Jesus with other philosophers, I cannot, at least at present, attend to, tho I should be glad if you, or some other person, would take it up.

With respect to one part of your letter to D Rush, which I thank you for sending me, you will allow me to express some surprize (tho it is not very extraordinary that, educated, and situated, as different men are, they should see any subject in different lights) that you should be of opinion, that Jesus never laid claim to a divine mission. It is an opinion that I do not remember ever to have heard before. By this means you, no doubt, make *him* to have been no imposter, but then you make many others to have been such, who yet appear to have been men of great integrity and piety; and who, besides having no advantage to expect from any scheme of an imposture, must have been less qualified to carry it on. If Mahomet could not be classed with imposters, is it at all probable that his immediate followers, who must then have been such, could have established his religion, as those of Jesus did his; and his disciples had originally as much ambition and jealousy as those of Mahomet, and yet they all pretended to act by authority from him. How came so many persons, hundreds in the first instance, and thousands presently after, to believe that Jesus *did* pretend to a divine mission, and to be satisfied, by some means or other, that his pretensions were well founded. What could have induced any Jew to abandon his favourite idea of their Messiah being a temporal prince, and to receive in that character one who disclaimed all worldly power? With respect to natural ability, or advantage of any other kind, the apostles, at least Paul, were upon a level with Jesus; and yet they all submitted to him as their leader, and as much after he was dead, as while he was living.—How came the Gnostics, the philosophers of the age, who despised the apostles as illiterate men, to admit the supposed high claims of Jesus, tho equally illiterate? There must have been a wonderful power of imposing upon mankind somewhere, and for no probable or rational end that we can discover, and this appears to me to be as great a miracle as any that is ascribed to Jesus; whereas the supposition that Jesus had a divine mission, and that he gave sufficient evidence of it solves every difficulty. It accounts for his superior knowledge and all the authority that he assumed, and makes the whole of the subsequent history consistent and natural, which no other hypothesis does. Without this the question of the people of Nazareth where Jesus was brought up, remains unsolved, *Whence has this man this wisdom?*

But I ask pardon for writing in this manner, and by no means wish to draw you into a controversy, or a correspondence on the subject; but suggest the hints for your private consideration.

I think myself greatly honoured by your repeated kind invitations, but fear that my health will not admit of my availing myself of them. With the truest attachment, I am yours sincerely,

J. PRIESTLEY

RC (DLC); endorsed by TJ as received 12 May [1803] and so recorded in SJL.

To Joseph Priestley

Washington, 29 Jan. 1804. "Your favor of Dec. 12 came duly to hand, as did the 2d. letter to Dr. Linn and the treatise on Phlogiston, for which I pray you to accept my thanks. The copy for Mr. Livingston has been delivered, together with your letter to him, to Mr. Harvie, my secretary, who departs in a day or two for Paris, and will deliver them himself to Mr. Livingston, whose attention to your matter cannot be doubted. I have also to add my thanks to Mr. Priestley, your son, for the copy of your Harmony, which I have gone through with great satisfaction. It is the first I have been able to meet with which is clear of those long repetitions of the same transaction as if it were a different one because related with some different circumstances.—I rejoice that you have undertaken the task of comparing the moral doctrines of Jesus with those of the ancient Philosophers. You are so much in possession of the whole subject that you will do it easier and better than any other person living. I think you cannot avoid giving, as preliminary to the comparison, a digest of his moral doctrines, extracted in his own words from the evangelists, and leaving out everything relative to his personal history and character. It would be short and precious. With a view to do this for my own satisfaction, I had sent to Philadelphia to get two testaments Greek of the same edition, and two English with a design to cut out the morsels of morality, and paste them on the leaves of a book, in the manner you describe as having been pursued in forming your Harmony. But I shall now get the thing done by better hands."

PrC (DLC).

Priestley's FAVOR OF DECEMBER 12 announced that he was undertaking a comparative study of the moral teachings of Jesus and the ancient philosophers, congratulated TJ upon the acquisition of Louisiana, and promised to forward several scientific and theological works to him. Priestley's 2d. LETTER TO DR. LINN was a defense of *Socrates and Jesus Compared* entitled *A Second Letter to the Revd. John Blair Linn . . . in Reply to His Defense of*

the *Doctrines of the Divinity of Christ and Atonement* (Northumberland, 1803). See Sowerby, comp., *Catalogue*, No. 1663. THE TREATISE ON PHLOGISTON was Priestley's *The Doctrine of Phlogiston Established, and that of the Composition of Water Refuted* (Northumberland, 1803). See same, No. 836. TJ actually received both of these works from John Vaughan of Philadelphia (Vaughan to TJ, 20 Dec. 1803). Priestley's HARMONY was *A Harmony of the Evangelists, in Greek . . .* (London, 1777)— *A Harmony of the Evangelists, in English*

... (London, 1780), another copy of which TJ had received the previous year. See Sowerby, comp., *Catalogue*, No. 1492. Priestley's MORAL DOCTRINES OF JESUS: *The*

Doctrines of Heathen Philosophy, Compared with Those of Revelation (Northumberland, 1804), printed posthumously. See same, No. 1528.

To Benjamin Rush

DEAR SIR   Monticello Aug. 8. 04.

Your favor of the 1st. inst. came to hand last night. The embarrasment of answering propositions for office negatively, and the inconveniencies which have sometimes arisen from answering affirmatively, even when the affirmative is intended, has led to the general rule of leaving the answer to be read in the act of appointment or non-appointment whenever either is manifested. I depart from the rule however in the present case, that no injury may arise from that suspension of opinion which would be removed at once by a communication of the fact that there is no probability that Colo. Monroe will quit his present station at any time now under contemplation. The departure of a person as his secretary, not long since, at his particular request, proves he has no such intention, and certainly we do not wish it, as his services give the most perfect satisfaction. We had begun by appointing secretaries of legation, for the purpose of giving young men opportunities of qualifying themselves for public service: but desireable and useful as this would have been, it's aptness to produce discord has obliged us to abandon it, and to leave the ministers to appoint their own private secretaries, whose dependance on their principal secures a compatibility of temper. I shall be happy to recieve your pamphlet, as I am whatever comes from you. I have also a little volume, a mere and faithful compilation which I shall some of these days ask you to read as containing the exemplification of what I advanced in a former letter as to the excellence of 'the Philosophy of Jesus of Nazareth.' Accept affectionate salutations & assurances of esteem & respect.

                                        TH: JEFFERSON

RC (Mrs. John S. Ames, North Easton, Mass., 1950). PrC (DLC).

According to TJ's Summary Journal of Letters, Rush's missing FAVOR OF THE 1ST. INST. requested the appointment of his son Richard as secretary to the American legation in London. In response to TJ's proposal that Rush read his LITTLE VOLUME, which was of course "The Philosophy of Jesus," Rush wrote: "I shall receive with

pleasure the publication you have promised me upon the character of the Messiah, but unless it advances it to divinity, and renders his *death* as well as his *life* necessary for the restoration of mankind, I shall not accord with its author. There is [a] writer of the name of Abbadie whose opinions are mine upon this subject. He is learned, ingenious, and logical, and perfectly free from enthusiasm. You will probably find it in the library of your Parish minister, or of some of the clergy in your neighbourhood" (Rush to TJ, 29 Aug. 1804). Rush referred to Jacques Abbadie (1654?-1727), a Protestant theologian who was the author of *Traité de la divinité de nôtre-seigneur Jé-* *sus-Christ* (Rotterdam, 1689). Since "The Philosophy of Jesus" could not meet Rush's exacting theological standards, TJ never sent it to him.

To Benjamin S. Barton

DEAR SIR   Washington Feb. 14. 05

Your favor of the 1st. inst. has been longer unanswered than I could have wished. The correspondence between Dr. Priestley and myself was unfrequent and short. His fear of encroaching on my public duties deprived me of communications from him which would have been always welcome. I have examined all his letters to me since Mar. 1801. (those preceding being at Monticello) and find they do not contain a single fact interesting to your object. I hardly suppose the following one to be so. Having been long anxious to see a fair and candid comparison made between the doctrines of the Greek and Roman Philosophers, and the genuine doctrines of Jesus, I pressed Dr. Priestley, early in 1803. to undertake that work. He at first declined it from the extent of the subject, his own age and infirmities: but he afterwards informed me that having viewed the subject more attentively and finding that his Common place book would refer him readily to the materials, he had undertaken it: and a little before his death he informed me he had finished it. I apprehend however that he meditated a 2d. part which should have given a view of the genuine doctrines of Jesus divested of those engrafted into his by false followers. I suppose this because it is wanting to compleat the work, and because I observe he calls what is published Part Ist. Accept my friendly salutations & assurances of great esteem & respect.   TH: JEFFERSON

RC (PHi); addressed: "Doctr. Benjamin S. Barton Philadelphia"; franked and post-marked: "WASHN. CITY FEB 14"; endorsed by Barton as received 18 Feb. 1805. PoC (DLC).

Barton's FAVOR announced that he was "revising for the press, my Eulogium (lately delivered before the Philosophical Society) on the late Dr. Priestley" and asked TJ for permission to use any of Priestley's letters to the president "that may be useful to me"

(Barton to TJ, 1 Feb. 1805). Although Barton's eulogy of Dr. Priestley was delivered at a special meeting of the American Philosophical Society on 24 Feb. 1804, there is no evidence that it was ever published (Am. Phil. Soc., *Trans.*, VI [1809], 190). Barton (1766-1815), a Pennsylvania physician and naturalist, was at this time in his career one of the Society's three vice-presidents. TJ was serving as president of the organization.

To James Fishback

Sir   Monticello Sep. 27. 09.

Your favor of June 5. came to hand in due time, and I have to acknolege my gratification at the friendly sentiments it breathes towards myself. We have been thrown into times of a peculiar character, and to work our way through them has required services and sacrifices from our countrymen generally, and, to their great honor, these have been generally exhibited, by every one in his sphere, and according to the opportunities afforded. With them I have been a fellow laborer, endeavoring to do faithfully the part allotted to me, as they did theirs; and it is a subject of mutual congratulation that, in a state of things, such as the world had never before seen, we have gotten on so far well: and my confidence in our present high functionaries, as well as in my countrymen generally leaves me without much fear for the future.

I thank you for the pamphlet you were so kind as to send me. At an earlier period of life I pursued enquiries of that kind with industry and care. Reading, reflection and time have convinced me[1] that the interests of society require the observation of those moral precepts only in which all religions agree, (for all forbid us to murder, steal, plunder, or bear false witness) and that we should not intermeddle with the particular dogmas in which all religions differ, and which are totally unconnected with morality. In all of them we see good men, and as many in one as another. The varieties in the structure and action of the human mind as in those of the body, are the work of our creator, against which it cannot be a religious duty to erect the standard of uniformity. The practice of morality being necessary for the well-being of society, he has taken care to impress it's precepts so indelibly on our hearts that they shall not be effaced by the subtleties of our brain. We all agree in the obligation of the moral precepts of Jesus, and no where will they be found delivered in greater purity than in his discourses. It is then a matter of principle with me to avoid disturbing the tranquility of others by the expression of any opinion on the innocent questions on which we schismatise.

On the subject of your pamphlet, and the mode of treating it, I permit myself only to observe the candor, moderation and ingenuity with which you appear to have sought truth. This is of good example, and worthy of commendation.[2] If all the writers and preachers on religious questions had been of the same temper, the history of the world would have been of much more pleasing aspect.

I thank you for the kindness towards myself which breathes through your letter. The first of all our consolations is that of having faithfully fulfilled our duties: the next, the approbation and good will of those who have witnessed it: and I pray you to accept my best wishes for your happiness, & the assurances of my respect.

Th: Jefferson

RC (NjP: Decoppet Collection). PoC (DLC); endorsed by TJ at head of text: "This, and not the preceding was sent." Dft (DLC); dated "Sep 09." The last is the text referred to in TJ's endorsement on the PoC as "not . . . sent." It is actually a fair copy of a missing composition draft that contains a number of variations from the RC, the most important of which are indicated in the textual notes below.

Fishback, a Kentucky doctor, lawyer, and newspaper editor, was a prominent Presbyterian layman who became a Baptist minister in 1816 and was one of the leaders in the struggle against political and religious liberalism in Kentucky. See Neils H. Sonne, *Liberal Kentucky, 1780-1828* (New York, 1939), p. 109-16, 235-38. His FAVOR OF JUNE 5. praised TJ's "patriotic efforts" on behalf of religious freedom in the United States and enclosed "a Pamphlet of my own production" on which he solicited TJ's opinion. Fishback's PAMPHLET was *A New and Candid Investigation of the Question, Is Revelation True?* (Lexington, Ky., 1809), in which he argued that human reason is an inadequate instrument for discovering religious truth and that divine revelation is the only valid source of true religion.

[1] From this point until the end of the second sentence in the next paragraph of the RC the Dft reads: "it is better to be quiet myself, and let others be quiet on these speculations. Every religion consists of moral precepts, and of dogmas. In the first they all agree. All forbid us to murder, steal, plunder, bear false witness &ca. and these are the articles necessary for the preservation of order, justice, and happiness in society. In their particular dogmas all differ; no two professing the same. These respect vestments, ceremonies, physical opinions, and metaphysical speculations, totally unconnected with morality, and unimportant to the legitimate objects of society. Yet these are the questions on which have hung the bitter schisms of Nazarenes, Socinians, Arians, Athanasians in former times, and now of Trinitarians, Unitarians, Catholics, Lutherans, Calvinists, Methodists, Baptists, Quakers &c. Among the Mahometans we are told that thousands fell victims to the dispute whether the first or second toe of Mahomet was longest; and what blood, how many human lives have the words 'this do in remembrance of me' cost the Christian world! We all agree in the obligation of the moral precepts of Jesus: but we schismatize and lose ourselves in subtleties about his nature, his conception maculate or immaculate, whether he was a god or not a god, whether his votaries are to be initiated by simple aspersion, by immersion, or without water; whether his priests must be robed in white, in black, or not robed at all; whether we are to use our own reason, or the reason of others, in the opinions we form, or as to the evidence we are to believe. It is on questions of this, and still less importance, that such oceans of human blood have been spilt, and whole regions of the earth have been desolated by wars and persecutions, in which human ingenuity has been exhausted in inventing new tortures for their brethren. It is time then to become sensible how insoluble these questions are by minds like ours, how unimportant, and how mischievous; and to consign them to the sleep of death, never to be awakened from it. The varieties in the structure and action of the human mind, as in those of the body, are the work of our creator, against which it cannot be a religious duty to erect the standard of uniformity. The practice of morality being necessary for the well being of society, he

has taken care to impress it's precepts so indelibly on our hearts, that they shall not be effaced by the whimsies of our brain. Hence we see good men in all religions, and as many in one as another. It is then a matter of principle with me to avoid disturbing the tranquility of others by the expression of any opinion on the ⟨*unimportant points*⟩ innocent questions on which we schismatize, and think it enough to hold fast to those moral precepts which are of the essence of Christianity, and of all other religions. No where are these to be found in greater purity than in the discourses of the great reformer of religion whom we follow.—I have been led into these reflections by your invitation to make observations on the subject of your pamphlet, as you have treated it. The only one I permit myself is on the candor, the moderation and the ingenuity with which you appear to have sought truth."

[2] Dft reads: "and worthy of ⟨*imitation*⟩ much commendation."

To William Baldwin

SIR Monticello Jan. 19. 1810.

Your's of the 7th. inst. has been duly recieved, with the pamphlet inclosed, for which I return you my thanks. Nothing can be more exactly and seriously true than what is there stated; that but a short time elapsed after the death of the great reformer of the Jewish religion before his principles were departed from by those who professed to be his special servants, and perverted into an engine for enslaving mankind, and aggrandizing their oppressors in church and state: that the purest system of morals ever before preached to man has been adulterated and sophisticated, by artificial constructions, into a mere contrivance to filch wealth and power to themselves, that rational men not being able to swallow their impious heresies, in order to force them down their throats, they raise the hue and cry of infidelity, while themselves are the greatest obstacles to the advancement of the real doctrines of Jesus, and do in fact constitute the real Anti-Christ.

You expect that your book will have some effect on the prejudices which the society of friends entertain against the present and late administrations. In this I think you will be disappointed. The Friends are men, formed with the same passions, and swayed by the same natural principles and prejudices as others. In cases where the passions are neutral, men will display their respect for the religious *professions* of their sect. But where their passions are enlisted, these *professions* are no obstacle. You observe very truly that both the late and present administration conducted the government on principles *professed* by the Friends. Our efforts to preserve peace, our measures as to the Indians, as to slavery, as to religious freedom, were all in consonance with their *professions*. Yet I never expected we should get a vote from them, and in this I was neither decieved nor disappointed. There is no riddle in this to those who do not suffer themselves to be duped by the *professions* of religious sectaries. The theory of American Quakerism is a very obvious one. The Mother-society is in England. It's members are English by birth and residence, devoted to their own country as good citizens ought to be. The Quakers of these states are colonies or filiations from the mother society, to whom that society sends it's yearly lessons. On these the filiated societies model their opinions, their conduct, their passions and attachments. A Quaker is essentially an Englishman, in whatever part of the earth he is born or lives. The outrages of Great Britain on our navigation and commerce have kept us in perpetual bickerings with her. The Quakers here have taken side against their own government; not on their *profession* of peace, for they saw that peace was our object also; but from devotion to the views of the Mother-society. In 1797. and 8. when an administration sought war with France the Quakers were the most clamorous for war. Their principle of peace, as a secondary one, yielded to the primary one of Adherence to the Friends in England, and what was patriotism in the Original became Treason in the Copy. On that occasion they obliged their good old leader, Mr. Pemberton, to erase his name from a petition to Congress, against war, which had been delivered to a Representative of Pensylvania, a member of the late and present administration. He accordingly permitted the old gentleman to erase his name. You must not therefore expect that your book will have any more effect on the society of Friends here, than on the English merchants settled among us. I apply this to the Friends in general, not universally. I know individuals among them as good patriots as we have. I thank you for the kind wishes & sentiments towards myself expressed in your letter, & sincerely wish to yourself the blessings of health & happiness.   TH: JEFFERSON

PoC (DLC); addressed at foot of text: "Mr. Samuel Kercheval"; endorsed by TJ: "not sent." Despite the address, internal evidence clearly demonstrates that TJ wrote this letter to William Baldwin, not Samuel Kercheval. TJ wrote in response to a 7 Jan. 1810 letter; yet there is no record of such a letter from Kercheval to TJ. However, Kercheval did write a 12 Dec. 1809 letter to TJ, which was received on 7 Jan. 1810, suggesting that TJ confused the letter he received from Kercheval on 7 Jan. with the one Baldwin actually wrote him on that date (see notes below). Moreover, TJ wrote two letters to Baldwin on 19 Jan. 1810, but posted only one of them. See TJ's SJL (DLC).

Baldwin (1779-1819), a graduate of the University of Pennsylvania who was practicing medicine in Wilmington, Del., subsequently became one of America's leading botanists. His letter OF THE 7TH. INST. enclosed "a copy of the Essays of Cerus and Amicus," which, Baldwin explained, "are now published principally with a view of having them extensively circulated among the *society of Friends* in the eastern part of the state of *Pennsylvania*, who have been too generally prejudiced against the *late Administration*, and whose prejudices still exist, against the *present*." THE PAMPHLET INCLOSED by Baldwin was [Cerus], *Observations on Infidelity, and the Religious and Political Systems of Europe, Compared with*

Those of the United States: Showing the In-
compatibility of Religion with the Despotism
of National Churches . . . to Which are Added

the Essays of Amicus on the Maryland
Church-Bill and Quakers' Petition (Wilmington, Del., 1809).

To John Adams

DEAR SIR   Monticello Aug. 22. 13.

Since my letter of June 27. I am in your debt for many; all of
which I have read with infinite delight. They open a wide field for
reflection; and offer subjects enough to occupy the mind and the
pen indefinitely. I must follow the good example you have set; and
when I have not time to take up every subject, take up a single one.
Your approbation of my outline to Dr. Priestly is a great gratification
to me; and I very much suspect that if thinking men would have
the courage to think for themselves, and to speak what they think,
it would be found they do not differ in religious opinions, as much
as is supposed. I remember to have heard Dr. Priestly say that if
all England would candidly examine themselves, and confess, they
would find that Unitarianism was really the religion of all: and I
observe a bill is now depending in parliament for the relief of Anti-
Trinitarians. It is too late in the day for men of sincerity to pretend
they believe in the Platonic mysticisms that three are one, and one
is three; and yet the one is not three, and the three are not one: to
divide mankind by a single letter into ὁμοöθσians and ὁμοιοθσians.
But this constitutes the craft, the power and the profit of the priests.
Sweep away their gossamer fabrics of factitious religion, and they
would catch no more flies. We should all then, like the quakers, live
without an order of priests, moralise for ourselves, follow the oracle
of conscience, and say nothing about what no man can understand,
nor therefore believe; for I suppose belief to be the assent of the
mind to an intelligible proposition.

It is with great pleasure I can inform you that Priestly finished
the comparative view of the doctrines of the Philosophers of antiquity, and of Jesus, before his death; and that it was printed soon
after; and, with still greater pleasure, that I can have a copy of his
work forwarded from Philadelphia, by a correspondent there, and
presented for your acceptance, by the same mail which carries you
this, or very soon after. The branch of the work which the title
announces is executed with learning and candor, as was every thing
Priestley wrote: but perhaps a little hastily; for he felt himself pressed
by the hand of death. The Abbé Batteux had in fact laid the foundation of this part, in his Causes premieres; with which he has given

us the originals of Ocellus, and Timaeus, who first committed the doctrines of Pythagoras to writing; and Enfield, to whom the Doctor refers, had done it more copiously. But he has omitted the important branch, which in your letter of Aug. 9. you say you have never seen executed, a comparison of the morality of the old testament with that of the new. And yet no two things were ever more unlike. I ought not to have asked him to give it. He dared not. He would have been eaten alive by his intolerant brethren, the Cannibal priests. And yet this was really the most interesting branch of the work.

Very soon after my letter to Doctr. Priestley, the subject being still in my mind, I had leisure, during an abstraction from business, for a day or two while on the road, to think a little more on it, and to sketch more fully than I had done to him, a Syllabus of the matter which I thought should enter into the work. I wrote it to Dr. Rush; and there ended all my labor on the subject; himself and Dr. Priestley being the only depositories of my secret. The fate of my letter to Priestley, after his death, was a warning to me on that of Dr. Rush; and at my request his family was so kind as to quiet me by returning my original letter and Syllabus. By this you will be sensible how much interest I take in keeping myself clear of religious disputes before the public; and especially of seeing my Syllabus disembowelled by the Aruspices of the modern Paganism. Yet I enclose it *to you* with entire confidence, free to be perused by yourself and Mrs. Adams, but by no one else; and to be returned to me.

You are right in supposing, in one of yours, that I had not read much of Priestley's Predestination, his No-soul system, or his controversy with Horsley. But I have read his Corruptions of Christianity, and Early opinions of Jesus, over and over again; and I rest on them, and on Middleton's writings, especially his letters from Rome, and to Waterland, as the basis of my own faith. These writings have never been answered, nor can be answered, by quoting historical proofs, as they have done. For these facts therefore I cling to their learning, so much superior to my own.

I now fly off in a tangent to another subject. Marshal, in the 1st. vol. of his history, c. 3. pa. 180. ascribes the petition to the king of 1774. (1 Journ. Congr. 67.) to the pen of Richard Henry Lee. I think myself certain it was not written by him, as well from what I recollect to have heard, as from the internal evidence of style. His was loose, vague, frothy, rhetorical. He was a poorer writer than his brother Arthur; and Arthur's standing may be seen in his Monitor's letters, to ensure the sale of which they took the precaution of tacking to them a new edition of the Farmer's letters: like Mezentius who 'mortua jungebat corpora vivis.' You were of the committee, and can tell me who wrote this petition: and who wrote the Address to the inhabitants of the colonies ib. 45. Of the papers of July 1775 I recollect well that Mr. Dickinson drew the petition to the king, ib. 149. I think Robt. R. Livingston drew the address to the Inhabitants of Great Britain, ib. 152. Am I right in this? And who drew the Address to the people of Ireland, ib. 180.? On these questions, I ask of your memory to help mine. Ever and affectionately your's.   TH: JEFFERSON

P.S. Miss Lomax, daughter of one of our friends of 1776, lately dead, now here on a visit, asks permission to consign to you a memorial of the family respect for you: not done with the pencil, the burine or the chissel, but with the only instrument habitual to her, the humble scissars. You will find it inclosed.

RC (MHi: AM); endorsed by Adams as answered 14 Sep. 1813. PoC (DLC). Enclosures: TJ to Benjamin Rush, 21 Apr. 1803, and the "Syllabus"; see notes to TJ to Benjamin Rush, 21 Apr. 1803.

TJ's OUTLINE TO DR. PRIESTLEY was his 9 Apr. 1803 letter to Dr. Joseph Priestley, printed above. Adams had read this letter in Thomas Belsham, *Memoirs of . . . Theophilus Lindsey* (London, 1812), and had praised it in a 16 July 1813 letter to TJ. ὁμοόθσιANS and ὁμοιοθσιANS: those of the same substance and those of similar substance. The work by the ABBÉ BATTEUX was Charles Batteux, *Histoire des causes premiers, ou exposition sommaire des pensées de philosophes sur les principes des êtres* (Paris, 1769). See Sowerby, comp., *Catalogue*, No. 1293. The works that in TJ's time were ascribed to the Pythagorean philosophers OCELLUS and TIMAEUS are now widely regarded as either spurious or as the work of later writers (Catherine B. Avery, ed., *The New Century Classical Handbook* [New York, 1962], p. 760, 1101). PRIESTLEY'S PREDESTINATION has not been identified.

His NO-SOUL SYSTEM was *Disquisitions Relating to Matter and Spirit. To Which is Added, The History of the Philosophical Doctrine Concerning the Origin of the Soul and the Nature of Matter* (London, 1777), and his CONTROVERSY WITH HORSLEY may be found in *Letters to Dr. Horsley, in Answer to His Animadversions on the History of the Corruptions of Christianity . . .* (London, 1783). Priestley's CORRUPTIONS OF CHRISTIANITY was *A History of the Corruptions of Christianity*, 2 vols. (Birmingham, 1782), and his EARLY OPINIONS OF JESUS was *An History of Early Opinions Concerning Jesus Christ . . .; Proving that the Christian Church was at First Unitarian*, 2 vols. (Birmingham, 1786). See Sowerby, comp., *Catalogue*, Nos. 1526-27. MIDDLETON'S WRITINGS were contained in *The Miscellaneous Works of the Late Reverend and Learned Conyers Middleton . . .*, 4 vols. (London, 1752). See same, No. 1525. Marshall's HISTORY was John Marshall, *The Life of George Washington*, 5 vols. (Philadelphia, 1804-07). See same, No. 496. MORTUA JUNGEBAT CORPORA VIVIS: "bound dead bodies to the living."

To William Canby

SIR   Monticello Sep. 18. 13.

I have duly recieved your favor of Aug. 27. Am sensible of the kind intentions from which it flows, and truly thankful for them.

The more so as they could only be the result of a favorable estimate of my public course. During a long life, as much devoted to study as a faithful transaction of the trusts committed to me would permit, no subject has occupied more of my consideration than our relations with all the beings around us, our duties to them, and our future prospects. After reading and hearing every thing which probably can be suggested respecting them, I have formed the best judgment I could as to the course they prescribe, and in the due observance of that course, I have no recollections which give me uneasiness. An eloquent preacher of your religious society, Richard Motte, in a discourse of much unction and pathos, is said to have exclaimed aloud to his congregation that he did not believe there was a Quaker, Presbyterian, Methodist or Baptist in heaven. Having paused to give his audience time to stare and to wonder, he added, that in heaven, God knew no distinctions, but considered all good men as his children and as brethren of the same family. I believe, with the Quaker preacher, that he who steadily observes those moral precepts in which all religions concur, will never be questioned, at the gates of heaven, as to the dogmas in which they all differ. That on entering there, all these are left behind us, and the Aristideses and Catos, the Penns and Tillotsons, Presbyterians and Papists, will find themselves united in all principles which are in concert with the reason of the supreme mind. Of all the systems of morality antient or modern which have come under my observation, none appear to me so pure as that of Jesus. He who follows this steadily need not, I think, be uneasy, altho' he cannot comprehend the subtleties and mysteries erected on his doctrines by those who, calling themselves his special followers and favorites, would make him come into the world to lay snares for all understandings but theirs. These metaphysical heads, usurping the judgment seat of god, denounce as his enemies all who cannot percieve the Geometrical logic of Euclid in the demonstrations of St. Athanasius that three are one, and one is three; and yet that the one is not three, nor the three one. In all essential points, you and I are of the same religion; and I am too old to go into enquiries and changes as to the unessential. Repeating therefore my thankfulness for the kind concern you have been so good as to express, I salute you with friendship and brotherly esteem.

TH: JEFFERSON

PoC (DLC). Tr (NjP: Straus Autograph Collection); in the hand of Ellen Wayles Randolph and endorsed: "Religion creed of the wise."

Canby (1748-1830), a prominent Quaker miller in Wilmington, Del., had been trying for a decade to convert TJ to Christianity (Henry S. Canby, *Family History* [Cambridge, Mass., 1945], p. 33-34; Canby to

TJ, 27 May 1802, 1 Feb. 1803, 24 Mch. 1808). His FAVOR OF AUG. 27. expressed the wish that TJ would embrace Christianity and thereby win eternal salvation, observing in part: "I have for years at times felt affection toward thee, with a wish for thy Salvation; to wit the attainment while on this stage of time (in the Natural Body), of a suitable portion of divine life, for otherways we know little more than the life of Nature, and therein are in danger of becoming inferior to the Beasts which perish, in consequence of declining the offers of divine life, made to every rational being." The present letter is TJ's only known written response to Canby.

To John Adams

DEAR SIR   Monticello Oct. 12. 13.

Since mine of Aug. 22. I have recieved your favors of Aug. 16. Sep. 2. 14. 15. and [22] and Mrs. Adams's of Sep. 20. I now send you, according to your request a copy of the Syllabus. To fill up this skeleton with arteries, with veins, with nerves, muscles and flesh, is really beyond my time and information. Whoever could undertake it would find great aid in Enfield's judicious abridgment of Brucker's history of Philosophy, in which he has reduced 5. or 6. quarto vols. of 1000. pages each of Latin closely printed, to two moderate 8vos. of English, open, type.

To compare the morals of the old, with those of the new testament, would require an attentive study of the former, a search thro' all it's books for it's precepts, and through all it's history for it's practices, and the principles they prove. As commentaries too on these, the philosophy of the Hebrews must be enquired into. Their Mishna, their Gemara, Cabbala, Jezirah, Sohar, Cosri and their Talmud must be examined and understood, in order to do them full justice. Brucker, it should seem, has gone deeply into these Repositories of their ethics, and Enfield, his epitomiser, concludes in these words. 'Ethics were so little studied among the Jews, that, in their whole compilation called the Talmud, there is only one treatise on moral subjects.—Their books of Morals chiefly consisted in a minute enumeration of duties. From the law of Moses were deduced 613. precepts, which were divided into two classes, affirmative and negative, 248 in the former, and 365 in the latter.—It may serve to give the reader some idea of the low state of moral philosophy among the Jews in the Middle age, to add, that of the 248. affirmative precepts, only 3. were considered as obligatory upon women; and that, in order to obtain salvation, it was judged sufficient to fulfill any one single law in the hour of death; the observance of the rest being deemed necessary, only to increase the felicity of the future

[351]

life. What a wretched depravity of sentiment and manners must have prevailed before such corrupt maxims could have obtained credit! It is impossible to collect from these writings a consistent series of moral Doctrine.' [1] Enfield B. 4. chap. 3. It was the reformation of this 'wretched depravity' of morals which Jesus undertook. In extracting the pure principles which he taught, we should have to strip off the artificial vestments in which they have been muffled by priests, who have travestied them into various forms, as instruments of riches and power to them. We must dismiss the Platonists and Plotinists, the Stagyrites and Gamalielites, the Eclectics the Gnostics and Scholastics their essences and emanations, their Logos and Demi-urgos, Aeons and Daemons male and female, with a long train of &c. &c. &c. or, shall I say at once, of Nonsense. We must reduce our volume to the simple evangelists, select, even from them, the very words only of Jesus, paring off the Amphibologisms into which they have been led by forgetting often, or not understanding, what had fallen from him, by giving their own misconceptions as his dicta, and expressing unintelligibly for others what they had not understood themselves. There will be found remaining the most sublime and benevolent code of morals which has ever been offered to man. I have performed this operation for my own use, by cutting verse by verse out of the printed book, and arranging, the matter which is evidently his, and which is as easily distinguishable as diamonds in a dunghill. The result is an 8vo. of 46. pages of pure and unsophisticated doctrines, such as were professed and acted on by the *unlettered* apostles, the Apostolic fathers, and the Christians of the 1st. century. Their Platonising successors indeed, in after times, in order to legitimate the corruptions which they had incorporated into the doctrines of Jesus, found it necessary to disavow the primitive Christians, who had taken their principles from the mouth of Jesus himself, of his Apostles, and the Fathers cotemporary with them. They excommunicated their followers as heretics, branding them with the opprobrious name of Ebionites or Beggars.

For a comparison of the Graecian philosophy with that of Jesus, materials might be largely drawn from the same source. Enfield gives a history, and detailed account of the opinions and principles of the different sects. These relate to

the gods, their natures, grades, places and powers;

the demi-gods and daemons, and their agency with man;

the Universe, it's structure, extent, production and duration;[2]

the origin of things from the elements of fire, water, air and earth;

the human soul, it's essence and derivation;

the summum bonum, and finis bonorum; with a thousand idle dreams and fancies on these and other subjects the knolege of which is witheld from man, leaving but a short chapter for his moral duties, and the principal section of that given to what he owes himself, to precepts for rendering him impassible, and unassailable by the evils of life, and for preserving his mind in a state of constant serenity.

Such a canvas is too broad for the age of seventy, and especially of one whose chief occupations have been in the practical business of life. We must leave therefore to others, younger and more learned than we are, to prepare this euthanasia for Platonic Christianity, and it's restoration to the primitive simplicity of it's founder. I think you give a just outline of the theism of the three religions when you say that the principle of the Hebrew was the fear, of the Gentile the honor, and of the Christian the love of God.

An expression in your letter of Sep. 14. that 'the human understanding is a revelation from it's maker' gives the best solution, that I believe can be given, of the question, What did Socrates mean by his Daemon? He was too wise to believe, and too honest to pretend that he had real and familiar converse with a superior[3] and invisible being. He probably considered the suggestions of his conscience, or reason, as revelations, or inspirations from the Supreme mind, bestowed, on important occasions, by a special superintending providence.

I acknolege all the merit of the hymn of Cleanthes to Jupiter, which you ascribe to it. It is as highly sublime as a chaste and correct imagination can permit itself to go. Yet in the contemplation of a being so superlative, the hyperbolic flights of the Psalmist may often be followed with approbation, even with rapture; and I have no hesitation in giving him the palm over all the Hymnists of every language, and of every time. Turn to the 148th. psalm in Brady and Tate's version. Have such conceptions been ever before expressed? Their version of the 15th. psalm is more to be esteemed for it's pithiness, than it's poetry. Even Sternhold, the leaden Sternhold, kindles, in a single instance, with the sublimity of his original, and expresses the majesty of God descending on the earth, in terms not unworthy of the subject.

'The Lord descended from above
And underneath his feet he cast
On Cherubim and Seraphim
And on the wings of mighty winds
And bowed the heav'ns most high;
The darkness of the sky.
Full royally he rode;
Came flying all abroad.

Psalm xviii. 9.10.

The Latin versions of this passage by Buchanan and by Johnston, are but mediocres, but the Greek of Duport is worthy of quotation.

Ουρανον αγκλινας κατεβη̣. ὑπο ποσσι δ᾽ ἐοισιν
Ἀλυς ἀμφι μελαινα χυθη και νυξ ερεβεννη.
῾Ριμφα ποτᾶτο Χερουβῳ οχευμενος, ὡσπερ εφ᾽ ἱππῳ
Ἱπτατο δε πτερυγεσσι πολυπλαγκτου ανεμοιο.

The best collection of these psalms is that of the Octagonian dissenters of Liverpool in their printed Form of prayer; but they are not always the best versions. Indeed bad is the best of the English versions; not a ray of poetical genius having ever been employed on them. And how much depends on this may be seen by comparing Brady and Tate's XVth. psalm with Blacklock's Justum et tenacem propositi virum of Horace, quoted in Hume's history Car. 2. ch. 65. A translation of David in this style, or in that of Pompei's Cleanthes, might give us some idea of the merit of the original. The character too of the poetry of these hymns is singular to us. Written in Monostichs, each divided into strophe and antistrophe, the sentiment of the 1st. member responded with amplification or antithesis in the second.

On the subject of the Postscript of yours of Aug. 16. and of Mrs. Adams's letter, I am silent. I know the depth of the affliction it has caused, and can sympathise with it the more sensibly, inasmuch as there is no degree of affliction, produced by the loss of those dear to us which experience has not taught me to estimate. I have ever found time and silence the only medecine, and these but assuage, they never can suppress, the deep-drawn sigh which recollection for ever brings up, until recollection and life are extinguished together. Ever & affectionately yours, TH: JEFFERSON

P.S. Your's of Sep. __⁴ just recieved.

RC (MHi: AM); endorsed by Adams: "Syllabus inclosed. Ansd. Nov. 25th [i.e., 14th]." PoC (DLC). Enclosure: Ellen Wayles Randolph's copy of the "Syllabus"; see notes to TJ to Benjamin Rush, 21 Apr. 1803.

ENFIELD'S JUDICIOUS ABRIDGMENT: William Enfield, *The History of Philosophy, from the Earliest Times to the Beginning of the Present Century; Drawn up from Brucker's Historia Critica Philosophiae*, 2 vols. (Dublin, 1792). See Sowerby, comp., *Catalogue*, No. 1337. BRADY AND TATE'S VERSION: Nahum Tate and Nicholas Brady, *A New Version of the Psalms of David, Fitted* to the Tunes in Churches (London, 1696). TJ owned a 1773 edition of this work printed in London. See same, No. 1510. LEADEN STERNHOLD: Thomas Sternhold and others, *The Whole Book of Psalmes Collected into Englysche Meter* (London, 1564). The editions of the works by BUCHANAN and JOHNSTON as well as the GREEK OF DUPORT to which TJ refers are George Buchanan and James Duport, *Psalmorum Davidicorum Metaphrasis Graecis versibus contexta per Jacobum Duportum Cantabrigiensem. Cui in oppositis paginis respondens accessit Paraphrasis Poetica Latina auctore Georgio Buchanano* (London, 1742), and Arthur Johnston, *Psalmorum Davidis*

Paraphrasis poetica et Canticorum Evangelicorum . . . (London, 1741). See Sowerby, comp., *Catalogue*, Nos. 4398-99. COLLECTION OF THE OCTAGONIAN DISSENTERS: *A Form of Prayer, and a New Collection of Psalms, for the Use of a Congregation of Protestant Dissenters in Liverpool* (Liverpool, 1763). See same, No. 1513. JUSTUM ET TENACEM PROPOSITI VIRUM: "a man just and steadfast of purpose." HUME'S HISTORY: David Hume, *The History of England, from the Invasion of Julius Caesar to the Revolution in 1688*, 8 vols. (London, 1790-91). See Sowerby, comp., *Catalogue*,

No. 370. The SUBJECT OF THE POSTSCRIPT of Adams' 16 Aug. 1813 letter was the death of his daughter Abigail Adams Smith.

¹ TJ used dashes in this quotation to indicate ellipses.

² PoC reads "extent and duration." TJ altered the RC to read as above.

³ TJ initially concluded this sentence with the phrase "converse with a superior power" and then altered it to read as above.

⁴ Adams had dated this letter "Quincy Sept. 1813."

To Thomas Law

DEAR SIR   Poplar Forest near Lynchburg. June 13. 14.

The copy of your Second thoughts on Instinctive impulses with the letter accompanying it, was recieved just as I was setting out on a journey to this place, two or three days distant from Monticello. I brought it with me, and read it with great satisfaction; and with the more, as it contained exactly my own creed on the foundation of morality in man. It is really curious that, on a question so fundamental, such a variety of opinions should have prevailed among men; and those too of the most exemplary virtue and first order of understanding. It shews how necessary was the care of the Creator in making the moral principle so much a part of our constitution as that no errors of reasoning or of speculation might lead us astray from it's observance in practice. Of all the theories on this question, the most whimsical seems to have been that of Woollaston, who considers *truth* as the foundation of morality. The thief who steals your guinea does wrong only inasmuch as he acts a lie, in using your guinea as if it were his own. Truth is certainly a branch of morality, and a very important one to society. But, presented as it's foundation, it is as if a tree, taken up by the roots, had it's stem reversed in the air, and one of it's branches planted in the ground.— Some have made the *love of god* the foundation of morality. This too is but a branch of our moral duties, which are generally divided into duties to god, and duties to man. If we did a good act merely from the love of god, and a belief that it is pleasing to him, whence arises the morality of the Atheist? It is idle to say as some do, that no such being exists. We have the same evidence of the fact as of most of those we act on, to wit, their own affirmations, and their reasonings in support of them. I have observed indeed generally that, while in protestant countries the defections¹ from the Platonic

Christianity of the priests is to Deism, in Catholic countries they are to Atheism. Diderot, Dalembert, D'Holbach, Condorcet, are known to have been among the most virtuous of men. Their virtue then must have had some other foundation than the love of god.

The το καλον of others is founded in a different faculty, that of taste, which is not even a branch of morality. We have indeed an innate sense of what we call beautiful: but that is exercised chiefly on subjects addressed to the fancy, whether thro' the eye, in visible forms, as landscape, animal figure, dress, drapery, architecture, the composition of colours &c. or to the imagination directly, as imagery, style, or measure in prose or poetry, or whatever else constitutes the domain of criticism or taste, a faculty entirely distinct from the moral one. Self-interest, or rather Self love, or *Egoism*, has been more plausibly substituted as the basis of morality. But I consider our relations with others as constituting the boundaries of morality. With ourselves we stand on the ground of identity, not of relation; which last, requiring two subjects, excludes self-love confined to a single one.[2] To ourselves, in strict language, we can owe no duties, obligation requiring also two parties. Self-love therefore is no part of morality. Indeed it is exactly it's counterpart. It is the sole antagonist of virtue, leading us constantly by our propensities to self-gratification in violation of our moral duties to others.[2] Accordingly it is against this enemy that are erected the batteries of moralists and religionists, as the only obstacle to the practice of morality. Take from man his selfish propensities, and he can have nothing to seduce him from the practice of virtue. Or subdue those propensities by education, instruction, or restraint, and virtue remains without a competitor. Egoism, in a broader sense, has been thus presented as the source of moral action. It has been said that we feed the hungry, clothe the naked, bind up the wounds of the man beaten by thieves, pour oil and wine into them, set him on our own beast, and bring him to the inn, because we recieve ourselves pleasure from these acts. So Helvetius, one of the best men on earth, and the most ingenious advocate of this principle, after defining 'interest' to mean, not merely that which is pecuniary, but whatever may procure us pleasure or withdraw us from pain, [de l'Esprit. 2.1.] says [ib. 2.2.] 'the humane man is he to whom the sight of misfortune is insupportable and who, to rescue himself from this spectacle, is forced to succour the unfortunate object.' This indeed is true. But it is one step short of the ultimate question. These good acts give us pleasure: but how happens it that they give us pleasure? Because nature hath implanted in our breasts a love of others, a sense of duty to them, a moral instinct in short, which prompts us irresistibly to feel and to succour their distresses; and protests against the language of Helvetius [ib. 2.5.] 'what other motive than self interest could determine a man to generous actions? It is as impossible for him to love what is good for the sake of good, as to love evil for the sake of evil.' The creator would indeed have been a bungling artist,[3] had he intended man for a social animal, without planting in him social dispositions. It is true they are not planted in every man; because there is no rule without exceptions; but it is false reasoning which converts exceptions into the general rule. Some men are born without the organs of sight, or of hearing, or without hands. Yet it would be wrong to say that man is born without these faculties; and sight, hearing and hands may with truth enter into the general definition of Man. The want or imperfection of the moral sense in some men, like the want or imperfection of the senses of sight and hearing in others, is no proof that it is a general characteristic of the species. When it is wanting we endeavor to supply the defect by education, by appeals to reason and calculation, by presenting to the being so unhappily conformed other motives to do good, and to eschew evil; such as the love, or the hatred or rejection of those among whom he lives and whose society is necessary to his happiness, and even existence; demonstrations by sound calculation that honesty promotes interest in the long run; the rewards and penalties established by the laws; and ultimately the prospects of a future state of retribution for the evil as well as the good done while here. These are the correctives which are supplied by education, and which exercise the functions of the moralist, the preacher and legislator: and they lead into a course of correct action all those whose depravity is not too profound to be eradicated. Some have argued against the existence of a moral sense, by saying that if nature had given us such a sense, impelling us to virtuous actions, and warning us against those which are vicious, then nature must also have designated, by some particular ear-marks, the two sets of actions which are, in themselves, the one virtuous, and the other vicious: whereas we find in fact, that the same actions are deemed virtuous in one country, and vicious in another. The answer is that nature has constituted *utility* to man the standard and test of virtue. Men living in different countries, under different circumstances, different habits, and regimens, may have different utilities. The same act therefore may be useful, and consequently virtuous, in one country, which is injurious and vicious in another differently circumstanced. I sincerely then believe with you in the general existence of a moral instinct. I think it the brightest gem with which the human character is studded; and the want of it as more degrading than the most hideous of the bodily deformities. I am happy in reviewing the roll of associates in this principle which you present in your 2d. letter, some of which I had not before met with. To these might be added Ld. Kaims, one of the ablest of our advocates, who goes so far as to say, in his Principles of Natural religion, that a man owes no duty to which he is not urged by some impulsive feeling. This is correct if referred to the standard of general feeling in the given case, and not to the feeling of a single individual. Perhaps I may misquote him, it being fifty years since I read his book.

The leisure and solitude of my situation here has led me to the indiscretion of taxing you with a long letter on a subject whereon nothing new can be offered you. I will indulge myself no further than to repeat the assurances of my continued esteem & respect.

TH: JEFFERSON

RC (ViU); slightly mutilated; a few missing letters supplied. PoC (DLC); TJ added "Thomas Law esq." at foot of text after PoC was completed; since this text was somewhat faint, especially at the beginning of some lines, TJ clarified a good many words by overwriting, suggesting the importance he attached to this letter. All brackets in the text are his.

Law (1759-1834), son of the Anglican bishop of Carlisle, England, served as a revenue collector with the East India Company before moving to the United States in 1793, where he married a granddaughter of Martha Washington, corresponded regularly with TJ, and became a leading advocate of the establishment of a national currency. His *Second Thoughts on Instinctive Impulses* (Philadelphia, 1813), was an effort, in his words, to "develop a theory of moral sensations into a regular science, founded on primordial, universal, invariable principles." See Sowerby, comp., *Catalogue*, No. 3250. THE LETTER ACCOMPANYING this pamphlet, was Law to TJ, 3 May 1814. WOOLLASTON: William Wollaston (1660-1724), an English natural philosopher whose theory of morality is set

forth in *The Religion of Nature Delineated* . . . (London, 1722), the seventh edition of which, printed in Glasgow in 1746, was owned by TJ. See Sowerby, comp., *Catalogue*, No. 1252. The work by HELVETIUS quoted in this letter was probably part of the ten-volume set of "Oeuvres d'Helvetius *in petit format*" that TJ had acquired in 1803 (same, No. 1242). YOUR 2D. LETTER: Law's *Second Thoughts* was divided into letters rather than chapters. TJ owned LD. KAIMS, *Essays on the Principles of Morality and Natural Religion* (Edinburgh, 1751). See same, No. 1254.

[1] TJ first wrote "deflections" and then altered it to read as above.

[2] In the margin of the RC opposite the preceding two sentences there is a vertical line that was presumably drawn by Law to mark these passages.

[3] The words "bungling artist" are deleted from the RC in a different ink from the rest of the text but are untouched in the PoC. This alteration was certainly not made by TJ and probably not by Law, who subsequently expressed approval of TJ's letter (Law to TJ, 12 July 1814).

To John Adams

Monticello, 5 July 1814. Acknowledges receipt of "yours of Mar. 14" and is saddened by the news of Adams' ill health. Rejoices in the downfall of Napoleon and discusses prospects for peace between the United States and Great Britain.

"I am just returned from one of my long absences, having been at my other home for five weeks past. Having more leisure there than here for reading, I amused myself with reading seriously Plato's republic. I am wrong however in calling it amusement, for it was the heaviest task-work I ever went through. I had occasionally before taken up some of his other works, but scarcely ever had patience to go through a whole dialogue. While wading thro' the whimsies, the puerilities, and unintelligible jargon of this work, I laid it down often to ask myself how it could have been that the world should have so long consented to give reputation to such nonsense as this? How the soi-disant Christian world indeed should have done it, is a piece of historical curiosity. But how could the Roman good sense do it? And particularly how could Cicero bestow such eulogies on Plato? Altho' Cicero did not wield the dense logic of Demosthenes, yet he was able, learned, laborious, practised in the business of the world, and honest. He could not be the dupe of mere style, of which he was himself the first master in the world. With the Moderns, I think, it is rather a matter of fashion and authority. Education is chiefly in the hands of persons who, from their profession, have an interest in the reputation and the dreams of Plato. They give the tone while at school, and few, in their after-years, have occasion to revise their college opinions. But fashion and authority apart, and bringing Plato to the test of reason, take from him his sophisms, futilities, and incomprehensibilities, and what remains? In truth he is one of the race of genuine Sophists, who has escaped the oblivion of his brethren, first by the elegance of his diction, but chiefly by the adoption and incorporation of his whimsies into the body of artificial Christianity. His foggy mind, is for ever presenting the semblances of objects which, half seen thro' a mist, can be defined neither in form or dimension. Yet this which should have consigned him to early oblivion really procured him immortality of fame and reverence. The Christian priesthood, finding the doctrines of Christ levelled to every understanding, and too plain to need explanation,[1] saw, in the mysticisms of Plato, materials with which they might build up an artificial system which might, from it's indistinctness, admit everlasting controversy, give employment for their order, and introduce it to profit, power and pre-eminence. The doctrines which flowed from the lips of Jesus himself are within the comprehension of a child; but thousands of volumes have not yet explained the Platonisms engrafted on them: and for this obvious reason that nonsense can never be explained. Their purposes however are answered. Plato is canonised; and it is now deemed as impious to question his merits as those of an Apostle of Jesus. He is peculiarly appealed to as an advocate of the immortality of the soul; and yet I will venture to say that were there no better arguments than his in proof of it, not a man in the world would believe it. It is fortunate for us that Platonic republicanism has not obtained the same favor as Platonic Christianity; or we should now have been all living, men, women and children, pell mell together, like the beasts of the field or forest. Yet 'Plato is a great Philosopher,' said La Fontaine. But says Fontenelle 'do you find his ideas very clear'?—'Oh no! he is of an obscurity impenetrable.'—'Do you not find him full of contradictions?'—'Certainly,' replied La Fontaine, 'he is but a Sophist.' Yet immediately after, he exclaims again, 'Oh Plato was a great Philosopher.'—Socrates had reason indeed to complain of the misrepresentations of Plato; for in truth his dialogues are libels on Socrates."—Apologizes for "dosing you with these Ante-diluvian topics" and concludes by stressing the need for properly educating the rising generation.

RC (MHi: AM); addressed: "John Adams late President of the US. Quincy Massachusets"; franked and postmarked: "Milton Va 7 July"; endorsed by Adams: "ansd." PoC (DLC).

Adams' letter of MAR. 14 was actually dated Feb. 1814, but contained a 3 Mch. postscript.

[1] TJ first wrote "understanding" and then altered it to read as above.

To Miles King

SIR   Monticello Sep. 26. 14.

I duly recieved your letter of Aug. 20. and I thank you for it, because I believe it was written with kind intentions, and a personal concern for my future happiness. Whether the particular revelation, which you suppose to have been made to yourself were real or imaginary, your reason alone is the competent judge. For, dispute as long as we will on religious tenets, our reason at last must ultimately decide, as it is the only oracle which god has given us to determine between what really comes from him, and the phantasms of a disordered or deluded imagination. When he means to make a personal revelation he carries conviction of it's authenticity to the reason he has bestowed as the umpire of truth. You believe you have been favored with such a special communication. Your reason, not mine, is to judge of this: and if it shall be his pleasure to favor me with a like admonition, I shall obey it with the same fidelity with which I would obey his known will in all cases. Hitherto I have been under the guidance of that portion of reason which he has thought proper to deal out to me. I have followed it faithfully in all important cases, to such a degree at least as leaves me without uneasiness; and if on minor occasions I have erred from it's dictates, I have trust in him who made us what we are, and knows it was not his plan to make us always unerring. He has formed us moral agents. Not that, in the perfection of his state, he can feel pain or pleasure from any thing we may do: he is far above our power: but that we may promote the happiness of those with whom he has placed us in society, by acting honestly towards all, benevolently to those who fall within our way, respecting sacredly their rights bodily and mental, and cherishing especially their freedom of conscience, as we value our own. I must ever believe that religion substantially good which produces an honest life, and we have been authorised by one, whom you and I equally respect, to judge of the tree by it's fruit. Our particular principles of religion are a subject of accountability to our god alone. I enquire after no man's, and trouble none with mine: nor is it given to us in this life to know whether your's or mine, our friend's or our foe's are exactly the right. Nay, we have heard it said that there is not a quaker or a baptist, a presbyterian or an episcopalian, a catholic or a protestant in heaven: that, on entering that gate, we leave those badges of schism behind, and find ourselves united in those principles only in which god has united us all. Let us not be uneasy then about the different roads we may pursue, as believing them the shortest, to that our last abode: but, following the guidance of a good conscience, let us be happy in the hope that, by these different paths, we shall all meet in the end— and that you and I may there meet and embrace is my earnest prayer: and with this assurance I salute you with brotherly esteem and respect. TH: JEFFERSON

PoC (DLC).

Miles King's closely written, eleven-page LETTER OF AUG. 20 was a fervent plea to TJ to embrace the "religion of the gospel of our Lord Jesus Christ," not only to achieve personal salvation, but also to serve as an example to the American people, whose lack of strong religious faith, King believed, was the ultimate source of the reverses they were suffering in the War of 1812. In order to lend force to his plea, King, a "Methodist preacher" in Mathews County, Va., who claimed that he had been divinely inspired to write to TJ, gave a long account of his own spiritual evolution from the "luxurious life of debauch and intrigue" he had led during his career as a merchant ship captain and U.S. Navy officer to his relatively recent conversion to Methodism. "As a Methodist preacher I now write to you my dear Sir," King noted, "not so much for the purpose of persuading you to become a Member of our church, tho we be Methodists, as to intreat your espousal of the christian System of Salvation—and to be so far a Methodist as to be Methodical in religious worship—in Devotion, and every Known duty whether it relates to the life that now is—or that which is soon to come—for without Method none will be Saved under our dispensation. My prayer to God! now is that you may be disposed by his grace to seek untill you shall find Christ Jesus [. . .] by faith revealed in you the hope of Glory! ere you go hence and be no more seen on Earth! for the place that Knows you now will Soon Know you no More for Ever! and do my friend and illustrious fellow citizen, timely consider, even now lay it close to your heart, that God! hath commanded all men every where to repent, because he hath appointed a day in the which he will Judge this world in Righteousness, by that man (God-man) whom he hath Ordained, Jesus Christ! whereof he hath given an assurance to all men in that he hath raised him up from the dead!"

From Charles Clay

C. CLAY TO MR. JEFFERSON   Dec. 20. 1814.

Reflecting on an expression of yours relative to an Idea Sometimes entertained by you of Compressing the Moral doctrines taught by Jesus of Nazareth in the Gospels, divested of all other Matters into a small and regular system of the purest morality ever taught to Mankind, and meritting the highest praise, and most worthy the Strictest attention, &c. &c. however laudable may be your Views and meritorious your intentions in such a nice and critical (delicate) undertaking, I cannot help entertaining doubts and fears for the final issue, how it may effect your future character and reputation on the page of history as a Patriot, legislator and sound Philosopher. The Metaphysical sophystry of the Day have drawn its adepts into such a Variety of strange whims and Vagaries, such niceties and refinements of reasoning and diction, and such amazing strange, novel, and paradoxical results from such premises, that I feel sensibly for the final event, should you be induced to permit yourself to send forth such a piece to the public, lest they might not Sufficiently appreciate your good intentions, but ascribe it to views as inimical to the christian religion in particular, and eventually to all religion from divine Authority, which I am persuaded you Can have no intention of doing, for when we consider that whatever may occasionally have been its excesses, extravagances, or abusives, it is by far better to be as it is, than be altogether without any, and that no System of morality however pure it might be, yet without the sanction of divine authority stampt upon it, would have sufficient weight on Vulgar minds to ensure an Observance internal and external, notwithstanding the excellent beauty of Holiness, and the inticing Charms of Virtue all lovely as she might appear to Noble Minds when fairly exhibited in her pure simple and natural form, divested of all insignia.—My fears are, that should your performance not exactly meet the approbation of the public, (both now and hereafter), that your Name will be degraded from the Venerable Council of true, genuine, Useful Philosophy; and Condemned to be rankled with the wild Sophisters of Jacobinism, the Theosophies of Masonry, with Martinists, Swedenborgers, and Rosicrusians, with the Epopts and Magi of Illuminism &c. which Phantastic kind of beings, future Historians will most assuredly denominate by some opprobrious epithet, as the Maniacs of Philosophy &c.—And it certainly may be expected that the whole of your numerous Enemies on the Northern and eastern parts of the U.S. with all their Friends, Disciples, followers and associates through out America; (and who it must be Confessed possess Considerable influence in the public education and Consequently in forming the Opinion of the rising generation) should the performance not exactly Coincide with their Ideas and meet their entire approbation, even in the Minutiæ of diction (which it is highly probable it would not) they would greedily seize the Occasion, and raise the hue and Cry after you through the world, and all the Canaille of America and Europe wuld be found barking at your heels! Except assurances of respect & esteem.

C. CLAY

[362]

RC (MHi); endorsed by TJ as received 16 Jan. 1815.

Charles Clay (d. 1824), a Bedford County, Va., farmer who had once been an Anglican minister in charge of St. Anne's parish in Albemarle County, 1769-1785, was a longtime friend and neighbor of TJ (Bishop [William] Meade, *Old Churches, Ministers, and Families of Virginia* [Philadelphia, 1900], II, 48-50).

To Charles Clay

DEAR SIR   Monticello Jan. 29. 15.

Your letter of Dec. 20. was 4. weeks on it's way to me. I thank you for it: for altho founded on a misconception, it is evidence of that friendly concern for my peace and welfare which I have ever believed you to feel. Of publishing a book on religion, my dear Sir, I never had an idea. I should as soon think of writing for the reformation of Bedlam, as of the world of religious sects. Of these there must be at least ten thousand, every individual of every one of which believes all are wrong but his own. To undertake to bring them all right, would be like undertaking, single handed, to fell the forests of America. Probably you have heard me say I had taken the four evangelists, had cut out from them every text they had recorded of the moral precepts of Jesus, and arranged them in a certain order, and altho' they appeared but as fragments, yet fragments of the most sublime edifice of morality which had ever been exhibited to man. This I have probably mentioned to you, because it is true; and the idea of it's publication may have suggested itself as an inference of your own mind. I not only write nothing on religion, but rarely permit myself to speak on it, and never but in a reasonable society. I have probably said more to you than to any other person, because we have had more hours of conversation in duetto in our meetings at the Forest. I abuse the priests indeed, who have so much abused the pure and holy doctrines of their master, and who have laid me under no obligations of reticence as to the tricks of their trade. The genuine system of Jesus, and the artificial structures they have erected to make him the instrument of wealth, power, and preeminence to themselves are as distinct things in my view as light and darkness: and, while I have classed them with soothsayers and necromancers, I place him among the greatest of the reformers of morals, and scourges of priest-craft, that have ever existed. They felt him as such, and never rested till they silenced him by death. But his heresies against Judaism prevailing in the long run, the priests have tacked about, and rebuilt upon them the temple which he destroyed, as splendid, as profitable, and as imposing as that.

Government, as well as religion, has furnished it's schisms, it's persecutions, and it's devices for fattening idleness on the earnings of the people. It has it's hierarchy of emperors, kings, princes and nobles, as that has of popes, cardinals, archbishops, bishops, and priests. In short, Cannibals are not to be found in the wilds of America only, but are revelling on the blood of every living people. Turning then from this loathsome combination of church and state, and weeping over the follies of our fellow-men, who yield themselves the willing dupes and drudges of these Mountebanks, I consider reformation and redress as desperate, and abandon them to the Quixotism of more enthusiastic minds.

I have recieved from Philadelphia by mail, the spectacles you had desired, and now forward them by the same conveyance, as equally safe and more in time, than were they to await my own going. In a separate case is a compleat set of glasses from early use to old age. I think the pair now in the frames will suit your eyes, but should they not, you will easily change them by the screws. I believe the largest numbers are the smallest magnifiers, but am not certain. Trial will readily ascertain it. You must do me the favor to accept them as a token of my friendship & with them the assurance of my great esteem & respect.   TH: JEFFERSON

PoC (DLC); slightly worn at right edge.

To Charles Thomson

MY DEAR AND ANTIENT FRIEND   Monticello Jan. 9. 15. [i.e. 1816]

An acquaintance of 52. years, for I think ours dates from 1764. calls for an interchange of notice now and then that we remain in existence, the monuments of another age, and examples of a friendship unaffected by the jarring elements, by which we have been surrounded, of revolutions, of government, of party and of opinion. I am reminded of this duty by the receipt, thro' our friend Dr. Patterson, of your Synopsis of the four Evangelists. I had procured it as soon as I saw it advertized, and had become familiar with it's use, but this copy is the more valued as it comes from your hand. This work bears the stamp of that accuracy which marks every thing from you, and will be useful to those who, not taking things on trust, recur for themselves to the fountain of pure morals. I too have made a wee little book, from the same materials, which I call the Philosophy of Jesus. It is a paradigma of his doctrines, made by cutting the texts out of the book, and arranging them on the pages of a blank book, in a certain order of time or subject. A more beautiful or precious morsel of ethics I have never seen. It is a document in proof that *I* am a *real Christian*, that is to say, a disciple of the doctrines of Jesus, very different from the Platonists, who call *me* infidel, and *themselves* Christians and preachers of the gospel, while they draw all their characteristic dogmas from what it's Author never said nor saw. They have compounded from the heathen mysteries a system beyond the comprehension of man, of which the great reformer of the vicious ethics and deism of the Jews, were he to return on earth, would not recognise one feature. If I had time I would add to my little book the Greek, Latin and French texts, in columns side by side, and I wish I could subjoin a translation of Gassendi's Syntagma of the doctrines of Epicurus, which, notwithstanding the calumnies of the Stoics, and caricatures of Cicero, is the most rational system remaining of the philosophy of the ancients, as frugal of vicious indulgence, and fruitful of virtue as the hyperbolical extravagancies of his rival sects.

I retain good health, am rather feeble to walk much, but ride with ease, passing two or three hours a day on horseback, and every three or four months taking, in a carriage, a journey of 90. miles to a distant possession, where I pass a good deal of my time. My eyes need the aid of glasses by night, and with small print in the day also; my hearing not quite so sensible as it used to be; no tooth shaking yet, but shivering and shrinking in body from the cold we now experience, my thermometer having been as low as 12.° this morning. My greatest oppression is a correspondence afflictingly laborious, the extent of which I have been long endeavoring to curtail. This keeps me at the drudgery of the writing table all the prime hours of the day, leaving for the gratification of my appetite for reading only what I can steal from the hours of sleep. Could I reduce this epistolary corvée within the limits of my friends, and affairs, and give the time redeemed from it to reading and reflection, to history, ethics, mathematics, my life would be as happy as the infirmities of age would admit, and I should look to it's consummation with the composure of one 'qui summum nec metuit diem nec optat.'

So much as to myself; and I have given you this string of egotisms in the hope of drawing a similar one from yourself. I have heard from others that you retain your health, a good degree of activity, and all the vivacity and chearfulness of your mind. But I wish to learn it more minutely from yourself. How has time affected your health, your strength, your faculties and spirits? What are your amusements literary and social? Tell me every thing about yourself, because all will be interesting to one who retains for you ever the same constant & affectionate friendship & respect.

Tн: Jefferson

RC (DLC: Charles Thomson Papers); misdated 1815 but recorded in SJL under 9 Jan. 1816; addressed: "Charles Thompson esq. near Philadelphia"; franked and postmarked: "Milton Va 16 Jany." As the RC is slightly damaged, several words have been supplied from PoC (DLC).

The synopsis in question was Charles Thomson, *A Synopsis of the Four Evangelists; or, A Regular History of the Conception, Birth, Doctrine, Miracles, Death, Resurrection, and Ascension of Jesus, in the Words of the Evangelists* (Philadelphia, 1815). Acting on instructions from Thomson, the former secretary of the Continental Congress who was also a noted biblical scholar, Dr. Robert Patterson had sent TJ a copy of the *Synopsis* (Patterson to TJ, 24 Nov. 1815). GASSENDI'S SYNTAGMA was Pierre Gassendi, *Syntagma Epicuri Philosophiae* (The Hague, 1659). QUI SUMMUM NEC METUIT DIEM NEC OPTAT: "Who neither fears the last day nor hopes for it"— an adaptation of Marcus Valerius Mar-

tialis, *Epigramata* (Amsterdam, 1701), 47, 1. ult.

This letter to Thomson proved to be a source of embarrassment and annoyance to TJ. For some reason the letter itself did not reach the eighty-seven-year-old Thomson until April 1816, at which time he was suffering the effects of a paralytic stroke (Thomson to TJ, 16 May 1816). While in this condition Thomson left the letter in Dr. Patterson's home and proceeded to give a garbled version of it to friends that left them with the impression that TJ had expressed a much more favorable opinion of orthodox Christianity than was in fact the case (Thomson to TJ, undated). As a result, rumors began to circulate in Philadelphia and elsewhere that TJ had converted to Christianity and was about to publish a book on the subject. For TJ's sometimes stern denials of these reports, see his letters to Margaret Bayard Smith, 6 Aug. 1816, and to George Logan, 12 Nov. 1816, printed below.

From Francis Adrian Van der Kemp

Sɪʀ   Oldenbarneveld 24 March 1816.

The many condescending proofs, which I received from your politeness imbue me with the confidence to Sollicit another favour from your kindness. I know too well, I can have no claims, but that, which originates in your indulgence, and in your ardent wish to promote the indagation of truth. About three years past I Spend a few days with my old respected friend at Quincy, whom you, perhaps, know, that continues to favour me with his affectionate esteem. Various topics of literature were then freely discussed, and as I enjoy'd his full confidence, Some of a more Serious cast. He had then lately received from you a *Syllabus*, exhibiting your view on a most momentous Subject. Developing it in part, he favoured me at last with its perusal for a few moments; I was Surprised with this new point of view and deemed it deserving a more full consideration. I requested a copy: this was peremtorily refused, as He was not at liberty to keep one for himself, and was resolved not to violate this Sacred truth. Its memory was nearly erased from my mind, at least its traces were so faint, that recollection was not powerful enough to call up again its Summary. This Spring I received, with a parcel of Books, among whom *The Month: Repos. of Theol: and Gen: Literat:* which by its candour would entertain you in a moment of leisure, Belsham's Mem. of my late friend Th. Lindsey in which Pag. 539 I once more did see your Views of Christianity. Some what in a cloud, I wrote on the blank page at P. 539 "I have Seen this view with Surprise and delight, and regret, that I was not permitted to copy it. It Showeth an unprejudiced Inquirer, and a Sincere lover of truth."

Actuated by the Same motives, which impelled you to that communication, I now Sollicit, to grant me the favour of the Same Sight, with which you honoured my friend, under what restrictions, you may please to command. I will engage to adhere faithfully to these, even, if required, to return it uncopied. I request in Such a case only the permission, of extracting its leading features. But could you look at it as so much interesting, as I consider it, then you would allow me its copying, with the Liberty to send it to my correspondents in England, for insertion in the Month. Rev. when it shall open the way for its more full and impartial discussion. I would forbear to hint even at your name, till you self should have given leave. I doubt not or it must do good.

Having in view, if my days are prolonged, to draw up a history of J.C. it would be of great use to me, to contemplate the whole in this new point. If after all prudence dictates to decline my demand, I shall not be hurted by it, but then yet I should not regret my application, if by it you was induced to communicate this plan for discussion, to one of your European friends, and then Great Brittain again must be the spot where it shall appear.

I was yesterday gratified with a few lines of my old respected friend. His Strength fails, his Lady is on the decline, and Shall, I apprehend, Sink under this Severe attack of illness, and He would not Survive Her long. She is indeed an accomplished woman! So my old friends go away—Pentionary de Gyzelaer, my oldest friend Dr. Toulmin, at the time, he intended, as his legacy, to publish my corrected Sketch on the Achaic Republic—Both gone! and if those Worthies follow, I am nearly left alone.

I expect, ere long, the criticisms of de Witt Clinton upon my *Philosophical Researches* which you have seen in embryo, and which my young friend C. Eliot, after the correction of the Idiom, intended to publish, had he not been prevented by death. Now they remain with the rest of my lucubrations here, to be burned in the tomb of the Capulets.

I am informed by my Correspondents in Europe, that my Sketch on the Moral and Physical causes, which I corrected and enlarged by the hints with which you honoured me, begins to attract Some notice. I Should rejoyce, if such a momentous work was undertaken; then I Should reap a large and honourable recompence.

I dare not encroach longer on your precious time, but confide, that you will not misinterpret the Liberty, which I have taken. Permit me without any further apology to assure you, that I remain with unabated respect and the highest consideration Sir! your most obed: humble Servant,   Fr. Adr. van der Kemp

RC (DLC); endorsed by TJ as received 9 Apr. 1816 and so recorded in SJL.

Van der Kemp never wrote his projected HISTORY OF J. C. (Henry F. Jackson, *Scholar in the Wilderness, Francis Adrian Van der Kemp* [Syracuse, N.Y., 1963], p. 241-42). The SKETCH ON THE ACHAIC REPUBLIC was an unpublished history of the Achaean league of cities (280-146 B.C.) in which Van der Kemp sought to convince Americans that maintaining a balanced government was the firmest guarantee of republicanism (same, p. 176-85). Van der Kemp also failed to find a publisher for his PHILOSOPHICAL RESEARCHES, a lengthy treatise on natural history in which, among other things, he discussed TJ's *Notes on the State of Virginia* (same, p. 158-70). Van der Kemp's SKETCH ON THE MORAL AND PHYSICAL CAUSES was the outline of a projected history entitled "Moral and Physical Causes of the Revolutionary Spirit in the Latter Part of the 18th Century, with their Probable Issue on both Continents." The outline was published in the October 1813 issue of the *General Repository and Review*, a Boston periodical; the history itself was never written (same, p. 235-38). For TJ's HINTS on this "Sketch," see TJ to Van der Kemp, 22 Mch. 1812.

To Francis Adrian Van der Kemp

SIR   Poplar Forest near Lynchburg Apr. 25. 16.

Your favor of Mar. 24. was handed to me just as I was setting out on a journey of time and distance, which will explain the date of this both as to time and place.—The Syllabus, which is the subject of your letter, was addressed to a friend to whom I had promised a more detailed view. But finding I should never have time for that, I sent him what I thought should be the Outlines of such a work. The same subject entering sometimes into the correspondence between Mr. Adams and myself, I sent him a copy of it. The friend to whom it had been first addressed dying soon after, I asked from his family the return of the original, as a confidential communication, which they kindly sent me. So that no copy of it, but that in possession of Mr. Adams, now exists out of my own hands. I have used this caution, lest it should get out in connection with my name; and I was unwilling to draw on myself a swarm of insects, whose buz is more disquieting than their bite.—As an abstract thing, and without any intimation from what quarter derived, I can have no objection to it's being committed to the consideration of the world. I believe it may even do good by producing discussion, and finally a true view of the merits of this great reformer. Pursuing the same ideas after writing the Syllabus, I made, for my own satisfaction, an Extract from the Evangelists of the texts of his morals, selecting those only whose style and spirit proved them genuine, and his own: and they are as distinguishable from the matter in which they are imbedded as diamonds in dunghills. A more precious morsel of ethics was never seen. It was too hastily done however, being the work of one or two evenings only, while I lived at Washington, overwhelmed with other business: and it is my intention to go over it again at more leisure. This shall be the work of the ensuing winter. I gave it the title of 'The Philosophy of Jesus extracted from the text of the Evangelists.'—To this Syllabus and Extract, if a history of his life can be added, written with the same view of the subject, the world will see, after the fogs shall be dispelled, in which for 14. centuries he has been inveloped by Jugglers to make money of him, when the genuine character shall be exhibited, which they have dressed up in the rags of an Impostor, the world, I say, will at length see the immortal merit of this first of human Sages. I rejoice that you think of undertaking this work. It is one I have long wished to see written on the scale of a Laertius or a Nepos. Nor can it be a work of labor, or of volume. For his journeyings from Judaea to Samaria, and Samaria to Galilee, do not cover much country; and the incidents of his life require little research. They are all at hand, and need only to be put into human dress; noticing such only as are within the physical laws of nature, and offending none by a denial, or even a mention, of what is not. If the Syllabus and Extract (which is short) either in substance, or at large, are worth a place under the same cover with your biography, they are at your service. I ask one only condition, that no possibility shall be admitted of my name being even intimated with the publication. If done in England, as you seem to contemplate, there will be the less likelihood of my being thought of. I shall be much gratified to learn that you pursue your intention of writing the life of Jesus, and pray to accept the assurances of my great respect and esteem.   TH: JEFFERSON

RC (NBuHi); not recorded in SJL. Although TJ mentioned no enclosure, he did in fact enclose a copy of his 21 Apr. 1803 letter to Benjamin Rush and the "Syllabus" (Van der Kemp to TJ, 4 June 1816, printed below). PoC (DLC).

Diogenes LAERTIUS (200-250) and Cornelius NEPOS (100-125 B.C.) were the authors of biographical sketches of noted ancient philosophers and statesmen that were primarily designed to reveal the characters of their subjects rather than to give factually accurate accounts of their lives and times. See Sowerby, comp., *Catalogue*, Nos. 31-33, 70-73; Sir Paul Harvey, *The Oxford Companion to Classical Literature* (Oxford, 1937), p. 146, 286.

From Francis Adrian Van der Kemp

SIR   Oldenbarneveld 4 June 1816.

Accept my Sincerest thanks for the distinguished proof of your confidential esteem, with which you have been pleased to gratify me. I Suppose I consult your wishes to copy it, and send it in my handwriting to my friend in England, for publication in the *Month. Repos. of Theol.* with the expressed request, that neither he or his friends by insinuation or allusion should drop a hint with respect to the presumtive Author, but invite a fair discussion of this interesting Subject, except leave to act in a contrary course was obtained from me in expressed words.

I know from experience, my master Van der Marck Prof. at Law, having been a victim to a persecuting clergy, not because he was not Orthodox, which he was indeed in a Superlative degree, but because he resisted the Hierarchy, and would not Submit to clerical power. And had I not received this lesson in my youth, the warnings of my friend Adams, before I crossed the Atlantic, not to meddle here with topics of controversy, would have been Solemn enough, to make me avoid that rock, and generally, with one or two exceptions, I Steered free. A Sketch of the hist. of Calvin and Servetus was inserted in the Vol. of the Monthl. Repos. for 1810, but yet, incedi per ignes.

An estimate of the doctrine of Jezus, and a view of his history, on the proposed plan, are two desirable Subjects, requiring more candour than learning, an unbiassed mind, and ardent love of truth. Such an investigation, even if it is not at first carried to perfection must effectually promote the Gospel-cause, which, in my opinion, Stands Stedfast, on a rock.

All heterogeneous materials ought to be carefully set aside, nothing precariously assumed, and from one undisputed or proved fact proceeded to the next. The Sublime doctrine of a first wise and good Being, the pure and elevated moral doctrine, with the certainty of a future life, contain the Summary of the Christ: Revelation. The remaining are hay and Stubbles. You presume, that according with this plan, I have adopted the Devine interposition—miracles—the revival of a man—died on the cross. Without this last point, I cannot perceive, that with all the excellence of that doctrine above others, we have advanced one Single Step farther than before. Immortality remains desirable, but cannot be proved.

On this Subject you will permit me a few words more. In my youth, educated as others, but Surrounded with young men of Superior Talents, I soon rejected what, though not examined, appeared absurd, inquired for my Self, and ransacked all that was written on the Subject in France and England. Soon I was convinced that truth was not the only aim of the opposers, neither was allways at their Side. An utter Stranger to polemical Divinity, as what I had learnd from the catechism, well armed with preparatory knowledge of Languages, hist. and Antiquities, I resolved to enquire in the truth. I became persuaded of the hist. truth of Christianity, now I proceeded to examine its doctrine. If it had a divine origine, it must be so plain "that any man, of the meanest capacities, but with a sound head and honest heart, could discover it with ease." With this axiom, taken for granted, I supposed, the four Evang: and Acts must contain this doctrine. These I would endeavour to read, as if they were Send me and I had lived in those times, however with the allowance, that even now, they ought to have the Same effect. All what I did not plainly understand, at first, by an attent perusal, I passed by. This was not for me. At the end of my enquiry, the doctrine I had gathered, was plain and Simple. I renewed the perusal, Several times, without further progress, and have Since forty years, having more than once repeated this critical examination, not gathered a more ample Stock; by this, you must perceive that I am no proper person to enter the list of the Champions of divinity. Neither am I longing to obtain that distinction.

I hope your life may be Spared to finish your plan, of which I anticipate, that it must do good. Several years past I Send to my old friend Dr. Toulmin a life of Jezus which, as he informed me then, never reached him. I cannot repair that loss, as by the Sale of my large Library, before I left Europe, retaining only a few remnants of ancient and modern Literature and history and Philosophy, I would be unable to retrace that plan. But, as I possess many Separate fragments, relating to this Subject, if my days are prolonged, I may yet, and it is my intention, institute an Inquiry—"what there is in the Jewish writings about a Messiah, what opinions the cotemporaries of Jezus friends and foes had of him, and what he instilled in his disciples, what they learned of him in Public." You will say, this is not an easy task, and in this I agree, but I deem it feasible.

I include a copy of the Letter which I send to England to accompany it and am confident that my Correspondents shall make no abuse of it by any hints, even the most distant.

Are you acquainted with Goethens ingenious conjecture, "that not one word of what we call the Decalogues, was written on the two Tables?" It is in 14 vol. of his Schriften. If unknown to you, and you wish to see it, I shall make a translation, as soon the Season of labouring, to which I must Submit, is over, and the fall or winter permits me to return to my Study. Permit me to Sollicit the continuance of your favourable regard and believe, that I remain with Sentiments of high respect Sir! Your most obed: and obliged Sert.,

FR. ADR. VAN DER KEMP

RC (DLC); endorsed by TJ as received 19 June 1816 and so recorded in SJL. Enclosure: a text (missing) of Van der Kemp's 1 July 1816 letter to the editor of the *Monthly Repository*; see notes below.

TJ's 21 Apr. 1803 letter to Benjamin Rush and the accompanying "Syllabus" constituted the DISTINGUISHED PROOF OF YOUR CONFIDENTIAL ESTEEM. Van der Kemp arranged for the publication of these two items, suitably altered by TJ so as to disguise any trace of his authorship, in *The Monthly Repository of Theology and General Literature*, XI (Oct. 1816), 573-74, together with an introductory letter of his own to the editor of this London Unitarian periodical which also carefully concealed TJ's identity. However, Van der Kemp must have been less cautious in his private correspondence with the editor of the *Monthly Repository*, for the letter to Rush and the "Syllabus" appeared in print with a prefatory editorial note stating that they were the work of "an eminent American Statesman, whose name we are not at liberty to mention, but who will probably be recognized by such of our readers as are acquainted with the characters of the leading men in the American revolution" (same, p. 573). With the aid of this clue, John

Quincy Adams, then serving as American ambassador to London, immediately recognized both documents as TJ's work and so informed his parents in Massachusetts (John Quincy Adams to Abigail Adams, 19 Nov. 1816, MHi: AM). For a while TJ feared that this editorial indiscretion would reveal his authorship of these documents to the world, but there is no evidence that any other reader of the *Monthly Repository* guessed his secret, perhaps because the periodical was not widely known in America (Van der Kemp to TJ, 20 Feb. 1817 and 30 Mch. 1817; TJ to Van der Kemp, 16 Mch. 1817 and 1 May 1817).

The COPY OF THE LETTER WHICH I SEND TO ENGLAND was evidently an early draft (missing) of Van der Kemp's introductory letter to the editor of the *Monthly Repository*, which was printed under the date 1 July 1816 with TJ's letter to Rush and the "Syllabus."

Goethe made this INGENIOUS CONJECTURE in a 1773 essay entitled "Zwo wichtige bisher unerörterte Biblische Fragen zum erstenmal gründlich beantwortet" (Goethe, *Schriften*, 4 vols. in 2 [Karlsruhe, 1778-80], IV, 29-50). TJ and John Adams had already discussed this CONJECTURE some years before (Adams to TJ, 14 Nov. 1813, and TJ to Adams, 24 Jan. 1814).

From Francis Adrian Van der Kemp

SIR   Oldenbarneveld 14 July 1816.

The distinguished proof of your esteem, with which you favoured and gratified me, when you honoured me with your letter of Apr.

25. induces me to take the liberty of Sending you a few lines more. I am pleased to Suppose, that my last has not been unacceptable and that you approved the course, which I have taken with the papers with whom I was entrusted. These are now on their way to Old England. Since I wrote my last I received a highly valuable parcel of books from there, of which I doubt not, are Several would be perused by you with delight: they are written in that Spirit which recommend themselves to elevated minds. Among these were Kenricks discourses and several of Belsham's works. Was I so fortunate to live in your neighbourhood, I should not hesitate with their communication, in the full confidence, that this would be acceptable. But the same unavailing wish I have often indulged with my old friend at Quincey, and yet, I was once unexpectedly, blessed with the opportunity of visiting him.

Among these Theological works is one excentric production, which I regret, that I cannot communicate to either of you, as it is a masterly performance in burlesque, viz. a defence of the orthodox System, against Unitarian Heretics "a new way of answering old heresies by *Basanistes*." He not only defends a Triune God, but defends a *Quaternity*. Moses is the fourth person! The third ed: has appeared.

Did I live nearer your residence I should flatter my self, that you might communicate with me your proposed lucubrations, for your next winter amusement. Now I hope, when you have accomplished this momentous task, you will condescend to favour me with its outlines. Permit me now a few words on the Syllabus, which I have perused again and again, and I do not retract my former favorable opinion of it. I hope, it may be seen in the same point of view by my Brittish friends, and I am Satisfied its publishing must eventually have a good effect.

Upon what grounds do you assert that the Mosaic Religion did imbue degrading and injurious ideas of God and his attributes?

Why do you Suppose that the reason of Jezus had not attained the maximum of his energy?

In what point was his System of moral duties deficient? and in what point were his doctrines defective?

How could he emphatically, by what I understand to a clear conviction, preach the doctrine of a future state, if his dead and resurrection are not above Suspicion?

To my last query it is required that I explain, that on my opinion it is the basis of the Christian revelation, the ground of all my future hopes. As I am persuaded, that man perish by death, as well as beast, it may be desirable, it may be made plausible, that he should be immortal. But this too is the utmost, and I see no incongruity, that it takes no place even admitting, an intelligent good Being governing the universe. But a dark veil on the human existence is drawn away, if his existence is to be continued, if he shall revive again, with his former consciousness. Of this gospel truth I am firmly persuaded. But the ground of my conviction is that Jezus was a man, in every respect, that he proclaimed true doctrine, that he died, and was, in its confirmation, restored again to life.

I know not, if we shall agree in so far, but then I have one solid ground of consolation more, or some arguments must have made a deeper impression on your mind, which lost their efficacy on mine. It matters not in my opinion, if we adopt the Souls immateriality or not, whatever this may be, without the evidence of Jezus resurrection. I should believe that both are perishable, or, to soften this harsh language, I should not be able to foster my solid hope, upon my continued existence, although I might loung for it.

If my friend Dr. W. Willoughby returns next winter to Congress, it might not be amiss, to give him Basanistes as a guide to Monticello. He wished to pay his respect to you, and deserves in every regard to be favoured with your kind reception, being a man of sterling worth. Grant me the privilege, that I may continue to assure you that I remain with high consideration Sir! your most obed: and obliged Sert.,   FR. ADR. VAN DER KEMP

RC (MHi); endorsed by TJ as received 26 July 1816 and so recorded in SJL.

These specific DISCOURSES by John Kenrick and WORKS by Thomas Belsham, two English Unitarian ministers, have not been identified. The MASTERLY PERFORMANCE in question was Basanistes, AIPE-ΣΕΩΝ ΑΝΑΣΤΑΣΙΣ: or, A New Way of Deciding old Controversies, 3d. ed. (London 1815). "Basanistes," a leading English Unitarian periodical reported, "is said to be a clergyman of the Established Church" (The Monthly Repository of Theology and General Literature, XI [May 1816], 288). DR. W. WILLOUGHBY was Westel Willoughby, Jr. (1769-1844), a New York physician and judge who served in the U.S. House of Representatives, 1815-1817.

To Francis Adrian Van der Kemp

DEAR SIR   Monticello July 30. 16.

Your favor of July 14. is recieved, and I am entirely satisfied with the disposition you have made of the Syllabus, keeping my name unconnected with it, as I am sure you have done. I should really be gratified to see a full and fair examination of the ground it takes. I believe it to be the only ground on which reason and truth can take their stand, and that only against which we are told that the gates of hell shall not finally prevail. Yet I have little expectation that the affirmative can be freely maintained in England. We know it could not here. For altho' we have freedom of religious opinion by law, we are yet under the inquisition of public opinion: and in England it would have both law and public opinion to encounter. The love of peace, and a want of either time or taste for these disquisitions, induce silence on my part as to the contents of this paper, and all explanations and discussions which might arise out of it; and this must be my apology for observing the same silence on the questions of your letter. I leave the thing to the evidence of the books on which it claims to be founded, and with which I am persuaded you are more familiar than myself.—Altho' I rarely waste time in reading on theological subjects, as mangled by our Pseudo-Christians, yet I can readily suppose Basanistos may be amusing. Ridicule is the only weapon which can be used against unintelligible propositions. Ideas must be distinct before reason can act upon them; and no man ever had a distinct idea of the trinity. It is the mere Abracadabra of the mountebanks calling themselves the priests of Jesus. If it could be understood it would not answer their purpose. Their security is in their faculty of shedding darkness, like the scuttle fish, thro' the element in which they move, and making it impenetrable to the eye of a pursuing enemy. And there they will skulk, until some rational creed can occupy the void which the obliteration of their duperies would leave in the minds of our honest and unsuspecting brethren. Whenever this shall take place, I believe that Christianism may be universal and eternal. I salute you with great esteem and respect.

TH: JEFFERSON

RC (NBuHi); address cover mutilated, with loss of frank; addressed to Van der Kemp "at Oldenbarnevelt near Trenton, New York"; postmarked "Milton Va 31 July." PoC (DLC).

To Margaret Bayard Smith

Monticello. Aug. 6. 16

I have recieved, dear Madam, your very friendly letter of July 21. and Assure you that I feel with deep sensibility it's kind expressions towards my self, and the more as from a person than whom no other's could be more in sympathy with my own affections. I often call to mind the occasions of knowing your worth, which the societies of Washington furnished; and none more than those derived from your much valued visit to Monticello. I recognise the same motives of goodness in the solicitude you express on the rumor supposed to proceed from a letter of mine to Charles Thomson on the subject of the Christian religion. It is true that, in writing to the translator of the Bible and Testament, that subject was mentioned: but equally so that no adherence to any particular mode of Christianity was there expressed; nor any change of opinions suggested. A change from what? The priests indeed have heretofore thought proper to ascribe to me religious, or rather antireligious sentiments, of their own fabric, but such as soothed their resentments against the Act of Virginia for establishing religious freedom. They wished him to be thought Atheist, Deist, or Devil, who could advocate freedom from their religious dictations. But I have ever thought religion a concern purely between our god and our consciences, for which we were accountable to him, and not to the priests. I never told my own religion, nor scrutinised that of another. I never attempted to make a convert, nor wished to change another's creed. I have ever judged of the religion of others by their lives: and by this test, my dear Madam, I have been satisfied yours must be an excellent one, to have produced a life of such exemplary virtue and correctness. For it is in our lives, and not from our words, that our religion must be read. By the same test the world must judge me. But this does not satisfy the priesthood. They must have a positive, a declared assent to all their interested absurdities. My opinion is that there would never have been an infidel, if there had never been a priest. The artificial structures they have built on the purest of all moral systems, for the purpose of deriving from it pence and power, revolts those who think for themselves, and who read in that system only what is really there. These therefore they brand with such nicknames as their enmity chuses gratuitously to impute. I have left the world, in silence, to judge of causes from their effects: and I am consoled in this course, my dear friend, when I percieve the candor with which I am judged by your justice and discernment; and that, notwithstanding the slanders of the Saints, my fellow-citizens have thought me worthy of trusts. The imputations of irreligion having spent their force, they think an imputation of change might now be turned to account as a boulster for their duperies. I shall leave them, as heretofore to grope on in the dark.

Our family at Monticello is all in good health; Ellen speaking of you with affection, and Mrs. Randolph always regretting the accident which so far deprived her of the happiness of your former visit. She still cherishes the hope of some future renewal of that kindness; in which we all join her, as in the assurances of affectionate attachment and respect.   Th: Jefferson

RC (DLC: J. Henley Smith Papers); addressed: "Mrs. M. Harrison Smith to the care of Mr. Samuel Boyd Pine street Philadelphia"; franked and postmarked: "CHARLOTville Va Aug 7"; docketed: "Dead Letters"; "not found Ar."

Margaret Bayard Smith (1778-1844), a Washington social leader and novelist, was the wife of Samuel Harrison Smith, the editor from 1800 to 1810 of the *National Intelligencer and Washington Advertiser*, a highly partisan Jeffersonian newspaper.

Despite her own Federalist proclivities, Mrs. Smith had been a close friend of TJ and his family during TJ's presidency. Her VERY FRIENDLY FAVOR OF JULY 21. sought to ascertain the truth of "a rumour which has lately become the topic of conversation; which is, that in a letter which you have written to Mr. Charles Thompson, you have express'd opinions so highly favorable to the christian religion, that they amount to a profession of faith."

From Francis Adrian Van der Kemp

DEAR SIR   Oldenbarneveld 1 Nov. 1816.

Reperusing your interesting Syllabus I have recalled in my mind a train of thoughts, which I brought in writing about twenty years past and Send them, for his criticisms, to my old friend Joshua Toulmin of Taunton, father of the judge in the Missisippi Territory, which treatise has been irrecoverably lost on its passage to England.

Having hurted my right leg, in my garden, by carelessness, which through neglect of it has compelled me to leave of working for a few days, I employ'd this leisure time in digesting a plan, upon which, en gros, with my desirable modifications, an interesting work might be executed. I shall send a copy to Mss-bay. It might be, that one of its worthies was willing to undertake the task. It would require a thorough acquaintance with ancient history, an unbiassed mind, and willingness to pay homage to truth, whatever it might be discovered, a vast deal of time, and a well provided Library: from these requisites, to which you might join others, you perceive I can not be the man.

I did not hesitate to use your own expressions, as the Syllabus was in many respect the ground work, and shall be gratified, if you can find it proper, to remove the defects, and Supply the weak parts with props. By this, another may be enabled to raise an elegant Superstructure.

Dr. W. Willoughby, member of Congress, eminent as a Physician and respected by all parties, and beloved by all who knew, desired to be introduced to Monticello. Perhaps I shall be so free in sending him a Letter of introduction, when he returns to Washington. Permit

me to assure you, that I remain with high respect and consideration
Dear Sir! your obed. and obliged St., FR. ADR. VANDERKEMP

P.S. May I Sollicit, if you published any thing else besides your
Valuable Notes, to gratify me with a copy?

ENCLOSURE

Memoirs
respecting the person and doctrine of J. C.
Compiled from S. S.

Outlines

Part. i

Preliminary discussions
  Developement of the general principles of nat: Religion.
  Inquiry in the Authenticity of the S. S., of the Jewish writings—the LXX.
    Examination of *Astruc's* hypothesis, arguments, objections, of Goethen's.
  Delineation of the Jewish nation, character, *remarquable periods*, under the
    Patriarchs, the *Legislation of Moses*, under the judges, kings, before, in,
    and after the *Babylonian captivity*, after the *destruction* of Jeruzalem, deg-
    radation, dispersion and preservation as a distinct People.
  Religion of the Jews
    Theism—morality
    Examination of their principles and correctness.
General view of the heathen world before the Christian æra
  Ancient Philosophers—Oriental, Greece, Rome, Indian, Chinese.
    Merits and *defects.*
  Comparison with the Jews

Part. ii

Life, Character, doctrine of Jezus.
Preliminary observations
Inquiry in the authenticity of the S. s. *Arguments, objections.*
  Particular discussions—Inspiration &c. Rules of criticism &c.
Concise view of the various Systems of Divinity among christians.
  Inquiry in the authenticity of the first Chapt. of Matthew and Luke.
  Apparition of angels—hymns of Simeon—Hana
  Miraculous conception and *birth.*
  Inquiry in its usefulness—necessity.
Chronological observations with regard to the time of the birth of Jezus.
  Discussion of the arguments pleaded for Jezus being more than a man—of
    being a Spiritual head of the pious—*being* a proof of his high dignity.
  Examination of various passages of S. S. 2 King. IV. 16. Jes. IX. 5/6 &c.
    of God preparing him a body—not according the ordinary Laws of Nature
    Hebr. X. 5. made of a *woman* Gal. IV. 4. not of a *Virgin* Matth. xi. 9.
    &c.
General observation.
"All what is necessary to believe and to do, to Secure our happiness, must have

been So clearly revealed, as to be understood without any difficulty by any one of a Sound judgment and a Sincere heart."

Consequences.

Discussion

i. What Messiah was expected by the Jews?
   a. Consideration of the Jewish Prophecies.
   b. application of these.

ii. What ideas entertained the Jews of Jezus?
   a. His *enemies*—and *impartial observers*
   b. his *friends* and *disciples.*

iii. With what ideas did Jezus imbue his Disciples about himself?

iv. Causes of the different conceptions among his followers.
   Oriental Philosophy—Gnosticism—Platonism.

Corollary

The fundamental part of the Christian Revelation is, the *Divine Mission* of Jezus—not his person—character—
Requisites—Examination.

Part. iii

Life of Jezus of Nazareth
   Great outlines
   His *person, character, views, doctrine, Success*

i. Was he really a man?

Conclusion from Adam's creation considered Luke i. 1/2. Where is thy Father Jo. viii. 19 comp. with 27. He followed his Father's trade Marc. vi. 3. His progress in mental endowments, though without a liberal education, gradual Luc. ii. 42/52 ii Sam. 3 vs. 24-26. 1 Cor. xv. 22. comp: with Gen: ii. 7.

Did Jezus exist before his birth? Examination of Jo. i. 18. ἐις τον κολπου. "In conviviis dilectissime Solebant in sinu ejus accumbere, qui convivii Princeps esset["] (Grotius, Elsner). εν κολπῳ τινος ειυφι by which Summa familiaritas et censi horum cum aliquo communicatio is intended. It is used of married Deut xiii. 6. xxviii. 54-6.

ii. Had Jezus a human body and soul? Was he man, an Angelic being or Man-God?

   Concessions—by Orthodox—Skeptics.

§18 That Jezus had a real *human nature*, with *all* its frailties, sin excepted, having been conceived in the body of the beatified Virgin Mary, by the power of the holy ghost, without the concurrence of man, and has not only adopted human nature in regard to the body, but a real *human Soul* too, to become a real man, because this was necessary, as body and Soul were lost.

§19. Jezus human nature did loose *nothing* of her properties by her *inseparable* union and junction with the Godhead, but he remained a creature, had a beginning of existence, being of a finite nature, preserving every thing, which belongs to a real body, and, though by its resurrection it *became* immortal, the reality of his human nature was not altered, because, our salvation and resurrection were depending from the reality of the body.

But these two natures have been *so* conjointed in *one* person, that *even* by the death of Jezus they have not been separated: so was, what he, dying, recommended in the hands of his Father, a *real human Spirit*, who departed from his body: but, in the mean time, the Godhead remained allways conjoined with the human part, *even then*, as it laid in the tomb, and the Godhead did not cease to be in him, even as she was, when he *was* a babe, although she for some time did not reveal herself.—*Confessn. of the Ref.* Church Synod. Dort. 1618/9

That he in body and soul, during his *whole* life, but particularly at the *end of his life* bore the wrath of God against the Sin of the whole human race—Heidelb. catech. answ. to Q 37. Comp: with the 2. art. of the church of England 1562.

For if the divine essence, or godhead, did not enter *into the womb of the* Virgin, when was it, that that fulness of the Godhead, which dwelled in him bodily col. ii. 9. did enter into him.—Rob. Clayton Bish. of Clogher's Vindic. of the O. & N. T. Lett. v. Pag. 446. Lond. 1759.

(b) *Skeptics*—Eulogiums.

ii *Character of Jezus*—the most *innocent*—the most *benevolent* the most eloquent and sublime. His courage, prudence, wisdom, humility, Philanthropy.

    Consideration of his forbidding to declare himself the Messiah.

    Matth xii. 20 Marc. xviii. 29/30 Luc. ix. 20-25.

    His devout temper—in prayer—compassion—filial obedience. Luc. ii. 42 Love and delight in the service of God.

iii *His views and doctrine.*

    Personal, in regard to *mankind.*

    Pure Theism, nature and attributes of God.

    Perfect morality, the most benevolent and Sublime that ever was taught.

    Comparison with that of other Philosophers: *ancient modern:*—with *Moses* and *Mahomet.*

    Belief in a future state—unquestionable proof of its certainty.

Miracles: definition—Requisites—end, not for ostentation but, to attain a great end, to evince beyond doubt the interposition of *All-mighty power.* Their *defence*, extent.

iv. *Success* of his enterprize.

    Obstacles, disadvantages

    Prejudices among the great, the Scientific, the Vulgar.

His doctrine not committed in writing, his disciples illiterate men.

    Consideration of the state of Christianity upon the hypothesis—"that he was an Enthusiast or Impostor, so too his disciples."

    Conclusion—Prognostic.

RC (DLC); endorsed by TJ as received 21 Nov. 1816 and so recorded in SJL. TJ also noted in his endorsement the following topics for his reply: "Syllabus Dr. Willoughby Any thing except Notes?" Enclosure: "Memoirs . . . of J.C." Van der Kemp also sent a text of this enclosure to John Adams with a letter of 4 Nov. 1816 (MHi: AM).

ASTRUC'S HYPOTHESIS, as Van der Kemp explained to John Adams, "is that Moses writings have in great part been compiled from ancient traditions, hist. fragments, monuments and genealogies" (Van der Kemp to Adams, 4 Nov. 1816, in MHi: AM). Jean Astruc (1684-1766), a French physician who occasionally dabbled in theology, advanced this seminal hypothesis in *Conjectures sur les mémoires originaux dont il paroi que Moyse s'est servi pour composer le livre de la Génèse* (Brussels, 1753).

ἐις του κολπου . . . IS INTENDED: "In the bosom: 'At banquets the favorites used to recline in the bosom of the one who presided over the banquet['] (Grotius, Elsner). To be in someone's bosom: by which the closest possible intimacy and the sharing of the wealth of these with someone is intended."

To George Logan

DEAR SIR   Poplar Forest near Lynchburg Nov. 12. 16.

I recieved your favor of Oct. 16. at this place, where I pass much of my time, very distant from Monticello. I am quite astonished at the idea which seems to have got abroad; that I propose publishing something on the subject of religion. And this is said to have arisen from a letter of mine to my friend Charles Thompson, in which certainly there is no trace of such an idea. When we see religion split into so many thousands of sects, and I may say Christianity itself divided into it's thousands also, who are disputing, anathematising, and where the laws permit, burning and torturing one another for abstractions which no one of them understand, and which are indeed beyond the comprehension of the human mind, into which of the chambers of this Bedlam would a man wish to thrust himself. The sum of all religion as expressed by it's best preacher, 'fear god and love thy neighbor,' contains no mystery, needs no explanation—but this wont do. It gives no scope to make dupes; priests could not live by it. Your ideas of the moral obligations of governments are perfectly correct. The man who is dishonest as a statesman would be a dishonest man in any station. It is strangely absurd to suppose that a million of human beings collected together are not under the same moral laws which bind each of them separately. It is a great consolation to me that our government, as it cherishes most it's duties to it's own citizens, so is it the most exact in it's moral conduct towards other nations. I do not believe that in the four administrations which have taken place, there has been a single instance of departure from good faith towards other nations. We may sometimes have mistaken our rights, or made an erroneous estimate of the actions of others, but no voluntary wrong can be imputed to us. In this respect England exhibits the most remarkable phaenomenom in the universe in the contrast between the profligacy of it's government and the probity of it's citizens. And accordingly it is now exhibiting an example of the truth of the maxim that virtue and interest are inseparable. It ends, as might have been expected, in the ruin of it's people. But this ruin will fall heaviest, as it ought to fall, on that hereditary aristocracy which has for generations been preparing the catastrophe. I hope we shall take warning from the example and crush in it's birth the aristocracy of our monied corporations which dare already to challenge our government to a trial of strength, and to bid defiance to the laws of their country. Present me respectfully to Mrs. Logan and to yourself my friendly & respectful salutation.   TH: JEFFERSON

APPENDIX

PoC (DLC).

George Logan (1753-1821), a wealthy Pennsylvania Quaker and strict pacifist who had personally undertaken controversial peace missions to Paris in 1798 and to London in 1810, served in the U.S. Senate, 1801-1807, and was a frequent correspondent of TJ. His FAVOR OF OCT. 16. argued the need to apply Christian moral principles to the conduct of politics and stated: "I contemplate with great satisfaction the publication of your system of ethicks extracted from the holy scriptures, as tending to support the correct maxim— that religion should influence the political as well as the moral conduct of man, strictly complying with the sacred injunction, of doing unto others whatever we desire others to do unto us." In writing this letter, Logan obviously had some knowledge of TJ's letter to Charles Thomson of 9 Jan. 1816 (printed above).

Soon after dispatching this letter, TJ received from Joseph Delaplaine of Philadelphia an even more graphic account of the rumors to which his correspondence with Thomson had given rise. Delaplaine, who was seeking biographical information for a sketch of TJ that was to appear in the second volume of *Delaplaine's Repository of the Lives and Portraits of Distinguished American Characters*, 2 vols. (Philadelphia, 1816-17), noted: "I have been several times recently, to see the honorable Charles Thomson. He spoke of you freely. It appears that one of your letters gave him great delight. It is that, in which you speak of the scriptures &c. After this, I will not conceal from you the fact, and it is now no secret, that your letter to Mr. Thomson as well as one to another gentleman in another quarter, near Philada., has been quoted. Genl. Wilkinson said to me a few days ago 'Sir, I am happy to learn that Mr. Jefferson has written to a gentleman that he has become a disciple or follower of Jesus Christ.' To be brief, it is in general circulation, and a current opinion and belief, that you have avowed yourself a *perfect believer* in the Christian Religion and that you believe in the *Divinity of our saviour*. This has gained such ground that Genl. Wilkinson, has given it a place, he told me a few days ago, in his work which will be published in 2 or 3 weeks.—I mention these things, dear sir, in a frank, open manner, to enable you to know, if you have not already heard, what the people say in this quarter on this subject. And I can say that the Religious world in this quarter, are daily congratulating each other, on what they call, your happy change of Religious belief.—On this subject, Dear sir, I beg leave to say one word. I had been requested by their possessors and others to look at these letters spoken of, but from my great regard for you, have declined doing so, unless I should receive your approbation, which I shall not ask for. But I beg leave to say, dear sir, that inasmuch as the respectable gentlemen to whom you have written, believe that your letters justify and authorize them to promulgate what has been mentioned, can I ask from you on the subject of Religion precisely that which you believe, for the purpose of introducing it in your life, not for the world, however, in the way of quotation, but in general terms. I know well, that if the change in your Religious faith, so spoken of by these gentlemen, is mentioned in the Repository, it will give a tone and currency to the book, in a certain quarter, and in the Religious world, that will produce great and lasting benefits to me" (Delaplaine to TJ, 23 Nov. 1816).

In reply TJ flatly refused to comply with Delaplaine's request that he elucidate his religious beliefs: "To the enquiries in your's of Nov. 23. I answer 'say nothing of my religion. It is known to my god and myself alone. It's evidence before the world is to be sought in my life. If that has been honest and dutiful to society the religion which has regulated it cannot be a bad one' " (TJ to Delaplaine, 25 Dec. 1816). In consequence, the account of TJ's life that was printed in *Delaplaine's Repository* made no mention of his religious beliefs.

The other GENTLEMAN . . . NEAR PHILADA. mentioned by Delaplaine was probably Dr. Robert Patterson, in whose home Charles Thomson inadvertently left the letter TJ had written to him on 9 Jan. 1816. In any event, the only letter of the sort described by Delaplaine that TJ is known to have written to someone in or around Philadelphia in 1816 is the one to Thomson.

To Francis Adrian Van der Kemp

DEAR SIR   Poplar Forest near Lynchburg Nov. 24. 16.

I recieve your favor of Nov. 1. at this place at which I make occasionally a temporary residence; and I have perused with great satisfaction the magnificent skeleton you inclose me of what would indeed be a compleat Encyclopedia of Christian philosophy. It's execution would require a Newton in physics a Locke in metaphysics, and one who to a possession of all history, adds a judgment and candor to estimate it's evidence and credibility in proportion to the character of the facts it presents and he should have a long life before him. I fear we shall not see this canvas filled in our day, and that we must be contented to have all this light blaze upon us when the curtain shall be removed which limits our mortal sight. I had however persuaded myself to hope that we should have from your own pen, one branch of this great work, the mortal biography of Jesus. This candidly and rationally written, without any regard to sectarian dogmas, would reconcile to his character a weighty multitude who do not properly estimate it; and would lay the foundation of a genuine christianity.

You ask if I have ever published any thing but the Notes on Virginia? Nothing but official State papers, except a pamphlet at the commencement of our difference with England and on that subject, and another at the close of the revolution proposing the introduction of our decimal money, of neither of which do I possess a copy.—Should a curiosity to see our part of the union tempt your friend Dr. Willoughby to come as far as Monticello, I shall be very happy to recieve him there and to shew my respect for his worth as well as for your recommendation of it. Accept the assurance of my great esteem and consideration.   TH: JEFFERSON

RC (NBuHi). PoC (DLC).

To Charles Thomson

MY VERY DEAR AND ANTIENT FRIEND   Monticello Jan. 29. 17.

I learnt from your last letter, with much affliction, the severe and singular attack your health has lately sustained; but it's equally singular and sudden restoration confirms my confidence in the strength of your constitution of body and mind, and my conclusion that neither has recieved hurt, and that you are still ours for a long time to come. We have both much to be thankful for in the soundness of our physical organisation, and something for self-approbation in the order and regularity of life by which it has been preserved. Your preceding letter had given me no cause to doubt the continued strength of your mind; and, were it not that I am always peculiarly gratified by hearing from you, I should regret you had thought the incident with Mr. Delaplaine worth an explanation. He wrote to me on the subject of my letter to you of Jan. 9. 1816. and asked me questions which I answer only to one being. To himself therefore I replied 'say nothing of my religion; it is known to my god and myself alone. It's evidence before the world is to be sought in my life. If that has been honest and dutiful to society, the religion which has regulated it cannot be a bad one.' It is a singular anxiety which some people have that we should all think alike. Would the world be more beautiful were all our faces alike? Were our tempers, our talents, our tastes, our forms, our wishes, aversions and pursuits cast exactly in the same mould? If no varieties existed in the animal, vegetable, or mineral creation,[1] but all were strictly uniform, catholic and orthodox, what a world of physical and moral monotony would it be! These are the absurdities into which those run who usurp the throne of god, and dictate to him what he should have done. May they, with all their metaphysical riddles, appear before that tribunal with as clean hands and hearts as you and I shall. There, suspended in the scales of eternal justice, faith and works will shew their worth by their weight. God bless you and preserve you long in life & health.

Th: Jefferson

RC (DLC: Charles Thomson Papers); addressed: "Charles Thomson esq. near Philadelphia"; franked and postmarked: "Milton Va 29 Jan"; endorsed by Thomson as received 7 Feb. 1817. PoC (DLC).

Thomson's LAST LETTER described his recovery from a "paralytic stroke" and gave the following account of the INCIDENT WITH MR DELAPLAINE: "I have been thus particular to apologize for my answer to your letter, and for an Answer which I gave on the 9th. of Sept to what I deemed an impertinent question of Mr Delaplaine which has occasioned a very improper application to you. The case as far as I can now recollect was simply this—Among many other questions he asked me one which seemed to refer to the slanderous charges bandeid about respecting your infidelity and disbelief of Christianity. This roused my resentment and I wished to answer it by a sentence of your letter which at the instant occurred to my mind. On looking for the letter I could not find it. But after several questions I recollected that passage of your letter in which you informed me that you have employed some time in composing 'a wee little book which was a document in proof that you are a real Christian that is a disciple of the doctrines of Jesus Christ.' With these words I answered this question. He put several questions touching the meaning, but I answered all, with a repetition of the same words at the same time trying to recollect when or where I had lost the letter. At last it occurred to me that I had been in Philadelphia and had shewn the letter to Doct Patterson; I thereupon desired Mr. Delaplaine to call on Doct Patterson and inquire if I had left it there. This happened to have been the case. I had laid it on the table and forgot it: But Mr D. it seems construed the favour I asked into a grant of something to himself" (Thomson to TJ, ca. 5 Jan. 1817).

Thomson's PRECEDING LETTER expressed pleasure at the receipt of TJ's 9 Jan. 1816 letter, described the deteriorating state of his health, and discussed the merits of "Allen's history of Lewis and Clark's interesting expedition" (Thomson to TJ, 16 May 1816).

¹ TJ first wrote "world" and then changed it to "creation."

To Salma Hale

SIR   Monticello July 26. 18.

I thank you for the pamphlets you have been so kind as to send me, which I now return. They give a lively view of the state of religious dissension now prevailing in the North, and making it's way to the South. Most controversies begin with a discussion of principles; but soon degenerate into episodical, verbal, or personal cavils. Too much of this is seen in these pamphlets, and, as usual, those whose dogmas are the most unintelligible are the most angry. The truth is that Calvinism has introduced into the Christian religion more new absurdities than it's leader had purged it of old ones. Our saviour did not come into the world to save metaphysicians only. His doctrines are levelled to the simplest understandings and it is only by banishing Hierophantic mysteries and Scholastic subtleties, which they have nick-named Christianity, and getting back to the plain and unsophisticated precepts of Christ, that we become *real* Christians. The half reformation of Luther and Calvin did something towards a restoration of his genuine doctrines; the present contest will, I hope, compleat what they begun, and place us where the evangelists left us. I salute you with esteem and respect.

TH: JEFFERSON

PoC (DLC).

Hale (1787-1866), a New Hampshire printer, newspaper editor, and supreme court clerk, served in the U.S. House of Representatives, 1817-1819. TJ was responding to a letter from Hale of 13 July 1818, which stated in part: "I have collected and send you the pamphlets containing the Unitarian controversy which you expressed a desire to see when I visited you lately at Monticello. The whole impression being sold, I have been obliged to borrow two or three from a friend, and if you feel indifferent about retaining would oblige me by returning them." The specific PAMPHLETS he sent to TJ have not been identified.

To Thomas B. Parker

Monticello May 15. 19

I thank you, Sir, for the pamphlet you have been so kind as to send me on the reveries, not to say insanities of Calvin and Hopkins; yet the latter, I believe, is the proper term. Mr. Locke defines a madman to be one who has a kink in his head on some particular subject, which neither reason nor fact can untangle. Grant him that postulate, and he reasons as correctly as other men. This was the real condition of Calvin and Hopkins, on whom reasoning was wasted. The strait jacket alone was their proper remedy. You ask my opinion on this subject, but when we see so many Hopkinsonian religions in the world, all different, yet every one confident it is the only true one, a man must be very clear-sighted who can see the impression of the finger of God on any particular one of them. Were I to be the founder of a new sect, I would call them Apriarians, and, after the example of the bee, advise them to extract the honey of every sect. My fundamental principle would be the reverse of Calvin's, that we are to be saved by our good works which are within our power, and not by our faith which is not within our power. I salute you with respect and good-will.   TH: JEFFERSON

PoC (DLC).

TJ wrote this letter in response to one from Parker in which he revealed that "I have just published a small work against Calvin and Hopkins and have taken the liberty to forward you a copy of it presuming you to be a friend to the great cause of truth" (Parker to TJ, 12 Apr. 1819). The enclosed PAMPHLET was *The Trial: Calvin and Hopkins versus the Bible and Common Sense. By a Lover of Truth* (Boston, 1819). TJ subsequently refused a request by Parker for permission to publish this letter (Parker to TJ, 9 July 1819, and TJ to Parker, 2 Aug. 1819).

To Ezra Stiles Ely

Monticello June 25. 19.

Your favor Sir, of the 14th. has been duly recieved, and with it the book you were so kind as to forward to me. For this mark of attention be pleased to accept my thanks. The science of the human mind is curious, but it is one on which I have not indulged myself in much speculation. The times in which I have lived, and the scenes in which I have been engaged, have required me to keep the mind too much in action to have leisure to study minutely it's laws of action. I am therefore little qualified to give an opinion on the comparative worth of books on that subject, and little disposed to do it on any book. Your's has brought the science within a small compass and that is a merit of the 1st. order; and especially with one to whom the drudgery of letter writing often denies the leisure of reading a single page in a week. On looking over the summary of the contents of your book, it does not seem likely to bring into collision any of those sectarian differences which you suppose may exist between us. In that branch of religion which regards the moralities of life, and the duties of a social being, which teaches us to love our neighbors as ourselves, and to do good to all men, I am sure that you and I do not differ. We probably differ on that which relates to the dogmas of theology, the foundation of all sectarianism, and on which no two sects dream alike; for if they did they would then be of the same. You say you are a Calvinist. I am not. I am of a sect by myself, as far as I know. I am not a Jew: and therefore do not adopt their theology, which supposes the god of infinite justice to punish the sins of the fathers upon their children, unto the 3d. and 4th. generation: and the benevolent and sublime reformer of that religion has told us only that god is good and perfect, but has not defined him. I am therefore of his theology, believing that we have neither words nor ideas adequate to that definition. And if we could all, after his example, leave the subject as undefinable, we should all be of one sect, doers of good and eschewers of evil. No doctrines of his lead to schism. It is the speculations of crazy theologists which have made a Babel of a religion the most moral and sublime ever preached to man, and calculated to heal, and not to create differences. These religious animosities I impute to those who call themselves his ministers, and who engraft their casuistries on the stock of his simple precepts. I am sometimes more angry with them than is authorised by the blessed charities which he preached. To yourself I pray the acceptance of my great respect.

Th: Jefferson

PoC (DLC).

Ely (1786-1861), a graduate of Yale, was pastor of the Third Presbyterian Church in Philadelphia. His letter OF THE 14TH. asked TJ to "Permit a young Philosopher to present a veteran" with a copy of his *Conversations on the Science of the Human Mind* (Philadelphia, 1819) for possible use at the University of Virginia and noted that as "a Presbyterian, a Calvinist, and a man of common sense: I can, therefore, respect and esteem a literary man, of distinguished talents, and usefulness to his country, however I may differ from him, even in important theological opinions" (Ely to TJ, 14 June 1819).

To William Short

Dear Sir   Monticello Oct. 31. 19.

Your favor of the 21st. is recieved. My late illness, in which you are so kind as to feel an interest was produced by a spasmodic stricture of the ilium, which came upon me on the 7th. inst. The crisis was short, passed over favorably on the 4th. day, and I should soon have been well but that a dose of calomel and Jalap, in which were only 8. or 9. grains of the former brought on a salivation. Of this however nothing now remains but a little soreness of the mouth. I have been able to get on horseback for 3. or 4. days past.

As you say of yourself, I too am an Epicurean. I consider the genuine (not the imputed) doctrines of Epicurus as containing every thing rational in moral philosophy which Greece and Rome have left us. Epictetus indeed has given us what was good of the Stoics; all beyond, of their dogmas,[1] being hypocrisy and grimace. Their great crime was in their calumnies of Epicurus and misrepresentations of his doctrines: in which we lament to see the candid character of Cicero engaging as an accomplice. The merit of his philosophy is in the beauties of his style, diffuse, vapid, rhetorical, but enchanting. His prototype Plato, eloquent as himself, dealing out mysticisms incomprehensible to the human mind, has been deified by certain sects usurping the name of Christians; because, in his foggy conceptions, they found a basis of impenetrable darkness whereon to rear fabrications as delirious, of their own invention. These they fathered blasphemously on him whom they claimed as their founder, but who would disclaim them with the indignation which their caricatures of his religion so justly excite. Of Socrates we have nothing genuine but in the Memorabilia of Xenophon. For Plato makes him one of his Collocutors merely to cover his own whimsies under the mantle of his name; a liberty of which we are told Socrates himself complained. Seneca is indeed a fine moralist, disfiguring his work at times with some Stoicisms, and affecting too much of antithesis and point, yet giving us on the whole a great deal of sound and practical morality. But the greatest of all the Reformers of the depraved religion of his own country, was Jesus of Nazareth. Abstracting what is really his from the rubbish in which it is buried, easily distinguished by it's lustre from the dross of his biographers, and as separable from that as the diamond from the dung hill, we have the outlines of a system of the most sublime morality which has ever fallen from the lips of man: outlines which it is lamentable he did not live to fill up. Epictetus and Epicurus give us laws for governing ourselves, Jesus a supplement of the duties and charities we owe to others. The establishment of the innocent and genuine character of this benevolent[2] Moralist, and the rescuing it from the imputation of imposture, which has resulted from misconstructions of his words by his pretended votaries,[3] is a most desirable object, and one to which Priestly has successfully devoted his labors and learning. It would in time, it is to be hoped, effect a quiet euthanasia of the heresies of bigotry and fanaticism which have so long triumphed over human reason, and so generally and deeply afflicted mankind. But this work is to be begun by winnowing the grain from the chaff of the historians of his life. I have sometimes thought of translating Epictetus (for he has never been tolerably translated into English) of adding the genuine doctrines of Epicurus from the Syntagma of Gassendi, and an Abstract from the Evangelists of whatever has the stamp of the eloquence and fine imagination of Jesus. The last I attempted too hastily some 12. or 15. years ago. It was the work of 2. or 3. nights only at Washington, after getting thro' the evening task of reading the letters and papers of the day.—But with one foot in the grave, these are now idle projects for me. My business is to beguile the wearisomness of declining life, as I endeavor to do, by the delights of classical reading and of Mathematical truths, and by the consolations of a sound philosophy, equally indifferent to hope and fear.[4]

I take the liberty of observing that you are not a true disciple of our master Epicurus, in indulging the indolence to which you say you are yielding. One of his canons, you know, was that 'that indulgence which prevents a greater pleasure, or produces a greater pain, is to be avoided.' Your love of repose will lead, in it's progress, to a suspension of healthy exercise, a relaxation of mind, an indifference to every thing around you, and finally to a debility of body and hebetude of mind, the farthest of all things from the happiness which the well regulated indulgences of Epicurus ensure. Fortitude, you know, is one of his four cardinal virtues. That teaches us to meet and surmount difficulties; not to fly from them, like cowards, and to fly too in vain, for they will meet and arrest us at every turn of our road. Weigh this matter well; brace yourself up; take a seat with Correa, and come and see the finest portion of your country which, if you have not forgotten, you still do not know, because it is no longer the same as when you knew it. It will add much to the happiness of my recovery to be able to recieve Correa and yourself, and to prove the estimation in which I hold you both. Come too and see our incipient University, which has advanced with great activity this year. By the end of the next we shall have elegant accomodations for 7. professors, and the year following the professors themselves. No secondary character will be recieved among them. Either the ablest which America or Europe can furnish, or none at all. They will give us the selected society of a great city separated from the dissipations and levities of it's ephemeral insects.

I am glad the bust of Condorcet has been saved and so well placed. His genius should be before us; while the lamentable, but singular act of ingratitude which tarnished his latter days, may be thrown behind us.

I will place under this a Syllabus of the doctrines of Epicurus, somewhat in the lapidary style, which I wrote some 20. years ago. A like one of the philosophy of Jesus, of nearly the same age, is too long to be copied. *Vale, et tibi persuade carissimum te esse mihi.*

Th: Jefferson

A Syllabus of the doctrines of Epicurus.

Physical. The Universe eternal.

It's parts, great and small, interchangeable.

Matter and Void alone.

Motion inherent in matter, which is weighty and declining.

Eternal circulation of the elements of bodies.

Gods, an order of beings next superior to man.

enjoying, in their sphere, their own felicities;

but not medling with the concerns of the scale of

beings below them.

Moral. Happiness the aim of life.

Virtue the foundation of happiness;

Utility the test of virtue.

Pleasure active and In-dolent.

In-dolence is the absence of pain, the true felicity.

Active, consists in agreeable motion

It is not happiness, but the means to produce it.

Thus the absence of hunger is an article of

felicity; eating the means to obtain it.

The Summum bonum is to be not pained in body, nor troubled in mind.

i.e. In-dolence of body, tranquility of mind.

To procure tranquility of mind we must avoid desire and fear the two principal diseases of the mind.

Man is a free agent.

Virtue consists in

1. Prudence. 2. Temperance. 3. Fortitude. 4. Justice.

To which are opposed

1. Folly.   2. Desire.   3. Fear.   4. Deciept.

RC (ViW); endorsed by Short as received 8 Nov. 1819. PoC (DLC). After finishing the PoC, TJ made a significant alteration in the text, for which see note 3 below.

William Short's FAVOR OF THE 21ST. concluded with the observation that "I have so far adopted the principles of Epicurus (who, after all I am inclined to believe, was the wisest of the ancient Philosophers, as he is certainly the least understood and the most calumniated among them) as to consult my ease towards the attainment of happiness in this poor world, poor even in making the best of it" (Short to TJ, 21 Oct. 1819).

TJ was undoubtedly encouraged to make AN ABSTRACT FROM THE EVANGELISTS by Short's response to this letter. "But to return to yourself, my dear sir," Short wrote, "I see with real pains that you have no intention of continuing the abstract from the Evangelists which you begun at Washington. The reason you give for confining yourself to classical reading and mathematical truths should not, I should think, operate against this agreeable task—and if agreeable to you, I know nothing which could be more so, and at the same time more useful to others. You observe that what is genuine is easily distinguished from the rubbish in which it is buried—if so, it is an irresistible reason for your continuing the work—for others, it would seem, have not found it thus distinguishable—and I fear I should be of the number if I were to undertake this study. It would cost you but little trouble on a fair edition of this book, if you would by more lines mark off what appeared to you thus manifestly genuine" (Short to TJ, 1 Dec. 1819).

The Abbé Joseph CORREA de Serra (1750-1823), a Portuguese priest and natural scientist who served as his country's minister plenipotentiary to the United States, 1816-1820, was a highly valued friend of TJ and a frequent visitor to Monticello during his stay in America (Richard B. Davis, "The Abbé Correa in America, 1812-1820," Amer. Phil. Soc., *Trans.*, new ser., XLV [1955], 90-121).

[1] TJ first wrote "doctrines" and then altered it to read as above.

[2] TJ first wrote "great" and then altered it to read as above.

[3] After the RC had been dispatched, TJ altered this part of the PoC to read as follows: "imposture, which has resulted from artificial systems, invented by Ultra-Christian sects, unauthorised by a single word ever uttered by him is a most desirable object." Then, at the foot of the page, keyed by an asterisk to "artificial systems," TJ added the following: "e.g. the immaculate conception of Jesus, his deification, the creation of the world by him, his miraculous powers, his resurrection and visible ascension, his corporeal presence in the Eucharist, the Trinity, original sin, atonement, regeneration, election, orders of Hierarchy, &c."

[4] The words "equally indifferent to hope and fear" were crowded in at the end of the line, obviously after TJ had begun the following paragraph.

To William Short

DEAR SIR   Monticello Apr. 13. 20.

Your favor of Mar. 27. is recieved, and my grandaughter Ellen has undertaken to copy the Syllabus, which will therefore be inclosed. It was originally written to Dr. Rush. On his death, fearing that the inquisition of the public might get hold of it, I asked the return of it from the family, which they kindly complied with. At the request of another friend, I had given him a copy. He lent it to his friend to read, who copied it, and in a few months it appeared in the theological magazine of London. Happily that repository is scarcely known in this country; and the Syllabus therefore is still a secret, and in your hands I am sure it will continue so.

But while this Syllabus is meant to place the character of Jesus in it's true and high light, as no imposter himself, but a great Reformer of the Hebrew code of religion, it is not to be understood that I am with him in all his doctrines. I am a Materialist; he takes the side of spiritualism: he preaches the efficacy of repentance towards forgiveness of sin, I require a counterpoise of good works to redeem it &c. &c. It is the innocence of his character, the purity and sublimity of his moral precepts, the eloquence of his inculcations, the beauty of the apologues in which he conveys them, that I so much admire; sometimes indeed needing indulgence to Eastern hyperbolism. My eulogies too may be founded on a postulate which all may not be ready to grant. Among the sayings and discourses imputed to him by his biographers, I find many passages of fine imagination, correct morality, and of the most lovely benevolence: and others again of so much ignorance, so much absurdity, so much untruth, charlatanism, and imposture, as to pronounce it impossible that such contradictions should have proceeded from the same being. I separate therefore the gold from the dross; restore to him the former, and leave the latter to the stupidity of some, and roguery of others of his disciples. Of this band of dupes and impostors, Paul was the great Coryphaeus, and first corrupter of the doctrines of Jesus. These palpable interpolations and falsifications of his doctrines led me to try to sift them apart. I found the work obvious and easy, and that his part composed the most beautiful morsel of morality which has been given to us by man. The Syllabus is therefore of *his* doctrines, not *all* of *mine*. I read them as I do those of other antient and modern moralists, with a mixture of approbation and dissent.

I rejoice, with you, to see an encoraging spirit of internal improvement prevailing in the states. The opinion I have ever expressed of the advantages of a Western communication through the James river, I still entertain, and that the Cayuga is the most promising of the links of communication.—The history of our University you know. So far, 7 of the 10 pavilions destined for the Professors, and about 30 dormitories will be compleated this year, and 3. others, with 6. Hotels for boarding, and 70. other dormitories will be compleated the next year, and the whole be in readiness then to recieve those who are to occupy them. But means to bring these into place, and to set the machine into motion, must come from the legislature. An opposition in the mean time has been got up. That of our alma mater William and Mary, is not of much weight. She must descend into the secondary rank of academies of preparation for the University. The serious enemies are the priests of the different religious sects, to whose spells on the human mind it's improvement is ominous. Their pulpits are now resounding with denunciations against the appointment of Dr. Cooper whom they charge as a Monotheist in opposition to their tritheism. Hostile as these sects are in every other point, to one another, they unite in maintaining their mystical theogony against those who believe there is one god only. The Presbyterian clergy are loudest, the most intolerant of all sects, the most tyrannical, and ambitious; ready at the word of the lawgiver, if such a word could be now obtained, to put the torch to the pile, and to rekindle in this virgin hemisphere, the flames in which their oracle Calvin consumed the poor Servetus, because he could not find in his Euclid the proposition which has demonstrated that three are one, and one is three, nor subscribe to that of Calvin that magistrates have a right to exterminate all heretics to Calvinistic creed. They pant to reestablish *by law* that holy inquisition, which they can now only infuse into *public opinion*. We have most unwisely committed to the hierophants of our particular superstition, the direction of public opinion, that lord of the Universe. We have given them stated and privileged days to collect and catechise us, opportunities of delivering their oracles to the people in mass, and of moulding their minds as wax in the hollow of their hands. But, in despite of their fulminations against endeavors to enlighten the general mind, to improve the reason of the people, and encorage them in the use of it, the liberality of this state will support this institution, and give fair play to the cultivation of reason.—Can you ever find a more eligible occasion of visiting once more your native country, than that of accompanying Mr. Correa, and of seeing with him this beautiful and hopeful institution in ovo?

Altho' I had laid down, as a law to myself, never to write, talk, or even think of politics, to know nothing of public affairs and therefore had ceased to read newspapers, yet the Missouri question arroused and filled me with alarm. The old schism of federal and republican, threatened nothing, because it existed in every state, and united them together by the fraternism of party. But the co-incidence of a marked principle, moral and political, with a geographical line, once concieved, I feared would never more be obliterated from the mind; that it would be recurring on every occasion and renewing irritations, until it would kindle such mutual and mortal hatred, as to render separation preferable to eternal discord. I have been among the most sanguine in believing that our Union would be of long duration. I now doubt it much, and see the event at no great distance, and the direct consequence of this question: not by the line which has been so confidently counted on. The laws of nature controul this: but by the Potomak, Ohio, and Missouri, or more probably the Missisipi upwards to our Northern boundary. My only comfort and confidence is that I shall not live to see this: and I envy not the present generation the glory of throwing away the fruits of their fathers sacrifices of life and fortune, and of rendering desperate the experiment which was to decide ultimately whether man is capable of self government? This treason against human hope will signalize their epoch in future history, as the counterpart of the medal of their predecessors.

You kindly enquire after my health. There is nothing in it immediately threatening, but swelled legs, which are kept down mechanically by bandages from the toe to the knee. These I have worn for 6. months, but the tendency to turgidity may proceed from debility alone. I can walk the round of my garden; not more. But I ride 6. or 8. miles a day without fatigue. I shall set out to Poplar Forest within 3. or 4. days; a journey from which my physician augurs much good. I salute you with constant and affectionate friendship and respect.

Th: JEFFERSON

RC (ViW); endorsed by Short as received 21 Apr. and answered 2 May 1820. PoC (DLC). Enclosure: Ellen Wayles Randolph's copy of the "Syllabus"; see notes to TJ to Benjamin Rush, 21 Apr. 1803.

Short's FAVOR OF MAR. 27. discussed the University of Virginia, the Missouri controversy, and internal improvements in the United States, and stated that, provided TJ employed an amanuensis, "I would then have no scruple in begging you to send me the syllabus of the Philosophy of Jesus, which you found too long to copy; and which, indeed, I would not have at the price of that trouble to you" (Short to TJ, 27 Mar. 1820).

Short, TJ's longtime friend and protégé, described his reaction to the "Syllabus" the following month: "I had the very sincere pleasure of receiving some days ago your kind favor of the 18th. ulto. covering the syllabus. It has been a source to me of much gratification and instruction also. The subject has been always one on which I have postponed to aim at information, because I felt *in limine* the conviction that it was

impossible to attain such a degree of certainty as would be satisfactory to me. Whilst therefore I was persuaded that those who were relying on their dogmas as demonstrated truths, were under an error, thought it best for me not to lose my time or my trouble in endeavoring to dissipate that error, as I could offer only doubt and uncertainty in its place. Your view of the subject as relative to the Christian system is the most satisfactory that I have met with, and I am glad to learn that you found it easy to separate what was really of Jesus, from that which belongs to his biographers. I have never myself so far occupied myself with the subject as to make that research, although I was always satisfied that all which was attributed to him could not really be his. Be so good as to offer to Miss Ellen on my part my most respectful thanks for the trouble she has been so good as to take on this occasion. And I beg you to remain persuaded that this syllabus shall be kept for my sole use, and not be allowed to get into hands that might make an improper use of it" (Short to TJ, 2 May 1820).

To William Short

Monticello Aug. 4. 20.

DEAR SIR

I owe you a letter for your favor of June 29. which was recieved in due time, and there being no subject of the day of particular interest I will make this a supplement to mine of Apr. 13. My aim in that was to justify the character of Jesus against the fictions of his pseudo-followers which have exposed him to the inference of being an impostor. For if we could believe that he really countenanced the follies, the falsehoods and the Charlatinisms which his biographers father on him, and admit the misconstructions, interpolations and theorisations of the fathers of the early, and fanatics of the latter ages, the conclusion would be irresistible by every sound mind, that he was an impostor. I give no credit to their falsifications of his actions and doctrines; and, to rescue his character, the postulate in my letter asked only what is granted in reading every other historian. When Livy or Siculus, for example, tell us things which coincide with our experience of the order of nature, we credit them on their word, and place their narrations among the records of credible history. But when they tell us of calves speaking, of statues sweating blood, and other things against the course of nature, we reject these as fables, not belonging to history. In like manner, when an historian, speaking of a character well known and established on satisfactory testimony imputes to it things incompatible with that character, we reject them without hesitation, and assent to that only of which we have better evidence. Had Plutarch informed us that Caesar and Cicero passed their whole lives in religious exercises, and abstinence from the affairs of the world, we should reject what was so inconsistent with their established characters, still crediting what he relates in conformity with our ideas of them. So again, the superlative wisdom of Socrates is testified by all antiquity, and placed on ground not to be questioned. When therefore Plato puts into his mouth such fancies, such paralogisms[1] and sophisms as a schoolboy would be ashamed of, we conclude they were the whimsies of Plato's own foggy brain, and acquit Socrates of puerilities so unlike his character. (Speaking of Plato I will add that no writer antient or modern has bewildered the world with more ignes fatui than this renowned philosopher, in Ethics, in Politics and Physics. In the latter, to specify a single example, compare his views of the animal economy, in his Timaeus, with those of Mrs. Bryan in her Conversations on chemistry, and weigh the science of the canonised philosopher against the good sense of the unassuming lady. But Plato's visions have furnished a basis for endless systems of mystical theology, and he is therefore all but adopted as a Christian saint.— It is surely time for men to think for themselves, and to throw off the authority of names so artificially magnified. But to return from this parenthesis, I say that) this free exercise of reason is all I ask for the vindication of the character of Jesus. We find in the writings of his biographers matter of two distinct descriptions. First a ground work of vulgar ignorance, of things impossible, of superstitions, fanaticisms, and fabrications. Intermixed with these again are sublime ideas of the supreme being, aphorisms and precepts of the purest morality and benevolence, sanctioned by a life of humility, innocence, and simplicity of manners, neglect of riches, absence of worldly ambition and honors, with an eloquence and persuasiveness which have not been surpassed. These could not be inventions of the grovelling authors who relate them. They are far beyond the powers of their feeble minds. They shew that there was a character, the subject of their history, whose splendid conceptions were above all suspicion of being interpolations from their hands. Can we be at a loss in separating such materials, and ascribing each to it's genuine author? The difference is obvious to the eye and to the understanding, and we may read, as we run, to each his part; and I will venture to affirm that he who, as I have done, will undertake to winnow this grain from it's chaff, will find it not to require a moment's consideration. The parts fall asunder of themselves as would those of an image of metal and clay.

There are, I acknolege, passages not free from objection, which we may with probability ascribe to Jesus himself; but claiming indulgence from the circumstances under which he acted. His object was the reformation of some articles in the religion of the Jews, as taught by Moses. That Seer had presented, for the object of their worship, a being of terrific character, cruel, vindictive, capricious and unjust. Jesus, taking for his type the best qualities of the human head and heart, wisdom, justice, goodness, and adding to them power, ascribed all of these but in infinite perfection, to the supreme being, and formed him really worthy of their adoration. Moses had either not believed in a future state of existence, or had not thought it essential to be explicitly taught to his people. Jesus inculcated that doctrine with emphasis and precision. Moses had bound the Jews to many idle ceremonies, mummeries and observances of no effect towards producing the social utilities which constitute the essence of virtue. Jesus exposed their futility and insignificance. The one instilled into his people the most anti-social spirit towards other nations; the other preached philanthropy and universal charity and benevolence.—The office of reformer of the superstitions of a nation is ever dangerous. Jesus had to walk on the perilous confines of reason and religion: and a step to right or left might place him within the gripe of the priests of the superstition, a bloodthirsty race, as cruel and remorseless as the being whom they represented as the family god of Abraham, of Isaac and of Jacob, and the local god of Israel. They were constantly laying snares too to entangle him in the web of the law. He was justifiable therefore in avoiding these by evasions, by sophisms, by misconstructions and misapplications of scraps of the prophets, and in defending himself with these their own weapons as sufficient, ad homines, at least. That Jesus did not mean to impose himself on mankind as the son of god physically speaking I have been convinced by the writings of men more learned than myself in that lore. But that he might conscientiously believe himself inspired from above, is very possible. The whole religion of the Jews, inculcated on him from his infancy, was founded in the belief of divine inspiration. The fumes of the most disordered imaginations were recorded in their religious code, as special communications of the deity; and as it could not but happen that, in the course of ages, events would now and then turn up to which some of these vague rhapsodies might be accomodated by the aid of allegories, figures, types, and other tricks upon words, they have not only preserved their credit with the Jews of all subsequent times, but are the foundation of much of the religions of those who have schismatised from them. Elevated by the enthusiasm of a warm and pure heart, conscious of the high strains of an eloquence which had not been taught him, he might readily mistake the coruscations of his own fine genius for inspirations of an higher order. This belief carried therefore no more personal imputation, than the belief of Socrates that himself was under the care and admonitions of a guardian daemon. And how many of our wisest men still believe in the reality of these inspirations, while perfectly sane on all other subjects. Excusing therefore, on these considerations, those passages in the gospels which seem to bear marks of weakness in Jesus, ascribing to him what alone is consistent with the great and pure character of which the same writings furnish proofs, and to their proper authors their own trivialities and imbecilities, I think myself authorised to conclude the purity and distinction of his character in opposition to the impostures which those authors would fix upon him: and that the postulate of my former letter is no more than is granted in all other historical works.

M. Correa is here on his farewell visit to us. He has been much pleased with the plan and progress of our University and has given some valuable hints for it's botanical branch. He goes to do, I hope, much good in his new country; the public instruction there, as I understand, being within the department destined for him. He is not without dissatisfaction, and reasonable dissatisfaction too with the piracies of Baltimore: but his justice and friendly dispositions will, I am sure, distinguish between the iniquities of that den of plunder and corruption, and the sound principles[2] of our country at large, and of our government especially. From many conversations with him I hope he sees, and will promote, in his new situation, the advantages of a cordial fraternisation among all the American nations, and the importance of their coalescing in an American system of policy, totally independant of, and unconnected with that of Europe. The day is not distant when we may formally require a meridian of partition thro' the ocean which separates the two hemispheres, on the hither side of which no European gun shall ever be heard, nor an American on the other: and when, during the rage of the eternal wars of Europe, the lion and the lamb, within our regions, shall lie down together in peace. The excess[3] of population in Europe, and want of room, render war, in their opinion, necessary to keep down that[4] excess of numbers. Here, room is abundant, population scanty, and peace the necessary means[5] for producing men, to whom the redundant soil is offering the means of life and happiness. The principles of society there and here then are radically different: and I hope no American patriot will ever lose sight of the essential policy of interdicting in the seas and territories of both americas the ferocious and sanguinary contests of Europe. I wish to see this coalition begun. I am earnest for an agreement with the maritime powers of Europe, assigning them the task[6] of keeping down the piracies of their seas and the cannibalisms of the African coast, and to us the suppression of the same enormities within our seas: and for this purpose I should rejoice to see the fleets of Brazil and the US. riding together, as brethren of the same family, and pursuing the same object.[7] And indeed it would be of happy augury to begin at once this concert of action here, on the invitation of either to the other government, while the way might be preparing for withdrawing our cruisers from Europe, and preventing naval collisions there which daily endanger our peace.

Turning to another part of your letter, I do not think the obstacles insuperable which you state as opposed to your visit to us. From one of the persons mentioned, I never heard a sentiment but of esteem for you: and I am certain you would be recieved with kindness and cordiality. But still the call may be omitted without notice. The mountain lies between his residence and the mail road, and occludes the expectation of transient visits. I am equally ignorant of any dispositions not substantially friendly to you in the other person. But the alibi there gives you ten free months in the year. But if the visit is to be but once in your life, I would suppress my impatience and consent it should be made a year or two hence. Because, by that time our University will be compleated and in full action: and you would recieve the satisfaction, in the final adieu to your native state, of seeing that she would retain her equal standing in the sisterhood of our republics. However, come now, come then, or come when you please. Your visit will give me the gratification I feel in every opportunity of proving to you the sincerity of my friendship and respect for you. TH: JEFFERSON

RC (ViW); addressed in TJ's hand: "William Short esquire Philadelphia"; readdressed in another hand: "Shrewsbury New Jersey"; franked and postmarked: "Milton Va 11 Augt"; "New-York Aug 16"; "Phila 21 Aug"; endorsed by Short as received 23 Aug. 1820. PoC (DLC); several words interlined and word endings added after execution of PoC in order to clarify text as in RC. Tr (DLC); in TJ's hand and headed: "Extract of a letter from Th: Jefferson to a friend dated Aug. 4. 1820." TJ enclosed a text of the Tr, which consists of a slightly variant version of the next to last paragraph of this letter, with a 24 Oct. 1820 letter to the Abbé Correa, who was then on the verge of leaving the United States to serve as a counselor of state in Brazil (DLC).

Short's FAVOR OF JUNE 29. dealt mainly with the case of Levett Harris, who wanted to visit TJ at Monticello to assure him that he was innocent of the charges of corruption that had been brought against him in connection with his service as consul in St. Petersburg, and merely referred in passing to the "Syllabus," noting that "I have read it over and over again; always with delight and instruction, and a renewed sense of my obligation to your amiable grandaughter as well as to yourself" (Short to TJ, 29 June

1820). Although *Conversations on Chemistry; in which the Elements of that Science are Familiarly Explained and Illustrated by Experiments*, 2 vols. (London, 1806), an anonymously published work written especially for young women, was often ascribed to Mrs. Margaret BRYAN, it was in fact the work of Jane Marcet. See Sowerby, comp., *Catalogue*, No. 837. The PIRACIES OF BALTIMORE was a reference to the practice whereby Uruguayan rebels commissioned privateers in that port to prey upon Portuguese shipping. The Abbé Correa had sought in vain to end these depredations during his tenure as Portugal's minister plenipotentiary to the United States (Richard B. Davis, "The Abbé Correa in America, 1812-1820," Am. Phil. Soc., *Trans.*, new ser., XLV [1955], 105-07).

[1] After the RC had been dispatched, TJ altered this passage in the PoC to read: "into his mouth such paralogisms, such quibbles on words and sophisms as a schoolboy would be ashamed of."

[2] "dispositions" in Tr.

[3] "surplus" in Tr.

[4] "their" in Tr.

[5] "state" in Tr.

[6] "duty" in Tr.

[7] "and having the same interests" in Tr.

To John Adams

Monticello, 15 Aug. 1820. Discusses at length "a critique on this institution in your North American Review of January last. . . . But enough of criticism: let me turn to your puzzling letter of May 12. on matter, spirit, motion &c. It's croud of scepticisms kept me from sleep. I read it, and laid it down: read it, and laid it down, again and again: and to give rest to my mind, I was obliged to recur ultimately to my habitual anodyne, 'I feel: therefore I exist.' I feel bodies which are not myself: there are other existencies then. I call them *matter*. I feel them changing place. This gives me *motion*. Where there is an absence of matter, I call it *void*, or *nothing*, or *immaterial space*. On the basis of sensation, of matter and motion, we may erect the fabric of all the certainties we can have or need. I can concieve *thought* to be an action of a particular organisation of matter, formed for that purpose by it's creator, as well as that *attraction* is an action of matter, or *magnetism* of loadstone. When he who denies to the Creator the power of endowing matter with the mode of action called *thinking* shall shew how he could endow the Sun with the mode of action called *attraction*, which reins the planets in the tract of their orbits, or how an absence of matter can have a will, and, by that will, put matter into motion, then the materialist may be lawfully required to explain the process by which matter exercises the faculty of thinking. When once we quit the basis of sensation, all is in the wind. To talk of *immaterial* existences is to talk of *nothings*. To say that the human soul, angels, god, are immaterial, is to say they are *nothings*, or that there is no god, no angels, no soul. I cannot reason otherwise: but I believe I am supported in my creed of materialism by Locke, Tracy, and Stewart.[1] At what age of the[2] Christian church this heresy of *immaterialism*, this masked atheism, crept in, I do not know.[3] But a heresy it certainly is. Jesus taught nothing of it. He told us indeed that 'God is a spirit,' but he has not defined what a spirit is, nor said that it is not *matter*. And the antient fathers generally, if not universally,[4] held it to be matter: light and thin indeed, an etherial gas; but still matter.[5] Origen says 'Deus reapse corporalis est; sed graviorum tantum corporum ratione, incorporeus.' Tertullian 'quid enim deus nisi corpus?' and again 'quis negabit deum esse corpus? Etsi deus spiritus, spiritus etiam corpus est, sui generis, in sua effigie.' St. Justin Martyr 'το Θειον φαμεν ειναι ασωματον ουκ ότι ασωματου—επειδη δε το μη κρατεισθαι ύπο τινος, του κρατεισθαι τιμιωτερον εστι, δια τουτο καλουμεν αυτον ασωματον.' And St. Macarius, speaking of angels says 'quamvis enim subtilia sint, tamen in substantiâ, formâ et figurâ, secundum tenuitatem naturae eorum, corpora sunt tenuia.' And St. Austin, St. Basil, Lactantius, Tatian, Athenagoras and others, with whose writings I pretend not a familiarity, are said by those who are, to deliver the same doctrine. Turn to your Ocellus d'Argens 97. 105. and to his Timaeus 17. for these quotations. In England these Immaterialists might have been burnt until the 29. Car. 2. when the writ de haeretico comburendo was abolished: and here until the revolution, that statute not having extended to us. All heresies being now done away with us, these schismatists are merely atheists, differing from the material Atheist only in their belief that 'nothing made something,' and from the material deist who believes that matter alone can operate on matter.—Rejecting all organs of information therefore but my senses, I rid myself of the Pyrrhonisms with which an indulgence in speculations hyperphysical and antiphysical so uselessly occupy and disquiet the mind. A single sense may indeed be sometimes decieved, but rarely: and never all our senses together, with their faculty of reasoning. They evidence realities; and there are enough of these for all the purposes of life, without plunging into the fathomless abyss of dreams and phantasms. I am satisfied, and sufficiently occupied with the things which are, without tormenting or troubling myself about those which may indeed be, but of which I have no evidence. I am sure that I really know many, many, things, and none more surely than that I love you with all my heart, and pray for the continuance of your life until you shall be tired of it yourself."

RC (MHi: AM). PoC (DLC). After posting the RC, TJ made several significant alterations in the PoC that are described in the notes below.

The CRITIQUE of the University of Virginia was an unsigned review of *Proceedings and Report of the Commissioners for the University of Virginia, presented 8th of December 1818* (Richmond, 1818) in the *North American Review*, x (Jan. 1820), 115-37.

The section of this letter containing TJ's quotations from ORIGEN, TERTULLIAN, ST. JUSTIN MARTYR, and ST. MACURIUS may be read as: "Origen says, 'God is in very fact corporeal, but, by reason of so much heavier bodies, incorporeal.' Tertullian, 'for what is God, except body?' and again, 'Who will deny that God is body? Although God is spirit, yet spirit is body, of his own nature, in his own image.' St. Justin Martyr says, 'We say that the divinity is without body, not because it is bodyless, but since the state of not being bounded by anything is a more honorable one than that of being bounded, for this reason we call him body-

less.' And St. Macurius, speaking of angels, says, 'For although their bodies are of light texture, nevertheless in substance, form, and figure, their bodies are rare, according to the rarity of their nature.' "

For the editions of the works of OCELLUS and TIMAEUS by Jean Baptiste de Bouer, marquis d'Argens, to which TJ refers, see *Catalogue: President Jefferson's Library*, Washington, D.C., 1829, lots 418-19.

¹ TJ altered the last part of this sentence in the PoC to read "by the Lockes, the Tracys, and the Stewarts."

² TJ inserted an asterisk at this point in the PoC to serve as a key to the following marginal note: "that of Athanasius and the Council of Nicaea anno 324."

³ TJ altered the last part of this sentence in the PoC to read "I do not exactly know."

⁴ TJ changed "if not universally" in the PoC to "of the three first centuries."

⁵ TJ wrote "Enfield VI. 3" in the margin of the PoC next to the line where this sentence ends and "ib." next to the following line, beginning "graviorum tantum."

To Jared Sparks

SIR   Monticello Nov. 4. 20.

Your favor of Sep. 18. is just recieved, with the book accompanying it. It's delay was owing to that of the box of books from Mr. Guegan, in which it was packed. Being just setting out on a journey I have time only to look over the summary of contents. In this I see nothing in which I am likely to differ materially from you. I hold the precepts of Jesus, as delivered by himself, to be the most pure, benevolent, and sublime which have ever been preached to man. I adhere to the principles of the first age; and consider all subsequent innovations as corruptions of his religion, having no foundation in what came from him. The metaphisical insanities of Athanasius, of Loyola, and of Calvin, are to my understanding, mere relapses into polytheism, differing from paganism only by being more unintelligble. The religion of Jesus is founded on the Unity of God, and this principle chiefly, gave it triumph over the rabble of heathen gods then acknoleged. Thinking men of all nations rallied readily to the doctrine of one only god, and embraced it with the pure morals which Jesus inculcated. If the freedom of religion, guaranteed to us by law *in theory*, can ever rise *in practice* under the overbearing inquisition of public opinion, truth will prevail over fanaticism, and the genuine doctrines of Jesus, so long perverted by his pseudo-priests, will again be restored to their original purity. This reformation will advance with the other improvements of the human mind but too late for me to witness it. Accept my thanks for your book, in which I shall read with pleasure your developements of the subject, and with them the assurance of my high respect.

TH: JEFFERSON

RC (MH); addressed: "The revd. Jared Sparks Baltimore"; franked and post-marked: "CHARLOTville Nov 7." PoC (DLC).

Sparks (1789-1866), then Unitarian minister of the First Independent Church in Baltimore, subsequently became famous for his pioneering efforts in the fields of the history of the American Revolution and historical editing. He produced over one hundred volumes of works, including editions of the correspondence of Washington, Franklin, Gouverneur Morris, and assorted Revolutionary diplomats that were once considered monuments of American historical scholarship but that have since fallen into low repute because of Sparks' faulty editorial techniques. His FAVOR OF SEP. 18. asked for TJ's assistance in writing a biography of the American explorer John Ledyard and enclosed a copy of Sparks' *Letters on the Ministry, Ritual, and Doctrines of the Protestant Episcopal Church* (Baltimore, 1820), remarking that "should you have leisure and inclination to look it over, I trust you will not be displeased with its manner and spirit." See *Catalogue: Jefferson's Library*, 1829, lot 530.

To Timothy Pickering

Monticello Feb. 27. 21.

I have recieved, Sir, your favor of the 12th. and I assure you I recieved it with pleasure. It is true as you say that we have differed in political opinions; but I can say with equal truth, that I never suffered a political to become a personal difference. I have been left on this ground by some friends whom I dearly loved, but I was never the first to separate. With some others, of politics different from mine, I have continued in the warmest friendship to this day, and to all, and to yourself particuiarly, I have ever done moral justice.

I thank you for Mr. Channing's discourse, which you have been so kind as to forward me. It is not yet at hand, but is doubtless on it's way. I had recieved it thro' another channel, and read it with high satisfaction. No one sees with greater pleasure than myself the progress of reason in it's advances towards rational Christianity.

When we shall have done away the incomprehensible jargon of the Trinitarian arithmetic, that three are one, and one is three; when we shall have knocked down the artificial scaffolding, reared to mask from view the simple structure of Jesus, when, in short, we shall have unlearned every thing which has been taught since his day, and got back to the pure and simple doctrines he inculcated, we shall then be truly and worthily his disciples: and my opinion is that if nothing had ever been added to what flowed purely from his lips, the whole world would at this day have been Christian. I know that the case you cite, of Dr. Drake, has been a common one. The religion-builders have so distorted and deformed the doctrines of Jesus, so muffled them in mysticisms, fancies and falsehoods, have caricatured[1] them into forms so monstrous and inconcievable, as to shock reasonable thinkers, to revolt them against the whole, and drive them rashly to pronounce it's founder an impostor. Had there never been a Commentator, there never would have been an infidel. In the present advance of truth, which we both approve, I do not know that you and I may think alike on all points. As the Creator has made no two faces alike, so no two minds, and probably no two creeds. We well know that among Unitarians themselves there are strong shades of difference, as between Doctors Price and Priestley for example. So there may be peculiarities in your creed and in mine. They are honestly formed without doubt. I do not wish to trouble the world with mine, nor to be troubled for them. These accounts are to be settled only with him who made us; and to him we leave it, with charity for all others, of whom also he is the only rightful and competent judge. I have little doubt that the whole of our country will soon be rallied to the Unity of the Creator, and, I hope, to the pure doctrines of Jesus also.

In saying to you so much, and without reserve, on a subject on which I never permit myself to go before the public, I know that I am safe against the infidelities which have so often betrayed my letters to the strictures of those for whom they were not written, and to whom I never meant to commit my peace. To yourself I wish every happiness, and will conclude, as you have done, in the same simple style of antiquity, da operam ut Valeas. Hoc mihi gratius facere nihil potes. 　　　　　　　　　　　Th: Jefferson

RC (MHi: Pickering Papers); addressed: "Timothy Pickering esquire Salem Mass."; franked and postmarked: "charlotville Mar 3"; endorsed by Pickering as received 10 Mch. 1821 and as "In answer to mine—topic, *Christianity*." PoC (DLC).

Pickering (1745-1829), who had served as secretary of state under John Adams and then as a U.S. Senator from Massachusetts, was a staunch Federalist who was otherwise a harsh critic of TJ, as evidenced by his effort in 1823 to denigrate TJ's achievement in drafting the Declaration of Independence. His FAVOR OF THE 12TH. sought to elicit a profession of faith by TJ in the Unitarian religion, laying great emphasis on the recent conversion to that creed of a young skeptic from New York named Dr. Drake (Pickering to TJ, 12 Feb. 1821). MR. CHANNING'S DISCOURSE was William Ellery Channing, *A Sermon Delivered at the Ordination of the Rev. Jared Sparks, to the Pastoral Care of the First Independent Church in Baltimore* (Boston, 1819), one of the key documents in the history of American Unitarianism.

[1] TJ first wrote "perverted" and then altered it to read as above.

To Thomas Whittemore

Monticello June 5. 22.

I thank you, Sir, for the pamphlets you have been so kind as to send me, and am happy to learn that the doctrine of Jesus, that there is but one God, is advancing prosperously among our fellow-citizens. Had his doctrines, pure as they came from himself, been never sophisticated for unworthy purposes, the whole civilised world would at this day have formed but a single sect. You ask my opinion on the items of doctrine in your catechism. I have never permitted myself to meditate a specified creed. These formulas have been the bane and ruin of the Christian church, it's own fatal invention which, thro' so many ages, made of Christendom a slaughter house, and at this day divides it into Casts of inextinguishable hatred to one another. Witness the present internecine rage of all other sects against the Unitarian. The religions of antiquity had no particular formulas of creed, those of the modern world none; except those of the religionists calling themselves Christians, and even among these, the Quakers have none. And hence alone the harmony the quiet, the brotherly affections, the exemplary and unschismatising society of the Friends. And I hope the Unitarians will follow their happy example.—With these sentiments of the mischiefs of creeds and Confessions of faith, I am sure you will excuse my not giving opinions on the items of any particular one; and that you will accept at the same time the assurance of the high respect and consideration which I bear to it's author.

TH: JEFFERSON

RC (MMet); endorsed by Whittemore: "One of these chatechisms was sent to Mr. Jefferson. He had taken much interest in religion, as avowed by the liberal sects. He noticed the little work as follows." PoC (DLC).

Whittemore (1800-1861), a Universalist minister who had recently become pastor of a church in Cambridgeport, Mass., subsequently enjoyed a varied career as a Universalist theologian, Massachusetts state legislator, magazine editor, and businessman. TJ was writing in response to a 22 May 1822 letter from Whittemore (missing). Although the PAMPHLETS Whittemore sent to TJ have not been identified, the enclosed CATECHISM was Whittemore's *An Epitome of Scripture Doctrine, Comprised in a Catechism for the Use of Children* (Boston, 1821.)

To Benjamin Waterhouse

DEAR SIR   Monticello June 26. 22.

I have recieved and read with thankfulness and pleasure your denunciation of the abuses of tobacco and wine. Yet however sound in it's principles, I expect it will be but a sermon to the wind. You will find it as difficult to inculcate these sanative precepts on the sensualists of the present day, as to convince an Athanasian that there is but one God. I wish success to both attempts, and am happy to learn from you that the latter, at least, is making progress, and the more rapidly in proportion as our Platonising Christians[1] make more stir and noise about it.

The doctrines of Jesus are simple, and tend all to the happiness of man.

1. that there is one God, and he all-perfect:
2. that there is a future state of rewards and punishments:
3. that to love God with all thy heart, and thy neighbor as thyself, is the sum of religion.

These are the great points on which he endeavored to reform the religion of the Jews. But compare with these the demoralising dogmas of Calvin.

1. that there are three Gods:
2. that good works, or the love of our neighbor are nothing:
3. that Faith is every thing; and the more incomprehensible the proposition, the more merit in it's faith:
4. that Reason in religion is of unlawful use:
5. that God, from the beginning, elected certain individuals to be saved, and certain others to be damned; and that no crimes of the former can damn them, no virtues of the latter save.

Now which of these is the true and charitable Christian? He who believes and acts on the simple doctrines of Jesus? or the impious dogmatists of Athanasius and Calvin? Verily, I say that these are the false shepherds, foretold as to enter, not by the door into the sheep-fold, but to climb up some other way.[2] They are mere Usurpers of the Christian name, teaching a Counter-religion, made up of the deliria of crazy imaginations, as foreign from Christianity as is that of Mahomet. Their blasphemies have driven thinking men into infidelity, who have too hastily rejected the supposed Author himself, with the horrors so falsely imputed to him. Had the doctrines of Jesus been preached always as purely as they came from his lips, the whole civilised world would now have been Christian. I rejoice that in this blessed country of free enquiry and belief, which has surrendered it's creed and conscience to neither kings nor priests, the genuine doctrine of one only God is reviving, and I trust that there is not a *young man* now living in the US. who will not die an Unitarian.

But much I fear that when this great truth shall be re-established, it's Votaries will fall into the fatal error of fabricating formulas of creed, and Confessions of faith, the engines which so soon[3] destroyed the religion of Jesus, and made of Christendom a mere Aceldama: that they will give up morals for mysteries,[4] and Jesus for Plato. How much wiser are the Quakers, who, agreeing in the fundamental doctrine of the gospel, schismatize about no mysteries, and keeping within the pale of Common sense, suffer no speculative differences of opinion, any more than of feature, to impair the love of their brethren. Be this the wisdom of Unitarians; this the holy mantle which shall cover within it's charitable circumference all who believe in one God, and who love their neighbor.—I conclude my sermon with sincere assurances of my friendly esteem and respect.

TH: JEFFERSON

RC (MH-M). Dft (DLC).

Waterhouse (1754-1846), a graduate of the University of Leyden and a former professor of physics at Harvard, was a pioneer in the use of vaccination in America and an ardent Unitarian. He had written TJ about the growing conflict between Calvinists and Unitarians in New England and enclosed "a copy from my last edition of the Lecture on the *pernicious effects of Tobacco*, and of the other strand in that same cord, *ardent Spirits, on young subjects*" (Waterhouse to TJ, 8 June 1822).

[1] In the Dft, TJ first wrote "anti-Christian Maniacs" and then altered it to read as above.

[2] In the Dft, TJ first wrote "Verily I say that these are the false shepherds foretold as entering not by the door but climbing up some other way" and then altered it to read as above.

[3] In the Dft, TJ first wrote "first destroyed" and then altered it to read as above.

[4] In the Dft, TJ first wrote "morals for metaphysics" and then altered it to read as above.

To Benjamin Waterhouse

DEAR SIR   Monticello July 19. 22.

An antiently dislocated, and now stiffening wrist makes writing an operation so slow and painful to me that I should not so soon have troubled you with an acknolegement of your favor of the 8th. but for the request it contained of my consent to the publication of my letter of June 26. No, my dear Sir, not for the world. Into what a nest of hornets would it thrust my head! The genus irretabile vatum, on whom argument is lost, and reason is, by themselves, disclaimed in matters of religion. Don Quixot undertook to redress the bodily wrongs[1] of the world, but the redressment of mental vagaries would be an enterprise more than Quixotic. I should as soon undertake to bring the crazy skulls of Bedlam to sound understanding, as to inculcate reason into that of an Athanasian. I am old, and tranquility is now my summum bonum. Keep me therefore from the fire and faggots of Calvin and his victim Servetus. Happy in the prospect of a restoration of primitive Christianity, I must leave to younger Athletes to encounter and lop off the false branches which have been engrafted into it by the mythologists of the middle and modern ages.

I am not aware of the peculiar resistance to Unitarianism which you ascribe to Pensylvania. When I lived in Philadelphia there was a respectable congregation of that sect, with a meeting house and regular service which I attended, and in which Dr. Priestley officiated to numerous audiences. Baltimore has one or two churches, and their Pastor, author of an inestimable book on this subject, was elected Chaplain to the late Congress. That doctrine has not yet been preached to us: but the breeze begins to be felt which precedes the storm; and fanaticism is all in a bustle, shutting it's doors and windows to keep it out. But it will come, and will drive before it the foggy mists of Platonism which have so long obscured our Atmosphere. I am in hopes that some of the disciples of your institution will become missionaries to us, of these doctrines truly evangelical, and open our eyes to what has been so long hidden from them. A bold and eloquent preacher would be no where listened to with more freedom than in this state, nor with more firmness of mind. They might need a preparatory discourse on the text of 'prove all things, hold fast that which is good' in order to unlearn the lesson that reason is an unlawful guide in religion. They might startle on being first awaked from the dreams of the night, but they would rub their eyes at once and look the spectres boldly in the face. The preacher might be excluded by our hierophants from their churches and meeting houses, but would be attended in the fields by whole acres of hearers and thinkers. Missionaries from Cambridge would soon be greeted with more welcome, than from the tritheistical school of Andover. Such are my wishes, such would be my welcomes, warm and cordial as the assurances of my esteem and respect for you.   TH: JEFFERSON

RC (MeHi); addressed: "Doctr. Benjamin Waterhouse Cambridge Mass."; franked and postmarked: "CHARLOTville July 20." PoC (DLC).

Jared Sparks was the Baltimore minister who was ELECTED CHAPLAIN TO THE LATE CONGRESS.

Despite TJ's express wish to preserve the confidentiality of MY LETTER OF JUNE 26, a partial text of it was published after Waterhouse imprudently showed it to some friends. As a result of a report spread by one of these friends, erroneous accounts of the letter appeared in several Massachusetts papers, prompting Waterhouse to publish the following item, which first appeared in the *Boston Patriot* and later in the *Richmond Enquirer*:

A MISTAKE RECTIFIED

It has been asserted, from memory, in some of the papers, that in letters from "the great philosopher and statesman of the south," to a literary gentleman of eminence in this neighborhood, "that if the religion of JESUS had always been preached, in its original simplicity and power, there would not at this moment have been a single human being who was not a Christian." This is not exactly so expressed by the illustrious writer.—His words are: "Their blasphemies, [the corruptors of Christianity] have driven thinking men into infidelity; who have, too hastily, rejected the supposed author HIMSELF, with the horrors so falsely imputed to HIM. Had the doctrines of JESUS been preached always as purely as they came from his lips, the whole civilized world would now have been Christian. I rejoice that in this blessed country of free inquiry and belief, which has surrendered its creed and conscience to neither kings nor priests, the genuine doctrine of ONE GOD is reviving. But much I fear that when this great truth shall be established, its votaries will fall into the fatal errors of fabricating formulas of creed and confessions of faith, the engines which so soon destroyed the religion of JESUS, and made of Christendom a mere Akaldama."—The letters are in Mr. Jefferson's happiest style and amply refute the calumnies of his political enemies respecting his opinion of the Christian religion and its immaculate author.

(*Richmond Enquirer*, 6 Sep. 1822; Waterhouse to TJ, 14 Sep. 1822; TJ to Waterhouse, 15 Oct. 1822).

Perhaps because of TJ's failure to rebuke him for his indiscretion, Waterhouse next circulated copies of TJ's letters of 26 June and 19 July 1822 among some of the doctor's Unitarian friends in Massachusetts. As the following extract from a letter of Timothy Pickering indicates, some of those who read the letters were deeply disappointed by TJ's refusal to publicize his religious views: "I thank you for giving me an opportunity of reading Mr. Jefferson's letters on the subject of religion. I return them, with that of his correspondent, Dr. Waterhouse.—A man standing on the edge of his grave, ought to be sincere: I hope this of Mr. Jefferson's expressions. He has read the New Testament with some diligence. Has he nevertheless passed this sentence unobserved? 'Whosoever shall be ashamed of me and of my words, of him shall the son of man be ashamed, when he shall come in his own glory, and in his father's, and of the holy angels.'—He forbids the publication of his letter: 'No, my dear sir, not for the world. Into what a nest of hornets would it thrust my head?' He dreads an attack from the clergy—'the genus irritabile vatum—on whom argument is lost.' Now if rational believers, who have in other ways acquired distinction and influence, refuse to let their religious sentiments be publicly known, on what ground does he rest his opinion, 'that there is not a *young man* now living in the U.S. who will not die a unitarian?'—His apology is that he is old, and tranquillity is now his summum bonum; and he must leave to younger athletes to encounter the 'hornets.'—Yet he can enter on the 'arena' of politics; and vau[n]t afresh his false notions of government; and affect a jealousy of federalists, should they be admitted into the republican camp: that is, should they be allowed to participate, *officially*, in supporting the constitution which they framed, and in administering the government which they organized under it, and for a series of years practically and faithfully conducted; notwithstanding the opposition of the host of antifederalists, himself at their head" (Pickering to Joseph May, 6 Feb. 1823, MHi: Pickering Papers).

¹ TJ first wrote "grievances" and then altered it to read as above.

To James Smith

SIR   Monticello Dec. 8. 22.

I have to thank you for your pamphlets on the subject of Unitarianism, and to express my gratification with your efforts for the revival of primitive Christianity in your quarter. No historical fact is better established than that the doctrine of one god, pure and uncompounded was that of the early ages of Christianity; and was among the efficacious doctrines which gave it triumph over the polytheism of the antients, sickened with the absurdities of their own theology. Nor was the unity of the supreme being ousted from the Christian creed by the force of reason, but by the sword of civil government wielded at the will of the fanatic Athanasius. The hocus-pocus phantasm of a god like another Cerberus with one body and three heads had it's birth and growth in the blood of thousands and thousands of martyrs. And a strong proof of the solidity of the primitive faith is it's restoration as soon as a nation arises which vindicates to itself the freedom of religious opinion, and it's eternal divorce from the civil authority. The pure and simple unity of the creator of the universe is now all but ascendant in the Eastern states; it is dawning in the West, and advancing towards the South; and I confidently expect that the present generation will see Unitarianism become the general religion of the United states. The Eastern presses are giving us many excellent pieces on the subject, and Priestly's learned writings on it are, or should be in every hand. In fact the Athanasian paradox that one is three, and three but one is so incomprehensible to the human mind that no candid man can say he has any idea of it, and how can he believe what presents no idea. He who thinks he does only decieves himself. He proves also that man, once surrendering his reason, has no remaining guard against absurdities the most monstrous, and like a ship without rudder is the sport of every wind. With such persons gullability which they call faith takes the helm from the hand of reason and the mind becomes a wreck.

I write with freedom, because, while I claim a right to believe in one god, if so my reason tells me, I yield as freely to others that of believing in three. Both religions I find make honest men, and that is the only point society has any authority to look to—altho' this mutual freedom should produce mutual indulgence, yet I wish not to be brought in question before the public on this or any other subject, and I pray you to consider me as writing under that trust. I take no part in controversies religious or political. At the age of 80. tranquility is the greatest good of life, and the strongest of our desires that of dying in the good will of all mankind. And with the assurances of all my good will to Unitarian & Trinitarian, to whig & tory accept for yourself that of my entire respect.

TH: JEFFERSON

PoC (DLC).

TJ was writing in response to the Rev. James Smith's letter of 4 Nov. 1822. The PAMPHLETS ON THE SUBJECT OF UNITARIANISM were *James Smith's Vindication for Resisting the Ecclesiastical Power and Authority of their Episcopal Dignity, Michael Ellis & David Young; to Which is Added, a Short Sketch on the Government of God in the Church and a Few Thoughts on Infant Justification; Also, The Doctrine of Christian Perfection and Sanctification Impartially Examined* (Clinton, Ohio, 1814), actually two pamphlets in one. According to his letter and pamphlets, Smith, a resident of Mount Vernon, Ohio, was a former Methodist Episcopal minister and longtime admirer of TJ who, having rejected the doctrine of the Trinity, had "long since abandoned priestly dominion, and entirely shelter under the mild and peaceable Gospel of Jesus Christ, the most perfect model of Republicanism in the Universe."

To John Adams

DEAR SIR   Monticello. April 11. 23.

The wishes expressed, in your last favor, that I may continue in life and health until I become a Calvinist, at least in his exclamation of '*mon Dieu!* jusque à quand'! would make me immortal. I can never join Calvin in addressing *his god*. He was indeed an Atheist, which I can never be; or rather his religion was Daemonism. If ever man worshipped a false god, he did. The being described in his 5. points is not the God whom you and I acknolege and adore, the Creator and benevolent governor of the world; but a dæmon of malignant spirit. It would be more pardonable to believe in no god at all, than to blaspheme him by the atrocious attributes of Calvin. Indeed I think that every Christian sect gives a great handle to Atheism by their general dogma that, without a revelation, there would not be sufficient proof of the being of a god. Now one sixth of mankind only are supposed to be Christians: the other five sixths then, who do not believe in the Jewish and Christian revelation, are without a knolege of the existence of a god! This gives compleatly a gain de cause to the disciples of Ocellus, Timaeus, Spinosa, Diderot and D'Holbach. The argument which they rest on as triumphant and unanswerable is that, in every hypothesis of Cosmogony you must admit an eternal pre-existence of something; and according to the rule of sound philosophy, you are never to employ two principles to solve a difficulty when one will suffice. They say then that it is more simple to believe at once in the eternal pre-existence of the world, as it is now going on, and may for ever go on by the principle of reproduction which we see and witness, than to believe in the eternal pre-existence of an ulterior cause, or Creator of the world, a being whom we see not, and know not, of whose form substance and mode or place of existence, or of action no sense informs us, no power of the mind enables us to delineate or comprehend. On the contrary I hold (without appeal to revelation) that when we take a view of the Universe, in it's parts general or particular, it is impossible for the human mind not to percieve and feel a conviction of design, consummate skill, and indefinite power in every atom of it's composition. The movements of the heavenly bodies, so exactly held in their course by the balance of centrifugal and centripetal forces, the structure of our earth itself, with it's distribution of lands, waters and atmosphere, animal and vegetable bodies, examined in all their minutest particles, insects mere atoms of life, yet as perfectly organised as man or mammoth, the mineral substances, their generation and uses, it is impossible, I say, for the human mind not to believe that there is, in all this, design, cause and effect, up to an ultimate cause, a fabricator of all things from matter and motion, their preserver and regulator while permitted to exist in their present forms, and their regenerator into new and other forms. We see, too, evident proofs of the necessity of a superintending power to maintain the Universe in it's course and order. Stars, well known, have disappeared, new ones have come into view, comets, in their incalculable courses, may run foul of suns and planets and require renovation under other laws; certain races of animals are become extinct; and, were there no restoring power, all existences might extinguish successively, one by one, until all should be reduced to a shapeless chaos. So irresistible are these evidences of an intelligent and powerful Agent that, of the infinite numbers of men who have existed thro' all time, they have believed, in the proportion of a million at least to Unit, in the hypothesis of an eternal pre-existence of a creator, rather than in that of a self-existent Universe. Surely this unanimous sentiment renders this more probable than that of the few in the other hypothesis. Some early Christians indeed have believed in the coeternal pre-existance of both the Creator and the world, without changing their relation of cause and effect. That this was the opinion of St. Thomas, we are informed by Cardinal Toleto, in these words 'Deus ab æterno fuit jam omnipotens, sicut cum produxit mundum. Ab æterno potuit producere mundum.—Si sol ab æterno esset, lumen ab æterno esset; et si pes, similiter vestigium. At lumen et vestigium effectus sunt efficientis solis et pedis; potuit ergo cum causâ æterno effectus coæterna esse. Cujus sententiæ est S. Thomas Theologorum primus.' Cardinal Toleta.

Of the nature of this being we know nothing. Jesus tells us that 'God is a spirit.' 4. John 24. but without defining what a spirit is 'πνευμα ὁ Θεος.' Down to the 3d. century we know that it was still deemed material; but of a lighter subtler matter than our gross bodies. So says Origen. 'Deus igitur, cui anima similis est, juxta Originem, reapte corporalis est; sed graviorum tantum ratione corporum incorporeus.' These are the words of Huet in his commentary on Origen. Origen himself says 'appelatio ἀσωματον apud nostros scriptores est inusitata et incognita.' So also Tertullian 'quis autem negabit Deum esse corpus, etsi deus spiritus? Spiritus etiam corporis sui generis, in suâ effigie.' Tertullian. These two fathers were of the 3d. century. Calvin's character of this supreme being seems chiefly copied from that of the Jews. But the reformation of these blasphemous attributes, and substitution of those more worthy, pure and sublime, seems to have been the chief object of Jesus in his discources to the Jews: and his doctrine of the Cosmogony of the world is very clearly laid down in the 3 first verses of the 1st. chapter of John, in these words, 'ἐν αρχη ἦν ὁ λόγος, καὶ ὁ λόγος ἦν πρὸς τὸν Θεόν, καὶ Θεος ἦν ὁ λόγος. Οὗτος ἦν ἐν ἀρχη πρὸς τὸν Θεόν. Πάντα δε᾽ αντοῦ ἐγένετο. Καὶ χωρὶς αὐτοῦ ἐγένετο οὐδὲ ἓν, ὅ γέγονεν.' Which truly translated means 'in the beginning God existed, and reason [or mind] was with God, and that mind was God. This was in the beginning with God. All things were created by it, and without it was made not one thing which was made.' Yet this text, so plainly declaring the doctrine of Jesus that the world was created by the supreme, intelligent being, has been perverted by modern Christians to build up a second person of their tritheism by a mistranslation of the word λογος. One of it's legitimate meanings indeed is 'a word.' But, in that sense, it makes an unmeaning jargon: while the other meaning 'reason,' equally legitimate, explains rationally the eternal preexistence of God, and his creation of the world. Knowing how incomprehensible it was that 'a word,' the mere action or articulation of the voice and organs of speech could create a world, they undertake to make of this articulation a second preexisting being, and ascribe to him, and not to God, the creation of the universe. The Atheist here plumes himself on the uselessness of such a God, and the simpler hypothesis of a self-existent universe. The truth is that the greatest enemies to the doctrines of Jesus are those calling themselves the expositors of them, who have perverted them for the structure of a system of fancy absolutely incomprehensible, and without any foundation in his genuine words. And the day will come when the mystical generation of Jesus, by the supreme being as his father in the womb of a virgin will be classed with the fable of the generation of Minerva in the brain of Jupiter. But we may hope that the dawn of reason and freedom of thought in these

United States will do away all this artificial scaffolding, and restore to us the primitive and genuine doctrines of this the most venerated reformer of human errors.

So much for your quotation of Calvin's 'mon dieu! jusqu' a quand' in which, when addressed to the God of Jesus, and our God, I join you cordially, and await his time and will with more readiness than reluctance. May we meet there again, in Congress, with our antient Colleagues, and recieve with them the seal of approbation 'Well done, good and faithful servants.'   TH: JEFFERSON

RC (DLC); brackets in text are TJ's.

CARDINAL TOLETA was Francisco Cardinal Toledo (1532-1596), author of numerous commentaries on St. Thomas Aquinas and Aristotle. DEUS AB AETERNO: "God has been omnipotent forever, just as when he made the world. He has had the power to make the world forever. If the sun were in existence forever, light would have been in existence forever; and if a foot then likewise a footprint. But light and footprint are the effects of an efficient sun and foot; therefore the effect has had the power to be co-eternal with the eternal cause.

Of this opinion is St. Thomas, the first of the theologians." DEUS IGITUR: "God, therefore, to whom the soul is similar, in consequence of its origins, is in reality corporeal; but He is incorporeal in comparison with so much heavier bodies." HUET was Pierre Daniel Huet (1630-1721), bishop of Avranches and author of *Origenis in Sacras Scripturas Commentaria*...(Cologne, 1685). APPELATIO: "The word ἀσωματον among our writers, is not used or known." QUIS AUTEM: "Yet who will deny that God is body, although God is spirit? Indeed He is spirit of His own type of body, in His own image."

To John Davis

Monticello Jan. 18. 24.

I thank you, Sir, for the copy you were so kind as to send me of the revd. Mr. Bancroft's Unitarian sermons. I have read them with great satisfaction, and always rejoice in efforts to restore us to primitive Christianity, in all the simplicity in which it came from the lips of Jesus. Had it never been sophisticated by the subtleties of Commentators, nor paraphrased into meanings totally foreign to it's character, it would at this day have been the religion of the whole civilized world. But the metaphysical abstractions of Athanasius, and the maniac ravings of Calvin, tinctured plentifully with the foggy dreams of Plato, have so loaded it with absurdities and incomprehensibilities, as to drive into infidelity men who had not time, patience, or opportunity to strip it of it's meretricious trappings, and to see it in all it's native simplicity and purity. I trust however that the same free exercise of private judgment which gave us our political reformation will extend it's effects to that of religion, which the present volume is well calculated to encourage and promote.

Not wishing to give offence to those who differ from me in opinion, nor to be implicated in a theological controversy, I have to pray that this letter may not get into print, and to assure you of my great respect and good will.   TH: JEFFERSON

PoC (DLC).

Davis (1787-1854), a Worcester, Mass., lawyer who graduated from Yale and was in 1824 a legal partner of Levi Lincoln, TJ's attorney general, subsequently served Massachusetts as a U.S. Representative, U.S. Senator, and governor (William Lincoln, *History of Worcester, Mass.* [Worcester, 1862], p. 206-07). He had written: "Having understood that you are friendly to the exertions which have for some years been making in this part of our Country to reestablish the christian religion upon its primitive basis, and to purify its doc-

trines from the creeds and dogmas of Athanasius and Calvin, I have taken the liberty to send you by mail (this being the only mode of communication of which I can avail myself) a volume of sermons delivered before the second parish in this town by the Revd. Dr. Bancroft its minister" (Davis to TJ, 3 Jan. 1824). MR. BANCROFT'S UNITARIAN SERMONS : Aaron Bancroft, *Sermons on those Doctrines of the Gospel, and on those Constituent Principles of the Church, which Christian Professors have Made the Subject of Controversy* (Worcester, Mass., 1822).

To George Thacher

SIR   Monticello Jan. 26. 24.

I have read with much satisfaction the Sermon of Mr. Pierpoint which you have been so kind as to send me, and am much pleased with the spirit of brotherly forbearance in matters of religion which it breathes, and the sound distinction it inculcates between the things which belong to us to judge, and those which do not. If all Christian sects would rally to the Sermon in the mount, make that the central point of Union in religion, and the stamp of genuine Christianity, (since it gives us all the precepts of our duties to one another) why should we further ask, with the text of our sermon, 'What think *ye* of Christ'? And if one should answer 'he is a member of the Godhead,' another 'he is a being of eternal pre-existence,' a third 'he was a man divinely inspired,' a fourth 'he was the Herald of truths reformatory of the religions of mankind in general, but more immediately of that of his own countrymen, impressing them with more sublime and more worthy ideas of the Supreme being, teaching them the doctrine of a future state of rewards and punishments, and inculcating the love of mankind, instead of the anti-social spirit with which the Jews viewed all other nations,' What right, or what interest has either of these respondents to claim pre-eminence for his dogma, and, usurping the judgment-seat of God, to condemn all the others to his wrath? In this case, I say with the wiser heathen 'deorum injuriae, diis curae.'

You press me to consent to the publication of my sentiments and suppose they might have effect even on Sectarian bigotry. But have they not the Gospel? If they hear not that, and the charities it teacheth, neither will they be persuaded though one rose from the dead. Such is the malignity of religious antipathies that, altho' the laws will no longer permit them, with Calvin, to burn those who are not exactly of their Creed, they raise the Hue and cry of Heresy against them, place them under the ban of public opinion, and shut them out from all the kind affections of society. I must pray permission therefore to continue in quiet during the short time remaining to me: and, at a time of life when the afflictions of the body weigh heavily enough, not to superadd those which corrode the spirit also, and might weaken it's resignation to continuance in a joyless state of being which providence may yet destine. With these sentiments accept those of good will and respect to yourself.

TH: JEFFERSON

PoC (DLC).

Thacher (1754-1824), a lawyer who graduated from Harvard in 1776 and served as associate justice of the Massachusetts Supreme Court, 1801-1824, was a Federalist in politics and a deist sympathetic to Unitarianism in religion. He had written TJ that Dr. Benjamin Waterhouse had read to him TJ's letters to Waterhouse of 26 June and 19 July 1822, and he urged TJ to consent to their publication, arguing that this "would promote the cause of what we consider *important truth*, and redound to your present and future fame" (Thacher to TJ, 6 Jan. 1824). The SERMON OF MR. PIERPOINT was John Pierpont, *What Think Ye of Christ? A Sermon, Preached at Newburyport, Sunday, October 26, 1823* (Cambridge, Mass., 1823).

To Alexander Smyth

DEAR SIR   Monticello Jan. 17. 25.

I have duly recieved 4 proof sheets of your explanation of the Apocalypse, with your letters of Dec. 29. and Jan. 8. in the last of which you request that, so soon as I shall be of opinion that the explanation you have given is correct, I would express it in a letter to you. From this you must be so good as to excuse me, because I make it an invariable rule to decline ever giving opinions on new publications in any case whatever. No man on earth has less taste or talent for criticism than myself, and least and last of all should I undertake to criticise works on the Apocalypse. It is between 50. and 60. years since I read it, and I then considered it as merely the ravings of a Maniac, no more worthy, nor capable of explanation than the incoherences of our own nightly dreams. I was therefore well pleased to see, in your first proof-sheet, that it was said to be not the production of St. John, but of Cerinthus, a century after the death of that Apostle. Yet the change of the Author's name does not lessen the extravagances of the composition, and come they from whomsoever they may, I cannot so far respect them as to consider them as an allegorical narrative of events, past or subsequent. There is not coherence enough in them to countenance any suite of rational ideas. You will judge therefore from this how impossible I think it that either your explanation, or that of any man in the heavens above, or on the earth beneath, can be a correct one. What has no meaning admits no explanation. And pardon me if I say, with the candor of friendship, that I think your time too valuable, and your understanding of too high an order, to be wasted on these paralogisms. You will percieve, I hope, also that I do not consider them as revelations of the supreme being, whom I would not so far blaspheme as to impute to him a pretension of revelation, couched at the same time in terms which, he would know, were never to be understood by those to whom they were addressed. In the candor of these observations, I hope you will see proofs of the confidence, esteem and respect which I truly entertain for you.　　　　TH: J

PoC (DLC).

Smyth (1765-1830), a Virginia lawyer and soldier who had had a checkered career as a brigadier general in the U.S. Army during the War of 1812, was elected to a number of terms in the Virginia state legislature both before and after that conflict and also served in the U.S. House of Representatives, 1817-1825. His EXPLANATION OF THE APOCALYPSE was *An Explanation of the Apocalypse, or Revelation of St. John* (Washington, D.C., 1825), in which he argued that the Apocalypse was written in the second century by St. Irenaeus, not in the first by St. John the Apostle, and therefore should be excluded from the canon of Scripture *(Catalogue: Jefferson's Library*, 1829, lot 543). Smyth's LETTERS OF DEC. 29. AND JAN. 8. forwarded proof sheets of parts of this pamphlet to TJ and solicited his endorsement of it.

INDEX

INDEX

book on Christianity, 22-3, 27, 29, 327-9, 337, 340, 342; adopts demythologized version of Christianity, 23-5, 39-42, 331-6; criticizes corruptions of Christianity, 23-5, 41-2, 331, 333, 345, 352, 363, 365, 388-9, 391n, 403, 413; praises Jesus' teachings on God, 24, 39, 41, 328, 334, 387, 396, 400, 401-2, 405, 411-2; corresponds with John Adams on religious subjects, 31-2; denies reported conversion to orthodox Christianity, 33-4, 366n, 375-7, 381, 382n, 384; urges Van der Kemp to write life of Jesus, 34-6, 368-9, 383; attitude toward Unitarianism, 36, 385, 401-9, 413-5; and Evangelists, 38, 328, 333, 392, 396-7; and Jesus' materialism and spiritualism, 38n, 391-2; and doctrine of immaculate conception, 41, 391n; and existence of hell, 41, 116; differs with Jesus' teachings, 41n, 391-2; and doctrine of Atonement, 42, 391n; and doctrine of election, 42, 391n; and doctrine of real presence in Eucharist, 42, 391n; and validity of ecclesiastical hierarchy, 42, 391n; note on legal charge against Jesus, 286-7, 312-3; promises to send statement of religious creed to Rush, 318, 320, 327; requests confidentiality for religious beliefs, 330, 331, 337-8, 403, 406-7, 409, 414, 415; attitude toward Quakers, 345-6, 347, 350, 404, 406; urged not to publish book on religion, 361-3; refuses to publish book on religion, 363, 381; criticizes Hopkins, 385-6; on faith, 386; on works, 386; on forgiveness of sins, 392; historical approach of to New Testament, 395-7; and spirit, 399-400, 411-2; opinion of Apocalypse, 415-6
Jesus Christ: attitudes toward divinity of, 6-7, 15, 17n, 33-4, 41, 42, 331, 339-40, 366n, 382n, 391n, 396-7; praised as great moral teacher, 15-6, 21, 23-5, 36, 40, 41, 328, 330, 332-4, 343, 344n-5n, 350, 352, 363, 385, 387-9, 391-2, 395-7, 400, 401-2, 405, 411-2, 414-5; compared to Socrates, 20-1, 327, 330; Arian view of, 36n; Socinian view of, 36n; regarded as spiritualist by TJ, 38n, 391-2; TJ's note on legal charge against, 286-7, 312-3

Jews: TJ's attitude toward, 11, 22-3, 24, 41, 328, 332, 351-2, 387, 396-7, 405, 412; mentioned, 6
John, St.: TJ's attitude toward, 38; on God as spirit, 411, 412; Apocalypse, 415-6. See also Evangelists
Johnson, Jacob: edition of New Testament used by TJ, 126
Johnston, Arthur: Psalmorum Davidis, 354
Julian the Apostate, 46, 335n
Jupiter, 353, 412
Justinian: Digesta, 286-7, 312-3
Justin Martyr, St., 400, 401n

Kames, Henry Home, Lord: influences TJ's view of moral sense, 8; conversion of to Christianity, 318; Essays on the Principles of Morality and Natural Religion, 358
Kenrick, John, 373, 374n
Kercheval, Samuel, 346n
King, Miles: letter to, 360-1
Krueger, Paul, ed.: Corpus Iuris Civilis, 313

La Bletterie, Jean Phillipe René de: Life of the Emperor Julian, 46, 335n
Lacey, John F.: and publication of "Life and Morals of Jesus," 126
Lactantius Firmianus, Lucius Caelius, 400
Laertius, Diogenes, 369, 370n
La Fontaine, Jean de, 359
Law, Thomas: letter to, 355-8; Second Thoughts on Instinctive Impulses, 355, 358n
Ledyard, John, 402n
Lee, Arthur, 348
Lee, Richard Henry, 348
Letter from Rome (Conyers Middleton): influences TJ's religious views, 15n, 348
Letters on the Ministry, Ritual, and Doctrines of the Protestant Episcopal Church (Jared Sparks): received by TJ, 401; mentioned, 402n, 407
Letters to Dr. Horsley (Joseph Priestley), 348, 349n
Letter to Dr. Waterland (Conyers Middleton): influences TJ's religious views, 15n, 348
Leusden, Johannes, 126
"Life and Morals of Jesus": provenance of, 30-8; compilation of, 37-8, 47-8; transcription of, 46; editorial note on, 125-6

INDEX

Life of George Washington (John Marshall), 348, 349n
Life of the Emperor Julian (Jean Phillipe René de La Bletterie), 46, 335n
Lincoln, Levi: letters to, 336, 337-8; sent copy of "Syllabus" and letter to Rush, 25, 336
Lindsey, Theophilus: letter from Priestley quoted, 329n
Linn, John Blair, 340
Linn, William: *Serious Considerations on the Election of a President*, 11
Literary Bible of Thomas Jefferson (ed. Gilbert Chinard), 6-7, 8-9
Livingston, Robert R., 340, 349
Livy, 6-7, 395
Locke, John, 383, 385, 400
Logan, George: letter to, 381-2
Lomax, Miss, 349
Loyola, St. Ignatius of, 401
Luke, St.: TJ's attitude toward, 38. *See also* Evangelists
Luther, Martin, 385

Macarius, St., 400, 401n
Madison, James: letter to quoted, 118; mentioned, 336n
Madison, Rev. James, 320, 321
Marcet, Jane: *Conversations on Chemistry*, 395, 399n
Mark, St.: TJ's attitude toward, 38. *See also* Evangelists
Marshall, John: *Life of George Washington*, 348, 349n
Martialis, Marcus Valerius: *Epigrammata*, 366n
Mason, John M.: *Voice of Warning, to Christians*, 10, 11
Matthew, St.: TJ's attitude toward, 38. *See also* Evangelists
Mayo, Frederick A.: and "Life and Morals of Jesus," 38, 125
Mazzei, Philip, 10, 320, 321
Memoirs of Theophilus Lindsey (Thomas Belsham): contains TJ's letter to Priestley, 31, 34, 329n, 349n, 367
"Memoirs respecting J.C." (Francis Adrian Van der Kemp), 378-80
Memorabilia (Xenophon), 388
Mezentius, 348-9
Middleton, Conyers: *Letter from Rome* and *Letter to Dr. Waterland*, 15n, 348; *Miscellaneous Works*, 349n
Minerva, 412
miracles: rejected by TJ, 6, 16, 41,

391n; accepted by Priestley, 15; validity questioned by Middleton, 15n
Miscellaneous Works (Conyers Middleton), 349n
Missouri crisis, 393-4
Mohammed, 339, 344n, 405
Monroe, James, 21, 341
Montanus, Benedictus Arias, 126
Monthly Repository of Theology and General Literature: contains "Syllabus" and letter to Rush, 35, 335n, 372n; mentioned, 367
Moore, Clement C.: *Observations upon Certain Passages in Mr. Jefferson's Notes on Virginia*, 12; *Night before Christmas*, 12n
morality: TJ on, 343, 344n-5n, 350, 355-8, 387; Wollaston's theory of, 355; Helvetius' theory of, 356-7
Morse, Jedidiah, 329n
Moses, 351, 373, 380n, 396
Motte, Richard, 350

Nepos, Cornelius, 369, 370n
New and Candid Investigation of the Question, Is Revelation True? (James Fishback), 343-4
Newcome, Archbishop William: *Harmony in Greek of the Gospels*, 37
New Orleans, La., 21
New Testament: editions used by TJ to compile "Life and Morals of Jesus," 27, 30-1, 126, 340; editions used by TJ to compile "Philosophy of Jesus," 27, 45, 340. *See also* Table of New Testament Passages
Newton, Isaac, 383
New Version of the Psalms of David (Nicholas Brady and Nahum Tate), 353, 354
New Way of Deciding Old Controversies ("Basanistes"), 373, 374n, 375
Nicaea, Council of, 401n
Norfolk, Va., 319
North American Review, 399, 401n
Notes on the State of Virginia: quoted, 6-7, 9; criticized, 10-2; criticizes Christianity, 42; appendix to, 327; mentioned, 383

Observations on Infidelity ("Cerus"): TJ's comments on, 345-6; mentioned, 346n-7n
Observations upon Certain Passages in Mr. Jefferson's Notes on Virginia (Clement C. Moore), 12

INDEX

Randolph, Martha Jefferson (Mrs.) Thomas Mann Randolph, Jr., daughter of TJ): letter to quoted, 335n; sent copy of "Syllabus" and letter to Rush, 25, 334n-5n; holds Grierson edition of New Testament, 46; takes custody of "Life and Morals of Jesus," 125

Randolph, Sarah Nicholas: takes custody of "Life and Morals of Jesus," 125

Randolph, Thomas Jefferson: *Memoir of Thomas Jefferson*, 3n; on TJ's reluctance to discuss religion, 4n; on "Philosophy of Jesus," 45; takes custody of "Life and Morals of Jesus," 125

Reibelt, J. P.: letter to quoted, 30

religion, freedom of: supported by TJ, 9-10, 19, 42, 320, 374-5; in England, 375; in U.S., 375

Religion of Nature Delineated (William Wollaston), 358n

Repository of Lives and Portraits of Distinguished American Characters (Joseph Delaplaine), 382n

Republic (Plato): TJ's comments on, 359

republicanism: TJ's concern for survival of in U.S., 13-4; and Christianity, 16-30, 318, 321-4; British roots of, 322-3

Richmond Enquirer, 408n

Rittenhouse, David, 337

Robinson, Moses: letter to, 324-5; letter to quoted, 19

Rush, Benjamin: letters to, 319-21, 331-6, 341-2; letters from, 317-9, 321-4, 338; letters to quoted, 17, 18, 23-4, 334n; letters from quoted, 18, 341n-2n; and relationship between Christianity and republicanism, 16-9, 318, 321-4; letter to Elhanan Winchester quoted, 17; describes TJ's religious beliefs, 17n; sent copy of "Syllabus" and letter, 23-5, 331, 334n; reaction to "Syllabus," 25-6, 338; reaction to TJ's offer to send "Philosophy of Jesus," 28-9, 341n-2n; on titles, 317-8; promised statement of TJ's religious creed, 318, 320, 327; on cities, 321

Rush, John, 322

Rush, Richard, 341n

Rutledge, Edward: letter to quoted, 14

Second Letter to the Revd. John Blair Linn (Joseph Priestley), 340

Second Thoughts on Instinctive Impulses (Thomas Law), 355, 358n

Sedition Act, 13

Seneca: moral teachings, 8, 388; TJ's attitude toward, 328, 332; works, 332

Serious Considerations on the Election of a President (William Linn), 11

Sermon Delivered at Ordination of Rev. Jared Sparks (William Ellery Channing), 402, 404n

Sermons on Doctrines of the Gospel (Aaron Bancroft), 413, 414n

Servetus, Michael, 393, 407

Short, William: letters to, 387-91, 391-4, 394-9; letters to quoted, 37, 39, 41-2, 115; letters from quoted, 37, 390n, 391n, 394n, 399n; inspires TJ to compile "Life and Morals of Jesus," 36-8, 391n; attitude toward Epicurus, 37, 390n; and "Syllabus," 335n, 391, 394n, 399n

Siculus. *See* Calpurnius Siculus

Smith, Abigail Adams (Mrs. William Stephens Smith), 354, 355n

Smith, J.: edition of New Testament used by TJ, 30-1, 126

Smith, James: letter to, 408-10; letter to quoted, 36, 40, 42; *Vindication*, 408-10

Smith, Margaret Bayard (Mrs. Samuel Harrison Smith): letter to, 375-7; letter to quoted, 33

Smith, Thomas Jefferson: letter to quoted, 40-1

Smith, William L.: *The Pretensions of Thomas Jefferson to the Presidency Examined*, 10n

Smithsonian Institution: acquires "Life and Morals of Jesus," 125-6

Smyth, Alexander: letter to, 415-6; *Explanation of the Apocalypse*, 415-6

Socinianism, 16, 36n

Socrates: compared to Jesus, 20-1, 327, 330; TJ's attitude toward, 328, 332; fails to record teachings, 333; divine inspiration of denied by TJ, 353, 397; complains of Plato, 359, 388; *Memorabilia* of by Xenophon, 388; wisdom of, 395

Socrates and Jesus Compared (Joseph Priestley): influences TJ's religious views, 20-1, 327, 330, 331, 334n,

TABLE OF
NEW TESTAMENT PASSAGES

Library of Congress Cataloging in Publication Data

Jefferson, Thomas, 1743-1826.
Jefferson's extracts from the Gospels.

(Papers of Thomas Jefferson. Second series)
Includes index.   1. Bible. N.T. Gospels—Criticism,
interpretation, etc. I. Adams, Dickinson, W.
II. Lester, Ruth W. III. Bible. N.T. Gospels.
IV. Title. V. Series.
BS2549.J5J43 1983   226'.1   82-61371
ISBN 0-691-04699-9

Library of Congress Cataloging in Publication Data

Jefferson, Thomas, 1743-1826.
Jefferson's extracts from the Gospels.

(Papers of Thomas Jefferson. Second series)
Includes index.   1. Bible. N.T. Gospels—Criticism,
interpretation, etc. I. Adams, Dickinson, W.
II. Lester, Ruth W. III. Bible. N.T. Gospels.
IV. Title. V. Series.
BS2549.J5J43 1983   226'.1   82-61371
ISBN 0-691-04699-9